5/5/22

*'A good hotel is where
the guest comes first'*

Hilary Rubinstein, founding editor
(1926–2012)

The Mason's Arms, Branscombe © Chetwode Ram Associates

CONTENTS

www.goodhotelguide.com

Our website has many handy features to help you get the most out of your Guide.

- Explore offers and discounts
- View special collections
- Read the latest news
- Search for a hotel near you
- Search for a hotel near a particular destination
- Submit a review
- Join the Good Hotel Guide Readers' Club
- Order a copy of the printed Guide

DESKTOP

TABLET

SMARTPHONE

Make it even easier to get on the Good Hotel Guide website while you're on the go: add an icon to the home screen of your iPhone or iPad for one-touch smartphone access. Go to **www.goodhotelguide.com** on your mobile browser. Tap on the rectangle with an arrow pointing upwards, at the bottom of the screen. Then tap on the + sign ('Add to Home Screen') that pops up.

INTRODUCTION

As we enter our 42nd year, the Guide is now older than both the president of France and prime minister of New Zealand. As with those two countries it also has a fresh face holding the reins. As the new editor I will ensure it remains a knowledgeable companion for the discerning traveller, exactly as it was when launched by Hilary Rubinstein in 1977. We championed an outstanding welcome and decent service then. We still do now.

In this time of smoke and mirrors, when old certainties are constantly being questioned, we continue to adhere to the values that have underpinned the Guide for more than four decades. Impartial inspections, personal recommendations and rigorous research inform every one of the 865 entries in this publication. We have never accepted payment or complimentary hospitality from a hotel keen to be included in these pages. Commerce has never tainted our integrity.

Of course, we couldn't do this without you. It is simply beyond our means to inspect each property every year, so readers' reports are indispensable. The more the merrier. Your honest praise and criticism illuminate a property's strengths – and its weaknesses. As regular guests paying your way, you are the acid test of a hotel's performance.

Our ranks include hotels, inns, restaurants-with-rooms, B&Bs and guest houses. Some inhabit vibrant cities, others enjoy glorious rural isolation; some are swaddled by mountains, others gaze across salt marsh and sea. Many are family owned and managed; at least two serve divine devilled kidneys for breakfast. César-winning hotels, selected on the basis of favourable reports over the year, are on top of their game, but only four hotels have graced every single issue since we first published in 1978: Ballymaloe, Currarevagh House, Lastingham Grange and Rothay Manor.

Alongside the print edition, we warmly embrace the new. The Good Hotel Guide website allows you to search for accommodation suitable for everyone from dog owners and golfers to romantics and history buffs. Who knows? Some hotels may suit all four. It also contains nearly 500 of our favourite places on the Continent and further afield, along with many offers and special breaks.

Wherever the road takes you this year, I do hope the Guide adds to the enjoyment of your travels.

Ian Belcher
July 2018

HOW TO USE THE GOOD HOTEL GUIDE

MAIN ENTRY

The 428 main entries, which are given a full page each, are those we believe to be the best of their type in Great Britain and Ireland.

Colour bands identify each country;
London has its own section.

Hotels are listed alphabetically under the name of the town or village.

The maps at the back of the book are divided into grids for easy reference. A small house indicates a main entry, a triangle a Shortlist one.

An index at the back lists hotels by hotel name.

This hotel is making its first appearance, is returning after an absence, or has been upgraded from the Shortlist.

We name readers who have endorsed a hotel; we do not name inspectors, readers who ask to remain anonymous, or those who have written a critical report.

This hotel has agreed to give Guide readers a 25% discount off its normal bed-and-breakfast rate for one night only, subject to availability. Terms and conditions apply.

We try to indicate whether a hotel can accommodate wheelchair-users. It's always worth calling the hotel to check the details of wheelchair access.

The panel provides the contact details, number of bedrooms and facilities.

We give the range of room or B&B prices for 2019, or the 2018 prices when we went to press. The price for dinner is for a set meal, or the average cost of three courses from an à la carte menu.

Sample entry panel

www.goodhotelguide.com · ENGLAND · 101

BISHOP'S CASTLE Shropshire · Map 3:C4

THE CASTLE HOTEL · NEW

Built on the bailey of a hilltop castle, this dog-friendly hotel overlooks 'a lovely town in stunning countryside'. A sister to Pen-y-Dyffryn, Oswestry (see entry), it has gained a full entry after Guide inspectors called: Beyond 'a little patio with water feature', the interior is 'a pleasing mix of traditional country pub and a more contemporary, sleek style'. A master bedroom had 'comfortable armchairs, a roomy bathroom with bath and shower over'. All rooms are individually styled; some with in-room bath; others with walk-in rain shower. Three bar/dining areas had 'open fires in cosy spaces', where dinner was 'comfort food, ideal for walkers'. Curried peppers, courgettes and hazelnut loaf with raita and 'a good portion of vegetables', proved 'a cut above pub food', as did chicken stuffed with garlic mushrooms, leek and Shropshire Blue sauce, while vanilla panna cotta with mixed berries was 'outstanding'. In the morning, tables were attractively set in the panelled dining room for a breakfast of avocado toast, poached egg, smoked salmon; 'perfectly cooked eggs Benedict'. In summer 'an upper-level patio with ornamental pond would be truly lovely, with wonderful views'. (David Lowe, Anne Sprason, and others)

25% DISCOUNT VOUCHERS

Market Square
Bishop's Castle
SY9 5BN

T: 01588 638403
E: stay@thecastlehotelbishops castle.co.uk
W: www.thecastlehotelbishops castle.co.uk

BEDROOMS 12.
OPEN all year except 25 Dec.
FACILITIES 3 bar areas, dining room, free Wi-Fi, in-room TV (Freeview), in-room spa treatments, patio, terrace, garden, parking, bicycle storage, bars and restaurant wheelchair accessible.
BACKGROUND MUSIC in bar areas.
LOCATION in small market town centre.
CHILDREN all ages welcomed.
DOGS allowed in bedrooms, bar, at owner's side at meal times in dog-friendly areas, not in restaurant, dog welcome box, no charge.
CREDIT CARDS Mastercard, Visa.
PRICES [2018] per room B&B single £100–£115, double £110–£195, D,B&B single £127–£142, double £165–£250. À la carte £30. 1-night bookings sometimes refused Sat.

HOW TO USE THE GOOD HOTEL GUIDE

SHORTLIST ENTRY

The Shortlist includes untested new entries and places we think should be appropriate in areas where we have limited choice. It also includes some hotels about which we have not had recent reports. There are no photographs; many of the hotels have chosen to be included, with pictures, on our website.

In some cases we list the entry under the nearest town.

These are abbreviated descriptions listing the essential facilities.

This hotel has agreed to give Guide readers a 25% discount off its normal bed-and-breakfast rate for one night only, subject to availability. Terms and conditions apply.

Many readers tell us they find background music irritating. We tell you if music is played and where you might encounter it.

Dinner prices are either for a set menu or an estimate of the likely price of a three-course meal.

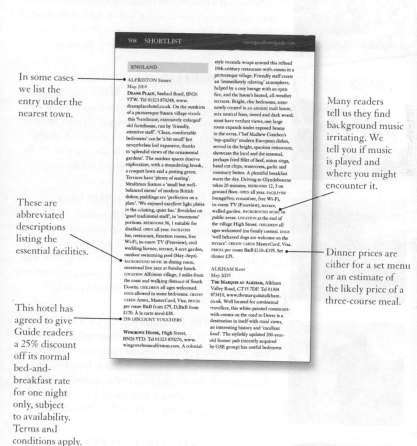

508   SHORTLIST   www.goodhotelguide.com

ENGLAND

ALFRISTON Sussex
Map 2:E4
DEANS PLACE, Seaford Road, BN26
5TW. Tel 01323 870248, www.
deansplacehotel.co.uk. On the outskirts
of a picturesque Sussex village stands
this 'handsome, extensively enlarged'
old farmhouse, run by 'friendly,
attentive staff'. 'Clean, comfortable
bedrooms' can be 'a bit small' but
nevertheless feel expansive, thanks
to 'splendid views of the ornamental
gardens'. The outdoor spaces deserve
exploration, with a meandering brook,
a croquet lawn and a putting green.
Terraces have 'plenty of seating'.
Mealtimes feature a 'small but well-
balanced menu' of modern British
dishes; puddings are 'perfection on a
plate'. 'We enjoyed excellent light plates
in the relaxing, quiet bar.' Breakfast on
'good traditional stuff', in 'enormous'
portions. BEDROOMS 36, 1 suitable for
disabled. OPEN all year. FACILITIES
bar, restaurant, function rooms, free
Wi-Fi, in-room TV (Freeview), civil
wedding licence, terrace, 4-acre garden,
outdoor swimming pool (May–Sept).
BACKGROUND MUSIC in dining room,
occasional live jazz at Sunday lunch.
LOCATION Alfriston village, 3 miles from
the coast and walking distance of South
Downs. CHILDREN all ages welcomed.
DOGS allowed in some bedrooms. CREDIT
CARDS Amex, MasterCard, Visa. PRICES
per room B&B from £75, D,B&B from
£170. À la carte meal £38.
25% DISCOUNT VOUCHERS

WINGROVE HOUSE, High Street,
BN26 5TD. Tel 01323 870276, www.
wingrovehousealfriston.com. A colonial-
style veranda wraps around this refined
19th-century restaurant-with-rooms in a
picturesque village. Friendly staff create
an 'immediately relaxing' atmosphere,
helped by a cosy lounge with an open
fire, and the house's heated, all-weather
terraces. Bright, chic bedrooms, some
newly created in an ancient malt house,
mix neutral hues, tweed and dark wood;
most have verdant views; one large
room expands under exposed beams
in the eaves. Chef Mathew Comben's
'top-quality' modern European dishes,
served in the bright, spacious restaurant,
showcase the local and the seasonal,
perhaps fried fillet of beef, onion rings,
hand cut chips, watercress, garlic and
rosemary butter. A plentiful breakfast
starts the day. Driving to Glyndebourne
takes 20 minutes. BEDROOMS 12, 3 on
ground floor. OPEN all year. FACILITIES
lounge/bar, restaurant, free Wi-Fi,
in-room TV (Freeview), terrace,
walled garden. BACKGROUND MUSIC in
public areas. LOCATION at the end of
the village High Street. CHILDREN all
ages welcomed (no family rooms). DOGS
'well behaved dogs are welcome on the
terrace'. CREDIT CARDS MasterCard, Visa.
PRICES per room B&B £110–£195. Set
dinner £35.

ALKHAM Kent
Map 2:D5
THE MARQUIS AT ALKHAM, Alkham
Valley Road, CT15 7DF. Tel 01304
873410, www.themarquisatalkham.
co.uk. Well located for continental
travellers, this white-painted restaurant-
with-rooms on the road to Dover is a
destination in itself for rural views,
an interesting history and 'excellent
food'. The stylishly updated 200-year-
old former pub (recently acquired
by GSE group) has restful bedrooms

CÉSARS 2019

We give our César awards to the ten best hotels of the year. Named after César Ritz, the most celebrated of hoteliers, these are the Oscars of hotel-keeping.

❦ NEWCOMER OF THE YEAR
Pentonbridge Inn, Penton
Gifted young chefs Jake and Cassie White have transformed a remote and run-down Cumbrian pub into an exciting gourmet destination within sight of the Scottish border. Each smart bedroom is named after an infamous clan of Border Reivers – a daring departure.

❦ LUXURY HOTEL OF THE YEAR
Kinloch Lodge, Sleat
There are glorious loch views from bedrooms filled with antiques, at Lord and Lady Macdonald's former hunting lodge on Skye. Ancestral portraits abound. A ghillie organises fishing and stalking, while chef Marcello Tully cooks Michelin-starred fare. Speed, bonny boat!

❦ SEASIDE HOTEL OF THE YEAR
The Nare, Veryan-in-Roseland
With its spa, its pools, balconies and sub-tropical gardens overlooking sandy Carne Beach, Toby Ashworth's hotel is the perfect mix of family-friendliness and luxury. Top marks for Cornish cream teas, local seafood, a talented new chef, smiling staff and traditional values.

❦ COUNTRY HOUSE HOTEL OF THE YEAR
Tudor Farmhouse, Clearwell
Hari and Colin Fell have created luxurious contemporary accommodation within historic, rustic farm buildings. Eggs from the ducks and hens in the paddock, vegetables from the kitchen garden, wild garlic foraged from the Forest of Dean supply chef Rob Cox's 20-mile menus.

❦ B&B OF THE YEAR
Stoberry House, Wells
The bedrooms are luxurious, breakfast is exceptional at Tim and Frances Meeres Young's 18th-century coach house overlooking the cathedral city. From the hosts' attention to the smallest detail, to the beautifully landscaped gardens, this is a labour of love.

🏆 ROMANTIC HOTEL OF THE YEAR
The Salutation, Sandwich
There is a pleasurable away-from-it-all feeling at this
Queen Anne-style Lutyens house with 'secret garden', on
the edge of a jewel of a medieval town. New owners John
and Dorothy Fothergill have refurbished with great style.
Food and service win high praise.

🏆 INN OF THE YEAR
The Star Inn, Harome
This chocolate-box-pretty-thatched village inn is infused
with wit – the bar filled with odds and ends; a billiard
table at the foot of a bed – but chef/patron Andrew Pern's
Michelin-starred cooking is seriously good. One room has
both spa bath and piano.

🏆 SCOTTISH HOTEL OF THE YEAR
Knockendarroch Hotel, Pitlochry
Struan and Louise Lothian spare no effort to please guests
at their friendly hotel. Fires burn in comfy lounges. There's
a cabinet of whiskies; rooms with balcony, with books, a
four-poster, binoculars, loch views; a daily-changing menu
of superb cooking.

🏆 WELSH RESTAURANT-WITH-ROOMS
OF THE YEAR
Restaurant James Sommerin, Penarth
Superb sea views, contemporary design and acclaimed
Michelin-starred cooking prove to be winning ingredients
at Louise and James Sommerin's family-run enterprise on
the Severn estuary.

🏆 IRISH HOTEL OF THE YEAR
Gregans Castle Hotel, Ballyvaughan
A generosity of spirit infuses Simon Haden and Frederieke
McMurray's Georgian country house, with magical views
across the Burren to Galway Bay. Elegant interiors are
filled with antiques, modern art, fresh garden flowers.
The cooking is unpretentious but imaginative.

REPORT OF THE YEAR COMPETITION

Readers' contributions are the lifeblood of the Good Hotel Guide. Everyone who writes to us is a potential winner of the Report of the Year competition. Each year we single out the writers of the most helpful reports. These correspondents win a copy of the Guide and an invitation to our annual launch party in October.

This year's winners are:
Robert Cooper of Oxton
Ian & Barbara Dewey of Bathampton (Bath)
Chris Elliot of Wanshurst Green
Brian Griffiths of Honley
David Hampshire of Stoke Wood (Stoke Poges)
Bob & Jean Henry of Linton (Wetherby)
Trevor Lockwood of Manaccan (Helston)
Ian McGiver of Bedford
Chris & Erika Savory of Lyme Regis
Tessa Stuart of London

JOIN THE GOOD HOTEL GUIDE READERS' CLUB

Send us a review of your favourite hotel.
As a member of the club, you will be entitled to:
- A pre-publication discount offer
- Personal advice on hotels
- Advice if you are in dispute with a hotel
- Monthly emailed Guide newsletter

The writers of the ten best reviews will each win a free copy of the Guide and an invitation to our launch party. And the winner of our monthly web competition will win a free night, dinner and breakfast for two at one of the Guide's top hotels.

Send your review via
our website: www.goodhotelguide.com
or email: editor@goodhotelguide.com
or fax: 020 7602 4182
or write to:
Good Hotel Guide
50 Addison Avenue
London W11 4QP
England

EDITOR'S CHOICE

Herb garden spa treatments, 18th-century oak trees and a cat called Sir Godfrey are just some of the features that make these our favourite hotels in various categories this year. Turn to the full entry for the bigger picture.

No 112

The Raeburn, Edinburgh

THE ELMS
ABBERLEY
The name scarcely does justice to this gracious Queen Anne mansion turned luxury hotel and spa in landscaped grounds. Under new ownership, it impressed Guide inspectors from the moment they stepped into the stunning hallway. (Page 70)

BROOKS COUNTRY HOUSE
ROSS-ON-WYE
The creative owners have made over Georgian Pengethley Manor, with a beguiling mix of grandeur and fun. It stands in parkland complete with vineyard. Choose a house room or a horsebox – and get the nosebag on for hearty Herefordshire fare. (Page 278)

BAYARDS COVE INN
DARTMOUTH
There is a warm welcome at this former merchant's house turned pub-with-rooms, behind a half-timbered facade, near the waterfront. Winding stairs lead to bedrooms with low, beamed ceilings. Inspectors enjoyed local crab in a lovely, pub atmosphere. (Page 154)

THE PUNCH BOWL INN
CROSTHWAITE
Rooms at this popular gastropub in a pretty Lakeland village are named after past vicars of the adjacent church. The young chef works with Cumbrian produce to create dishes that pack a punch. Comfy sofas, a log burner, beamed ceilings, bags of atmosphere. (Page 152)

THE GUNTON ARMS
THORPE MARKET
Damien Hirst in the ladies' loo, David Bailey in the gents', a deer park strewn with sculptures… This pub delights art-lovers and novelty-seekers. Under the dining room's arched wooden ceiling, an open fire serves for grilling and smoking. (Page 315)

THE RAEBURN
EDINBURGH
Boutique rooms with rainforest shower and perhaps a roll-top bath, a library, bar, brasserie and terrace, friendly staff and Georgian elegance all come together as one harmonious whole at this family-run hotel just a 15-minute stroll from the city centre. (Page 363)

TWR Y FELIN HOTEL
ST DAVIDS
A former temperance hotel built around a working windmill has been transformed, at vast expense, into 'Wales's first contemporary art hotel'. A showcase for local, seasonal Welsh produce and for over 100 pieces of specially commissioned art. (Page 448)

SUMMER LODGE
EVERSHOT
Thomas Hardy, with his architect's hat on, had a hand in extending this former dower house, today an exceptionally well-run hotel. Rooms have such pleasing touches as fresh flowers, fruit and shortbread. There is high-quality cooking, too. (Page 171)

BLUE HAYES
ST IVES
Unabashedly luxurious, this 1920s retreat on the hill above Porthminster Beach impressed our inspector in every detail, from the hospitality tray's fresh milk and bone china teapot, to the chef's way with local seafood, to breakfast's devilled kidneys. (Page 283)

THE WELLINGTON ARMS
BAUGHURST
A former hunting lodge today delights as a comfy country pub. Bedrooms have espresso machine and minibar. There are honey bees, laying hens, home-grown and local produce – and Wellington teapots with a knitted cosy to buy as a souvenir. (Page 90)

CASTLE LESLIE
GLASLOUGH
A 1,000-acre estate with lakes and
woodland surrounds this Victorian pile. It
is filled with paintings, antiques – a grand
piano, a della Robbia fireplace. Every
bedroom has its own story. Eagle's Nest
has a balcony with lake views. (Page 473)

GLENAPP CASTLE
BALLANTRAE
Sea-facing rooms at this Victorian fantasy
castle in landscaped grounds, gaze across
the Firth of Clyde to Ailsa Craig. Some
have a half-tester bed. Order a cocktail
in teapot in the restored tea rooms in the
walled garden. (Page 352)

LIME WOOD
LYNDHURST
A mansion in the New Forest, a stellar
clientele, sublime Italian food – could you
get more romantic? Apparently, yes. Lime
Wood now has 'the UK's sexiest bedroom',
a cabin cantilevered over a small lake with
a private island and alfresco bath and
wood-vurning stove. (Page 224)

HARTWELL HOUSE
AYLESBURY
Louis XVIII paid £500 a year to house his
court in exile at this sublime mansion in
an Arcadian landscape. For a little less you
can spend two nights in a Royal Four-
Poster room filled with paintings and
antiques. (Page 77)

DRAKES
BRIGHTON
For Jane Austen Brighton was a 'scene of
dissipation and vice'. So much the better
for an amorous weekend! Sybarites
choose a room with a freestanding bath
in the floor-to-ceiling window, at this
Regency hotel with sea-facing cocktail
bar. (Page 119)

THE PAINSWICK
PAINSWICK
For that dream date, here is a Palladian
mansion with Italianate loggia and
glamorous cocktail bar in a picturesque
Cotswolds village. George's suite has a
four-poster, a sitting room with log burner,
a stone balcony with blissful views.
(Page 257)

STRATTONS
SWAFFHAM
Theatrical bedrooms set the scene for
seduction at this Palladian-villa. There's
the opulent Red Room, with Jacobean
four-poster bed; Opium with free-standing
bath; exotic Fantouche and Venetian
murals in Seagull and Boudoir. (Page 307)

THE PORTOBELLO
LONDON
In raffish Notting Hill of rom-com
fame, this wacky boutique hotel offers
everything for couples, from 'cosy doubles'
with exotic murals to 'signature rooms',
one with circular bed, another with a
four-poster from Hampton Court Palace.
(Page 61)

PRESTONFIELD
EDINBURGH
Lady Anne Dick, former chatelaine of
this 16th-century mansion, scandalised
polite Edinburgh society with her 'coarse'
verses and cross-dressing, and there is still
something deliciously louche about all
the swags and velvets and sumptuousness
here. (Page 362)

PEN-Y-DYFFRYN
OSWESTRY
Long walks in tranquil countryside, tea by
a blazing log fire, a bedroom with a double
spa bath or private stone-walled patio…
This small hotel close to the Welsh border
offers a perfect getaway à deux. (Page 252)

Drakes, Brighton

Gilpin Hotel and Lake House, Windermere

LIME WOOD
LYNDHURST

Spa days and holidays are spent in luxury at this New Forest hotel. There is a mud house, an outdoor hot pool, sauna and rooftop gym, with healthy food in Raw & Cured, all in a tranquil forest setting. (Page 224)

CLIVEDEN HOUSE
TAPLOW

Surely one of Britain's most beautiful spas lies within old brick walls in the gardens of this Italianate mansion. Facilities include an indoor and (notorious) outdoor pool, a gym, hot tubs – an easy drive from London. (Page 310)

ST BRIDES SPA HOTEL
SAUNDERSFOOT

A warm, salt-water infinity pool overlooking the bay is a highlight of this coastal hotel's spa. Double treatment rooms have full-height sliding windows to let in the sea breezes and soothing sound of the waves. (Page 449)

THE ROYAL CRESCENT HOTEL AND SPA
BATH

Guests don robes and flip-flops to relax and sip champagne with lunch at this luxury hotel's spa garden. The bath house has a relaxation pool, vitality pool, salt-infused sauna and a blossom steam room. (Page 89)

CONGHAM HALL
KING'S LYNN

Fragrant herbs and flowers from the renowned herb garden infuse signature treatments in the Secret Garden Spa at this Georgian mansion. There's a pool with floor-to-ceiling windows, a thermal suite, an outdoor hot tub. (Page 202)

BARNSLEY HOUSE
BARNSLEY

Cotswold stone and beams create indoor–outdoor harmony at the spa in the garden of this manor house. There is a choice of music in treatment rooms, a herbaceous sauna, a lounge overlooking the outdoor, heated hydrotherapy pool. (Page 81)

GILPIN HOTEL AND LAKE HOUSE
WINDERMERE

Cedar-clad spa lodges at Gilpin Hotel have a treatment area, steam room, outdoor sauna and hot tub. Lake House guests can book treatments in the Jetty Spa, in a tree canopy overlooking a lake. (Page 340)

PARK HOUSE
BEPTON

Day guests, members and hotel residents pass through a marble shower before dipping in a mother-of-pearl indoor pool at this Edwardian country house's spa. They can also bathe in the outdoor pool, use sauna or steam rooms. (Page 95)

ILSINGTON COUNTRY HOUSE
ILSINGTON

This Dartmoor country house hotel's spa draws inspiration from Tibet, with soothing sounds, scents and music. There's a hydrotherapy pool, steam room, sauna, and poolside 'kubel dusche' – a bucket of ice water to tip over yourself. (Page 199)

SEAHAM HALL
SEAHAM

A dramatic swimming pool with massage stations and a floor-to-ceiling glass wall overlooking the verdant grounds, an Asian herbal sanarium and an Indian steam room with amethyst crystals lie at the heart of this Georgian mansion's award-winning spa. (Page 290)

THE GEORGE
YARMOUTH

On a shingle beach lapped by the waves, with sea-facing conservatory restaurant and terrace, this smart Guide newcomer occupies a historic town house between castle and pier. Many rooms have Solent or harbour views. (Page 344)

THE SEASIDE BOARDING HOUSE
BURTON BRADSTOCK

On Chesil Beach, drawing inspiration from Edward Hopper's Cape Cod, this is a hip but laid-back operation. All bedrooms have a sea view. You can eat on the terrace – crab sandwiches, home-made ices, Dorset cream tea. (Page 131)

TRESANTON
ST MAWES

All bedrooms have views across Falmouth Bay to St Anthony's lighthouse, at Olga Polizzi's relaxed but stylish hotel. You can sail aboard a vintage yacht or just hang out in the Beach Club, lunch on oysters or a crab sandwich with champagne. (Page 287)

TREGLOS HOTEL
CONSTANTINE BAY

There is a real holiday vibe at this family-run, family-friendly hotel, with many sea-facing bedrooms, golf course, spa, partner surf school ('coasteering', kayaking, stand-up paddleboarding), and seafood platter lunches served on the deck. (Page 148)

ARTIST RESIDENCE
BRIGHTON

From sea-view balcony rooms to the basement Bunkhouse and 'Below Deck', this Regency seafront hotel is as cool and quirky as Brighton itself. Breakfast in The Set includes scrambled rare-breed Cacklebean eggs with local smoked mackerel. (Page 118)

THE WHITE HORSE
BRANCASTER STAITHE

There are Brancaster oysters and beer-battered cod on the bar menu at this family-run inn with views across the salt marshes to the sea. Close by are miles of unspoilt honey-hued sandy beaches, perfect for kite-surfing. (Page 116)

THE CARY ARMS
BABBACOMBE

You can arrive by sea and moor at this secluded hotel, which clings to the cliffs above the Teign estuary. Beach huts in tropical coastal gardens have wall-to-wall glass doors, a sunbathing deck, views across Lyme Bay. (Page 78)

ARGYLL HOTEL
ISLE OF IONA

The best tables in the sun lounge gaze across the water to Mull at this owner-run hotel occupying a row of crofters' cottages. Menus embrace locally caught fish, hand-creeled langoustines, crab and lobster, organic garden produce. (Page 372)

TREFEDDIAN
ABERDYFI

A hotel for family holidays, not boutique or trendy, but relaxed, with the beach just across the road, sea-facing lounges, packed lunches to order, children's supper, tea on the terrace, a putting green, and good, old-fashioned hospitality. (Page 415)

HELL BAY
BRYHER

Outside, calm protected beaches and dreamy views of outlying islets. Inside, rooms with a breezy New England style, an acclaimed collection of Cornish art and a menu highlighting gloriously fresh produce from the Isles of Scilly. Its crab shack is a popular summer fixture. (Page 128)

Tresanton, St Mawes

THE MASH INN
RADNAGE

There is rural peace without, a happy buzz within, as guests tuck in to Jon Parry's no-choice menus at Nick Mash's reinvented village inn. Meat and fish sizzle on a bespoke wood-fired grill. Vegetables are fresh from the garden. Simply brilliant. (Page 269)

LITTLE BARWICK HOUSE
BARWICK

Classically inspired food and an exceptional wine list win praise at Emma and Tim Ford's Georgian country house. Airy, comfortable bedrooms have flowers and shortbread. There are gardens, warm hospitality and an excellent breakfast. A place to relax. (Page 82)

JSW
PETERSFIELD

Guests arrive for Jake Saul Watkins's memorable Michelin-starred cooking (perhaps a tasting or vegetarian menu), sleep in comfort, awake to freshly squeezed orange juice and pastries from Paris. (Page 264)

TUDDENHAM MILL
TUDDENHAM

The name sounds folksy, but this 17th-century converted mill has contemporary rooms with perhaps an alfresco hot tub or a Philippe Starck bath. Chef/patron Lee Bye's cooking is ambitious; breakfasts are first class. (Page 322)

THE THREE CHIMNEYS AND THE HOUSE OVER-BY
DUNVEGAN

Long-standing owners Shirley and Eddie Spear are welcoming hosts at their loch-side island retreat. Suites are generously equipped. Chef Scott Davies uses excellent local produce in his highly creative cooking. (Page 361)

LAKE ISLE
UPPINGHAM

Not on lake-lapped Innisfree but in a Rutland market town, Richard Burton's romantically named former shop, with bijou bedrooms, rates highly for gourmet cooking. Chef Stuart Mead has a sure touch with local, seasonal ingredients. Breakfast includes fishcakes and fresh juice. (Page 326)

THE NEPTUNE
OLD HUNSTANTON

Kevin Mangeolles's Michelin-starred menus at this former coaching inn delighted Guide regulars this year. Pork and game are from surrounding estates, fish and shellfish locally landed. Jacki Mangeolles is welcoming front-of-house. Full marks for enthusiasm. (Page 249)

BARLEY BREE
MUTHILL

Modern French cuisine, local produce and warm Scottish hospitality are the prime ingredients at Alison and Fabrice Bouteloup's former coaching inn. He cooks with flair (perhaps brisket of beef sous vide); she is a wine expert. (Page 384)

TYDDYN LLAN
LLANDRILLO

'We're not a hotel,' say Susan and Bryan Webb, but rooms at their rural stone house are of a high standard, while Mr Webb's Michelin-starred cooking showcases the best of seasonal Welsh produce. (Page 436)

THE HARDWICK
ABERGAVENNY

Stephen and Joanna Terry alchemised a grotty roadside pub into an establishment that inspires readers to make return visits. Alongside Mr Terry's first-rate menu, offering plenty of choice at a fair price, there are modern, well-equipped bedrooms. (Page 417)

The Three Chimneys and the House Over-By, Dunvegan

Prince Hall, Two Bridges

TRIGONY HOUSE
THORNHILL
Walkies start at the door of this former sporting lodge, where dogs enjoy gourmet treats and have access to house and grounds. A free bed, towels, bowls and breakfast sausage are offered. Extras include a dog-sitter and spa therapies. (Page 406)

WELLINGTON ARMS
BAUGHURST
Your four-legged friend is allowed even in the dining room at this relaxed, happy place on the North Wessex Downs. Water bowls, luxury dog food and chews are provided. Just don't let dogs worry the resident Jacob's sheep. (Page 90)

PRINCE HALL
TWO BRIDGES
With Dartmoor on the doorstep, treats, bowls, towels, outside tap and more, dogs enjoy a princely welcome at this manor-house hotel. Dogs are allowed in the bistro, and up to two stay free (£15 for a three-dog night). (Page 323)

MOOR OF RANNOCH HOTEL
RANNOCH STATION
Dogs (maximum two) stay free in any bedroom and have the run of this remote hotel surrounded by romantic wilderness. There is a hose pipe for mucky pups, towels for soggy dogs, cushions by the fire, a sausage for breakfast. (Page 396)

CASTLE HOTEL
BISHOP'S CASTLE
A mat, bowl, towel, lead and treats are all provided at this town hotel amid great walking country. You can eat in the dog-friendly bar and use the large garden free of charge (but no dips in the pond, please). (Page 101)

FELIN FACH GRIFFIN
FELIN FACH
It was puppy love for a furry guest this year at this Welsh dining pub, where dogs are greeted with treats and allowed in the bar or under one restaurant table. Resident dogs Max and Lottie enjoy a game; maps are available for walks. (Page 431)

THE WENTWORTH
ALDEBURGH
It costs just £2 a night for a dog to stay at this friendly seafront hotel. The restaurant and (in summer) the main beach are out of bounds, but bounding is allowed on nearby beaches. You can eat together in the bar, the conservatory or alfresco. (Page 71)

THE TRADDOCK
AUSTWICK
Dog-owners can choose any room or suite for £5 a dog-night (maximum two), and eat in the bar, at this hotel in the Yorkshire Dales. In prime walking country, it has washing facilities for when you return after mud larks. (Page 76)

TALLAND BAY HOTEL
TALLAND-BY-LOOE
Most rooms are dog-friendly at this fun hotel between beach and countryside. You can dine with your canine companion in the brasserie or on the terrace. A £12.50 nightly charge includes a banger for breakfast and a chicken dinner. (Page 309)

LORDS OF THE MANOR
UPPER SLAUGHTER
Home-baked biscuits, blankets, treats, toys and acres of grounds await lucky mutts at this smart hotel in the heart of the Cotswolds. Pampered pooches are allowed in public rooms (not the dining room) and in specially prepared bedrooms for £30 a night. (Page 325)

GRAVETYE MANOR
EAST GRINSTEAD

A romantic Elizabethan manor house in well-tended gardens, Michelin-starred cooking in a dramatic glass-walled new dining room, log fires in comfy lounges, and every imaginable comfort combine at this perennial Guide favourite. (Page 161)

JUDGES
YARM

Tried and trusted, this Victorian mansion is filled with antiques, books, oil paintings. Clubby armchairs are drawn up to roaring fires. From complimentary sherry and a teddy bear, to the turn-down service and morning cup of tea, here is pure, old-fashioned comfort. (Page 343)

ASKHAM HALL
PENRITH

The Lowther family's Grade I listed ancestral home has a relaxed, house-party feel, with historic and personal touches – old photographs, a priest hole, perhaps a four-poster or antique bath, topiary garden and free-ranging livestock. Great food and wine, too. (Page 258)

LANGAR HALL
LANGAR

One of the Guide's most characterful hotels, this apricot-washed Georgian mansion might be a private house, with its many idiosyncratic charms. Antique clocks tick. Walls are hung with artworks. Pretty, old-fashioned, individually styled bedrooms overlook magical grounds. (Page 206)

BROCKENCOTE HALL
CHADDESLEY CORBETT

Guests drive through woodland to discover this château-style Victorian mansion with a romantic lake, fountain and ancient dovecote. Afternoon tea can be taken by the fire in a panelled library hung with oil paintings. Elegant bedrooms are supplied with all comforts. (Page 138)

BALLATHIE HOUSE
KINCLAVEN

Country sports are a big attraction at this turreted Victorian country house and estate on the River Tay. Anglers are in their element. Deer roam the grounds. It is family run, filled with antiques, a pleasing mix of grandeur and comfort. (Page 375)

LLANGOED HALL
LLYSWEN

The late Sir Bernard Ashley's art collection still adorns this Jacobean mansion remodelled by Clough Williams Ellis. An Edwardian house-party atmosphere prevails, with fresh flowers, new-laid eggs from happy hens, elderflower champagne at afternoon tea. (Page 441)

TEMPLE HOUSE
BALLYMOTE

Guests gather for drinks by a log fire before sitting down together to dine, house-party style, at this classic Georgian mansion in parkland overlooking medieval castle ruins. Antiques, hunting prints, a stag's head and fossil collection make for interesting browsing. (Page 465)

LYMPSTONE MANOR
EXMOUTH

Celebrity chef Michael Caines's perfectionism is everywhere apparent in this beautifully restored Georgian mansion on the Exe estuary. From watercolours and water colours (an estuary-inspired palette) to Michelin-starred cooking, everything is tiptop. (Page 172)

HARE AND HOUNDS
TETBURY

Wooded grounds surround this Victorian Cotswold stone house, built by the founder of neighbouring Westonbirt Arboretum. Interiors are stylish, but log fires, tweedy armchairs and a library of curios lend a private-house feel. Well-mannered hounds are welcome. (Page 314)

Askham Hall, Penrith

Hambleton Hall, Hambleton

HOTEL ENDSLEIGH
MILTON ABBOT
Olga Polizzi's ducal fishing lodge stands in an 18th-century arcadia laid out by Humphry Repton, with the River Tamar running through. Discover streams, pools, cascades, ravines, a shell house and grotto, and one of England's longest herbaceous borders. (Page 233)

BODYSGALLEN HALL AND SPA
LLANDUDNO
Guests can wander more than 200 acres of parkland, pleasure grounds and gardens at this Jacobean manor house. Garden tours take in a rare 17th-century box parterre. There are woodland walks, a lily pond, a cascade, specimen trees, a prolific walled kitchen garden. (Page 437)

BOATH HOUSE
AULDEARN
An ornamental trout lake, wildflower meadow, streams and formal plantings surround this Georgian mansion. The walled garden supplies organic fruit and vegetables for the table; bees and hens do their bit for breakfast. (Page 351)

CLIVEDEN HOUSE
TAPLOW
Sir Charles Barry's Italianate mansion overlooking the Thames stands amid pleasure grounds, with a yew maze, rose garden, a Japanese water garden, a parterre laid out by John Fleming, pioneer of 'carpet bedding' – and Britain's most notorious swimming pool. (Page 310)

CONGHAM HALL
KING'S LYNN
With more than 400 varieties of herbs, the herb garden at this Georgian country house is a great attraction for students of all things culinary and physic, while supplying kitchen and spa. Best experienced with the heady aromas found at dawn or dusk. (Page 202)

THE SALUTATION
SANDWICH
The 'Secret Garden', laid out by Lutyens, architect of this Queen Anne-style house, is revealed to the paying public and hotel residents. Designed as a series of 'rooms', the walled garden includes a poplar, holm oak and meadow walk, wet meadow, tropical and jungle garden. (Page 289)

HAMBLETON HALL
HAMBLETON
The owners of this former hunting lodge have created a glorious patchwork on 17 south-facing acres, with a parterre, ornamental ponds, mature trees, statues and topiary, bordering Rutland Water. Lovely in all seasons. (Page 182)

HILTON PARK
CLONES
Oaks grown from acorns planted in 1752 to commemorate an ancestor's marriage, champion beeches, a kitchen garden and a rose garden created by Victorian landscaper Ninian Niven, can all be found in the park and pleasure grounds of this very special stately home. (Page 471)

GOLDSTONE HALL
MARKET DRAYTON
One of the UK's largest hotel kitchen gardens, reclaimed from wilderness, supplies the kitchen with a wealth of produce at this Georgian manor house. There is a herb walkway, a walled garden with double-tiered herbaceous border, a riot of colour all summer long. (Page 226)

LONGUEVILLE MANOR
ST SAVIOUR
From 1863, the Rev Christian (aka WB) Bateman landscaped the grounds around this ancient manor house, with lake, specimen trees, kitchen garden. They remain much as he designed them – though with the addition of a pool, jogging trails and spa. (Page 459)

GLENFINNAN HOUSE HOTEL
GLENFINNAN

A lawn reaches down to the Loch Shiel shoreline from this 18th-century stone mansion, with views across the water towards a monument to Bonnie Prince Charlie and Ben Nevis. Roaming red deer add to the drama. (Page 367)

THE SCARLET
MAWGAN PORTH

Most bedrooms have a seaward balcony and floor-to-ceiling windows at this serene, coolly contemporary adults-only hotel. There is a sea-view restaurant, while the decked terrace, reed-bed swimming pool and hot tub are within sight of the beach. (Page 230)

THE COTTAGE IN THE WOOD
BRAITHWAITE

Mountain-view rooms gaze out towards Skiddaw at this restaurant-with-rooms in England's only true mountain forest, while the garden view ones may offer a glimpse of red squirrels. Dining room and terrace also enjoy memorable vistas of the verdant surroundings. (Page 114)

ROMNEY BAY HOUSE
NEW ROMNEY

Between the Strait of Dover and Littlestone Golf Club, this glamorous house, built for a Hollywood actress, is surrounded by the flat, sheep-studded expanse of Romney Marsh – not a pretty-pretty landscape, but one that has stirred many a literary imagination. (Page 239)

TEMPLE HOUSE
BALLYMOTE

Bedrooms overlook a 1,000-acre estate at this grand but lived-in ancestral home, with terrace gardens, sheep-grazed pastures, native woodlands carpeted with bluebells in the springtime, and, beside the lake, the ivy-covered ruins of a medieval Knights Templar castle. (Page 465)

THE PIG ON THE BEACH
STUDLAND

Guests can choose a view of countryside, or of the sea towards Old Harry chalk-stack rocks and the Isle of Wight, at this Gothic, turreted former aristocrat's holiday home. Thatched bothies overlook the trademark kitchen garden. (Page 305)

THE FOVERAN
ST OLA

The light-filled dining room at this restaurant-with-rooms offers stirring vistas across Scapa Flow to the southern Orkney islands. The luminous, big-sky landscape is all around, and, late in the season, the northern lights may loom into view. (Page 398)

LLANTHONY PRIORY
LLANTHONY

Romantic priory ruins that once inspired JMW Turner stand in a wild and wonderful setting, swaddled by the Vale of Ewyas in the Black Mountains. This hotel occupies former cloisteral buildings. Norman arches frame wooded hillsides. (Page 440)

THE ATLANTIC HOTEL
ST BRELADE

Full-height windows and balconies afford spectacular views across landscaped gardens to the ocean at this upmarket hotel. Connoisseurs of golf landscaping might prefer to overlook James Braid's La Moye course. The sunsets do not require Photoshop. (Page 456)

THE BLAKENEY HOTEL
BLAKENEY

Many bedrooms, some with balcony, look across estuary and salt marsh towards Blakeney Point, an Area of Outstanding Natural Beauty, at this family-friendly, quayside hotel. The first-floor lounge has panoramic views; boat trips reveal the local seals. (Page 102)

The Scarlet, Mawgan Porth

The Quay House, Clifden

38 ST GILES
NORWICH

A stroll from castle and cathedral, this lovely house, built in 1700, is run as a very special B&B. From tea and cake on arrival to beautifully appointed rooms and excellent breakfast, every aspect pleases. (Page 247)

BROOKS GUESTHOUSE
BRISTOL

Guests sleep in a smart, conventional bedroom or an aluminium retro caravan on the Astroturf roof at this former office block turned friendly, unfussy city base. Breakfast brings bacon butties, smoked salmon bagels, eggs Benedict. Local restaurants abound. (Page 122)

THE ROSELEIGH
BUXTON

Choose a bay-windowed front room at this handsomely furnished Victorian guest house, and enjoy views over the lake of the Pavilion Gardens, designed by Joseph (Crystal Palace) Paxton. A comfortable, traditional, stylish and professional operation. (Page 132)

THE OLD RECTORY
HASTINGS

Designer chic and witty caprice abound at this former rectory with beautiful lounges and lovely walled garden. Rooms are supplied with home-baked biscuits, own-label toiletries. At breakfast there are smoothies, home-cured kippers, bread fresh from the oven. (Page 186)

THE HACK & SPADE
WHASHTON

So close to Scotch Corner, yet so peaceful, this former Georgian ale-house-cum-Victorian pub is now a fine B&B, rustic without, chic within. Bathrooms have a rainfall shower, aromatherapy toiletries. High praise for the full Yorkshire breakfast. (Page 334)

CHAPEL HOUSE
PENZANCE

A Georgian house, once an admiral's home, is run with care and pride as a B&B. Rooms are highly individual – one bathroom has a retractable glass roof. From tea and cake on arrival to Sunday brunch's kedgeree, everything is tiptop. (Page 262)

ST CUTHBERT'S HOUSE
SEAHOUSES

A former Presbyterian church dedicated to the patron saint of northern England is today an award-winning B&B and music venue. Rooms have an espresso machine, posh toiletries. Breakfast includes kippers from the famous local smokehouse. (Page 292)

COES FAEN
BARMOUTH

A literally ground-breaking B&B (the entrance hall incorporates a rock outcrop, with water trickling into a pool) has been fashioned from a Victorian lodge. Each bedroom has a unique spa feature. Tuscan-style dinner is served four nights a week. (Page 421)

THE QUAY HOUSE
CLIFDEN

Warm and genuine hosts encourage a relaxed and happy ethos at this former harbourmaster's house filled with antiques and curios. In the morning there is breakfast cake, freshly squeezed orange juice, perfect poached eggs. (Page 469)

CRAIGATIN HOUSE AND COURTYARD
PITLOCHRY

A Victorian former doctor's house has been made over as a splendid B&B by its hospitable, hands-on owners. Rooms have contemporary styling. Breakfast brings fruits from the garden (berry compote, apple pancakes), omelette Arnold Bennett. (Page 387)

BROOKS COUNTRY HOUSE
ROSS-ON-WYE
Doubles at £59, a four-poster room from
£99, a three-course dinner for £29…
Gracious country house living is nowhere
more affordable and fun than at Carla and
Andrew Brooks's welcoming Georgian
mansion. All this and wines from the
vineyard. (Page 278)

KILLIANE CASTLE COUNTRY
HOUSE & FARM
DRINAGH
A 17th-century farmhouse grafted on to
a 15th-century castle, in lovely grounds, is
run by the Mernagh family as a wonderful
guest house. Newcomers are welcomed
with home-baked biscuits. Doubles start at
just €120; breakfasts are a treat. (Page 472)

THE CEILIDH PLACE
ULLAPOOL
A night in the bunkhouse, fish and
chips in the café and a glass of Chilean
Sauvignon will set you back £42.15 at
Jean Urquhart's fun music venue and
bookshop-with-rooms. A good bedroom
won't break the bank either. (Page 409)

THE BLACK SWAN
RAVENSTONEDALE
Double rooms start from £95 at Louise
Dinnes's Victorian pub-with-rooms in
an Eden Valley conservation village. It's
ideal for fell walkers and ramblers, with a
comfy lounge and superior pub food; fish
and chips for £12. (Page 271)

THISTLEYHAUGH FARM
LONGHORSLEY
An ideal base for exploring the
Northumberland coast, the Nelless
family's Georgian farmhouse B&B sits
amid their organic livestock farm. Doubles
cost £100, singles from £70, including a
hearty breakfast (Craster kippers, local
sausages, free-range eggs). (Page 217)

AYNSOME MANOR
CARTMEL
Hosts Chris and Andrea Varley's take
great care of guests at their Lake District
manor house. Comfortable rooms start
at under £100, and at night the daily
changing menu of locally sourced fare
costs from £23.95. (Page 137)

NO. 33
HUNSTANTON
Guests arriving at Jeanne Whittome's
stylish B&B are offered afternoon tea and
a discount voucher for sister business
Thornham Deli, which supplies breakfast
bagels, smoked salmon and cream cheese.
Doubles priced from £95, £85 for single
occupancy. (Page 196)

THE OLD RECTORY AT STEWTON
LOUTH
Linda and Alan Palmer are perfect hosts
at their Georgian-style Victorian B&B
swaddled by lawns and mature trees.
Rooms start at £50 for single occupancy,
doubles from £75. A generous breakfast is
served 'within reason, as late as you like'.
(Page 220)

DOLFFANOG FAWR
TYWYN
There are views of lake and mountain
from Alex Yorke and Lorraine Hinkins's
Snowdonia B&B. Rooms (from £90 single,
£110 double) are supplied with smart
toiletries. Breakfast, and a four-course
dinner four nights a week, win plaudits.
(Page 451)

TREREIFE
PENZANCE
The Le Grice family's ancestral home
in parkland is filled with antiques and
portraits but the atmosphere is welcoming.
Each bedroom is named after a romantic
poet; a double can be had for a mere £80.
(Page 263)

The Black Swan, Ravenstonedale

The Pipe and Glass Inn, South Dalton

THE PUNCH BOWL INN
CROSTHWAITE

You can sleep in a four-poster bed made of reclaimed elm at this atmospheric 300-year-old inn in a pretty south Lakeland village inn. The chef makes inventive use of prime Cumbrian produce. Vegetarians have a field day. (Page 152)

BEECH HOUSE & OLIVE BRANCH
CLIPSHAM

Readers write of the fun at this village pub/restaurant, but the food is seriously good. Options include tapas and creative, modern British fare, with fresh produce from the kitchen garden. The pub's bedrooms in Beech House are rather glamorous. (Page 147)

THE OLD COASTGUARD
MOUSEHOLE

Casual chic, a laid-back vibe and local art are the style at this former coastguard's station turned dining pub in a picture-postcard fishing village. Enjoy Cornish produce, clever cooking, foraging walks, yoga weekends and sub-tropical gardens. (Page 234)

THE GREYHOUND INN
LETCOMBE REGIS

Real ale, wine tastings, jazz evenings and quiz nights assure this 18th-century pub of a local following. The friendly staff, superior pub fare and smart rooms supplied with freshly baked biscuits make it a Guide shoo-in. (Page 209)

THE GUNTON ARMS
THORPE MARKET

Venison from the surrounding deer park appears on the daily-changing menus at this extraordinary converted country house near Cromer, crammed with Victorian paintings, vintage novelties and Brit Art. One room has a marble bathroom from Egypt. (Page 315)

THE COLONSAY
COLONSAY

There are quiz nights and live music at the sole hostelry on this remote island. Simple bedrooms have views of hillside and sea, across to neighbouring Jura. A new chef is making waves. Why not come for the annual book festival? (Page 358)

THE BILDESTON CROWN
BILDESTON

Ancient timbers, a roaring fire in winter, alfresco dining in summer, characterful bedrooms (one with antique four-poster), the chef's ways with local produce and an excellent breakfast won over our inspectors in 2018 at this historic coaching inn. (Page 100)

THE PIPE AND GLASS INN
SOUTH DALTON

Beyond a beamed bar serving hand-pulled Yorkshire ales, there are menus for children, for vegetarians, for everyone, in the Michelin-starred restaurant at this friendly former coaching inn. Jazzy, high-spec bedrooms surround a herb garden. (Page 299)

THE CAT INN
WEST HOATHLY

A log fire warms the bar of this popular 16th-century pub, its oak beams hung with pewter mugs. There is pub grub of the highest order, freshly decorated bedrooms, each with a Nespresso coffee machine, a good breakfast. The terrace and herb garden are the cat's whiskers. (Page 333)

GLENELG INN
GLENELG

You can eat in the garden overlooking the Sound of Sleat, or cosily in the bar, at this traditional inn and music venue in a remote and beautiful landscape. The young chef works magic with local produce. (Page 366)

Bedruthan Hotel and Spa, Mawgan Porth

MOONFLEET MANOR
FLEET
Family rooms, all-weather play facilities, beaches for fossil hunts, a crèche, babysitters, a baby pool, flexible meal options, treatment rooms and adult-only dining keep all generations in clover at this country manor house close to Chesil Beach. (Page 175)

FOWEY HALL
FOWEY
'There's Toad Hall…' said the Rat, '…one of the nicest houses in these parts.' Nice, indeed. And with so much laid on for kids at this manor house (said to have been Kenneth Graham's model for Toad Hall), parents can truly relax. (Page 176)

AUGILL CASTLE
KIRKBY STEPHEN
Children thrill to stay in this fantasy castle with its free-and-easy ethos. Books and games, a cinema, flexible meal times, tennis, a playground and 'Little Cooks' school add up to a recipe for a happy holiday. (Page 203)

BEDRUTHAN HOTEL AND SPA
MAWGAN PORTH
Baby and Toddler and Toddler and Time Out breaks are available at this super-family-friendly, Scandi-style seaside hotel. Children's menus and sophisticated dining, a happy, laid-back vibe and plenty of activities keep everyone entertained. (Page 229)

BALLYVOLANE HOUSE
CASTLELYONS
The relaxed, welcoming atmosphere at this Georgian country house on a working farm makes everyone feel instantly at home. Young guests have woods to explore, a tree house to discover, animals to feed, new-laid eggs to collect. (Page 468)

GLENAPP CASTLE
BALLANTRAE
Wellies of all sizes await outdoor types at this Scottish baronial castle on the Ayrshire coast. Take a boat trip with a picnic to see seabirds on Ailsa Craig, roam woodlands, go mountain biking, play tennis, quoits, giant pick-up-sticks. (Page 352)

STAR CASTLE
ST MARY'S
Now here is the real thing, an Elizabethan stone house within star-shaped fortress walls. Tim the boatman offers sea trips. You can swim in the indoor pool, play tennis, go horse riding, hire an electric Scilly Cart or take afternoon tea on the ramparts. (Page 285)

THE GROVE
NARBERTH
A fairy trail beguiles little ones at this Georgian mansion in gardens and woodland. With boules, croquet, bike rides, an Iron Age settlement and sandy beaches, you'll never hear 'I'm bored!' Family suites and early supper are available. (Page 442)

LONGUEVILLE MANOR
ST SAVIOUR
It's one long round of pleasure for kids at this Jersey manor-house hotel, with nature trails and treasure hunts, cookery classes and tennis lessons, beaches and pool. Babysitting and baby listening allow carefree evening dining. (Page 459)

ROSE & CROWN
SNETTISHAM
From bangers and mash and knickerbocker glory, to a walled garden with climbing frame, early suppers, high chairs, cots, crayons and colouring books, children are more than merely tolerated at this fun 14th-century pub. (Page 297)

THE CREGGANS INN
STRACHUR
From a stroll along the Loch Fyne shore, to exploring enchanted Puck's Glen, broad leaf and conifer forests and waterfalls, great walks start at the door of this friendly inn, or are just a short drive away. (Page 401)

THE PEACOCK AT ROWSLEY
ROWSLEY
Whether exploring the estate around medieval Haddon Hall, or tackling more challenging terrain in the Peak District national park, walkers are in their element at Lord and Lady Manners's 17th-century hotel. Ask reception for their walks folder. (Page 280)

FARLAM HALL
BRAMPTON
Thoughtful route guides to local walks have been compiled by the long-time owners of this manor house hotel near the top of the North Pennines and just three miles from coast-to-coast Hadrian's Wall Path. (Page 115)

LEATHES HEAD HOTEL
BORROWDALE
Guests can order a picnic before setting out from this Edwardian country house hotel, perhaps to follow a waymarked path ten miles around Derwentwater, or to climb to the top of Catbells for panoramic views. (Page 107)

TREVALSA COURT
MEVAGISSEY
Steps from the Coastal Path, this friendly small hotel offers a variety of walking and strolling options. Head across country to the Lost Gardens of Heligan – lost no more – and return for a Cornish cream tea. (Page 232)

BRYNIAU GOLAU
BALA
You can take a scenic walk around Bala lake, pick up a family or heritage trail, head for hill or mountain, from this lovely Snowdonia B&B. A good breakfast sets you up; drying facilities await your return. (Page 420)

STELLA MARIS
BALLYCASTLE
You pass a blow hole on the walk to the sea stack of Downpatrick Head, topped with the ruins of a church founded by St Patrick. One of many thrilling forays from this hotel on the Wild Atlantic Way. (Page 464)

TIMBERSTONE
CLEE STANTON
Tea and biscuits await Rover's return to this dog-friendly rural B&B, after a day roaming the blue remembered hills of Shropshire, visiting Ironbridge Gorge, or browsing the specialist food shops in nearby Ludlow. (Page 146)

THE PLOUGH
KELMSCOTT
You can pick up the Thames Path from this welcoming pub-with-rooms in the William Morris heartlands, perhaps to walk to Lechlade, or past a pretty lock-keeper's cottage, for a crafty pint in The Trout at Tadpole Bridge. (Page 200)

DUNKERY BEACON
WOOTTON COURTENAY
From this Edwardian hunting lodge, walkers climb to the top of the eponymous beacon hill, or pick up the Coleridge Way across Exmoor towards Lynmouth or Nether Stowey in the footsteps of the great poet. How romantic is that! (Page 342)

Dunkery Beacon, Wootton Courtenay

The Pig on the Beach, Studland

HAZLITT'S
LONDON

A cluster of Soho Georgian houses here combine as a boutique hotel brimming with wit and studied eccentricity – antiques and curios, oil paintings, throne loos, books, busts, vintage beds. Public rooms are patrolled by Sir Godfrey the cat. (Page 57)

THE OLD RAILWAY STATION
PETWORTH

Just the ticket for train buffs! Guests check in at the former parcels office at this beautiful disused station, sleep in a colonial style bedroom, or a Pullman carriage with Edwardian fittings, take breakfast in the waiting room. (Page 265)

THE PIG ON THE BEACH
STUDLAND

Whimsical touches at this neo-Gothic fantasy include wood carvings from a Portuguese palace, a coat of arms prop from Pirates of the Caribbean. Sleep in a shepherd's hut, a thatched dovecote or a room with a loo with a view. (Page 305)

THE STAR INN
HAROME

There is a piano in room 8 at this estimable restaurant-with-rooms, should you wish to practise the Moonlight Sonata at dead of night. Or pot the black at the snooker table in room 5. Michelin-starred cooking raises more smiles. (Page 184)

THE GEORGE
STAMFORD

The gallows sign no longer hangs across the road from this historic inn, but the old waiting rooms are still marked 'London' and 'York', from its days as a stagecoach stop. Look out for the portrait and walking sticks of England's one-time heaviest man. (Page 302)

ST CUTHBERT'S HOUSE
SEAHOUSES

At breakfast, raise your eyes from your oak-smoked kipper to admire the pillars and old harmonium in the former sanctuary at this deconsecrated Presbyterian church, now an award-winning B&B and music venue. (Page 292)

KNOCKINAAM LODGE
PORTPATRICK

Churchill loved his long, hot baths. Book the room he slept in at this former coastal hunting lodge (where he laid plans for D-Day with Eisenhower), and you can wallow in the very same enamelled concrete tub. (Page 394)

ROUNDWOOD HOUSE
MOUNTRATH

Many hotels have a 'library', sometimes just a token bookshelf, but in the grounds of this Georgian mansion and lovable, idiosyncratic hotel, a galleried library contains a thousand tomes dedicated to the evolution of civilisation. (Page 482)

THE DIAL HOUSE
REEPHAM

More than a thousand weird and wonderful objects are for sale at this Grand-Tour-themed small hotel, eclectically furnished throughout. Sleep in the Raj room; buy a white elephant, enter the Natural History room through a display case door. (Page 272)

LEWTRENCHARD MANOR
LEWDOWN

Renaissance woodwork. An ornate Jacobean plaster ceiling. A Rococo fireplace flanked by putti. The extravagant 19th-century rebuilding of an ancient manor house was the work of squire, parson and prolific writer Sabine Baring-Gould. (Page 210)

GRAVETYE MANOR
EAST GRINSTEAD
Built by ironmaster for his bride, this Elizabethan manor house in lovely gardens laid out by William Robinson is as romantic a venue as you could wish. Exclusive use is available for parties of up to 60, with the wedding breakfast in the glass-walled dining room. (Page 161)

LANGAR HALL
LANGAR
Ceremonies are held in the Indian room, garden room or dining room at this apricot-washed mansion in beautiful grounds in the Vale of Belvoir. Small, informal weddings and partnerships are a speciality. (Page 206)

THE BINGHAM
RICHMOND-UPON-THAMES
You can book the garden and garden rooms, and choose anything from canapés to buffet to barbecue at this romantic riverside hotel. Packages include 'Summer Whirlwind', 'Small and Intimate', and exclusive use. (Page 276)

FISCHER'S AT BASLOW HALL
BASLOW
Readers who spent their wedding night at this stone manor house on the edge of the Chatsworth estate loved it so much that they returned this year for their 12th anniversary. Ceremonies in drawing room or study. (Page 84)

PRESTONFIELD
EDINBURGH
Throw a party in the circular stables ballroom at this 17th-century mansion, or go for something more intimate in the Stuart Room or Italian room. Then how about a night to remember in a silver-leaf sleigh bed in a room with an antique chaise longue and trompe l'oeil drapery? (Page 362)

TEMPLE HOUSE
BALLYMOTE
A family home for centuries, this Georgian mansion has witnessed many splendid wedding celebrations. Vast period rooms and a ruined Knights Templar castle by the lake – imagine those photos – are the icing on the cake. (Page 465)

THE HORN OF PLENTY
TAVISTOCK
The name doesn't lie. There's plenty of good cheer, from falcons to fireworks, for guests at this 19th-century mansion. With four rooms for civil ceremonies, and a host of atmospheric local churches, celebrations can embrace the main house or use a marquee for large parties. (Page 311)

SEAHAM HALL
SEAHAM
Lord Byron married Annabella Milbanke at this Georgian mansion turned spa hotel. The union didn't fare well, but the hotel's wedding packages, named after their brilliant daughter, Ada Lovelace, include everything from use of the ballroom to champagne. (Page 290).

ASSEMBLY HOUSE
NORWICH
You can hire the Grand Hall, the Ballroom, the Music Room, or a less flamboyant space at this landmark Georgian building replete with chandeliers. Best of all, book exclusive use and bag the bridal suite with tester bed. (Page 245)

JESMOND DENE HOUSE
NEWCASTLE UPON TYNE
From the Apartment, hosting ten guests, to the panelled Great Hall for up to 120, from a small supper to a banquet, cakes, flowers, photographers, magicians, all can be arranged at this 19th-century stone mansion in woodland. (Page 241)

Seaham Hall, Seaham

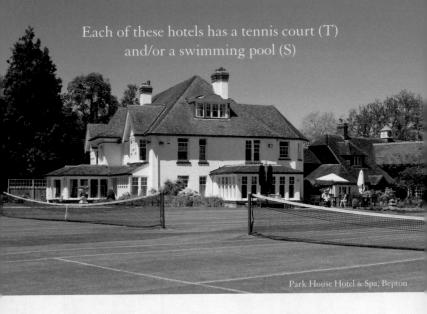

Each of these hotels has a tennis court (T)
and/or a swimming pool (S)

Park House Hotel & Spa, Bepton

ENGLAND
The Elms,
  Abberley (T,S)
Hartwell House & Spa,
  Aylesbury (T,S)
Park House Hotel & Spa,
  Bepton (T,S)
Burgh Island Hotel,
  Bigbury-on-Sea (T,S)
The Blakeney Hotel,
  Blakeney (S)
Widbrook Grange,
  Bradford-on-Avon (S)
Woolley Grange,
  Bradford-on-Avon (S)
The Lygon Arms,
  Broadway (S)
Hell Bay Hotel,
  Bryher (S)
Brockencote Hall,
  Chaddesley Corbett (T)
Tor Cottage,
  Chillaton (S)
Treglos Hotel,
  Constantine Bay (S)

Corse Lawn House,
  Corse Lawn (T,S)
The Rectory Hotel,
  Crudwell (S)
Dart Marina,
  Dartmouth (S)
Old Whyly,
  East Hoathly (T,S)
The Grand Hotel,
  Eastbourne (S)
Starborough Manor,
  Edenbridge (T,S)
Summer Lodge,
  Evershot (T,S)
Moonfleet Manor,
  Fleet (S)
Fowey Hall,
  Fowey (S)
Hambleton Hall,
  Hambleton (T,S)
The Pheasant,
  Harome (S)
Congham Hall,
  King's Lynn (S)
Augill Castle,
  Kirkby Stephen (T)

Lime Wood,
  Lyndhurst (S)
Bedruthan Hotel and Spa,
  Mawgan Porth (T,S)
The Scarlet,
  Mawgan Porth (S)
Mullion Cove Hotel,
  Mullion Cove (S)
Chewton Glen,
  New Milton (T,S)
The Old Rectory,
  Norwich (S)
Askham Hall,
  Penrith (S)
Brooks Country House,
  Ross-on-Wye (S)
Star Castle,
  St Mary's (T,S)
Soar Mill Cove Hotel,
  Salcombe (T,S)
Seaham Hall,
  Seaham (S)
Plumber Manor,
  Sturminster Newton (T)
Cliveden House,
  Taplow (T,S)
Calcot Manor,
  Tetbury (T,S)
The Royal Hotel,
  Ventnor (S)
The Nare,
  Veryan-in-Roseland (T,S)
Gilpin Hotel and Lake House,
  Windermere (S)
Middlethorpe Hall & Spa,
  York (S)

SCOTLAND
Glenapp Castle,
  Ballantrae (T)
Shieldaig Lodge,
  Gairloch (T)
Douneside House,
  Tarland (T,S)

WALES
Trefeddian Hotel,
  Aberdyfi (T,S)
Porth Tocyn,
  Abersoch (T,S)
Gliffaes,
  Crickhowell (T)
Bodysgallen Hall & Spa,
  Llandudno (T,S)
The Lake,
  Llangammarch Wells (T,S)

CHANNEL ISLANDS
The White House,
  Herm (T,S)
The Atlantic Hotel,
  St Brelade (T,S)
Greenhills,
  St Peter (S)
Longueville Manor,
  St Saviour (T,S)

IRELAND
Ballyvolane House,
  Castlelyons (T)
Killiane Castle,
  Drinagh (T)
Castle Leslie,
  Glaslough (T)
Marlfield House,
  Gorey (T)
Rosleague Manor,
  Letterfrack (T)
Currarevagh House,
  Oughterard (T)
Rathmullan House,
  Rathmullan (T,S)
Coopershill,
  Riverstown (T)
Ballymaloe House,
  Shanagarry (T,S)

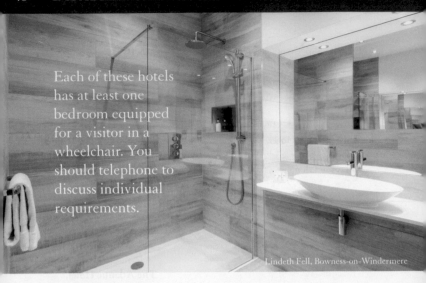

Each of these hotels has at least one bedroom equipped for a visitor in a wheelchair. You should telephone to discuss individual requirements.

Lindeth Fell, Bowness-on-Windermere

LONDON

The Goring

The Zetter

The Zetter Townhouse,
Marylebone

The Zetter Townhouse,
Clerkenwell

ENGLAND

The Elms,
Abberley

The Wentworth,
Aldeburgh

Rothay Manor,
Ambleside

Hartwell House & Spa,
Aylesbury

Red Lion Inn,
Babcary

Barnsley House,
Barnsley

The Cavendish,
Baslow

No. 15 Great Pulteney,
Bath

Park House,
Bepton

The Blakeney Hotel,
Blakeney

The Lord Crewe Arms,
Blanchland

The Crown Hotel,
Blandford Forum

Leathes Head Hotel,
Borrowdale

The Millstream,
Bosham

Lindeth Fell,
Bowness-on-Windermere

Widbrook Grange,
Bradford-on-Avon

Woolley Grange,
Bradford-on-Avon

The White Horse,
Brancaster Staithe

The Mason's Arms,
Branscombe

The Lygon Arms,
Broadway

The Pig in the Forest,
Brockenhurst

Hell Bay Hotel,
Bryher

The Gallivant,
Camber

Pendragon Country House,
Camelford

Blackmore Farm,
Cannington

Brockencote Hall,
Chaddesley Corbett

Crouchers,
Chichester

Captain's Club Hotel,
Christchurch

Kings Head Hotel,
Cirencester

Beech House & Olive Branch,
Clipsham

Treglos Hotel,
Constantine Bay

Hipping Hall,
Cowan Bridge

Clow Beck House,
Croft-on-Tees

Dart Marina,
Dartmouth

Dedham Hall,
Dedham

The Red Lion Freehouse,
East Chisenbury

The Grand Hotel,
Eastbourne

Eckington Manor,
Eckington

Summer Lodge,
Evershot

Lympstone Manor,
Exmouth

The Carpenters Arms,
Felixkirk

Fowey Hall,
Fowey

The Pig at Combe,
Gittisham

Forest Side,
Grasmere

The Pheasant,
Harome

Castle House,
Hereford

Battlesteads,
Hexham

No. 33,
Hunstanton

The Howard Arms,
Ilmington

Congham Hall,
King's Lynn

Augill Castle,
Kirkby Stephen

Northcote,
Langho

Lewtrenchard Manor,
Lewdown

Lime Wood,
Lyndhurst

Sands Hotel,
Margate

The Old Rectory Hotel,
Martinhoe

Bedruthan Hotel and Spa,
Mawgan Porth

The Scarlet,
Mawgan Porth

Hotel Endsleigh,
Milton Abbot

Chewton Glen,
New Milton

Jesmond Dene House,
Newcastle upon Tyne

The Packhorse Inn,
Newmarket

Beechwood Hotel,
North Walsham

The Assembly House,
Norwich

Hart's Hotel,
Nottingham

Old Bank,
Oxford

Old Parsonage,
Oxford

Tebay Services Hotel,
Penrith

The Pig near Bath,
Pensford

The Old Railway Station,
Petworth

The Yorke Arms,
Ramsgill-in-Nidderdale

The Black Swan,
Ravenstonedale

The Coach House at
Middleton Lodge,
Richmond

Brooks Country House,
Ross-on-Wye

Boskerris Hotel,
St Ives

Idle Rocks,
St Mawes

Soar Mill Cove Hotel,
Salcombe

Seaham Hall,
Seaham

St Cuthbert's House,
Seahouses

La Fleur de Lys,
Shaftesbury

Brocco on the Park,
Sheffield

Hotel Riviera,
Sidmouth

The Rose & Crown,
Snettisham

The Pipe and Glass Inn,
South Dalton

The Crown,
Stoke by Nayland

Plumber Manor,
Sturminster Newton

The Royal Oak,
Swallowcliffe

Cliveden House,
Taplow

The Horn of Plenty,
Tavistock

Calcot Manor,
Tetbury

The Hare and Hounds,
Tetbury

The Gunton Arms,
Thorpe Market

Briarfields,
Titchwell

Titchwell Manor,
Titchwell
Tuddenham Mill,
Tuddenham
The Royal Hotel,
Ventnor
The Nare,
Veryan-in-Roseland
The Inn at West End,
West End
The Crescent Turner Hotel,
Whitstable
Gilpin Hotel and Lake House,
Windermere
The George,
Yarmouth
Middlethorpe Hall & Spa,
York

SCOTLAND

Loch Melfort Hotel,
Arduaine
Boath House,
Auldearn
Glenapp Castle,
Ballantrae
Coul House,
Contin
The Three Chimneys and The House Over-By,
Dunvegan
Prestonfield,
Edinburgh
The Raeburn,
Edinburgh
The Glenelg Inn,
Glenelg
Ballathie House,
Kinclaven
Kylesku Hotel,
Kylesku
Langass Lodge,
Locheport
The Albannach,
Lochinver
The Peat Inn,
Peat Inn
Craigatin House and Courtyard,
Pitlochry
The Green Park,
Pitlochry
Viewfield House,
Portree
Kinloch Lodge,
Sleat
The Inn at Loch Tummel,
Strathtummel
Douneside House,
Tarland

Tiroran House,
Tiroran

WALES

Harbourmaster Hotel,
Aberaeron
Trefeddian Hotel,
Aberdyfi
The Hardwick,
Abergavenny
Coes Faen,
Barmouth
The Bull,
Beaumaris
Gliffaes,
Crickhowell
Penbontbren,
Glynarthen
Tyddyn Llan,
Llandrillo
Bodysgallen Hall & Spa,
Llandudno
The Lake,
Llangammarch Wells
The Grove,
Narberth
Restaurant James Sommerin,
Penarth
Twr y Felin Hotel,
St David
St Brides Spa Hotel,
Saundersfoot

CHANNEL ISLANDS

Greenhills,
St Peter

IRELAND

The Mustard Seed at Echo Lodge,
Ballingarry
Stella Maris,
Ballycastle
Gregans Castle Hotel,
Ballyvaughan
The Quay House,
Clifden
Castle Leslie,
Glaslough
Brook Lane Hotel,
Kenmare
No.1 Pery Square,
Limerick
Viewmount House,
Longford
Rathmullan House,
Rathmullan
Ballymaloe House,
Shanagarry

LONDON

The Thames at sunset

LONDON

Map 2:D4

ARTIST RESIDENCE LONDON

♛ Previous César winner

In an area of white stucco terraces, a Victorian former pub relives as a hip hotel for people who know what is good and know what they like. One of four (see index) created by Charlotte and Justin Salisbury, it is 'quirky and full of character', with upcycled materials and vintage furniture used to stylish effect. From first-floor 'small' doubles to suites, rooms have air conditioning, well-stocked minibar, a Roberts radio; the best have an espresso machine. The Loft has a sitting area, French-style bath and walk-in shower, while the Art Deco-style Club Suite has leather club armchairs, velvet sofa, freestanding roll-top bath and walk-in shower. 'The details are well thought through', from lighting, to plug sockets, to storage. There is a basement cocktail bar, while, at street level, the Cambridge Street Kitchen dispenses food all day. Breakfast choices include spiced porridge, avocado toast, freshly baked pastries. For a light lunch, perhaps a grass-fed burger, or spiced cauliflower with bulgur wheat, pomegranate, raisins and minted yogurt. At night, Elliot Miller cooks such dishes as halibut, mussels, pak choi, salty fingers, coconut and lemongrass broth.

52 Cambridge Street
London
SW1V 4QQ

T: 020 3019 8610
E: london@artistresidence.co.uk
W: www.artistresidence.co.uk/
  our-hotels/london/

BEDROOMS: 10. 2 suites.
OPEN: all year.
FACILITIES: cocktail bar, restaurant, club room lounge, games/private dining room, small 'hidden' garden, free Wi-Fi, in-room TV (Freeview), unsuitable for disabled.
BACKGROUND MUSIC: in public areas.
LOCATION: Pimlico, underground Pimlico.
CHILDREN: all ages welcomed, cot available for larger rooms, no extra beds for children sharing.
DOGS: only allowed in the restaurant.
CREDIT CARDS: Amex, MasterCard, Visa.
PRICES: [2018] room £190–£450. Cooked breakfast from £7, full English £12, à la carte £40. 1-night bookings sometimes refused weekends.

SEE ALSO SHORTLIST

LONDON

Map 2:D4

THE CAPITAL

With its classic red brick facade, smartly suited doormen and Knightsbridge location, the hotel has offered the same 'splendid', intimate hospitality for almost half a century. Managed by Joanne Taylor-Stagg (the Levin family no longer has any connection with the hotel), its 'professional but unstuffy, helpful' staff go the extra mile. 'The top-hatted doorman ran out on the street, hailed a taxi and rode it back to hold the door open for us. What service!' Generally spacious rooms – small doubles suit a single guest – blend antiques with elegant fabrics, but one of The Capital's trump cards is its restaurant, frequented by royals. New head chef Andrew Sawyer works alongside Nathan Outlaw to create seasonal seafood menus including chilli-cured monkfish; brill, Porthilly sauce and cabbage: 'We could appreciate why it has a Michelin star.' Breakfast, including 'eggs Benedict with wonderfully dark-orange egg yolk', won equal plaudits, as did afternoon tea's colour-coded sandwiches: 'green bread for cucumber, pink for smoked salmon'. For more casual dining, try sister hotel The Levin, next door (see entry). (Jill and Mike Bennett)

22–24 Basil Street
London
SW3 1AT

T: 020 7589 5171
E: reservations@capitalhotel.co.uk
W: www.capitalhotel.co.uk

BEDROOMS: 49. 9 suites.
OPEN: all year, restaurant closed Sun.
FACILITIES: lift, sitting room, bar, restaurant, free Wi-Fi, in-room TV (Sky), access to nearby health club/spa, restaurant wheelchair accessible.
BACKGROUND MUSIC: in public areas.
LOCATION: central, underground Knightsbridge, private car park.
CHILDREN: all ages welcomed.
DOGS: not allowed.
CREDIT CARDS: all major cards.
PRICES: [2018] per room B&B from £340, D,B&B from £480. Set lunch menus £33–£39, à la carte £69 (plus 12½% discretionary service charge).

SEE ALSO SHORTLIST

LONDON

Map 2:D4

DURRANTS

♔ Previous César winner

Close to the hurly-burly of Marylebone High Street, the Miller family's hotel 'remains a well-polished haven of rather eccentric good care'. Its walls host gilt-framed paintings and 'gleaming brass rails', chambermaids wear 'neat period uniform', there are 'quiet corners where one can read in peace'. 'It is solid, respectable, unchanging,' writes a returning visitor in 2018. Of course, over the years, there have been tweaks within the Georgian walls. The refurbished 'comfortable' bedrooms display classical and antique furniture, harmonious prints; each has a hand-made bed, a flat-screen television, high-end toiletries in the neat bathroom. The quietest overlook a mews at the rear. In the wood-panelled dining room, the 'only music is the contented murmur of diners. The rare roast beef, carved from a trolley, was some of the best I have enjoyed anywhere.' The 'excellent' breakfast offers good healthy options and cooked fare including a 'cheese omelette, light and airy'. One reader's room had a faulty cistern and loo seat; 'I forgave them because they are courteous, welcoming, convenient, and slightly batty.' (Robert Cooper, Keith Salway, and others)

26–32 George Street
London
W1H 5BJ

T: 020 7935 8131
E: enquiries@durrantshotel.co.uk
W: www.durrantshotel.co.uk

BEDROOMS: 92. 7 on ground floor.
OPEN: all year, restaurant closed 25 Dec evening.
FACILITIES: lifts, bar, restaurant, lounge, function rooms, free Wi-Fi, in-room TV (Freeview), use of nearby fitness club, public areas wheelchair accessible, no adapted toilet.
BACKGROUND MUSIC: none.
LOCATION: off Oxford Street, underground Bond Street, Baker Street.
CHILDREN: all ages welcomed.
DOGS: allowed in George bar.
CREDIT CARDS: Amex, MasterCard, Visa.
PRICES: [2018] per room B&B single from £165, double from £250. Set menu £24, à la carte £45.

SEE ALSO SHORTLIST

LONDON

Map 2:D4

THE GORING

A royal warrant and a Michelin star are but two accolades held by London's last grand Edwardian hotel, still run by the family that built it. Fourth-generation owner Jeremy Goring has edged it into the 21st century, but it retains the traditional values of a golden age. 'Guests are politely reminded that mobile phones and laptops are not welcome in the public rooms,' writes a reader this year. A vintage lift with 'highly polished brass plates' bears guests up to luxurious bedrooms, some with silk-lined walls and views of the one-acre garden, an oasis so close to Buckingham Palace. Shoes left out overnight were returned 'in a stout and elegant cardboard box, every pair individually wrapped in tissue paper'. The dining room, designed by David Linley, lit at night by Swarovski chandeliers, was, oddly, one cold day, rather chilly. Here chef Shay Cooper's Michelin-starred dishes showcase fine British produce, perhaps Cornish cod, Jersey Royals, asparagus, peas, cockle and bacon velouté; aged sirloin of beef, pickled red onions, smoked cauliflower, wild garlic oil. Breakfast has 'full waiter service with not a self-service counter in sight'. (Harry and Annette Medcalf)

15 Beeston Place
London
SW1W 0JW

T: 020 7396 9000
E: reception@thegoring.com
W: www.thegoring.com

BEDROOMS: 69. 2 suitable for disabled.
OPEN: all year.
FACILITIES: lifts, lounge, bar, restaurant, private dining rooms, free Wi-Fi, in-room TV (Sky), civil wedding licence, business centre, fitness room, veranda, 1-acre garden (croquet), public rooms wheelchair accessible, adapted toilet.
BACKGROUND MUSIC: none.
LOCATION: Belgravia, mews parking, underground Victoria.
CHILDREN: all ages welcomed.
DOGS: only assistance dogs allowed.
CREDIT CARDS: all major cards.
PRICES: [2018] B&B single from £455, double from £485, D,B&B double from £520. À la carte (3 courses) from £64, pre-theatre dinner (2 courses) £37.

SEE ALSO SHORTLIST

LONDON

THE GRAZING GOAT

In one of those atmospheric London entities – a street that feels like a village in the heart of the capital – this hip pub-with-rooms assumes the role of community hub, yet has 'a great location', within minutes of frenetic Oxford Street. Large French doors welcome visitors into a room with an exposed steel joist, open fireplaces and mounted antlers. There, and one floor up in the dining room, all pale wood panelling and contemporary earth tones, chef Leigh Hartnett's 'largish' all-day menu offers 'good' seasonal British gastropub fare, perhaps Cardington grass-fed rib-eye, truffle and Parmesan fries, Béarnaise sauce. The pub downstairs may be busy, but upstairs, calm reigns in the 'thoughtfully furnished' bedrooms, where a rustic yet chic mood is evoked in coir mats, tastefully muted hues, beams and vintage prints. There are posh teas, a cafetière with ground coffee, filtered water, free-range hangers and an 'excellent' bathroom, with 'especially good' Aesop toiletries. 'We had rooftop views from our beautiful top-floor room.' At breakfast, charged separately, perhaps porridge, coconut, chia seeds, apple compote; smoked ham hock, poached egg. The Orange, in Pimlico, is a sister inn (see entry).

6 New Quebec Street
London
W1H 7RQ

T: 020 7724 7243
E: reservations@thegrazinggoat.
co.uk
W: www.thegrazinggoat.co.uk

BEDROOMS: 8.
OPEN: all year.
FACILITIES: bar, dining room, patio, free Wi-Fi, in-room TV, bar wheelchair accessible.
BACKGROUND MUSIC: all day in bar.
LOCATION: central, underground Marble Arch.
CHILDREN: all ages welcomed.
DOGS: allowed in public rooms, not in bedrooms.
CREDIT CARDS: Amex, MasterCard, Visa.
PRICES: [2018] room £210–£250. À la carte £40, breakfast mains from £8.

SEE ALSO SHORTLIST

LONDON

Map 2:D4

HAZLITT'S

'Exquisitely refurbished.' Peter McKay and
Douglas Blain have cultivated 'an oasis of
civilisation' within a decadent cluster of Soho's
Georgian houses. At least one had been a
depressed boarding house where lived and died
essayist William Hazlitt, who lends his name. It
is now alive with whimsical curios, proper china
for afternoon tea and Sir Godfrey, the resident
cat. His namesake would no doubt have savoured
the honesty bar's locally made gin. Elsewhere, the
sloping floors and throne loos have been retained,
but electricity replaces most of the candles.
Sumptuous bedrooms and suites, all antiques and
period artwork, revel in the unexpected; not the
lovely but often-seen roll-top baths or romantic
ornate beds, but the gilt-framed plasma TV, a
Jacobean love seat disguising a loo, a spring-
loaded dressing table. Rooms at the front have
triple-glazed windows; some lighter sleepers
may prefer a rear room. Twenty-four-hour room
service with pastas, deli baguettes and light bites,
includes breakfast, as lavish as one likes. For
everything else, the steakhouses, vegan ice-cream
parlours, and the stages of Soho are steps away.
(See also The Rookery, main entry, and Batty
Langley's, Shortlist.)

6 Frith Street
London
W1D 3JA

T: 020 7434 1771
E: reservations@hazlitts.co.uk
W: www.hazlittshotel.com

BEDROOMS: 30. 2 on ground floor.
OPEN: all year.
FACILITIES: lift, library, private
lounge/meeting room, free Wi-Fi,
in-room TV (Sky), public rooms
wheelchair accessible, adapted toilet.
BACKGROUND MUSIC: none.
LOCATION: centre of Soho,
underground Tottenham Court
Road, Leicester Square.
CHILDREN: all ages welcomed.
DOGS: not allowed.
CREDIT CARDS: Amex, Mastercard,
Visa.
PRICES: [2018] per room B&B from
£288, D,B&B from £338. À la carte
£25.

SEE ALSO SHORTLIST

LONDON

Map 2:D4

THE LEVIN

Location, location, location; the small but
perfectly formed Levin is just a credit card toss
from Harrods, close to the designer stores and
cultural hubs of Knightsbridge and a stroll
from the green lungs of Hyde Park. Guests laud
the accommodating, knowledgeable service,
overseen by general manager Joanne Taylor-
Stagg, who also runs the larger luxurious sibling,
The Capital, a couple of doors away (see entry).
They also praise the stylish interiors, lurking
behind the red brick facade with echoes of a
New York town house, from the pale duck
egg blue lobby with Art Nouveau flourishes
to the striking light installation plunging
five floors through the stairwell. Rooms mix
crisp yet warm contemporary interiors with
Designers Guild fabrics, marble bathrooms and
Nespresso machines; light-washed junior suites
overlook Basil Street with sofa beds for children,
while higher and rear rooms may be quieter.
Continental breakfast is served in the lobby –
more significant options await at The Capital
– while the bright yet discreet basement bistro
offers informal all-day dining, perhaps spinach,
blue cheese and red onion frittata, or chicken
and leek pie.

28 Basil Street
London
SW3 1AS

T: 020 7589 6286
E: reservations@thelevinhotel.co.uk
W: www.thelevinhotel.co.uk

BEDROOMS: 12.
OPEN: all year.
FACILITIES: lobby, library, bar/
brasserie, free Wi-Fi, in-room TV
(Sky), access to nearby health club/
spa, unsuitable for disabled.
BACKGROUND MUSIC: in restaurant
and lobby.
LOCATION: central, underground
Knightsbridge.
CHILDREN: all ages welcomed.
DOGS: only guide dogs allowed.
CREDIT CARDS: all major cards.
PRICES: [2018] per room B&B
(continental) from £277. À la
carte £25.

SEE ALSO SHORTLIST

LONDON

Map 2:D4

NUMBER SIXTEEN

♀ Previous César winner

Close to the designer names of Fulham Road and museums of South Kensington, this 'conveniently situated' accommodation is a 'home-away-from-home' with 'helpful, courteous staff'. One of Tim and Kit Kemp's Firmdale group of relaxed boutique hotels, its classic white stucco facade gives few clues to the bold yet harmonious interiors within. The bedrooms, many washed with light through large period windows, sport fresh, modern design including colourful padded headboards, writing desks, and granite and oak bathrooms, supplied with house toiletries and robes. Some rooms have stacked bookshelves, antique furnishings, or open on to a wrought iron balcony. Downstairs two drawing rooms, one evoking winter, the other summer, have striking prints and vast sofas, leading in to an airy, high-ceilinged Orangery with hand-picked artwork. Beyond, a zen-like garden contains a slate sculpture, mosaics and a fish pond planted with water lilies. Afternoon tea defies its name by being served all day, while a concise lunch and supper menu offers the likes of stone bass, garlic and chilli kale, parsley butter. Breakfast brings a buffet and cooked options, either in-room or in the Orangery.

16 Sumner Place
London
SW7 3EG

T: 020 7589 5232
E: sixteen@firmdale.com
W: www.firmdalehotels.com/hotels/london/number-sixteen/

BEDROOMS: 41. 1 on ground floor.
OPEN: all year.
FACILITIES: drawing room, library, conservatory, free Wi-Fi, in-room TV (Sky), civil wedding licence, garden.
BACKGROUND MUSIC: in library.
LOCATION: Kensington, underground South Kensington.
CHILDREN: all ages welcomed.
DOGS: small dogs sometimes allowed (phone to discuss).
CREDIT CARDS: Amex, MasterCard, Visa.
PRICES: [2018] B&B £220–£540, room only single from £180, double from £276. Continental breakfast £18, à la carte from £25.

SEE ALSO SHORTLIST

LONDON

Map 2:D4

THE ORANGE

'An informal alternative' to Pimlico's pricey
traditional hotels, The Orange is more like
staying above a local pub – albeit a classy,
artfully distressed local with an upmarket
clientele. Sloane Square is just a five-minute
walk away. In the ground floor's spacious bar
– 'surprisingly busy even on a Monday night' –
exposed wood abounds: in the window frames,
furniture and ceiling timbers, alongside muted
hues, vintage posters. There are over 30 wines by
the glass, local craft beers. Here, and one floor
up, in the light, airy dining room with views of
Orange Square, the 'well-presented' seasonal
modern menu (British ingredients, European
flourishes) includes such dishes as poached chalk
stream trout, brown crab fritters, seaweed, sorrel
hollandaise. Rising still further up narrow stairs,
the 'beautifully crafted' top-floor bedrooms have
calming earth tones, high ceilings, king-size
beds and bathrooms in marble and limed oak.
'We had the largest, on the corner overlooking
Pimlico Road. There was some (inevitable)
noise.' Breakfast, in the bar, brings continental
and cooked options. There is a small rustic roof
terrace. The family-run Cubitt House group
also own The Grazing Goat, London (see entry).

37 Pimlico Road
London
SW1W 8NE

T: 020 7881 9844
E: reservations@theorange.co.uk
W: theorange.co.uk

BEDROOMS: 4.
OPEN: all year.
FACILITIES: restaurant, 2 bars, private
dining rooms, free Wi-Fi, in-room
TV.
BACKGROUND MUSIC: in public areas.
LOCATION: Pimlico, underground
Sloane Square.
CHILDREN: all ages welcomed.
DOGS: not allowed.
CREDIT CARDS: Amex, MasterCard,
Visa.
PRICES: [2018] per room B&B
£205–£240. À la carte £40.

SEE ALSO SHORTLIST

LONDON

Map 2:D4

PORTOBELLO HOTEL

It may have put its years of rock'n'roll excess behind it, but this hotel on 'an elegant street in Notting Hill' has lost none of its eclectic charm. Occupying two adjoining classical mansions, it was acquired in 2014 by the Curious group of hotels (see Guide website, Canal House, Amsterdam), who retained and polished its quirky elements. All bedrooms have air conditioning, a minibar, espresso machine, smart smellies. 'Beautifully coloured' attic box rooms are presented as singles (in a previous less tasteful incarnation, one inspired a screenwriter to pen a gory scene in the movie Alien), while 'cosy' doubles have exotic murals; some have French windows, a wrought iron balcony over the private garden, an in-room bath. Best are the 'splendid' rooms, with bathtub and separate shower, a large sitting area, garden views, but most famous are the 'signature' category, one with a four-poster from Hampton Court Palace, another with a Victorian bathing machine. There is a magnificent drawing room, a well-stocked honesty bar. Breakfast brings porridge, muesli, cold meats and cheeses, smoked salmon, hot dishes at extra charge, served on pretty, mismatched china from Portobello Road market.

22 Stanley Gardens
London
W11 2NG

T: 020 7727 2777
E: stay@portobellohotel.com
W: www.portobellohotel.com

BEDROOMS: 21.
OPEN: all year.
FACILITIES: lift, drawing room/breakfast room with honesty bar, free Wi-Fi, in-room TV, unsuitable for disabled.
BACKGROUND MUSIC: 'chill-out' in drawing room.
LOCATION: Notting Hill, underground Notting Hill Gate.
CHILDREN: not under 16.
DOGS: not allowed.
CREDIT CARDS: Amex, MasterCard, Visa.
PRICES: [2018] per room B&B (continental) single from £195, double £295–£444. Cooked breakfast £6–£10.

SEE ALSO SHORTLIST

LONDON

Map 2:D4

THE ROOKERY

Along a narrow lane, a lamb-chop toss from
Smithfield market, Clerkenwell's hubbub
surrenders to the 'club-like' calm of Peter McKay
and Douglas Blain's tumble of 18th-century
houses. The self-proclaimed 'old buffoons' are
also responsible for Hazlitt's (see entry) and Batty
Langley's (see Shortlist), so they are modest as
well as talented hoteliers. The interconnected
properties sport antique furniture, wood panelling
and stone flags; gilt-framed mirrors sit alongside
Turneresque landscapes and heritage paint tones.
Each air-conditioned room is named after a
former raffish resident. There are 17th-century
carved oak beds, period four-posters, heavy silk
curtains and vintage shutters. The two-storey
penthouse has a sitting room beneath a 40-foot
spire. Even the most authentic restoration takes a
few liberties, however. The bathrooms – unheard
of in most Georgian houses – are 'immaculate',
with 'throne loos', roll-top baths and that staple
of an 18th-century fop, fine toiletries. There's an
honesty bar in the Conservatory, and room-service
menu, including an extensive breakfast. Several
decent restaurants lurk nearby, frequented by city
types. The days when a rookery was slang for an
urban slum are long gone.

12 Peter's Lane
London
EC1M 6DS

T: 020 7336 0931
E: reservations@rookery.co.uk
W: www.rookeryhotel.com

BEDROOMS: 33. 1 on ground floor.
OPEN: all year.
FACILITIES: conservatory lounge,
meeting rooms, free Wi-Fi, in-room
TV (Sky), small patio garden,
unsuitable for disabled.
BACKGROUND MUSIC: none.
LOCATION: Clerkenwell,
underground Farringdon, Barbican.
CHILDREN: all ages welcomed.
DOGS: not allowed.
CREDIT CARDS: Amex, MasterCard,
Visa.
PRICES: [2018] per room B&B from
£170. À la carte (from limited room-
service menu) £28.

SEE ALSO SHORTLIST

LONDON

Map 2:D4

SAN DOMENICO HOUSE

A step across the threshold transports visitors from London's busy centre to the luxury of an Italian palazzo. The Pugliese owners, the Melpignano family, have converted a couple of Chelsea's Victorian red brick-and-stone town houses into a lavishly styled hotel that prizes tranquillity and comfort. 'Charming staff could not have been more helpful' for one reader's 'delightful stay'. The interiors played their part too, with a marbled lobby leading into a refined world of ornate fireplaces and antiques, oil paintings and gilt-framed mirrors, ormolu and putti. Grand bedrooms, individually designed, have rich fabrics, eclectic antiques and spoiling toiletries in a marble bathroom; each has air conditioning; several have a balcony or terrace. Grander rooms might have a mezzanine seating area; a bespoke four-poster bed; a walk-in wardrobe. The day starts with freshly squeezed orange juice and good pastries – a morning ritual that can be moved out to the terrace on clement days. There is plenty on the doorstep to tempt guests – the Royal Court Theatre, bustling King's Road, many restaurants – but expansive room-service menus offer a serene alternative. More reports, please.

29–31 Draycott Place
London
SW3 2SH

T: 020 7581 5757
E: info@sandomenicohouse.com
W: www.sandomenicohouse.com

BEDROOMS: 19.
OPEN: all year.
FACILITIES: lounge, breakfast room, roof terrace, free Wi-Fi, in-room TV (Freeview), unsuitable for disabled.
BACKGROUND MUSIC: in lounge and breakfast room.
LOCATION: Chelsea, underground Sloane Square.
CHILDREN: all ages welcomed.
DOGS: not allowed.
CREDIT CARDS: all major cards.
PRICES: [2018] room from £255. Breakfast from £18.

SEE ALSO SHORTLIST

LONDON

Map 2:D4

THE VICTORIA

'Convenient for Heathrow,' wrote readers flying from Australia. They so 'loved the feel' of this gastropub with rooms half a mile from Richmond Park, that they were planning a return visit. Part of chef/owner Paul Merrett's small Jolly Fine Pubs group, it is as jolly as it is fine, family-friendly and relaxed. Mr Merrett is passionate about food ethics, and every Monday the pub goes vegetarian, from breakfast through to night – although every day brings interesting veggie options. An imaginative bar menu includes such choices as vegetable spring rolls; a Moroccan spiced lamb burger; steak, bacon and ale pie. From the à la carte menu: peppered thighs of corn-fed chicken, crispy new potatoes, tomato and green olive dressing; butternut squash, roasted pepper and apricot tagine, couscous, smashed avocado, toasted pitta. Beyond the conservatory dining room the walled garden's outdoor kitchen hosts summertime grills. Smart contemporary bedrooms, in 'cool shades of lilac, biscuit and sea green', have an espresso machine, home-baked biscuits, mineral water. The room price includes a 'great' continental breakfast, or a cooked one, perhaps a Lincolnshire sausage bap; smoked salmon; eggs Benedict with Serrano ham. (GP)

10 West Temple Sheen
London
SW14 7RT

T: 020 8876 4238
E: reservations@victoriasheen.co.uk
W: victoriasheen.co.uk

BEDROOMS: 7. 3 on ground floor.
OPEN: all year.
FACILITIES: bar, lounge, restaurant, free Wi-Fi, in-room TV, garden, play area, unsuitable for disabled.
BACKGROUND MUSIC: in pub and dining room, occasional live music events.
LOCATION: Mortlake, 10 mins' walk from Waterloo/Clapham Jct, car park.
CHILDREN: all ages welcomed.
DOGS: allowed in pub and garden.
CREDIT CARDS: MasterCard, Visa.
PRICES: [2018] per room B&B £135 (continental breakfast), £140 (cooked). À la carte £33 (plus discretionary 12½% service charge).

SEE ALSO SHORTLIST

LONDON

Map 2:D4

THE ZETTER

Handy for the Square Mile and the West End, this hip hotel conversion of a Victorian warehouse, in its 15th year, is on its best form yet. Rooftop studios, with oak flooring, private patio and panoramic city views, have been refurbished in the past year. The best deluxe rooftop suites have an alfresco bath. 'Reimagined' furniture draws inspiration from the building heritage (just reimagine!). All bedrooms have mood lighting, an honesty tray, Penguin paperbacks, individually controlled air conditioning, a rain-dance shower, smart toiletries, 24-hour room service. For children there are colouring books and crayons, mini-bathrobes. The atmosphere at ground level is warm and inclusive, with food and drink served all day. Breakfast choices include brioche, kippers, poached egg on avocado toast. At lunch maybe a club sandwich or Zetter burger. At dinner, chef Ben Boeynaems's 'surprisingly good-value, three-course menus include such dishes as Dingley Dell pork chop, fermented turnip, cime di rapa, black truffle; pan-roasted Cornish cod, wakame potatoes, creamed mussels, sea herbs. Sister Townhouse hotels are across the square and in Marylebone (see next two entries).

25% DISCOUNT VOUCHERS

St John's Square
London
EC1M 5RJ

T: 020 7324 4444
E: info@thezetter.com
W: www.thezetter.com

BEDROOMS: 59. 2 suitable for disabled.
OPEN: all year.
FACILITIES: 2 lifts, atrium, bar/restaurant, terrace (alfresco dining) free Wi-Fi, in-room TV (Freeview, some with Smart TV), in-room spa treatments, reduced rates at local gym, bicycles to borrow. NCP 5 mins' walk, public areas wheelchair accessible, adapted toilet.
BACKGROUND MUSIC: in bar and restaurant.
LOCATION: Clerkenwell, NCP garage 5 mins' walk, underground Farringdon.
CHILDREN: all ages welcomed.
DOGS: only guide dogs allowed.
CREDIT CARDS: Amex, MasterCard, Visa.
PRICES: [2018] room £150–£558. Breakfast buffet £15.50, full English £12, à la carte £35.

SEE ALSO SHORTLIST

LONDON
Map 2:D4

THE ZETTER TOWNHOUSE CLERKENWELL

♥ Previous César winner

A theatrical verve and 'exceptionally nice staff' at this Clerkenwell Georgian town house have visitors 'raving about it'. It stands, 'spotlessly clean', a mere cobbled square away from the original Zetter (see previous entry). The town house is styled as the eclectic private home of a pleasantly dotty Great-Aunt Wilhelmina. In the apothecary-style bar, her favourite gin cocktails are crafted by a resident mixologist, using tinctures and home-made cordials. Her front room is a jumble of winged and button-backed armchairs, knick-knacks, a parasol-wielding cat, oil paintings; a 'brilliantly quirky' feast for the eyes. This year saw the launch of afternoon tea with the great-aunt joined by Uncle Seymour, who offers heartier treats (truffled sausage roll, devilled eggs) to compliment Wilhelmina's dainty finger sandwiches, freshly baked scones and frilly vanilla choux. At dinner, the neighbourhood has plenty of popular options. The bedrooms, equally eccentric, have welcoming comforts: stacks of books, fluffy robes and slippers, hot-water bottles in hand-knitted covers; a 'proper cascade shower', quality toiletries in the bathroom. Breakfast is served in the lounge. (PM)

49–50 St John's Square
London
EC1V 4JJ

T: 020 7324 4567
E: reservations@thezetter.com
W: www.thezettertownhouse.com/clerkenwell

BEDROOMS: 13. 1 suitable for disabled.
OPEN: all year.
FACILITIES: cocktail lounge, private dining room, games room, free Wi-Fi, in-room TV (terrestrial).
BACKGROUND MUSIC: all day in cocktail lounge.
LOCATION: Clerkenwell, underground Farringdon.
CHILDREN: all ages welcomed.
DOGS: assistance dogs only.
CREDIT CARDS: Amex, MasterCard, Visa.
PRICES: [2018] room £258–£582. Continental breakfast Mon–Fri £15; cooked breakfast delivered by room service Sat, Sun, £10.50. À la carte £35.

SEE ALSO SHORTLIST

LONDON

Map 2:D4

THE ZETTER TOWNHOUSE MARYLEBONE

This delightful 'dotty' hotel was once home to that Victorian purveyor of nonsense verse Edward Lear. It is today the domain of 'wicked Uncle Seymour', a character dreamed up by owners Mark Sainsbury and Michael Benyan, and no doubt a pal of the Pobble who had no toes. Guests suspend disbelief as they settle in for afternoon tea or cocktails in Seymour's Parlour, with its leather sofas, red-painted walls crammed with artwork, clocks and trophies from Seymour's Grand Tour. The third in the Zetter stable (see entries for The Zetter and the Zetter Townhouse Clerkenwell), it has 'a decidedly masculine feel'. It all sounds bonkers, but everything has been cleverly thought out for guests' comfort and pleasure. Bedrooms, with monsoon showers (walk-in or over a bath), have a minibar, ground coffee, organic teas, bathrobes, slippers, hot-water bottles, novels... A rooftop apartment has a terrace and an open-air bath. There are exotic bespoke cocktails like Uncle Seymour's Tea, sharing boards and snacks – a pork pie with home-made piccalilli, Scotch egg, goat's cheese toastie. Breakfast brings a continental spread, organic porridge, smoked salmon, the full English.

25% DISCOUNT VOUCHERS

28–30 Seymour Street
London
W1H 7JB

T: 020 7324 4544
E: reservations@thezetter.com
W: www.thezettertownhouse.com
/marylebone

BEDROOMS: 24. 2 suitable for disabled.
OPEN: all year.
FACILITIES: lift, cocktail lounge/restaurant, free Wi-Fi, in-room TV (terrestrial).
BACKGROUND MUSIC: all day in cocktail lounge.
LOCATION: central, underground Marble Arch.
CHILDREN: all ages welcomed.
DOGS: only guide dogs allowed.
CREDIT CARDS: Amex, MasterCard, Visa.
PRICES: [2018] room B&B £270–£882. Continental buffet £15.50, full English £16, à la carte £35.

SEE ALSO SHORTLIST

ENGLAND

Cranborne Chase, Dorset

ABBERLEY Worcestershire

Map 3:C5

THE ELMS

NEW

'Very enjoyable; a place for relaxing weekends and special occasions,' say Guide inspectors of the 'beautifully proportioned Queen Anne mansion in spacious grounds'. The Elms, under the new ownership of Tim Jenkins, has a 'wow factor entrance: an impressive hall with large case clock, warming fire and grand staircase; at the top a stunning stained glass half-dome'. Happily it's style with substance and 'young, friendly staff on top of things'. Our 'five-star' arrival included 'a chatty receptionist greeting, luggage carried upstairs' and George the cat; 'très soigné, he wanders the corridors checking on the cleaners'. The 'vast' room, Apricot, had 'solid, old brown furniture, two pink armchairs and good bedside lamps' and 'a big outlook over the croquet lawn'; the bathroom had an over-bath shower and 'plenty of space for toiletries'. There's a 'superb' bar – 'rather clubby with open fire, old books and interesting objects' – while chef John Brandon's 'inventive, temptingly presented' dinner included Iberico pork, apple and parsnips with cabbage and bacon. The 'enjoyable breakfast had a huge variety of cooked choices with kippers, vegetarian, carb-free and detox dishes'.

Stockton Road
Abberley
WR6 6AT

T: 01299 896666
E: info@theelmshotel.co.uk
W: www.theelmshotel.co.uk

BEDROOMS: 23. 6 within coach house annexe, 1 suitable for disabled.
OPEN: all year.
FACILITIES: drawing room, bar, café, dining room, free Wi-Fi, in-room TV (Freeview), civil wedding licence, spa, swimming pool (12-metre), 10-acre gardens (tennis court, croquet lawn).
BACKGROUND MUSIC: all day in front hall, bar, café and spa, restaurant during opening hours.
LOCATION: 11 miles SW of Kidderminster.
CHILDREN: all ages welcomed.
DOGS: allowed in coach house annexe rooms (£15 per night), on lead in bar and lounge.
CREDIT CARDS: Amex, Mastercard, Visa.
PRICES: [2018] per room B&B £115–£375, D,B&B £191–£451. À la carte £43. 1-night bookings refused peak weekends.

ALDEBURGH Suffolk

Map 2:C6

THE WENTWORTH

'Aldeburgh is such a delightful place, made
perfect by having the Wentworth.' Praise from
a trusted reader for Michael Pritt's Victorian
hotel across the road from the shingle beach.
'We return every year, always to the same
welcome, and many of the staff have been there
for years.' The late Joyce Grenfell, a summer
visitor, would no doubt have said the same.
The ethos is self-professedly 'old-fashioned'.
Mr Pritt (whose grandfather took over the
then Wentworth Castle in 1920) 'makes sure
standards never drop, and people feel at ease'.
Manager Chris Holden is also of long standing.
Interiors are a smart blend of the traditional and
the contemporary. There are sea views from
the lounges, the front terrace, and many of the
individually designed bedrooms, while rooms in
Darfield House, behind, have use of a courtyard
garden. Four rooms were recently refurbished.
Light lunches (Suffolk sausages, Wentworth
fishcakes) are served in the bar, while in the
restaurant, at dinner, Tim Keeble's 'consistently
good' cooking includes such dishes as herb-
crusted hake fillet; braised lamb shank, tomato
ragout, rosemary polenta. (Simon Rodway)

25% DISCOUNT VOUCHERS

Wentworth Road
Aldeburgh
IP15 5BD

T: 01728 452312
E: stay@wentworth-aldeburgh.
   co.uk
W: www.wentworth-aldeburgh.
   com

BEDROOMS: 35. 7 in Darfield House
opposite, 5 on ground floor, 1
suitable for disabled.
OPEN: all year except 7–17 Jan.
FACILITIES: 2 lounges, bar,
restaurant, private dining room,
conference room, free Wi-Fi,
in-room TV (Freeview), 2 terrace
gardens, courtyard garden, public
rooms wheelchair accessible.
BACKGROUND MUSIC: none.
LOCATION: seafront, 5 mins' walk
from centre.
CHILDREN: all ages welcomed.
DOGS: allowed in bedrooms (£2 per
dog per night) and public rooms,
not in restaurant.
CREDIT CARDS: all major cards.
PRICES: [2018] per room B&B
£110–£320, D,B&B £130–£360. Set
dinner £22–£28. 1-night bookings
refused Sat.

AMBLESIDE Cumbria

Map 4: inset C2

ROTHAY MANOR

Jamie and Jenna Shail continue to make improvements to their early 19th-century manor house. It stands in wooded grounds on the edge of Ambleside, with views to Wansfell Pike. 'Comfortable, well-equipped' bedrooms have modern decor, seating area, smart toiletries; the best balcony rooms have an espresso machine, mini-fridge, Herdwick wool carpet, handmade bed, bespoke bathroom. In the 'modern grey, minimalist, smart and cool dining room', new chef Daniel McGeorge works with seasonal, locally sourced ingredients to create such dishes as Herdwick lamb loin and shoulder, Jerusalem artichoke, Cévennes onion, globe artichoke, cured spinach; turbot, fennel, haricots blancs, bitter lemon, camomile beurre blanc. Simpler fare – burgers, salads, sandwiches – and afternoon tea are served in the lounges, while dogs can join owners chowing down at breakfast and dinner in the Brathay lounge. Under the steady management of Peter Sinclair, service remains 'attentive and friendly'. Outside, a murmur of traffic can be heard from the road, but it dies down at night. Special-interest breaks – bridge, chess, painting, garden visits – are a regular feature. (P and SG)

25% DISCOUNT VOUCHERS

Rothay Bridge
Ambleside
LA22 0EH

T: 015394 33605
E: hotel@rothaymanor.co.uk
W: www.rothaymanor.co.uk

BEDROOMS: 19. 2 in bungalow in the grounds, 1 suitable for disabled.
OPEN: all year except 3 weeks Jan.
FACILITIES: lounge, drawing room, bar, 2 dining rooms, free Wi-Fi, in-room TV (Sky), civil wedding licence, 1-acre garden (croquet), free entry to local leisure centre, public rooms wheelchair accessible.
BACKGROUND MUSIC: all day in bar and restaurant.
LOCATION: ¼ mile SW of Ambleside.
CHILDREN: all ages welcomed.
DOGS: allowed in 4 bedrooms, in 2 lounges, not in bar or restaurant, £20 per dog per stay.
CREDIT CARDS: Amex, MasterCard, Visa.
PRICES: [2018] per room B&B £130–£275, D,B&B £215–£365. Dinner £38–£45 (2 or 3 courses), 9-course tasting menu £65. Normally min. 2-night bookings Sat.

SEE ALSO SHORTLIST

AMPLEFORTH Yorkshire

Map 4:D4

SHALLOWDALE HOUSE

We have readers who return year after year to this 'delightful, comfortable' B&B with panoramic views across the North Yorkshire countryside. 'Warm', 'friendly', 'restful', they write of it. Natural hosts Phillip Gill and Anton van der Horst devote time and attention to guests, greeting returnees 'as old friends', baking cakes for tea by the fire, squeezing oranges for breakfast. The architect-designed 1960s house, with big picture windows, stands on a south-facing hillside, more and more at one with a garden densely planted by Anton with shrubs, roses, honeysuckle. The public rooms are filled with antiques and objets d'art. Bright, spacious, spotless bedrooms – one with double-aspect windows – are supplied with luxury toiletries, fresh milk for morning coffee. At night Phillip cooks a four-course dinner of fresh, seasonal produce, with wines available from a well-chosen list. Perhaps local asparagus, pancetta-wrapped guineafowl, panna cotta, then a cheeseboard, served at tables set with silverware and crisp linen. In the morning there are Craster kippers, local sausages, home-made jams – and, in prospect, maybe a drive to York or to the romantic ruins of Rievaulx Abbey. (AW)

West End
Ampleforth
YO62 4DY

T: 01439 788325
E: stay@shallowdalehouse.co.uk
W: www.shallowdalehouse.co.uk

BEDROOMS: 3.
OPEN: all year except Christmas/New Year, 'occasionally at other times'.
FACILITIES: drawing room, dining room, sitting room/library, in-room TV (Freeview), 2½-acre gardens, unsuitable for disabled.
BACKGROUND MUSIC: none.
LOCATION: edge of village.
CHILDREN: not under 12.
DOGS: not allowed.
CREDIT CARDS: MasterCard, Visa.
PRICES: [2018] per room B&B single £110–£135, double £130–£164, D,B&B double £224–£260. Set dinner £48 (min. 48 hours' notice). 1-night bookings occasionally refused weekends.

ARUNDEL Sussex

Map 2:E3

THE TOWN HOUSE

'Opposite the walls of the castle in this ancient market town', Lee and Katie Williams run their Regency town house as 'a top-notch, great-value' restaurant-with-rooms. You might step straight off the street into the restaurant, where our inspectors marvelled at the 'ornate walnut, carved and gilded, 16th-century Florentine ceiling, worthy of a visit in its own right' (and 'probably worth more than the entire building', they hazard). An alternative side entrance and steep stairs lead to 'clean, comfortable' bedrooms. Bay has a four-poster, a balcony and views of the castle walls. A rear-facing room was 'well appointed', with generous storage, real clothes hangers, a 'clean, modern bathroom'. The bed, just shy of six feet, 'could have been longer – our only real niggle'. The dinner menu, too, is 'relatively short', but 'well thought out'. After a complimentary glass of champagne, 'delicious' home-baked focaccia arrived, orders were taken. Pigeon on a bed of macaroni cheese, and scallops with seasonal baby vegetables, were among dishes 'of good size, cooked to perfection'. Service by Lee Williams and his son, Harry, was 'attentive and friendly'. 'There's no better location from which to explore Arundel.'

65 High Street
Arundel
BN18 9AJ

T: 01903 883847
E: enquiries@thetownhouse.co.uk
W: www.thetownhouse.co.uk

BEDROOMS: 5.
OPEN: all year except 25/26 Dec, 1 Jan, restaurant closed Sun/Mon.
FACILITIES: restaurant, free Wi-Fi, in-room TV (Freeview), unsuitable for disabled.
BACKGROUND MUSIC: in restaurant.
LOCATION: top end of High Street.
CHILDREN: all ages welcomed.
DOGS: only guide dogs allowed.
CREDIT CARDS: Diners, MasterCard, Visa.
PRICES: [2018] per room B&B £110–£150 (2-room family suite £190), D,B&B (mid-week) £150–£190. Set dinner £28–£33. 1-night bookings refused weekends in high season.

AUSTWICK Yorkshire

Map 4:D3

AUSTWICK HALL

Guests step straight into a 'grand entrance hall' at this B&B in a village in the Yorkshire Dales national park. Built in the 17th century and extended in the 19th, the house reputedly began as a 16th-century pele tower. A Guide stalwart arriving in the rain thought the facade 'impressive' but slightly austere, yet beyond the Tuscan porch all was exuberance. 'Kind and dedicated owners' Michael Pearson and Eric Culley have filled the interiors with antiques, ethnic art, paintings and curios – here a stag's head, there 'a delightful youthful portrait of Mendelssohn'. An imperial staircase sweeps up to four bedrooms, one with a four-poster, one with a half-tester bed, all with swags, drapes, art and artefacts, maybe a Buddha or carved tigers by an original fireplace, armchairs and sofas… Opulence continues in big en suite bathrooms, each with roll-top bath, three with a separate shower. At breakfast, perfectly cooked free-range eggs are from the resident hens. Beyond the Italianate gardens, woodland walks and a sculpture trail await discovery. All this and a wood-fired hot tub for outdoor bathing. For dinner you need look no further than the Traddock (see next entry). (RG)

Townhead Lane
Austwick
LA2 8BS

T: 01524 251794
E: info@austwickhall.co.uk
W: www.austwickhall.co.uk

BEDROOMS: 4.
OPEN: all year.
FACILITIES: hall, drawing room, dining room, free Wi-Fi, in-room TV (Freeview), 14-acre gardens, hot tub, unsuitable for disabled.
BACKGROUND MUSIC: none.
LOCATION: edge of village.
CHILDREN: not under 16.
DOGS: not allowed.
CREDIT CARDS: MasterCard, Visa.
PRICES: [2018] per room B&B single £110–£140, double £125–£155. 1-night bookings refused bank holiday weekends.

AUSTWICK Yorkshire

THE TRADDOCK

Ω Previous César winner

'One of my favourites.' 'Deserves a glowing account.' Readers are full of praise for the Reynolds family's dog-friendly, people-friendly hotel in the Dales. The Georgian house, built on a trading paddock (hence tr'addock) and extended in Victorian times, is 'very comfortable', with 'plenty of spaces for wet-weather days' in lounges with log fires. The staff are commendably helpful. A couple coming in from the rain 'had our kit whisked away for drying'. Bedrooms have 'tasteful furniture', rich fabrics, antiques, luxury toiletries. You can choose a bath or shower – or both. Town Head, under the eaves, has mood lighting, a limestone-tiled bathroom, cast iron bath, walk-in shower, widescreen views. Double-aspect Gordale has an in-room, roll-top bath. All rooms have fresh fruit, home-made biscuits, bottled water. The new chef, Matthew Horsfall, cooks such dishes as Yorkshire short rib, caramelised onion, heritage carrot, pomme mousseline, bone marrow, parsley sauce. Breakfast brings Manx kippers, eggs Benedict with honey-glazed ham, smoked haddock. 'Excellent for walking, cycling, fishing', with packed lunches and picnic hampers to order. (F Kuhlmann, ML)

25% DISCOUNT VOUCHERS

Austwick
LA2 8BY

T: 01524 251224
E: info@thetraddock.co.uk
W: www.thetraddock.co.uk

BEDROOMS: 12. 1 on ground floor.
OPEN: all year.
FACILITIES: 3 lounges, bar, 2 dining rooms, function facilities, free Wi-Fi, in-room TV (Freeview), 1½-acre grounds (sun deck), unsuitable for disabled, only ground-floor restaurant wheelchair accessible.
BACKGROUND MUSIC: in public areas except 1 lounge.
LOCATION: 4 miles NW of Settle.
CHILDREN: all ages welcomed.
DOGS: allowed in bedrooms and on lead in public rooms, not in dining rooms, but owners may eat in bar area with their dogs (£5 per dog per night).
CREDIT CARDS: MasterCard, Visa.
PRICES: [2018] per room B&B single £100–£290, double £110–£300, D,B&B double £169–£370. À la carte £35. 1-night bookings refused Sat.

AYLESBURY Buckinghamshire

Map 2:C3

HARTWELL HOUSE

In a Georgian Arcadia, this Jacobean mansion, refashioned in the 1700s, was the palatial refuge of the exiled Louis XVIII and his court. Public rooms are filled with antiques, oil paintings, flowers. A staircase adorned with statues leads up to lavish suites and spacious bedrooms supplied with freshly baked biscuits. A top-floor room was 'excellent, large and light', with a shared roof terrace; a room in the stables annexe is 'perfectly good', though less grand than those in the main house. 'Everything hangs together with style, confidence and attention to detail,' writes a reader this year, praising 'the relaxed friendliness and a sense that nothing is too much trouble'. Smart dress is expected in the dining rooms, where head chef Daniel Robertson's cooking is modern and inventive. 'I particularly liked the venison infused with hibiscus.' A less happy reader found his meal 'bland', while, on an off night, a party of 20 caused kitchen and service to falter. Some other quibbles ('cold, bendy' breakfast toast, a mojito with no mojo). However, all agree that the National Trust maintains the house and grounds in high style. (Matthew Caminer, and others).

Oxford Road
Aylesbury
HP17 8NR

T: 01296 747444
E: info@hartwell-house.com
W: www.hartwell-house.com

BEDROOMS: 48. 16 in stable block a short walk away, some on ground floor., 1 (main house) suitable for disabled.
OPEN: all year, closed for lunch Mon/Tues.
FACILITIES: great hall, morning room, drawing room, library, 2 dining rooms, function facilities, free Wi-Fi, in-room TV (Sky, Freeview), civil wedding licence, spa (swimming pool, 8 by 16 metres), 94 acres of gardens and parkland, tennis, public rooms wheelchair accessible.
BACKGROUND MUSIC: none.
LOCATION: 2 miles W of Aylesbury.
CHILDREN: not under 6.
DOGS: allowed in some bedrooms in stable block with access to grounds.
CREDIT CARDS: all major cards.
PRICES: per room B&B £200–£750. À la carte £51.

BABBACOMBE Devon

Map 1:D5

THE CARY ARMS

At the end of a 'precipitous, twisty descent', 'courageous' visitors are rewarded with 'unrestricted views and a genuine, good-humoured welcome' at Lana de Savary's 'fabulously secluded' cliff-face hotel. A seaside air drifts through the 'unpretentious' building, which bears nautical ephemera, binoculars and New England colours. A log stove in the rustic bar is ideal for when the breeze becomes nippy, and for recovering from the English Channel's sharp bite. Children and dogs are warmly welcomed (buckets and spades for the former, a 'high-quality dinner and well-produced guide of local walks' for the latter). 'Spacious, attractive' bedrooms look out to sea; all but one have a private terrace or balcony. Chic beach huts, each with a light, bright interior and private terrace, pepper a sheltered, sunny spot in the grounds. The dining room specialises in seafood (perhaps the 'succulent' prawn, crayfish and rocket pancake), paired with an 'eminently quaffable' wine list – 'not gourmet, but beautifully cooked'. Fine weather opens up the tempting prospect of eating on the terrace, where hangs a bell 'with a request that it be rung when dolphins are spotted'. Moorings are available on the Teign estuary, for guests arriving by sea.

Beach Road
Babbacombe
TQ1 3LX

T: 01803 327110
E: enquiries@caryarms.co.uk
W: www.caryarms.co.uk

BEDROOMS: 16. 2 on ground floor, 8 in beach huts and suites, 2 in cottages. Plus 3 self-catering cottages.
OPEN: all year.
FACILITIES: lounge, bar, restaurant, conservatory, free Wi-Fi, in-room TV (Freeview), civil wedding licence, spa (treatment rooms, plunge pool, mini-gym, steam room, sun deck), garden, terraces.
BACKGROUND MUSIC: all day in bar.
LOCATION: by beach, 2¼ miles N of Torquay harbour.
CHILDREN: all ages welcomed.
DOGS: allowed in some rooms, not in conservatory.
CREDIT CARDS: Amex, MasterCard, Visa.
PRICES: per room B&B from £245. À la carte £30. 1-night bookings sometimes refused.

BABCARY Somerset

Map 1:C6

THE RED LION

With its rough-cut stone exterior and thatch, the Red Lion is outwardly the archetypal olde worlde pub – 'but,' say trusted readers, 'in our granddaughter's terminology, the place rocks.' In the cosy bar, with beams, flagstones and open fire, a blackboard announces that it's Pimm's o'clock and advertises the Bellini of the day. The operation is 'aimed at the younger audience', yet also 'caters very satisfactorily for the older generation'. The staff 'go out of their way to please'. Bedrooms, in a timber-clad building across the garden, are 'immaculate', painted in restful shades, with 'stylish furniture' and 'delicate abstract' works by an artist friend. At wood tables in the dining room – 'no frills or flowers' – chef Jake Tutill's menus (24 hours from field to fork) include such dishes as lamb cutlets, mini shepherd's pie, carrot purée; 'cleverly presented pork with crackling strips'. Fish is from British waters, maybe pan-fried hake, shellfish risotto, sea lettuce, sauce vierge. On summer weekends pizzas are cooked alfresco. Breakfast, served in the Den – 'effectively a very smart café' – is 'entirely satisfactory' if simple, with local free-range eggs.

Babcary
TA11 7ED

T: 01458 223230
E: info@redlionbabcary.co.uk
W: www.redlionbabcary.co.uk

BEDROOMS: 6. All in converted barn, 1, on ground floor, suitable for disabled.
OPEN: all year.
FACILITIES: bar, snug, restaurant, private dining room, meeting/function facilities, free Wi-Fi, in-room TV (BT), farm shop, garden (play area, marquee for wedding parties), bar is wheelchair accessible.
BACKGROUND MUSIC: in bar area, regular live music nights.
LOCATION: 5 miles E of Somerton.
CHILDREN: all ages welcomed.
DOGS: allowed in bars only.
CREDIT CARDS: all major cards.
PRICES: [2018] per room B&B single £95–£105, double £115–£125. À la carte £29.

BAINBRIDGE Yorkshire

Map 4:C3

LOW MILL GUEST HOUSE

A unique, centuries-old working waterwheel helps generate business for Jane and Neil McNair's 'warm and welcoming' guest house in the Yorkshire Dales national park. The late 18th-century corn mill has been sympathetically refurbished, showcasing its mighty stone walls, huge beams and original equipment. Ask the 'friendly, relaxed' hosts for a tour to see the restored mechanics in action, 'it's astonishing'. Quirky touches add personality, including colourful patchwork sofas and a life-size bulldog statue. Enormous Workshop bedroom has a wood-burning stove, freestanding copper bath and operating machinery; Kiln has historic earthenware drying tiles. All rooms have a king-size or emperor bed. The 'delicious' menus use local 'home-made produce in abundance'; eggs from neighbours' hens, fish from Whitby, meat from nearby farms. Typical dishes: spiced Dales lamb rump, sweet potato chips; Carricks smoked salmon, beetroot fritters, horseradish cream. Craft beers come from Yorkshire. 'Generous dinner portions, and a comprehensive selection at breakfast, fuelled us to enjoy the magnificent walking straight from the door.' (Christine and Philip Bright, and others)

Low Mill
Bainbridge
DL8 3EF

T: 01969 650553
E: lowmillguesthouse@gmail.com
W: www.lowmillguesthouse.co.uk

BEDROOMS: 3.
OPEN: all year except Christmas–27 Dec, dinners served three nights a week (check in advance).
FACILITIES: lounge, dining room, free Wi-Fi, in-room TV (Freeview), ¼-acre riverside garden with seating, secure bicycle storage, unsuitable for disabled.
BACKGROUND MUSIC: none.
LOCATION: 5 miles E of Hawes.
CHILDREN: not under 12.
DOGS: allowed in bedrooms, not in dining room, on lead in other public areas.
CREDIT CARDS: MasterCard, Visa.
PRICES: [2018] per room B&B single £75–£135, double £110–£180. Dinner £22–£28. 1-night bookings refused some Sats, bank holidays.

SEE ALSO SHORTLIST

BARNSLEY Gloucestershire

Map 3:E6

BARNSLEY HOUSE

Henry VIII gave the manor of Barnsley to each wife in turn – the old romantic! – before it passed to the Bourchier family, who built this Cotswold stone house in the 1690s. It is today an upmarket hotel and spa with 'a relaxed feel and lovely setting'. 'Beautiful bedrooms', decorated in natural tones, come with biscuits, magazines, mineral water. Some deluxe rooms, overlooking gardens laid out by former resident and garden designer Rosemary Verey, have side-by-side baths and walk-in shower. The Rosemary Verey suite has a private courtyard, conservatory and grotto. The Stableyard suites are 'not for the old or infirm': 'a steep flight of steps' separates bedroom from bathroom and seating area. A bath 'the size of a small swimming pool' was a mobility challenge in itself. In the Potager restaurant, Francesco Volgo's cooking is inspired by the seasons and produce from the kitchen garden, perhaps chicken breast, sweetcorn pancakes, bacon, sprouting broccoli. Cheaper fare is available in The Village Pub (see Shortlist). Staff are 'polite, attentive and plentiful', while an 'excellent breakfast' includes free-range eggs from the house hens. Calcot Manor, Tetbury (see entry) is a sister enterprise.

Barnsley
GL7 5EE

T: 01285 740000
E: info@barnsleyhouse.com
W: www.barnsleyhouse.com

BEDROOMS: 18. 7 in stableyard, 4 in courtyard, 1 in cottage, 1 suitable for disabled.
OPEN: all year.
FACILITIES: 2 lounges, bar, restaurant, cinema, meeting room, free Wi-Fi, in-room TV (Sky, Freeview), civil wedding licence, terrace, 11-acre garden (spa, outdoor hydrotherapy pool), restaurant and lounge wheelchair accessible.
BACKGROUND MUSIC: 'easy listening' in lounge and restaurant.
LOCATION: 5 miles NE of Cirencester.
CHILDREN: not under 14.
DOGS: allowed in stableyard rooms, not in grounds or public areas.
CREDIT CARDS: Amex, MasterCard, Visa.
PRICES: [2018] per room B&B single £181–£621, double £199–£621. À la carte £42. 1-night bookings sometimes refused.

SEE ALSO SHORTLIST

BARWICK Somerset

Map 1:C6

LITTLE BARWICK HOUSE

25% DISCOUNT VOUCHERS

'So relaxing and homely, but with style and much attention to detail', Emma and Tim Ford's 'absolutely delightful', 'tranquil' restaurant-with-rooms is the 'complete package', say Guide readers this year. The 'handsome old' Georgian country house is set in 'peaceful, secluded gardens' including a towering cedar tree where guests take afternoon tea. 'I couldn't believe it's only a mile from Yeovil but in the depths of the country.' Acclaimed service is courtesy of an 'attentive hostess' and 'pleasant well-trained staff'. 'Lovely', airy bedrooms have a country house feel; comfortable beds, sash windows, home-made shortbread, and 'free-range coat-hangers', although 'some guests might baulk at the number of scatter cushions' (one reader counted 13). In the crisply smart restaurant, the 'amazing cuisine' of Tim Ford and son Olly uses seasonal, mainly local, ingredients for dishes such as Cornish red mullet fillet, basil-crushed new potatoes, saffron sauce; saddle of wild roe deer, beetroot purée, savoy cabbage, rösti. The acclaimed wine list offers exceptional wines by the glass. 'Our first visit and not our last.' (Mary Coles, Ross Urquhart, Zara Elliot, Michael Cross, Lindsay Hunt)

Rexes Hollow Lane
Barwick
BA22 9TD

T: 01935 423902
E: info@littlebarwick.co.uk
W: www.littlebarwickhouse.co.uk

BEDROOMS: 7. 1 for week-long let.
OPEN: all year except Christmas Day, New Year and 3 weeks in Jan, also closed Sun, Mon and Tues lunchtime.
FACILITIES: 2 lounges, restaurant, conservatory, free Wi-Fi, in-room TV (Freeview), 3½-acre garden (terrace, paddock), restaurant wheelchair accessible.
BACKGROUND MUSIC: none.
LOCATION: ¾ mile outside Yeovil.
CHILDREN: not under 5.
DOGS: allowed in bedrooms, sitting rooms, only assistance dogs in restaurant.
CREDIT CARDS: MasterCard, Visa.
PRICES: [2018] per person B&B £60–£95 (double room, single occupancy £85–£155), D,B&B double £120–£150. Set 3-course dinner £55. 1-night bookings sometimes refused at weekends.

BASLOW Derbyshire

Map 3:A6

THE CAVENDISH

Owned by the Duke and Duchess of Devonshire, and sitting within the Chatsworth Estate, this smart hotel is a great base for exploring the Peak District. The building – an inn since 1700 – has been extended and updated. Superior rooms, some with a four-poster, some with an original iron fireplace, occupy the oldest part. They have antiques, artwork; a new bathroom (part of a recent refurbishment). 'Beautiful and stylish' so-called 'standard' rooms in the Devonshire Wing have also been updated. New rooms in a restored coach house have a four-poster, and antiques hand-picked from Chatsworth House. All rooms are supplied with ground coffee, 'shortbread and fresh milk in a jug refilled every day'. In the fine-dining restaurant, Alan Hill's menus include such dishes as breast, haggis and shoulder of Chatsworth Estate lamb. Guests can eat less formally in the Garden Room, perhaps honey-roast Derbyshire ham, egg and hand-cut chips; smoked ham-hock burger; meatballs with linguine. The service is 'friendly without being over-familiar'. At breakfast there are organic Chatsworth yogurts, locally smoked kippers, Scottish smoked haddock, eggs Benedict with Lincolnshire ham. (SW)

Church Lane
Baslow
DE45 1SP

T: 01246 582311
E: info@cavendish-hotel.net
W: www.cavendish-hotel.net

BEDROOMS: 28. 2 on ground floor, 4 in converted coach house, 2 suitable for disabled.
OPEN: all year.
FACILITIES: lounge/bar, 2 restaurants, 2 private dining rooms, function facilities, free Wi-Fi, in-room TV (Freeview), civil wedding licence, ½-acre grounds (putting green), public rooms wheelchair accessible.
BACKGROUND MUSIC: background in Garden Room only.
LOCATION: on edge of village.
CHILDREN: all ages welcomed.
DOGS: only guide dogs allowed.
CREDIT CARDS: Amex, MasterCard, Visa.
PRICES: [2018] per room B&B single £194–£251, double £269–£399, D,B&B double £379–£509. Set menus £55. 1-night bookings sometimes refused at weekends.

BASLOW Derbyshire

FISCHER'S AT BASLOW HALL

'The hotel, its staff and food were exquisite,' a reader writes of an anniversary visit to Max and Susan Fischer's stone manor house, in a village on the fringe of Chatsworth Park. A shady drive leads to the house, built in 1907 in rich Jacobean style. 'Very comfortable and well-appointed' main-house bedrooms, replete with swags and drapes and luxury toiletries, overlook a garden with clipped yews and box hedges, flower borders, pond and arboretum. 'Spacious and extremely comfortable' Garden Rooms, in contemporary style, have their own private walled garden. From this luxurious base, guests can explore the Peak District, returning for dinner in the dining room, the new wine room or at chef Rupert Rowley's tasting bench. 'Fischer's certainly deserves the Michelin star and other accolades' for such dishes as Derbyshire pork jowl, piccalilli, langoustine, grilled pak choi – or, from the vegetarian menu, mushroom risotto, truffle mascarpone. Many ingredients are home-grown. At breakfast there's freshly squeezed juice, honey from the Baslow Hall bees. For a gastropub lunch, look no further than Rowley's down the road. (Stan Buchanan, Robert Cave)

Calver Road
Baslow
DE45 1RR

T: 01246 583259
E: reservations@fischers-
baslowhall.co.uk
W: www.fischers-baslowhall.co.uk

BEDROOMS: 11. 5 in Garden House, 4 on ground floor suitable for disabled.
OPEN: all year except 25/26 Dec,
FACILITIES: lounge/bar, main dining room, dawing room, wine room, function facilities, free Wi-Fi, in-room TV (Freeview), civil wedding licence, 5-acre grounds, restaurant wheelchair accessible.
BACKGROUND MUSIC: in bar/lounge.
LOCATION: edge of village, 5 miles NE of Bakewell.
CHILDREN: all ages welcome, no under-8s in restaurant.
DOGS: not allowed.
CREDIT CARDS: Amex, MasterCard, Visa.
PRICES: [2018] per room B&B single £185–225, double £260–£325, D,B&B £367–£482. Set menu £65–£79, tasting menu £88, à la carte £78.50.

BASSENTHWAITE LAKE Cumbria

Map 4: inset C2

THE PHEASANT

Far from the hurrying world, this former coaching inn stands amid Wordsworth's northern Lakes. The pace slows at the 'comfortable' country hotel flanked by wooded hillsides, mature gardens and a babbling beck, where 'nothing was too much trouble; service was most attentive'. It's also a dog-friendly haven, with an abundance of local walks for pooches of all stamina. After an exploration of the perimeters, the oak-panelled, pubby bar welcomes dogs and their owners to rest by the fire over a soothing beverage. Homely bedrooms have further welcoming touches (china tea service, locally made biscuits), chintzy fabrics and 'a really good bathroom'. Come dinnertime, Cumbria-sourced dishes are enough to placate the peckish and feed the famished. Find simple fare in the 'informal' bistro, such as cottage pie, cheese-glazed mash, pickled red cabbage, buttered greens; and 'well-cooked, artistically presented' options in chef Jonathan Bell's 'elegant' restaurant, perhaps fillet of sea bass with braised squid, warm king prawn salad, sauce vierge. A crackling fire at breakfast gets the day off to a warm start. (Derek Lambert, JS).

25% DISCOUNT VOUCHERS

Bassenthwaite Lake
CA13 9YE

T: 017687 76234
E: info@the-pheasant.co.uk
W: www.the-pheasant.co.uk

BEDROOMS: 15. 2 on ground floor in lodge.
OPEN: all year except 25 Dec, restaurant closed Sun eve and Mon.
FACILITIES: 2 lounges, bar, bistro, restaurant, private dining room, free Wi-Fi, in-room TV (Freeview), 40-acre grounds, lake 200 yds (fishing), access to nearby spa, pool and treatment rooms.
BACKGROUND MUSIC: in bistro during opening hours only.
LOCATION: 5 miles E of Cockermouth, ¼ mile off A66 to Keswick.
CHILDREN: not under 8.
DOGS: allowed in some bedrooms (£10 charge), public rooms.
CREDIT CARDS: MasterCard, Visa.
PRICES: [2018] per room B&B £110–£210. Set menu (restaurant) £45, à la carte (bistro) £30. 1-night bookings occasionally refused Sat.

BATH Somerset   Map 2:D1

APSLEY HOUSE

Rumoured to have been built for his mistress by
the Duke of Wellington, although less imposing
than its Hyde Park Corner namesake (aka No.
1, London), this is a fine Georgian house, run
as a B&B by Nicholas and Claire Potts. Elegant
bedrooms offer a range of options. Several
have an ornate four-poster, such as The Beau,
accessed from the garden, while Waterloo has a
bathroom with slipper bath and walk-in shower.
Copenhagen, recalling the Iron Duke's horse,
can combine with Mornington as a family suite.
'Most rooms have views across Bath to the hills
beyond.' It's all managed by the 'delightful'
Miroslav Mikula and Katarzyna Kowalczyk.
The 'spacious and comfortable lounge' is
beautifully proportioned, furnished with
antiques, paintings, a grand piano and perfectly
coordinated Chesterfield. Here a fire burns on
cold days, and guests can help themselves from
the honesty bar – a proper counter, not just a
sideboard tray. Breakfast, served in the lofty,
light-filled dining room at tables laid with white
linen and silverware, embraces locally sourced
eggs, sausages and bacon. On fine days, a drink
in the south-facing garden is a singular pleasure.
More reports, please.

141 Newbridge Hill
Bath
BA1 3PT

T: 01225 336966
E: info@apsley-house.co.uk
W: www.apsley-house.co.uk

BEDROOMS: 12. 1 on ground floor,
plus 1 self-catering 2-bedroom
apartment.
OPEN: all year except 24–26 Dec,
6–10 Jan.
FACILITIES: drawing room, dining
room, free Wi-Fi, in-room TV
(Freeview), ¼-acre garden, parking,
unsuitable for disabled.
BACKGROUND MUSIC: Classic FM in
drawing and dining rooms.
LOCATION: 1¼ miles W of city centre.
CHILDREN: all ages welcomed.
DOGS: only guide dogs allowed.
CREDIT CARDS: MasterCard, Visa.
PRICES: [2018] per room B&B single
£99–£250, double £99–£280. 1-night
bookings refused Sat in peak season.

SEE ALSO SHORTLIST

BATH Somerset

NO.15 GREAT PULTENEY

'There are chandeliers all over' at Christa and Ian Taylor's latest addition to the Bath hotel scene – the old Carfax, run formerly by the Salvation Army, now spiffed up to the nines, with the addition of a small spa. On 'a really lovely street', behind the classical Georgian facade of three town houses, it has 'stylish, contemporary' interiors designed in 'a quirky, imaginative and creative way' by and for the Taylors. Wherever you turn, your eye lights upon some artwork or curiosity – 'shells, fans, musical instruments, hats, magic lantern slides…' But there is substance too. From compact bedrooms on the (top) Artist's Floor, some with an original mural, through smart Coach House accommodation, to the Hideaway Suite with a hot tub and steam room/shower, all have super-comfortable beds, an espresso machine, complimentary snacks. 'We had a delightful room with excellent facilities. They are also very welcoming of dogs.' Service is highly praised. In the café, Oliver Clarke's short menus include such dishes as crispy beef cheek, Roscoff onion, bone marrow crumb. Breakfast delivers pastries, artisan meats and cheeses, eggs every which way. (Chris Savory, C and GJ)

15 Great Pulteney Street
Bath
BA2 4BR

T: 01225 807015
E: enquiries@no15greatpulteney.co.uk
W: www.no15greatpulteney.co.uk

BEDROOMS: 40. 8 in coach house, 1 suitable for disabled.
OPEN: all year, café closed Mon, Tues (open for dinner Wed–Sat, brunch on Sun).
FACILITIES: lift, lounge, bar, café, private dining room, free Wi-Fi, in-room TV (Sky), spa, small garden terrace, limited parking (charge), public rooms wheelchair accessible.
BACKGROUND MUSIC: all day in public areas.
LOCATION: central.
CHILDREN: all ages welcomed.
DOGS: allowed in bedrooms, bar, not in restaurant.
CREDIT CARDS: Amex, MasterCard, Visa.
PRICES: [2018] per room B&B £149 –£370. À la carte £24. 1-night bookings sometimes refused at weekends.

SEE ALSO SHORTLIST

BATH Somerset

Map 2:D1

THE QUEENSBERRY

Close to the Assembly Rooms and other Bath glories, in 'an unsurpassed situation' yet 'so quiet', Laurence and Helen Beere's hotel is smart and getting smarter, with bedrooms and bathrooms receiving a designer make-over. Beautifully proportioned junior suites occupy the first-floor drawing rooms of the four Georgian houses that combine to make the whole. The four-poster suite has a modern four-poster and double walk-through shower, while some deluxe doubles can accommodate a child's roll-away bed. Contemporary decor and furnishings combine happily with original features. In Old Q bar, the spirit of John Douglas, Marquess of Queensberry, is larkily evoked with a list of contemporary Queensberry Rules – no stilts, pogo sticks, audible obscenities or shouting into mobile phones… ('But Old Q was the notorious 4th duke,' a pedant writes; don't spoil the fun, we say.) Here you can take a club sandwich, a ploughman's platter, while in the Olive Tree restaurant, Chris Cleghorn creates tasting menus for omnivores, vegetarians, vegans (order à la carte if you prefer). A typical dish: brill on the bone, artichoke, mustard, button mushroom, sea herbs. Service is 'happy, relaxed, positive, friendly'.

4–7 Russel Street
Bath
BA1 2QF

T: 01225 447928
E: reservations@thequeensberry.
co.uk
W: www.thequeensberry.co.uk

BEDROOMS: 29. Some on ground floor.
OPEN: all year, restaurant closed Mon evening.
FACILITIES: lift, residents' drawing room, bar, 2 sitting rooms, restaurant, meeting room, free Wi-Fi, in-room TV (Freeview), 4 linked courtyard gardens, unsuitable for disabled.
BACKGROUND MUSIC: in restaurant and bar.
LOCATION: near Assembly Rooms.
CHILDREN: all ages welcomed.
DOGS: assistance dogs only.
CREDIT CARDS: Amex, MasterCard, Visa.
PRICES: [2018] per room B&B £125–£475. Tasting menus £68–£85, à la carte £55. 1-night bookings sometimes refused weekends.

SEE ALSO SHORTLIST

BATH Somerset

Map 2:D1

THE ROYAL CRESCENT HOTEL & SPA

'Behind the dramatic facade lies a beautiful garden,' writes a reader in praise of this hotel and spa with its green oasis at the centre of a divine Georgian crescent. Public rooms are filled with antiques, while the 'well-equipped and spotlessly clean' bedrooms occupy the main house and garden buildings. Deluxe suites, some with a four-poster, have a bath and shower, a separate sitting room. Food is available all day in the Montagu bar, the name recalling Elizabeth Montagu, Queen of the Blue Stockings, who held court here in the 18th century. In the wisteria-draped Dower House restaurant (no jeans or trainers; blue stockings welcome), David Campbell cooks such modern dishes as roasted brill, salt cod, purple sprouting broccoli, artichoke, lemon, clams – with appealing separate menus for vegetarians and children. 'The tasting menu was outstanding.' A wide choice at breakfast includes a healthy juice (freshly squeezed orange; cucumber, ginger, apple and celery), spiced muesli or organic porridge, through Manx kippers, to a cholesterol-loading full English with Stornoway black pudding, hog's pudding, organic sausages and free-range eggs. (Robert Cooper)

16 Royal Crescent
Bath
BA1 2LS

T: 01225 823333
E: info@royalcrescent.co.uk
W: www.royalcrescent.co.uk

BEDROOMS: 45. 10 in Dower House, 14 in annexes, 8 on ground floor.
OPEN: all year.
FACILITIES: lift, bar, drawing room, library, restaurant, function facilities, free Wi-Fi, in-room TV (Sky, Freeview), civil wedding licence, 1-acre garden, spa (12-metre pool, gym, sauna, treatment rooms), public rooms wheelchair accessible.
BACKGROUND MUSIC: in library and restaurant.
LOCATION: ½ mile from High Street.
CHILDREN: all ages welcomed.
DOGS: allowed in some bedrooms, public rooms, not in restaurant or bar.
CREDIT CARDS: Amex, MasterCard, Visa.
PRICES: [2018] per room B&B from £360. À la carte £65, tasting menu £75. Min. 2-night stay weekends in peak season.

SEE ALSO SHORTLIST

BAUGHURST Hampshire

Map 2:D2

THE WELLINGTON ARMS NEW

'The immaculate and well-laid-out garden gave the promise of the outstanding stay to come,' write readers this year, of a night at Simon Page and Jason King's 'amazing', dog-friendly pub. Inside the 18th-century former hunting lodge on the North Wessex Downs, there was 'a friendly welcome, a comfy, country atmosphere'. In the kitchen, Jason King works with local meat and game, home-grown herbs, fruit and vegetables to create such deceptively 'unfussy' dishes as pot pie of red-wine-braised roe deer and root vegetables, under a flaky pastry lid. The beamed bedrooms have bespoke oak furniture, goose-down bedding and a rain shower, alongside an espresso machine, minibar, home-made biscuits, 'lovely' toiletries and waffle robes. 'In the morning, we opened the curtains to quiet fields of grazing horses.' At breakfast, 'delicious' choices include free-range eggs from the pub's hens, honey from the apiary, oak-smoked salmon; bashed avocado with chilli flakes on fresh-baked sourdough, or French toast with crisp bacon, blueberries and maple syrup. You can even buy a memento of your visit to the inn – a souvenir teapot and mohair cosy knitted by Simon's mum. (Robert and Ros Harcourt)

Baughurst Road
Baughurst
RG26 5LP

T: 0118 982 0110
E: hello@thewellingtonarms.com
W: www.thewellingtonarms.com

BEDROOMS: 4. 3 in converted outbuildings.
OPEN: all year, restaurant closed Sun night.
FACILITIES: bar, restaurant, free Wi-Fi, in-room TV (Freeview), 1-acre garden, parking.
BACKGROUND MUSIC: in bar and restaurant.
LOCATION: equidistant between Reading, Basingstoke and Newbury.
CHILDREN: all ages welcomed.
DOGS: allowed.
CREDIT CARDS: MasterCard, Visa.
PRICES: (2018) per room B&B £110–£200. À la carte £35.

BEAMINSTER Dorset

Map 1:C6

THE OLLEROD

In March 2018, the then owners sold what was Bridge House to Silvana Bandini and Chris Staines, she a former general manager at The Pig near Bath, he a one-time executive chef at the Abbey Hotel, Bath. And if that sounds like a grand game of musical chairs, now that the music has stopped we expect good things. A proposed redecoration should be well advanced, and the hotel has become more restaurant-led (Mr Staines held a Michelin star in London). Bedrooms are individually styled, with good linens, waffle robes, organic toiletries. The building is characterful, with mullioned windows, flagstone floors, beams. The 'biggest drawback' is the road that runs past the door, yet traffic noise was not a problem, say Guide inspectors. In the crepuscular dining room, Mr Staines 'gives modern British cooking a Dorset focus' in menus that include small plates, interesting vegetarian choices (broccoli orzo 'risotto', charred purple sprouting broccoli, kale, toasted almonds). 'Breakfast in a nice garden room had a small buffet with delicious apricot and prune compote, excellent pain au chocolat and croissants, a good kipper.' 'Everyone was so friendly.' Reports, please.

3 Prout Bridge
Beaminster
DT8 3AY

T: 01308 862200
E: hello@theollerod.co.uk
W: www.theollerod.co.uk

BEDROOMS: 13. 4 in coach house, 4 on ground floor.
OPEN: all year.
FACILITIES: hall/reception, lounge, bar, sun room, conservatory, restaurant, free Wi-Fi, in-room TV (Freeview), civil wedding licence, ¼-acre walled garden, terrace, unsuitable for disabled.
BACKGROUND MUSIC: in public rooms.
LOCATION: 100 yards from centre.
CHILDREN: all ages welcomed.
DOGS: allowed in 2 bedrooms and lounge, not in restaurant (£15 per dog per night)
CREDIT CARDS: Amex, MasterCard, Visa.
PRICES: [2018] per room B&B £100–£280 (single occupancy rates, 7 days' notice required). À la carte meal £40.

BEAULIEU Hampshire

Map 2:E2

THE MASTER BUILDER'S

'New Forest ponies or long-horned cattle may stage an ambush at the driveway entrance', but regular Guide readers were happy to take the risk in 2018 to visit this 'unpretentious, friendly hotel'. On a tranquil lane, with lawns reaching to the Beaulieu river, the Georgian shipbuilder's house has a 'lovely setting' and 'delightful staff'. In the main house, bedrooms might have a carved-wood four-poster, vintage prints, while in the Henry Adams wing, they are white, bright with splashes of coastal blue. 'Our modern, comfortable and tastefully furnished room had a nautical but not over-insistent theme.' Another reader found his room 'on the small side'. Guests can venture into the old village directly from the Yachtsman's bar, where staff in Breton stripes bring platters, pizzas, pub classics. In the airy dining room, with its many plants and pastel green decor, chef Alicia Storey's 'very good' seasonal dishes include sole meunière, asparagus, samphire, brown butter sauce. 'Breakfast overlooking the ancient shipyard where Nelson's fleet was built is a fine start to any day.' The Bull and Swan at Burghley, Stamford (see Shortlist), has the same owners. (Lindsay Hunt and John Fisher, LR)

Buckler's Hard
Beaulieu
SO42 7XB

T: 01590 616253
E: enquiries@themasterbuilders.co.uk
W: www.themasterbuilders.co.uk

BEDROOMS: 26, 18 in Henry Adams wing.
OPEN: all year.
FACILITIES: lounge, bar, restaurant, terrace, free Wi-Fi, in-room TV (Freeview), civil wedding licence, ½-acre garden, bar and restaurant wheelchair accessible, no adapted toilet.
BACKGROUND MUSIC: in bar and restaurant.
LOCATION: 6 miles NE of Lymington.
CHILDREN: all ages welcomed.
DOGS: allowed in 9 bedrooms, lounge, Yachtman's bar, not in restaurant.
CREDIT CARDS: Amex, MasterCard, Visa.
PRICES: [2018] per room B&B single from £100, double from £120, D,B&B double from £160. À la carte £45.

BEAULIEU Hampshire

Map 2:E2

MONTAGU ARMS

'We had breakfast in the restaurant overlooking the most attractive garden,' write readers, well pleased with this hotel in a New Forest village on Beaulieu Water. They had arrived the night before in a downpour, and found the reception 'dark and gloomy', the place 'apparently deserted'. What a difference a day makes! By morning, 'The sun was out… The hotel was full and had a definite buzz   The staff were helpful and attentive, the public rooms and sitting-out areas in the garden comfortable, our room was comfortable and well equipped.' Interiors are traditional, with oak panelling, brick fireplaces, leaded windows. Some bedrooms have a four-poster or half-tester bed and, if 'not of the latest design', they are characterful. In a converted barn, two duplex suites have freestanding bath and private terrace. In the restaurant, 'the food is delicious, the ambience great'. Chef Matthew Tomkinson exploits the organic kitchen garden to create such dishes as roast saddle of Everleigh Farm venison, home-grown artichokes, red wine-braised salsify and venison 'hotpot'. At breakfast, eggs are from the hotel hens. 'We would definitely go back.' (Robert Cooper, Monty Knight-Olds)

25% DISCOUNT VOUCHERS

Palace Lane
Beaulieu
SO42 7ZL

T: 01590 612324
E: reservations@
   montaguarmshotel.co.uk
W: www.montaguarmshotel.co.uk

BEDROOMS: 24. 2 new Hayloft suites.
OPEN: all year, Terrace restaurant closed Mon, Tues lunch.
FACILITIES: lounge, conservatory, library/bar/brasserie, restaurant, free Wi-Fi, in-room TV (Freeview), civil wedding licence, 3-acre garden, access to spa at Careys Manor (6 miles away), public rooms wheelchair accessible.
BACKGROUND MUSIC: Classic FM all day in reception.
LOCATION: village centre.
CHILDREN: all ages welcomed.
DOGS: assistance dogs allowed.
CREDIT CARDS: Amex, MasterCard, Visa.
PRICES: [2018] per room B&B £189–£399, D,B&B £289–£499. À la carte from £28 (Monty's Inn), £70 (Terrace restaurant). 1-night bookings sometimes refused.

BEESANDS Devon

THE CRICKET INN `NEW`

In an 'absolutely beautiful position' overlooking Start Bay, Rachel and Nigel Heath's 19th-century village fishermen's inn is 'a relaxing place to stay', writes a trusted reader this year. To reach it by car, you must negotiate 'narrow lanes, steep hills and sharp bends' – or walk there via the South West Coast Path. The names on the doors of the sea-facing bedrooms echo the cricket theme, but, within, the style is breezy, nautical New England. Oval has 'a seat in the large bay window and panoramic views'. Identical Trueman and Botham have a king-size four-poster. Downstairs, the friendly hosts are 'much in evidence'. The bar, adorned with old photographs, stocks real ales and award-winning ciders. You can eat in the restaurant or beachside, on wooden benches, from son Scott Heath's simple menus, ranging from fish and chips, to freshly caught lobster and scallops, or sardines with harissa and a charcoal-grilled steak if you fancy something fiery or beefy. 'The food was very good, especially the fresh fish (nice to see it was not the same every night). Breakfasts were excellent, and freshly cooked.' (Lynn Wildgoose)

Beesands
Kingbridge
TQ7 2EN

T: 01548 580215
E: enquiries@thecricketinn.com
W: thecricketinn.com

BEDROOMS: 7. 4 in extension.
OPEN: closed Christmas Day.
FACILITIES: bar, restaurant (alfresco dining), private dining facilities, free (intermittent) Wi-Fi, in-room TV (Freeview), parking, restaurant and bar wheelchair accessible.
BACKGROUND MUSIC: all day.
LOCATION: in village, on South West Coast Path.
CHILDREN: all ages welcomed.
DOGS: allowed (in bar only).
CREDIT CARDS: MasterCard, Visa.
PRICES: [2018] per room B&B £110–£150, D,B&B £150–£190. Min. 2-night stay preferred at weekends.

BEPTON Sussex

Map 2:E3

PARK HOUSE, HOTEL & SPA

'We much enjoyed our stay,' writes a reader this year, of this Edwardian country house hotel in 'grounds of a sporty nature'. The tennis courts, croquet lawn, bowling and putting greens are 'in immaculate condition'. Run by the O'Brien family for six decades, this is a professional operation hosting corporate events, yet retaining a relaxed ambience. Bedrooms are pretty and traditional, supplied with bathrobes, slippers, good toiletries and home-made biscuits. With 24-hour room service, staff spring into action when you call. 'They were very helpful, they remade our bed with super sheets and a beautiful blanket,' continues our reader, spurning a duvet. And the room? 'Comfortable', with 'an excellent, large and long bath'. Downstairs, 'there was a huge lounge for relaxing before and after eating. Also a large bar with good views over the golf course.' The kitchen, under executive chef Callum Keir, wins praise for modern dishes, with the emphasis on seasonal and local ingredients, for instance, loin and belly of pork, pickled cauliflower, snow peas. 'Very good dinner with super amuse-bouche… We would very definitely stay again.' (John Barnes, MW)

Bepton
GU29 0JB

T: 01730 819000
E: reservations@parkhousehotel.com
W: www.parkhousehotel.com

BEDROOMS: 21. 5 on ground floor, 1 suitable for disabled, 9 in cottages in grounds.
OPEN: all year, except 23–27 Dec.
FACILITIES: drawing room, bar, dining room, conservatory, function rooms, free Wi-Fi, in-room TV (Sky), civil wedding licence, 10-acre grounds, spa, heated swimming pools, tennis, pitch and putt, 6-hole 18-tee golf course, public rooms wheelchair accessible.
BACKGROUND MUSIC: background in dining room/conservatory.
LOCATION: village centre.
CHILDREN: all ages welcomed.
DOGS: well-behaved dogs allowed in some bedrooms with access to gardens, not in public rooms.
CREDIT CARDS: Amex, MasterCard, Visa.
PRICES: [2018] per room B&B from £150, D,B&B from £230. Set dinner £45. Min. 2-night stay Fri/Sat.

BEVERLEY Yorkshire

NEWBEGIN HOUSE

'Perfect hosts' Nuala and Walter Sweeney
clearly enjoy welcoming guests to their
'beautiful Georgian house' in a market town
dominated by its sublime Gothic minster.
Trusted Guide readers found 'a home from
home', occupied by three generations of
Sweeneys and their dog. The bedrooms have
paintings and antiques, and are supplied with
those extra touches that speak of pride in the
operation: fresh milk in a mini-fridge, biscuits,
chocolate, good china. The largest and most fun,
the double-length Drawing Room, has a sofa,
armchairs, original fireplaces, mantel clocks
and overmantel mirrors, crammed bookshelves,
knick-knacks and photos, even a rocking horse.
It reminded one reader of 'a nursery or library';
the shutters should screen out 'intermittent'
traffic noise. Iveson and its bathroom offer
'wonderful views' of the walled garden, with
potager, ponds, a waterfall. This room has a
claw-footed bath, but no shower – 'peaceful'
Appleton has both. Breakfast brings 'a wide
choice' of local produce – a full Yorkshire, fresh
fruit salad. The town centre, with Saturday
market and independent restaurants, is two
minutes' walk away. (S and JJ, and others)

10 Newbegin
Beverley
HU17 8EG

T: 01482 888880
E: wsweeney@wsweeney.karoo.
co.uk.
W: www.newbeginhousebbbeverley.
co.uk/

BEDROOMS: 3.
OPEN: all year except when owners
take a holiday.
FACILITIES: sitting room, dining
room, small conference facilities,
free Wi-Fi, in-room TV (Freeview),
walled garden, unsuitable for
disabled.
BACKGROUND MUSIC: none.
LOCATION: central.
CHILDREN: all ages welcomed.
DOGS: not allowed.
CREDIT CARDS: none accepted.
PRICES: B&B per room single £60,
double £90. 1-night bookings
refused during the Early Music
Festival and the Folk Festival.

BIGBURY-ON-SEA Devon

Map 1:D4

BURGH ISLAND HOTEL

♔ Previous César winner

New owner Giles Fuchs has ambitious plans for this gleaming white Art Deco hotel, much loved by readers. They include a spa, private members' club and refurbished local inn. Mr Fuchs, who made a fortune renting out office space, wants to restore Burgh Island to its former glory as the most luxurious hotel west of the Ritz. We hope it will remain 'one of a kind', 'a place to dance and dream', the service and style, as ever, 'classical and sophisticated'. The sea tractor still ferries guests across the sands. Morning tea and coffee are brought to period-style bedrooms named after notable former guests, and supplied with chocolates, fluffy bathrobes, bespoke toiletries. Some have a balcony, most a lovely sea view. You can hire Agatha Christie's beach writing retreat, or a dog-friendly apartment above the 700-year-old Pilchard Inn; drink cocktails in the Palm Court bar; don best bib and tucker for a three-course dinner in The Ballroom. There is less-formal dining in the Ganges restaurant, Captain's Cabin and inn. A dip in the natural seawater Mermaid Pool is a perfect start to the day. Reports, please.

Burgh Island
Bigbury-on-Sea
TQ7 4BG

T: 01548 810514
E: reception@burghisland.com
W: www.burghisland.com

BEDROOMS: 25. 1 suite in Beach House in grounds, apartment above Pilchard Inn.
OPEN: all year.
FACILITIES: lift, bar, 2 restaurants, ballroom, sun lounge, billiard room, private dining room, spa, free Wi-Fi (public areas, most bedrooms), civil wedding licence, 17-acre grounds on 26-acre island (30-metre natural sea bathing pool), tennis court.
BACKGROUND MUSIC: period music in public rooms, live music Wed and Sat with dinner in ballroom.
LOCATION: off Bigbury beach. private garages on mainland.
CHILDREN: not under 5, no under-13s at dinner.
DOGS: not allowed in hotel.
CREDIT CARDS: MasterCard, Visa.
PRICES: [2018] per room D,B&B single £310, double £420–£700. 1-night bookings refused Sat, some bank holidays.

BIGBURY-ON-SEA Devon   Map 1:D4

THE HENLEY

'As superb and lovely as ever', Martyn Scarterfield and Petra Lampe's Edwardian holiday cottage turned guest house is 'a home-away-from-home' for many devoted returning visitors. 'We've been coming here for years… It is all so relaxing and comfortable.' A cliff path leads to the sandy beach on the Avon estuary, 'wonderful for dogs (and humans)'. In public rooms there are potted plants in superabundance, paintings, books, flowers, a wood-burning stove. Bedrooms are entirely traditional. The owners' Labrador is 'as welcoming as his owners'. 'Caspar still waits outside our door every morning to greet our dogs (and have biscuits).' The dining room, with rattan chairs, potted palms, estuary views through a wall of windows, has the airy feel of a conservatory. Here, for residents only, Martyn cooks a limited-choice three-course dinner with local produce and locally landed fish. Typical dishes: fillet steak, Madeira and peppercorn sauce; pan-fried John Dory, lemongrass, marinated prawns. 'The food is much better than at many London restaurants.' At breakfast there are Aune Valley bacon and sausages, poached kippers, eggs Benedict, smoked salmon. Overall 'absolute heaven!' (Simon Rodway, and others)

Folly Hill
Bigbury-on-Sea
TQ7 4AR

T: 01548 810240
E: thehenleyhotel@btconnect.com
W: www.thehenleyhotel.co.uk

BEDROOMS: 5.
OPEN: Mar–end Oct.
FACILITIES: 2 lounges, dining room, reception, free Wi-Fi, in-room TV (Freeview), small terraced garden (steps to beach, golf, sailing, fishing), Coastal Path nearby, unsuitable for disabled.
BACKGROUND MUSIC: jazz/classical in the evenings in lounge, dining room.
LOCATION: 5 miles S of Modbury.
CHILDREN: not under 12.
DOGS: allowed in bedrooms (not on bed), lounges, not in dining room.
CREDIT CARDS: Amex, MasterCard, Visa.
PRICES: [2018] per room B&B single £95–£100, double £127–£166, D,B&B (2-night min.) single £125–£130, double £188–£218. Set dinner £36. 1-night bookings sometimes refused weekends.

BIGGIN-BY-HARTINGTON Derbyshire

Map 3·B6

BIGGIN HALL

'We were welcomed with a complimentary Pimm's,' write Guide insiders, who dined at James Moffett's historic stone manor house in the Peak District national park. And if it seems churlish to note that the Pimm's could have been colder, they add; 'This was our only criticism.' In two lounges, 'a jolly atmosphere' prevailed. In the large dining room – 'divided into several areas, each with a log fire' – the efficient team served residents and locals. 'The meal was really good in a refreshingly unpretentious way.' Leek and potato soup, sea bream with a potato cake, hot pot, and panna cotta were enjoyed. The 'good accommodation' includes traditionally styled bedrooms in the main house and outbuildings. We do hear niggles (a cold room, a rushed dinner), but our readers love the spirit of the enterprise, the 'undeniable charm', such nice touches as a fridge with fresh milk, the offer of a free packed lunch, with 'really good, freshly made sandwiches'. Walkers can pick up trails from the extensive grounds. A returning guest in 2018 concludes, 'Not posh but straightforward. Amazing value.' (Derek Lambert, SP, DL, and others)

Main Street
Biggin-by-Hartington
SK17 0DH

T: 01298 84451
E: enquiries@bigginhall.co.uk
W: www.bigginhall.co.uk

BEDROOMS: 21. 13 in annexes, some on ground floor.
OPEN: all year, restaurant closed Mon lunch.
FACILITIES: sitting room, library, dining room, meeting room, free Wi-Fi (in sitting rooms, some bedrooms), in-room TV (Freeview), civil wedding licence, 8-acre grounds (croquet), River Dove 1½ miles, restaurant wheelchair accessible.
BACKGROUND MUSIC: none.
LOCATION: 8 miles N of Ashbourne.
CHILDREN: not under 12.
DOGS: allowed in courtyard and bothy bedrooms free of charge (unless for damage), not in main house.
CREDIT CARDS: MasterCard, Visa.
PRICES: [2018] per room B&B £80–£160, D,B&B £130–£210. À la carte £28. 1-night bookings sometimes refused Sat, peak season.

BILDESTON Suffolk   Map 2:C5

THE BILDESTON CROWN   **NEW**

25% DISCOUNT VOUCHERS

'In a peaceful village near Lavenham', this 15th-century former merchant's house and coaching inn is 'full of character, warm, intimate, relaxed'. It is run as their own business by Hayley and Chris Lee, manager and head chef. After a 'super-friendly check-in', Guide inspectors were shown to a room on the second floor, where 'the low ceiling has lots of beams and the warning "Duck"'. Fresh milk was brought in a glass bottle. A 'good-sized' bathroom had a large bath and separate walk-in shower, with strong water pressure, 'stylish soaps'. All rooms are 'characterful and colourful', with perhaps a playful touch – doggy wallpaper, a tartan carpet, one has an antique four-poster. In the candlelit restaurant, Chris Lee's 'interesting menus' include such dishes as local pheasant Kiev; fish stew with aïoli; chargrilled Red Poll rump steak; Nedging lamb supplied by the building's owner, James Buckle, local farmer and businessman. 'A light, fluffy banoffee pie was the highlight.' At breakfast 'a bread basket arrived with a small, warm doughnut in the middle. Fresh orange juice was brought to the table. Eggs Florentine was delicious.'

104 High Street
Bildeston
IP7 7EB

T: 01449 740510
E: reception@thebildestoncrown.co.uk
W: www.thebildestoncrown.com

BEDROOMS: 12.
OPEN: all year, no accommodation 24–26 Dec, New Year's Day.
FACILITIES: 2 bars, restaurant, 2 private dining areas, lift, free Wi-Fi, in-room TV (Freeview), courtyard, 3 small patios, parking, mobile phone reception variable, restaurant and bar wheelchair accessible, adapted toilet.
BACKGROUND MUSIC: in public areas.
LOCATION: village centre 10 mins' drive from centre.
CHILDREN: all ages welcomed.
DOGS: allowed in some rooms and in bar, not in restaurant.
CREDIT CARDS: Amex, MasterCard, Visa.
PRICES: [2018] per room B&B £80–£175. À la carte £40.

BISHOP'S CASTLE Shropshire

Map 3:C4

THE CASTLE HOTEL

NEW

Built on the bailey of a hilltop castle, this dog-friendly hotel overlooks 'a lovely town in stunning countryside'. A sister to Pen-y-Dyffryn, Oswestry (see entry), it has gained a full entry after Guide inspectors called. Beyond 'a little patio with water feature', the interior is 'a pleasing mix of traditional country pub and a more contemporary, sleek style'. A master bedroom had 'comfortable armchairs, a roomy bathroom with bath and shower over'. All rooms are individually styled; some with in-room bath; others with walk-in rain shower. Three bar/dining areas had 'open fires in cosy spaces', where dinner was 'comfort food, ideal for walkers'. Curried peppers, courgettes and hazelnut loaf with raita and 'a good portion of vegetables', proved 'a cut above pub food', as did chicken stuffed with garlic mushrooms, leek and Shropshire Blue sauce, while vanilla panna cotta with mixed berries was 'outstanding'. In the morning, tables were attractively set in the panelled dining room for a breakfast of avocado toast, poached egg, smoked salmon; 'perfectly cooked eggs Benedict'. In summer 'an upper-level patio with ornamental pond would be truly lovely, with wonderful views'. (David Lowe, Anne Sprason, and others)

25% DISCOUNT VOUCHERS

Market Square
Bishop's Castle
SY9 5BN

T: 01588 638403
E: stay@thecastlehotelbishops
castle.co.uk
W: www.thecastlehotelbishops
castle.co.uk

BEDROOMS: 12.
OPEN: all year except 25 Dec.
FACILITIES: 3 bar areas, dining room, free Wi-Fi, in-room TV (Freeview), in-room spa treatments, patio, terrace, garden, parking, bicycle storage, bars and restaurant wheelchair accessible.
BACKGROUND MUSIC: in bar areas.
LOCATION: in small market town centre.
CHILDREN: all ages welcomed.
DOGS: allowed in bedrooms, bar, at owner's side at meal times in dog-friendly areas, not in restaurant, dog welcome box, no charge.
CREDIT CARDS: Mastercard, Visa.
PRICES: [2018] per room B&B single £100–£115, double £110–£195, D,B&B single £127–£142, double £165–£250. À la carte £30. 1-night bookings sometimes refused Sat.

BLAKENEY Norfolk

Map 2:A5

THE BLAKENEY HOTEL

Previous César winner

Standing quayside, overlooking estuary and salt
marshes, in a coastal village of flint cottages,
gift shops and galleries, Emma Stannard's hotel
is ideal for outdoorsy family holidays. With
crabbing, mud sliding, seal-watching trips
and sandy beaches, there is plenty to entertain
children. The 'welcoming staff make it clear
that they like looking after people', writes a
reader this year; they are 'universally friendly
and efficient'. The 'relaxing, comfy lounges' have
'wonderful views'. Bedrooms are contemporary,
'tastefully decorated'. Some interconnect. The
more expensive have additional features, cafetière
coffee, perhaps a four-poster, a balcony, a garden
patio. 'Delicious, locally sourced food' is available
for most of the day, with sandwiches from the
bar. In the restaurant, 'ambitious' seasonal menus,
'with some unusual combinations', include such
dishes as slow-cooked belly pork, Parmentier
potatoes, green beans, sage jus. 'Dinner is up
there with the best', the wine list is 'first rate'. The
'marvellous breakfast suits all tastes', and when
it rains, the games room offers table tennis, pool,
darts. It isn't cheap, but 'we will return for sure'.
(Andrew Warren, Patsi Ryan)

The Quay
Blakeney
NR25 7NE

T: 01263 740797
E: reception@blakeneyhotel.co.uk
W: www.blakeneyhotel.co.uk

BEDROOMS: 64. 16 in Granary annexe
opposite, some on ground floor, 1
suitable for disabled.
OPEN: all year.
FACILITIES: lift, lounges, bar,
restaurant, free Wi-Fi, in-room
TV (Freeview), function facilities,
heated indoor swimming pool (15
by 5 metres), steam room, sauna,
mini-gym, games room, terrace,
¼-acre walled garden, public rooms
wheelchair accessible, adapted toilet.
BACKGROUND MUSIC: none.
LOCATION: on the quay.
CHILDREN: all ages welcomed.
DOGS: allowed in some bedrooms,
not in public rooms.
CREDIT CARDS: Amex, MasterCard,
Visa.
PRICES: [2018] per person B&B
£118–£187, D,B&B (2-night min.)
£130–£205. À la carte £32. 1-night
bookings sometimes refused
weekends, bank holidays.

BLANCHLAND Co. Durham

Map 4:B3

THE LORD CREWE ARMS

♥ Previous César winner

A 'lovely drive over moors' leads to this hotel in a North Pennines village built from the stone of a dissolved 12th-century abbey. The hotel itself occupies surviving monastic buildings, including the abbot's lodge, in gardens leading down to the River Derwent. Part of the Calcot group (see entry for Calcot Manor, Tetbury), it has been 'very stylishly' made over while maintaining its historic character. Today's visitor finds flagstone floors, 'a maze of corridors', 'an enormous fire on which meats are sometimes grilled', a 'dark crypt bar', beams and barrel-vaulted ceilings. Bedrooms, in the main building, former miners' cottages and 'another interesting old building', The Angel, opposite, blend contemporary style with original features. They range from 'cosy' to 'suites' via 'canny' and 'champion' ('our champion room had books, magazines, an espresso machine, home-made biscuits, fudge, a walker's pack and umbrella'). In the upstairs Bishop's Dining Room, Simon Hicks uses local and home-grown produce in such dishes as Ayrshire mutton banger, lamb chop, whipped tatties, wild garlic; Durham rare breed pork chop, naughty beans. Breakfast brings fresh juice, toast-your-own crumpets, eggs from the hotel's hens.

The Square
Blanchland
DH8 9SP

T: 01434 675469
E: enquiries@lordcrewearms
   blanchland.co.uk
W: www.lordcrewearms
   blanchland.co.uk

BEDROOMS: 21. 7 in adjacent miners' cottages, 10 in The Angel across road, some on ground floor, 1 suitable for disabled.
OPEN: all year.
FACILITIES: 2 lounges, restaurant, Gatehouse events space, free Wi-Fi, in-room TV (Freeview), civil wedding licence, beer garden,
BACKGROUND MUSIC: in dining room and bar.
LOCATION: in Blanchland village on the B6306, 9 miles S of Hexham.
CHILDREN: all ages welcomed.
DOGS: 'well-behaved dogs' allowed in bedrooms, public rooms, not in dining room.
CREDIT CARDS: Amex, MasterCard, Visa.
PRICES: [2018] per room B&B single £99–£200, double £119–£224.
À la carte £32.

BLANDFORD FORUM Dorset

Map 2:E1

THE CROWN HOTEL

'A handsome Georgian house' and former coaching inn, overlooking the River Stour meadows in a market town, is today 'a very pleasant hotel' with 'super staff' and the ghost of a cloaked highwayman. Although owned by the 'well-regarded' brewers Hall & Woodhouse, it doesn't feel the least bit corporate. 'A great L-shaped room goes from a dining space to a long bar, to a kind of gentleman's snug' with leather sofas, a log-burner, battered hardback books, sporting trophies (silverware, not animal parts). 'A mini-piazza with tables and umbrellas' comes into its own when the sun shines. 'A twin bedroom was, in fact, two rooms, with a small foyer and stylish, expensively appointed bathroom. The outstanding decor included Farrow & Ball paintwork, expensive wall coverings, interesting portraits and engravings.' As well as the bar there's a formal dining room, its walls crowded with paintings. Typical à la carte dishes: chicken and wild mushroom pie; vegan shepherd's pie; rib-eye steak; Badger beer-battered fish and chips. Breakfast includes smashed avocado on toast, croque-monsieur, an interesting veggie option, the full 'Drayman's' with sautéed potatoes and Beanz. (RO, Mary Woods)

West Street
Blandford Forum
DT11 7AJ

T: 01258 456626
E: crownhotel.reception@hall-woodhouse.co.uk
W: crownhotelblandford.co.uk

BEDROOMS: 27. 1 suitable for disabled.
OPEN: all year.
FACILITIES: lift, bar, common room, restaurant, function suite, free Wi-Fi, in-room Smart TV (Freeview), civil wedding licence, garden terrace, public areas wheelchair accessible, adapted toilet.
BACKGROUND MUSIC: none.
LOCATION: edge of town centre, 1 min. from High Street.
CHILDREN: all ages welcomed.
DOGS: allowed in some bedrooms by prior arrangement for an additional charge, not in restaurant.
CREDIT CARDS: Amex, MasterCard, Visa.
PRICES: [2018] per room B&B £80–£170. À la carte £40.

BLEDINGTON Gloucestershire

Map 3:D6

THE KING'S HEAD INN

Ducks glide on a brook that bisects a village green, overlooked by a Cotswold stone pub owned by Nicola and Archie Orr-Ewing, who also manage the Swan Inn at Swinbrook (see Shortlist). A Guide inspector, stepping inside, was greeted by 'friendly, very amenable staff', and shown to 'an elegantly decorated room in a quiet courtyard area away from the main building'. Flagstone floors, a firm bed, 'good-quality linen', nice lighting and an espresso machine found approval. In the bathroom, a shower 'produced a nice, strong jet of water'. Rooms in the old inn are smaller. All have handmade, own-brand toiletries. Back in the bar, 'soft lighting' added to a 'relaxed and cosy' atmosphere, 'made all the warmer by a large open fire'. In the restaurant, Mike Tozer's menus draw on seasonal, local, free-range and organic produce, beef from the family farm. Dishes range from pub classics (burgers, haddock and chips) to traditional British with a European spin. Maybe lamb chump, garden peas, mint, spinach risotto, tenderstem broccoli, jus. A 'wide choice' at breakfast includes 'delicious, thick, creamy yogurt', 'outstanding' eggs Benedict, locally smoked ham.

The Green
Bledington
OX7 6XQ

T: 01608 658365
E: info@kingsheadinn.net
W: www.thekingsheadinn.net

BEDROOMS: 12. 6 in courtyard annexe, some on ground floor.
OPEN: all year except 25/26 Dec.
FACILITIES: bar, restaurant, snug, courtyard, free Wi-Fi, in-room TV (Freeview), children's play area, unsuitable for disabled.
BACKGROUND MUSIC: most of the day, in bar.
LOCATION: on village green.
CHILDREN: all ages welcomed.
DOGS: allowed in bar and certain bedrooms by arrangement, not in restaurant.
CREDIT CARDS: MasterCard, Visa.
PRICES: [2018] per room B&B single £80–£105, double £110–£140. À la carte £35. 1-night bookings refused Sat.

BORROWDALE Cumbria

Map 4: inset C2

HAZEL BANK

⚜ Previous César winner

Gary and Donna MacRae take evident pride
in their hotel in its own wooded grounds,
perched above this hamlet in the Borrowdale
valley. It has views of Scafell Pike and Great
Gable. 'We had a lovely, relaxing stay in this
gorgeous country house,' writes a reader. 'Such
a beautiful setting. The service was outstanding
and the food was delicious.' 'Gary MacRae
is a delightful host,' reports a trusted Guide
correspondent, who had a comfortable room,
Bowfell, and was mightily impressed by the
bathroom: the 'beautiful wall tiling', underfloor
heating, anti-mist mirror, big bath and 'copious
supplies' of posh toiletries. At 7 pm guests gather
for canapés and a four-course meal cooked by
Mrs MacRae and chef David Jackson, with
good choices at each course. Maybe a warm
goat's cheese tart, passion fruit sorbet, cradle of
Lakeland Herdwick lamb, crème brûlée with
garden-grown strawberry and rhubarb compote.
At breakfast there are omelettes, kippers,
Cumberland sausage, of course. Walks start
from the door, and guests may ask for a packed
lunch ('terrific sandwiches'). (Michael Gwinnell,
Mike and Barbara Clegg, and others)

Borrowdale
Keswick
CA12 5XB

T: 017687 77248
E: info@hazelbankhotel.co.uk
W: www.hazelbankhotel.co.uk

BEDROOMS: 7. 1 on ground floor with
walk-in shower.
OPEN: all year except 15 Dec–24 Jan.
FACILITIES: lounge, dining room,
drying room, free Wi-Fi, in-room
TV (Freeview), 4-acre grounds
(croquet, woodland walks).
BACKGROUND MUSIC: none.
LOCATION: 6 miles S of Keswick on
B5289 to Borrowdale.
CHILDREN: not under 16.
DOGS: not allowed.
CREDIT CARDS: MasterCard, Visa.
PRICES: [2018] per person B&B
£55–£90. À la carte £32. Min.
2-night bookings except by special
arrangement.

BORROWDALE Cumbria

Map 4: inset C2

LEATHES HEAD HOTEL

Cumbrian comforts abound at this 'well-kept' Edwardian country house hotel, in three-acre grounds in a 'beautiful setting' in the Borrowdale valley. Laura Dadulak joins this year as manager. There are binoculars in the lounge, and a 'pretty terrace' to take in the valley and fell views. A roaring fire in the lounge keeps the chill away on cold days while, in fine weather, parasols on the terrace provide shade for a soothing cuppa after one of the 'many lovely walks'. For stronger rejuvenation, Graphite, the oak and slate bar ('very "boutique hotel"'), stocks local gins and ales, and has a topographical map of the surrounding landscape etched into its counter top, allowing you to plan your next day's trek. In the newly refurbished restaurant, the modern British menu highlights produce grown, reared and foraged in Cumbria including vegetables from an on-site greenhouse. Chef Noel Breaks serves dishes such as Borrowdale venison and gnocchi, with rainbow chard, girolles, turnip; daily-changing ravioli. Bedrooms, individually styled and variously sized, have garden, lake or countryside views. 'Our good-size room had a brand new bathroom.' Breakfast has American pancakes, egg and soldiers. (ST)

25% DISCOUNT VOUCHERS

Borrowdale
Keswick
CA12 5UY

T: 01768 777247
E: reservations@leatheshead.co.uk
W: www.leatheshead.co.uk

BEDROOMS: 11. Some on ground floor, 1 suitable for disabled.
OPEN: all year.
FACILITIES: lounge, conservatory, bar, dining room, free Wi-Fi, in-room TV (Freeview), civil wedding licence, drying room, terrace, 3-acre grounds.
BACKGROUND MUSIC: in bar and dining room.
LOCATION: 4½ miles S of Keswick.
CHILDREN: not under 15.
DOGS: allowed in some bedrooms and public areas.
CREDIT CARDS: all major cards.
PRICES: [2018] per room B&B £100–£190, D,B&B £160–£285. À la carte £45.

BOSCASTLE Cornwall

Map 1:C3

THE OLD RECTORY

'What a super place to stay for tackling some of the Coastal Path; it ticks all possible boxes,' writes a Guide inspector in 2018 of Sally and Chris Searle's historic B&B. 'Cheerful, chatty but never intrusive', Sally, whose grandmother grew up in the rectory, is a 'mine of information on Thomas Hardy' – the author stayed here in 1870 while planning the renovation of St Juliot's church, returning years later to pen some notable poetry. Rooms have 'real comfort and charm'. Emma's, with its original fireplace and loo ('a working museum piece'), overlooks a 'super garden with lots of early camellias'; Mr Hardy's, where the writer slept, is 'smaller but still cosy and comfy'. All four rooms have 'organic smellies', proper wardrobe hangers, and a tea tray with fresh milk, 'delicious home-made shortbread' and a teapot. However, after a mix-up with their booking, regular readers in 2018 found their room to be 'mournful'.Locally sourced ingredients, some from Sally's walled kitchen garden, fuel a vast breakfast selection with 'four smoked fishes, along with massive veggie and carnivore selections that set you up for a long cliff walk' – or perhaps a short stroll across three fields to St Juliot's.

St Juliot
Boscastle
PL35 0BT

T: 01840 250225
E: sally@stjuliot.com
W: www.stjuliot.com

BEDROOMS: 4. 1 in stables (connected to house via conservatory).
OPEN: normally Feb–end Oct, 'but please check'.
FACILITIES: sitting room, breakfast room, conservatory, free Wi-Fi, in-room TV (Freeview), 3-acre garden (croquet lawn, 'lookout', walled kitchen garden), unsuitable for disabled.
BACKGROUND MUSIC: none.
LOCATION: 2 miles NE of Boscastle.
CHILDREN: not under 12.
DOGS: up to 2 allowed, only in stable room (£10 per stay).
CREDIT CARDS: MasterCard, Visa.
PRICES: [2018] per room B&B single £56–£99, double £70–£115. 1-night bookings only accepted if a late vacancy or quiet period.

BOSHAM Sussex

Map 2:E3

THE MILLSTREAM

'The enthusiastic welcome immediately made us feel at home again.' In a pretty coastal village near Chichester harbour, the Wild family's traditional red brick hotel has grown from three 17th-century workmen's cottages. Some guests may find it old-fashioned, and a room in the modern extension was disliked, but regular visitors over many years praise its 'high standards and immaculate upkeep'. A 'nice, cosy atmosphere' is retained thanks to its many long-serving staff members. Rooms vary in size and decor, but all greet visitors with biscuits, bathrobes and fresh milk in the fridge. Many of the newly refurbished rooms have patio doors on to the lawn, or look across the gardens where, in clement weather, there are tables for afternoon tea. On colder days, the 'very comfortable' lounge provides a refuge from the elements, and a good place to relax before supper in Marwick's brasserie or Neil Hiskey's modern restaurant. 'We had blue cheese soufflé followed by Thai prawn curry. Both were superb.' Breakfast is a 'treat'. 'We wouldn't stay anywhere else when we're theatre-hopping in Chichester.' (Brian and Gwen Thomas, and others)

Bosham Lane
Bosham
PO18 8HL

T: 01243 573234
E: info@millstream-hotel.co.uk
W: www.millstreamhotel.com

BEDROOMS: 35. 2 in cottage, 7 on ground floor, 2 suitable for disabled.
OPEN: all year.
FACILITIES: lounge, bar, restaurant (pianist Sat eve), brasserie, conference room, free Wi-Fi, in-room TV (Freeview), civil wedding licence, front lawn (alfresco dining), residents' garden (stream, gazebo).
BACKGROUND MUSIC: all day in bar, lounge and restaurants.
LOCATION: 4 miles W of Chichester.
CHILDREN: all ages welcomed.
DOGS: not allowed.
CREDIT CARDS: MasterCard, Visa.
PRICES: [2018] per room B&B £135–£245, D,B&B £180–£310. À la carte £39. 1-night bookings sometimes refused Sat.

BOURTON-ON-THE-HILL Gloucestershire   Map 3:D6

HORSE AND GROOM

Close to Batsford Park, once home to the
Mitfords, and its arboretum, this Cotswold-stone
Georgian inn remains friendly and affordable
after a seamless transition from private ownership
to the Cirrus Inns group in 2016. The five
bedrooms are individually styled, supplied with
cafetière coffee, a teapot, home-baked biscuits,
smart bathroom products. 'Our standard double
looked down towards the Evenlode valley and
Moreton-in-Marsh. It was a good size with a
generous bathroom (retro fittings), a bath with
shower over. Heavy interlined blinds cut out the
light and dimmed the noise from the road; we
slept well.' All rooms are on the first floor, but
the lie of the land means that one, with French
windows, opens on to the garden. In the bar and
dining room, the daily-changing menu reflects
what is good, local and available. Maybe 'delicious
twice-cooked goat's cheese soufflé, well-presented
free-range chicken supreme, crushed potatoes'. A
vegan option, maybe asparagus and flageolet bean
risotto. 'Breakfast had a small buffet (with pastries
and two home-made preserves but boring orange
juice). The cooked bacon, egg and sausage was
excellent.' (Desmond and Jenny Balmer)

25% DISCOUNT VOUCHERS

Bourton-on-the-Hill
GL56 9AQ

T: 01386 700413
E: enquiries@horseandgroom.info
W: www.horseandgroom.info

BEDROOMS: 5.
OPEN: all year except Christmas/
New Year, restaurant closed
Sun eve except on bank holiday
weekends.
FACILITIES: bar/restaurant, free
Wi-Fi, in-room TV (Freeview),
1-acre garden, public rooms
wheelchair accessible (toilets
upstairs).
BACKGROUND MUSIC: none.
LOCATION: village centre.
CHILDREN: all ages welcomed.
DOGS: allowed in most bedrooms
('small additional charge') and in
bar, not in dining room.
CREDIT CARDS: MasterCard, Visa.
PRICES: [2018] per room B&B
£110–£195. À la carte £30. 1-night
bookings refused weekends.

BOWNESS-ON-WINDERMERE Cumbria   Map 4: inset C2

LINDETH FELL

'Lovely owners', the 'charming and friendly' Kennedy family, lay on a cream tea for new arrivals at their wisteria-draped Edwardian country house, run as a luxury B&B. It sits in grounds laid out by nurseryman and garden designer Thomas Mawson, and melts into the landscape, against a backdrop of the fells swaddling Lake Windermere. Bedrooms range from snug singles to spacious, traditionally styled doubles with lake views. All are warmly elegant, and supplied with an espresso machine, decanter of sherry, smart toiletries. A generous breakfast includes home-made yogurt and marmalade, French pastries; perhaps a Cumberland grill, kippers or Finnan haddock, or full veggie with free-range eggs. Soup and sandwiches are served all day, with wines from a short list, while from 12 to 8 pm, with notice, you can order a cheese, meat or fish platter. Sunday lunch can also be pre-booked. Sitting on the terrace when the rhododendrons are in full cry, you may not want to tear yourself away, unless for spa treatments in Windermere, or a meal at The Punch Bowl in Crosthwaite (see entry), well worth the 15-minute drive.

Lyth Valley Road
Bowness-on-Windermere
LA23 3JP

T: 01539 443286
E: kennedy@lindethfell.co.uk
W: www.lindethfell.co.uk

BEDROOMS: 14. 1, on ground floor, suitable for disabled.
OPEN: all year except 24–26 Dec, 2 Jan–8 Feb, open for New Year.
FACILITIES: 2 lounges, bar, entrance hall with seating, dining room, free Wi-Fi, in-room TV (Freeview), 7-acre grounds (terrace, gardens, croquet, putting, bowls, tarn), complimentary access to local gym, spa and pool, 5 mins' drive away.
BACKGROUND MUSIC: classical music in dining room and bar.
LOCATION: 1 mile S of Bowness.
CHILDREN: all ages welcomed.
DOGS: only assistance dogs allowed.
CREDIT CARDS: MasterCard, Visa.
PRICES: [2018] per room B&B single £95–£187, double £190–£250. Pre-ordered Sunday lunch £24, evening platters £14.50. 1-night bookings sometimes refused weekends.

SEE ALSO SHORTLIST

BRADFORD-ON-AVON Wiltshire   Map 2:D1

WIDBROOK GRANGE   **NEW**

A sheep made out of scrap metal and spark plugs, 'old farm vehicles and delivery floats' are part of the fun at Jane and Peter Wragg's Georgian farmhouse, which gains a full Guide entry this year. Our inspectors were greeted by the 'welcoming, enthusiastic' manager, and shown to an outbuilding room with 'beamed ceiling, a huge bed, crisp bedlinen, leather wing armchair'; it was 'warm on a very cold night'. A large bathroom had 'amazing painted tiles', a good over-bath shower, Bramley toiletries. An umbrella was provided for the walk to the main house, where rooms have such 'endlessly inventive features' as 'a washbasin over an old Pashley bike'. A stone-flagged bar led off a 'lovely, slightly clubby sitting room with tweedy fabrics, leather and wood'. At dinner, chef Sandor Szucs's menus include such 'exceptionally interesting dishes' as rosemary-marinated lamb, smoked root vegetables, sage polenta, black garlic jus; from the vegan menu, salt-baked celeriac, quinoa risotto, grilled heritage carrots, glazed candy beetroot, salsa verde. After a dip in the indoor pool, we enjoyed breakfast with 'excellent smoked salmon and scrambled eggs'. Sister pub The Boat House, opposite, overlooks the marina.

Widbrook
Bradford-on-Avon
BA15 1UH

T: 01225 864750
E: stay@widbrookgrange.co.uk
W: www.widbrookgrange.co.uk

BEDROOMS: 19. Some in courtyard, 1 suitable for disabled.
OPEN: all year.
FACILITIES: bar, snug, restaurant, free Wi-Fi, in-room TV (Freeview), civil wedding licence, function facilities, 11-acre grounds, 11-metre indoor heated swimming pool, gym, giant chess, parking, public rooms wheelchair accessible.
BACKGROUND MUSIC: soft, in dining room.
LOCATION: 2 miles south of Bradford-on-Avon.
CHILDREN: all ages welcomed.
DOGS: allowed in courtyard bedrooms (£15 per dog per night) and public rooms, except restaurant.
CREDIT CARDS: Amex, MasterCard, Visa.
PRICES: [2018] per room B&B £105–£220, family room £170–£235. À la carte £32.

SEE ALSO SHORTLIST

BRADFORD-ON-AVON Wiltshire

Map 2:D1

WOOLLEY GRANGE

'As soon as we arrived, the kids got started on the Woolley Grange Sheep Challenge treasure hunt,' writes a Guide insider after a stay at this 'beautiful Jacobean manor house in lovely grounds'. Part of Nigel Chapman's Luxury Family Hotels group, it has 'scores of considerate little touches' making for real child-friendliness: 'space to run around, fairy houses, a hidden glockenspiel, swing ball, cricket, badminton…' Comfy sitting rooms with log fires are patrolled by resident spaniel Rex, while bedrooms – some in annexes – are traditionally styled, including doubles, trebles, and suites such as the Hayloft, with sitting room and two bedrooms, sleeping seven. At night families might take an early supper together, or children have high tea before parents sit down to a candlelit dinner. Chef Jethro Lawrence uses seasonal produce from local suppliers and the kitchen garden, in such dishes as confit duck leg, pancetta, shallot potato cake, garlic kale, caramelised red onion, demi-glace. At breakfast, guests devour the morning's newsletter over such 'delicious' dishes as poached eggs and spinach on a toasted muffin. 'Friendly staff went out of their way to be helpful.' (AR-T)

Woolley Green
Bradford-on-Avon
BA15 1TX

T: 01225 864705
E: info@woolleygrangehotel.co.uk
W: www.woolleygrangehotel.co.uk

BEDROOMS: 25. 11 in annexes, 2 on ground floor, 1 suitable for disabled.
OPEN: all year.
FACILITIES: 2 lounges, 2 restaurants, cinema, 2 private dining rooms, free Wi-Fi, in-room TV (Freeview), crèche, play room, spa, heated indoor and outdoor swimming pools, civil wedding licence, 14-acre grounds, wheelchair accessible.
BACKGROUND MUSIC: in restaurants.
LOCATION: 1 mile NE of Bradford-on-Avon, 8½ miles SE of Bath.
CHILDREN: all ages welcomed.
DOGS: allowed in bedrooms and public rooms, not in restaurants.
CREDIT CARDS: Amex, MasterCard, Visa.
PRICES: [2018] per room B&B £120–£560, D,B&B £190–£650. À la carte £40. 1-night bookings sometimes refused weekends.

SEE ALSO SHORTLIST

BRAITHWAITE Cumbria

THE COTTAGE IN THE WOOD

'Stunning views' towards Skiddaw, and glimpses of red squirrels, are served with the 'superb dinner' at Kath and Liam Berney's 'idyllic' restaurant-with-rooms on the Whinlatter Pass. The Cottage in question is a 17th-century coaching inn; the Wood is England's only true mountain forest. 'The owners have translated their passion and hard work through to the staff. The enthusiasm is addictive,' report readers in 2018. 'It was like staying with friends.' New chef Ben Wilkinson's northern European-style dishes reflect the wooded Lakeland location, often with a pine-infused flavour. The Herdwick hogget remains a perennial favourite. 'The tasting menu was superb; the wines exquisite.' In some rooms, original features sit alongside slick, contemporary flourishes. While those in the main house can be small, even 'tiny', they have 'all the comforts'. The loft room allows stargazing from your bed, while the 'generously proportioned, luxurious' garden room offers a seating area and striking wet room. 'A lot of thoughtful touches' is the conclusion of two readers, who, at breakfast, were asked 'if they preferred their scrambled eggs creamy or firmer – the first time that has ever happened!'. (Neil Leaver, RO, and others)

Magic Hill
Braithwaite
CA12 5TW

T: 017687 78409
E: relax@thecottageinthewood.co.uk
W: www.thecottageinthewood.co.uk

BEDROOMS: 9. 1 in the garden with separate entrance.
OPEN: all year except 25/26 Dec, 2nd and 3rd week Jan, restaurant closed Mon.
FACILITIES: lounge, restaurant, free Wi-Fi, in-room TV (Freeview), drying room, secure bicycle storage, terraced garden, 2 acres of woodland, restaurant and public areas wheelchair accessible, adapted toilet.
BACKGROUND MUSIC: none.
LOCATION: 5 miles NW of Keswick.
CHILDREN: not under 10.
DOGS: not allowed.
CREDIT CARDS: MasterCard, Visa.
PRICES: [2018] per room B&B single £96, double £96–£220, D,B&B double £200–£290. Set menu £45, tasting menu £65. 1-night bookings refused weekends.

BRAMPTON Cumbria   Map 4:B3

FARLAM HALL

'This continues to be a very dependable oasis,' writes a trusted reader and regular visitor to this country house hotel (Relais & Châteaux), between the North Pennines Area of Outstanding Natural Beauty and Hadrian's Wall World Heritage site. It has been run by the Quinion family since 1975 with some staff having worked at the property for over 30 years, and offers 'a truly exceptional experience'. The interiors of the creeper-clad bay-fronted manor house are traditional and elegant, with marble fireplaces, paintings, antiques and ornaments. Guests arriving in the afternoon are served tea and home-made cakes in one of the lounges. Bedrooms, mainly in peachy shades, are large and comfortable, with armchairs, sofas, garden views. Those in the stables are reached via an exterior stone staircase – ideal if you've been out late on the razzle. From the dining room, tall windows look on to an ornamental lake. Dinner, at 8 pm, includes such 'beautifully cooked' dishes as Yorkshire venison, juniper and port wine sauce (give notice if you're vegetarian). Farlam, concludes our reader, is 'one of those now endangered species, a Proper Hotel'.
(Chris Savory)

25% DISCOUNT VOUCHERS

Hallbankgate
Brampton
CA8 2NG

T: 01697 746234
E: farlam@farlamhall.co.uk
W: www.farlamhall.co.uk

BEDROOMS: 12. 2 on ground floor, 1 in stables 3 mins' walk from house.
OPEN: all year except 24–31 Dec (restaurant open Christmas Eve), 7–25 Jan.
FACILITIES: 2 lounges, restaurant, free Wi-Fi, in-room TV (Freeview), civil wedding licence, 6-acre grounds, unsuitable for disabled.
BACKGROUND MUSIC: none.
LOCATION: on A689, 2½ miles SE of Brampton (not in Farlam village).
CHILDREN: not under 5.
DOGS: allowed in bedrooms (not unattended) and public rooms, not in restaurant.
CREDIT CARDS: Amex, MasterCard, Visa.
PRICES: [2018] per room B&B single £165–£195, double £211–£271, D,B&B double £310–£370. Set dinner £50. 1-night bookings refused over New Year period.

BRANCASTER STAITHE Norfolk

THE WHITE HORSE

♉ Previous César winner

'One of my favourite hotels,' writes a trusted reader, after nights at the Nye family's inn with views across salt marshes to the sea. 'Good location, nice room, excellent food. It has it all.' Bedrooms are contemporary in style, decorated in light coastal colours. A split-level room at the top has a balcony and telescope, while dog-friendly annexe rooms have a private terrace, a wood-floored entrance for muddy mutts and boots. 'We had a big room overlooking the sea marsh, providing great birdwatching opportunities when the tide was out.' Chef Fran Hartshorne cooks ambitious food in the regulars' bar, and a menu strong on local produce for the restaurant, along with the glass-walled conservatory and decked terrace. For instance, salt marsh lamb, fish and shellfish, inventive vegetarian options (celeriac, foraged wild garlic, apple, potato, leaves, Havensfield fried hen's egg). 'Halibut, plaice, stone bass were all excellent – and I can very highly recommend the lemon tart.' Staff are 'young, efficient and friendly'. Breakfast brought 'decent fruit, good croissants, a perfect poached egg'. Walkers can pick up the Coastal Path at the bottom of the garden. (Peter Anderson)

Main Road
Brancaster Staithe
PE31 8BY

T: 01485 210262
E: reception@whitehorsebrancaster.co.uk
W: www.whitehorsebrancaster.co.uk

BEDROOMS: 15. 8 on ground floor in annexe, 1 suitable for disabled.
OPEN: all year.
FACILITIES: public bar, open-plan lounge areas, conservatory restaurant, dining-room, free Wi-Fi, in-room TV (Freeview), ½-acre garden (terrace, covered sunken garden), in-room therapies, public rooms wheelchair accessible, adapted toilet.
BACKGROUND MUSIC: 'subtle' in restaurant.
LOCATION: centre of village.
CHILDREN: all ages welcomed.
DOGS: allowed in garden rooms (£10 per night), bar.
CREDIT CARDS: MasterCard, Visa.
PRICES: [2018] per room B&B £120–£200, D,B&B (Sun–Thurs in low season only, except bank hols and school hols) £170–£250. À la carte £30.

BRANSCOMBE Devon

Map 1:C5

THE MASON'S ARMS

NEW

It was all go at this whitewashed, 14th-century former cider house in Britain's longest village, when a trusted reader arrived at 1 pm. 'The place was heaving with guests, but the deputy manager immediately welcomed us, taking us through check-in at a splendid but thoughtful rate of knots.' The front garden, with tables and thatch parasols, overlooks the mile-long main street which leads down, past picturesque thatched cottages, to the South West Coast Path and a shingle beach. Upgraded to a full entry this year, the popular inn's affordable, cottage-style pub bedrooms vary in size. 'Ours was lovely and large, with a huge bathroom, but only one tiny window overlooking the car park.' Reading lighting and soundproofing were 'very good'. Dog-friendly, ground-floor cottage rooms have antiques, bath and shower. Best are Branscombe rooms, with perhaps a four-poster, French doors, countryside views. Long menus of good pub fare include a hand-pressed, chargrilled beef burger on brioche, steamed Exe mussels, several vegetarian options. Alison Ede, who manages for St Austell Brewery Hotels & Inns, oversees the 'efficient and welcoming staff', kept busy serving food and drinks throughout the day. (Susan Jenkinson)

Branscombe
EX12 3DJ

T: 01297 680300
E: masonsarms@staustellbrewery.co.uk
W: www.masonsarms.co.uk

BEDROOMS: 27. 14 in cottages, 1 suitable for disabled.
OPEN: all year.
FACILITIES: bar, restaurant, free Wi-Fi (in main bar), in-room TV, garden with outdoor seating, public rooms wheelchair accessible, adapted toilet (reached via outside route).
BACKGROUND MUSIC: none.
LOCATION: village centre.
CHILDREN: all ages welcomed.
DOGS: allowed in ground-floor cottage rooms by arrangement (£10 per dog per night).
CREDIT CARDS: Diners, MasterCard, Visa.
PRICES: [2018] per room B&B £85–£150. À la carte £26.

BRIGHTON Sussex

Map 2:E4

ARTIST RESIDENCE BRIGHTON

Charlotte and Justin Salisbury's eclectic hotel
distils relaxed, creative Brighton into a cool
Regency town house. Original artwork, murals
and limited edition prints decorate bedrooms,
many of which overlook the seafront. One Guide
reader this year enjoyed Room 21's 'perfect
view', and 'big Le Creuset mugs for the excellent
tea and fresh milk; a perfect shared treat in the
freestanding bath – who needs champagne?'
Less praise, however, for the few coat-hangers
and 'standard non-fluffy towels'. Quirky
vintage completes the look. An apartment with
kitchenette was added next door in 2018, but
readers recommend trying new chef Dan Kenny's
'good, reasonably priced' tapas menu in the Set
bar, which also serves cocktails and craft beers.
'The pork and cheese croquette; squid bun; and
potatoes and buttermilk, were really tasty. Sweet
items (malted marshmallows, blood orange
madeleines) were delicious.' Seasonal tasting
menus with fashionably basic descriptions – trout
crab, mussel – are served in the Set restaurant.
An inventive breakfast menu includes porridge
with maple pecans, turmeric-soaked apricots,
chia seeds and toasted cocoa nibs. (Kevin and
Victoria Seymour)

34 Regency Square
Brighton
BN1 2FJ

T: 01273 324302
E: brighton@artistresidence.co.uk
W: www.artistresidence.co.uk/
   our-hotels/brighton/

BEDROOMS: 25. 2 in The Apartment
in building next door.
OPEN: all year, restaurant closed
25/26 Dec.
FACILITIES: lift, lounge, 2 bars,
restaurant, ping-pong/meeting
room, free Wi-Fi, in-room TV
(Freeview), unsuitable for disabled.
BACKGROUND MUSIC: in public areas.
LOCATION: town centre.
CHILDREN: not under 16.
DOGS: allowed in some bedrooms
and in the Set bar.
CREDIT CARDS: Amex, MasterCard,
Visa.
PRICES: [2018] room only double
£85–£350. Min. 2-night stay at
weekends.

SEE ALSO SHORTLIST

BRIGHTON Sussex

Map 2:E4

DRAKES

'Exquisite' was the verdict of a regular reader on a belated return to this ultra-chic hotel on the resort's Regency seafront. All the rooms are individually styled. Some are on the attic floor, there's a good-value single, a ground-floor en suite with double monsoon wet room. 'Bijou' city-facing rooms have a freestanding bath and wet room. Most glamorous are the feature rooms, with a freestanding bath in the floor-to-ceiling window offering pier views – particularly glorious at dusk. But at all hours, rooms have cafetière coffee (fresh milk and espresso delivered on request), glossy magazines, still and sparkling water, complimentary branded slippers and toiletry gift packs. The sea-facing cocktail bar is open to non-residents in licensing hours – and around the clock to resident guests. In 'the best restaurant in Brighton', chef Andy Vitez wins high praise for his modern European dishes including pan-fried Barbary duck breast, mulled wine-poached pears, dark chocolate, confit leg bonbon; mushroom and vegetable Wellington with truffle cream sauce. Breakfast choices range from full English with handmade sausages, through free-range eggs Benedict, smoked haddock and salmon, to field mushrooms on toast. (DB)

25% DISCOUNT VOUCHERS

43–44 Marine Parade
Brighton
BN2 1PE

T: 01273 696934
E: info@drakesofbrighton.com
W: www.drakesofbrighton.com

BEDROOMS: 20.
OPEN: all year.
FACILITIES: lounge/bar, restaurant, meeting/private dining room, free Wi-Fi, in-room TV (Sky), civil wedding licence, off-road parking, unsuitable for disabled.
BACKGROUND MUSIC: in bar and restaurant.
LOCATION: ½ mile from centre, on seafront.
CHILDREN: all ages welcomed.
DOGS: only assistance dogs allowed.
CREDIT CARDS: Amex, MasterCard, Visa.
PRICES: [2018] room only £120–£360, D,B&B £185–£365. Breakfast £7.50–£15, tasting menu £65, set menu £36–£48. Min. 2-night stay Fri/Sat or Sat/Sun, but check availability.

SEE ALSO SHORTLIST

BRILL Buckinghamshire

Map 2:C3

THE POINTER

NEW

In the hilltop village that inspired JRR Tolkien's Bree, this red brick pub-and-restaurant-with-rooms is a logical extension to new owner Harry Aubrey-Fletcher's farm. Staff are 'exceptionally friendly', say inspectors in 2018. 'Simply stylish, very comfortable' bedrooms are in a building opposite. A ground-floor room had a large bathroom with slipper bath, 'very good walk-in shower'. The modern rustic style embraces 'chunky oak furniture, sisal carpet, ornately carved wood panels over the bed'. The window overlooked the road; upstairs rooms are smaller but more private. In the restaurant and the 'large, lovely garden', chef James Graham's menus have fish and vegetarian options, but carnivores have a field day, with the owner's livestock (and organic vegetable garden) supplying the kitchen – a classic example of farm-to-fork. 'Very good bread' arrived with butter and beef dripping, a 'refreshing taster of tomato and cucumber'. Roast turbot, with wild garlic and pea fricassée, was 'fantastic'; hay-baked shoulder and rack of lamb 'immaculately cooked'. Breakfast brought a good buffet, 'perfectly cooked' eggs Florentine. Verdict: 'High prices, but high standards. And if you're after a bargain, Bicester outlet village is nearby.'

27 Church Street
Brill
HP18 9RT

T: 01844 238339
E: office@thepointerbrill.co.uk
W: thepointerbrill.co.uk

BEDROOMS: 4. In annexe opposite, 2 on ground floor.
OPEN: all year, closed Mon.
FACILITIES: restaurant, bar, garden, free Wi-Fi in main building, in-room TV, bar (not restaurant) wheelchair accessible, adapted toilet.
BACKGROUND MUSIC: soft instrumental or vocal.
LOCATION: near village centre.
CHILDREN: all ages welcomed.
DOGS: allowed in bedrooms (£20 per dog per night), in bar, but not in restaurant.
CREDIT CARDS: MasterCard, Visa.
PRICES: [2018] per room B&B £130–£185. À la carte £43, set menu (Tues–Fri) £18–£22.50.

BRISTOL

Map 1:B6

BACKWELL HOUSE NEW

There is make-do-and-mend on a grand scale at the Hobbs family's classical Georgian mansion, incorporating upcycled materials mostly salvaged on site. Beyond the portico, 'the impression is of a very elegant mansion converted into a modern, chic hotel', say our inspectors, who were greeted by 'welcoming and helpful' staff. 'Reception rooms maintain the original house's grandeur.' From the 'dramatic entrance hall', an 'elegant stone staircase sweeps up' to bedrooms with maybe a reconditioned, in-room copper bathtub, a basin fashioned from concrete-filled vintage suitcases. All are 'well equipped, with luxurious bedding, cafetière, fresh milk and rural views. 'Our room had no wardrobe, just a shelf and rail with hangers' (that's the make-do bit). The bathroom had 'a striking punched copper sink'. The 'focal point' bar sports recycled wood from the kitchen floor, while in the dining room, 'bread was warm from the oven, a perfect companion to wonderfully smooth duck liver pâté'. Chef Josh Hutson's chicken supreme and fondant potatoes had 'a colourful sweep of tarragon sauce'. Everything was 'sourced locally from organic farms'. Breakfast brought 'light and buttery scrambled eggs'.

Farleigh Road
Bristol
BS48 3QA

T: 0117 325 1110
E: enquiries@backwellhouse.co.uk
w: backwellhouse.co.uk

BEDROOMS: 9.
OPEN: all year except Christmas (phone for details).
FACILITIES: bar, lounge, breakfast room, restaurant (closed Sun eve), conservatory, meeting room/snug, free Wi-Fi, in-room TV (Freeview), civil wedding licence, cinema room, ornamental walled garden, parking, public rooms wheelchair accessible, adapted toilet.
BACKGROUND MUSIC: in public areas.
LOCATION: in the country, 8 miles from Bristol.
CHILDREN: not under 12.
DOGS: not allowed.
CREDIT CARDS: all major credit cards.
PRICES: [2018] per room B&B £95–£245. Set dinner £24.50–£30.

BRISTOL

BROOKS GUESTHOUSE

Owners Carla and Andrew Brooks have made
a foray into the country (see entry for Brooks
Country House, Ross-on-Wye), but everything
ticks over nicely back at their 'impressive' city
B&B. It occupies a converted 1960s office block
in the old town, by St Nicholas market, a stroll
from the harbour with its waterside eateries. The
unfussy style mixes bare floorboards with leather
sofas, moulded plastic chairs, an honesty bar.
Bedrooms have controllable heating, shutters,
efficient bathroom, hospitality tray, wine glasses, a
Roberts radio. Some overlook the Mediterranean-
style courtyard. A novel option, especially fun for
children, is to take one of the Airstream camper
vans on the Astroturf-covered roof. One, sleeping
four, had 'a good-size double bed', two small
singles, good bedding and towels, a powerful
shower, 'great lighting including colour-changing
strips'. When the seagulls sound reveille it is time
for breakfast in the open-plan kitchen, including
organic yogurts, 'lovely jams, marmalade and
juices', home-made granola, fruit compote, the
full English, bacon butties, smoked-salmon
bagels. 'The staff were very friendly, taking time
to ask the children how they liked staying on the
roof.' It was 'very good value'.

Exchange Avenue
Bristol
BS1 1UB

T: 0117 930 0066
E: info@brooksguesthousebristol.
   com
W: www.brooksguesthousebristol.
   com

BEDROOMS: 27. 4 in Airstream
caravans on roof.
OPEN: all year except 24–26 Dec.
FACILITIES: lift, lounge/breakfast
room, honesty bar, free Wi-Fi,
in-room TV (Freeview), courtyard
garden.
BACKGROUND MUSIC: contemporary
in lounge and breakfast area.
LOCATION: central, next to
St Nicholas Market.
CHILDREN: all ages welcomed.
DOGS: not allowed.
CREDIT CARDS: MasterCard, Visa.
PRICES: [2018] per room B&B single
£89–£149, double £99–£169. Min.
2-night stay Sat.

BRISTOL

Map 1:B6

NUMBER THIRTY EIGHT CLIFTON

♀ Previous César winner

Whichever room you choose at Adam Dorrien-Smith's stylish B&B, you are assured of a view. The bay-fronted Georgian merchant's house stands high on the hill, looking out over Clifton Downs to the fore, and across the city at the rear, to the docks and distant hills. Each room is shipshape and Bristol fashionable, with an 'excellent bathroom', luxury toiletries, waffle dressing gowns, a minibar – rather importantly, as the much-praised 'attentive staff' disappear in mid-evening, so you have to let yourself in and attend to your own needs. Wood-panelled bedroom walls are painted in mostly muted, always restful colours. Some have a sleigh bed, perhaps a roll-top copper bath or a separate bath and shower. You can take a cream tea or a cocktail by the log-burner in the sitting room, or on the roof terrace, feeling on top of the world. With the acquisition of the next-door property, since last year two new suites have been added, and a meeting space/private dining room. At breakfast there are pastries, fresh fruit, granola, smoked salmon, a locally sourced full English with roasted vine tomatoes. More reports, please.

38 Upper Belgrave Road
Bristol
BS8 2XN

T: 0117 946 6905
E: info@number38clifton.com
W: www.number38clifton.com

BEDROOMS: 11.
OPEN: all year.
FACILITIES: lounge, breakfast room, meeting space, free Wi-Fi, in-room TV (Freeview), terrace, limited number of parking permits on request, unsuitable for disabled.
BACKGROUND MUSIC: in public areas 8 am–8 pm.
LOCATION: 2½ miles from city centre.
CHILDREN: not under 13.
DOGS: not allowed.
CREDIT CARDS: all major cards.
PRICES: [2018] per room B&B single £115–£235, double £130–£265.

BROADWAY Worcestershire

Map 3:D6

THE BROADWAY HOTEL

'Twin sentinel clipped yews' stand at the
entrance of this 15th-century hotel, part of the
Cotswolds Inns and Hotels group. It is 'friendly
and personal', says a Guide inspector, 'but with
clearly professionally trained management'. An
equestrian theme in bedrooms is inspired by the
proximity of Cheltenham. Our room, Golden
Miller (five times Gold Cup winner in the 1930s),
was light and relaxing, with a raftered ceiling,
latticed casements, horsey-print headboard and
cushions.' The small bathroom had Molton
Brown toiletries; the washbasin, with capricious
taps, was in the bedroom. There are larger rooms
too: Desert Orchid has a four-poster, wallpaper
imitating book-lined shelves. Light meals are
served in the double-height Jockey bar, with 'a
sort of minstrels' gallery arrangement', 'bespoke
wallpaper of stags' heads', an open fireplace,
tasteful seating. The conservatory-style Tattersalls
Brasserie has 'voguish decor' (unfussy neutrals,
pendant lights) and serves 'modern, fairly
elaborate' dishes, including lamb rump roasted
with fennel seed, burnt aubergine, black garlic,
braised leeks, lentils, cumin. Breakfast delivers
smoked salmon; buttermilk pancakes with bacon;
crushed avocado on granary sourdough.

25% DISCOUNT VOUCHERS

The Green
Broadway
WR12 7AA

T: 01386 852401
E: info@broadwayhotel.info
W: www.cotswold-inns-hotels.
co.uk/the-broadway-hotel/

BEDROOMS: 19. 1 on ground floor,
2 self-catering cottages nearby.
OPEN: all year.
FACILITIES: sitting room, bar,
brasserie, free Wi-Fi, in-room
TV (Freeview), courtyard, garden
(residents-only terrace), car park,
unsuitable for disabled.
BACKGROUND MUSIC: ambient in
public areas.
LOCATION: village centre, 'best to
request a parking space before you
arrive, especially in summer'.
CHILDREN: all ages welcomed.
DOGS: well-behaved dogs allowed in
some bedrooms and in public areas,
not in restaurant.
CREDIT CARDS: Amex, MasterCard,
Visa.
PRICES: [2018] per room B&B
£190–£260, D,B&B £258–£328. À la
carte £39.

SEE ALSO SHORTLIST

BROADWAY Worcestershire

Map 3:D6

THE LYGON ARMS NEW

In 'lovely Cotswold stone buildings around a pretty courtyard', this mostly 16th-century former coaching inn has had a stylish make-over. 'Its historic and quirky features have been enhanced with beautiful fabrics and colours,' say the nominators in 2018. There are several relaxing lounges. 'We had a tiny sitting room and fire to ourselves, where we enjoyed cocktails.' A wide choice of bedrooms too. Ground-floor courtyard suites open on to an individual terrace garden, while the Great Chamber Suite has a vaulted ceiling, antique furniture and heirlooms. The 'relaxed informal' atmosphere is helped by 'friendly, efficient staff' in 'smart jeans'. Food is served all day in the lounges and bar, but the place to dine is the Bar and Grill, with barrel ceiling and minstrels' gallery, where chef Ales Maurer's seasonal British dishes include Gower salt marsh lamb; Cotswold ale-battered cod; Buckland tomato, courgette and basil risotto. Breakfast has free-range eggs, good pastries, French toast with salted caramel crème fraîche. In the same inclusive spirit that saw both Charles I and Oliver Cromwell accommodated in the Civil War, children and dogs are made welcome. (Sarah and Trevor Beeton)

High Street
Broadway
WR12 7DU

T: 01386 852 255
E: reservations@lygonarmshotel.co.uk
W: www.lygonarmshotel.co.uk

BEDROOMS: 86. 26 on ground floor, 2 suitable for disabled.
OPEN: all year.
FACILITIES: 7 lounge areas, wine bar/restaurant, bar/grill, in-room TV (Freeview), free Wi-Fi, civil wedding licence, 3-acre garden, indoor pool, spa, public areas (not spa) wheelchair accessible, adapted toilet.
BACKGROUND MUSIC: in lounges.
LOCATION: village centre.
CHILDREN: all ages welcomed.
DOGS: min. 1-year-old allowed in some bedrooms, all lounges.
CREDIT CARDS: Amex, MasterCard, Visa.
PRICES: [2018] per room B&B £240–£460, D,B&B £300–£520. À la carte £35. 1-night bookings sometimes refused Sat, always at Christmas/New Year.
SEE ALSO SHORTLIST

BROADWAY Worcestershire

RUSSELL'S

A 17th-century mellow stone building overlooking the 'broad way' with its cafés, antique shops and milling tourists, is run as a well-regarded restaurant-with-rooms by Andrew and Gaynor Riley. The building once served as the workshop of furniture designer Sir Gordon Russell, and guests have free access to the design museum set up in his name. An oak-panelled staircase, built by Russell himself, leads to some of the bedrooms (two are on the ground floor). Some have beams, bare stone walls, a sloping ceiling, leaded windows. The best is huge, with a separate sitting area, whirlpool bath and walk-through shower, ceiling spots, a hurricane lantern. All are 'rather special in their own way', with a natural stone bathroom complete with robes and smart toiletries. In the kitchen, former senior sous-chef George (Jorge) Santos has been promoted to head chef, cooking a daily-changing menu of local produce. Typical dishes, stone bass, smoked bone marrow arancini, savoy cabbage, spätzle, black tiger prawn, shellfish bisque – or a vegetarian option, Evesham butternut squash, violet potato and spinach tart, roasted mixed squash, pumpkin purée, toasted seeds. Breakfast is 'cooked well and accurately'.

The Green
Broadway
WR12 7DT

T: 01386 853555
E: info@russellsofbroadway.co.uk
W: www.russellsofbroadway.co.uk

BEDROOMS: 7. 3 in adjoining building, 2 on ground floor.
OPEN: all year, restaurant closed Sun night and bank holiday Mon.
FACILITIES: residents' lounge, bar, restaurant, private dining room, free Wi-Fi, in-room TV (Freeview), patio (heating, meal service), restaurant and bar wheelchair accessible.
BACKGROUND MUSIC: in restaurant.
LOCATION: village centre.
CHILDREN: all ages welcomed, under-2s stay free, extra bed £15.
DOGS: allowed in certain bedrooms, public rooms.
CREDIT CARDS: Amex, MasterCard, Visa.
PRICES: [2018] per room B&B £130–£300. Set dinner (Mon–Fri) £24, à la carte £50. 1-night bookings refused weekends.

SEE ALSO SHORTLIST

BROCKENHURST Hampshire

Map 2:E2

THE PIG IN THE FOREST

A New Forest shooting lodge hosts mother Pig – the first of Robin Hutson's expanding chain of family-friendly Pig hotels (see index). It sets the tone with shabby-chic public spaces, a relaxed vibe and 'delightful staff who really make the place'. 'They couldn't have been more helpful with our baby.' Smaller, tastefully neutral rooms have a walk-in monsoon shower, larger ones a freestanding bath as well. Family rooms have a bunk for children, a log-burner. Cosy lodges in the grounds sport timber-clad interiors. In 2018 Guide inspectors found their room 'expensive' given the lack of space and storage, and the 'ridiculously small bedside tables'. However, in the high-ceilinged dining room, extending into a plant- and herb-filled conservatory, the cooking is 'truly outstanding; original without being pretentious'. Menus include foraged ingredients and produce from the 'huge, wonderful' kitchen garden, with plenty for vegetarians, fish fanciers and carnivores alike – perhaps Romsey lamb breast and cured neck, garden lettuce, blackcurrant leaf oil. The breakfast buffet's 'huge choice' is 'truly a feast', while cooked dishes 'sound tempting'. 'We are such fans.' (Anna and Bill Brewer, and others)

Beaulieu Road
Brockenhurst
SO42 7QL

T: 01590 622354
F: info@thepighotel.com
W: www.thepighotel.com

BEDROOMS: 31. 10 in stable block (100 yds), some on ground floor, 2 lodges and a cabin in the garden, 1 suitable for disabled.
OPEN: all year.
FACILITIES: lounge, library, bar, restaurant, free Wi-Fi, in-room TV (Freeview), civil wedding licence, treatment rooms, kitchen garden, 6-acre grounds, public rooms wheelchair accessible, adapted toilet.
BACKGROUND MUSIC: in public areas.
LOCATION: 1 mile E of Brockenhurst village.
CHILDREN: all ages welcomed.
DOGS: not allowed.
CREDIT CARDS: Amex, MasterCard, Visa.
PRICES: [2018] room £155–£395. Breakfast £10–£15, à la carte £35. 1-night bookings refused at weekends, Christmas, New Year.

SEE ALSO SHORTLIST

BRYHER Isles of Scilly

Map 1: inset C1

HELL BAY HOTEL

♔ Previous César winner

'The surrounds are dramatic, the interiors pretty spectacular too.' Readers report much to enjoy at Robert Dorrien-Smith's gloriously isolated island hotel. The 'simply stunning' location offers protected beaches, outlying islets and, on the exposed west coast, relentless Atlantic swells (next stop Canada). Inside, in the bar, lounge and dining room, the acclaimed collection of Cornish art includes works by Dame Barbara Hepworth, Patrick Heron and Sir Terry Frost. Forged from a cluster of converted cottages and clapboard chalets, some with a balcony, the hotel has a New England vibe helped by airy, uncluttered rooms with pastels, creams and coastal paintings. In the 'simple, light-washed' restaurant, chef Richard Kearsley uses Tresco beef, Bryher crab and Isles of Scilly vegetables in daily-changing 'wow factor' menus including such dishes as roasted sea bass, saffron, mussel and herb broth. Time the tides right and food stalls pop up on the seabed between the islands. More regular, 'rather pricey' summer crab shack nights are held in a converted outbuilding, dedicated to crabs, mussels, scallops and Eton mess. 'Well worth the trip.' (FF, IB)

Bryher
TR23 0PR

T: 01720 422947
E: contactus@hellbay.co.uk
W: www.hellbay.co.uk

BEDROOMS: 25 suites. In 5 buildings, some on ground floor, 1 suitable for disabled.
OPEN: mid-Mar–mid-Oct.
FACILITIES: lounge, games room, bar, 2 dining rooms, free Wi-Fi, in-room TV (Freeview), gym, grounds (heated swimming pool, 15 by 10 metres, playground, par-3 golf course), beach 75 yds, public rooms wheelchair accessible, adapted toilet (island access by ferry).
BACKGROUND MUSIC: none.
LOCATION: W coast of island, boat from St Mary's (reached by boat/plane from mainland).
CHILDREN: all ages welcomed.
DOGS: allowed (charge), not in restaurant.
CREDIT CARDS: MasterCard, Visa.
PRICES: [2018] per room B&B single £175–£450, double £190–£630, D,B&B £280–£720. Set dinner £48, Min. 2-night bookings at weekends.

BUDE Cornwall

Map 1:C3

THE BEACH

With its cocktail bar and sea-facing terrace, Susie and Will Daniel's buzzy hotel overlooking Summerleaze surfers' beach is 'a mecca for the young of Bude'. The Victorian building has been given a smart, contemporary facelift. The 'very good' bedrooms vary in size, and are individually decorated in New England style, with limed oak furniture, Lloyd Loom chairs. A regular reader on a third visit found the staff 'as welcoming and friendly as before'. In the restaurant, classically trained chef Joe Simmonds uses locally grown – and caught – produce in such dishes as roasted wild sea bass, crab and potato doughnut, confit garlic, grilled leeks, garlic and lemon yogurt, poached leeks and coriander, shallot and spring onion dressing. For veggies, maybe beetroot pesto macaroni, pickled and roast root vegetables, toasted hazelnuts, goat's cheese. 'We found the meals filling and beautifully cooked.' Another reader was not pleased to have to eat in the 'noisy bar', while the restaurant was being used for a wine tasting, but, for our returnee, it was still 'a wonderful experience drinking wine in the bar in the evening'. (Frank G Millen, and others)

25% DISCOUNT VOUCHERS

Summerleaze Crescent
Bude
EX23 8HJ

T: 01288 389800
E: enquiries@thebeachatbude.co.uk
W: www.thebeachatbude.co.uk

BEDROOMS: 18. 1 on ground floor, 1 new family suite.
OPEN: all year except Christmas.
FACILITIES: lift, bar, lounge area, restaurant, free Wi-Fi, in-room TV (Freeview), terrace, ground floor wheelchair accessible.
BACKGROUND MUSIC: all day in public areas.
LOCATION: above Summerleaze beach.
CHILDREN: all ages welcomed.
DOGS: not allowed except on terrace.
CREDIT CARDS: Amex, MasterCard, Visa.
PRICES: [2018] per room B&B £150–£254, D,B&B £207–£315. À la carte £30.50.

BURFORD Oxfordshire

Map 3:D6

THE LAMB INN

On a tranquil side street in a picture-postcard
market town on the River Windrush, this
higgledy-piggledy old inn pleased Guide
inspectors with its 'classic Cotswold ambience'.
Part of the small Cotswold Inns and Hotels
group, it occupies former weavers' cottages, built
in the 15th century, reincarnated as an inn around
1700. Log fires burn in a chain of cosy lounges
with stacked bookshelves, log baskets, deep
sofas and a 'popular afternoon tea'. Rooms, some
recently refurbished, are anything but standard:
some have beams, one a four-poster, all come
with home-baked flapjacks, a Nespresso machine,
posh toiletries, a jar of Cotswold lavender. Allium
has an enormous, dual-aspect bathroom with
plasma-screen TV and roll-top bath; it can be
twinned with dog-friendly Rosie, which has a
private garden and entrance. You can eat in the
bar, lounges and walled garden (perhaps venison
pie, fish and chips), or the more formal restaurant,
where the three-course menu includes 'a stand-
out scallop starter'; grilled Herdwick lamb
rack; 'heavenly mango sorbet', all 'beautifully
presented'. Breakfast provides freshly squeezed
juices, home-made Drambuie marmalade,
'excellent sausages'. (MC, and others)

Sheep Street
Burford
OX18 4LR

T: 01993 823155
E: info@lambinn-burford.co.uk
W: www.cotswold-inns-hotels.
  co.uk/the-lamb-inn/

BEDROOMS: 17. 1 with private
garden, 1 on ground floor.
OPEN: all year.
FACILITIES: 2 lounges, bar,
restaurant, free Wi-Fi, in-room
TV (Freeview), courtyard, ½-acre
walled garden.
BACKGROUND MUSIC: subtle in all
public areas.
LOCATION: 500 yds from High Street.
CHILDREN: all ages welcomed.
DOGS: allowed by prior arrangement
in some bedrooms, bar, lounges,
garden, not in restaurant (£15 per
dog per night).
CREDIT CARDS: Amex, MasterCard,
Visa.
PRICES: [2018] per room B&B single
£180–£200, double £190–£300. Set
dinner £45 (£39 for residents if
booked in advance).

SEE ALSO SHORTLIST

BURTON BRADSTOCK Dorset

Map 1:D6

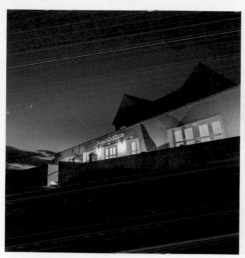

THE SEASIDE BOARDING HOUSE

White walls, pleasant staff, bright sunshine, blue, blue sky, sparkling sea just over the road…' For one reader this year, everything hit the spot at this cool small hotel overlooking Lyme Bay. Owners Mary-Lou Sturridge and Tony Mackintosh, formerly of London's Groucho Club, who transformed a shabby B&B into a stylish destination, continue to draw inspiration from British Edwardian hotels and Edward Hopper's Cape Cod. Pristine bedrooms, all with sea views, come with a radio, books from the cosy library. Bathrooms have a shower or claw-footed bath. The food is 'excellent, tasty', unfussy, allowing local ingredients to shine. There is an all-day bar menu including crab sandwich, home-made ice cream, Dorset cream tea. The restaurant's 'very good menus' are devised by Alastair Little with head chef Dan Richards (a typical dish: tranche of turbot, haricot beans, preserved lemon dressing). On fine days, the place to eat is on the terrace, serenaded by the surf. The breakfast menu runs from the full Monty, via kippers, to avocado on toast. 'Not often have I sent a "rave review", but I can't wait to return.' (Minda Alexander)

Cliff Road
Burton Bradstock
DT6 4RB

T: 01308 897 205
E: info@theseasideboardinghouse.com
W: theseasideboardinghouse.com

BEDROOMS: 9.
OPEN: all year.
FACILITIES: cocktail bar, restaurant, library, function facilities, in-room TV on request, free Wi-Fi, civil wedding licence, terrace, lawn, restaurant and bar wheelchair accessible.
BACKGROUND MUSIC: 'classical music' in bar.
LOCATION: ½ mile from village centre, 3½ miles SE of Bridport.
CHILDREN: all ages welcomed.
DOGS: allowed in some bedrooms, bar, library and on terrace, not in restaurant.
CREDIT CARDS: Amex, MasterCard, Visa.
PRICES: [2018] per room B&B £215–£265. À la carte £35. 1-night bookings sometimes refused at busy times.

BUXTON Greater Manchester　　Map 4:E3

THE ROSELEIGH

Gazing across the lake in Buxton's 'elegant, well-wooded main park', the Victorian B&B's 'fine premises' earned a return visit and more praise from trusted Guide correspondents. Welcoming, 'helpful' owners, Gerard and Maggi Heelan, two former tour leaders well versed in the charms of the Peak District, provided informed local assistance during 'another excellent stay'. Roseleigh's bedrooms – front ones overlook the Pavilion Gardens – offer traditional decoration with richly patterned curtains; some with wingback chairs or antique-style brass bed, alongside thoughtful touches from bathroom flannels to 'non-thieves coat-hangers'. The 'very useful sitting room', with warm red hues, leather sofa and armchairs, is stocked with guides, maps and history books to plan next day's adventures. Add in well-regarded breakfasts with a hurrah for the bacon if not the foil-wrapped butter, and this is a good base for exploring the area from Chatsworth, 30 minutes' drive away, to Haddon Hall and Castleton's caverns, or Georgian Buxton itself: 'We were there during the festival when they were full, very busy, and very good. We quickly booked the same four nights for the following year.' (Stephen and Pauline Glover)

19 Broad Walk
Buxton
SK17 6JR

T: 01298 24904
E: enquiries@roseleighhotel.co.uk
W: roseleighhotel.co.uk

BEDROOMS: 14. 1 on ground floor.
OPEN: all year except 9 Dec–24 Jan.
FACILITIES: lounge (computer for guests' use), breakfast room, free Wi-Fi, in-room TV (Freeview), parking, unsuitable for disabled.
BACKGROUND MUSIC: classical/baroque in breakfast room.
LOCATION: central.
CHILDREN: not under 6.
DOGS: not allowed.
CREDIT CARDS: MasterCard, Visa.
PRICES: [2018] per person B&B single from £42, double £35–£50.

CAMBER Sussex

THE GALLIVANT

There is much to like at Harry Cragoe's roadside restaurant-with-rooms, which takes its inspiration from California beach motels, and adds a dash of Scandinavia. Bedrooms are contemporary, with coastal-inspired colours, rather minimal storage space. Some have French doors opening on to the garden, some a fenced private deck, but all offer fresh milk, an eclectic choice of books and a Bakelite telephone. A grumble this year about a bathroom (no window or extractor fan; heated towel rail didn't work). There have been big changes, though, with the addition of a new summer house dining room. There is a sitting room with open fire, a reading room, a copper-topped bar. Seasonal menus showcase local ingredients: maybe lamb from the Romney salt marshes, confit potatoes, broccoli; South Coast brill, Jerusalem artichoke, crispy chicken. Breakfast brings home-baked banana walnut bread, home-made jams, continental hams, kedgeree, Gallivant sausages and home-cured bacon – bloody Mary from the 'recovery station'. Climb the towering dunes opposite to overlook 'seemingly endless sandy beaches in one direction – the shocking pink and bright blue of Pontins Holiday Park in the other'. (R and BS)

New Lydd Road
Camber
TN31 7RB

T: 01797 225057
E: enquiries@thegallivant.co.uk
W: www.thegallivant.co.uk

BEDROOMS: 20. All on ground floor, some suitable for disabled.
OPEN: all year.
FACILITIES: bar, sitting room, reading room, restaurant, private dining room, free Wi-Fi, in-room TV (Freeview), civil wedding licence, function facilities, beach hut spa treatment room, terrace, car park, coastal garden, restaurant and bar wheelchair accessible.
BACKGROUND MUSIC: in bar and restaurant.
LOCATION: 3¾ miles SE of Rye.
CHILDREN: all ages welcomed.
DOGS: allowed in some bedrooms, bar, terrace, not in dining room, not on furniture.
CREDIT CARDS: MasterCard, Visa.
PRICES: [2018] per room B&B £135–£235, D,B&B £205–£305. À la carte £38, daily specials menu (Wed–Sat) £24–£28.

CAMBRIDGE Cambridgeshire   Map 2:B4

DUKE HOUSE

Once the student digs of the Duke of Gloucester, Liz and Rob Cameron's boutique B&B is in a 'perfect' situation to explore the city colleges and architectural delights on foot. After dealing with reservations 'very professionally', 'helpful' Liz sorted out parking logistics 'so family could meet us in the parking restricted area, within walking distance of the whole city', writes one grateful reader after a visit this year. Interiors are 'beautifully presented', with 'warm, well-lit' bedrooms offering 'bottles of in-house branded toiletries', waffle robes and 'good bedlinen'. Original features include wooden shutters, brass fittings and, in Gloucester room, an original Victorian fireplace. Stargazers will enjoy the Cambridge mini-suite, with a telescope and private balcony. Where possible, breakfast is seasonal and locally sourced from the nearby market and bakery, with apple juice from Watergull Orchards, salmon cured in Bottisham. 'It was everything one could wish for.' For later, 'Liz recommended a superb pub, The Clarendon Arms. We had pot-roasted partridge, beautifully cooked.' Tea, coffee and something sweet is served in the elegant Duchess sitting room. (Michael Brown, SW, and others)

1 Victoria Street
Cambridge
CB1 1JP

T: 01223 314773
E: info@dukehousecambridge.
   co.uk
W: www.dukehousecambridge.
   co.uk

BEDROOMS: 5. 1 in adjacent cottage, plus self-catering apartment.
OPEN: all year.
FACILITIES: sitting room, breakfast room with courtyard, balcony, free Wi-Fi, in-room TV (Freeview), limited parking (by arrangement).
BACKGROUND MUSIC: none.
LOCATION: city centre.
CHILDREN: babies, and over-10s welcomed.
DOGS: not allowed.
CREDIT CARDS: Diners, MasterCard, Visa.
PRICES: [2018] per room B&B £125–£250. 1-night bookings refused weekends.

SEE ALSO SHORTLIST

CAMELFORD Cornwall

Map 1:C3

PENDRAGON COUNTRY HOUSE

'Simply outstanding, bordering on the spectacular,' writes a regular visitor to this Victorian former rectory with views of Dartmoor and Bodmin Moor. 'We've discovered a real gem here!' writes a newcomer. The owners, Nigel and Sharon Reed, are 'perfect hosts, full of helpful advice regarding local attractions', among them Tintagel Castle, legendary birthplace of King Arthur, son of Uther Pendragon. An Arthurian theme continues in the bedrooms. Bedivere and Lamorak each have a four-poster bed, Tristram a French-style sleigh bed (king-size, of course) and Cornish tin ceiling. At night the host cooks a 'superb' dinner, while his wife is in charge of desserts, both making use of 'fresh, natural, locally sourced ingredients' to create the likes of slow-roasted, pressed belly of pork with cider reduction jus; rhubarb fool with cinnamon-glazed wafers. Breakfast is 'a real treat', with 'scrumptious' locally caught kippers, home-made bread and jams, Cornish butter, Davidstow Cheddar, Cornish ham, Pendragon rarebit. You can bring your horse; there are stables next door. Packed lunches can be ordered for days on the hoof. (Chris Davison, William Blair, Ian McGiver)

25% DISCOUNT VOUCHERS

Old Vicarage Hill
Camelford
PL32 9XR

T: 01840 261131
E: enquiries@pendragoncountry
house.com
W: www.pendragoncountryhouse.
com

BEDROOMS: 7. 1 on ground floor suitable for disabled, with wet room and dedicated parking.
OPEN: all year except Christmas, restaurant closed Sun eve.
FACILITIES: sitting room, lounge with honesty bar, dining room, games room (pool table), free Wi-Fi, in-room TV (Freeview), 1¾ -acre grounds.
BACKGROUND MUSIC: none.
LOCATION: 3½ miles NE of Camelford.
CHILDREN: all ages welcomed.
DOGS: allowed in ground-floor bedroom, lounge but not restaurant, except guide dogs (£5 per night).
CREDIT CARDS: all major cards.
PRICES: [2018] per room B&B single £65–£75, double £95–£150, D,B&B single £90–£100, double £145–£200, Set menu £25–£35.

CANNINGTON Somerset

Map 1:B5

BLACKMORE FARM

Breakfast is served at a carved oak refectory table by the Great Hall's massive log fire at Ann and Ian Dyer's B&B in a manor house with private chapel. Surrounded by the family farm at the foot of the Quantocks, it has a suit of armour, medieval pikes and halberds – but no battleaxes, just 'a friendly atmosphere' and 'old-fashioned hospitality'. The house is 'amazing', an architectural treasure trove of oak panelling, ogee-headed doors and lancet arch windows, built around the reign of Richard III. In the main house there are two huge four-poster rooms; a suite with stairs to sitting room and bathroom, while in a barn conversion, suites have fridge, toaster, microwave. The Cider Press, sleeping four, has a kitchen, patio and small garden, while two can fit snugly into the shepherd's hut. All come with fresh milk (this is a dairy farm). Free-range breakfast eggs are from Blackmore's hens, bread is from the village bakery, bacon and sausages from award-winning butcher Pyne's of Somerset. The farm shop/café has soups, quiches, home-made cakes, cream teas. For dinner, the village pub is a stroll away.

Blackmore Lane
Cannington
TA5 2NE

T: 01278 653442
E: dyerfarm@aol.com
W: www.blackmorefarm.co.uk

BEDROOMS: 10. 6 on ground floor in annexes, 1 in shepherd's hut in grounds, 1 suitable for disabled.
OPEN: all year.
FACILITIES: lounge/TV room, Great Hall/breakfast room, free Wi-Fi, in-room TV (Freeview), 1-acre garden (stream, coarse fishing), children's play area, farm shop/café, lounge and dining room wheelchair accessible.
BACKGROUND MUSIC: none.
LOCATION: 3 miles W of Bridgwater.
CHILDREN: all ages welcomed.
DOGS: allowed in some bedrooms by prior arrangement, not in public rooms.
CREDIT CARDS: Diners, MasterCard, Visa.
PRICES: [2018] per room B&B single £75–£90, double £130–£140. 1-night bookings refused bank holiday weekends.

CARTMEL Cumbria

Map 4: inset C2

AYNSOME MANOR

Warm hospitality, centuries-old architecture and 'beautiful countryside' again delighted loyal fans of this 'exceptionally good-value oasis of peace and tranquillity'. Christopher and Andrea Varley are the second-generation owners of the Cumbrian manor house – former home of descendants of the aristocratic founder of Cartmel's Norman priory. 'Chris and his team looked after us so well,' wrote regular Guide readers. 'They combine efficiency with first-class service in a friendly, unobtrusive manner.' Rooms, which some guests found a tad tired, also pleased: 'Ours was a good size, with excellent lighting, ample storage, although boiler noise might irritate some.' A folder of nearby walks was appreciated, as was the upstairs lounge, 'the ideal venue to relax over coffee and talk with other guests'. Admired features included the spiral cantilevered staircase and, no doubt, the elegant Georgian dining room where chef Gordon Topp offers his locally sourced country house menu including oven-baked fillet of Fleetwood cod topped with a prawn, shallot and caper berry butter; 'a joy to have a good vegetable selection served separately'. Breakfast was 'excellent' (Bob and Jean Henry, DR)

25% DISCOUNT VOUCHERS

Aynsome Lane
Cartmel
LA11 6HH

T: 01539 536653
E: aynsomemanor@btconnect.com
W: www.aynsomemanorhotel.co.uk

BEDROOMS: 12. 2 in cottage (with lounge) across courtyard.
OPEN: all year except 23–27 Dec, 2–30 Jan, lunch served Sun only, Sun dinner for residents only.
FACILITIES: 2 lounges, bar, dining room, free Wi-Fi, in-room TV (Freeview), ½-acre garden, unsuitable for disabled.
BACKGROUND MUSIC: none.
LOCATION: ¾ mile N of village.
CHILDREN: all ages welcomed.
DOGS: allowed, not in public rooms or unattended in bedrooms (£7 nightly charge).
CREDIT CARDS: Amex, MasterCard, Visa.
PRICES: [2018] per room B&B £95–£160, D,B&B £162–£199. Set dinner £30. 1-night bookings occasionally refused weekends.

CHADDESLEY CORBETT Worcestershire   Map 3:C5

BROCKENCOTE HALL

A drive through woodland brings visitors to 'a romantic lake, a spectacular dovecote, a splendid fountain', and what looks, for all the world, like a Loire château. Built for a wealthy local mayor in 1869, it is 'a beautiful place', say trusted readers this year and, as a hotel, 'top of the tree'. A spacious, 'elegantly furnished' bedroom came with a fridge, milk and bottled water. The bathroom had 'a really large china bathtub' and a walk-in shower, 'first-class toiletries'. Afternoon tea and pre-dinner drinks can be taken in a panelled library hung with oil paintings, in the conservatory/bar, or alfresco on the terrace. In the dining room, chef Tim Jenkins creates regularly changing menus (including one for vegetarians), with seasonal, local, traceable ingredients. Crab cannelloni was 'delicious and beautifully presented', venison with roasted Jerusalem artichokes 'perfectly cooked'. Breakfast brings a good buffet, 'scrambled eggs generously draped round by good smoked salmon'. Another trusted reader fared less well in the post-New Year doldrums, but still found this a 'relaxing place' with 'excellent, welcoming staff and a good personal feel… We would certainly stay again.' (Francine and Ian Walsh, Sue Jenkinson)

Chaddesley Corbett
DY10 4PY

T: 01562 777876
E: info@brockencotehall.com
W: www.brockencotehall.com

BEDROOMS: 21. Some on ground floor, 1 suitable for disabled.
OPEN: all year.
FACILITIES: lift, hall, lounge, conservatory, bar, library, restaurant, function facilities, free Wi-Fi, in-room TV (Freeview), civil wedding licence, 72-acre grounds (gardens, lake, fishing, croquet, tennis), public rooms wheelchair accessible, adapted toilet.
BACKGROUND MUSIC: all day in public areas.
LOCATION: 3 miles SE of Kidderminster.
CHILDREN: all ages welcomed.
DOGS: not allowed.
CREDIT CARDS: Amex, MasterCard, Visa.
PRICES: [2018] per room B&B single from £105, double £170–£390, D,B&B double £225–£355. Set dinner (market menu) £49, fixed-price à la carte £45–£60.

CHESTER Cheshire

Map 3:A4

EDGAR HOUSE

On the broad promenade of the ancient wall of
this 'lovely city', overlooking the River Dee, Tim
Mills and Michael Stephen's Georgian villa has
been made over in a spirit of exuberance. Bold
interiors have been 'well designed without losing
a sense of integrity'. Bedrooms are idiosyncratic.
A dual-aspect room has a balcony, comfy seating
overlooking a weir, a custom-made, 'four-poster-
inspired' bed; in the bathroom, a freestanding
bath with waterfall spout and separate rain
shower. A junior suite has a vaulted, beamed
ceiling, exposed brick, an in-room copper bath.
Other fun touches: a hospitality bar in a black-
painted telephone kiosk; paintings by the forger
John Myatt, such as 'Matisse's' Yellow Odalisque.
Service is good from first to last: 'Case whisked
up to the room while we were checking in,
carried to door on departure.' In Twenty2
restaurant, at night, the new chef Joanna
Środka's tasting menu changes every six weeks
and kicks off with canapés and champagne. An
example: pumpkin soup; scallops, mango, crispy
pancetta/beetroot and goat's cheese salad; duck/
wild mushroom risotto; sorbet hazelnut délice;
apple tarte Tatin. Breakfast brings granola, fresh
fruit, eggs Royale and more.

22 City Walls
Chester
CH1 1SB

T: 01244 347007
E: hello@edgarhouse.co.uk
W: www.edgarhouse.co.uk

BEDROOMS: 7.
OPEN: all year, restaurant closed
Mon and Tues.
FACILITIES: garden lounge, mini-
cinema, restaurant, free Wi-Fi, in-
room TV (Freeview), sun terrace,
riverside garden (alfresco meals),
free allocated parking, unsuitable
for disabled.
BACKGROUND MUSIC: Classic FM in
lounge.
LOCATION: central, on the river.
CHILDREN: not under 14.
DOGS: not allowed in hotel, but
welcome in garden and when
dining outside.
CREDIT CARDS: MasterCard, Visa.
PRICES: [2018] per room B&B
£189–£269, D,B&B £280–£359.
Tasting menu £59. Min. 2-night stay
when incl. Sat.

SEE ALSO SHORTLIST

CHETTLE Dorset

Map 2:E1

CASTLEMAN

'Set in a period property, this hotel pampers
its clients like friends, and captures an age
of country house hospitality,' write readers
this year, of Barbara Garnsworthy's former
dower house in a feudal village. The hybrid
building began life as a 17th-century farmhouse,
growing over the years to acquire 19th-century
drawing rooms, Regency plasterwork and
a Jacobean fireplace. 'If you're looking for a
trendy boutique hotel, this is not for you!' The
ambience is that of a family home. There are
antiques and oil paintings in abundance, 'a
comprehensive library'. Bedrooms are spacious,
handsomely furnished, perhaps with four-
poster, cheval glass, Victorian wardrobe. The
daily-changing menu includes such dishes as
smoked cod, sorrel, white wine and cream;
pork medallions, glazed shallots and port. 'You
wait with bated breath as the menu rolls off the
press at about 7 pm. The quality of the food
is outstanding and superb value for money.'
At breakfast, 'you start with freshly squeezed
orange juice, then enjoy whatever you would
like cooked for you'. A good base for golf and
country sports, while walks start at the door.
(Bob and Jean Henry)

Chettle
Blandford Forum
DT11 8DB

T: 01258 830096
E: enquiry@castlemanhotel.co.uk
W: www.castlemanhotel.co.uk

BEDROOMS: 8. 1 family room.
OPEN: Mar–end Jan, except 25/26,
31 Dec, restaurant closed midday
except Sun.
FACILITIES: 2 drawing rooms, bar,
restaurant, free Wi-Fi, in-room TV
(Freeview), 2-acre grounds (stables
for visiting horses), riding, fishing,
shooting, cycling nearby, restaurant
wheelchair accessible.
BACKGROUND MUSIC: none.
LOCATION: village, 1 mile off A354
Salisbury–Blandford.
CHILDREN: all ages welcomed.
DOGS: only guide dogs.
CREDIT CARDS: MasterCard, Visa.
PRICES: [2018] per room B&B single
£80, double £105–£120, D,B&B
double (midweek only) £135–£155.
À la carte £33.

CHICHESTER Sussex

Map 2:E3

CROUCHERS

With Chichester in one direction, the pristine sands of West Wittering in the other, guests at Lloyd van Rooyen and Gavin Wilson's smart, contemporary hotel have the best of both worlds. Described as a 'restaurant, bar and country hotel', it was created from a farmhouse and outbuilding, and it backs on to fields. While one reader reported road noise in a room in the main building, another wrote that bedrooms, 'in new cottages, clustered around the restaurant', are 'totally quiet in the dark hours'. They vary in size and particulars. 'Cosy' rooms are, indeed, small. By contrast, ground-floor luxe rooms have a king-size four-poster and private patio. One has a whirlpool bath. All are 'spotless; done out in impeccable taste' with a 'state-of-the-art bathroom', fleecy towels, good toiletries. The oak-beamed restaurant, 'obviously very popular with local diners', has 'pleasant and effective' waiting staff. Sample dishes: poached rump of lamb, Szechwan pepper and mint crust, kumquats, potato and lamb shoulder terrine; celeriac, kohlrabi and pea cannelloni, shallots, carrots, almond, dill. Food is served all day in the bar. Breakfast offers an 'adequate buffet', interesting cooked options.

Birdham Road
Chichester
PO20 7EH

T: 01243 784995
E: enquiries@crouchershotel.co.uk
w: www.crouchershotel.co.uk

BEDROOMS: 26. 23 in converted coach house, barn and stables, 10 with patio, 2 suitable for disabled.
OPEN: all year.
FACILITIES: lounge, bar, restaurant, free Wi-Fi, in-room TV (Freeview), civil wedding licence/function facilities, courtyard, 2-acre garden, restaurant and bar wheelchair accessible with adapted toilet.
BACKGROUND MUSIC: in public areas.
LOCATION: 3 miles S of town centre.
CHILDREN: all ages welcomed.
DOGS: allowed in some bedrooms, bar, not in restaurant.
CREDIT CARDS: Amex, MasterCard, Visa.
PRICES: [2018] per room B&B £111–£250, D,B&B £158–£297. Set menus £18–£24, à la carte £37.

SEE ALSO SHORTLIST

CHILLATON Devon

Map 1:D3

TOR COTTAGE

A trug of sparkling wine, organic home-made fudge, fresh fruit and flowers awaits guests at the 'lovely' Maureen Rowlatt's rather special B&B by a stream, in a private valley on the edge of Dartmoor. It is ideal for those who want to come and go independently. Apart from one cottage room, the accommodation is in garden bedsits, each with open fire or log-burner and secluded terrace, a microwave with grill, plates and crockery. One of these, Laughing Waters, is done out in New England style, with patchwork quilt, maple furnishings, its own garden and woodland. It has decking with hardwood furniture and a patio heater, cooking area with gas barbecue, veranda. The heated outdoor swimming pool is available for morning dips. Picnic platters of sandwiches, pastries, desserts and cheeses can be ordered in advance. Breakfast is served in the main house, from a menu that includes a compote of prunes and apricots, home-made muesli, Greek yogurt, kedgeree (a rare treat), scrambled eggs with mushrooms, the full English with Devon pork sausages, and a vegetarian grill. Where to dine out in the evening? Ask Maureen or see the Guide map.

Chillaton
PL16 0JE

T: 01822 860248
E: info@torcottage.co.uk
W: www.torcottage.co.uk

BEDROOMS: 5. 4 in garden.
OPEN: Feb–mid-Dec.
FACILITIES: sitting room, large conservatory, free Wi-Fi in reception and public areas, in-room TV (Freeview), 28-acre grounds (2-acre garden, heated outdoor swimming pool, 12 by 6 metres, May–Sept until 11.30 am and evenings by arrangement) with pool house, river (fishing ½ mile), unsuitable for disabled.
BACKGROUND MUSIC: none.
LOCATION: ½ mile S of Chillaton, 6½ miles N of Tavistock.
CHILDREN: not under 15.
DOGS: only guide dogs allowed.
CREDIT CARDS: MasterCard, Visa.
PRICES: [2018] per room B&B single £98, double £150–£170. Platters £32 for two. Normally min. 2 nights, 'but check availability'.

CHRISTCHURCH Dorset

Map 2:E2

CAPTAIN'S CLUB HOTEL

It is as if a cruise liner had docked on the banks of Dorset's Stour several years ago, to the sound of popping corks, and everyone liked it so much that they'd stayed. Robert Wilson and Tim Lloyd's sleek hotel is a do-as-you-please, go-as-you-please operation, with moorings for guests who like messing about in boats. Watery light floods through floor-to-ceiling windows as you gaze out at an ever-changing riverscape. Accommodation is in 'state rooms', suites and family apartments with fully equipped kitchen. All have smart TV, espresso machine, contemporary decor. Grazing options include 'light bites' in the newly refurbished Quay bar and on the terrace (mini-fishcakes, sausage rolls, pakoras), any-time meals in the Club Lounge (fish and chips, burgers, risotto). At lunch and dinner, chef Andrew Gault uses 'quality ingredients' in extensive menus of such dishes as moules marinière, seafood linguine, bavette steak. After an 'enjoyable' breakfast, guests can relax in the spa or simply step 'ashore' and stroll to the historic walled city centre. In the afternoon, perhaps a boat trip to the Isle of Wight for a champagne tea. (LG)

Wick Ferry
Christchurch
BH23 1HU

T: 01202 475111
E: enquiries@captainsclubhotel.
com
W: www.captainsclubhotel.com

BEDROOMS: 29. 2 suitable for disabled.
OPEN: all year.
FACILITIES: lifts, open-plan bar/lounge/restaurant, function facilities, free Wi-Fi, in-room TV (Sky, Freeview), civil wedding licence, riverside terrace, spa (hydrotherapy pool, treatments, sauna), moorings for guests.
BACKGROUND MUSIC: in public areas, live music some evenings.
LOCATION: on the river.
CHILDREN: all ages welcomed.
DOGS: allowed in some suites, on terrace and small area of lounge (£20 per dog per night).
CREDIT CARDS: MasterCard, Visa.
PRICES: per room B&B doubles from £159, suites £219–£549. Set menu £20–£24, à la carte £40. 1-night bookings normally refused Sat.

CIRENCESTER Gloucestershire

Map 3:E5

KINGS HEAD HOTEL

In its deepest fabric 14th-century, this former coaching inn could, by the 1860s, boast of its hot and cold baths; a more recent revamp has gone much further. Owners Mark and Alison Booth spent £7 million on a seven-year refurbishment, creating an 'atmospheric, stylish hotel with many original features', including a 'unique spa in its ancient vaulted basement'. Chic, updated bedrooms have 'harmonious earthy hues, eclectic art', an espresso machine, a mini-fridge with fresh milk. Choices include an 'indulgent' room with a four-poster, an in-room copper bathtub, and a 'feature' room with exposed brick or medieval beams. The restaurant, on the ground floor, is 'open plan, with an adjacent bar area, complete with sofas, a wood-burning stove'. From the 'pleasingly knowledgeable sommelier' to 'friendly, informal' waiting staff, there is 'an obvious desire to get things right'. In the seasonal British menu, 'outstanding quality ingredients' shine in such dishes as marinated lamb rump, fricassée of chorizo, broad beans, Parmentier potatoes, balsamic and mint; market fish of the day; pumpkin and sage ravioli. Breakfast brings freshly squeezed orange juice, Gloucester Old Spot sausages. (IB, and others)

24 Market Place
Cirencester
GL7 2NR

T: 01285 700900
E: info@kingshead-hotel.co.uk
W: kingshead-hotel.co.uk

BEDROOMS: 46. 1 suitable for disabled. 6 apartments.
OPEN: all year.
FACILITIES: lifts, lounge/bar, restaurant, study, meeting/private dining rooms, free Wi-Fi, in-room TV (Freeview), civil wedding licence, spa (treatments, steam room, sauna), roof terrace, public rooms wheelchair accessible, adapted toilet.
BACKGROUND MUSIC: in public areas.
LOCATION: town centre, limited secure parking (£15 a day).
CHILDREN: all ages welcomed.
DOGS: allowed by arrangement in some bedrooms (£20 per dog per night), lounge, not in restaurant.
CREDIT CARDS: MasterCard, Visa.
PRICES: [2018] per room B&B £114–£409, D,B&B £134–£449. À la carte £35. 1-night bookings sometimes refused.

CLEARWELL Gloucestershire

Map 3:D4

♔TUDOR FARMHOUSE

César award: country house hotel of the year

'A lovely little hotel,' writes a reader on a return visit to Hari and Colin Fell's ingeniously converted farm buildings in the Forest of Dean. Another reader, on arrival, was impressed by the 'pleasant garden', and a 'warm welcome'. The bedrooms are all comfortable and contemporary, with espresso machine, and fresh milk in a minibar. A mid-price room, 'up a steep, twisty staircase', was 'lovely, with superbly comfortable bed', armchairs, a desk. 'Decor was the currently fashionable grey, with a sisal carpet, which sounds clinical, but it wasn't.' The bathroom was 'magnificent, as big as the bedroom, with roll-top bath taking centre stage, and a splendid shower'. In the 'atmospheric dining room', chef Rob Cox works with locally produced and home-grown ingredients, rare breed meats, eggs from the hens in the paddock, to create his 'outstanding' 20-mile menus. Typical mains: longhorn beef rump, ox cheek, celeriac, horseradish and shallot confit with red wine sauce; poached halibut, leeks, thyme gnocchi, wild mushrooms, chive and cream sauce. Service is 'leisurely and friendly', breakfast 'equally good, with an ample selection'. (Peter Anderson, Andrew and Moira Kleissner)

High Street
Clearwell
GL16 8JS

T: 01594 833046
E: info@tudorfarmhousehotel.co.uk
W: www.tudorfarmhousehotel.co.uk

BEDROOMS: 20. 8 on ground floor, 4 in farmhouse, 9 in barn, 7 in cider house.
OPEN: all year.
FACILITIES: lounge, bar, 2 dining rooms, free Wi-Fi, in-room TV (Freeview), 14-acre grounds (garden, ancient grassland).
BACKGROUND MUSIC: in restaurant and lounge at lunch and dinner.
LOCATION: 7 miles SE of Monmouth.
CHILDREN: all ages welcomed.
DOGS: allowed in 3 bedrooms, grounds, not in public rooms.
CREDIT CARDS: Amex, MasterCard, Visa.
PRICES: [2018] per room B&B £130–£250, D,B&B £210–£330. Tasting menu £60, à la carte £35–£50. Min. 2-night stay at weekends.

CLEE STANTON Shropshire

Map 3:C5

TIMBERSTONE

'Timberstone remains a great favourite,' writes a Guide regular this year after staying at Tracey Baylis and Alex Read's B&B in the undulating landscape immortalised by AE Housman. 'We were treated with courtesy and respect by every member of staff.' Forged from two 300-year-old stone cottages, it has room names reflecting the Clee Hills mining history. Slate has hill views, oak beams, bathroom with double-ended bath and separate shower. Clay, in a contemporary extension, has French doors on to a balcony overlooking the verdant surroundings; Dhustone – still quarried on Titterstone Clee nearby – has a bathroom with bath and separate slate shower. All rooms have king-size bed, organic smellies, shortbread, tea/coffee facilities. Downstairs, sofas, books and a wood-burner keep it cosy in the open-plan sitting/dining room, where Tracey, who previously worked for Michelin-starred chef Shaun Hill, cooks 'imaginative, well-presented' dinners on request, perhaps duck breast, red wine, blackcurrant. Breakfast brings kippers, home-baked bread, free-range eggs every way including spicy Mexican. Walks start from the front door, while the sauna and reflexology therapies soothe aching limbs. (David Bartley)

25% DISCOUNT VOUCHERS

Lackstone Lane
Clee Stanton
SY8 3EL

T: 01584 823519
E: timberstone1@hotmail.com
W: www.timberstoneludlow.co.uk

BEDROOMS: 4. Plus summer house retreat in summer.
OPEN: all year.
FACILITIES: lounge/dining room, conservatory, free Wi-Fi, in-room TV (Freeview), ½-acre garden, treatment room, unsuitable for disabled.
BACKGROUND MUSIC: none.
LOCATION: 5 miles NE of Ludlow.
CHILDREN: all ages welcomed.
DOGS: allowed by arrangement, not in dining room.
CREDIT CARDS: MasterCard, Visa.
PRICES: [2018] per room B&B single £85, double £100. Set menus £25–£30.

CLIPSHAM Rutland

Map 2:A3

BEECH HOUSE & OLIVE BRANCH

♕ Previous César winner

'We collected the room key from a young lady dressed in the uniform of checked shirt and jeans. Everyone was so cheerful, I assumed something humorous had taken place.' Readers had a fun stay at Ben Jones and Sean Hope's Beech House, across a quiet road from their village pub/restaurant. Another Guide regular found it 'as excellent as ever' in 2018. Aubergine bedroom had 'the style of a mini-Claridge's', with 'Art Deco picture frames and lights', a bathroom with 'great Art Deco fittings'. There was cafetière coffee, fresh milk in a fridge on the landing. It was chilly on arrival, a fact they put down to their late booking. 'We drew the heavy curtains, turned up the radiator and went for some grub.' Smart thinking! Chef Sean Hope's 'fantastic' food includes tapas, specials from the blackboard (whole baked plaice, roast chicken ballottine), vegetarian options and a set gourmet menu. For example: sweetcorn soup, almond and chilli dressing; chicken breast, new potatoes, spring vegetable broth; elderflower panna cotta…) An 'excellent locally sourced breakfast' includes 'fresh oranges for your juice along with a little squeezer', 'superb kedgeree'. (Mary Milne-Day, RS)

Main Street
Clipsham
LE15 7SH

T: 01780 410355
E: beechhouse@theolivebranchpub.com
W: www.theolivebranchpub.com

BEDROOMS: 6. 2 on ground floor, family room (also suitable for disabled) in annexe.
OPEN: all year, pub closed evening 25 Dec and 1 Jan.
FACILITIES: pub, dining room, breakfast room, free Wi-Fi, in-room TV (Freeview, Netflix), small terrace, garden, public rooms wheelchair accessible, adapted toilet.
BACKGROUND MUSIC: classical/jazz in pub.
LOCATION: in village 7 miles NW of Stamford.
CHILDREN: all ages welcomed.
DOGS: allowed in ground-floor bedrooms and bar.
CREDIT CARDS: MasterCard, Visa.
PRICES: [2018] per room B&B £115–£205, D,B&B £175–£260. Set 5-course dinner £32.50, à la carte £36.

CONSTANTINE BAY Cornwall   Map 1:D2

TREGLOS HOTEL   **NEW**

The Barlows were not present to welcome Mrs Simpson, who stayed here when Edward VIII visited Cornwall – the family has run the place for only 50 years. What began as a four-bedroomed Victorian house with views across the bay, has grown over decades into a holiday hotel, promoted to a full entry this year on the recommendation of trusted readers. 'It's always a pleasure to return here… Comfortable room with a terrace overlooking the bay, sunshine every day, good food, swimming pool…' The hospitality and welcome are universally praised. 'The staff were absolutely superb, professional, pleased to do anything to make our stay relaxing and happy.' 'Our room was spacious, pleasantly furnished and well equipped.' With landscaped gardens, a spa, golf course and children's playground, there is plenty to keep the family entertained. 'A self-service cold table for first course, on three nights a week, was exceptional and had an abundance of seafood.' Breakfast brings 'a splendid array of fruits… good, freshly cooked food'. A bedroom with a balcony and sea view is clearly the best choice. (Bill Wood, Sue and John Jenkinson, Mary Coles)

Beach Road
St Merryn, nr Padstow
Constantine Bay
PL28 8JH

T: Tel 01841 520727,
E: stay@tregloshotel.com
W: www.tregloshotel.com

BEDROOMS: 42. 1 on ground floor, 2 suitable for disabled, plus self-catering apartments in grounds.
OPEN: Mar–Nov.
FACILITIES: lift, 2 lounges, bar, conservatory, restaurant (smart/casual dress after 7 pm), children's den, games room, free Wi-Fi (variable signal), in-room TV (Freeview), 1-acre grounds, sunken garden, indoor swimming pool, spa.
BACKGROUND MUSIC: in bar and restaurant in early evening.
LOCATION: 3 miles W of Padstow.
CHILDREN: all ages welcomed.
DOGS: allowed in some bedrooms, conservatory when not otherwise in use, on lead in grounds.
CREDIT CARDS: MasterCard, Visa.
PRICES: [2018] per room B&B £157–£232. Set dinner £40. 2-night min. stay during peak periods.

CORSE LAWN Gloucestershire

Map 3:D5

CORSE LAWN HOUSE

'We stumbled across the hotel quite by accident – oh, serendipity! We plan to return.' Newcomers this year to the Hine family's 'gracious' pink brick Queen Anne coaching inn join a loyal following, with praise for its 'old-fashioned values, excellent food and attentive staff'. Another reader in 2018 lauded the 'beautifully maintained and furnished interiors'. Now in her fifth decade at the helm, Baba Hine, with son Giles, is a 'benign presence'. 'The Edwardian decor is wonderfully quirky. Our generously proportioned bedroom had a comfortable king-size bed, pleasant sitting area, large bathroom and French doors leading to a large terrace.' All the rooms have leaf teas, 'proper coffee', shortbread, fruit and fresh milk; most enjoy leafy views. Dine in the bistro overlooking a sweeping willow, or in the restaurant where long-standing chef Martin Kinahan cooks 'outstanding' dishes; perhaps 'melt-in-the-mouth venison', or globe artichoke with wild mushrooms off the vegan menu. 'The cheese trolley was superb.' A 'near-perfect' breakfast includes home-made muesli, 'deftly cooked' sausages. 'They sent us on our way happy and delightfully replete.' (Brian Griffiths, and others)

Corse Lawn
GL19 4LZ

T: 01452 780771
E: enquiries@corselawn.com
W: www.corselawn.com

BEDROOMS: 18. 5 on ground floor (step free).
OPEN: all year except 24–26 Dec.
FACILITIES: 2 drawing rooms, snug bar, restaurant, bistro, private dining/meeting rooms, free Wi-Fi, in-room TV (Sky, BT, Freeview), civil wedding licence, 12-acre grounds (croquet, tennis, indoor heated swimming pool, 20 by 10 metres).
BACKGROUND MUSIC: none.
LOCATION: 5 miles SW of Tewkesbury on B4211.
CHILDREN: all ages welcomed.
DOGS: allowed in bedrooms, on lead in public rooms, not in eating areas.
CREDIT CARDS: Amex, MasterCard, Visa.
PRICES: [2018] per room B&B from £140, D,B&B from £200. Set dinner (restaurant) £34, (bistro) £24, à la carte £35.

COWAN BRIDGE Lancashire

Map 4: inset D2

HIPPING HALL

'A wonderful place,' write readers this year, of Andrew Wildsmith's first venture, between Lake District and Yorkshire Dales. Mr Wildsmith planned a career in chemistry, but instead chose alchemy, creating here a luxurious yet relaxed hotel, before working his magic at The Ryebeck, Bowness-on-Windermere (see Shortlist), and at Forest Side, Grasmere (see main entry). Dating back to the 15th century, Hipping Hall's dining room was once its Great Hall. It has oak ships' beams and an open fireplace; a well is embedded in the conservatory floor. Recently redesigned bedrooms, in the main house, cottage and stables, have paint pigments created by local artists, using natural mineral colours. A refurbished stables suite was 'splendid, with a good bed, nice, large bathroom and a pleasant sitting room'. An outdoor seating area had views over 'fine countryside, with sheep on the nearby hill'. At dinner, chef Oli Martin cooks fortnightly-changing tasting menus for carnivores and vegetarians, capturing 'the quintessence' of local ingredients in such 'outstanding' dishes as Cumbrian red deer venison loin, hay-baked turnip, yeasted crab apple; smoked Ashcroft's beetroot, sheep yogurt curd, sunflower seed. 'Memorable.' (David Grant, AD)

Cowan Bridge
LA6 2JJ

T: 01524 271187
E: info@hippinghall.com
W: www.hippinghall.com

BEDROOMS: 15. 3 in cottage, 5 in converted stables, 1 room suitable for disabled.
OPEN: all year.
FACILITIES: lounge, orangery, bar, restaurant, 'chef's kitchen', wedding/function facilities, free Wi-Fi in bedrooms and most public areas, in-room TV (Freeview), civil wedding licence, 12-acre grounds, orangery, restaurant and lounge wheelchair accessible.
BACKGROUND MUSIC: in lounge, restaurant.
LOCATION: 2 miles SE of Kirkby Lonsdale, on A65.
CHILDREN: all ages welcomed.
DOGS: well-behaved dogs allowed in stable bedrooms (max 2) and orangery.
CREDIT CARDS: Amex, MasterCard, Visa.
PRICES: [2018] per room B&B £179–£269, D,B&B £279–£379. Set dinner £60–£80.

CROFT-ON-TEES Yorkshire

Map 4:C4

CLOW BECK HOUSE

Heather and David Armstrong are warm
and accommodating hosts at this 'fascinating'
hotel, occupying a farmhouse and rustic-
looking, purpose-built annexes. Clow Beck
would have been known to the boy Charles
Lutwidge Dodgson, aka Lewis Carroll, who
lived at the village rectory and reputedly
wrote 'Jabberwocky' there. The Armstrongs'
guests can take tea in the hotel lounge or, on
frabjous days, sit out under a tumtum tree in
the 'beautiful, well-cared-for' gardens with
topiary and duck ponds. Most bedrooms are in
the annexes. The styling is idiosyncratic, tending
to the traditional, sometimes a bit quirky, with
rather homey antiques and many personal
touches. Each room (one reader felt theirs a little
'dreary') has a fridge, fresh milk, chocolates,
home-made biscuits 'well worth getting fat for',
posh toiletries, postcards and an umbrella. In
the evening, Heather serves drinks and canapés
before David's hearty dinner. Maybe local fillet
steak with melted Yorkshire Blue, or one of
several vegetarian options, followed by a proper
pudding or Yorkshire cheeses, in the beamed
dining room. Breakfast delivers local produce,
home-made breads and jam.

Monk End Farm
Croft-on-Tees
DL2 2SP

T: 01325 721075
E: reservations@clowbeckhouse.
co.uk
W: www.clowbeckhouse.co.uk

BEDROOMS: 10. 1 in main building,
9 in garden buildings, some on
ground floor, 1 suitable for disabled.
OPEN: all year except Christmas and
New Year.
FACILITIES: lounge, restaurant, free
Wi-Fi, in-room TV (Freeview),
small conference facilities, 2-acre
grounds on 100-acre farm.
BACKGROUND MUSIC: classical, 'easy
listening' in restaurant.
LOCATION: 3 miles SE of Darlington.
CHILDREN: all ages welcomed.
DOGS: not allowed.
CREDIT CARDS: Amex, MasterCard,
Visa.
PRICES: [2018] per room B&B single
£90, double £140. À la carte £37.

CROSTHWAITE Cumbria   Map 4: inset C2

THE PUNCH BOWL   [NEW]

'Always a favourite' of Guide friends in the
north, Richard Rose's 300-year-old pub-with-
rooms is in 'one of the prettiest villages in
south Lakeland'. It is promoted to a full entry
this year. 'Lots of atmosphere, particularly in
the front room with the wood-burning stove.'
Bedrooms are 'comfortable and very reasonably
priced'. Their names recall past vicars of St
Mary's church next door. All bedrooms have a
Roberts radio, flat-screen TV, heated limestone
bathroom floor, freestanding roll-top bath (two
baths in the case of Noble, which occupies the
entire top storey, under the eaves). Cooper has
a four-poster bed built from reclaimed elm.
Arthur Bridgeman Quin, 'a great young chef
with good ideas', uses local, seasonal produce
to pack a punch with such dishes as Cumbrian
fillet steak, braised cheek, red wine jus, roast
shallot, horseradish vinegar, creamed potato –
and, from a separate veggie menu, caramelised
carrot fondants, orange and cardamom sauce,
baby leeks, sautéed potatoes. 'He also does a
mean rare roast beef with all the trimmings.'
Guests may ask to be woken with tea or coffee.
(Stephanie Thompson and Keith Sutton,
David Peel)

Crosthwaite
Lyth Valleyl
Cumbria
LA8 8HR

T: 01539 568237
E: info@the-punchbowl.co.uk
W: www.the-punchbowl.co.uk

BEDROOMS: 9.
OPEN: all year.
FACILITIES: bar, bar dining area,
restaurant, free Wi-Fi i, in-room
TV (Freeview), civil wedding
licence, 2 terraces, parking, bar and
restaurant wheelchair accessible.
BACKGROUND MUSIC: in public areas.
LOCATION: 5 miles W of Kendal,
via A5074.
CHILDREN: all ages welcomed.
DOGS: allowed in bar only.
CREDIT CARDS: Amex, MasterCard,
Visa.
PRICES: [2018] per room B&B
£110–£320. À la carte £35. 1-night
bookings usually refused 25 Dec,
31 Dec.

CRUDWELL Wiltshire

Map 3:E5

THE RECTORY HOTEL   NEW

'We only called in for coffee, but were shown
around by enthusiastic staff… and came away
thinking what a wonderful place.' A reader
was impressed by this Georgian country house
hotel, set back from the road, in lovely gardens.
Bought by music industry executive Alex Payne
in 2016, it has received a designer make-over.
The result, more House Beautiful than Acid
House, has not sacrificed period charm, say
inspectors, while 'the addition of a cocktail bar
is a great improvement'. Individually styled
bedrooms are priced according to size. 'We
didn't find our "small" room small at all. It had
a very comfortable king-size bed and two large
windows', no wardrobe, just hooks. All have a
Roberts radio, Bramley toiletries, home-made
shortbread, cafetière and ground coffee; fresh
milk is in a fridge on the landing. A big shower
head promised more than it delivered. Some
rooms have an in-bedroom freestanding bath. In
the 'coolly elegant' restaurant, Antony Ely cooks
such 'excellent, creative dishes' as butter-roasted
Wiltshire mallard, Jerusalem artichoke, red
cabbage, pickled blackberries. There is further
inventive cooking in sister establishment The
Potting Shed, opposite. (David Haigh, and others)

Crudwell
SN16 9EP

T: 01666 577194
E: reception@therectoryhotel.com
W: www.therectoryhotel.com

BEDROOMS: 18. 3 in cottage in
garden.
OPEN: all year, restaurant closed
lunchtime.
FACILITIES: living room, drawing
room, dining room, card room, bar,
in-room TV (Freeview), free Wi-Fi,
meeting facilities, civil wedding
licence, 3-acre garden, heated
outdoor swimming pool (10 by 15
metres, May–Oct), restaurant and
bar wheelchair accessible.
BACKGROUND MUSIC: sometimes, in
public areas.
LOCATION: 4 miles N of Malmesbury.
CHILDREN: all ages welcomed.
DOGS: allowed in 3 bedrooms and
public rooms, not in dining room.
CREDIT CARDS: all major cards.
PRICES: [2018] per room B&B
£120–£230. Set dinner £27–£33.
À la carte £35. Min. 2-night
bookings at weekends.

DARTMOUTH Devon

Map 1:D4

BAYARDS COVE INN

NEW

'Tucked away at the end of the main street of this idyllic town, seconds from the water's edge', Charles Deuchar's pub-with-rooms is a medieval merchant's house in a 17th-century shell. It looks as Tudor as you please, with its 'chocolate-box-perfect entrance'. 'You check in at the bar,' explains a Guide insider this year. 'We could not have been greeted more warmly, and felt instantly at home.' A winding staircase (mind your head on the beams) led to a 'charmingly decorated' bedroom with 'uneven walls and floor, extremely comfy bed, sofa, coffee table, home-made shortbread'. For families, there are suites and a triple room. Views are, variously, of the River Dart, the cove and Dartmouth Castle. By day, bar food (a ploughman's, toasties, mussels), cakes and coffees are served in the 'lovely atmosphere of the pub'. At dinner, 'we both had fresh local crab, then a superfood salad and a seafood risotto. I liked the menu's local credentials and the option for lighter meals.' Breakfast, served obligingly early, brought 'excellent smoked salmon and scrambled eggs'. Overall, 'I was enchanted.'

27 Lower Street
Dartmouth
TQ6 9AN

T: 01803 839278
E: info@bayardscoveinn.co.uk
W: www.bayardscoveinn.co.uk

BEDROOMS: 7. 2 family suites.
OPEN: all year.
FACILITIES: bar, restaurant, free Wi-Fi, in-room TV (Freeview), bicycle storage, private parking nearby (reservation required, £15 per day), public areas wheelchair accessible, adapted toilet.
BACKGROUND MUSIC: in public areas.
LOCATION: in centre, close to waterfront.
CHILDREN: all ages welcomed.
DOGS: allowed throughout (£12 per dog per night).
CREDIT CARDS: all major cards.
PRICES: [2018] per person B&B single £90–£195, double £95–£200. À la carte £35. Min. 2-night stay at weekends.

SEE ALSO SHORTLIST

DARTMOUTH Devon

Map 1:D4

DART MARINA

'Completely wonderful in every way.' 'One of our absolute favourites.' Readers give the thumbs-up to Richard Seton's spa hotel overlooking the River Dart. 'The lovely thing is that it doesn't stand still – they are always looking to improve.' Indeed, since last year a new wing of balcony suites has been added and the balconies on standard rooms have been replaced. Each room has a river view, perhaps sliding glass doors or French doors. Newly refurbished, pet-friendly ground-floor rooms have a handmade bed, wet room with drench shower; outdoor seating. The decor is contemporary and smart. 'Fabulous staff', under the 'ever-present' manager, Paul Downing, are 'very helpful and eager to please'. Guests can order a seafood platter for sharing on the waterside terrace, hoping for a glimpse of a grey seal. At dinner, chef Peter Alcroft cooks such sophisticated dishes as pan-fried pollack, trio of beetroot, rösti, samphire and crab velouté. More simple options include West Country steaks with hand-cut chips. Breakfasts are judged 'second to none', though one reader did not care for the orange juice. (Ian Malone, Eric and Mary Woods, G Griffiths)

Sandquay Road
Dartmouth
TQ6 9PH

T: 01803 832580
E: reception@dartmarina.com
W: www.dartmarina.com

BEDROOMS: 49. 4 on ground floor, 1 suitable for disabled, plus 4 apartments.
OPEN: all year.
FACILITIES: lounge/bar, restaurant, free Wi-Fi, in-room TV (Freeview), river-front lawn, spa (heated indoor swimming pool, 8 by 4 metres, gym), lounge and restaurant wheelchair accessible.
BACKGROUND MUSIC: in restaurant and lounge/bar during the day.
LOCATION: on waterfront.
CHILDREN: all ages welcomed.
DOGS: allowed in some bedrooms and lounge, not in restaurant.
CREDIT CARDS: MasterCard, Visa.
PRICES: [2018] per room B&B double £210–£470, D,B&B an additional £35 per person. À la carte £37. 1-night bookings usually refused weekends at peak times.

SEE ALSO SHORTLIST

DEDHAM Essex

Map 2:C5

DEDHAM HALL & FOUNTAIN HOUSE RESTAURANT

In the heart of Constable country, Wendy and Jim Sartin's ancient manor house is a hotspot for painting courses. But artists aren't its only appreciative guests. 'The whole family enjoyed our stay,' write Guide readers, approving the 'friendly owners', the 'cosy parlours' with fire and beamed ceiling, the 'simply and nicely decorated rooms'. A Guide inspector on arrival had a delightful welcome from a kitten who jumped into his car; he glimpsed rabbits skittering in 'overgrown' gardens brimming with lupins, poppies, old-fashioned roses. The cottage-style bedrooms, some with exposed timbers, some in converted barns around the studio, have 'comfortable beds, high-quality linen', hand-woven rugs. At night Wendy Sartin cooks for residents only, a frequently changing menu of simple, locally sourced dishes, served in 'generous' portions. For instance: beef fillet slices, wild mushrooms, red wine. Service is fleet and polite. At breakfast, the vintage china comes out for excellent fruit compote, home-made bread, perfect scrambled eggs. Our readers had an excellent lunch at The Sun Inn, but that's another story (see next entry). (RG, T and SR)

25% DISCOUNT VOUCHERS

Brook Street
Dedham
CO7 6AD

T: 01206 323027
E: sarton@dedhamhall.demon.co.uk
W: www.dedhamhall.co.uk

BEDROOMS: 20. 16 in annexe around art studio, some on ground floor, suitable for disabled.
OPEN: all year except Christmas–New Year.
FACILITIES: 2 lounges, bar, dining room, restaurant, studio, free Wi-Fi, in-room TV, 6-acre grounds (pond, gardens), lounge and dining room wheelchair accessible.
BACKGROUND MUSIC: none.
LOCATION: end of village High Street (set back from road).
CHILDREN: all ages welcomed.
DOGS: allowed in some bedrooms, not in public rooms.
CREDIT CARDS: MasterCard, Visa.
PRICES: [2018] per room B&B single £75, double £120, D,B&B double £105–£180. À la carte/fixed-price dinner £35.

DEDHAM Essex

Map 2:C5

THE SUN INN

'A convivial local gathering spot', Piers Baker's 15th-century timber-framed inn stands 'in a prime situation' in 'this endearing village of variously coloured houses' in Constable country. There have been changes since last year (new furniture in bar and dining room), but it is still the quintessential village pub, with oak beams and open fires in bar, lounge and restaurant. Access to two of the bedrooms is via the terrace, up an Elizabethan staircase. Rooms vary in size. Some overlook the garden, some the street and St Mary's Church with its soothing chimes. Constable, at the front, has a bay window and half-tester bed. The bar menu now goes beyond sandwiches, while in the dining room, Jack Levine's cooking is, as ever, modern English pub fare with Italian gusto, served in 'copious portions'. Maybe artichoke risotto with confit garlic, or 'a cucina-povera-inspired dish of Sutton Hoot chicken involtini with butter beans and chorizo'. 'A sweet, jiggly panacotta went perfectly with stewed rhubarb.' After an 'exceptional breakfast (freshly squeezed orange, 'perfect' omelettes), it's not two miles on foot, along and across the Stour, to Flatford Mill.

25% DISCOUNT VOUCHERS

High Street
Dedham
CO7 6DF

T: 01206 323351
E: office@thesuninndedham.com
W: www.thesuninndedham.com

BEDROOMS: 7. 2 across the terrace, approached by Elizabethan staircase.
OPEN: all year except 25/26 Dec.
FACILITIES: lounge, bar, dining room, free Wi-Fi, in-room TV (Freeview), 1-acre walled garden (covered terrace seating 40, children's play area, garden bar), unsuitable for disabled.
BACKGROUND MUSIC: background all day in public areas.
LOCATION: village centre.
CHILDREN: all ages welcomed.
DOGS: in bar, and in guest bedrooms by arrangement and subject to terms and conditions, not in dining room. .
CREDIT CARDS: Amex, MasterCard, Visa.
PRICES: [2018] per room B&B single £90–£130, double £145, D,B&B double £200. À la carte £28.50.

DODDISCOMBSLEIGH Devon   Map 1:C4

THE NOBODY INN

Previous César winner

A 'time capsule of ancient England', Sue
Burdge's venerable former dwelling house has
been the village pub and hub since 1837. 'An
exquisite example of a Devon inn', its 'beguiling'
bar all 'low beams and parchment-stained
walls, prints and pictures, guns, swords and
old maps'. One reader was reminded of a film
set – a Carry On, to judge by a report from
other regular contributors, who squashed into
the smallest room, with a four-foot bed and
'ancient mattress'; 'by moving a chest of drawers
we pulled the bed out far enough to get in on
both sides'. A larger, 'still quite small' room,
has 'a nice outlook and a big, comfortable bed',
a shower room. But the best choice is large and
still very affordable, with an 'enormous bed' and
'wonderfully appointed bathroom'. All rooms
have a decanter of sherry. Staff are welcoming.
The list of whiskies runs to hundreds. In a 'bar-
cum-dining room area', food can be somewhat
hit and miss. The steak and ale NoBody pie was
'heavenly', while haddock and chips had 'soggy
batter'. Breakfast is 'superb', the experience
'memorable'. (EM, and others)

Doddiscombsleigh
EX6 7PS

T: 01647 252394
E: info@nobodyinn.co.uk
W: www.nobodyinn.co.uk

BEDROOMS: 5.
OPEN: all year except 24/25 Dec, 31
Dec, 1 Jan, restaurant closed Sun,
Mon.
FACILITIES: 2 bars, restaurant, free
Wi-Fi (improving but may be
patchy), in-room TV (Freeview),
garden, patio, parking, dining room
wheelchair accessible.
BACKGROUND MUSIC: none.
LOCATION: in village 8 miles SW of
Exeter.
CHILDREN: not under 5.
DOGS: allowed, on lead, in bar only.
CREDIT CARDS: MasterCard, Visa.
PRICES: [2018] per room B&B single
£59–£85, double £79–£110, D,B&B
single £79–£105, double £110–£135.
À la carte £32.

DUNSTER Somerset

Map 1:B5

THE LUTTRELL ARMS HOTEL

In a medieval village dominated by a hilltop castle, between Exmoor national park and the coast, Nigel and Anne Way's historic hotel is showing its age – in all the best ways. Dating in parts from the 1400s, it retains such original features as latticed casement windows, carved stone mullions, a 17th-century plaster ceiling. Bedrooms range from smallish 'standard', through 'superior', with a terrace on to the garden, to 'feature', with perhaps an antique four-poster, a hammerbeam roof, sheepskins, a stag's head, a sarcophagus-like carved fireplace. The whole operation, from 'seamless' check-in to the presentation of a very reasonable bill, impressed a fellow hotelier on a busman's holiday. 'The bedroom was spacious and warm', with a seating area – the style 'absolutely suited to a very nice coaching inn'. Food is served all day in the busy bar, the lounge and the walled 'secret' garden (signs point the way). Barrie Tucker's ambitious cooking in Psalter's restaurant showcases local produce for such dishes as seared venison loin, butternut squash purée, roasted fig, Jerusalem artichoke, puffed wild rice, cherry sauce. Vegetarian options are similarly inventive. 'We'll be back.'

32–36 High Street
Dunster
TA24 6SG

T: 01643 821555
E: enquiry@luttrellarms.co.uk
W: www.luttrellarms.co.uk

BEDROOMS: 28. Some on ground floor.
OPEN: all year.
FACILITIES: lounge, bar, restaurant, function rooms, free Wi-Fi, in-room TV (Freeview), civil wedding licence, courtyard, garden (alfresco dining), bar and restaurant wheelchair accessible.
BACKGROUND MUSIC: in restaurant.
LOCATION: village centre, 3½ miles SE of Minehead.
CHILDREN: all ages welcomed.
DOGS: allowed in most bedrooms, bar, not in restaurant.
CREDIT CARDS: Amex, MasterCard, Visa.
PRICES: [2018] per room B&B single £105, double £150–£220, D,B&B double £185–£300. À la carte £32. Min. 2-night stay at weekends.

EAST CHISENBURY Wiltshire

Map 2:D2

THE RED LION FREEHOUSE

♥ Previous César winner

Readers this year 'ran out of superlatives' after a 'rather splendid visit' to this thatched gastropub in 'a delightful village'. The bar is pure country local, with beams, exposed brick, log-burner, wooden tables and chairs – if you want just a pint and a pickled egg, that's fine. But the big attraction is the Michelin-starred modern British cooking of chef/proprietors Guy and Brittany Manning, using the freshest local and home-grown ingredients. Our readers enjoyed 'truly scrumptious' Cornish crab tart; carrot and sweet potato velouté; pumpkin risotto; slow-cooked lamb shoulder, charred leeks, mash, lamb sauce; crème brûlée. The staff are 'friendly and on the ball'. In fine weather you can eat alfresco in the garden. Bedrooms, in the Troutbeck Guesthouse, a bungalow across the road, are 'decorated with enthusiasm and flair'. Each has a private deck overlooking a peaceful stretch of the River Avon. Dog-friendly Manser room was 'very well appointed, with excellent bathroom'. At breakfast there are eggs from the Red Lion's rescued hens, a 'splendid full English', smoked salmon, home-made breads and jams, all 'beautifully presented'. (Chris and Erica Savory, J T-P)

East Chisenbury
SN9 6AQ

T: 01980 671124
E: troutbeck@redlionfreehouse.com
W: www.redlionfreehouse.com

BEDROOMS: 5. On ground floor, in adjacent building; 1 (with wet room) suitable for disabled.
OPEN: all year, kitchen closed Sun evening, all day Mon/Tues.
FACILITIES: bar/restaurant, private dining room, free Wi-Fi, in-room TV (Freeview), 1-acre garden.
BACKGROUND MUSIC: in pub/restaurant.
LOCATION: in village, 6 miles S of Pewsey.
CHILDREN: all ages welcomed.
DOGS: allowed.
CREDIT CARDS: Amex, MasterCard, Visa.
PRICES: [2018] per room B&B £160–£245, D,B&B £195–£260. À la carte £43.

EAST GRINSTEAD Sussex

Map 2:D4

GRAVETYE MANOR

♛ Previous César winner

'We have become addicted to this place,' write trusted readers, following a return visit to this recently 'spruced-up' Elizabethan manor house (Relais & Châteaux). 'The staff go to great lengths to make your stay memorable, the welcome is always warm, the service impeccable.' From classic doubles to deluxe four-poster rooms, the accommodation is 'superb'. 'The style varies from traditional Tudor to smart, modern but equally cosy.' A 'generous hospitality tray' includes a coffee-maker and 'delicious home-made biscuits'. 'Huge log fires' burn in comfortable lounges, while in the 'wonderfully airy' new restaurant, with floor-to-ceiling glass walls that open on to a garden patio, is 'absolutely spectacular, a tour de force'. It hosts Michelin-starred chef George Blogg's 'exquisite' dishes, highlighting orchard, kitchen garden and local produce. 'Our excellent carpaccio starter was followed by a delicious lobster done two ways.' Breakfast is 'a total joy' with 'perfectly cooked eggs', pastries, 'whatever you like'. The 'breathtaking' gardens were laid out by William Robinson, pioneer of the natural English style, over his 50-year tenure, from 1885. (Francine and Ian Walsh, Bill Bennett)

Vowels Lane
East Grinstead
RH19 4LJ

T: 01342 810567
E: info@gravetyemanor.co.uk
W: www.gravetyemanor.co.uk

BEDROOMS: 17.
OPEN: all year.
FACILITIES: 2 lounges, bar, restaurant, 2 private dining rooms, free Wi-Fi, in-room TV (Sky), civil wedding licence, 1,000-acre grounds (woodland, ornamental and kitchen gardens, meadow, orchard, lake, croquet lawn, glasshouses), only restaurant wheelchair accessible.
BACKGROUND MUSIC: in bar in evening.
LOCATION: 4 miles SW of East Grinstead.
CHILDREN: not under 7.
DOGS: not allowed.
CREDIT CARDS: Amex, MasterCard, Visa.
PRICES: [2018] per room B&B £278–£850. Set dinner £35–£50, tasting menu £90, seasonal menu £75. 1-night bookings sometimes refused at weekends.

EAST HOATHLY Sussex

Map 2:E4

OLD WHYLY

'As wonderful as ever,' writes a regular visitor to Sarah Burgoyne's 'charmingly run' Grade II listed, red brick Georgian manor house adjoining a private estate, close to Lewes. Glyndebourne is a ten-minute drive away (picnics can be provided). 'A beautiful house, glorious garden [with a secluded outdoor pool and wisteria-draped pool house, a hard tennis court, lake, rose-covered pergola], comfortable rooms.' There are lovely views from the traditionally styled bedrooms (two en suite, two with private bathroom), all supplied with wool blankets, Egyptian cotton or Irish linen sheets. Fine china is brought out for tea and cakes served in a drawing room filled with paintings, books, photographs and family possessions. Here, later, guests will gather for aperitifs, before a 'delicious dinner' in the candlelit dining room – or alfresco on warm evenings – prepared by the hostess, who trained in cookery and flower-arranging in Paris. Perhaps curried squash soup; duck breast, port sauce, red cabbage; dark chocolate flan, lime cream. Breakfast includes eggs from the hens, honey from the orchard's hives, poached pears from its trees. (Catrin Treadwell)

London Road
East Hoathly
BN8 6EL

T: 01825 840216
E: stay@oldwhyly.co.uk
W: www.oldwhyly.co.uk

BEDROOMS: 4.
OPEN: all year.
FACILITIES: drawing room, dining room, free Wi-Fi, in-room TV (Freeview), 4-acre garden, heated outdoor swimming pool (14 by 7 metres), tennis, unsuitable for disabled.
BACKGROUND MUSIC: none.
LOCATION: 1 mile N of village.
CHILDREN: all ages welcomed.
DOGS: allowed in drawing room, not in dining room or unattended in bedrooms.
CREDIT CARDS: none.
PRICES: [2018] per room B&B £98–£150, D,B&B £136–£188. Set dinner £38, hamper £40 per person. 1-night bookings may be refused at weekends in summer season.

EASTBOURNE Sussex

Map 2:E4

BELLE TOUT LIGHTHOUSE

'Great place. Wonderful breakfast.' A thumbs-up this year from visitors to David and Barbara Shaw's unusual B&B, at a decommissioned granite lighthouse in a 'dramatic, empty landscape' in the South Downs national park. First impressions are stark: 'not a tree, not a flower'. But within, a friendly welcome awaits at the upstairs reception. Most of the accommodation is in an adjacent house. The Keeper's Loft, in the lighthouse itself, has brick walls, a fireplace, a ladder to climb to your bunk bed. The other bedrooms are contemporary and pristine. The lounge and breakfast room share the open-plan second floor – a cosy space, with 'lots of leather sofas, a grandfather clock, a working fire, fresh flowers', views of Beachy Head and the Seven Sisters. Here, guests gather at 5 pm for complimentary drinks, 'a clever way to make newcomers feel at home in this remote situation'. Some buy supper from the delicatessen in the nearest village, East Dean, while others head there for the ancient Tiger Inn. For the true lighthouse experience, you need to ascend to the lantern on a dark, star-filled night.

Beachy Head Road
Eastbourne
BN20 0AE

T: 01323 423185
E: info@belletout.co.uk
W: www.belletout.co.uk

BEDROOMS: 6. 5 in house, 1 in lighthouse (bunk bed).
OPEN: all year except Christmas/New Year.
FACILITIES: 2 lounges, breakfast room, free Wi-Fi (in some rooms and some public areas), in-room TV (Freeview), terrace, garden, unsuitable for disabled.
BACKGROUND MUSIC: none.
LOCATION: 3 miles W of Eastbourne, 2 miles S of East Dean village (pub, deli).
CHILDREN: not under 15.
DOGS: not allowed.
CREDIT CARDS: MasterCard, Visa.
PRICES: [2018] per room B&B £160–£240. Min. 2 nights, though 1-night bookings may be accepted (check for availability in the week before proposed stay).

EASTBOURNE Sussex

THE GRAND HOTEL

Once a month a string quartet serenades afternoon tea at this Victorian seafront hotel nicknamed 'The White Palace'. Grand it may be, but stuffy it isn't – and it is 'obviously popular with families'. Trusted Guide readers' Master Suite this year had 'super sea views', a 'spacious' sitting room with sofa, armchairs, a breakfast table by the window. Despite some 'shortcomings' (a 'puny' shower, lack of storage in a second, single bedroom), 'we really liked it'. Shoes left outside were returned, 'beautifully polished, in a shoe bag'. 'Freshly made, delicious sandwiches', delivered by room service, justified the 30-minute wait. Extras included fresh fruit, shortbread, a small decanter of sherry. At dinner in the refurbished Mirabelle restaurant, new chef Stephanie Malvoisin's fine-dining menus include such dishes as halibut fillet, sweet potato crisp, apple and carrot cider cream sauce; for veggies, maybe aubergine cheesecake. In the Garden restaurant the style is slightly simpler, perhaps braised blade of beef, creamed potato, root vegetable medley, French beans, onion gravy. Breakfast choices include a full English, full Mediterranean (chorizo, pancetta), grilled kippers, oak-smoked haddock. (Michael Gwinnell, VRS)

King Edwards Parade
Eastbourne
BN21 4EQ

T: 01323 412345
E: enquiries@grandeastbourne.com
W: www.grandeastbourne.com

BEDROOMS: 152. 1 suitable for disabled.
OPEN: all year, Mirabelle restaurant closed first 2 weeks Jan.
FACILITIES: 5 lounges, bar, 2 restaurants, extensive function facilities, lifts, free Wi-Fi, in-room TV (BT, Freeview), civil wedding licence, terrace, spa/health club (indoor and outdoor pools), 2-acre garden, public areas wheelchair accessible, adapted toilets.
BACKGROUND MUSIC: in restaurants, live music at weekends.
LOCATION: seafront, outside centre.
CHILDREN: all ages welcomed.
DOGS: allowed ('strictly controlled') in bedrooms, not in public rooms.
CREDIT CARDS: all major cards.
PRICES: [2018] per room B&B £165–£730, D,B&B £239–£804. Set dinner £46 (Mirabelle), £42 (Garden).

ECKINGTON Worcestershire

ECKINGTON MANOR

With its own farm, orchard, vegetable and herb gardens, food is at the heart of everything at Judy Gardner's restored restaurant-with-rooms, occupying a half-timbered farmhouse and rustic outbuildings. Compact, ground-floor 'classic' bedrooms have a shower room, designer features. More expensive rooms might have oak beams, a wood-burning stove, an in-room, freestanding roll-top bath. A reader this year found a classic room in the cider mill a bit cramped, 'somewhat claustrophobic'. It had 'no window, just two skylights'. That said, 'it was beautifully decorated, with silk wallpaper, two dining chairs'. The bathroom was 'nicely finished and had a powerful shower'. The highlight of his stay was dinner in the restaurant, where former MasterChef: The Professionals winner Mark Stinchcombe and his wife, Sue, win acclaim for their 'elaborately presented, delicious food'. A signature dish of rib-eye of beef, braised shin, heritage carrot, marrow-bone crust, charcoal emulsion, was 'exceptionally tasty; a great combination'. Service, in the dining room and reception, is 'first class'. At breakfast, commercial jams and juices may disappoint, but there is 'a very nice selection of prepared food and good cooked dishes'. (Steven Hur)

Hammock Road
Eckington
WR10 3BJ

T: 01386 751600
E: info@eckingtonmanor.co.uk
W: www.eckingtonmanor.co.uk

BEDROOMS: 17. All in courtyard annexes, 1 suitable for disabled.
OPEN: all year except 25/26 Dec, restaurant closed Sun evening, Mon, Tues.
FACILITIES: lift, 2 sitting rooms (one with bar area), restaurant, function rooms, free Wi-Fi, in-room TV (Freeview), civil wedding licence, cookery school, 260-acre grounds (lawns, herb garden, orchard, working farm), public areas wheelchair accessible, adapted toilet.
BACKGROUND MUSIC: in garden bar and restaurant.
LOCATION: 4 miles SW of Pershore.
CHILDREN: not under 8.
DOGS: allowed in 2 bedrooms, not in public rooms.
CREDIT CARDS: Amex, MasterCard, Visa.
PRICES: [2018] per room B&B £179–£279. Set dinner £48.

EDENBRIDGE Kent

Map 2:D4

STARBOROUGH MANOR

'We had a lovely stay, a real treat.' Guide inspectors could find nothing to fault at Daisy and Clive Hayley's Georgian manor house B&B, remodelled in the late 1900s. Approached by a tree-lined drive, it stands in well-tended grounds overlooking Starborough Castle – an 18th-century neo-Gothic garden house on a moated artificial island. A surprise upgrade to the honeymoon suite, a 'gorgeous, high-ceilinged room with beautiful painted antique furniture, an enormous bed and large bathroom', surely contributed to the positive view. It is 'usually used only for special events' (honeymoons, indeed – this is a popular wedding venue). The guest bedrooms in normal use are prettily, traditionally furnished, each with its own style, and with posh bathroom products. Ashdown Forest, Winnie the Pooh's old stomping ground, is nearby, and when it's time for food, the friendly, forthcoming hosts will advise on where to eat, or you can hire dining room and kitchen. A 'very good breakfast' is served in the 'lovely large kitchen, at a long table', and might include baked cinnamon plums, Greek yogurt, local butcher's sausages, scrambled eggs with smoked salmon.

Moor Lane
Edenbridge
TN8 5QY

T: 01732 862152
E: daisy@starboroughmanor.co.uk
W: starboroughmanor.co.uk

BEDROOMS: 4 (incl. 1 suite with 2 bedrooms, 4 sharing).
OPEN: all year.
FACILITIES: 2 sitting rooms, dining room, kitchen/breakfast room, laundry for guests' use, function facilities, free Wi-Fi, in-room TV (Freeview), 4-acre gardens in 13-acre grounds (parkland, tennis, heated outdoor swimming pool in season), unsuitable for disabled.
BACKGROUND MUSIC: none.
LOCATION: 1½ miles W of Edenbridge.
CHILDREN: all ages welcomed.
DOGS: not allowed.
CREDIT CARDS: Amex, MasterCard, Visa.
PRICES: [2018] per room B&B single £90–£110, double £140, family room from £220. 1-night bookings usually refused weekends in summer.

SEE ALSO SHORTLIST

EGTON BRIDGE Yorkshire

Map 4:C5

BROOM HOUSE AT EGTON BRIDGE

'Just outside a picturesque little village', host to an annual gooseberry show, in the North York Moors national park, this 'high-quality B&B' is run by owners Georgina and Michael Curnow. Bedrooms vary in size, from a compact attic room with views over the Esk valley and moors, to a dual-aspect room with a sofa in front of a feature fireplace. The May Barn, with private access, has a ground-floor sitting room, double bedroom, wet room and patio; a first-floor double with exposed beams and stonework, a travertine bathroom, walk-in shower, a roll-top bath with a view. 'Decor was modern, clean, like an upmarket barn conversion... Farrow & Ball-type colours.' All rooms are supplied with hospitality tray, good toiletries. Breakfast, cooked by Michael, is 'good, with attention paid to local sourcing'. Scrambled eggs, a test of timing, were perfectly done – but, says a reader, guests staying for a few days might appreciate more choice. It is a ten-minute walk to the pub, across the river by stepping stones, a ten-minute drive to Whitby, for fans of Dracula (the ruined abbey), and fish and chips (the Magpie).

Broom House Lane
Egton Bridge
YO21 1XD

T: 07423 636783
E: mail@broom-house.co.uk
W: broom-house.co.uk

BEDROOMS: 9. 2 (1 on ground floor) in converted barn suite.
OPEN: Mar–Nov.
FACILITIES: lounge, breakfast room, free Wi-Fi, in-room TV (Freeview), 1-acre garden.
BACKGROUND MUSIC: in breakfast room.
LOCATION: ½ mile W of village.
CHILDREN: all ages welcomed (by arrangement).
DOGS: not allowed.
CREDIT CARDS: MasterCard, Visa.
PRICES: [2018] per room B&B £89–£200. Min. 2-night bookings preferred at weekends.

EMSWORTH Hampshire   Map 2:E3

36 ON THE QUAY

☙ Previous César winner

A 17th-century house, 'in a delightful position opposite the quay', in an 'attractive little town', is today run as a smart restaurant-with-rooms. The long-time owners, Karen and Ramon Farthing, are now partners with Gary and Martina Pearce, manager and chef respectively. Light, airy, 'beautifully decorated, spotless' bedrooms, some with centuries-old exposed timbers, offer views of an arm of Chichester harbour or a tidal millpond. 'Comfortable accommodation,' says a reader, but it is for Mr Pearce's cooking, above all, that people come. His style is modern British with European influences. Ingredients are locally produced or foraged (sea buckthorn from the shore, cèpes and chanterelles from the South Downs). Menus offer four choices at each of three courses. Perhaps smoked eel, hazelnut and eel mousse, apple terrine, potato and eel croquette, apple and eel sauce; pan-fried red mullet, sand carrots, confit chicken, pickled amaranth, spiced red wine sauce; parfait of Hayling Island honey, frozen yogurt rocks, salted lemon curd, sumac meringue. Next morning, a continental breakfast. PG Wodehouse once rented a cottage in Emsworth named Threepwood; 'Plum' fans will make the connections.

47 South Street
Emsworth
PO10 7EG

T: 01243 375592
E: info@36onthequay.co.uk
W: www.36onthequay.co.uk

BEDROOMS: 4.
OPEN: all year except 24–28 Dec, 1 week May, 1 week Oct; restaurant closed Sun/Mon.
FACILITIES: bar area, restaurant, free Wi-Fi, in-room TV (Freeview), small terrace, limited parking, restaurant wheelchair accessible, adapted toilet.
BACKGROUND MUSIC: none.
LOCATION: on harbour.
CHILDREN: all ages welcomed.
DOGS: not allowed.
CREDIT CARDS: Amex, MasterCard, Visa.
PRICES: [2018] per room B&B single £75–£110, double £110–£200. À la carte £48–£58, tasting menu £65.

ERMINGTON Devon

Map 1:D4

PLANTATION HOUSE

In the rolling South Hams countryside, Richard Hendey's Georgian rectory turned small hotel is 'a delightful place to stay, peaceful and friendly'. Interiors are smart and contemporary. The 'beautifully furnished' bedrooms are supplied with such thoughtful extras as home-made cake on arrival, cafetière coffee, fresh fruit, biscuits, garden flowers, a hot-water bottle for chilly nights. Bathrooms have underfloor heating, luxury toiletries. 'The perfect host', Mr Hendey also cooks ('he seems to be everywhere'), with John Raines and Josh Tolley, using locally farmed, raised or caught, and home-grown produce in 'perfectly balanced' dishes. For instance, roast rack, braised shoulder and crackling of lamb on a shallot and Merlot jus, toasted barley risotto, roast vegetables. The kitchen will happily cater for vegetarians or anyone with special dietary requirements, given notice. 'The food is uncommonly good, despite the difficulties of making gluten-free dishes for me.' Breakfast brings freshly squeezed orange juice, leaf tea, a fruit platter with yogurt, Agen prunes, smoked haddock, boiled eggs with asparagus and soldiers, bubble and squeak, or the 'full Devon'. (J Balson, MC)

25% DISCOUNT VOUCHERS

Totnes Road
Ermington
PL21 9NS

T: 01548 831100
E: info@plantationhousehotel.co.uk
W: www.plantationhousehotel.co.uk

BEDROOMS: 8.
OPEN: all year, restaurant closed midday, some Sun evenings.
FACILITIES: lounge/bar, 2 dining rooms, free Wi-Fi, in-room TV (Freeview), in-room massage, terrace, 1-acre garden, only restaurant suitable for wheelchair.
BACKGROUND MUSIC: in public rooms 'whenever required or when deemed suitable'.
LOCATION: 10 miles E of Plymouth.
CHILDREN: all ages welcomed.
DOGS: allowed in 1 bedroom, not in public rooms.
CREDIT CARDS: Amex, MasterCard, Visa.
PRICES: per room B&B single £95–£195, double £110–£230, D,B&B double £189–£309. Set dinner £39.50. 1-night bookings sometimes refused on bank holiday weekends.

EVERSHOT Dorset

Map 1:C6

THE ACORN INN

'Thomas Hardy's historic Acorn Inn,' reads the sign outside this 16th-century former coaching inn (it appears as The Sow and Acorn in *Tess*, and in two of Hardy's short stories). A sister to Summer Lodge, Evershot (see next entry), it is managed for Red Carnation Hotels by Richard and Natalie Legg, alongside 'friendly, helpful staff'. Readers this year chose one of three four-poster rooms (Tess, Hardy and Silverthorne). 'It was very colourful, the bedhead's blue fabric depicting charming people from an earlier age (maybe mid-Victorian to echo Hardy's era).' It was 'a bit small, we had difficulty knowing where to put our cases', but 'the bed was comfortable'; the bathroom had a walk-in shower, no bath. 'Snug' rooms are really snug. The loft suite has a double and a single room, lounge, both bath and shower. Downstairs, a dog-friendly pub with skittle alley combines with sophisticated dining. From chef Robert Ndungu's restaurant menu: roasted loin of Dorset lamb, slow-cooked shoulder, fondant potato, hispi cabbage and broad bean purée, thyme jus. 'Breakfast was excellent. Superb toast using bread from the bakery. Eggs and bacon scrumptious.' (John Barnes, ID)

28 Fore Street
Evershot
DT2 0JW

T: 01935 83228
E: stay@acorn-inn.co.uk
W: www.acorn-inn.co.uk

BEDROOMS: 10.
OPEN: all year.
FACILITIES: 2 bars, restaurant, lounge, free Wi-Fi, in-room TV (Sky, Freeview), skittle alley, beer garden, access to spa, gym at sister hotel opposite (£15 per day), bar and restaurant wheelchair accessible, toilet not adapted.
BACKGROUND MUSIC: in bar and restaurant.
LOCATION: in village, 10 miles S of Yeovil.
CHILDREN: all ages welcomed.
DOGS: allowed (£12 charge per dog per night, water bowls, towels, treats).
CREDIT CARDS: Amex, MasterCard, Visa.
PRICES: [2018] per room B&B £105–£230, D,B&B £175–£300. À la carte £35. Min. 2-night stay at weekends during peak season.

EVERSHOT Dorset

Map 1:C6

SUMMER LODGE

NEW

It had 'that "special" feel of a very good and well-run hotel', found a visitor to this country house hotel and spa (Relais & Châteaux) in deepest Thomas Hardy country. It is owned by Bea Tollman's Red Carnation group (see previous entry, Acorn Inn, Evershot) and, indeed, Hardy himself had a hand in extending what was then a dower house. Our reader was impressed by the welcome from manager Jack Mackenzie, and by a bedroom overlooking the gardens, which was 'beautifully furnished, with expensive drapes' and an 'excellent bathroom'. Extra touches included fresh flowers, fruit, shortbread. In the 'tastefully decorated' lounge 'a great log fire' blazed. The staff were 'helpful, courteous, professional, always with a smile'. In the dining room, Steven Titman's cooking was 'sheer joy and of such quality'. A typical dish: roast loin of Dorset lamb, braised shoulder 'shepherd's pie', savoy cabbage, rosemary jus. Breakfast in the conservatory was 'a delight', with freshly squeezed orange juice, spiced and marinated dried fruit, breads and pastries from the village bakery, local bacon and sausages. 'There is a lovely spa and pool, kitchen garden and formal garden.' (Ian Dewey)

9 Fore Street
Evershot
DT2 0JR

T: 01935 482000
E: summerlodge@rchmail.com
W: www.summerlodgehotel.co.uk

BEDROOMS: 24, 6 in coach house, 3 in courtyard house, 1 in honeymoon cottage, 1 on ground floor suitable for disabled, plus 4 in other cottages.
OPEN: all year.
FACILITIES: ramps, whisky lounge, drawing room, restaurant, conservatory, meeting room, free Wi-Fi, in-room TV (Sky), indoor swimming pool (11 by 6 metres), spa, civil wedding licence, 4-acre grounds (tennis), public rooms wheelchair accessible.
BACKGROUND MUSIC: 'easy listening' in bar/whisky lounge.
LOCATION: 10 miles S of Yeovil.
CHILDREN: over 7 welcomed.
DOGS: allowed in some bedrooms, whisky lounge.
CREDIT CARDS: Amex, MasterCard, Visa.
PRICES: [2018] per room B&B £215–£795, D,B&B £335–£915. Set dinner £54–£68.

EXMOUTH Devon   Map 1:D5

LYMPSTONE MANOR   NEW

Michael Caines's 'beautifully restored' Georgian
manor house stands in parkland beside the
luminous Exe estuary. The transformation
of a formerly dilapidated property has been
remarkable. A reader found luxury and
attention to detail everywhere, an atmosphere
'so quiet that, but for the deep-pile carpet, you
could hear a pin drop'. Yet it is coolly chic and
beautiful, not stuffy, with a palette inspired by
the estuary. A balconied bedroom had views
of the water, the Devon hills, and 'the most
comfortable bed we've slept on'. All bedrooms,
each named after an estuary bird, have works
by local watercolourist Rachel Toll, an espresso
machine, gin and tonic on a polished tray.
Some have a balcony, some a terrace with soak
tub and fire pit. In the dining rooms, the chef/
patron's 'search for perfection' is evident in
Michelin-starred signature menus and à la carte
dishes such as braised Brixham turbot, wild
mushroom, spinach, truffle butter sauce; loin
and confit shoulder of Darts Farm lamb, fennel
purée, mint, boulangère potato. Until wines from
the new vineyard come on stream, there are a
mere 600 bins to choose from. (Richard Barrett)

Courtlands Lane
Exmouth
EX8 3NZ

T: 01395 202040
E: info@lympstonemanor.co.uk
W: lympstonemanor.co.uk

BEDROOMS: 21. 5 on ground floor,
1 suitable for disabled.
OPEN: all year.
FACILITIES: 3 dining rooms, reception
lounge, lounge, bar, 28-acre grounds
(vineyard), in-room TV (Freeview),
free Wi-Fi, civil wedding licence,
public areas wheelchair accessible,
adapted toilet.
BACKGROUND MUSIC: all day in public
rooms.
LOCATION: 1 mile N of Exmouth,
¼ mile off A376.
CHILDREN: all ages welcome (no
under-5s in restaurant).
DOGS: in 2 bedrooms with separate
entrance, not in main house.
CREDIT CARDS: all major cards.
PRICES: [2018] per room D,B&B
single £415–£1,205, double
£565–£1,355. 8-course tasting menu
per person £145, seafood menu £135,
à la carte £125 (discretionary service
charge of 12½% is added to food).

FAVERSHAM Kent

Map 2.D5

READ'S

Veterans of the hospitality industry Rona and David Pitchford run Georgian Macknade Manor as an elegant restaurant-with-rooms. It stands back from the road, approached by an impressive gravel drive, in grounds shaded by lofty horse chestnut trees, cedars, laurels – hence the tree theme in the naming of the six large bedrooms. All are furnished with antiques. Dual-aspect Chestnut overlooks the front lawn, Laurel has a four-poster and original fireplace, Cedar a view of a majestic Cedar of Lebanon. Three rooms have a bath, one a shower; Chestnut and Cedar enjoy both. All the rooms are stylish and traditional, equipped for practical comfort. Classically trained Mr Pitchford has worked in kitchens since starting as a teenage commis chef at London's Dorchester. He uses produce from the walled kitchen garden alongside local game and meat in such dishes as Kentish lamb, potato hotpot, carrot purée, seasonal vegetables, while most of the fish arrives fresh from the Whitstable and Hythe quaysides. More vegetarian options would be appreciated but 'dishes ranged from good to very good indeed'. Breakfast, also cooked by the host, is reputedly excellent. We would welcome more reports.

Macknade Manor
Faversham
ME13 8XE

T: 01795 535344
E: enquiries@reads.com
W: www.reads.com

BEDROOMS: 6.
OPEN: all year except 4 days Christmas, first 2 weeks Jan, 2 weeks Sept, restaurant closed Sun/Mon.
FACILITIES: sitting room/bar, 3 dining rooms, free Wi-Fi, in-room TV (Freeview), civil wedding licence, 4-acre garden (terrace, outdoor dining), restaurant wheelchair accessible.
BACKGROUND MUSIC: none.
LOCATION: ½ mile SE of Faversham.
CHILDREN: all ages welcomed.
DOGS: allowed in bedrooms.
CREDIT CARDS: all major cards.
PRICES: [2018] per room B&B single £140–£195, double £180–£210, D,B&B single £185–£250, double £290–£320. Set dinner £60, tasting menu £65.

FELIXKIRK Yorkshire

Map 4:C4

THE CARPENTERS ARMS

'Excellent standards are being maintained,' confirms a Guide trusty this year, after staying at this village inn with rooms overlooking the Vale of Mowbray. One of two main-house bedrooms had 'a very comfortable king-size bed and spacious shower room'. Housekeeping was 'of the highest order'. Dog-friendly, ground-level rooms are ranged around a landscaped garden; each has a super-king-size bed, seating area, minibar, private terrace. Some rooms interconnect for family use. There are gun safes and drying wardrobes for country sports enthusiasts. The pub is part of Yorkshire-based Provenance Inns, which specialises in character village properties close to beautiful countryside. (See also Cleveland Tontine, Northallerton, in Shortlist.) In the dining room, with 'wonderful distant views', chef Lee Purcell's locally menus include produce from the company's Mount St John kitchen garden. For instance, roasted Dales lamb, charred leeks, creamed potato, rosemary jus. 'Food first rate, especially fennel and clam soup and twice-baked Yorkshire cheese soufflé; tasty steak; nothing fancy but well presented.' Breakfast includes rare-breed pork sausages, home-made black pudding. (Robert Gower)

Felixkirk
YO7 2DP

T: 01845 537369
E: enquiries@thecarpentersarms
felixkirk.com
W: thecarpentersarmsfelixkirk.com

BEDROOMS: 10. 8 in garden annexe, 1 suitable for disabled.
OPEN: all year.
FACILITIES: bar/sitting area, restaurant, private dining room, free Wi-Fi, in-room TV (Freeview), terrace (alfresco meals), garden, public rooms on ground floor wheelchair accessible, toilet adapted.
BACKGROUND MUSIC: 'generally at mealtimes' in bar and garden room.
LOCATION: in village 3 miles NE of Thirsk.
CHILDREN: all ages welcomed.
DOGS: welcomed in garden bedrooms, bar and some dining areas.
CREDIT CARDS: Amex, MasterCard, Visa.
PRICES: [2018] per room B&B £120–£200, D,B&B £175–£255. À la carte £30.

FLEET Dorset

Map 1:D6

MOONFLEET MANOR

Once used to billet D-Day troops, this revamped early 17th-century mansion now hosts 'young children, exhausted parents' and grandparents. A member of Luxury Family Hotels, it offers 'expert' care by 'extremely friendly' staff. 'For a weekend with three generations, it could not have been more suitable.' Facilities are 'excellent'. Grown-ups appreciate the spa, monitor listening service, and Sunday morning lie-ins when their broods are collected, fed and, under the gaze of Ofsted-registered nannies, make jewellery, dress up, have a ball – 'No guilt, it didn't feel like a dumping ground!' Close of play brings family movies at 6 pm, while in between, a soft play area, sand pit and ride-on toys for toddlers; an indoor football pitch, air hockey and geocaching for older ones. 'Spacious and comfortable' bedrooms, with family-friendly arrangements, are 'interestingly furnished' in a modern, colonial style. Flexible mealtimes include children's tea, family sittings and, after 7.30 pm, adult-only dining, where new chef Michael Culley creates such dishes as slow-braised Jurassic Coast beef, pearl onions, field mushrooms, braised red cabbage, creamy mashed potato. Breakfast was rated 'awesome' by one trusted five-year-old Guide insider.

Fleet Road
Fleet
DT3 4ED

T: 01305 786948
E: info@moonfleetmanorhotel.co.uk
W: www.moonfleetmanorhotel.co.uk

BEDROOMS: 36. 3 in coach house, 3 in villa, 3 on ground floor.
OPEN: all year.
FACILITIES: 2 lounges, family snug, restaurant, indoor playroom, crèche, cinema room, free Wi-Fi, in-room TV (Freeview), civil wedding licence, indoor swimming pools, terrace, 5-acre garden (play areas).
BACKGROUND MUSIC: contemporary in restaurant.
LOCATION: 7 miles W of Weymouth.
CHILDREN: all ages welcomed.
DOGS: allowed in bedrooms, on lead in public areas, not in restaurant or children's play areas.
CREDIT CARDS: Amex, MasterCard, Visa.
PRICES: [2018] per room B&B £120–£525, D,B&B £190–£595. À la carte £40. 1-night bookings sometimes refused.

FOWEY Cornwall   Map 1:D3

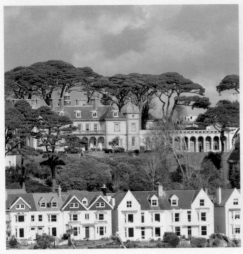

FOWEY HALL

♔ Previous César winner

A Victorian baroque showstopper, this manor
house stands on a steep hill in gardens above
the Fowey estuary. Part of the Luxury Family
Hotels group, 'it ticks all the luxury boxes', yet is
entirely child-friendly. Lofty public rooms filled
with antiques display many original features.
Bedrooms range from standard doubles (classic
in the main house, contemporary in the annexe)
to large family suites and interconnecting rooms
with seating area and two bathrooms. A reader
found many pleasing touches: 'A shoe-cleaning
service – amazing! Lovely log fires in the drawing
room. Loads of wellies in the porch. Delicious
nibbles with drinks…' Children's meals and light
snacks are served all day. There's a spa for adult
indulgence, while toddlers are entertained in the
Ofsted-registered crèche, and older siblings use
the indoor pool and games room, walk Bramble,
the dog, or feed the chickens. Once small children
are tucked up with the baby-listening device
engaged, chef James Parkinson takes over in the
fine-dining restaurant, turning locally fished and
farmed produce into such dishes as Cornish catch
of the day, sautéed potatoes, seasonal greens, herb
velouté. 'An outstanding place.'

Hanson Drive
Fowey
PL23 1ET

T: 01726 833866
E: info@foweyhallhotel.co.uk
W: www.foweyhallhotel.co.uk

BEDROOMS: 36. 8 in coach house,
some on ground floor, 2 suitable for
disabled.
OPEN: all year.
FACILITIES: 2 lounges, library/snug,
2 restaurants, free Wi-Fi, in-room
TV (Freeview), crèche, games
rooms, civil wedding licence, spa,
12-metre indoor swimming pool,
7-acre grounds (trampoline, zip
wire), public rooms wheelchair
accessible, adapted toilet.
BACKGROUND MUSIC: in restaurants.
LOCATION: ½ mile from town centre.
CHILDREN: all ages welcomed.
DOGS: allowed in main house
bedrooms (£15), not in restaurant.
CREDIT CARDS: Amex, MasterCard,
Visa.
PRICES: [2018] per room B&B
£140–£750. Set dinner £33–£43, à la
carte £43. 1-night bookings refused
at weekends.
SEE ALSO SHORTLIST

GITTISHAM Devon

Map 1:C5

THE PIG AT COMBE

'In its glory, in the very beautiful Otter valley', this Elizabethan manor house is the fifth member of Robin Hutson's Pig family. The rustic-chic style has seen hayloft and stable pressed into service as bedrooms. A stables room had an 'enormous half-tester' and spacious shower room. 'We were delighted that it retained much of its equine history,' write readers, although anyone who objects to the clip-clop of feet on a wooden staircase should review the options among main-house rooms, from 'cheap and cheerful' to 'big comfy luxe', to laundry and attic. Light falls through gorgeous leaded windows upon the Great Hall, now the main bar, with big, inviting sofas. As with all the Pigs, this hotel is veggie heaven, with local and kitchen-garden produce at the heart of the 'imaginative menus', whether in the conservatory restaurant or family-style in the garden folly. Maybe Barnstaple cauliflower risotto; Lyme Bay hake fillet, Teign mussels, shore veg, radishes, white wine sauce; Gibbins Farm 'Tomahawk' pork chop, creamy spinach, pancetta, mustard sauce. 'The staff are young, hard-working, extraordinarily enthusiastic.' Breakfast brings organic juices, free-range eggs, Dartmouth Smokehouse kippers. (Colin Honcy, TGR)

Gittisham
EX14 3AD

T: 01404 540400
E: reservations@thepighotel.com
W: www.thepighotel.com

BEDROOMS: 30. 10 in stable yard, 3 in cottages, 1 suitable for disabled.
OPEN: all year.
FACILITIES: bar, 2 lounges, restaurant, Folly (communal dining), alfresco drinking/eating area, meeting/private dining rooms, free Wi-Fi, in-room TV (Freeview), civil wedding licence, spa treatment rooms, terrace, 3,500-acre grounds (3 walled gardens), public rooms wheelchair accessible, adapted toilet.
BACKGROUND MUSIC: all day in public areas.
LOCATION: on outskirts of village.
CHILDREN: all ages welcomed.
DOGS: not allowed.
CREDIT CARDS: Amex, MasterCard, Visa.
PRICES: [2018] room £145–£500. À la carte £35, breakfast (per person) continental £11, buffet and cooked dishes £17.50. 1-night bookings sometimes refused.

GRASMERE Cumbria

FOREST SIDE

☙ Previous César winner

'It's difficult to pinpoint what makes this hotel
so special.' Atop a winding driveway, this Gothic
confection is 'light, airy, full of boutiquey charm
– and, naturally, has delightful views across
Grasmere'. 'Everything is elegantly understated
and themed around the Cumbrian landscape',
whether the decor or the award-winning
restaurant. 'Beautifully turned-out' bedrooms,
a touch on the small side, have a 'super-comfy'
bed and 'fantastic bathroom'. Guide readers
in 2018 repeat praise for the 'seamless' service
('particularly the easy accommodation of a
disabled member of our party') and 'superb'
dining. 'Dinner is a masterpiece.' The kitchen
opens on to the bustling restaurant floor,
where diners can watch Michelin-starred chef
Kevin Tickle bring marsh herbs, surf clams,
even squirrel pâté to the table, alongside
more traditional mains (perhaps a 'good slab'
of shorthorn rib) and an array of vegetarian
options. At breakfast, duck eggs, locally smoked
salmon and home-made granola start the day.
A stroll round the restored gardens and 'utterly
indulgent' tea complete the afternoon. 'Well run
from start to finish.' (Ralph Wilson, MW)

Keswick Road
Grasmere
LA22 9RN

T: 015394 35250
E: info@theforestside.com
W: www.theforestside.com

BEDROOMS: 20. 1 suitable for
disabled.
OPEN: all year, restaurant closed
midday Mon and Tues.
FACILITIES: lounges, bar, restaurant,
function/private dining rooms,
civil wedding licence, free Wi-Fi,
in-room TV (Freeview), terrace, 43-
acre grounds include 1-acre kitchen
garden.
BACKGROUND MUSIC: in public areas.
LOCATION: outskirts of village.
CHILDREN: all ages welcomed.
DOGS: allowed in some bedrooms
(max. 2 per room, £20 per dog,
includes welcome pack).
CREDIT CARDS: American Express,
MasterCard, Visa.
PRICES: [2018] per room B&B £229–
£369, D,B&B £329–£469. 10-course
tasting menu £95, à la carte £60.

SEE ALSO SHORTLIST

GRASMERE Cumbria

Map 4: inset C2

OAK BANK

'Such a comfortable place.' 'Peaceful and restful.' 'Great hotel.' Several of our readers are regulars at Glynis and Simon Wood's family-run Lakeland village hotel in the Wordsworth heartlands. 'Staff and management are very friendly, and keen to make guests feel at home.' Smart, contemporary bedrooms vary in size and facilities. All have a comfortable bed and luxury toiletries, bold patterned wallpaper and fabrics; some have a balcony. Views are variously of the garden, the River Rothay and surrounding mountains. There has been a change in the kitchen this year, with Matt Clarke – one-time sous-chef here – returning to take charge, carrying on a tradition of inventiveness and 'consistently high standards'. Typical dishes: salt-aged sirloin steak, dripping chips, tomato, ox-cheek-stuffed mushroom, bordelaise sauce; halibut, confit potato, artichoke monk's beard, brown butter hollandaise. The extensive breakfast menu includes such options as prunes steeped in Earl Grey tea, smoked haddock, kipper, omelettes, eggs Benedict, Scotch pancake with maple syrup, freshly baked pastries and the full Oak Bank grill. 'Would recommend staying here,' concludes a reader, succinctly. (William Swaddle, AM, FM, SA)

25% DISCOUNT VOUCHERS

Broadgate
Grasmere
LA22 9TA

T: 015394 35217
E: info@lakedistricthotel.co.uk
W: www.lakedistricthotel.co.uk

BEDROOMS: 13. 1 on ground floor.
OPEN: all year except 16–26 Dec, 6–24 Jan.
FACILITIES: lounge, bar, restaurant, conservatory dining room, free Wi-Fi, in-room TV (Freeview), ½-acre garden, unsuitable for disabled.
BACKGROUND MUSIC: classical at breakfast, 'easy listening' at dinner.
LOCATION: just outside village centre.
CHILDREN: all ages welcomed (not under 10 in restaurant or public rooms after 6 pm).
DOGS: allowed in 3 bedrooms, front lounge.
CREDIT CARDS: MasterCard, Visa.
PRICES: per room B&B single £55–£155, double £71–£171. À la carte £38, tasting menu £65. 1-night bookings usually refused weekends.

SEE ALSO SHORTLIST

GURNARD Isle of Wight

THE LITTLE GLOSTER   `NEW`

'There is always something to watch' from
Ben and Holly Cooke's restaurant-with-rooms
overlooking the Solent, 'up close to all the
yachting activity'. Guide inspectors, arriving in
the rain, could not enjoy the alfresco terrace,
'but even inside, one has the opportunity to
appreciate the views'. Bedrooms, 'furnished
in Scandinavian style – soft greys and whites',
occupy a separate building. Bay View room's
roof windows look towards Cowes; its bathroom
is rather narrow. 'A better bet', the Balcony
Suite has floor-to-ceiling windows and glass
doors, while the Garden Suite has a sitting room
and terrace. All have an espresso machine and
binoculars, 'generous selections of coffee, tea
(and jelly babies), fresh milk, bottled water'.
Ben Cooke's 'enjoyable' food includes snacks,
steaks, pastas and fish, making fine use of local
ingredients. 'We enjoyed a starter of Isle of
Wight crab on toast, lemon, fennel, chilli, mint;
pappardelle with slow-cooked ragout; chocolate,
fig and walnut brownie, salted caramel ice
cream. A barrel-cut steak was especially tender.'
Breakfast, ordered the night before, includes
'super juices', eggs Benedict, a 'well-cooked' full
English. 'The staff are very friendly and helpful.'

31 Marsh Road
Gurnard
PO31 8JQ

T: 01983 298776
E: office@thelittlegloster.com
W: www.thelittleglosterrooms.com

BEDROOMS: 3. All in adjoining
building.
OPEN: all year except 23–27 Dec, 1
Jan–second week Feb, restaurant
closed Sun evening, Mon–Wed
Oct–Apr.
FACILITIES: bar, restaurant, free
Wi-Fi, in-room TV (Freeview),
function facilities, garden, public
rooms wheelchair accessible.
BACKGROUND MUSIC: in dining room.
LOCATION: on the coast, a five-
minute drive west of Cowes.
CHILDREN: all ages welcomed.
DOGS: not allowed.
CREDIT CARDS: MasterCard, Visa.
PRICES: [2018] per room B&B
£130–£195. À la carte £35. 1-night
bookings sometimes refused.

HALNAKER Sussex

Map 2:E3

THE OLD STORE

Behind a 'gorgeous, checkerboard red-brick-and-stone facade', in a hamlet a mile from Goodwood and 'an easy, breezy drive from Chichester', the former village grocer's shop is run as a friendly B&B. Guests are welcomed with tea and home-made cake in a small sitting room dominated by 'a massive Victorian model train in a display case'. A room under the eaves was on the snug side, but the bed was 'incredibly comfortable'. The bathroom had a 'powerful and strong' walk-in shower, aromatherapy toiletries from a local soap-maker. In the morning, a buffet is laid out in a sunny, dual-aspect breakfast room with a window on to the garden. Full marks for 'really tasty apple juice', 'exceptionally good' muesli, strong cafetière coffee. Cooked items include local, organic, free-range eggs, locally made sausages, pancakes with bacon and maple syrup, home-made bread and marmalade. Let them know if you have special dietary requirements: Heather came up trumps for a vegan reader. In sum: it's not posh, it's not perfect, but 'an excellent bed, wonderful shower, great breakfast, accommodating, thoughtful hosts, all the things that make a stay worthwhile'.

Stane Street
Halnaker
PO18 0QL

T: 01243 531977
E: theoldstore4@aol.com
W: www.theoldstoreguesthouse.
co.uk

BEDROOMS: 7. 1 on ground floor with step between bathroom and bedroom.
OPEN: Mar–Dec.
FACILITIES: lounge, breakfast room, free Wi-Fi, in-room TV (Freeview), ¼-acre garden with seating.
BACKGROUND MUSIC: none.
LOCATION: 4 miles NE of Chichester.
CHILDREN: all ages welcomed.
DOGS: not allowed.
CREDIT CARDS: MasterCard, Visa.
PRICES: [2018] per person B&B single £63, double £89–£99, family from £110 (higher for Goodwood 'Festival of Speed' and 'Revival' meetings). 1-night bookings refused weekends, sometimes other nights in high season.

HAMBLETON Rutland

HAMBLETON HALL

♧ Previous César winner

'Perfection to the very last detail,' writes a reader
this year, of Tim and Stefa Hart's hotel (Relais
& Château) with landscaped gardens stretching
down to Rutland Water. 'Welcoming staff
and outstanding food and service.' 'A lovely,
civilised place,' adds a Guide regular in 2018.
'Faultless,' another endorses. The house was
built as a hunting lodge in 1881 for a wealthy
brewer, whose society-hostess sister Eva Astley
Cooper entertained the likes of Noël Coward
and Malcolm Sargent in the drawing room.
The bedrooms, individually designed by Stefa
Hart, have fresh flowers, stamped postcards,
biscuits from the hotel's celebrated bakery. The
restaurant has held its Michelin star since 1982,
with Aaron Patterson running the kitchen
since 1992. His modern European cooking
uses locally produced and foraged ingredients,
including fruit and vegetables from the kitchen
garden. For example, breast of Merrifield Farm
duck, mandarin, black beans. The grounds are
a colourful patchwork of topiary, ornamental
ponds, statuary and a parterre. A sister hotel is
Hart's, Nottingham (see entry). (Lee Menzies,
Sara HollowellRG, AB, RS)

Oakham
Hambleton
LE15 8TH

T: 01572 756991
E: hotel@hambletonhall.com
W: www.hambletonhall.com

BEDROOMS: 17. 2-bedroomed suite
in cottage.
OPEN: all year.
FACILITIES: lift, hall, drawing room/
bar, restaurant, 2 private dining
rooms, free Wi-Fi, in-room TV
(Sky), civil wedding licence, 17-
acre grounds (tennis, swimming
pool (heated May–Sept), croquet,
vegetable garden).
BACKGROUND MUSIC: none.
LOCATION: 3 miles SE of Oakham,
Rutland.
CHILDREN: all ages welcomed.
DOGS: allowed in bedrooms (not
unattended), hall, not in public
rooms.
CREDIT CARDS: all major cards.
PRICES: [2018] per room B&B single
£200, double £290–£600. Excluding
service, set dinner £73, tasting menu
£92. 1-night bookings normally
refused weekends (but call to
check).

HAROME Yorkshire

Map 4:D4

THE PHEASANT

'In a quiet part of the village, overlooking the duck pond', Jacquie Pern and Peter Neville's 'very comfortable hotel' finds favour with trusted readers. A wide choice of bedrooms includes a 'single' (with double bed), doubles and family suites, and the two-storey Pheasant Suite. A ground-floor room had 'tasteful decor, with a vivid abstract headboard set against patterned paper with gold birds and animal patterns'. There was milk in a small fridge, ground coffee, complimentary sloe gin, a 'spacious walk-in shower and Cowshed toiletries'. A 'luxuriously appointed lounge' was warmed by a 'designer wood-burner'. In the restaurant, chef/patron Peter Neville's cooking is 'consistently good – not least, home-baked olive and Parmesan rolls, locally cured salmon (carved at the table), and an inspired amuse-bouche of carrot soup with grated coconut'. For a main course perhaps herb-fed chicken, salt-baked celeriac, chanterelles, black truffle, lentil velouté. The 'outstanding' breakfast includes chilled, freshly squeezed orange juice, porridge with Yorkshire moors heather honey, freshly baked pastries, Hartlepool kippers, 'perfectly prepared scrambled eggs and fine tea'. (Bill Wood, Robert Gower)

Mill Street
Harome
YO62 5JG

T: 01439 771241
E: reservations@thepheasanthotel.
com
W: www.thepheasanthotel.com

BEDROOMS: 16. 3 on ground floor, 4 in courtyard, 1 in cottage, 1 room in hotel suitable for disabled.
OPEN: all year.
FACILITIES: bar, lounge, conservatory, restaurant, free Wi-Fi, in-room TV (Freeview), civil wedding licence, heated indoor swimming pool, terrace, public areas wheelchair accessible.
BACKGROUND MUSIC: in public areas.
LOCATION: village centre.
CHILDREN: all ages welcomed.
DOGS: allowed in 2 bedrooms, on terrace and in garden, not in public rooms.
CREDIT CARDS: MasterCard, Visa.
PRICES: [2018] per room B&B single £95–£240, double £180–£270, D,B&B double £260–£350. Tasting menu £75, à la carte £45.

HAROME Yorkshire

Map 4:D4

❦ THE STAR INN

César award: inn of the year

'Wow, what a wonderful place this is!' A regular reader lauded Andrew Pern's restaurant-with-rooms on the edge of the North York Moors, which has a Michelin star and ambience on tap. At the 14th-century thatched inn 'one sinks back and is looked after by the very pleasant staff'. Even the background music raised a gentle smile: 'I sat by the log stove with a whisky, enjoying the likes of Sinatra and Fitzgerald.' 'Lovely' hunting lodge-style bedrooms in converted farm buildings opposite are 'nicely decorated and spacious', with 'very quirky' touches – a rope-slung bed, a piano, a snooker table. In the restaurant, readers savoured Andrew Pern's 'exceptional, wonderfully tasting' dishes. The refined seasonal menus highlight local, foraged and home-grown ingredients, perhaps twice-baked Stinking Bishop cheese soufflé, red wine shallot relish, hay-roasted pear, grape verjus, crisp wheat; braised navarin of dry-aged Yorkshire Dales mutton, slow-roasted carrots, turnips, roast hazelnut and chicory salad. There are 'thoughtful' vegetarian and gluten-free options. Breakfast, served at 'a large round table, meant everyone chatted' and was 'among the best we have ever eaten'. (Steve Hur, Robert Cooper)

High Street
Harome
YO62 5JE

T: 01439 770397
E: reservations@
   thestarinnatharome.co.uk
W: www.thestaratharome.co.uk

BEDROOMS: 9. All in Cross House Lodge, opposite, 3 on ground floor.
OPEN: all year, restaurant closed midday Mon.
FACILITIES: lounge, restaurant, The Wheelhouse private dining room, free Wi-Fi, in-room TV (Freeview), civil wedding licence, terrace, 2-acre garden, restaurant wheelchair accessible.
BACKGROUND MUSIC: in lounge and dining room.
LOCATION: village centre.
CHILDREN: all ages welcomed.
DOGS: allowed in 3 bedrooms, in lounge with consent of other guests, not in restaurant or pub.
CREDIT CARDS: MasterCard, Visa.
PRICES: [2018] per room B&B £150–£260. Market menus £20–£25, tasting menu £85, à la carte £50.

HARWICH Essex

Map 2:C5

THE PIER AT HARWICH

On the quay, overlooking the Stour and Orwell estuaries, and with 'a compelling view over the boats and container ships on the water', the Milsom family's hotel is run by friendly young staff. The Victorian building, topped with a cupola, has a first-floor terrace behind iron lace for alfresco dining. 'Public spaces are decorated in a chic industrial style, with vintage shipping posters framed in fluorescent perspex.' A main-house room (some are in the annexe) was a fair size, with neutral decor and panorama of navy yard and church. Extras included 'quality tea and coffee, still and sparkling water, fresh milk and chilled glasses in a mini-fridge'. The bathroom was compact, with bathtub, shower curtain and rain shower head. Minor irritations: no handy socket for the kettle, squeaky floorboard. Light snacks are served by day in the Navyärd bar, while, in the split-level brasserie, there are steaks, chops, Norfolk mussels, Colchester rock oysters, Harwich crab (dressed, baked, devilled, 'when Gary the Crab can be bothered to fish!'). At breakfast there is house-smoked salmon, eggs Benedict, San Daniele ham.

The Quay
Harwich
CO12 3HH

T: 01255 241212
E: pier@milsomhotels.com
W: www.milsomhotels.com

BEDROOMS: 14. 7 in annexe, 1 on ground floor suitable for disabled.
OPEN: all year.
FACILITIES: bar, lounge (in annexe), restaurant, private dining room, small lift, free Wi-Fi, in-room TV (Sky, BT, Freeview), civil wedding licence, balcony, small front terrace, restaurant, bar wheelchair accessible.
BACKGROUND MUSIC: in the bar.
LOCATION: on quay, in old town.
CHILDREN: all ages welcomed.
DOGS: allowed in bedrooms, bar, lounge.
CREDIT CARDS: all major cards.
PRICES: [2018] per room B&B £135–£215. À la carte £35.

HASTINGS Sussex   Map 2:E5

THE OLD RECTORY

On the edge of the Old Town, designer Lionel
Copley has created a beautiful B&B in this Grade
II listed Georgian-cum-Victorian rectory. A
palette of muted blues and greys, stripped and
varnished floors and artistic flower arrangements
could be straight out of an interiors magazine,
with 'paintings, sculptures and hand-painted
wallpapers by local artists integrated into the
decor', but everywhere a sense of fun is apparent.
Ebenezer bedroom has a wall of Wedgwood
calendar plates, while Crown has a 'secret' loo
behind a bookcase, and a freestanding in-room
bath. Some rooms have a bathroom and separate
wet room. Those at the back overlook a lovely
walled garden. All come with milk, home-made
biscuits, 'Made by the Sea' toiletries, produced by
Mr Copley, co-owner of Swan House, Hastings
(see next entry). 'Guests are encouraged to use
the beautiful lounges, which have an honesty
bar, and an open fire for cold days.' A breakfast
of 'high-quality, local ingredients' has 'terrific
variety' – home-made muesli, home-baked
bread, fruit smoothie, home-cured bacon, kippers
with parsley butter, mushroom and parsley
omelette. Luxurious treatment rooms have been
added since last year. (A and BB)

Harold Road
Hastings
TN35 5ND

T: 01424 422410
E: info@theoldrectoryhastings.
   co.uk
W: www.theoldrectoryhastings.
   co.uk

BEDROOMS: 8. One 2-bed suite.
OPEN: all year except 1 week
Christmas, 1 week Jan, open for
New Year.
FACILITIES: 2 lounges (honesty bar),
breakfast room, treatment rooms,
sauna, free Wi-Fi, in-room TV
(Freeview), civil wedding licence,
1-acre walled garden, unsuitable for
disabled.
BACKGROUND MUSIC: in breakfast
room and main lounge.
LOCATION: edge of Old Town
(limited parking spaces,
complimentary permits).
CHILDREN: not under 10.
DOGS: not allowed.
CREDIT CARDS: Amex, MasterCard,
Visa.
PRICES: [2018] per room ssingle
£90–£175, double B&B £110–£175.
1-night bookings refused weekends.

HASTINGS Sussex

SWAN HOUSE

Tucked away in an Old Town cul-de-sac, a short stroll from the seafront, this early Tudor black-and-white house is run as a welcoming B&B. There's no reception – guests step straight into an open-plan lounge/breakfast room, with beamed ceilings, blonde linen sofas, big open fire and an honesty bar that pretends it's a bookcase. Owner Brendan McDonagh is 'entirely likeable, soft-spoken, welcoming' – he was 'very solicitous to a lone woman guest, talking about where she might go and what she might like to see'. In the same way, he happily advises on places for dinner. Pleasing designer touches are the work of his partner, Lionel Copley, owner of the nearby, more flamboyant, Old Rectory, Hastings (see previous entry). A ground-floor bedroom looks on to a pretty patio garden, while, on the top floor, two adjoining rooms with a roof terrace comprise the Renaissance Suite. Church Room overlooks the tower of St Clement's. All rooms have vintage furnishings, good bedlinen, beams, wonky floor. At a table laid with fresh flowers, breakfast, cooked by Brendan, includes local free-range eggs, kippers, smoked haddock, home-made 'baked beans', local strawberry and pomegranate jam.

25% DISCOUNT VOUCHERS

1 Hill Street
Hastings
TN34 3HU

T: 01424 430014
E: info@swanhousehastings.co.uk
W: www.swanhousehastings.co.uk

BEDROOMS: 5. 1 on ground floor, 2 adjoining.
OPEN: all year except 24–26 Dec.
FACILITIES: lounge/breakfast room, free Wi-Fi, in-room TV, patio garden, secure allocated parking a short walk away (permits supplied), unsuitable for disabled.
BACKGROUND MUSIC: none.
LOCATION: in old town, near seafront.
CHILDREN: 5 and upwards in Renaissance Suite, by prior arrangement.
DOGS: not allowed.
CREDIT CARDS: all major cards.
PRICES: [2018] per room B&B single £90–£95, double £120–£150. 1-night bookings usually refused weekends.

HATCH BEAUCHAMP Somerset

FROG STREET FARMHOUSE

'Such a peaceful, quiet place to stay. The log fire
was lit ready for our arrival.' A new endorsement
this year for 'perfect hosts' David and Louise
Farrance's wisteria-festooned B&B. 'They
are terrific hosts,' agrees a returning Guide
regular in 2018, 'continually seeking to improve
the property.' Dating from around 1436, the
traditional longhouse has been altered over the
centuries, but it has retained its character, beams
and 17th-century panelling. Returning guests
are 'treated like friends', new arrivals plied with
tea and home-made cake. The Orchard Suite
has two bedrooms and a family bathroom with
roll-top bath and corner shower. The Snug, over
two floors, has a separate entrance, a lounge
with log fire, an espresso machine and fridge. At
night, plates, cutlery and glasses can be supplied
for a take-away meal, but the local gastropub
is recommended. A 'great choice' at breakfast
includes summer tomatoes from the greenhouse,
and award-winning pork-and-marmalade
sausages, eggs laid by the Frog Street hens. It is
cooked on the Aga and served at a communal
table. 'I enjoyed talking to other guests. A perfect
break away.' (Tracey Bowden, Michael Gwinnell)

Hatch Beauchamp
TA3 6AF

T: 01823 481883
E: frogstreet@hotmail.com
W: www.frogstreet.co.uk

BEDROOMS: 4. 1 with private
entrance.
OPEN: all year except Dec.
FACILITIES: lounge, breakfast room,
free Wi-Fi, in-room TV (Sky),
150-acre grounds (½-acre garden,
farmland), unsuitable for disabled.
BACKGROUND MUSIC: none.
LOCATION: 6 miles SE of Taunton.
CHILDREN: all ages welcomed.
DOGS: not allowed.
CREDIT CARDS: all major cards.
PRICES: [2018] per person B&B
£4w–£90. 1-night bookings refused
weekends May–Sept.

HATHERSAGE Derbyshire

Map 3:A6

THE GEORGE HOTEL

A hotel of character in a Peak District village, The George is hundreds of years old. Owner Eric Marsh likes to say 500 – but the deeds prove only 300. He also oversees The Cavendish in Baslow (see entry) and, with his personal touch, inspires fierce loyalty. 'We've visited many times, it's still a favourite,' say Guide regulars in 2018. We hear a few complaints – a worn stair carpet, a botched food order, 'over-familiarity' from a waiter. Others feel the staff are 'very friendly, we had no problem with being called luv!' The rooms are 'perfectly adequate if a little short on storage'. Superior rooms have excellent beds, handmade furniture, luxury toiletries, robes, slippers. One suite has a four-poster and a stained-glass window. Fires burn in public rooms with beams and exposed stone. In the restaurant, chef Helen Haywood's three-course dinner menu is 'fine without being outstanding', with such dishes as spring chicken, purple potatoes, wild garlic, truffle cannelloni. 'Good breakfasts' include American-style pancakes with blueberry compote. 'It's not perfect but the pluses far outweigh the minuses. We will return.' (Peter Anderson, and others)'

25% DISCOUNT VOUCHERS

Main Road
Hathersage
S32 1BB

T: 01433 650436
E: info@george-hotel.net
W: www.george-hotel.net

BEDROOMS: 24.
OPEN: all year.
FACILITIES: lounge/bar, restaurant, 2 function rooms, free Wi-Fi, in-room TV, civil wedding licence, courtyard, restaurant wheelchair accessible, no adapted toilet.
BACKGROUND MUSIC: light jazz in restaurant.
LOCATION: in village centre, parking.
CHILDREN: all ages welcomed.
DOGS: not allowed.
CREDIT CARDS: Amex, MasterCard, Visa.
PRICES: [2018] per room B&B £115–£184. Set dinner £33.50–£39.95, early bird (6.30–7.30) £16.85–£20 (a 5% charge on goods and services is distributed directly to staff). 1-night bookings sometimes refused.

HEREFORD Herefordshire

Map 3:D4

CASTLE HOUSE

Hereford Castle is long gone, but ducks bob happily on the old moat beside the terraced garden of the Watkins family's hotel. A Regency villa (formerly two town houses), it is pleasingly in harmony with the 'congenial street scene'. There are further bedrooms at Number 25, a Georgian building. All are 'very well furnished', those in the main hotel in more traditional style. Some have direct garden access, fresh milk, a decanter of sherry, underfloor heating. The service is 'cheery', from 'intelligent, helpful' staff. 'Good but not outstanding' meals owe much to provenance, with the use of produce from Mr Watkins's own farm – fruit and vegetables from the kitchen garden, rare breed lamb, Hereford beef (not to mention cut flowers for the rooms). From creative menus put together by executive head chef Claire Nicholls, with head chef Gabor Katona, a typical dish might be pan-fried chalk-stream trout, Grenobloise sauce, almond tuile. In the bistro there is simpler fare. On sunny days, meals are served alfresco. Among the treasures in the cathedral, a stroll away, are the Mappa Mundi and a Magna Carta of 1217.

Castle Street
Hereford
HR1 2NW

T: 01432 356321
E: reception@castlehse.co.uk
W: www.castlehse.co.uk

BEDROOMS: 24. 8 in town house (a short walk away), some on ground floor, 1 suitable for disabled.
OPEN: all year.
FACILITIES: lift (in main house only), lounge, bar/bistro, restaurant, free Wi-Fi, in-room TV (Freeview), civil wedding licence, terraced garden, ground floor wheelchair accessible.
BACKGROUND MUSIC: occasionally in restaurant, bistro and reception.
LOCATION: central.
CHILDREN: all ages welcomed.
DOGS: not allowed except in garden, on a lead.
CREDIT CARDS: Amex, MasterCard, Visa.
PRICES: [2018] per room B&B single £140–£185, double £155–£250, D,B&B double £200–£305. Tasting menu £60, à la carte (restaurant) £40, (bistro) £30.

HETTON Yorkshire

Map 4:D3

THE ANGEL INN

NEW

'Arriving on a wet Sunday afternoon I was immediately made to feel welcome,' writes a trusted reader who spent four happy nights at this old drovers' inn in a Dales village. Run by mother and son Juliet and Pascal Watkins, it claims (with some reason) to have pioneered the gastropub concept. The bedrooms, in separate buildings, are highly individual. Meadow Studio, on the first floor of a converted barn, was 'beautifully furnished', with 'so many additional touches' – lamps lit, fresh milk in the minibar, a welcome note, a little box of truffles, ice cubes. Dinner is served in a beamed bar with log-burner, wooden chairs, benches, brassware, or more formally in the restaurant, 'all starched napery, silver service', but with 'a cosy, happy atmosphere'. Our reader 'pushed the boat out' with an amuse-bouche of tandoori duck pompom with piccalilli, then crab and goat's cheese tian, lobster thermidor, iced raspberry parfait with Chantilly cream: a 'truly perfect meal'. Breakfast involved freshly squeezed orange juice, smoked haddock in a lemony sauce, scrambled eggs, 'beautifully presented and absolutely delicious'. (Trevor Lockwood)

25% DISCOUNT VOUCHERS

Hetton
BD23 6LT

T: 01756 730263
E: info@angelhetton.co.uk
W: www.angelhetton.co.uk

BEDROOMS: 9 in Barn Lodgings and Sycamore Bank, 1 on ground floor.
OPEN: all year except 25 Dec.
FACILITIES: bar/brasserie, restaurant (2 rooms), private dining room, civil wedding licence, terrace (outside dining), wine shop, in-room TV (Freeview), free Wi-Fi, some public areas wheelchair accessible.
BACKGROUND MUSIC: none.
LOCATION: in centre of village, 5 miles N of Skipton.
CHILDREN: all ages welcomed.
DOGS: allowed in the snug and 2 bedrooms.
CREDIT CARDS: Amex, MasterCard, Visa.
PRICES: [2018] per room B&B single £135–£185, double £150–£200, D,B&B double from £230. À la carte £38, set menu £45, tasting menu £60.

HEXHAM Northumberland

Map 4:B3

BATTLESTEADS

♔ Previous César winner

Dee and Richard Slade's hybrid of pub and hotel in the empty reaches of Northumberland is liked for its unique blend of sustainable hospitality and astronomy. 'Our luxury lodge was superb, with every comfort,' wrote one regular Guide contributor. 'The most fastidious traveller would struggle to find fault.' Others enjoyed 'huge clean bedrooms with plenty of hot water for the large spa bath', the 'beautiful grounds' and 'amazing dark sky observatory'. They were a bigger hit than some of the service. 'Staff were most efficient, brisk and businesslike,' said one trusted correspondent, 'but a hotel needs someone who smiles at the guests.' Other frustrations: 'intrusive background music' and 'overdone eco-friendliness'. Far more appreciation for the 'good wholesome food' of chef Edward Shilton's mainly British modern menu, turning fine local produce, including bounty from the kitchen garden, into the likes of lamb shank, rich jus, mash and seasonal greens. 'After an excellent meal, a first-class bottle of organic wine, plus a visit to the moon, we slept like logs.' (Bob and Jean Henry, and others)

Wark-on-Tyne
Hexham
NE48 3LS

T: 01434 230209
E: info@battlesteads.com
W: www.battlesteads.com

BEDROOMS: 22. 4 on ground floor, 5 in lodge, 2 suitable for disabled.
OPEN: all year except 25 Dec.
FACILITIES: bar, dining room, function facilities, drying room, free Wi-Fi, in-room TV (Freeview), civil wedding licence, 2-acre grounds (walled garden, kitchen garden, dark sky observatory).
BACKGROUND MUSIC: in bar, restaurant.
LOCATION: 12 miles N of Hexham.
CHILDREN: all ages welcomed.
DOGS: allowed in public rooms, some bedrooms (£10 per night).
CREDIT CARDS: Amex, MasterCard, Visa.
PRICES: [2018] per room B&B from £120, D,B&B from £165. À la carte £33.

SEE ALSO SHORTLIST

HOLT Norfolk

Map 2:A5

MORSTON HALL

♀ Previous César winner

'An amazingly gorgeous hotel,' writes a reader this year, of Tracy and Galston Blackiston's restaurant-with-rooms, 'ideally located' for a seal trip to Blakeney Point. Bedrooms in the main house are in traditional country house style; those in the garden pavilion more contemporary, with separate sitting area and private terrace. 'Our room was excellent, with sheets and blankets, fresh milk in the minibar.' Bathroom lighting was 'a bit severe'. Some bathrooms have a spa bath, a monsoon shower. In the dining room overlooking the garden, guests sit down to a daily-changing menu of Michelin-starred cooking by Mr Blackiston and Greg Anderson. 'No choice, but the seven-plus-course dinner is delightful. Everything seems to be made on the premises, including delicious bread.' It is served with due ceremony, being 'indeed a sort of drama, with meticulously dressed staff producing items like clockwork'. Sample dishes: salt-baked celeriac, Baron Bigod cheese; Earl Stonham Wagyu beef, bordelaise sauce; hazelnut bavarois, chocolate sorbet. Breakfast delivers freshly squeezed orange juice, free-range eggs, home-smoked haddock – 'the best I've ever had'. (John Barnes)

The Street
Holt
NR25 7AA

T: 01263 741041
E: reception@morstonhall.com
W: www.morstonhall.com

BEDROOMS: 13. 6 on ground floor, 100 yds from house, in garden pavilion, 1, in main house, suitable for disabled.
OPEN: all year except 24–26 Dec, 1–31 Jan.
FACILITIES: reading lounge, sun lounge, conservatory, restaurant, free Wi-Fi, in-room TV (Freeview), civil wedding licence, 3-acre garden (pond, croquet), restaurant wheelchair accessible, adapted toilet.
BACKGROUND MUSIC: none.
LOCATION: 2 miles W of Blakeney.
CHILDREN: all ages welcomed.
DOGS: allowed in bedrooms, some public rooms, not in restaurant.
CREDIT CARDS: Amex, MasterCard, Visa.
PRICES: [2018] per person D,B&B single occupancy £255–£310, double £180–£210. Set dinner £75.

SEE ALSO SHORTLIST

HOPE Derbyshire

UNDERLEIGH HOUSE

A 19th-century cottage and barn combine as
one exceptional B&B on private land within
the Peak District national park. It is run with
enthusiasm, attention to detail and first-class
green credentials by 'helpful owners' Vivienne
and Philip Taylor. There is one double bedroom;
three suites, each with sitting room. All are
traditionally styled, equipped with a mini-fridge
and looking out on surrounding hills. A garden
suite has glazed doors on two sides, one opening
on to the patio and rose garden. Breakfast is a
social affair, served communally at a refectory
table laid with pretty china, in the former
'shippon' – no longer a lowly cattle shed, but a
cosy room with flagstone floor and grandfather
clock. It's 'quite a ceremony', as you are talked
through the house-recipe muesli, inventive
fruit compotes (maybe golden jumbo raisins
steeped in apple juice and ginger), home-made
jams, fresh-baked breads and croissants, before
an Aga-cooked full English with local black
pudding, free-range pork sausages, Cheshire
bacon, free-range eggs, or poached haddock. Let
them know ahead of time if you're vegetarian.
For dinner, we'd suggest The George Hotel at
Hathersage (see entry), a 12-minute drive away.

Lose Hill Lane
Hope
S33 6AF

T: 01433 621372
E: underleigh.house@btconnect.
   com
W: www.underleighhouse.co.uk

BEDROOMS: 4. 3 suites with a private
lounge.
OPEN: all year except mid-Dec to
mid-Feb.
FACILITIES: lounge, breakfast room,
free Wi-Fi, in-room TV (Freeview),
¼-acre garden, unsuitable for
disabled.
BACKGROUND MUSIC: none.
LOCATION: 1 mile N of Hope.
CHILDREN: not under 12.
DOGS: allowed in 1 suite by prior
arrangement, not in public rooms.
CREDIT CARDS: MasterCard, Amex
(payment by debit card preferred).
PRICES: [2018] per room B&B single
£75–£105, double £95–£125. 1-night
bookings normally refused Fri/Sat,
bank holidays.

HOUGH-ON-THE-HILL Lincolnshire   Map 2:A3

THE BROWNLOW ARMS

'A homely village pub within easy reach of the A1 and well worth the detour,' writes a trusted Guide reader after a three-night stay at Paul and Lorraine Willoughby's traditional inn. On cold days a log fire burns in the beamed bar, where winged armchairs are drawn up in the glow of table lamps. Lorraine Willoughby is 'the life and soul', 'a wonderfully hospitable figure, hugely energetic, exuding enthusiasm'. Bedrooms are traditionally styled, plush and cosy, with a mix of antique and contemporary furniture, complimentary biscuits and mineral water. 'We had a good-sized room, with a comfortable bed and large bathroom.' In the 'tastefully decorated restaurant, with its generously padded armchairs', chef Ruaraidh Bealby creates such imaginative dishes as pan-roasted, carved fillet of beef, wild mushroom ragout, wilted spinach, truffled mash, jus roti, crispy shallot rings. A vegan option might be roasted romero pepper stuffed with sun-dried tomato and pine nut risotto, tomato coulis, spiced chickpea salad. 'The food is excellent quality, locally sourced.' The staff are 'young and friendly'. Breakfast is 'appetising, promptly served and piping hot'. (Robert Gower, and others)

High Road
Hough-on-the-Hill
NG32 2AZ

T: 01400 250234
E: armsinn@yahoo.co.uk
W: www.thebrownlowarms.com

BEDROOMS: 5. 1 on ground floor in barn conversion.
OPEN: all year except 25/26 Dec, 31 Dec/1 Jan, restaurant closed Sun evening, Mon, Tues midday.
FACILITIES: bar, 3 dining rooms, free Wi-Fi, in-room TV (Freeview), unsuitable for disabled.
BACKGROUND MUSIC: in public areas.
LOCATION: rural, 2 miles E of town centre.
CHILDREN: no under-8s in the restaurant in the evening.
DOGS: only guide dogs allowed.
CREDIT CARDS: MasterCard, Visa.
PRICES: [2018] per room B&B single £75, double £110–£120, À la carte £50.

HUNSTANTON Norfolk

Map 2:A5

NO. 33

On a quiet residential street a stroll from the sea in a Victorian resort town, Jeanne Whittome's boutique B&B impressed readers with its 'bold, contemporary style'. New arrivals are offered complimentary tea and scones in the small sitting room. Bedrooms are well appointed, painted in restful shades of grey with perhaps a wall of designer wallpaper. All have a bath, a drench shower, cafetière coffee. One has a modern four-poster and a balcony, another a freestanding bath beside the original (not working) fireplace; a ground-floor room has its own courtyard. Readers say their large room was 'furnished to a high standard… Immaculate housekeeping made our visit a pleasure.' In the morning, in the stylish breakfast room with log-burner lit on cold days, there are free-range eggs, home-made granola, fresh breads, pastries, bagels and cream cheese from the owner's deli in nearby Thornham; the full English, smoked salmon, eggs Benedict. With notice they supply a gourmet hamper for days out exploring the breezy north Norfolk coast, or just lazing on the beach looking west over the Wash, right here in 'sunny Hunny'. (S and JM)

33 Northgate
Hunstanton
PE36 6AP

T: 01485 524352
E: reception@33hunstanton.co.uk
W: 33hunstanton.co.uk

BEDROOMS: 5. 1, on ground floor, suitable for disabled.
OPEN: all year.
FACILITIES: small sitting room, breakfast room, free Wi-Fi, in-room TV (Freeview), small garden.
BACKGROUND MUSIC: none.
LOCATION: town centre.
CHILDREN: all ages welcomed.
DOGS: allowed in bedrooms, not in dining room, max. 1 per room (£5 per night).
CREDIT CARDS: MasterCard, Visa.
PRICES: [2018] per room B&B single £85–£180, double £95–£190.

HUNTINGDON Cambridgeshire

Map 2:B4

THE OLD BRIDGE

On the banks of the River Ouse, Julia and John Hoskins's ivy-covered town house hotel impressed trusted readers, who enjoyed the buzz created by locals 'chatting over drinks' in the 'casual, cosy setting' of the bar. Individually styled bedrooms, blending traditional and 'bold contemporary' furnishings, are 'beautifully maintained', with perhaps a 'rich red chaise longue next to an original jet-black fireplace'. All have comfortable beds, wool mattress toppers, a power shower, perhaps a bath too, and good toiletries. Some rooms overlook garden and river, while triple glazing ensures serenity on the road front. Room 7 has a four-poster, a large, wallpapered bathroom with roll-top bath and separate shower. The two good-sized singles sport a marble bathroom. Mr Hoskins, a friendly, outgoing host and Master of Wine, runs the in-house wine shop. Tea and scones with organic cream are served all day in a lounge with a log fire and 'intimate clusters of seating'. In the restaurant, head chef Jack Woolner's cooking style is robust modern British – for instance, lamb rump, dauphinoise potatoes, savoy cabbage, pea purée, charred mushrooms. Breakfast is 'impressive', with 'a good selection of cooked dishes'.

1 High Street
Huntingdon
PE29 3TQ

T: 01480 424300
E: oldbridge@huntsbridge.co.uk
W: www.huntsbridge.com

BEDROOMS: 24. 2 on ground floor.
OPEN: all year.
FACILITIES: lounge, bar, restaurant, private dining room, wine shop, business centre, free Wi-Fi, in-room TV (Freeview), civil wedding licence, 1-acre grounds (riverside terrace, garden), fishing, jetty, boat trips, parking, unsuitable for disabled.
BACKGROUND MUSIC: none.
LOCATION: 500 yds from town centre, station 10 mins' walk.
CHILDREN: all ages welcomed.
DOGS: allowed in 2 bedrooms, lounge and bar, not in restaurant.
CREDIT CARDS: MasterCard, Visa.
PRICES: [2018] per room B&B single from £99, double £148–£230, D,B&B double £220–£320. À la carte £35.

ILMINGTON Warwickshire

Map 3:D6

THE HOWARD ARMS

On the 'picturesque green' of a 'peaceful and stunning' Cotswolds village, this 400-year-old inn was taken over in 2015 by two local families, providing a welcome breath of new life. There's a 'very friendly' welcome at the bar, where guests check in next to locals 'chatting casually' over pints of Old Hooky. Beams, flagstones, leather armchairs by a huge log fire, and 'wonderful old photographs' create a cosy atmosphere. Dinner is served on a mezzanine, with 'beautiful arched windows on to the green… quite an elegant affair'. Gareth Rufus's menus range from pub classics (steaks, beer-battered haddock) to 'more ambitious dishes' such as Cotswold White chicken supreme, leek and sage potato cake, crisp kale, roasted root vegetables, jus. Not every dish is faultless, say readers this year, though we hear praise for the 'rich, unctuous, savoury' steak and ale stew. Some rooms occupy a new annexe, some are under the eaves. All have bags of style, along with gingerbread and percolator coffee. 'Breakfast was good, especially the cooked selection, excellent scrambled egg, fresh orange juice, granary toast.' (Sue and John Jenkinson, A and BB)

Lower Green
Ilmington
CV36 4LT

T: 01608 682226
E: info@howardarms.com
W: www.howardarms.com

BEDROOMS: 8. 4 in extension, 1 on ground floor suitable for disabled.
OPEN: all year.
FACILITIES: snug, bar, restaurant, free Wi-Fi, in-room TV (Freeview), terrace, garden (alfresco dining), bar wheelchair accessible, toilet not adapted.
BACKGROUND MUSIC: all day in public areas.
LOCATION: 8 miles S of Stratford-upon-Avon, 6 miles NE of Chipping Campden.
CHILDREN: all ages welcomed.
DOGS: allowed in bar and on patio only.
CREDIT CARDS: MasterCard, Visa.
PRICES: [2018] per room B&B single £80–£130, double £110–£150. À la carte £32. 1-night bookings sometimes refused.

ILSINGTON Devon

ILSINGTON COUNTRY HOUSE `NEW`

On the edge of Dartmoor national park, with
views to granite Haytor, the Hassell family's
hotel is 'a little off the beaten tracks – but
worth finding'. Promoted to a full entry this
year, it has a spa for rejuvenation, lounges for
chess, a lawn for croquet. Bedrooms range
from the dog-friendly, ground-floor 'standard'
with garden access, through to 'deluxe', with
air conditioning, roll-top bath, two also with
walk-in shower. Family suites have a sitting
room with video games console. All rooms
have home-baked flapjacks. When the huge
grandfather clock in reception says it's time for
tea, there are scones, clotted cream, home-made
strawberry jam. An informal all-day menu
in the Blue Tiger (a riposte to the ubiquitous
Red Lion) includes 'simple but delicious' bistro
dishes served by 'pleasant and courteous staff'.
In the dining room, chef Mike O'Donnell's
modern British cooking finds favour. 'A
strength is the quality of the food. Highlights
included fillet of beef; hake with a perfect
smoked haddock risotto. The presentation was
excellent, and not at the expense of portion size.'
Breakfast brings new-laid eggs from resident
hens, home-smoked salmon. (Peter Anderson)

Ilsington
TQ13 9RR.

T: 01364 661452
E: hotel@ilsington.co.uk
W: www.ilsington.co.uk/Home

BEDROOMS: 25. 8 on ground floor.
OPEN: all year except 2–16 Jan.
FACILITIES: lift, 2 lounges, bar,
restaurant, Blue Tiger bistro,
conservatory, function facilities,
spa (fitness suite, sauna, heated
indoor swimming pool), free Wi-
Fi, in-room TV (Freeview), civil
wedding licence, 10-acre grounds,
public rooms wheelchair accessible,
adapted toilet.
BACKGROUND MUSIC: all day in bar, in
restaurant in the evening.
LOCATION: just W of village, 7 miles
NW of Newton Abbot.
CHILDREN: all ages welcomed.
DOGS: allowed in bar, ground-floor
bedrooms, conservatory, on lead in
garden, not in lounges, restaurants.
CREDIT CARDS: MasterCard, Visa.
PRICES: [2018] Per room B&B £135–
£230, D,B&B double £202–£317. Set
dinner £40, tasting menu (Fri, Sat)
£55. 1-night bookings refused some
weekends, bank hols, August.

KELMSCOTT Oxfordshire

Map 3:E6

THE PLOUGH

A popular pub-with-rooms in a tiny, 'beguiling' village close to the Thames, The Plough's warm welcome and foodie credentials are appreciated as much by locals (and their dogs) as by guests from farther afield. Owners Sebastian and Lana Snow, who also run The Five Alls, Lechlade (see Shortlist), have honed a contemporary rustic mood that complements the original 17th-century features; the bar has a flagstone floor, stone walls, mismatched tables and chairs, including a pommel horse repurposed 'from some ancient gymnasium'. The more formal restaurant with 'thoughtfully' spaced tables and 'two showpiece lamps created from bicycle frames' offers a daily-changing menu by Sebastian Snow and George Tauchman. 'Delicious, nicely presented' modern British dishes including scallops and bacon kebab, roast pepper relish, rocket leaf; crispy cracked pork, braised red cabbage, potato cake, sage and apple relish. There are 'interesting craft beers, a good wine list'. Upstairs, the compact, shabby-chic bedrooms have 'reasonable storage' and 'large, comfortable bed with good linen'. Light sleepers may want to avoid the four rooms above the bar or, as a Guide insider says, 'This is a pub where you are better to join in.'

Kelmscott
GL7 3HG

T: 01367 253543
E: info@theploughinnkelmscott.com
W: www.theploughinnkelmscott.com

BEDROOMS: 8.
OPEN: all year except 25 Dec, restaurant closed Mon eve and Sun from 6 pm (food service ends 3.30 pm).
FACILITIES: bar, restaurant, private dining room in Hideaway bar, free Wi-Fi, in-room TV (Freeview), garden (alfresco drinks and meals).
BACKGROUND MUSIC: all day in restaurant, Hideaway bar.
LOCATION: 3 miles E of Lechlade.
CHILDREN: all ages welcomed.
DOGS: allowed in all public rooms, not in bedrooms.
CREDIT CARDS: MasterCard, Visa.
PRICES: [2018] per room B&B single £90–£110, double £110–£140, D,B&B double £140. Set dinner (6 pm–7 pm Mon–Fri) £24, à la carte £30.

KING'S LYNN Norfolk

Map 2:A4

BANK HOUSE

Jeannette and Anthony Goodrich's investment has reaped a rich return, converting a former bank – albeit one in a Georgian Grade II* listed town house admired by Sir Nikolaus Pevsner – into a 'very attractive' boutique hotel. 'It sets out to be cool and modern,' writes a Guide regular who visited this year, 'but not at the expense of guests' comfort.' Or at the expense of the building's heritage – the brasserie occupies the Counting House, where the age-mellowed floorboards bear the dents of bank customers nervously shuffling their feet. No such anxiety today with residents cosseted by 'good, helpful' service in 'well-appointed, well-kept' rooms, of varying sizes, complete with magazines and home-made biscuits. The offer of a room well away from the popular, noisy bar was appreciated. In multiple dining areas, including a terrace overlooking the Ouse, chef Stuart Deuchars's acclaimed locally sourced modern British dishes include roast guineafowl supreme, chorizo lentil casserole, purple sprouting broccoli. Breakfast was 'excellent, with first-rate orange juice and coffee, a good kipper'. 'A most satisfactory stay.' Snettisham's Rose & Crown (see entry) has the same owners. (Anne Laurence Thackray)

King's Staithe Square
King's Lynn
PE30 1RD

T: 01553 660492
E: info@thebankhouse.co.uk
W: www.thebankhouse.co.uk

BEDROOMS: 12.
OPEN: all year.
FACILITIES: bar, 3 dining rooms, meeting/function rooms, vaulted cellars for private functions, free Wi-Fi, in-room TV (Freeview), riverside terrace, courtyard, all public rooms wheelchair accessible, adapted toilet.
BACKGROUND MUSIC: 'mellow jazz and offbeat pop' in public areas ('can be turned off on demand').
LOCATION: central.
CHILDREN: all ages welcomed.
DOGS: allowed in Counting House, bar, terrace and 2 bedrooms.
CREDIT CARDS: Amex, MasterCard, Visa.
PRICES: [2018] per room B&B £95–£220, D,B&B £125–£280. Pre-theatre dinner £15–£20, à la carte £28.

KING'S LYNN Norfolk

Map 2:A4

CONGHAM HALL

The herb garden is a major draw at this Georgian country house hotel set amid lawns, orchards and woodlands close to Sandringham. The 400 varieties of culinary and medicinal herbs supply treatments in the Secret Garden Spa, alongside flavourings and garnishes for the kitchen. Experienced hotelier Nicholas Dickinson, who has breathed new life into the former merchant's house, is 'much in evidence', say readers approvingly. Bedrooms, in the main property – some recently refurbished – and around the spa garden, blend classic and contemporary styles. All have slippers, bathrobes, an espresso machine, a larder with home-made biscuits, fresh milk. The dog-friendly garden rooms have a furnished terrace area, a luxury bathroom with freestanding bath and waterfall shower. Dandelion suite has an in-room feature bath, a balcony overlooking parkland, a wet room. There is a 'nice, understated lounge and library', and guests enjoy complimentary access to the slick contemporary spa. In the light, airy dining room, chef James O'Connor's seasonal locally sourced menus include such dishes as grilled haunch of venison, pumpkin purée, savoy cabbage, blackcurrant, thyme. To stay here is 'a delight'.

25% DISCOUNT VOUCHERS

Lynn Road
King's Lynn
PE32 1AH

T: 01485 600250
E: info@conghamhallhotel.co.uk
W: www.conghamhallhotel.co.uk

BEDROOMS: 26. 6 garden rooms, 1 suitable for disabled.
OPEN: all year, 4-day package at Christmas, 3-day at New Year.
FACILITIES: sitting room, bar, library, restaurant, free Wi-Fi, in-room TV (Freeview), civil wedding licence, conference facilities, terrace, spa, 12-metre swimming pool, 30-acre grounds, herb garden, public areas wheelchair accessible, adapted toilet.
BACKGROUND MUSIC: 'mellow' in bar and restaurant.
LOCATION: 6 miles E of King's Lynn.
CHILDREN: all ages welcomed.
DOGS: allowed in some bedrooms, public rooms.
CREDIT CARDS: MasterCard, Visa.
PRICES: [2018] per room B&B £165–350, D,B&B £229–£399, room only (Mon–Thurs) £135–£320. Continental breakfast £8, cooked £15, à la carte £36. 1-night bookings sometimes refused Sat.

KIRKBY STEPHEN Cumbria

Map 4:C3

AUGILL CASTLE

✪ Previous César winner

We hear a perennial chorus of approval from fans of Wendy and Simon Bennett's child-friendly Victorian fantasy castle in the Eden valley, between Lake District and Yorkshire Dales. 'No pretentiousness, just welcoming staff.' 'A very personable hostess,' wrote one reader in 2018. 'It felt as if you were staying with a family friend.' Bedrooms are highly individual, with maybe a four-poster, corner cabinet of china, working fireplace, or turret wardrobe. 'Bathrooms appear ancient but have a big bath, a shower with copious hot water, good toiletries.' Annexe rooms have a patio or garden. 'Dinner at the large dining table with other guests was fun. The food was amazing.' 'Good home cooking,' writes an inspector, 'onion soup or pâté, roast lamb, fig tart or cheese.' 'Great breakfast choices, and special touches such as coffee, tea and home-made cake in the bar.' There are 'roaring fires, comfy sofas' in the Great Hall, drawing room, music room, library. 'My children loved the games room and cinema. How we wish we could have stayed longer.' (Dana and Charles Irons, Jan Wallace, Steven Williams, and many others)

Leacett Lane
Kirkby Stephen
CA17 4DE

T: 01768 341937
E: enquiries@stayinacastle.com
W: www.stayinacastle.com

BEDROOMS: 17. 2 on ground floor, 7 in converted stableyard, 2 in estate house, 1 suitable for disabled.
OPEN: all year, dinner served Fri/Sat, Sun–Thurs cold platters, daily children's suppers.
FACILITIES: hall, drawing room, library (honesty bar), sitting room, conservatory bar, dining room, cinema, free Wi-Fi, in-room TV (Freeview), civil wedding licence, 20-acre grounds (landscaped garden, tennis), public rooms wheelchair accessible, adapted toilet.
BACKGROUND MUSIC: none.
LOCATION: 3 miles NE of Kirkby Stephen.
CHILDREN: all ages welcomed.
DOGS: allowed in 2 bedrooms.
CREDIT CARDS: all major cards.
PRICES: [2018] per room B&B £160–£260. Set dinner £25–£30. 1-night bookings sometimes refused weekends.

LACOCK Wiltshire

Map 2:D1

SIGN OF THE ANGEL

'Little has changed over the centuries' at this Tudor coaching inn in a National Trust village. Familiar to Harry Potter fans as the Babberton Arms, it was once home to Isambard Kingdom Brunel. Owners Tom and Jack Nicholas and John Furby have renovated the interiors since taking over in 2014, but sacrificed nothing of the 'old-worldly' feel. Within, there are open fireplaces, creaky floors, low beams. A Guide inspector was shown by 'a pleasant young man' up 'narrow stairs' and through 'a charming, wood-panelled sitting room' to a bedroom with 'lots of comfortable seating', oak furniture, a large bath with a shower over, 'lovely pottery cups and saucers; home-made chocolate bites'. Downstairs there's a small bar and three dining areas. John Furby uses locally sourced ingredients in such 'refined and decorative' dishes as confit pheasant, potato hash cake, Jerusalem artichoke purée, buttered cabbage, mulled pear sauce; 'really delicious baked gooseberry and hazelnut frangipane with lavender ice cream'. Breakfast is 'excellent', though background music won't please everyone. Outside, 'a delightful orchard garden is bordered by a stream with a bridge leading to a field'.

6 Church Street
Lacock
SN15 2LB

T: 01249 730230
E: info@signoftheangel.co.uk
W: www.signoftheangel.co.uk

BEDROOMS: 5.
OPEN: all year except Sun evening, all day Mon.
FACILITIES: small bar, 3 dining rooms, residents' sitting room, private dining room, free Wi-Fi, no mobile phone signal, cottage garden (alfresco drinking and eating), restaurant and garden wheelchair accessible.
BACKGROUND MUSIC: background music in restaurant, radio option in sitting room.
LOCATION: in village, 4 miles S of Chippenham.
CHILDREN: all ages welcomed.
DOGS: allowed in bedrooms (£15 charge), public rooms.
CREDIT CARDS: Amex, MasterCard, Visa.
PRICES: [2018] per room B&B single £80–£110, double £110–£150. À la carte £36.

LANCASTER Lancashire

Map 4:D2

THE ASHTON

Former TV set decorator James Gray has
created a super-stylish B&B in a Georgian
house just down from Williamson Park with
its crowning Ashton Memorial. 'We could not
rate it more highly,' writes a reader this year,
helping its promotion to a full entry. 'James
is the most charming and diligent host, the
decor is wonderful and the rooms are most
comfortable, with every amenity you could wish
for.' Each bedroom has its own contemporary
chic look, home-baked biscuits, sherry, ground
coffee, a luxury bathroom, perhaps a double
rainfall shower. You can curl up with one of
the many interior design books in the snug
sitting room, with tea and home-baked cake
provided each afternoon. On weekdays, in a
dining room painted invisible green (that restful
shade beloved of the likes of Humphry Repton
to disguise fence and trellis), guests can enjoy a
home-cooked supper (maybe cassoulet, a curry
or chilli) and a glass of wine, while weekends
bring a champagne high tea. The breakfast
sideboard is set with juices, compote, granola,
freshly baked bread and brioche, while cooked
dishes include locally made sausages, locally
smoked salmon. (John Moulton)

Well House
Lancaster
LA1 3JJ

T: 01524 684600
E: stay@theashtonlancaster.com
W: www.theashtonlancaster.com

BEDROOMS: 5.
OPEN: all year except Sun, 24–26, 31
Dec, 1 Jan.
FACILITIES: lobby, lounge (honesty
bar), dining room, free Wi-Fi, in-
room TV (Freeview), 1-acre garden,
parking.
BACKGROUND MUSIC: in dining room.
LOCATION: 1 mile E of city centre.
CHILDREN: not under 6.
DOGS: allowed in 2 bedrooms, public
rooms.
CREDIT CARDS: Amex, MasterCard,
Visa.
PRICES: [2018] per room B&B single
£115–£135, double £135–£185.
Simple weekday supper with glass
of wine £20, champagne high tea
Sat and Sun £35. 1-night bookings
refused bank holiday weekends,
single Sun,

SEE ALSO SHORTLIST

LANGAR Nottinghamshire

Map 2:A3

LANGAR HALL

Readers 'had a really lovely, relaxing stay' at Lila Arora's apricot-washed Georgian mansion, approached by an avenue of lime trees amid sheep-grazed pastures. Ms Arora is the granddaughter of the late chatelaine, Imogen Skirving, whose personality still infuses the place. The atmosphere is that of an elegant but lived-in private home, filled with paintings, antique clocks, ornaments, crammed bookcases. Your bedroom might have a four-poster, a rocking chair, Staffordshire china dogs on the mantelpiece. Cartland is the very feminine room Dame Barbara favoured. Three rooms are in a wing reached via the church garden at the rear. At dinner, Gary Booth's fixed-price menus include such dishes as fillet of Blackberry Farm beef, caramelised hispi cabbage, tempura oyster. Its 'pleasant, cheerful young staff' are perhaps not yet up to speed, 'so service was a bit dilatory'. After confusion over soufflé and soup, other Guide regulars described it as 'eccentric but willing'. A minor grumble, however. In sum: 'Great room. Magical grounds, as well as lots of history.' (Peter and Anne Davies, NP, PJ, A and CR)

Church Lane
Langar
NG13 9HG

T: 01949 860559
E: info@langarhall.co.uk
W: www.langarhall.com

BEDROOMS: 13. 1 on ground floor, 3 in annexe, 1 in garden chalet, 1 pod.
OPEN: all year.
FACILITIES: Study/sitting room, bar, garden room, main dining room, Indian room, free Wi-Fi, in-room TV (Freeview), civil wedding licence, 30-acre grounds (gardens, children's play area), restaurant wheelchair accessible.
BACKGROUND MUSIC: at lunch and dinner.
LOCATION: 12 miles SE of Nottingham.
CHILDREN: all ages welcomed.
DOGS: in bedrooms, sitting room and bar, not in restaurant.
CREDIT CARDS: Amex, MasterCard, Visa.
PRICES: [2018] per room B&B single £110–£180, double £125–£225. Set dinner (Fri, Sat) £54.50, other nights £37.50–£42.50.

LANGHO Lancashire

NORTHCOTE

Craig Bancroft's extended Victorian country house hotel in the Ribble valley has held a Michelin star since 1996, under former chef/director Nigel Haworth, and now Lisa Allen. It is above all a gourmet destination, but has other considerable charms. Bedrooms have bold, modern designer decor, turn-down service, daily newspaper, a minibar. Classic rooms have a shower, while some superior and deluxe rooms have both bath and walk-in shower. Those in the Garden Lodge, with lounge and pantry kitchen, have a balcony or terrace. There are 'several comfortable public rooms', log fires, a cocktail bar, 'a convivial atmosphere'. Biodynamic fruit and vegetables from the kitchen garden (it grows over 90 varieties) grace such dishes as roast Cumbrian lamb cutlet, sticky sweetbread, wild garlic barley, wood-roasted leek; roasted sea bass 'Véronique', spring vegetables, grape. A 'comprehensive breakfast menu' includes house smoothies; coconut yogurt with chia seeds and berries; avocado on sourdough; Lancashire cheese soufflé; Finnan haddock; Cumberland sausage. You can take a cookery course, discover 'one of Lancashire's lesser-known stunning areas' or climb Pendle Hill and 'explore the witches' territory'.

Northcote Road
Langho
BB6 8BE

T: 01254 240555
E: reception@northcote.com
W: www.northcote.com/

BEDROOMS: 26. 8 in garden lodge, 8 on ground floor, 2 suitable for disabled.
OPEN: all year.
FACILITIES: lift, 2 lounges, cocktail bar, restaurant, private dining/meeting room, chef's table, cookery courses, free Wi-Fi, in-room TV (Sky), civil wedding licence, 3-acre garden, public areas wheelchair accessible, adapted toilet.
BACKGROUND MUSIC: evening in bar.
LOCATION: 5½ miles N of Blackburn, on A59.
CHILDREN: all ages welcomed.
DOGS: not allowed.
CREDIT CARDS: Amex, MasterCard, Visa.
PRICES: [2018] per room B&B single £240–£585, double £280–£650, D,B&B double £335–£800. À la carte £75, tasting menu £85, vegetarian £65 (guests must dine in the restaurant Sat and Sun).

LASTINGHAM Yorkshire

LASTINGHAM GRANGE

'The Wood family continues to run this little hotel like a vocation,' say readers this year, having visited regularly for over three decades. 'It's a very special, nurturing place to escape ordinary life for a while.' The creeper-clad, extended 16th-century farmhouse, swaddled by ten acres of pretty gardens, and on the fringe of the North York Moors, is owned by brothers Bertie and Tom, and mother Jane. A 'friendly welcome' reveals traditional interiors – a grandfather clock, dark wood dresser, floral bedspreads in 'comfortable' rooms. 'Peace and quiet enveloped and refreshed us. It's like going on a retreat, but with lashings of creature comforts.' The 'warm, hospitable' hosts are clearly used to walkers. 'We returned soaking wet to have all our outer clothes kindly taken to a drying room, while we drank tea and ate well-deserved scones.' Indeed, ravenous appetites are well catered for by a daily-changing, locally sourced menu, perhaps Lastingham smoked trout, horseradish sauce; roast rack of Kirkbymoorside lamb, Yorkshire sauce. 'We had such enormous tender steaks we felt too full for pudding... but chose the light, delicately flavoured raspberries in elderflower jelly: a perfect finale.' (Mr and Mrs Judson)

High Street
Lastingham
YO62 6TH

T: 01751 417345
E: reservations@lastinghamgrange.com
W: www.lastinghamgrange.com

BEDROOMS: 11. Plus self-catering cottage in village.
OPEN: 6 Mar–19 Nov.
FACILITIES: hall, lounge, dining room, laundry facilities, free Wi-Fi, in-room TV (Freeview), 10-acre grounds (terrace, garden, orchard, croquet, boules), restaurant wheelchair accessible, toilet not fully adapted.
BACKGROUND MUSIC: none.
LOCATION: 5 miles NE of Kirkbymoorside.
CHILDREN: all ages welcomed.
DOGS: allowed in bedrooms with prior consent, lounge, garden but not in dining room.
CREDIT CARDS: Amex, MasterCard, Visa.
PRICES: [2018] per room B&B single £140–£170, double £150–£210, D,B&B double £225–£280.À la carte £42.

LETCOMBE REGIS Oxfordshire
Map 2:C2

THE GREYHOUND INN

'A truly wonderful place to stay,' writes an approving guest, who savoured the 18th-century red brick pub as much as Greyhound regulars do their pints of Titanic Plum Porter. Placed at the heart of the village community by local owners Martyn Reed and Catriona Galbraith, it holds wine tastings, jazz evenings and quizzes. Its 'great, friendly staff' extend a fine welcome. 'The manager helped us with luggage in the rain and led us to our room, explaining everything.' Upstairs accommodation – 'no traffic noise; occasional sound from the bar but not lasting until late' – includes two family suites, one under the Georgian eaves. 'Our exceptionally comfortable room had a sitting area, fresh milk with home-made biscuits, and a stunning bathroom with luxury toiletrics.' Food is served in three areas off the main bar with mellow wood, muted hues and brick fireplaces. Chef Phil Currie's 'delicious imaginative' dinners include slow-braised beef short rib, roast carrot, cured turnips, horseradish and parsley croquette, while breakfast offers 'good cooked dishes'; fuel for a windblown yomp up Uffington's White Horse Hill. (Amanda Tarrant, and others)

25% DISCOUNT VOUCHERS

Main Street
Letcombe Regis
OX12 9JL

T: 01235 771969
E: info@thegreyhoundletcombe.
co.uk
W: www.thegreyhoundletcombe.
co.uk

BEDROOMS: 8.
OPEN: all year except 24/25 Dec,
Mon lunchtime.
FACILITIES: bar with snug, 3 dining
rooms (1 available for private
dining/meetings), function room,
free Wi-Fi, in-room TV (Freeview),
garden, only bar/restaurant, garden
and toilet suitable for wheelchairs.
BACKGROUND MUSIC: occasionally in
public rooms.
LOCATION: in village, 2 miles SW of
Wantage.
CHILDREN: all ages welcomed.
DOGS: allowed in 2 bedrooms, bar,
garden, not dining rooms.
CREDIT CARDS: MasterCard, Visa.
PRICES: [2018] per room B&B single
£75–£125, double £90–£140. À la
carte £24–£35, 2-course Midweek
Fix dinner (Wed) £12.50.

LEWDOWN Devon   Map 1:C3

LEWTRENCHARD MANOR

'Can only talk in superlatives,' writes a reader
this year of Sue and James Murray's historic
manor house. It stands in parkland laid out
by Walter Sarel amid gently rolling Dartmoor
countryside. The hall chimneypiece is dated
1626, but the building is largely the creation of
the Revd Sabine Baring-Gould, best known for
penning 'Onward Christian Soldiers'. Our reader
was knocked out by 'the ambience... the friendly
and efficient welcome... the beauty and style of
the house... Three magnificent fireplaces, all lit
and roaring, creating a great atmosphere.' Public
rooms are filled with antiques and paintings.
'Impeccably furnished' bedrooms have 'high-
quality antiques' – not least, a four-poster that
once belonged to Charles I's beloved queen,
Henrietta Maria. In the dining room, with dark
panelling and ornate plaster ceiling, canapés are
a prelude to Matthew Peryer's cooking using
produce from local suppliers and the walled
kitchen garden. 'Presentation and quality were of
the highest order.' A typical dish: citrus-roasted
pollack, parsley root, Cornish cider, steamed
mussels, clams. 'Breakfast saw freshly squeezed
orange juice, quality local bacon, scrambled eggs
to match.' (Ian Dewey)

Lewdown
EX20 4PN

T: 01566 783222
E: info@lewtrenchard.co.uk
W: www.lewtrenchard.co.uk

BEDROOMS: 14. 1 in folly, 4 with
separate entrance, 1 suitable for
disabled.
OPEN: all year.
FACILITIES: front-hall lounge,
bar, library, restaurant, function
facilities, free Wi-Fi, in-room TV
(Freeview), civil wedding licence,
12-acre gardens.
BACKGROUND MUSIC: none.
LOCATION: rural, 10 miles N of
Tavistock.
CHILDREN: all ages welcomed.
DOGS: allowed in bedrooms (not
unattended), in public rooms, but
not in restaurant or kitchen garden.
CREDIT CARDS: Amex, MasterCard,
Visa.
PRICES: [2018] per room B&B single
£165–£235, double £200–£280,
D,B&B double £290–£370. Set
dinner £50, tasting menu £69.
1-night bookings sometimes refused
Sat in high season, bank holidays.

LICHFIELD Staffordshire

Map 2:A2

NETHERSTOWE HOUSE

On the outskirts of a cathedral city, Ben
Heathcote runs a former Georgian mill house-
turned-wool and lace manufactory as a small
hotel. Main-house bedrooms, some named
after Lichfield's finest, are traditionally, even
whimsically styled. Whether Dr Johnson would
have cared for lilac and cream decor with
accents of gold, or freestanding roll-top bath
with Aquavision TV and separate shower, we
can only guess but, as a 25-cups-a-day man, he'd
have approved of the afternoon tea. Indeed,
this may well be the meal to go for. 'We arrived
to find a dining room full of people enjoying
an excellent tea,' writes a Guide regular (who
was later troubled by a skylight window 'with
no way of keeping out the light', in a small but
otherwise fine room in the adjacent lodge).
While light grazing bites are served in the
Cheese and Wine cellar – one trusted reader
had them delivered to a serviced apartment
in the annexe – there is no cooked dinner. But
then, as Dr Johnson reasoned, supper is but a
turnpike we must pass through on the way to
bed. (MG, and others)

Netherstowe Lane
Lichfield
WS13 6AY

T: 01543 254270
E: info@netherstowehouse.com
W: www.netherstowehouse.com

BEDROOMS: 16. 7 in adjacent lodge,
5 on ground floor, plus 8 serviced
apartments in annexe.
OPEN: all year.
FACILITIES: 2 lounges, bar, 2 dining
rooms, private dining room, free
Wi-Fi, in-room TV (Freeview),
gym, 1-acre grounds.
BACKGROUND MUSIC: in restaurant
and lounges.
LOCATION: 1 mile N of city centre.
CHILDREN: not under 12 in hotel,
but all ages welcomed in serviced
apartments.
DOGS: only assistance dogs allowed.
CREDIT CARDS: Amex, MasterCard,
Visa.
PRICES: [2018] per room B&B
£110–£195.

SEE ALSO SHORTLIST

LIFTON Devon

Map 1:C3

THE ARUNDELL ARMS

'No wonder Adam has such a loyal clientele,' wrote a regular Guide reader after this year's visit to the country sports hotel, a mere fly cast from Dartmoor. Owned by Adam Fox-Edwards – it has been in his family for over half a century – the Arundell Arms has 'excellent, well-trained staff', 'cosy, comfortable rooms' with antiques, fluffy towels and upmarket toiletries, and an inviting atmosphere. 'All was warm and cosy, in tasteful country house style.' The 'glorious' residents' sitting room raised a particularly broad grin. 'A roaring fire is so very enticing and, oh bliss, comes with a comfy sofa for reading the papers.' Menus, courtesy of long-serving chef Steve Pidgeon, showcase fine local produce from the kitchen garden to guests' catches on the hotel's 20-mile Tamar beat. Perhaps pan-fried turbot with a fricassée of Brixham scallops, saffron potatoes, tomatoes, leeks and chives. 'The five-course tasting menu with accompanying wines for £50. Amazing.' Breakfast met 'previous high expectations'. It all comes with a side serving of history; the tackle room is a 250-year-old cockfighting pit, the annexe a Victorian tailor's shop. (Abigail Kirby-Harris)

25% DISCOUNT VOUCHERS

Fore Street
Lifton
PL16 0AA

T: 01566 784666
E: reservations@arundellarms.com
W: www.arundellarms.com

BEDROOMS: 27. 4 on ground floor, 4 in adjacent Church Cottage.
OPEN: all year.
FACILITIES: lounge, bar, village pub, restaurant, brasserie, private dining rooms, conference rooms, free Wi-Fi, in-room TV (Freeview), skittle alley, civil wedding licence, 1-acre garden, lake, 20 miles fishing rights on River Tamar and tributaries, unsuitable for disabled.
BACKGROUND MUSIC: none.
LOCATION: 3 miles E of Launceston.
CHILDREN: all ages welcomed.
DOGS: allowed in bedrooms and some public rooms, not in restaurant.
CREDIT CARDS: Amex, MasterCard, Visa.
PRICES: [2018] per room B&B single from £120, double £160–£195, D,B&B single from £150, double £260–£295. Tasting menu £49.50, à la carte £35.

LIVERPOOL Merseyside

Map 4:E2

2 BLACKBURNE TERRACE

'Everything perfect. A real find in this wonderful city.' Our readers are impressed with this chic B&B, in the Georgian quarter, between the two cathedrals. The 'very warm hosts', interior designer Glenn Whitter and his musician wife, Sarah, have filled their meticulously restored 1820s mansion with contemporary furniture, antiques, 'interesting' artwork and architectural photographs. A 'calm, relaxing' oasis, on a cobbled drive behind a screen of lime trees, it is 'within walking distance of Liverpool's attractions'. The bedrooms, with graceful Georgian proportions, are 'wonderfully quiet', carpeted, supplied with hand-made chocolates, a nip or two of artisan gin, fresh milk, luxury toiletries, bathrobes, slippers. One has a velvet sleigh bed and blue velvet sofa, an in-room, freestanding bath, a shower room, views of the Anglican cathedral. A former reception room, with wrought iron balcony, has a French classic sofa, a marble bathroom. Bedlinen is 'of the highest quality'. Breakfast begins with a generous buffet, and is served at a table set with silverware, porcelain and cut crystal. Cooked dishes include kippers, smoked salmon, the full English. (AT)

2 Blackburne Terrace
Liverpool
L8 7PJ

T: 0151 708 5474
E: info@2bbt.co.uk
W: www.2blackburneterrace.com

BEDROOMS: 4.
OPEN: all year.
FACILITIES: drawing room, dining room, free Wi-Fi, in-room smart TV (Freeview), walled garden, unsuitable for disabled.
BACKGROUND MUSIC: background classical at breakfast.
LOCATION: city centre.
CHILDREN: not under 10.
DOGS: not allowed.
CREDIT CARDS: MasterCard, Visa.
PRICES: [2018] per room B&B £150–£290.

SEE ALSO SHORTLIST

LODSWORTH Sussex

THE HALFWAY BRIDGE

'A comfortable, cosy place with nice rooms to curl up in', Sam and Janet Bakose's 250-year-old inn stands on the A272 between Midhurst and Petworth, in the South Downs national park. Guide inspectors stepping into the bar on a cold night were greeted by 'the gentle scent of a small log fire', and shown to a large room with 'handsome old beams' in the converted stables, across a country lane. 'All the essentials had been carefully considered: a desk and sofa, lots of storage, good lighting, fridge, fresh milk, still and sparkling water, biscuits, locally produced toiletries.' Fortified by books and cable TV, 'on a soggy Saturday we were content to hunker down all afternoon'. After dark, motion-sensor lights showed the way to the restaurant, where tea lights burned on window sills. New head chef Sven Wiege cooks such imaginative but accessible dishes as braised ox cheek bourguignon, potato terrine, braised red cabbage, button onions, parsnip crisp, pancetta and mushroom sauce. Breakfast brings 'moreish home-made berry compote, lovely chunky toast, good bacon', smoked salmon, 'creamy' scrambled eggs. Golfers can take their pick of nearby courses.

Lodsworth
GU28 9BP

T: 01798 861281
E: enquiries@halfwaybridge.co.uk
W: www.halfwaybridge.co.uk

BEDROOMS: 7. In converted barns, 165 yds from main building.
OPEN: all year.
FACILITIES: bar, restaurant, free Wi-Fi, in-room TV (Freeview), bar terrace, small beer garden, unsuitable for disabled.
BACKGROUND MUSIC: 'quiet' in bar and restaurant.
LOCATION: 3 miles W of Petworth, on A272.
CHILDREN: all ages welcomed.
DOGS: allowed in bar area only.
CREDIT CARDS: Amex, MasterCard, Visa.
PRICES: [2018] per room B&B single £90–£155, double £145–£230. Set menu £23.50, à la carte £32. 1-night bookings may be refused weekends.

LONG MELFORD Suffolk

Map 2:C5

LONG MELFORD SWAN & MELFORD HOUSE

In the middle of a pretty village, this 'intimate' restaurant-with-rooms is liked for its 'high-quality' accommodation and 'excellent food'. It is part of the family-run Stuart Inns group; its 'buzzy' restaurant sees antique hunters, drawn by surrounding emporiums, rub shoulders with gourmands enjoying 'creative, well-presented meals'. A characteristic dish: wild boar, potato-black pudding pressé, hen of the woods, Calvados apple. Bedrooms are within rolling distance, above the restaurant or in Melford House next door. (No staff remain overnight.) 'Boldly furnished, with lovely details', each room is a little different. Sizes may vary, but each has a super-king-size bed, still and sparkling water, fruit and home-made brownies. One large suite has a generous copper bath in the master bedroom, and a separate sitting area with a pull-out sofa. Breakfast, served in the bar, or the 'lovely garden', delivers fresh orange juice followed by the likes of avocado on sourdough toast; eggs Benedict with Suffolk ham; grilled kippers from Pinney's of Orford. That 'delightfully nutty granola' can be bought in the Duck Deli next door. (AW, and others)

Hall Street
Long Melford
CO10 9JQ

T: 01787 464545
E: info@longmelfordswan.co.uk
W: www.longmelfordswan.co.uk

BEDROOMS: 7. 4 in adjacent Melford House, 2 on ground floor.
OPEN: all year.
FACILITIES: bar, restaurant, deli, free Wi-Fi, in-room TV (Freeview), garden.
BACKGROUND MUSIC: all day in public areas.
LOCATION: village centre.
CHILDREN: all ages welcomed.
DOGS: allowed in bar only.
CREDIT CARDS: Amex, MasterCard, Visa.
PRICES: [2018] per room B&B single £95–£190, double £155–£210, D,B&B double £220–£300. À la carte £35.

LONG SUTTON Somerset

Map 1:C6

THE DEVONSHIRE ARMS

An air of a country gentleman's private study filters through this rural 19th-century hunting lodge, with appealing nods to the rural pursuits that might occupy him. Returning Guide readers in 2018 found everything at Philip Mepham's 'well-located' inn 'as good as ever'. Throughout, the country-contemporary design – squashy armchairs, wood panelling in rich heritage tones, hand-painted wallpaper – sits comfortably with flagstone floors and exposed timber. Still the village hub, its open-plan bar and restaurant serves hand-pumped local ales and ciders before a crackling log fire. However, 'the food is a real attraction. We thoroughly enjoyed smoked salmon with celeriac remoulade, and blue cheese mousse starters. The confit duck leg with red cabbage, mash and greens was faultless. For dessert: an excellent lemon posset with blueberry compote.' At night, modern bedrooms are 'quiet'. 'Our big, comfortable room overlooked the village green with a good-sized four-poster; in the big bathroom, our only gripe was that the large bath takes ages to fill.' At breakfast, fine cooked options include 'very good sausages and croissants'. 'A nice hotel, in a great location, we will return.' (Peter Anderson)

Long Sutton
TA10 9LP

T: 01458 241271
E: info@thedevonshirearms.com
W: www.thedevonshirearms.com

BEDROOMS: 9. 2, on ground floor, in annexe behind main building.
OPEN: all year except 25/26 Dec.
FACILITIES: open-plan bar and restaurant, private dining room, free Wi-Fi, in-room TV (Freeview), courtyard, garden (croquet lawn, vegetable garden), public areas wheelchair accessible, no adapted toilet.
BACKGROUND MUSIC: in bar.
LOCATION: by the village green.
CHILDREN: all ages welcomed.
DOGS: allowed in bar only.
CREDIT CARDS: MasterCard, Visa.
PRICES: [2018] per room B&B single £90–£160, double £100–£160, D,B&B double £170–£220. À la carte £30. 1-night bookings sometimes refused weekends.

LONGHORSLEY Northumberland

Map 4:B3

THISTLEYHAUGH FARM

♔ Previous César winner

'Wonderful location in rural Northumberland. Friendly, peaceful; superb dinners and a lovely breakfast.' Everything hit the sweet spot for one reader this year, at this Georgian farmhouse on the fringe of an organic livestock farm on Northumberland's River Coquet. The Nelless family has farmed here for three generations, and now Enid and daughter-in-law Zoë are welcoming hostesses, 'creating a home-from-home'. Spacious, pretty bedrooms, traditionally styled with antiques and paintings, are supplied with fresh milk and home-made biscuits, while fires burn in cosy lounges. At breakfast – and at dinner, for those who wish – guests sit down together around a beautifully set, polished table. The day might start with local sausages, home-cured bacon, free-range eggs, kippers from Craster. If there is anything you particularly want, readers report, just ask and the Nellesses will provide it next day. The wild and remote countryside offers memorable drives to gloriously photogenic Bamburgh Castle and ruined Dunstanburgh. A glass of sherry awaits your return, before a home-cooked three-course meal, perhaps roast lamb or chicken, a fruit Pavlova. (Philip Bright)

Longhorsley
NE65 8RG

T: 01665 570629
E: thistleyhaugh@hotmail.com
W: www.thistleyhaugh.co.uk

BEDROOMS: 4.
OPEN: Feb–Christmas.
FACILITIES: 2 lounges, garden room, dining room, free Wi-Fi, in-room TV (Freeview), ¼-acre garden (summer house), fishing, shooting, golf, riding nearby.
BACKGROUND MUSIC: none.
LOCATION: 10 miles N of Morpeth, W of A697.
CHILDREN: all ages welcomed.
DOGS: not allowed (kennels nearby).
CREDIT CARDS: MasterCard, Visa.
PRICES: [2018] per room B&B single £70–£90, double £100.

LOOE Cornwall

TRELASKE HOTEL & RESTAURANT

Hazel Billington and Ross Lewin are the 'excellent hosts' of this 'absolutely fantastic hotel' that has guests returning year after year. 'The standard remains high every time we visit.' Near the historic port of Looe, the landscape of Cornish wild-flower meadows and woodland is an 'enchanting' backdrop to 'excellent food', 'clean, spacious rooms' and 'second-to-none service', praise guests this year. 'Hazel's attention to detail leaves other establishments wanting.' Rooms in the main house have a soft, modern palette; 'each has a private balcony and is designed to give total privacy', while two in a garden annexe suit a family. The 'extensive grounds' ensure 'utter peace and quiet' at night. Dinner 'is a fish lover's paradise' with Ross Lewin, 'a superb chef', serving 'day-boat' fish and shellfish on a 'deliciously innovative' daily-changing menu, perhaps white crab meat, pink grapefruit, potato rösti. Meat and vegetarian dishes include 'melt-in-the-mouth beef stew'; warmed goat's cheese salad. A 'generous' breakfast includes home-made spiced muesli, fresh fruit, 'a fabulous full English'. The hosts offer ready advice on day-trips to the local coast. (Yvonne Waite, CF, and others)

Polperro Road
Looe
PL13 2JS

T: 01503 262159
E: info@trelaske.co.uk
W: www.trelaske.co.uk

BEDROOMS: 7. 4 garden rooms, on ground floor, in adjacent building.
OPEN: Mar–Nov.
FACILITIES: 2 lounges, dining room, free Wi-Fi (in main house), in-room TV (Freeview), function facilities, terrace (summer barbecues), 4-acre grounds, bar and restaurant wheelchair accessible.
BACKGROUND MUSIC: in lounge bar and restaurant.
LOCATION: 2 miles W of Looe, 3 miles NE of Polperro.
CHILDREN: all ages welcomed.
DOGS: allowed in 2 bedrooms (£7.50 per night), not in public rooms.
CREDIT CARDS: MasterCard, Visa.
PRICES: [2018] per room B&B £110–£130, D,B&B £165–£190. Set dinner £30–£35. 1-night bookings sometimes refused.

SEE ALSO SHORTLIST

LORTON Cumbria

Map 4: inset C2

NEW HOUSE FARM

A 'wonderful hot tub in the grounds' is one of the unexpected delights of Hazel Thompson's B&B in the Vale of Lorton, close to Loweswater, Buttermere and Crummock Water. The 'new' house and adjoining barn are Grade II listed, 18th-century, surrounded by open fields, woods and streams, against a theatrical backdrop of the Lakeland fells. All bedrooms are highly individual and well appointed. Both the Old Dairy and the Stable have a solid-oak four-poster – Old Dairy also sports a Victorian-style bathroom and double-ended freestanding slipper bath. Three spacious main-house rooms have similar character, including Swinside with a double power shower and body jets. On cold days, a huge open fire burns in the tearoom with tables in the old cow byres, where light lunches, cakes and ice creams are served from spring to autumn. It closes for weddings and events, so phone ahead instead of swinging by for tea – or Cumberland ham, Solway shrimps, or Whitby scampi and chips. There's a beamed residents' lounge with deep fireside sofas, substantial cooked breakfasts, while Wordsworth's birthplace, Cockermouth, with restaurants and Jennings brewery, is just six miles away. (JS)

Lorton
CA13 9UU

T: 07841 159818
E: hazel@newhouse-farm.co.uk
W: www.newhouse-farm.com

BEDROOMS: 5. 1 in stable, 1 in Old Dairy.
OPEN: all year.
FACILITIES: entrance hall, 2 lounges, dining room, free Wi-Fi, civil wedding licence, 17-acre grounds (garden, hot tub, streams, woods, field, lake and river, safe bathing 2 miles), unsuitable for disabled.
BACKGROUND MUSIC: none.
LOCATION: on B5289, 2 miles S of Lorton.
CHILDREN: not under 6.
DOGS: 'clean and dry' dogs with own bed allowed in bedrooms (£20 per night), not in public rooms.
CREDIT CARDS: MasterCard, Visa.
PRICES: [2018] per room B&B £120–£180. 1-night bookings usually refused weekends in peak season.

LOUTH Lincolnshire

THE OLD RECTORY AT STEWTON

Guests in 2018 praise the 'outstanding hospitality and attention to detail at this gem of a B&B'. 'Charming' hosts Alan and Linda Palmer's Georgian-style early Victorian house stands among lawns and mature trees at the end of a country lane. The 'deeply peaceful setting' teems with wildlife: squirrels and foxes, while flocks of birds leave birdwatchers twitching. At night, the only sound is the snuffle of badgers. Spacious, country-style bedrooms may have a four-poster bed; roll-top bath in a bathroom down a short staircase. Families with small children are well accommodated in suites with a private sitting room. 'Our very comfortable room was spotlessly clean.' Deep leather sofas, books and paintings fill the sitting room. Whether an early riser or more leisurely starter, breakfast 'is taken seriously'. Served in the 'lovely conservatory', a hearty feast of Lincolnshire sausages, free-range eggs, kippers, smoked haddock – plus good vegetarian options – is an 'excellent' start to the day. There are great walks ('with or without a dog') from the door; ask the hosts about nearby trails and wilder coastal hikes. 'Extraordinary value for money.' (Allan and Pat Hope)

Stewton
Louth
LN11 8SF

T: 01507 328063
E: alanjpalmer100@aol.com
W: www.louthbedandbreakfast.co.uk

BEDROOMS: 3,
OPEN: all year except Christmas–New Year.
FACILITIES: sitting room, breakfast room, conservatory, free Wi-Fi, in-room TV (Freeview), 3-acre garden, unsuitable for disabled.
BACKGROUND MUSIC: none.
LOCATION: in the countryside, 2½ miles SE of Louth.
CHILDREN: all ages welcomed.
DOGS: 'well-trained' dogs allowed in 1 bedroom (£10 charge, owners provide bedding and food), public rooms.
CREDIT CARDS: MasterCard, Visa.
PRICES: [2018] per room B&B single £50, double £75–£85.

LOWER BOCKHAMPTON Dorset
Map 1:D6

YALBURY COTTAGE

Surrounded by woodland and fields in the heart of Hardy's Wessex, Jamie and Ariane Jones's 'olde-worlde' thatched hotel offers 'a charming and very comfortable stay'. On a visit this year, Guide regulars found the hosts 'warm and welcoming', their service 'personal and friendly'. Jamie Jones's 'quite outstanding' classical French dinners, perhaps mustard- and herb-crusted cannon of Tolpuddle lamb, almond potato, spring cabbage, tarragon sauce; pan-fried fillet of Dorset sea bass, crushed new potato, fresh peas, lemon butter sauce, are served amid stone walls, inglenooks and oak-beamed ceilings. Breakfast included fresh croissants, home-made lemon curd and a 'good range of cooked options including Bridport kippers'. Some might find the decor 'a little folksy', and in 2018 readers reported a night-storage heater left their room 'like an oven' in late afternoon, while a fan heater made for a 'very chilly' bathroom in the morning. Overall, however, praise for the 'clean and tidy country-style' bedroom with 'lots of spare bedding, still and sparkling water, a long shoehorn (bliss), excellent coffee and home-made brownies'. 'We would certainly return.' (Lindsay Hunt and John Fisher, Peter Anderson, SR, and others)

Lower Bockhampton
DT2 8PZ

T: 01305 262382
E: enquiries@yalburycottage.com
W: www.yalburycottage.com

BEDROOMS: 8. 6 on ground floor.
OPEN: all year except 23 Dec–18 Jan.
FACILITIES: lounge, restaurant, free Wi-Fi, in-room TV (Freeview), garden with outdoor seating.
BACKGROUND MUSIC: 'easy listening' in lounge in evening..
LOCATION: 2 miles E of Dorchester.
CHILDREN: all ages welcomed, no under-12s in restaurant after 8 pm.
DOGS: allowed in bedrooms, lounge, not in restaurant.
CREDIT CARDS: MasterCard, Visa.
PRICES: [2018] per room B&B £75–£99, D,B&B £99–£165. À la carte £39.50.

LUDLOW Shropshire

Map 3:C4

OLD DOWNTON LODGE

Barns and stables – some medieval – surround a
courtyard laid out as parterre gardens, at Willem
and Pippa Vlok's restaurant-with-rooms, deep
in the Shropshire countryside. The buildings
offer 'gorgeous, cosy' accommodation, says a
reader this year, retaining rustic features – beams,
bare brick or stone. Each room is individually
styled, perhaps with a modern oak four-poster;
all are 'tasteful, calm, understated'. Some have
been updated since last year, with showers
added to bathrooms. Most are approached by a
flight of steps. The lounge playfully exploits its
working past as stables; stall timbers have been
used to provide seating, alongside 'lots of oak
furnishing', a log-burner and honesty bar. The
breakfast/dining room dates back to the Norman
Conquest, with 'dovecote windows, a large
tapestry and heavy metal candelabra'; baronial
chic, if you will. Here guests choose between
chef Karl Martin's tasting menus or a market
menu with either/or choices including stone bass,
keta caviar, wild rice, chives; duck, squash, kale,
grape, seeds. It's 'absolutely fabulous', 'special
occasion' food, but perhaps not for hikers or
trenchermen. Breakfast is 'farmhouse, local and
wholesome'. (Cath Jacob)

25% DISCOUNT VOUCHERS

Downton on the Rock
Ludlow
SY8 2HU

T: 01568 771826
E: bookings@olddowntonlodge.
  com
W: www.olddowntonlodge.com

BEDROOMS: 10. In buildings around
courtyard.
OPEN: all year, except Christmas,
restaurant closed Sun, Mon.
FACILITIES: sitting room, dining
room, 'museum' (function room),
free Wi-Fi, in-room TV (Freeview),
civil wedding licence, 1-acre
courtyard, two Tesla electric car
chargers, unsuitable for disabled.
BACKGROUND MUSIC: soft classical in
sitting room and dining room.
LOCATION: 6 miles W of Ludlow.
CHILDREN: over 12 only.
DOGS: allowed in some bedrooms
by prior arrangement, not in public
rooms.
CREDIT CARDS: Amex, MasterCard,
Visa.
PRICES: [2018] per room B&B £155–
£345, D, B&B from £215. 3-course
market menu £50, tasting menus6
courses £59, 9 courses £75.

LYMINGTON Hampshire

Map 2:E2

BRITANNIA HOUSE

Guests are full of 'high praise' for Tobias
Feilke's 'personal' hospitality at his 'homely'
B&B close to Lymington quay. Tobi 'made us
feel very welcome', finding time for a 'friendly
chat' and carrying cases up to the bedroom. As
with each of the five rooms, it was 'certainly
not bland'. The Courtyard Suite has pistachio
walls, Doric columns, classical art; the Britannia
has gold-and-black furnishings, a wrought iron
bed with a tasselled canopy; the bright, airy
two-storey apartment has enormous windows
and a balcony gazing across the quay to the Isle
of Wight. The decor is lavish throughout the
building, which, apart from a brief spell, has
been welcoming guests since opening in 1865.
Quirky features abound, from a wall decorated
with hats – fedoras and trilbies to conical coolies
– to a suit of armour, while a cosy lounge has
lush drapes, warm rich hues, plump sofas and
a marble fireplace. In the country-style kitchen
with green settle and botanical prints, a satisfied
reader reports the owner cooked an 'exceptional'
breakfast, with a continental buffet followed by
a full English. Vegans and vegetarians should
give advance notice.

Station Street
Lymington
SO41 3BA

T: 01590 672091
E: enquiries@britannia-house.com
W: www.britannia-house.com

BEDROOMS: 5. 2 on ground floor, one
2-storey apartment.
OPEN: all year.
FACILITIES: lounge, kitchen/breakfast
room, free Wi-Fi, in-room TV
(Freeview), courtyard garden,
parking, unsuitable for disabled.
BACKGROUND MUSIC: none.
LOCATION: 2 mins' walk from High
Street/quayside, close to station.
CHILDREN: not under 8.
DOGS: not allowed.
CREDIT CARDS: MasterCard, Visa.
PRICES: [2018] per room B&B single
£95–£124, double £95–£129. 1-night
bookings refused weekends.

LYNDHURST Hampshire

Map 2:E2

LIME WOOD

'At night, surrounded by floodlit cedars and oaks, it felt like a movie set,' writes one reader this year, after visiting the luxury New Forest retreat. Almost correct. The mellow-stone mansion, apart from a tiny original section, is a 21st-century recreation of a Georgian property. So theatrics, but no drama, just 'friendly, professional' staff and a 'gloriously relaxed' atmosphere in the 'delightful' public spaces sprinkled liberally with artwork. The main house's 'tasteful' rooms have coolly casual categories: eaves, cosy, spacious. Around the grounds, a thread of rustic family cottages, and two-storey suites and lodges with fireplace, dining area and forest or estate views. New this year, a linear timber-clad hideaway, cantilevered over the small lake, as if Frank Lloyd Wright had designed a log cabin. Wellies, waterproofs and bikes are provided, but may well be ignored for the acclaimed spa's soft grey robes. In the 'elegant, softly lit' restaurant, Luke Holder and Angela Hartnett's seasonal, locally sourced Italian fare includes such dishes as velvet crab, blood orange, fennel and basil risotto. Breakfast brings a 'terrific' buffet, or cooked options: smoked haddock, steak and eggs. (IB, and others)

Beaulieu Road
Lyndhurst
SO43 7FZ

T: 02380 287177
E: info@limewood.co.uk
W: www.limewoodhotel.co.uk

BEDROOMS: 32. 5 on ground floor, 2 suitable for disabled, 16 in pavilions and cottages in the grounds.
OPEN: all year.
FACILITIES: lifts, 2 bars, 3 lounges, 2 restaurants, private dining rooms, free Wi-Fi, in-room TV (Freeview), civil wedding licence, spa (16-metre swimming pool), 14-acre gardens (outdoor hot pool), cookery school, public rooms wheelchair accessible, adapted toilet.
BACKGROUND MUSIC: all day in public areas.
LOCATION: in New Forest, 12 miles SW of Southampton.
CHILDREN: all ages welcomed.
DOGS: allowed in outside bedrooms, not in main house.
CREDIT CARDS: MasterCard, Visa.
PRICES: [2018] room from £385. Breakfast £16.50–£25, à la carte £65. 1-night bookings refused most weekends, bank holidays.

MARGATE Kent

SANDS HOTEL

Sea and sand are steps away from this 'fantastic', well-located Victorian hotel, standing on the crescent bay of one of Kent's original resort towns. Nick Conington's 'very friendly' staff merit particular praise. A 'smart renovation' embraces the hotel's origins, with 'impeccably maintained' original features (yellow-and-blue stained glass, filigree-bound balconies) and the muted colours of the sea. Floor-to-ceiling windows in the 'striking, contemporary' dining room, and pretty bedroom balconies yield 'marvellous sunset views'. Bedrooms are 'airy, peaceful', and have 'a touch of glam' (ornate mirrors, crystal-studded light switches). 'Our spacious superior room, overlooking the sands, had a bathroom with his-and-hers basins.' Attic rooms have a parapet balcony separated by tidy rows of plants. Light sleepers in beachfront rooms may need earplugs. Minor niggles in 2018: some sloppy housekeeping, a repeatedly faulty room key. New chef Eddy Seys's seasonal, locally sourced dishes include seared scallops, mushroom broth, croutons; Sands bouillabaisse. For afters, a tramp along the seafront, an ice cream from the downstairs gelateria. 'We enjoyed our stay.' (Debbie Pullman, MG)

16 Marine Drive
Margate
CT9 1DH

T: 01843 228228
E: enquiries@sandshotelmargate.
co.uk
W: www.sandshotelmargate.co.uk

BEDROOMS: 20. 1 suitable for disabled.
OPEN: all year.
FACILITIES: lift, bar, restaurant, free Wi-Fi, in-room TV (Freeview), civil wedding licence, roof terrace, ice-cream parlour, public areas wheelchair accessible.
BACKGROUND MUSIC: varied, in public areas.
LOCATION: town centre.
CHILDREN: all ages welcomed.
DOGS: not allowed.
CREDIT CARDS: Amex, MasterCard, Visa.
PRICES: [2018] per room B&B £140–£180, D,B&B £230–£290. À la carte £40.

SEE ALSO SHORTLIST

MARKET DRAYTON Shropshire   Map 3:B5

GOLDSTONE HALL

For 'a quiet weekend in a friendly, characterful hotel among bucolic surroundings', John and Sue Cushing's red brick Georgian manor 'fits the bill perfectly'. One of its trump cards is the 'extraordinary' kitchen garden, source of most of Goldstone's vegetables and summer fruit, along with 100 different herbs – part of grounds developed by John's mother that open to the public each year under the National Garden scheme. Indoors, a Guide insider enjoyed plenty of 'bright, peaceful' lounges with upright leather chairs and sofas, a couple of them with a fireplace, while the 'smallish' beamed Arts and Crafts-style dining room has a fireplace, 'nicely separated tables', starched white linen. It is the stage for new chef David Jones's 'beautifully presented' dishes, perhaps loin of rabbit, broad beans, asparagus, morels, shoulder bon bons, pickled potatoes with a local cheese platter. A 'delicious breakfast' includes freshly squeezed juices, and an 'excellent vegetarian cooked option'. In 'tastefully furnished' bedrooms 'super-comfy' beds provide 'an excellent night's sleep'. Bathrobes, fresh milk, home-baked biscuits are provided. Grapevines have been planted in the garden, promising a tasty addition to the autumn cheese board.

Goldstone Road
Market Drayton
TF9 2NA

T: 01630 661202
E: enquiries@goldstonehall.com
W: www.goldstonehall.com

BEDROOMS: 12.
OPEN: all year except Christmas.
FACILITIES: bar, lounge, drawing room, dining room, orangery, free Wi-Fi, in-room TV (Sky, Freeview), function facilities, civil wedding licence, 5 acres of grounds (walled garden, kitchen garden).
BACKGROUND MUSIC: in bar and dining room.
LOCATION: 5 miles S of Market Drayton.
CHILDREN: all ages welcomed.
DOGS: not allowed.
CREDIT CARDS: Amex, MasterCard, Visa.
PRICES: [2018] per room B&B single £95–£115, double £150–£180, D,B&B single £138–£158, double £246–£276. Set dinner £48.50.

MARTINHOE Devon

MARTINHOE Devon

Map 1:B4

HEDDON'S GATE HOTEL

Perfect peace reigns within this friendly hotel at the end of a quarter-mile drive, swaddled by a densely wooded river valley on the western edge of Exmoor national park. Owners Mark and Pat Cowell spare no effort to make their guests happy – 'We could not have felt better cared for,' 'We felt totally spoilt,' say readers. Those returning in the afternoon – from walking the South West Coastal Path, say, or from swimming off secluded Heddon's Mouth beach – are offered tea and coffee in the lounge, or on the west-facing sun terrace. Most of the 11 individually styled bedrooms, named after trees in the grounds, occupy the original Victorian house; three more contemporary rooms are in a newer wing. Chestnut has 'a Victorian wooden bed, a large bathroom with bath and separate shower'. Menus are unpretentious – soups, pastas; cider-braised pork, pancetta, roasted apple; poached plaice with asparagus; braised local beef brisket medallion, wild mushroom and spinach potato rösti – but chef Justin Dunn 'likes the challenge' of cooking something special on request. Breakfast brings packet cereals but 'wonderful berry compotes'. (DO, J and MB)

25% DISCOUNT VOUCHERS

Martinhoe
EX31 4PZ

T: 01598 763481
E: stay@heddonsgatehotel.co.uk
W: www.heddonsgatehotel.co.uk

BEDROOMS: 11.
OPEN: 15 Mar–11 Nov, restaurant closed Sun and Mon, group bookings over Christmas and New Year.
FACILITIES: lounge, bar, TV room, library, breakfast/dining room, free Wi-Fi, in-room TV (Freeview), no mobile phone signal (guests may use landline free of charge), sun terrace, 2½-acre grounds, unsuitable for disabled.
BACKGROUND MUSIC: in dining room at dinner.
LOCATION: 6 miles W of Lynton.
CHILDREN: all ages welcomed.
DOGS: allowed in bedrooms (not unattended), and in public rooms, except dining room.
CREDIT CARDS: Amex, MasterCard, Visa.
PRICES: [2018] per room B&B single £50–£60, double £110–£150, D,B&B double £140–£180. À la carte £28.

MARTINHOE Devon

Map 1:B4

THE OLD RECTORY HOTEL

♔ Previous César winner

'It's clear why so many guests return again and again.' Huw Rees and Sam Prosser's converted Georgian rectory, in large, well-maintained grounds, 'is a haven of rural peace within easy reach of Exmoor and the sea'. 'The hosts are very welcoming and accommodating.' Guests this year 'were delighted that drinks are a sociable event – be it afternoon tea with home-made cakes or pre-prandial drinks in the conservatory'. 'Superbly appointed' bedrooms, in the main building and converted coach house, have muted hues, a 'large, comfortable bed'; those overlooking the garden are serenaded by its waterfall and stream. Pleasing extras include cafetière coffee, posh toiletries and spring water. Michael Caine acolyte Thomas Frost took over the kitchen this year. His modern British menu features just-landed fish and garden-fresh produce. 'Well-cooked, interesting dishes, served by cheerful staff' might include smoked duck, asparagus salad, sesame dressing; Devon beef, chateaubriand sauce. 'Breakfast has plenty of choice': fresh fruit smoothies; mushroom eggs Florentine; bacon from traditional breeds. Afterwards, the Exmoor coast beckons. (IM, and others)

25% DISCOUNT VOUCHERS

Berry's Ground Lane
Martinhoe
EX31 4QT

T: 01598 763368
E: reception@oldrectoryhotel.co.uk
W: www.oldrectoryhotel.co.uk

BEDROOMS: 11, 2 on ground floor, 3 in coach house, some suitable for disabled.
OPEN: Mar–early Nov.
FACILITIES: 2 lounges, orangery, dining room, free Wi-Fi, in-room TV (Freeview), 3-acre grounds, public rooms including restaurant wheelchair accessible.
BACKGROUND MUSIC: 'very quiet' in dining room.
LOCATION: 4 miles W of Lynton.
CHILDREN: not under 14.
DOGS: not allowed.
CREDIT CARDS: Amex, MasterCard, Visa.
PRICES: [2018] per room B&B single £165–£195, double £180–£210, D,B&B single £175, double £220. À la carte £35, 1-night bookings sometimes refused at weekends.

MAWGAN PORTH Cornwall

Map 1:D2

BEDRUTHAN HOTEL AND SPA

♋ Previous César winner

In a hillside location with 'stunning sea views', this supremely family-friendly hotel has something for everyone – indeed, everything for everyone. There is a lot going on here, with a theatre, pottery studio, gallery, art and design fairs – and the beach below for surf lessons. The ambience is happy and relaxed. 'The staff really make your stay' with their 'lovely attitude'. 'We were all made welcome.' 'A well-oiled operation.' The decor is Scandi-inspired, with acres of sofas, floor-to-ceiling windows, an open fire. Two hours of free childcare daily (lunch provided in the 11.30–1.30 session) leaves parents free to take advantage of the spa and sensory garden, or to enjoy cocktails in the bar or on the terrace. Rooms are supplied with fresh milk and mains-powered cool box. The more expensive have a sea view. The Wild Café serves cream teas, burgers, wood-fired pizzas. In the more sophisticated Herring, daily-changing menus include such dishes as red gurnard, salsify, spring onions, warm potted crab. The adults-only Scarlet (see next entry) is a sister hotel in every sense, owned by the same three sisters.

Mawgan Porth
TR8 4BU

T: 01637 860860
E: stay@bedruthan.com
W: www.bedruthan.com

BEDROOMS: 101. 1 suitable for disabled, apartment suites in separate block.
OPEN: all year except 3 weeks Jan.
FACILITIES: lift, bar, restaurant, café, relaxation lounge, shop and art gallery, free Wi-Fi, in-room TV (Freeview), indoor and outdoor play areas, spa (indoor swimming pool), civil wedding licence, 5-acre grounds (3 heated swimming pools, tennis, playing field), several public areas wheelchair accessible.
BACKGROUND MUSIC: 'laid-back' in restaurant, café and bar.
LOCATION: 4 miles NE of Newquay.
CHILDREN: all ages welcomed.
DOGS: allowed in some bedrooms, some public areas (£12 per night).
CREDIT CARDS: MasterCard, Visa.
PRICES: [2018] per room B&B single from £95, double from £160, D,B&B from £206. Set dinner £28–£38.

MAWGAN PORTH Cornwall

THE SCARLET

While families whoop it up at sister hotel
Bedruthan (see previous entry), grown-ups enjoy
the serenity at this adults-only hotel and spa. A
reader was impressed on arrival by valet parking,
'a comprehensive guided tour', complimentary
tea and coffee. He admired the design ('modern,
clean lines, interesting artwork and lighting are
achievable anywhere; here it's exciting') and
the eco-friendly credentials. 'I could go on: the
restaurant, the peace, the views… the charming
young staff.' Bedrooms, most with floor-to-ceiling
windows, have a terrace, balcony or courtyard
garden; all enjoy sea views. 'Ours was very
comfortable (wonderful mattress), bath in the
bedroom (not sure about that) and power shower.'
At dinner, chef Mike Francis cooks imaginative
dishes such as pan-roasted cod, crispy oyster,
Jerusalem artichoke, cavolo nero, salsa verde. One
reader raved, another found the restaurant low on
choice and slow on speed. Others in 2018 agreed:
'the cooking wasn't up to the standard of the
rest of the superb hotel; flavours were generally
bland.' Breakfast has more healthy than cooked
options but if you want something special, ask.
(Richard Barrett, ANR)

Tredragon Road
Mawgan Porth
TR8 4DQ

T: 01637 861800
E: stay@scarlethotel.co.uk
W: www.scarlethotel.co.uk

BEDROOMS: 37. 2 suitable for
disabled.
OPEN: all year except 2–31 Jan, house
parties Christmas (4 days) and New
Year (3 days).
FACILITIES: lift, 2 lounges, bar, library,
restaurant, free Wi-Fi, in-room
TV (Freeview), civil wedding
licence, spa (indoor swimming pool,
outdoor swimming pool, seaweed
baths, terrace, meadow garden,
public areas wheelchair accessible,
adapted toilet.
BACKGROUND MUSIC: all day in bar
and restaurant.
LOCATION: 4 miles NE of Newquay.
CHILDREN: not under 16.
DOGS: allowed in selected bedrooms,
some public areas.
CREDIT CARDS: MasterCard, Visa.
PRICES: [2018] per room B&B single
£240–£410, double £260–£480.
Set dinner £50. 1-night bookings
refused Fri/Sat.

MELLS Somerset

Map 2:D1

THE TALBOT INN

⚜ Previous César winner

'A rustic gem in an unspoilt village', this ancient coaching inn, built around a cobbled yard, is a sister to The Beckford Arms, Tisbury (see entry). 'It is equal to its sibling for comfort, cuisine and care of its guests,' says a reader, 'but closer to its origins in an agricultural community.' Bedrooms have a smart, contemporary style, some with a modern four-poster, an in-room, roll-top bath; one, with its own entrance and staircase, has a vaulted, beamed ceiling. All display works by local artists and are supplied with good-quality toiletries. A sitting room in a converted tithe barn, with a mural depicting the magic of the area, doubles as a cinema for locals and residents on some Saturday nights. In 'a sequence of homely rooms', chef Richard Peacocke's food includes bar snacks, pub classics and seasonal menus based on local and home-grown produce. A typical dish, Mangalitsa pork loin, hispi cabbage, creamed pearl barley, bacon, charred shallot. At weekends the coach house hosts charcoal grills. One reader this year complains of a tough steak, while another says everything is 'prepared with care and attention'. (J and RG)

Selwood Street
Mells
BA11 3PN

T: 01373 812254
E: info@talbotinn.com
W: www.talbotinn.com

BEDROOMS: 8. 1 on ground floor.
OPEN: all year except 25 Dec.
FACILITIES: sitting room, bar, restaurant, coach house grill room, free Wi-Fi, in-room Smart TV (including Freeview), courtyard, garden, kitchen table cookery school.
BACKGROUND MUSIC: in public areas.
LOCATION: in village.
CHILDREN: all ages welcomed.
DOGS: allowed in 1 bedroom (£10 one-off charge), and in all public areas.
CREDIT CARDS: MasterCard, Visa.
PRICES: [2018] per room B&B £100–£160 (family suite £200). À la carte £30. 1-night bookings refused at weekends.

MEVAGISSEY Cornwall

Map 1:D2

TREVALSA COURT

John and Susan Gladwin's 'very pleasant' small
hotel 'preserves a different world' filled with
'delicious' cream teas and 'glorious' walks along
the Coastal Path. Trevalsa is Cornish for 'house on
the cliff', hence the 'wonderful' vistas 'extending
right along the Cornish coast into Devon, with
Dartmoor in the far background'. Interiors blend
the tastefully neutral with rich bursts of colour,
while eclectic artworks range from traditional
seafaring to more contemporary. The clean lines
and a bright coastal vibe sit kindly with the
former grand home's oak-panelling, fireplaces
and granite mullioned windows. Books, games
and an open fire enhance colder months, a terrace,
overlooking the sub-tropical gardens takes
over on warmer days. The light airy bedrooms
are 'sophisticated' and 'well furnished'. 'Mine
was small but extremely comfortable, with a
spotless bathroom.' Most enjoy the sea view. Staff
are 'polite and helpful', while in the panelled
dining room, chef Adam Cawood's 'excellent'
modern British dishes include salmon, Jerusalem
artichoke, parsley crumb, monk's beard, kohlrabi
and avocado. An afternoon tea included home-
made scones, 'warmed, of course', and 'a generous
portion of clotted cream'. (MC, and others)

25% DISCOUNT VOUCHERS

School Hill
Mevagissey
PL26 6TH

T: 01726 842468
E: stay@trevalsa-hotel.co.uk
W: www.trevalsa-hotel.co.uk

BEDROOMS: 15. 3, plus family suite,
on ground floor.
OPEN: 10 Feb–20 Nov.
FACILITIES: lounge, bar, restaurant,
free Wi-Fi, in-room TV (Freeview),
2-acre garden, summer house,
public rooms wheelchair accessible.
BACKGROUND MUSIC: all day in bar.
LOCATION: on cliff-top, at edge of
village.
CHILDREN: all ages welcomed.
DOGS: allowed in bedrooms (not
unattended), not in restaurant, in
other public rooms with consent of
other guests.
CREDIT CARDS: Amex, MasterCard,
Visa.
PRICES: [2018] per room B&B
£70–£290, D,B&B £93–£345.
À la carte £34. 1-night bookings
refused high season.

MILTON ABBOT Devon

Map 1:D3

HOTEL ENDSLEIGH

🏵 Previous César winner

A Regency cottage-orné, built by Jeffry Wyatville as a fishing lodge for Georgiana, Duchess of Bedford, is run today in characteristic relaxed-chic style by Olga Polizzi (see also Tresanton, St Mawes). 'Staff are helpful and attentive, without being overbearing or unctuous – you're encouraged to feel like a house guest.' A mile-long drive bisects an Arcadia designed by Humphry Repton, with dells, streams, cascades and follies, the Tamar flowing through. The ambience is 'unpretentious, wholly enjoyable', say readers; it 'feeds the historical imagination'. Main-house bedrooms have their own personality, new and vintage furniture. Some have hand-painted wallpaper, perhaps a fireplace, a freestanding bath. Two stable suites have a wood-burning stove, pantry, timber floors. In the restaurant, chef Jose Graziosi uses seasonal produce, locally farmed or foraged, in modern British dishes with an Italian accent. For example: corn-fed chicken, dauphinoise potatoes, Jerusalem artichoke purée, kale, Chantenay carrots; wild mushroom risotto, watercress, pecorino. Breakfast brings freshly squeezed juices, home-made granola, grilled kipper, a full English. (A and HB)

25% DISCOUNT VOUCHERS

Milton Abbot
PL19 0PQ

T: 01822 870000
E: mail@hotelendsleigh.com
W: www.hotelendsleigh.com

BEDROOMS: 18. 1 on ground floor, 2 in stables, 1 in lodge (1 mile from main house). 1 suite suitable for disabled.
OPEN: all year.
FACILITIES: drawing room, library, card room, bar, 2 dining rooms, free Wi-Fi, in-room TV (Freeview), civil wedding licence, terraces, 108-acre estate (fishing, ghillie available), all public rooms wheelchair accessible, adapted toilet.
BACKGROUND MUSIC: none.
LOCATION: 7 miles NW of Tavistock.
CHILDREN: all ages welcomed.
DOGS: allowed in bedrooms, lounges, grounds, not in restaurant, or in library during afternoon tea.
CREDIT CARDS: Amex, MasterCard, Visa.
PRICES: [2018] per room B&B £180–£450, D,B&B £212–£544. Set dinner £28–£47. 1-night bookings refused Fri and Sat.

MOUSEHOLE Cornwall   Map 1: E1

THE OLD COASTGUARD

This 'youthful, buzzy' spot, say returning
guests this year, is liked for its 'good rooms,
friendly staff, excellent food – and no flashy
bits'. At their hotel (since Victorian times),
brothers Charles and Edmund Inkin let
laid-back comfort and carefree style float in
on sea breezes. The convivial bar is a popular
gathering spot for games night. Fancy something
more active? There are plenty of pursuits
(none trivial): mindful yoga weekends, playful
puppet workshops, 'wild' foraging walks. 'The
receptionist enthusiastically recommended good
running routes.' Jolly bedrooms have Cornish art,
lime-painted walls, a woollen blanket to wrap up
in when the salty air turns chilly. 'Our good-
sized room had a wonderful sea view, blocked
only slightly by the extension underneath.' The
lighting could have been brighter, however. In
the restaurant, Cornish produce, fresh from sea
and land, are the main feature: ray, swede,
spinach, crisp potato, café de Paris butter, curry
oil. Breakfast has scrambled eggs, home-made
muesli, apple juice from Polgoon, 'beautiful sea
views'. The Inkins' nearby Gurnard's Head,
Zennor, and Felin Fach Griffin, Felin Fach (see
entries), are similarly laid-back. (ME, and others)

The Parade
Mousehole
TR19 6PR

T: 01736 731222
E: bookings@oldcoastguardhotel.
  co.uk
W: www.oldcoastguardhotel.co.uk

BEDROOMS: 14.
OPEN: all year except 24/25 Dec.
FACILITIES: bar, sun lounge,
restaurant, free Wi-Fi, sea-facing
garden with path to beach,
restaurant and bar suitable for
disabled.
BACKGROUND MUSIC: Radio 4 at
breakfast, selected music at other
mealtimes.
LOCATION: 2-min. walk from village,
3 miles S of Newlyn.
CHILDREN: all ages welcomed.
DOGS: welcomed (treats, towels, dog
bowls), not allowed in dining room.
CREDIT CARDS: MasterCard, Visa.
PRICES: [2018] per room B&B single
from £105, double £140–£245, D,B&B
single £133, double £195–£300. Set
dinner £20–£25, à la carte £29.

MULLION COVE Cornwall

Map 1:E2

MULLION COVE HOTEL

On the cliff-top with 'fabulous views of Mounts Bay and down to Mullion Cove itself', the Grose family's dog-friendly hotel is 'as good as ever,' report Guide regulars in 2018. 'Staff were helpful, ever smiling; the housekeeping was faultless.' Built by the Great Western Railway, it retains the leisured, luxurious feel of the Edwardian age, while lacking nothing in modern comforts. Premier sea-view rooms have home-made biscuits, fresh fruit, bathrobes and slippers, while ground-floor sea-view garden suites have sliding patio doors. Bistro food is served all day in the bar, from sandwiches to steak and catch of the day (surf or turf). In the Atlantic View restaurant, Paul Stephens's 'constantly delicious' seasonal, daily menus exploit Cornish produce and fish. For instance, roasted fillet of sea trout, cocotte potatoes, samphire, basil oil red pepper purée. Vegetarian options are imaginative. Breakfast choices include eggs Benedict, smoked haddock, hash browns, scrambled tofu. 'Dinners were delightful, breakfasts excellent, and there was always a kindly greeting from whoever was on duty in the restaurant, the bar or reception.' (Peter Govier)

Cliff Road
Mullion Cove
TR12 7EP

T: 01326 240328
E: enquiries@mullion-cove.co.uk
W: www.mullion-cove.co.uk

BEDROOMS: 30. Some on ground floor.
OPEN: all year.
FACILITIES: lift, 3 lounges, bar, restaurant, free Wi-Fi, in-room TV (Freeview), 1-acre garden, 10-metre heated outdoor swimming pool, public areas wheelchair accessible.
BACKGROUND MUSIC: at meal times and in bar.
LOCATION: on edge of village
CHILDREN: all ages welcomed.
DOGS: allowed in some bedrooms, 1 lounge.
CREDIT CARDS: Amex, MasterCard, Visa.
PRICES: [2018] per room B&B single £85–£320, double £100–£335, D,B&B double £170–£405. Set dinner £42, à la carte £33. 1-night bookings sometimes refused Sat.

NEAR SAWREY Cumbria

Map 4: inset C2

EES WYKE COUNTRY HOUSE

'We will never tire of the stunning location, lovely rooms, superb food and excellent hospitality.' Praise in 2018 from readers for Richard Lee's Georgian country house overlooking Esthwaite Water. Others agree: 'A cosy hotel, fabulous views, friendly and helpful staff.' Beatrix Potter stayed three times on family holidays, when the house was called Lakefield; she bought her farmhouse close by, and thought Near Sawrey 'as nearly perfect a little place as I have ever lived in'. The lounges have the welcoming feel of a private home. The dining room and several bedrooms have views across the lake. Mr Lee's daily-changing menus include such dishes as roast duckling with thyme, ginger and honey sauce; grilled plaice, lemon, nut-brown butter. His 'dry sense of humour' amuses. 'When I complimented him on the sabayon sauce over ice cream and soft fruit, he murmured, "I just like the idea of hot custard over ice cream."' Breakfast includes home-baked pastries, freshly squeezed juices, local sausages. Fans will be sad to learn that the place is up for sale. Any buyer has 'a hard act to follow'. (Jenny and Ian Sherman, Alan and Nicky Brooks, AC)

Near Sawrey
LA22 0JZ

T: 015394 36393
E: mail@eeswyke.co.uk
W: www.eeswyke.co.uk

BEDROOMS: 8. 1 on ground floor. 6 en suite, 2 with separate private bathroom.
OPEN: all year, except Christmas.
FACILITIES: 2 lounges, restaurant, free Wi-Fi, in-room TV (Freeview), veranda, ½-acre garden, unsuitable for disabled.
BACKGROUND MUSIC: none.
LOCATION: edge of village 2½ miles SE of Hawkshead on B5285.
CHILDREN: not under 12.
DOGS: not allowed.
CREDIT CARDS: MasterCard, Visa.
PRICES: [2018] per room B&B single £65–£117, double £89–£155. Set dinner £30. 1-night bookings sometimes refused at weekends, bank holidays.

NETHER WESTCOTE Oxfordshire

Map 3:D6

THE FEATHERED NEST

♉ Previous César winner

Far-reaching views across sheep-spotted countryside spool away from this 'splendid' 300-year-old malthouse-turned-restaurant-with-rooms above the Evenlode valley. The panorama is an additional feather in the cap for owners Tony and Amanda Timmer, who gain praise for their 'warm welcome' and 'thoughtful hospitality' – as docs their 'Michelin-quality' restaurant. Raymond Blanc protégé chef Kuba Winkowski 'bakes, ferments, churns, cures, dry ages and smokes' everything in his 'stand-out' cuisine. His food is served in the 'pretty dining room' or out on the terrace and a minimalist approach is taken: scallops, air-dried ham, escabèche; celeriac, morels, egg yolk, wild garlic. 'His wonderful cooking deserves much wider recognition.' Downstairs, hand-pulled pints and a crackling fire in the popular, traditional pub (flagstone floors, sofas, cask-conditioned ales). Upstairs, 'well-equipped, spacious' bedrooms with a modern-rustic style; fresh flowers, plenty of books and magazines. 'Our room was lovely; we appreciated the strong walk-in shower, but the bath under the eaves was impractical for a tall person.' Next morning, a 'tasty breakfast'. (JH, and others)

Chipping Norton
Nether Westcote
OX7 6SD

T: 01993 833030
E: info@thefeatherednestinn.co.uk
W: www.thefeatherednestinn.co.uk

BEDROOMS: 4.
OPEN: closed 25 Dec, 2 weeks Feb, 2 weeks end of July, 1 week Oct, closed Mon/Tues/Wed apart from special trading days.
FACILITIES: 2 bars, small lounge, dining room, free Wi-Fi, in-room TV (Freeview), civil wedding licence, 45-acre grounds, restaurant and bar wheelchair accessible.
BACKGROUND MUSIC: in bar all day.
LOCATION: in hamlet, 5 miles S of Stow-on-the-Wold.
CHILDREN: 'all ages welcomed.
DOGS: allowed in bar, not in bedrooms.
CREDIT CARDS: Amex, MasterCard, Visa.
PRICES: [2018] per room B&B £245–£295, D,B&B £360–£410. Set dinner 4-course £65, 6-course £95.

NEW MILTON Hampshire

CHEWTON GLEN

After more than 50 years, this country house hotel
and spa on the edge of the New Forest still sets
the standard for luxury. From garden rooms with
balcony or terrace to tree-house suites with hot tub,
it has 'fabulous' accommodation. 'Everything is
taken care of from the minute you check in.' But
at this sister hotel to Cliveden House, Taplow (see
entry), luxury does not mean stuffy: 'It feels very
familiar – you're greeted with a smile and a hello.'
Staff are 'charming, efficient, friendly'. There are
children's welcome gifts, a kids' club, supervised
supper. All-day dining options include light bites in
The Pool bar, while The Kitchen restaurant (with
gleaming cookery school) serves informal fare.
In the dining room, executive head chef Simon
Addison and head chef Luke Matthews work
with local and home-grown produce to create
'memorable' dishes including Thai lobster curry;
slow-cooked ox cheek, celeriac and horseradish,
oxtail cromesquis. A rare note of dissent from a
Guide regular in 2018: a terrible breakfast croissant
and 'dinner service wasn't topnotch. Sky-high
prices lead to sky-high expectations, which are not
always fulfilled.' For most guests, however, it was
'perfect', 'super-relaxing'. (Debby Barry, Pauline
Weddell, and many more)

Christchurch Road
New Milton
BH25 6QS

T: 01425 275341
E: reservations@chewtonglen.com
W: www.chewtonglen.com

BEDROOMS: 72. 14 on ground floor,
14 tree-house suites in grounds,
1 suitable for disabled.
OPEN: all year.
FACILITIES: morning room, lounges,
bar, 2 restaurants, function rooms,
free Wi-Fi, in-room TV (Sky), civil
wedding licence, cookery school,
spa, indoor 17-metre swimming
pool, 130-acre grounds (outdoor
15-metre heated swimming pool,
tennis, par-3 golf course), public
rooms wheelchair accessible
BACKGROUND MUSIC: 'subtle' in
public areas.
LOCATION: on S edge of New Forest.
CHILDREN: all ages welcomed.
DOGS: allowed in tree-house suites,
on outdoor terraces.
CREDIT CARDS: Amex, MasterCard,
Visa.
PRICES: [2018] per room B&B
£370–£1,500, D,B&B £470–£1,620.
À la carte £60, tasting menu £70.

NEW ROMNEY Kent

Map 2:E5

ROMNEY BAY HOUSE

♀ Previous César winner

In the otherworldly landscape of Romney Marsh, this extraordinary 1920s house was built by Clough Williams Ellis for Hollywood actress Hedda Hopper. The isolated situation, between shingle beach and golf links, lend it special appeal. Run as a small hotel by Clinton and Lisa Lovell, 'it's very remote,' say readers who came for a honeymoon treat and were knocked out by the glamour. 'It's like walking on to the set of Poirot.' Guests gather at 7.30 for dinner at 8 pm, warmed by a log fire on cold days. 'We had drinks and delicious nibbles in the lounge and talked to two other couples.' A Guide regular in 2018 praised the 'warm welcome, nice staff'. On four nights a week, Mr Lovell, a classically trained chef, cooks a 'tasty, varied and beautifully presented' dinner. 'We had delicately flavoured salt marsh lamb. The service was beautiful.' The bedrooms – two with four-poster – are 'very comfortable', although one guest found the bathroom small, the decor 'a bit faded'. 'Romney Bay House marks the subtle but important difference between "smart casual" and "smart comfortable",' conclude other readers. (Gillian Rowe, IGC Farman, and others)

25% DISCOUNT VOUCHERS

Coast Road
New Romney
TN28 8QY

T: 01797 364747
E: enquiries@romneybayhouse
hotel.co.uk
w: www.romneybayhousehotel.
co.uk

BEDROOMS: 10.
OPEN: all year except Christmas and New Year, dining room open Tues/Wed/Fri/Sat evenings only.
FACILITIES: bar, sitting room, first-floor lounge with sea views, dining room, free Wi-Fi, in-room TV (Freeview), small function facilities, 1-acre garden, unsuitable for disabled.
BACKGROUND MUSIC: none.
LOCATION: 1½ miles from New Romney.
CHILDREN: not under 14.
DOGS: only registered guide dogs allowed.
CREDIT CARDS: Amex, MasterCard, Visa.
PRICES: [2018] per room B&B single £75–£95, double £95–£160. Set dinner £48. 1-night advance bookings refused weekends.

NEWBIGGIN-ON-LUNE Cumbria   Map 4:C3

BROWNBER HALL

Drawn by the possibilities for walking, climbing
and cycling, 'enthusiastic, hard-working'
Amanda Walker and Peter Jaques invite visitors
to share in Dales living at their lovingly restored
Victorian house. Guide inspectors praised the
many 'clever touches' from a thick, colourful
rope acting as the wall's handrail up the stairs,
to handmade cast iron wardrobes. Oblige the
'tempting' cakes, available in the reception
room (their sign says 'Please eat me'); carry on
into the book-lined sitting room, where drinks
are available from the vintage honesty bar, and
study the eclectic display of prints, watercolours,
etchings and photos. A curving staircase leads
up to 'well-designed' bedrooms, each with a
'comfortable' bed, 'good lighting' and 'plenty of
hot water'. A room at the front of the house will
let you wake to 'that wonderful view', all the
way to the North Pennines. Served in the 'light,
bright' dining room, on crisp linen, breakfast is
'excellent': 'delicious' local yogurt, fresh berries,
creamy scrambled eggs, 'proper' home-baked
sourdough bread, home-made marmalade –
splendid preparation for a hearty hike to the
Dales High Way, observed by resident red
squirrels and curious sheep.

Newbiggin-on-Lune
Cumbria
CA17 4NX

T: 01539 623208
E: enquiries@brownberhall.co.uk
W: www.brownberhall.co.uk

BEDROOMS: 8.
OPEN: all year except Christmas and
New Year.
FACILITIES: 2 lounges (log fire,
honesty bar), dining room, free
Wi-Fi, in-room TV (Freeview),
1-acre garden, bicycle storage,
unsuitable for disabled.
BACKGROUND MUSIC: all day in public
rooms.
LOCATION: 6¼ miles SW of Kirkby
Stephen – 'follow the hosts' clear
directions, not satnav'.
CHILDREN: all ages welcomed.
DOGS: allowed in 2 bedrooms, public
rooms.
CREDIT CARDS: MasterCard, Visa.
PRICES: [2018] per room B&B
£60–£180. 1-night bookings refused
on busy weekends.

NEWCASTLE UPON TYNE Tyne and Wear Map 4:B4

JESMOND DENE HOUSE

♥ Previous César winner

Above the dene (ravine with a stream), surrounded by 'attractive woodland', sits Peter Candler's 'impressive' 19th-century hotel. Guests praise the 'consistently attentive, friendly staff'; 'customer satisfaction is highly prized'. The rugged stone facade belies cosy interiors, where 'grand fireplaces' and 'comfortable seating' populate 'spacious' wood-panelled lounges. Chef Michael Penaluna's modern British dinner menu changes with the season. Typical dishes include 'small, but tasty' portions of Himalayan salt-aged flat-iron steak; mushroom, spinach, black truffle pithivier. 'The wine list is very good.' Bedrooms in the main house differ in size and shape – one might have a skylight or roof terrace; others large bay windows – while those in adjacent New House are cossetingly private. All have a supply of homely comforts including ground coffee, biscuits, fresh milk and good toiletries, and sport those contemporary essentials, a soft palette and lack of clutter. However, 'the bathroom could do with updating'. Breakfast, in a conservatory overlooking the garden, has 'an extensive buffet' and decent cooked options, along with 'pleasingly tart fresh orange juice'.

Jesmond Dene Road
Newcastle upon Tyne
NE2 2EY

T: 0191 212 3000
E: info@jesmonddenehouse.co.uk
W: www.jesmonddenehouse.co.uk

BEDROOMS: 40. 8 in adjacent New House, 2 suitable for disabled.
OPEN: all year.
FACILITIES: lift, lounge, cocktail bar, billiard room, restaurant, conference/function facilities, terrace, free Wi-Fi, in-room TV (Sky), civil wedding licence, parking, 2-acre garden, public areas accessible by wheelchair.
BACKGROUND MUSIC: in public areas and restaurant.
LOCATION: 2 miles from city centre.
CHILDREN: all ages welcomed.
DOGS: allowed in 1 New House bedroom.
CREDIT CARDS: Amex, MasterCard, Visa.
PRICES: [2018] per room B&B £113–£170, D,B&B £150–£270. Set dinner 2 courses £20, 3 courses £25, à la carte £45.

NEWMARKET Suffolk

THE PACKHORSE INN

A bit of country cool has turned a neglected
Victorian pub into a 'terrific' inn that retains its
village local cachet. Regular Guide readers this
year were 'charmed' by the staff and 'superb
food' at this 'jolly good joint', a member of Philip
Turner's Chestnut group. Antique paintings
of jockeys, flanking the entrance to the buzzy
former taproom beside a medieval packhorse
bridge, nod to nearby Newmarket Racecourse.
The 'well-decorated' bar and dining room are
chicly rustic, all scuffed wooden floors, country
tweeds and exposed brick. Spread across the main
building and the coach house, the bedrooms have
been decorated with 'great thought' ('though the
lighting had more style than substance'). Each has
cosy comforts, a goose-down duvet and mohair
throw on the large bed; a cascade shower and
freestanding bath in the well-equipped bathroom.
'There are no overnight staff (only an emergency
bell push).' At dinner, 'superb' modern European
cooking delivers roast Norfolk quail, pumpkin,
pickled walnut sauce; roast Denham estate
venison, salt-baked turnip, barley-and-mushroom
ragout. At breakfast, porridge and mixed berries,
Musk's sausages, streaky bacon, eggs all ways.
(John Barnes, and others)

Bridge Street
Newmarket
CB8 8SP

T: 01638 751818
E: info@thepackhorseinn.com
W: www.thepackhorseinn.com

BEDROOMS: 8. 4 on ground floor in
coach house suitable for disabled.
OPEN: all year.
FACILITIES: bar, restaurant, function
room, free Wi-Fi, in-room TV
(Freeview), courtyard.
BACKGROUND MUSIC: in public rooms.
LOCATION: opposite green in
Moulton village, 3 miles from
Newmarket.
CHILDREN: all ages welcomed.
DOGS: allowed in courtyard rooms
(£10 a night), restaurant and bar.
CREDIT CARDS: Amex, MasterCard,
Visa.
PRICES: [2018] per room B&B single
£85–£275, double £90–£275, D,B&B
double £130–£315. À la carte £40.

SEE ALSO SHORTLIST

NEWTON ABBOT Devon

Map 1:D4

THE ROCK INN

The tramway that once carried Dartmoor granite from the Stover Canal is no more, but this granite inn, built in 1820 along with quarry workers' cottages, still thrives. Set below Haytor rocks, it has been owned and run as a 'charming small hotel' by the Graves family since 1983. A trusted reader, who has known it for almost as long, assures us that it upholds its self-declared 'steadfastly traditional' values. Very affordable country-view rear-facing rooms look out over the moors. A front-facing garden-view room might have a four-poster. One room has a balcony, a large bathroom with bath and walk-in shower. All are traditionally styled, most with beams and other original features. Downstairs there are 'plenty of lovely, comfy' public rooms, supplied with books, board games, 'even jigsaw puzzles', while walkers are 'well catered for with maps and guidebooks'. Lunch, in the beamed bar, might be fish and chips, monkfish 'scampi', wild garlic linguine. At chef Josh Porter's dinner, served by 'attentive' staff, a short menu of imaginative dishes might include roasted bream fillet, bisque risotto, lemon, Parmesan, lovage oil. All the food is 'seriously good'. (DG)

Haytor Vale
Newton Abbot
TQ13 9XP

T: 01364 661305
E: enquiries@rock-inn.co.uk
W: www.rock-inn.co.uk

BEDROOMS: 9.
OPEN: all year except 25/26 Dec.
FACILITIES: bar, 3 dining rooms, lounge, free Wi-Fi, in-room TV (Freeview), ¼-acre garden, bar, 2 dining rooms, lounge wheelchair accessible, no adapted toilet.
BACKGROUND MUSIC: none.
LOCATION: 3 miles W of Bovey Tracey.
CHILDREN: all ages welcomed, not under 14 in main bar area.
DOGS: allowed in some bedrooms, bar, 1 dining room.
CREDIT CARDS: Diners, MasterCard, Visa.
PRICES: [2018] per room B&B single £80 (excl. weekends and bank hols), double £110–£170. À la carte £35 (fixed price £25, selected dishes from main menu). 1-night bookings sometimes refused.

NORTH WALSHAM Norfolk   Map 2:A6

BEECHWOOD HOTEL

'Well liked by traditionalists and locals', Emma
and Hugh Asher's creeper-smothered hotel in a
market town close to the coast was buzzing on
a Saturday night when Guide readers arrived.
'The door was opened for us, with offers to
carry our bags.' The bedroom had matching
curtains and bedcover, a large wardrobe, 'all
in good decorative order'. The bathroom had
a 'powerful walk-in shower, almost a water
cannon' and a freestanding bath. Some rooms
have a four-poster, some overlook lovely
gardens. In the bar, nuts, olives and warm
canapés were brought, as 'piano music drifted
from the dining room'. Photos in the lounge
recall that Agatha Christie stayed here often
when this was a private house. It is no mystery,
however, why 'the dining room was packed'.
Chef Steven Norgate, whose food attracts 'a
loyal following', wins praise for such dishes as
buttered tiger prawns, browned almonds, pea
shoot salad; halibut, wilted spinach, pea and
prawn risotto. 'There are terrific vegetarian
options – and it would be a crime not to go
for a pudding.' At breakfast, juices are freshly
squeezed, and the buffet and cooked dishes are
'top notch'. (MC, N and CH)

25% DISCOUNT VOUCHERS

20 Cromer Road
North Walsham
NR28 0HD

T: 01692 403231
E: info@beechwood-hotel.co.uk
W: www.beechwood-hotel.co.uk

BEDROOMS: 18. 4, on ground floor,
suitable for disabled.
OPEN: all year except 27/28 Dec.
FACILITIES: bar, 2 lounges,
restaurant, free Wi-Fi, in-room TV
(Freeview), 100-metre landscaped
garden (croquet).
BACKGROUND MUSIC: all day in public
rooms.
LOCATION: near town centre.
CHILDREN: all ages welcomed.
DOGS: allowed, not in restaurant.
CREDIT CARDS: Amex, MasterCard,
Visa.
PRICES: [2018] per room B&B single
£70, double £100–£175, single
occupancy of small double £90.
À la carte £40.

NORWICH Norfolk

Map 2:B5

THE ASSEMBLY HOUSE

Dripping with chandeliers, replete with plaster mouldings, this glorious Regency confection may have served as a camouflage factory in the Second World War, but these days it positively flaunts its opulence. An events venue hosting weddings, conferences and exhibitions, it serves food throughout the day to all comers, and has added a cookery school to its repertoire. Designer bedrooms in the east wing are 'fitted out most luxuriously and tastefully, with all mod cons'. Furniture is a mix of vintage and reproduction, 'a multi-coloured fabric headboard extending high up the wall, a glass chandelier'. Bathrooms have underfloor heating, a freestanding bath or daisy-head shower, decent toiletries. Six rooms have a small private garden. Breakfast includes omelette Arnold Bennett, huevos rancheros, a vegetarian fry-up with Norfolk rarebit. Later, one might look in for a Cromer crab sandwich or afternoon tea. Until 7 pm, the short supper menu includes such dishes as slow-cooked pork belly; butternut squash gnocchi; sirloin steak; Stilton and pear tart. 'Dining is less of a priority than event catering,' says a Guide insider, sensing a missed opportunity. But the Theatre Royal is next door, several good restaurants nearby.

Theatre Street
Norwich
NR2 1RQ

T: 01603 626402
E: admin@assemblyhousenorwich.co.uk
W: www.assemblyhousenorwich.co.uk

BEDROOMS: 11. All in St Mary's House extension, 6 with private garden, 2 suitable for disabled.
OPEN: all year.
FACILITIES: entrance hall, dining room, private dining and function rooms, civil wedding licence, free Wi-Fi, in-room TV (Sky, Freeview), 1-acre grounds, free permit parking, public rooms wheelchair accessible, adapted toilet.
BACKGROUND MUSIC: none.
LOCATION: central, car park permits for pay-and-display.
CHILDREN: all ages welcomed.
DOGS: not allowed.
CREDIT CARDS: Amex, MasterCard, Visa.
PRICES: [2018] per room B&B single £140–£240, double £170–£270. Fixed price supper £17–£22

SEE ALSO SHORTLIST

NORWICH Norfolk

Map 2:B5

THE OLD RECTORY

'Our praise for the very hospitable Chris and Sally Entwistle and their beautiful house,' writes one of many readers to commend this hotel. 'Excellent, welcoming and comfortable,' says another. An 'affable, chatty and warm' Mr Entwistle greeted Guide inspectors. Within the Georgian building, the style is 'traditional English', with 'lots of vintage porcelain character mugs on mantelpieces, classic pictures'. Bedrooms, in the rectory or Victorian coach house, are individually styled. Most have a garden view. Our inspectors' room 'felt a little old-fashioned, though not worn or shabby', with a 'spacious, comfortable seating area'; its 'good-sized' bathroom had a walk-in shower and a corner bath, 'which looked lovely but you couldn't lie down in it'. In the intimate dining room, James Perry cooks an 'imaginative, well-presented' three-course dinner. Perhaps medallions of Attleborough beef fillet, thyme mash, spiced greens, red wine, shallot and root vegetable sauce. Everything proved 'delicious', but one reader was surprised to find the same menu on consecutive nights. Breakfast included 'perfectly cooked porridge', 'plentiful and characterful' cooked dishes. (Keith Salway, Jill and Mike Bennett, and others)

103 Yarmouth Road
Norwich
NR7 0HF

T: 01603 700772
E: enquiries@oldrectorynorwich.com
W: www.oldrectorynorwich.com

BEDROOMS: 8. 3 in coach house.
OPEN: all year except Christmas/New Year, restaurant closed Sun and Mon.
FACILITIES: drawing room, conservatory, dining room, free Wi-Fi, in-room TV (Freeview), 1-acre garden, unheated swimming pool, unsuitable for disabled.
BACKGROUND MUSIC: classical/jazz in drawing room and dining room at night.
LOCATION: 2 miles E of Norwich.
CHILDREN: all ages welcomed.
DOGS: only assistance dogs allowed.
CREDIT CARDS: all major cards.
PRICES: [2018] per room B&B single £95–£150, double £125–£185, D,B&B add £28 per person. Set dinner £35. 1-night bookings refused Sat May–Sept.

SEE ALSO SHORTLIST

NORWICH Norfolk

Map 2:B5

38 ST GILES

In a 'lovely old building' a stroll from marketplace, cathedral and castle, this upmarket B&B is run with commitment and enthusiasm by father and daughter Dennis and Holly Bacon. Built in 1700 for the Gurney banking family, the house has many original features – fireplaces, ceiling friezes, wall panelling. The pristine and stylish bedrooms are supplied with fresh flowers, French toiletries. Spacious St Giles suite has a cast iron bed, glass doors to a bathroom with freestanding bath and separate shower area. Further accommodation, ideal for a family, is available in a Georgian town house and an apartment nearby. New arrivals are welcomed with tea and home-made cake in a sitting room with 'leather and green tweed chesterfield sofas, a table with reading material'. Breakfast, in the 'elegant dining room', is 'exceptional', with freshly squeezed orange juice, organic eggs, whisky-smoked salmon, Norfolk bacon, pancakes with Greek yogurt, maple syrup and berries, all served by 'pleasant, friendly young people'. Afterwards, 'there was no hurry to get us out. We wanted to explore. They stored our luggage and allowed us to leave our car in their car park until 3 pm.'

38 St Giles Street
Norwich
NR2 1LL

T: 01603 662944
E: booking@38stgiles.co.uk
W: www.38stgiles.co.uk

BEDROOMS: 12. 1 on ground floor, 4 in apartment and town house.
OPEN: all year except 24–28 Dec.
FACILITIES: breakfast room, lounge, free Wi-Fi, in-room TV (Freeview), courtyard garden, limited pre-booked private parking £15 per day, unsuitable for disabled.
BACKGROUND MUSIC: Radio 3 at breakfast.
LOCATION: central, limited private parking (advance booking, £15 per day).
CHILDREN: all ages welcomed.
DOGS: not allowed.
CREDIT CARDS: MasterCard, Visa.
PRICES: [2018] per room B&B single £95–£195, double £120–£245, town house (2 doubles) from £250, apartment (2 doubles) from £300.

SEE ALSO SHORTLIST

NOTTINGHAM Nottinghamshire   Map 2:A3

HART'S HOTEL

Returning guests in 2018 'enjoyed a relaxing time in warmth and comfort' at Tim Hart's purpose-built hotel, on the former ramparts of Nottingham's medieval castle. The 'universally helpful, friendly' staff were especially praised. In lieu of a lounge, there is the bar, where light bites can be ordered; a hillside garden is a cloistering spot for afternoon tea. The restaurant is housed in a separate building, just across the road. Chef Daniel Burridge whips up a 'high-quality, appetising' modern menu ('although only one of the mains changed daily'). The bedrooms 'aren't especially spacious', but have 'a comfortable bed and wonderful distant views across the city'. Breakfast is an event ('a dedicated staff member cuts and prepares toast using first-class bread from Hart's Hambleton Bakery'): 'freshly squeezed juice, spicy sausages, thick rashers of succulent bacon, perfect, molten scrambled egg; however, it was a red card for the cafetière in which a tea "of personality" was served, substituted by a teapot'. The central location 'makes it a clear choice for business travel and parents visiting offspring at university'. Hambleton Hall, Hambleton (see entry), has the same owners. (Robert Gower, and others)

Standard Hill
Nottingham
NG1 6GN

T: 0115 988 1900
E: reception@hartshotel.co.uk
W: www.hartsnottingham.co.uk

BEDROOMS: 32. 2 suitable for disabled.
OPEN: all year, restaurant closed 1 Jan.
FACILITIES: lift, reception/lobby with seating, bar, restaurant (30 yds), free Wi-Fi, in-room TV (Sky, Freeview), conference/banqueting facilities, small exercise room, civil wedding licence, courtyard, private garden, secure car park.
BACKGROUND MUSIC: 'light' in bar.
LOCATION: city centre.
CHILDREN: all ages welcomed.
DOGS: allowed in public rooms and bedrooms (not left unattended).
CREDIT CARDS: Amex, MasterCard, Visa.
PRICES: [2018] room from £134. Set dinner £24–£30, à la carte £38.

OLD HUNSTANTON Norfolk

Map 2:A5

THE NEPTUNE

'A restaurant-with-rooms – and a very good restaurant at that.' After visiting this year, a trusted reader sums up the appeal of Kevin (the chef) and Jacki Mangeolles's 18th-century former coaching inn. Michelin agrees, having awarded a star for the last nine years to contemporary British cuisine that exploits locally landed seafood, Norfolk pork and game from surrounding estates. 'Kevin even has time to come out of the kitchen and help serve', perhaps rabbit loin, confit of leg, hispi cabbage, carrot and ginger purée; gurnard fillets, Brancaster mussels, baked leek, pink fir apple potato, broccoli purée, salsify. 'The excellent hosts give personal attention to their guests – that always makes a hotel special.' Away from the dining room with its Lloyd Loom chairs, crisp white tablecloths and muted walls, there are light, airy, 'spotless', 'very comfortable' rooms with 'good bedside lighting and plenty of coat-hangers'. Breakfast includes home-baked croissants and decent cooked dishes. 'What comes across is Kevin and Jacki's undimmed enthusiasm. There's a genuine interest in food, constant search for new ideas, and no sign of complacency.' (Bill Wood, and others)

85 Old Hunstanton Road
Old Hunstanton
PE36 6HZ

T: 01485 532122
E: reservations@theneptune.co.uk
W: www.theneptune.co.uk

BEDROOMS: 4.
OPEN: all year, except 26 Dec, 3 weeks Jan, 1 week May, 1 week Nov, Mon.
FACILITIES: 2 bar areas, restaurant, free Wi-Fi, in-room TV (Freeview), unsuitable for disabled.
BACKGROUND MUSIC: in restaurant in evening.
LOCATION: village centre, on A149.
CHILDREN: not under 10.
DOGS: not allowed.
CREDIT CARDS: Amex, MasterCard, Visa.
PRICES: [2018] per room D,B&B £270–£300 (add £40 for tasting menus). Set menus £62–£78, à la carte £62. 1-night bookings sometimes refused Sat.

OLDSTEAD Yorkshire

Map 4:D4

THE BLACK SWAN
AT OLDSTEAD

♛ Previous César winner

'The progress made by a family of farmers who thought that they would like to run a restaurant is quite remarkable.' A reader reflects on the Banks family's transformation of a failing rural pub into a Michelin-starred restaurant-with-rooms. The concept is simple enough – work with what you grow, raise or forage; pick and pickle, age, ferment… But Tommy Banks pushes the boundaries of modern British cooking, with such dishes as langoustine and salted strawberry; raw deer with wild garlic; crapaudine beetroot slow-cooked in beef fat. According to a poll in 2017, this is the best restaurant in the world, no less. 'I wouldn't put it quite as high as that,' another reader demurs. And while 'the tasting menu was excellent', there was 'total confusion' over a booking. Still, the staff are 'charming, highly professional, helpful and knowledgeable'. In an annexe wing, ground-floor bedrooms overlook the kitchen garden, source of inspiration and extraordinary produce (even the lemons are home grown). Rooms in a nearby Georgian house have a feature bath and separate wet room. 'A delightful place to stay.' (Robert Cooper, Bill Wood, FM)

Oldstead
YO61 4BL

T: 01347 868387
E: reception@blackswanoldstead.co.uk
W: www.blackswanoldstead.co.uk

BEDROOMS: 9. 4, on ground floor, in annexe, 5 in Ashberry House, 50 yds away.
OPEN: all year except 23–27 Dec.
FACILITIES: bar, restaurant, private dining room, free Wi-Fi, in-room TV (Freeview), garden, 2-acre kitchen garden and orchard.
BACKGROUND MUSIC: in restaurant.
LOCATION: in village 7 miles E of Thirsk.
CHILDREN: not allowed to stay overnight, over 10 only in restaurant.
DOGS: not allowed.
CREDIT CARDS: MasterCard, Visa.
PRICES: [2018] per room D,B&B £390–£480. Tasting menu £98–£110.

ORFORD Suffolk

Map 2:C6

THE CROWN AND CASTLE

♔ Previous César winner

There have been changes at this 'comfortable, well-run' restaurant-with-rooms in a small coastal town dominated by its 12th-century castle. The Watsons have sold their interest to TA Collection, but indomitable Ruth Watson has been retained as food director, her voice coming through clear, conversational as ever, while erstwhile partner Tim Sunderland is at the helm of what is now TA's flagship. There may have been the odd changeover hiccup – a report of a disappointing room and undercooked lamb – but 'it was lovely as ever,' writes one regular visitor, 'same well-trained, friendly, welcoming staff'. Another fan on a return visit had a garden room, 'recently renovated', a bed 'particularly comfortable'. As Mrs Watson says, 'Really, nothing has changed.' In the refurbished dining room, staggered mealtimes allow guests to enjoy pre-dinner drinks in the 'tiny' bar. Locally sourced ingredients grace such 'excellent' dishes as Orford-landed skate, sautéed grapes and almonds, black butter. There are menus for vegetarians and vegans. 'Alan Bennett was a fellow guest – what more could you want?' (John Saul, Frances Thomas, Michael Gwinnell, and others)

Market Hill
Orford
IP12 2LJ

T: 01394 450205
E: info@crownandcastle.co.uk
W: www.crownandcastle.co.uk

BEDROOMS: 21. 10 (all on ground floor) in garden, 2 (on ground floor) in terrace, 1 in courtyard, 1 suite in stable block.
OPEN: all year.
FACILITIES: hall, bar, restaurant, private dining room (wheelchair access), free Wi-Fi, in-room TV (Freeview), limited on-site parking, ¼-acre garden.
BACKGROUND MUSIC: none.
LOCATION: market square, about 100 yds from the castle.
CHILDREN: not allowed to stay overnight.
DOGS: allowed in 5 garden rooms, at 'doggie table' in restaurant.
CREDIT CARDS: MasterCard, Visa.
PRICES: [2018] per room B&B £140–£250, D,B&B £200–£310. À la carte £38. 1-night bookings refused Fri/Sat.

OSWESTRY Shropshire

Map 3:B4

PEN-Y-DYFFRYN

'We always look forward to staying.' Miles and Audrey Hunter's 'tranquil' small hotel on the Welsh border received a flurry of praise from new and regular visitors this year. 'After a trying journey, we were ushered in by unfailingly pleasant staff. Memories of the drive were already fading by the time we reached our room.' In the 'warm, welcoming' lounge, daily newsletters, maps and guidebooks help plan the day, aided by log fires, newspapers and big armchairs. However, on a return visit in 2018, one Guide regular found the lounge 'still rather cold for relaxing'. Individually styled bedrooms, with newly upgraded en suite shower, are peaceful and 'spotless'. 'Our beautiful room had plenty of space, splendid views, a private terrace and an efficient bathroom with lovely toiletries.' Outdoor seating is a 'restful' place to while away the afternoon before (newly promoted) chef Alex Lloyd gives British concoctions a modern twist – 'a joy'. 'Breakfasts were as appetising as ever, with several new options since our last stay, including avocado on sourdough with grilled bacon. The poached eggs (my test for quality) were excellent.' 'I want to go back now!' (Bob and Jean Henry, Mary Hewson, and others)

25% DISCOUNT VOUCHERS

Rhydycroesau
Oswestry
SY10 7JD

T: 01691 653700
E: stay@peny.co.uk
W: www.peny.co.uk

BEDROOMS: 12. 4, each with patio, in coach house, 1 on ground floor.
OPEN: all year except Christmas.
FACILITIES: 2 lounges, bar, restaurant, free Wi-Fi, in-room TV (Freeview), 5-acre grounds (summer house, dog-walking area, fly-fishing pool).
BACKGROUND MUSIC: in evening in bar and restaurant.
LOCATION: 3 miles W of Oswestry.
CHILDREN: not under 3.
DOGS: allowed in some bedrooms, not in public rooms after 6.30 pm.
CREDIT CARDS: MasterCard, Visa.
PRICES: [2018] per person B&B £70–£105, D,B&B £97–£150, single occupancy £99–£120. Set menu £44. 1-night bookings occasionally refused Sat.

OXFORD Oxfordshire

Map 2:C2

OLD BANK HOTEL

♀ Previous César winner

A former draper's and mercer's-turned-bank, opposite the Bodleian Library, is these days a smart bar, restaurant and hotel. Owner Jeremy Mogford (see also next entry) founded the Browns restaurant chain in the 1970s. His interest in art and literature are here reflected in the inclusion of a library overlooking the Italianate garden terrace, and modern artwork from his private collection that adorn walls throughout. Since last year, several bedrooms have been 'refreshed'. A new rooftop room has panoramic city views. All have a handmade bed and marble bathroom, and are supplied with fresh flowers, a minibar and complimentary mineral water. There are no residents' lounges, but chef Rohan Kashid's food is served all day in the bar and Quod restaurant. 'We had a very pleasant meal in the courtyard,' write readers this year. 'Good, friendly service and cooking that was appetising without being sensational.' Typical choices: ricotta and spinach ravioli, wild nettles, pine nuts; shoulder of lamb, cannellini beans, anchovy, olive. Breakfast, served until 11 am, includes cold-pressed juices, banana pancakes, vanilla porridge, hand-picked crab and avocado on sourdough. (Robert Gower)

92–94 High Street
Oxford
OX1 4BJ

T: 01865 799599
E: reception@oldbank-hotel.co.uk
W: www.oldbank-hotel.co.uk

BEDROOMS: 42. 1 suitable for disabled.
OPEN: all year.
FACILITIES: lift, residents' library/bar, bar, dining terrace, 2 meeting/private dining rooms, free Wi-Fi, in-room TV (Freeview), small garden, use of bicycles, restaurant, bar wheelchair accessible, adapted toilet.
BACKGROUND MUSIC: in restaurant and reception area.
LOCATION: central, car park.
CHILDREN: all ages welcomed.
DOGS: allowed on terrace only.
CREDIT CARDS: Amex, MasterCard, Visa.
PRICES: [2018] room £195– £1,200. Breakfast à la carte (full English) £15, à la carte £40 (plus 12½% discretionary service charge). 1-night bookings refused at weekends in peak season.

SEE ALSO SHORTLIST

OXFORD Oxfordshire

OLD PARSONAGE HOTEL

'We visit Oxford every year and the Old Parsonage never disappoints.' The loyal returning visitor to Jeremy Mogford's 'excellent' upmarket hotel, with its artistic and literary flourishes, joins an eclectic list of residents. The much-extended 17th-century property has housed two mayors, a wig-maker, and a student called Oscar Wilde. In 2018, guests laud its 'good rooms, very good food and wine, first-class service and buzzy atmosphere'. Many original features, including the heavy oak door, the entrance hall's stone-arched fireplace and carved saints in the front window jambs, are complemented by contemporary architectural additions. The bright, modern glass-metal-and-wood library contains a thoughtfully curated book collection and photos of 1960s Oxford. 'One would like to spend days there, just reading and enjoying the decor.' The 'charming' restaurant has 'informal seating' and 'charcoal-grey walls hung with portraits'. New chef Allan McLaughlin gives a light touch to British classics, perhaps river trout fillet, heritage potatoes and crayfish tails. 'Comfortable' bedrooms are 'nicely furnished, well equipped and blissfully quiet – once the "sport" of campanology ceased at a nearby church'. (CR, and others)

1 Banbury Road
Oxford
OX2 6NN

T: 01865 310210
E: reception@oldparsonage-hotel.co.uk
W: www.oldparsonage-hotel.co.uk

BEDROOMS: 35. 10 on ground floor, 2 suitable for disabled.
OPEN: all year.
FACILITIES: lounge, library, bar/restaurant, free Wi-Fi, in-room TV (Freeview), civil wedding licence, terrace, rear garden with summerhouse, restaurant wheelchair accessible.
BACKGROUND MUSIC: 'very light' in restaurant and bar.
LOCATION: NE end of St Giles, small car park.
CHILDREN: all ages welcomed.
DOGS: allowed on terrace only.
CREDIT CARDS: Amex, MasterCard, Visa.
PRICES: [2018] per room B&B from £225, D,B&B from £299. À la carte £35 (plus 12½% discretionary service charge). 1-night bookings sometimes refused peak weekends.

SEE ALSO SHORTLIST

PADSTOW Cornwall

Map 1:D2

PADSTOW TOWNHOUSE

Not so much a restaurant-with-rooms as six rooms with two restaurants, this luxurious B&B is the creation of chef Paul Ainsworth and his wife, Emma. In a Georgian town house, six suites have been individually and opulently styled, with rich fabrics, modern artwork, perhaps a double rain-head shower, a separate lounge/dining area. Readers this year stayed in Honeycomb, with a wrought iron bed, gold and white double bath and double shower. 'Our room was serviced on every occasion we went out… fresh milk constantly replenished.' The honesty pantry operates as a 'deluxe tuckshop', where guests help themselves to home-made cake ('a little expensive at £6'), a Cornish cream tea, a glass of wine. 'We loved making our own cocktail with the huge array of ingredients.' There are bikes to borrow, picnic hampers to order. A chauffeured electric car zips you to breakfast, and maybe a Michelin-starred dinner down the hill at No. 6 (a typical dish: white crab, leek royale, jack shell gravy) or Italian fare at sister restaurant, Rojano's. 'Above all else, what will be remembered here was the outstanding level of service.' (Kevin and Victoria Seymour)

16–18 High Street
Padstow
PL28 8BB

T: 01841 550950
E: stay@padstowtownhouse.co.uk
W: www.padstowtownhouse.co.uk

BEDROOMS: 6. 2 on ground floor.
OPEN: all year except 24–26 Dec, 4 days Jan, open for New Year.
FACILITIES: honesty pantry, free Wi-Fi, in-room Smart TV, in-room spa treatments, electric car for guest transport, on-site car park.
BACKGROUND MUSIC: in reception and kitchen pantry area.
LOCATION: in old town, 5 mins' walk from harbour.
CHILDREN: not under 16.
DOGS: not allowed.
CREDIT CARDS: MasterCard, Visa.
PRICES: [2018] per suite B&B £280–£380. À la carte (Paul Ainsworth at No. 6) £75.

PADSTOW Cornwall

Map 1:D2

THE SEAFOOD RESTAURANT

You might find Cornish lamb on the menu at Rick and Jill Stein's flagship in a harbour town on the Camel estuary, but it is for fish and shellfish that fans have flocked since the chef transformed a dodgy nightclub into a basic hotel in 1975. After his countless TV appearances and cookbooks, that hotel has grown up to become a boutique restaurant-with-rooms. Coastal-inspired bedrooms are designed by Jill Stein. Guide insiders chose one with estuary view, good bed, 'large, comfy sofa', freestanding bath, separate shower. Even 'cosy' rooms have fresh milk, ground coffee, Stein biscuits, own-brand toiletries. Master rooms have a private terrace, perhaps a modern four-poster. In a 'spectacular' dining room hung with modern art, over-18s can perch at the seafood bar, while diners at tables enjoy chef Stephane Delourme's accomplished cooking, from hake and chips to turbot with hollandaise, Singapore chilli crab or tempting vegetarian options. Breakfast brings crab omelette, smoked haddock, grilled fish of the day. Then, should you want to 'eat out', you might sample the sister café, bistro, seafood bar or chippy – no wonder they call this Padstein! (Richard Creed)

Riverside
Padstow
PL28 8BY

T: 01841 532700
E: reservations@rickstein.com
W: www.rickstein.com/stay/
the-seafood-restaurant/

BEDROOMS: 16.
OPEN: all year except 24–26 Dec.
FACILITIES: lift, lounge, reading room, restaurant, free Wi-Fi, in-room TV (Freeview), restaurant and toilet wheelchair accessible.
BACKGROUND MUSIC: in restaurant.
LOCATION: town centre.
CHILDREN: all ages welcomed, not under 3 in restaurant.
DOGS: welcomed in some bedrooms (dog-sitting service).
CREDIT CARDS: Amex, MasterCard, Visa.
PRICES: [2018] per room B&B £165–£320, D,B&B from £235. À la carte £65. 1-night bookings refused Sat.

PAINSWICK Gloucestershire

THE PAINSWICK

'In a pretty south-Cotswolds village', this is a 'fun, relaxing place'. A Palladian mansion with Arts and Crafts refinements and an Italianate loggia, it was recently made over for the Calcot Collection (see Calcot Manor, Lord Crewe Arms). 'A splendid lounge had views out to the garden and a huge fireplace with a roaring log fire'; the cocktail bar was 'glamorous and exciting'. Bedrooms, some in separate wings, are decorated in restful, neutral shades. One suite has a log-burner, a stone balcony. One reader's room had 'mullioned windows looking over the garden and two terraces, to the valley and hills behind'. There was an espresso machine, while 'a little box called Chef's Delight held a cake and a biscuit'. At dinner in the 'large, high-ceilinged restaurant' or alfresco, new chef Jamie McCallum's imaginative cooking includes such dishes as rack of Cotswold lamb, crisp belly, roast artichoke, sand carrot, ricotta, morels; from the vegetarian menu, herb gnocchi, roast artichoke, purple sprouting broccoli. At breakfast, there are kippers, home-made crumpets, smoked salmon. Be aware: 'As it's on a steep slope, there are steps everywhere.' (JG, and others)

Kemps Lane
Painswick
GL6 6YB

T: 01452 813688
E: enquiries@thepainswick.co.uk
W: www.thepainswick.co.uk

BEDROOMS: 16. 7 in garden wing, 4 in chapel wing.
OPEN: all year.
FACILITIES: bar, lounge, restaurant, games room, private dining room, free Wi-Fi, in-room TV (Sky, Freeview), civil wedding licence, terrace, beauty treatment rooms, ¾-acre garden, unsuitable for disabled.
BACKGROUND MUSIC: all day in public areas.
LOCATION: in village 5 miles NE of Stroud.
CHILDREN: all ages welcomed.
DOGS: allowed in some garden rooms, on terrace, in lounge (£15 per night).
CREDIT CARDS: Amex, MasterCard, Visa.
PRICES: [2018] room £149–£404. Continental breakfast £6, cooked dishes £6–£12, à la carte dinner £40. 1-night bookings refused weekends.

PENRITH Cumbria

ASKHAM HALL

An easy-going atmosphere and oodles of
character filter through Charles Lowther's
dramatic ancestral home. As one Guide reader
contentedly observed, the discreet staff and
'shabby-chic style' contribute to its feeling
'more like staying at a grand house than a
hotel'. There is an honesty bar by the log fire,
stacks of modern art and old photographs.
The 'comfortable, classy' bedrooms have an
eclectic country house style: a four-poster
bed, an antique bath, a separate WC in an
old 'priest hole' carved into the wall, views
across the 17th-century topiary garden. In the
conservatory dining room, 'the food is excellent,
the staff friendly and attentive'. Richard Swales,
'a real wizard', serves 'delightfully balanced
and creative' combinations of unusual, locally
procured produce: perhaps home-reared
chicken, cauliflower cheese, truffle; followed
by geranium set cream, Yorkshire rhubarb,
blood orange and Campari granita. Don't miss
the quintessentially English terraces, woodland
walks or kitchen garden next to fields of goats,
ducks and rare-breed pigs. 'A wonderful
experience,' writes a reader in 2018. 'Heartily
recommended.' (K and JP)

Askham
Penrith
CA10 2PF

T: 01931 712350
E: enquiries@askhamhall.co.uk
W: www.askhamhall.co.uk

BEDROOMS: 18. 2 suitable for
disabled.
OPEN: all year except Christmas,
early Jan to mid-Feb, restaurant
closed Sun/Mon.
FACILITIES: drawing room, library,
billiard room, 3 dining rooms, free
Wi-Fi, in-room TV (Freeview),
civil wedding licence, 12-acre
grounds, spa, 10 by 5 metre heated
outdoor swimming pool (Apr–Oct),
restaurant suitable for disabled.
BACKGROUND MUSIC: in reception
rooms in evening.
LOCATION: 10 mins from Penrith
and junction 40 on M6.
CHILDREN: all ages welcomed.
DOGS: allowed in bedrooms and
public rooms, not in restaurant.
CREDIT CARDS: all major cards.
PRICES: [2018] per room B&B single
£138–£308, double £150–£320,
D,B&B £250–£420. À la carte £50.

SEE ALSO SHORTLIST

PENRITH Cumbria

Map 4: inset C2

TEBAY SERVICES HOTEL

'Comfortable, warm and reliable,' say readers this year, who stayed, on journeys north and south, at the Dunning family's hotel with farm shop off the M6. 'The staff are friendly and efficient, the rooms are simple but have all the necessary "functions" and great views over the Cumbrian moorlands, away from noise of motorway traffic.' In a modern, Alpine-inspired building, a big, informal lounge is the place to relax after hours on the road, with books and board games to amuse children. We hear regular praise for the sense of 'complete well-being', the 'special character', the 'comfortable' rooms. Since last year, double beds have been upgraded to super-king-size, single beds to ones with extra length; and classic rooms have a new carpet. 'Home-made biscuits were supplied with the tea tray.' The owners are hill farmers with a deep respect for produce and provenance. Their beef and lamb features in chef Garry Fothergill's seasonal menus, served in the restaurant with 'far-reaching views'. 'We enjoyed potted shrimps; pigeon; hogget lamb and mushroom.' 'Breakfast is buffet style but again serves quality foods. We will return.' (GC, S and MT, D and JB)

nr Orton
Penrith
CA10 3SB

T: 01539 624351
E: reservations@tebayserviceshotel.
   com
W: www.tebayserviceshotel.com

BEDROOMS: 51. 1 suitable for disabled.
OPEN: all year except Christmas.
FACILITIES: lounge with log fire, bar, mezzanine, restaurant, free Wi-Fi, in-room TV, function/conference facilities, farm shop, restaurant, bar and lounge wheelchair accessible, adapted toilet.
BACKGROUND MUSIC: none.
LOCATION: 2½ miles SW of Orton.
CHILDREN: all ages welcomed (family rooms with bunk beds).
DOGS: allowed in some bedrooms (£10 per dog per night, max. 2 dogs), and in one area of lounge.
CREDIT CARDS: Amex, MasterCard, Visa.
PRICES: [2018] per room B&B double £107–£149, family room £137–£144. À la carte £30.

SEE ALSO SHORTLIST

PENSFORD Somerset

THE PIG NEAR BATH

You know where you are with a Pig. The style set by Robin Hutson at The Pig in the Forest, Brockenhurst (see entry), is brilliantly carried off at this Georgian manor house in the Mendips. 'Now this is how to do shabby-chic! Staff, mostly young, are brilliant, the house is handsome and dignified but the atmosphere is buzzy.' Bedrooms have a walk-in monsoon shower, a Nespresso machine, a larder of snacks, 'loads of extras'. 'Ours was exceedingly comfortable, with views of free-range chickens on one side, free-range deer on the other.' The conservatory dining room has 'a greenhouse feel, with beetroot, lettuce and other seedlings "brought on" in pots'. A merry cacophony is created by the acoustics: 'Stone floors, brick walls, wooden tables, rusting metal chairs. An atmosphere place.' Chef Kamil Oseka uses produce from the Victorian greenhouses and walled kitchen garden in such dishes as day-boat plaice, lemon butter sauce, ruby chard, monk's beard; chargrilled pork cutlet, minted potato salad, fruit-cage currant sauce. At breakfast there is 'a fine range of breads and pastries'. (Lindsay Hunt and John Fisher, Andrew Butterworth, and others)

Hunstrete House
Pensford
BS39 4NS

T: 01761 490490
E: reservations@thepighotel.com
W: www.thepighotel.com

BEDROOMS: 29. 5 in gardens, some on ground floor, 1 suitable for disabled.
OPEN: all year.
FACILITIES: 2 lounges, bar, restaurant, snug, private dining room, free Wi-Fi, in-room TV (Freeview), civil wedding licence, treatment room, kitchen garden, wild flower meadow, deer park.
BACKGROUND MUSIC: all day in public areas.
LOCATION: 7 miles SW of Bath.
CHILDREN: all ages welcomed.
DOGS: not allowed.
CREDIT CARDS: Amex, MasterCard, Visa.
PRICES: [2018] room £155–£330. Breakfast £10–£15, à la carte £35. 1-night bookings refused weekends, Christmas/New Year.

PENTON Cumbria

Map 4:B2

♛PENTONBRIDGE INN   NEW

César award: newcomer of the year

'Jake and Cassie White have created a gourmet destination in a lonely pub at a crossroads just to the south of the Scottish moors,' write Guide inspectors this year. The pair worked as head chef and pastry chef for Marcus Wareing in London, and have 'completely refurbished' this formerly run-down pub. Most of the bedrooms are in the main building, some on the ground floor, some up 'imposing, glass-walled stairs'. Three are in a converted barn. 'Our first-floor room had fine countryside views, though the traditional old windows were set low so you had to sit down to see out. The bathroom had a large freestanding bath and separate wet-room shower.' All rooms have fresh flowers, freshly baked biscuits or home-made preserves to take home. They are attractive, but 'food is the raison d'être', whether 'interesting pub fare' (perhaps venison ragout with papardelle), or more ambitious dishes from the dining area's daily-changing menu – 'fabulous monkfish, mussels and beurre blanc', say, or 'perfect rare beef fillet, crushed Jersey Royals', kale from the Whites' Victorian kitchen garden at nearby Netherby Hall. 'This is a serious restaurant-with-rooms.'

Pentonbridge Inn
Penton
CA6 5QB

T: 01228 586636
E: info@pentonbridgeinn.co.uk
W: pentonbridgeinn.co.uk

BEDROOMS: 9. 3 in converted barn, covered walkway from reception, 3 on ground floor.
OPEN: all year, restaurant closed Mon/Tues.
FACILITIES: bar, restaurant, conservatory, free Wi-Fi, in-room TV (Freeview), bar and conservatory wheelchair accessible (restaurant menu available), adapted toilet.
BACKGROUND MUSIC: in bar and conservatory.
LOCATION: rural, 10 mins from Longtown.
CHILDREN: all ages welcomed.
DOGS: allowed in 8 bedrooms, bar and conservatory, not in restaurant.
CREDIT CARDS: Amex, MasterCard, Visa.
PRICES: [2018] per person B&B £99–£200, D,B&B £260. Set dinner £46, tasting menu £60, à la carte (pub) £30.

PENZANCE Cornwall

Map 1:E1

CHAPEL HOUSE

'I have travelled widely but never stayed in a place where I truly felt I was with a close friend.' Owner Susan Stuart 'has created a real treat', says a Guide regular after this year's visit to the 'beautifully restored listed house'. After 'a great welcome and offer of tea and chocolate or fruit cake, to a chilled glass of Prosecco to wish us well on our journey, she goes far beyond what one would expect' – including an introduction to the person behind the Tremenheere Sculpture Gardens. The former Georgian Admiral's house is now a 'beautifully appointed' B&B with contemporary and antique furniture, fresh flowers, and a calming coastal palette. Bedrooms are 'spacious and special, each one with a quirk'. A bathroom with retractable glass roof, contemporary four-poster, an egg-shaped in-room bath. 'Our room on the top floor had lovely harbour views even from the shower.' Susan's 'marvellous, impossibly good-value' communal dinner includes produce from local butchers, farmers, fishmongers and vineyards. Breakfast is fresh 'to the extent of the whole piece of fish being shown to my wife before cooking'. (David Soanes, David Britton)

Chapel Street
Penzance
TR18 4AQ

T: 01736 362024
E: hello@chapelhousepz.co.uk
W: www.chapelhousepz.co.uk

BEDROOMS: 6.
OPEN: all year, kitchen closed for dinner Sun–Thurs, but open for drinks all week.
FACILITIES: drawing room, open-plan kitchen/dining area, free Wi-Fi, in-room TV (Freeview), function facilities, terrace, garden, unsuitable for disabled.
BACKGROUND MUSIC: none.
LOCATION: town centre.
CHILDREN: all ages welcomed.
DOGS: allowed in bedrooms and public areas and in kitchen/dining area with consent of other guests.
CREDIT CARDS: MasterCard, Visa.
PRICES: [2018] per room B&B single £125–£165, double £150–£210. Set dinner £28. 1-night bookings refused 23 Dec–2 Jan, bank holiday weekends.

SEE ALSO SHORTLIST

PENZANCE Cornwall

Map 1:E1

TREREIFE

An Elizabethan farmhouse remodelled in the reign of Queen Anne, 'Treeve' has been home to the Le Grice family since 1796. The 'fantastic, large home' overlooks a large parterre in extensive parkland. Both house and gardens are opened for guided tours, and this is a popular wedding venue. Public rooms are filled with antiques – oak furniture, ancestral portraits, a grandfather clock. Guest bedrooms are named after literary figures of the Romantic era, associates of forebear Charles Valentine Le Grice. Two ground-floor courtyard rooms are dog-friendly, with Southey, recalling the author of the Goldilocks story, overlooking the garden. More glamorous are the two first-floor rooms in the main house. Coleridge, overlooking the parterre, is 'an amazing large room' with a roll-top bath. Wordsworth overlooks the garden on one side, a cobbled yard on the other. The cheapest, let's call it the Blake option, is a bell tent with log-burner and gas hob. At breakfast there is 'nothing fancy but everything you need', including jam from the fruits of the walled garden. A peach of a spot for exploring West Cornwall's beaches, galleries and cliff-top theatre. (ME)

Penzance
TR20 8TJ

T: 01736 362750
E: trereifepark@btconnect.com
W: trereifepark.co.uk

BEDROOMS: 4. 2 on ground floor. Plus 2 self-catering apartments, and bell tent for glamping.
OPEN: 1 Mar–20 Dec, self-catering all year.
FACILITIES: sitting room (honesty bar), dining room, free Wi-Fi, in-room TV (Freeview), civil wedding licence, 5-acre grounds (parterres, walled garden, woodland), parking, unsuitable for disabled.
BACKGROUND MUSIC: none.
LOCATION: 1¼ miles SW of Penzance.
CHILDREN: all ages welcomed.
DOGS: allowed in ground-floor bedrooms, not in public rooms.
CREDIT CARDS: all major cards.
PRICES: [2018] per room B&B £80–£160. Min. 2-night stay weekends June–Sept and for self-catering.

SEE ALSO SHORTLIST

PETERSFIELD Hampshire

Map 2:E3

JSW

'Stand-out' Michelin-starred food is at the core
of this 'elegant' restaurant-with-rooms in a
whitewashed 17th-century coaching inn on a
'pleasant, leafy street'. In the dining room, pared-
back styling (whites, creams, pale beams), life
portraits by chef/patron Jake Saul Watkins's sister,
'friendly, professional' staff and 'well-spaced
tables' create a contemplative space, the better to
appreciate the 'exquisitely presented' creations
without distraction. Local produce is used
wherever possible, including fish from the Solent,
fruit and vegetables from Hampshire. Particularly
memorable dishes for a Guide inspector in 2018
included 'the vibrant cured and poached salmon,
pickled cucumber, watercress'. Another reader
adored the 'buttery suckling pig with perfect
crackling; cheesecake with mango leather'. The
prodigious wine list has a tipple for every taste.
Uncluttered bedrooms 'up in the eaves' have
Nespresso machine, fresh milk in a Kilner jar, and
'comfortably firm bed with crisp, fresh bedding'.
Light sleepers may bring earplugs or request
a room overlooking the quiet courtyard. The
continental breakfast includes freshly squeezed
orange juice, pastries from Paris, 'home-made
lemon curd and pleasingly bitter marmalade'. (CS)

20 Dragon Street
Petersfield
GU31 4JJ

T: 01730 262030
E: jsw.restaurant@btconnect.com
W: jswrestaurant.com

BEDROOMS: 4.
OPEN: all year except Christmas and
New Year, 2 weeks Jan, 2 weeks
Apr, 2 weeks Sept, restaurant closed
Sun evening–Wed lunch.
FACILITIES: restaurant, function
room, free Wi-Fi, in-room TV
(Freeview), courtyard with outside
seating, restaurant suitable for
wheelchair, adapted toilet.
BACKGROUND MUSIC: none.
LOCATION: town centre.
CHILDREN: all ages welcomed.
DOGS: not allowed.
CREDIT CARDS: MasterCard, Visa.
PRICES: [2018] per room B&B
£125–£145, D,B&B £215–£355. Set
dinner £45–£55, tasting menus
£65–£90, à la carte £50. 1-night
bookings sometimes refused.

PETWORTH Sussex

Map 2:E3

THE OLD RAILWAY STATION

Now a 'gracious' B&B, this restored Victorian train station and princely Pullman carriages on disused tracks ooze the romance of travel's golden age. The station was built at the behest of the future Edward VII, a fan of nearby Goodwood. 'Warm, hands-on' Gudmund Olafsson and Catherine Stormont run the show with 'welcoming' staff. Visitors head to the former parcels office to check in, while the elegant former waiting room is an inviting sitting area. These 'charming, quirky spaces' have deep leather armchairs, period lanterns and furniture, paraphernalia and black-and-white photographs of the railway's heyday. 'Comfortable, well-furnished', colonial-style bedrooms, upstairs in the station building – one reached via a spiralling cast iron staircase – or in the thoughtfully finished carriages, have Edwardian fittings; a 'surprisingly spacious' bathroom. Cream teas and a 'wonderful' breakfast are served in the waiting room or outside under parasols on the old platform, next to lawns and verdant forest. A buzzy pub, just across the river and up the lane, is a good spot for evening meals (a torch is provided). Petworth's shops and eateries are five minutes' drive away. (JB)

Station Road
Petworth
GU28 0JF

T: 01798 342346
E: info@old-station.co.uk
W: www.old-station.co.uk

BEDROOMS: 10. 8 in Pullman carriages, 1 room suitable for disabled.
OPEN: all year except 23–26 Dec.
FACILITIES: lounge/bar/breakfast room, free Wi-Fi, in-room TV (Freeview), platform/terrace, 2-acre garden.
BACKGROUND MUSIC: 'soft '20s, '30s, '40s music' at breakfast.
LOCATION: 1½ miles S of Petworth.
CHILDREN: not under 10.
DOGS: not allowed.
CREDIT CARDS: Amex, MasterCard, Visa.
PRICES: [2018] per room B&B single £90–£128, double £120–£210. Min. 2-night bookings Fri and Sat.

PICKERING Yorkshire

THE WHITE SWAN

The Buchanan family has run this 'heart-warming' hotel for two generations, but, bar two short breaks, it has been a local hostelry since the 16th century. A popular spot in a 'delightful' market town on the edge of the North Yorkshire moors, it has 'naturally friendly' staff, 'smiling and helpful'. An old barn at the back of the courtyard is now the Bothy lounge, with oak beams, squashy sofas, a log-burning stove, books, games, an honesty bar and complimentary home-made biscuits. Bedrooms in the main building are traditional, some with stand-out pieces such as a Louis XVI super-king-size bed. More modern rooms in converted stables are 'extremely comfortable', 'airy, spacious', with a heated stone floor. In the cosy restaurant with flagstones, open fire and richly patterned wallpaper, Darren Clemmit's seasonal 'short and simple' menu is proudly local with 'Yorkshire proportions'. The owners are growing hand-dived scallops on their own area of seabed, and source meat from the renowned Ginger Pig farms – ask them to arrange a tour to see where your belly pork, sage and veal forcemeat, creamed onion, Cox's Pippin apple and buttery mash came from.

25% DISCOUNT VOUCHERS

Market Place
Pickering
YO18 7AA

T: 01751 472288
E: welcome@white-swan.co.uk
W: www.white-swan.co.uk

BEDROOMS: 21. 9 in annexe, on ground floor.
OPEN: all year.
FACILITIES: lounge, bar, restaurant, private dining room, Bothy residents' lounge/event room, free Wi-Fi, in-room TV (Freeview), small terrace (alfresco meals), snug, bar and lounge wheelchair accessible, toilet not adapted.
BACKGROUND MUSIC: none.
LOCATION: central.
CHILDREN: all ages welcomed.
DOGS: allowed in some bedrooms, bar and lounge, not in restaurant (owners may dine with dogs in snug).
CREDIT CARDS: Amex, MasterCard, Visa.
PRICES: [2018] per room B&B single £129–£199, double £159–£219, D,B&B double £219–£259. À la carte £38.

PORLOCK Somerset

THE OAKS

Tim and Anne Riley's small hotel stands serenely on a steep hillside on the edge of a village where the Exmoor national park meets the sea. Guide regulars arriving in 2018 'were warmly welcomed by Anne with tea and cake'. The Edwardian house is traditional and domestic, 'not in the least old-fashioned or faded'. Everywhere something catches the eye – statuary, a ginger jar collection, gently chiming clocks. An 'impressive' wine list' accompanies Anne Riley's 'generally excellent' home cooking, alongside 'highly professional service' and 'breathtaking views' – 'the changing light over the village is magical'. Dinner might include rose veal in cream mushroom sauce; a 'perfectly judged' pudding. The 'beautiful Melba toast and baked rolls' were particularly appreciated. Bedrooms are 'spacious' and airy; 'our bed was soft but comfortable'. Other readers lauded the 'large fluffy towels on a piping-hot bathroom rail'. Many rooms enjoy the same view as the restaurant; each has a mini-clock, a radio, ground coffee. Breakfast brings 'freshly squeezed orange juice, excellent porridge, good cafetière coffee and toasted home-made bread'. (Mike and Jill Bennett, and others).

Porlock
TA24 8ES

T: 01643 862265
E: info@oakshotel.co.uk
W: www.oakshotel.co.uk

BEDROOMS: 7.
OPEN: Easter–end Oct.
FACILITIES: 2 lounges, bar, restaurant, free Wi-Fi, in-room TV (Freeview), 1-acre garden, patio, pebble beach 1 mile, unsuitable for disabled.
BACKGROUND MUSIC: occasionally classical in the dining room.
LOCATION: edge of village.
CHILDREN: not under 8.
DOGS: not allowed.
CREDIT CARDS: MasterCard, Visa.
PRICES: [2018] per room D,B&B £250.

PORTSCATHO Cornwall

Map 1:E2

DRIFTWOOD HOTEL

♔ Previous César winner

'Wow! This was good.' A regular Guide reader
offered high praise after visiting Paul and Fiona
Robinson's 'delightful' hotel that gazes across
Gerrans Bay on the Roseland peninsula. Inside
all is airy and bright, with New England-style
decor; outside is a light-washed deck, above
a garden sprinkled with Adirondack chairs.
The atmosphere is 'stylish but informal', the
service 'attentive'. Two rooms occupy a nearby
weather-boarded cabin. 'Our room offered a
view over the garden to the sea, a comfy bed and
seating area', although 'the bathroom was a bit
small'. In the restaurant, Chris Eden has held
a Michelin star since 2012 for a locally sourced
menu, including such dishes as blonde ray wing,
Jerusalem artichoke, samphire, sunflower seeds
and thyme roasting juices. 'Superb food – we ate
in every night' (although with slight frustration
at paying extra for vegetables). Another reader
wished the food was 'a little simpler' but declared
the potato gnocchi with her John Dory 'a thing
of genius'. Breakfast was 'excellent'. Overall, 'it
isn't cheap but it is worth every penny. We will
return.' (Peter Anderson, and others)

Rosevine
Portscatho
TR2 5EW

T: 01872 580644
E: info@driftwoodhotel.co.uk
W: www.driftwoodhotel.co.uk

BEDROOMS: 15. 4 accessed via
courtyard, 2 in cabin (2 mins' walk).
OPEN: 1 Feb–8 Dec.
FACILITIES: bar, restaurant, drawing
room, snug, children's games room,
free Wi-Fi, in-room TV (Freeview),
7-acre grounds (terraced gardens,
private beach, safe bathing).
BACKGROUND MUSIC: all day in
restaurant and bar.
LOCATION: 1½ miles N of Portscatho.
CHILDREN: all ages welcomed.
DOGS: not allowed.
CREDIT CARDS: Amex, MasterCard,
Visa.
PRICES: [2018] per room B&B
£185–£300, D,B&B £240–£320.
Tasting menus £80–£100, à la carte
£70. 1-night bookings refused
weekends.

RADNAGE Buckinghamshire

Map 2:C3

THE MASH INN

♔ Previous César winner

'Food-focused readers will be happy' at this red brick Chilterns restaurant-with-rooms that offers a 'distinctive cooking style'. Owner Nick Mash, from a local family of farmers and greengrocers, has reinvented an old Georgian village inn. While the entrance and bar 'retain a timeless feel', the 'bright' dining room beyond partially opens on to a kitchen with wood-fired grill. Chef Jon Parry 'forages the woods, selects fresh produce from the garden, and draws from the family farm' to fuel seasonal menus with dishes such as lamb loin and sprouting broccoli; tranche of halibut and turmeric roast cauliflower. To go with dinner there is 'splendid bespoke ash and oak furniture', and garden doors, open in summer, providing bucolic views. 'We sat for a long time enjoying the silence,' write inspectors, 'watching the chef harvest vegetables from the raised beds.' Bedrooms have 'clean, modern decor', with grey and blue hues, bleached woods, king-size beds, a Roberts radio and Anglepoise lights. A simple approach – 'they say it is a place to lay your head after a good meal' – also taken with the 'fine breakfast', delivered on a tray to the room.

Horseshoe Road
Radnage
HP14 4EB

T: 01494 482440
E: hello@themashinn.com
W: themashinn.com

BEDROOMS: 6.
OPEN: all year, closed Sun, Mon, Tues.
FACILITIES: snug bar and dining area, semi-open-plan kitchen/dining room, free Wi-Fi, 2½-acre garden, restaurant wheelchair accessible.
BACKGROUND MUSIC: in public areas.
LOCATION: in hamlet 7 miles NW of High Wycombe.
CHILDREN: not under 16.
DOGS: allowed in bar.
CREDIT CARDS: MasterCard, Visa.
PRICES: [2018] per room B&B £110–£210. Tasting menu £80, daily set menu £55.

RAMSGILL-IN-NIDDERDALE Yorkshire Map 4:D3

THE YORKE ARMS

After more than two decades, Frances and Bill Atkins have sold their cherished, creeper-covered 18th-century stone coaching inn overlooking the green in a Dales village – but fans should take heart. New owner Jonathan Turner has initiated a programme of sensitive refurbishment, but otherwise, we are assured, it is business as usual. Michelin-starred chef Mrs Atkins is still in the kitchen, John Tullett remains as general manager, the team is going nowhere, so all's right with the world. Guests can expect the same 'wonderful food' and 'friendly, efficient service', as well as refreshed interiors. The 'comfortable' country-style bedrooms are a blend of traditional and contemporary furnishings. Two-storey courtyard apartments are a good option for a longer stay. All rooms have handmade treats and high-quality toiletries. A typical daily bar lunch menu runs from garden soup, via Whitby crab and Wensleydale soufflé, to fish and chips and beef fillet with portobello mushrooms, while at dinner the 'seasonal inspirations' menu brings such dishes as stuffed roast guineafowl, smoked tongue, borage, juniper; always a tempting vegetarian option. 'Not cheap, but worth it.' (Bill Wood, D and LH)

Ramsgill-in-Nidderdale
HG3 5RL

T: 01423 755243
E: enquiries@yorke-arms.co.uk
W: www.yorke-arms.co.uk

BEDROOMS: 18. 4 suites in courtyard, 1 suitable for disabled.
OPEN: all year except 25 Dec.
FACILITIES: lounge, bar, 2 dining rooms, 1 private dining room, free Wi-Fi in lounge and some bedrooms, in-room TV (Freeview), function facilities, 2-acre grounds.
BACKGROUND MUSIC: in public areas.
LOCATION: centre of village.
CHILDREN: not under 12.
DOGS: allowed in 1 bedroom, bar.
CREDIT CARDS: Amex, MasterCard, Visa.
PRICES: [2018] per room D,B&B single £275, double £375–£600. Dinner for non-residents £90.

RAVENSTONEDALE Cumbria

Map 4:C3

THE BLACK SWAN

♛ Previous César winner

A babbling brook etches a course past Louise
Dinnes's 'good-value, thoroughly dependable'
Victorian pub-with-rooms, where visitors find
'outstanding food' and 'welcoming, efficient
service'. The maze of cosy tartan-carpeted public
rooms has inviting comfy chairs, an open fire
and a relaxed, dog-friendly atmosphere. 'The
sort of place one could just sit in, happily tucked
away with a newspaper and a pint of cask ale or
a Cumbrian micro-distillery spirit.' Each nook
and cranny reveals something new: books, board
games, musical instruments. Served in these
spaces, chef Scott Fairweather's 'seriously good'
modern British menu offers the likes of celeriac
rösti, creamed cabbage, poached egg, Stilton;
chicken, sauce of black truffle, roasted onions,
pearl barley. Afterwards, comfortable nights in
a 'well-maintained' bedroom come with fresh
milk, handmade organic toiletries and fluffy
towels; some rooms have their own entrance
to keep Fido happy. The popular country inn
is surrounded by the fells – convenient for
ramblers and climbers, who can head south to
the Yorkshire Dales and west to the Lakes.
(RG, and others)

25% DISCOUNT VOUCHERS

Ravenstonedale
CA17 4NG

T: 015396 23204
E: enquiries@blackswanhotel.com
W: www.blackswanhotel.com

BEDROOMS: 16. 6 in annexe, 4 on
ground floor suitable for disabled.
Plus 3 'glamping' tents.
OPEN: all year.
FACILITIES: 2 bars, lounge, 2 dining
rooms, free Wi-Fi, in-room TV
(Freeview), beer garden in wooded
grounds, tennis and golf in village.
BACKGROUND MUSIC: in public areas
all day, but optional.
LOCATION: in village 5 miles SW of
Kirkby Stephen.
CHILDREN: all ages welcomed.
DOGS: allowed in 4 ground-floor
bedrooms, not in restaurant.
CREDIT CARDS: all major cards.
PRICES: [2018] per room B&B
single from £85, double £95–£165.
À la carte £30. 1-night bookings
sometimes refused.

REEPHAM Norfolk

Map 2:B5

THE DIAL HOUSE

While it maintains its 'eclectic, faultlessly tasteful' Grand Tour theme, there are changes afoot at this small hotel in a 'handsome red brick Georgian house'. New owners Andrew Jones and Hannah Springham are turning the spotlight on to its food. We expect good things. The couple own a popular Norwich restaurant, and Andrew Jones honed his chef's craft at Corrigan's of Mayfair. His seasonal British dishes are fuelled by fine Norfolk ingredients, often farm to fork on the same day. While menus are being developed as we go to press, an existing favourite of roast hake, white beans, Cromer crab, buttered courgette, will continue to feature. The informal dining room is receiving an elegant facelift, but other rooms are still 'a cornucopia of delightful furnishings and objects' – most of them for sale. The top-floor Raj room has a carved wood bed and elephant sculptures; the Natural History room is entered through a display case of travellers' curiosities, and the Africa room sports ethnic carvings and a vibrantly patterned bathtub at bed end. We hope the 'beautifully laid out breakfast' and 'lovely staff' will remain. More reports, please.

Market Place
Reepham
NR10 4JJ

T: 01603 879900
E: info@thedialhouse.org.uk
W: www.thedialhouse.org.uk

BEDROOMS: 8.
OPEN: all year.
FACILITIES: lounge, restaurant, private dining rooms, free Wi-Fi, in-room TV (Sky), terrace, public rooms wheelchair accessible, adapted toilet.
BACKGROUND MUSIC: jazz at dinner.
LOCATION: on main square.
CHILDREN: all ages welcomed.
DOGS: allowed on terrace only.
CREDIT CARDS: Amex, MasterCard, Visa.
PRICES: [2018] per room B&B £145–£190. À la carte £30.

RICHMOND Yorkshire

Map 4:C3

THE COACH HOUSE
AT MIDDLETON LODGE

♔ Previous César winner

Developments are afoot at this hotel, centred on
a Georgian coach house, 'in a glorious setting
on a huge estate with beautiful walled garden'.
The owner, James Allison, grew up in Palladian
Middleton Lodge; his architect partner, Rebecca
Tappin, was responsible for the hotel's design.
Beside the restored kitchen garden, three
Potting Shed bedrooms have been added, and
11 (mainly family) rooms are scheduled to open
in the Dovecote (a swimming pool is also being
built). The original bedrooms are in the coach
house and farmhouse, with ground-floor garden
rooms boasting a small private terrace. Trusted
readers found one of these rooms 'amazing', with
log-burning stove, underfloor heating, 'a huge,
very comfortable bed', a bathroom 'almost as big',
with a walk-in shower, a freestanding bath by the
window. A mid-priced room, 'up steep steps', was
less liked. The restaurant and bar occupy the lofty
stables. Chef Gareth Rayner's 'excellent dinner'
might include grilled cod, brassica, seaweed
butter; pork belly, cabbage, black pudding, apple.
Breakfast brings smoothies, pancakes, eggs
Benedict with York ham.

Kneeton Lane
Richmond
DL10 6NJ

T: 01325 377 977
E: info@middletonlodge.co.uk
W: middletonlodge.co.uk

BEDROOMS: 18. 3 in Potting Shed, 6
in farmhouse (a short walk away),
5 on ground floor, 1 suitable for
disabled. 11 more, in Dovecote, to
be completed late 2018.
OPEN: all year, set package stays over
Christmas/New Year.
FACILITIES: lounge, bar, snug,
restaurant, free Wi-Fi, in-room
TV (Sky), civil wedding licence,
treatment rooms, courtyard, garden
in 200-acre grounds, public rooms
wheelchair accessible, adapted toilet.
BACKGROUND MUSIC: in public areas.
LOCATION: 1 mile N of village.
CHILDREN: all ages welcomed.
DOGS: allowed in some bedrooms,
most public areas, not in restaurant.
CREDIT CARDS: MasterCard, Visa.
PRICES: [2018] per room B&B
£150–£200, D,B&B from £210.
À la carte £35.

SEE ALSO SHORTLIST

RICHMOND Yorkshire   Map 4:C3

THE FRENCHGATE RESTAURANT & HOTEL **NEW**

25% DISCOUNT VOUCHERS

A Georgian gentleman's residence and next-door Carolean town house combine as one hotel on cobbled Frenchgate. It enters the Guide this year on the recommendation of a Guide stalwart who received a 'friendly greeting from a young receptionist'. A comfortable single room had a 'small, modern en suite' with Swedish power shower. Other refurbished rooms have, variously, a bath, or bath and walk-in shower, a solid oak four-poster, views to the River Swale. Downstairs, there is 'a smallish lounge and bar area, a Georgian dining room with 18 covers at candlelit tables'. Owners David and Luiza Todd ensure 'it's a place which cares passionately about the quality of its food', and chef Lisa Miller clearly 'knows her craft'. A 'superb' dinner was 'original but not pretentious, not too pricey'. There were 'good olives, an amuse-bouche of thick tomato soup with basil oil, plus a pre-dessert of lemon posset with pine-nut crumble'. Main courses include roast loin of Swaledale lamb, potato dauphinoise, peas, broad beans, girolles, Iberico ham. Service is 'attentive and friendly'. Breakfast delivers 'freshly squeezed juice', smoked haddock, home-baked bread. (Robert Gower, A and CR)

59–61 Frenchgate
Richmond
DL10 7AE

T: 01748 822 087
E: info@thefrenchgate.co.uk
W: www.thefrenchgate.co.uk

BEDROOMS: 9, 1 on ground floor with 2 steps to en suite.
OPEN: all year.
FACILITIES: dining room, bar/terrace, lounge, free Wi-Fi, in-room TV (Freeview), civil wedding licence, small garden, public rooms wheelchair accessible, adapted toilet.
BACKGROUND MUSIC: soft jazz in public rooms.
LOCATION: 200 yds NE of town square.
CHILDREN: all ages welcomed.
DOGS: not allowed.
CREDIT CARDS: all major cards.
PRICES: [2018] per room B&B single £79–£178, double £138–£250, D,B&B double £206–£318. À la carte set-price menu £39.

SEE ALSO SHORTLIST

RICHMOND Yorkshire

Map 4:C3

MILLGATE HOUSE

♀ Previous César winner

'Silver, copper, glass, china, pictures, rugs' and other treasures are 'trustingly displayed' at Tim Culkin and Austin Lynch's 'wonderfully eccentric B&B' in a Georgian house, just off the town square. 'You would not want to be with children here,' report our inspectors this year. 'Clocks, clocks and more clocks are dotted around, several of them in every living room.' Bedrooms are furnished with antiques. One has a separate private bathroom, another an in-room shower and a separate, private WC. A spacious double room had 'a separate sitting room in which is an ancient oven/fireplace', a dresser laden with china, paperbacks, more china. A door led straight into the 'glorious' walled garden, with profuse plantings of shrub roses, clematis and ferns. An even better choice, perhaps, dual-aspect Room 1 has views over the garden towards the River Swale. Both of these have an en suite bathroom with bath and walk-in shower. At breakfast, 'served by a friendly lady', there was 'a generous buffet, delicious home-made marmalade, good poached egg on smoked haddock'. The hosts are proud of their list of past guests, including Joanna Trollope, Tom Courtenay, Alan Bennett.

3 Millgate
Richmond
DL10 4JN

T: 01748 823571
E: oztim@millgatehouse.demon.co.uk
W: www.millgatehouse.com

BEDROOMS: 6.
OPEN: all year.
FACILITIES: hall, drawing room, dining room, free Wi-Fi, in-room digital TV, ⅓-acre garden, unsuitable for disabled.
BACKGROUND MUSIC: occasional soft classical.
LOCATION: town centre.
CHILDREN: all ages welcomed.
DOGS: allowed in public rooms and bedrooms (not left unattended).
CREDIT CARDS: none.
PRICES: [2018] per room B&B £125–£165.

SEE ALSO SHORTLIST

RICHMOND-UPON-THAMES Surrey   Map 2:D3

BINGHAM

Tourists should 'forget fancy London hotels', say readers, and instead head out to Ruth and Samantha Trinder's hotel close to Richmond Park, with tranquil riverside garden and terrace. Originally two Georgian town houses, it was once home to Victorian poet 'Michael Field' (the nom de plume of Katherine Bradley) and Edith Cooper, her niece (and lover). True to its romantic past, it is a popular wedding venue. Bedrooms, several with a 'beautiful view of the Thames', have a mix of antique-market finds and contemporary furniture, cool, modern decor, bespoke bed frames, perhaps an in-room copper bath, a marble walk-in power shower. The bar has a menu of 'Bingham bites' with the likes of duck liver on toasted sourdough; cauliflower risotto with hazelnut crumble. In the coolly elegant restaurant, Andrew Cole's short seasonal British menus include such dishes as beef sirloin, asparagus, raw button mushrooms, wild garlic; cod, clams, sweet potato, spring onion, buttermilk sauce; potato dumplings, cauliflower, wild garlic, pickled morels. Guests can use the facilities at sister company bhuti, nearby (yoga, pilates, a vegan tearoom), or borrow a bike to see the park deer.

25% DISCOUNT VOUCHERS

61–63 Petersham Road
Richmond-upon-Thames
TW10 6UT

T: 020 8940 0902
E: info@thebingham.co.uk
W: www.thebingham.co.uk

BEDROOMS: 15.
OPEN: all year, restaurant closed Sun evening.
FACILITIES: bar, restaurant, function room, free Wi-Fi, in-room TV (Freeview), civil wedding licence, terrace, ½-acre garden, complimentary use of nearby wellness centre, public rooms wheelchair accessible, adapted toilet.
BACKGROUND MUSIC: in bar and restaurant.
LOCATION: ½ mile S of centre.
CHILDREN: all ages welcomed.
DOGS: allowed in some bedrooms, not in public areas.
CREDIT CARDS: Diners, MasterCard, Visa.
PRICES: [2018] B&B £179–£339, D,B&B £269–£429. Tasting menu £50, fixed-price à la carte £37–£45 (plus 12½% discretionary service charge).

ROMALDKIRK Co. Durham

Map 4:C3

THE ROSE AND CROWN

In a 'beautiful setting', beside the Saxon church in a 'picturesque' North Pennines village, Cheryl and Thomas Robinson's 18th-century inn is 'an absolute gem', loved especially by dog-owning readers. Bedrooms vary in style and character, with a mix of antique, locally made and modern furniture. Some have beams and exposed stone, while suites have a sofa bed for children. The more contemporary courtyard rooms have their own patio. All are supplied with ground coffee, biscuits, smart toiletries. 'The food is the star of the show', served in the candlelit oak-panelled dining room, or in the cosy bar with its log fire, horse brasses, hunting prints and settles. The Robinsons, who also own Headlam Hall in Darlington (see Shortlist), have farmed in Teesdale for four generations, and are passionate about seasonality, provenance and animal welfare. Head chef David Hunter is back in the kitchen this year, creating such dishes as pan-fried breast of woodpigeon, grilled pancetta, parsnip tartlet, juniper sauce. Breakfast choices include smoked haddock or honey-roasted ham, setting guests up for a hearty walk, perhaps to High Force waterfall. (AG, KJ)

25% DISCOUNT VOUCHERS

Romaldkirk
Barnard Castle
DL12 9EB

T: 01833 650213
E: hotel@rose-and-crown.co.uk
W: www.rose-and-crown.co.uk

BEDROOMS: 14. 2 in Monk's Cottage, 5 in rear courtyard, some on ground floor.
OPEN: all year except 23–28 Dec, no food served Mon lunchtime.
FACILITIES: 2 lounges, bar, Crown Room (bar meals), restaurant, free Wi-Fi, in-room TV (Freeview), boot room, fishing, grouse shooting, birdwatching nearby.
BACKGROUND MUSIC: all day and evening in restaurant.
LOCATION: village centre, 6 miles W of Barnard Castle.
CHILDREN: all ages welcomed.
DOGS: allowed in bedrooms and public rooms, except restaurant.
CREDIT CARDS: Amex, MasterCard, Visa.
PRICES: [2018] per room B&B £115–£205, D,B&B £175–£265. À la carte £40.

ROSS-ON-WYE Herefordshire

Map 3:D5

BROOKS COUNTRY HOUSE   NEW

Overlooking National Trust parkland, this Georgian country house has 'a real sense of grandeur', say inspectors in 2018. 'But all the details are welcoming and homely – the open front door, the flowers adorning mirrors and surfaces.' Entering the Guide this year, the 'very reasonably priced' hotel is a first rural foray for Carla and Andrew Brooks (see Brooks Bristol and Edinburgh). Interiors are filled with antiques, but the owners' sense of fun emerges in such 'amenities' as a photo booth and cast-off theatre costumes for dressing up. There are four-posters and a bunk in a vintage horsebox. Bedrooms in the main house and courtyard have Cole & Son wallpaper, perhaps a chandelier, roll-top bath and power shower. Coach house rooms are more rustic. 'Our courtyard room had a lobby area, good-sized bedroom and huge bathroom… For our dog: a beautiful bed, a water bowl and bag of treats.' Food is on the hearty side, for example Herefordshire ox liver, steak and triple-cooked chips. There are vegetables from the garden, eggs from the hens, wines from the vineyard. A busy nearby road doesn't interrupt the bucolic serenity. (ANR, and others)

Pengethley Park
Ross-on-Wye
HR9 6LL

T: 01989 730211
E: info@brookscountryhouse.com
W: www.brookscountryhouse.com

BEDROOMS: 27, 3 in coach house, 8 in courtyard, 3 in vintage horseboxes, 1 room suitable for disabled.
OPEN: all year.
FACILITIES: lounge, bar, restaurant, library, snooker room, games room, conference room, free Wi-Fi, in-room TV (Freeview), civil wedding licence, 15-acre garden, heated outdoor swimming pool (June–Sept), hot tub, sauna, public areas wheelchair accessible, adapted toilet.
BACKGROUND MUSIC: in public areas until 10 pm..
LOCATION: 4 miles N of Ross-on-Wye, 10 miles S of Hereford.
CHILDREN: all ages welcomed.
DOGS: allowed in 4 courtyard bedrooms, bar.
CREDIT CARDS: Amex, MasterCard, Visa.
PRICES: [2018] per room B&B £59–£119, D,B&B £90–£150. À la carte £23–£29.

ROSS-ON-WYE Herefordshire

WILTON COURT

From the moment of arrival at this Tudor manor house on the banks of the River Wye, say readers, 'we knew this was the place where we wanted to spend time'. Run today as a restaurant-with-rooms by Helen and Roger Wynn, the 'lovely old building' dates in parts from 1500, and was at one time a magistrates' court. Beneath the cosy, panelled library, formerly part of the courtroom, there is said to be a passage leading to what was the jail. Today's bedrooms offer a more hospitable sentence. Bright and traditional, some have exposed beams, William Morris wallpaper, an original fireplace, 'glorious river views'. All have good toiletries, kimonos, complimentary bottled water. 'The patio and garden area make a wonderful place to relax', observing gliding swans. In the Mulberry restaurant, head chef Rachael Williams cooks a weekly-changing, locally sourced menu with good choices for meat-eaters – perhaps her signature fillet of Herefordshire beef, lyonnaise potatoes, savoy cabbage, mustard cream sauce – alongside fish and vegetarian options. As we went to press we learnt that the hotel is up for sale. We await more reports. (B and JH)

25% DISCOUNT VOUCHERS

Wilton Lane
Ross-on-Wye
HR9 6AQ

T: 01989 562569
E: info@wiltoncourthotel.com
W: wiltoncourthotel.com

BEDROOMS: 11. 1 on ground floor.
OPEN: all year except first 2 weeks Jan.
FACILITIES: library, bar, restaurant, private dining room, free Wi-Fi, in-room TV (Freeview), ½-acre grounds, bar area and restaurant wheelchair accessible.
BACKGROUND MUSIC: in restaurant at mealtimes.
LOCATION: ½ mile from centre.
CHILDREN: all ages welcomed (cots, high chairs).
DOGS: allowed in all but 2 bedrooms and public rooms, not in restaurant (£5 per dog per night).
CREDIT CARDS: Amex, MasterCard, Visa.
PRICES: [2018] per room B&B single £110–£160, double £135–£195, D,B&B (min. 2 nights) double £185–£245. Set dinner £33, à la carte £45. 1-night bookings refused Sat in peak season.

ROWSLEY Derbyshire   Map 3:A6

THE PEACOCK AT ROWSLEY

Built in 1652 as a manor house, this stone inn
on the edge of the Peak District national park
is owned by Lord and Lady Manners of nearby
Haddon Hall. In springtime, festoons of white
wisteria and early roses frame leaded, mullioned
windows. Public rooms are filled with antiques,
paintings; ancestral portraits hang above blazing
fires. Trout in display cases in reception attest
to good fly-fishing in the River Derwent at
the bottom of the garden, and in the Wye
on the Haddon estate. Smart bedrooms, too,
have original artworks, perhaps a bespoke
four-poster; two are single, with shower room.
Marble bathrooms are supplied with good
toiletries. The cosy, beamed bar serves fish and
chips, sandwiches, Derbyshire burger of lamb
shoulder, while in the restaurant, chef Dan
Smith uses local produce and organic meat from
the estate in such dishes as beef fillet and cheek,
artichoke, spring cabbage, miso; lamb cutlet,
onion, broad beans, goat's curd, boulangère
potatoes. Staff are 'friendly and efficient', the
food is 'fantastic'. A credit, then, to the Manners
family, whose crest, a strutting peacock, is
rightly proud.

Bakewell Road
Rowsley
DE4 2EB

T: 01629 733518
E: reception@thepeacockatrowsley.
com
W: www.thepeacockatrowsley.co.uk

BEDROOMS: 15.
OPEN: all year except 24–26 Dec,
2 weeks Jan.
FACILITIES: lounge, bar, 2 dining
rooms, private dining/conference
room, free Wi-Fi, in-room TV
(Freeview, Apple TV), ½-acre
garden on the river, fishing rights
on rivers Wye and Derwent, public
areas wheelchair accessible.
BACKGROUND MUSIC: in public rooms.
LOCATION: village centre.
CHILDREN: not under 10 at
weekends.
DOGS: allowed in bedrooms only.
CREDIT CARDS: Amex, MasterCard,
Visa.
PRICES: [2018] per room B&B single
£130–£145, double £205–£310,
D,B&B single £160–£180, double
£285–£390. À la carte £65, tasting
menu £75. 1-night bookings
sometimes refused.

RYE Sussex

Map 2:E5

THE GEORGE IN RYE

Outwardly a Georgian coaching inn on the cobbled main street of the medieval town, Alex Clarke's 'absolutely lovely' hotel is 16th-century in its bones – the timbers from an Elizabethan galley. An 18th-century Act of Parliament wall clock still keeps time, and a fire burns in the entrance area, 'with very appealing-looking sofas and chairs'. The bedrooms, however, are a smart mix of traditional and contemporary, with bespoke furniture. Some have a four-poster, an in-room bath, 'fun touches' such as bookshelves jammed with Penguin Classics, 'a picture of a topless lady fishing' (call the PC police!). 'As it is an old building, you can hear footsteps from the room upstairs.' In this tourists' hotspot, the bar is almost too popular: 'We didn't try the highly recommended cocktails – defeated by the crowd.' In the 'tasteful' main dining room or alfresco, chef Josh Price cooks steaks and lobsters from a wood-charcoal grill, alongside the likes of Rye Bay seafood stew with locally landed fish, crevette, mussels, scallops, cavolo nero, tomato sauce and saffron aïoli. Breakfast options include poached pears, eggs Florentine, smoked kipper, field mushrooms on Pugliese toast. (AW, AR)

98 High Street
Rye
TN31 7JT

T: 01797 222114
E: reception@thegeorgeinrye.com
W: www.thegeorgeinrye.com

BEDROOMS: 34. 17 in annexe, some with private entrance.
OPEN: all year.
FACILITIES: lounge, bar, restaurant, function rooms, free Wi-Fi, in-room TV (Freeview), civil wedding licence, decked courtyard garden.
BACKGROUND MUSIC: in bar and restaurant.
LOCATION: town centre.
CHILDREN: all ages welcomed.
DOGS: allowed in bar only.
CREDIT CARDS: MasterCard, Visa.
PRICES: [2018] per room B&B £145–£245. À la carte £40.

SEE ALSO SHORTLIST

RYE Sussex

JEAKE'S HOUSE

'It's a lovely place to stay, with great character and charm.' Readers visiting Jenny Hadfield's 17th-century B&B 'as a little treat' to celebrate an occasion in 2018 'were made to feel special and right at home. Jenny and her team are wonderful hosts.' The ivy-covered former wool storehouse, on a pretty cobbled street, has remained unchanged for centuries. Its beamed bedrooms are 'charmingly higgledy-piggledy'; sloping floors and ceilings, and low beams, are de rigueur. 'You can feel the history all around you.' Some rooms overlook the wilds of Romney Marsh; others Rye's rooftops. 'The bed was so comfortable that we both slept like logs; there was ample seating and a well-equipped bathroom.' Downstairs, find crackling fires, wood-panelled walls hung with prints and oil paintings, antiques and a 'dramatic, glamorous bar' with an honesty box for drinks. Served in the 'handsome' galleried former chapel, 'breakfast is amazing' with Richard Martin's 'very good cooked dishes' of local sausages, oak-smoked haddock, potato rösti and devilled kidneys. A fount of local knowledge as well as tasty food, 'he was so helpful about Rye's attractions'. (Chris and Alison Brett, MEO, RO)

Mermaid Street
Rye
TN31 7ET

T: 01797 222828
E: stay@jeakeshouse.com
W: www.jeakeshouse.com

BEDROOMS: 11.
OPEN: all year.
FACILITIES: parlour, bar/library, breakfast room, free Wi-Fi, in-room TV (Freeview), unsuitable for disabled.
BACKGROUND MUSIC: chamber music in breakfast room.
LOCATION: central, private car park, 6 mins' walk away (charge for parking permit, advance booking).
CHILDREN: not under 8.
DOGS: allowed on leads and 'always supervised'.
CREDIT CARDS: MasterCard, Visa.
PRICES: [2018] per room B&B £95–£150. 1-night bookings sometimes refused Fri/Sat.

SEE ALSO SHORTLIST

ST IVES Cornwall

Map 1:D1

BLUE HAYES

NEW

Widescreen coastal views, 'calm, muted, clotted-cream colours' and 'delightful suntrap gardens' are a successful formula for Malcolm Herring's 'unashamedly luxurious' small hotel. 'It really does deliver,' reports a Guide inspector, following a visit in 2018 that saw the tastefully converted 1920s eyrie promoted to full entry. The six 'spacious' suites each have a -eapot and cafetière, bone china and fresh milk'. Alongside a 'big, comfy bed with top-quality linen', there are armchairs, a window table – 'meals are served there at no extra cost' – and a 'really large bathroom with enormous fluffy towels, bath, separate shower and nice smellies'. Staff are 'well trained, pleasant and welcoming: a joy!' Chef Nicola Martin's light, 'delicious but not very cheap' supper dishes embrace the West Country's natural bounty, perhaps a tian of smoked salmon and Cornish crab with horseradish and lemon mayo; seafood platter with St Ives Bay lobster, local crab and Atlantic prawns; followed by velvet cheesecake with local mead and Kahlúa. 'Lavish, magnificent' breakfast included 'my favourite devilled kidneys', and kippers. 'The tea tray's luxury but not home-made shortbread was the only possible fault.'

Trelyon Avenue
St Ives
TR26 2AD

T: 01736 797129
E: info@bluehayes.co.uk
W: www.bluehayes.co.uk

BEDROOMS: 6.
OPEN: Mar–Oct.
FACILITIES: 2 lounges, bar, dining room, free Wi-Fi, in-room TV (Freeview), small function facilities, room service, terrace, garden, parking, unsuitable for disabled.
BACKGROUND MUSIC: in bar and dining room only, during breakfast and supper.
LOCATION: ½ mile from centre of St Ives.
CHILDREN: not under 10.
DOGS: not allowed.
CREDIT CARDS: Amex, MasterCard, Visa.
PRICES: [2018] per room B&B single £150–£240, double £220–£300. Supper from £17. Min. 2-night stay, but check availability online.

SEE ALSO SHORTLIST

ST IVES Cornwall

Map 1:D1

BOSKERRIS HOTEL

For all its charms, arty St Ives is thronged in high summer, so Jonathan and Marianne Bassett's hillside hotel offers a bright, airy escape. Public spaces are open-plan, cool, chic, stripped back with light-washed creams and pastels, bare boards and glass doors opening on to a large sun-bleached deck overlooking Carbis Bay. Bedrooms are not huge, but even a standard family room had 'double-aspect windows with more than a glimpse of the sea, a huge shower', bunks in an adjoining room. All rooms are 'immaculate', with cafetière, fresh milk on request, luxury toiletries. Superior rooms have a roll-top bath and walk-in rain shower; the best has a two-person sunken bath in the room, plus a wet room. The staff 'go out of their way to give advice', including where to eat out. Alternatively, stay in for supper, as a Guide reader did, enjoying simple, unfussy Mediterranean-style dishes, perhaps heritage tomatoes, kiln-roast salmon, spicy soppressata; fish soup, rouille, mini-crostini. Breakfast options include ricotta hotcakes, oak-smoked salmon, a vegetarian full English with goat's cheese, field mushrooms, cherry vine tomatoes. (G and SB, and others)

Boskerris Road
St Ives
TR26 2NQ

T: 01736 795295
E: reservations@boskerrishotel.co.uk
W: www.boskerrishotel.co.uk

BEDROOMS: 15. 1, on ground floor, suitable for disabled.
OPEN: mid-Mar to mid-Nov, restaurant closed Sun, Mon.
FACILITIES: lounge, bar, breakfast room, supper room, free Wi-Fi, in-room TV (Freeview), decked terrace, massage and reflexology treatment room, 1½-acre garden, parking, public rooms wheelchair accessible.
BACKGROUND MUSIC: in public rooms.
LOCATION: 1½ miles from centre (20 mins' walk), close to station.
CHILDREN: not under 10.
DOGS: not allowed.
CREDIT CARDS: Amex, MasterCard, Visa.
PRICES: [2018] per room B&B single £120–£221, double £160–£295. À la carte £28. 1-night bookings refused in high season.

SEE ALSO SHORTLIST

ST MARY'S Isles of Scilly

STAR CASTLE

'High standards are maintained,' writes a devoted fan, following a New Year stay at the Francis family's hotel, forged from a 16th-century fortification. 'It was warm and cosy, with gorgeous flowers and an entertaining programme of activities.' Other guests report 'plenty of positives: helpful staff, great setting, delicious breakfasts'; 'fabulous historic features, in particular the dungeon bar'. There was praise for the castle's 'wonderful comfy bedrooms', but a mixed reception for one of its 'slightly Butlin's-style row of cabins'. It was 'nicely decorated with a comfortable, large bed', but also 'fairly small, with a rather jaded bathroom, and a view of bushes'. In the dining rooms, one a vine-hung conservatory, chef Billy Littlejohn's 'stupendous' modern British menus include the likes of sea bass fillet, chive and Parmesan risotto cake, carrot purée, asparagus spears, baby corn and chive velouté. Some wines are from the family vineyard. Vegan visitors were disappointed to find, despite assurances when booking, no dining options. Boating excursions are run on fine days, with 'well-stocked bookshelves and board games' for less clement weather. (Abigail Kirby-Harris, IB, and others)

25% DISCOUNT VOUCHERS

The Garrison
St Mary's
TR21 0JA

T: 01720 422317
E: info@star-castle.co.uk
W: www.star-castle.co.uk

BEDROOMS: 38. 27 in 2 garden wings.
OPEN: all year, B&B only Nov–mid-Feb, except Christmas–New Year (full service).
FACILITIES: lounge, bar, 2 restaurants, free Wi-Fi, in-room TV (Freeview), civil wedding licence, sun deck, 2-acre gardens, covered swimming pool (12 by 4 metres), vineyard, tennis, beach, golf nearby, unsuitable for disabled.
BACKGROUND MUSIC: none.
LOCATION: ¼ mile from town centre.
CHILDREN: all ages welcomed.
DOGS: allowed in garden rooms, not in restaurants or lounge.
CREDIT CARDS: Amex, MasterCard, Visa.
PRICES: [2018] per room B&B single £85–£157, double £160–£394, DB&B single £95–£185, double £180–£448. À la carte £42.

SEE ALSO SHORTLIST

ST MAWES Cornwall

Map 1:E2

IDLE ROCKS

'The situation, the view and interior are all marvellous,' writes a reader this year, of Karen and David Richards's 'superb hotel' (Relais & Château) right by the harbour wall in a fishing village on the Roseland peninsula. Built in 1907 and extended in the 1980s, it has bright-and-breezy, nautical-chic decor with lots of sea blues and bare floorboards. 'Coastal-inspired colours' continue in the bedrooms, most overlooking beach or harbour. A top-floor room had a 'wonderfully comfortable bed', but a shallow wardrobe and 'amazing but outsize' bedside lamps suggest that style can triumph over substance. Service is 'good, the 'staff are great', but one regular reader in 2018 'was disappointed' to be told he must have the full lunch menu when visiting for a light bite. Chef Guy Owen makes creative use of locally produced and foraged produce in cooking 'of the highest quality' served in the restaurant or bar, or on the terrace. Perhaps Ajax hake, mussels, saffron, gnocchi; pressed lamb breast, leek, ewe's curd, shimeji. The kids, meanwhile, can tuck into goujons and chips. One reader would have liked more variety and less richness but breakfast rates another 'marvellous'. (OT, and others)

Harbourside
St Mawes
TR2 5AN

T: 01326 270270
E: info@idlerocks.com
W: www.idlerocks.com

BEDROOMS: 19. 4 in adjacent cottage, 1 suitable for disabled.
OPEN: all year.
FACILITIES: lounge, restaurant, kids' room, boot room, free Wi-Fi, in-room TV (Sky), in-room treatments, waterside terrace, public areas wheelchair accessible, small car park.
BACKGROUND MUSIC: all day in public areas.
LOCATION: central, on the harbour.
CHILDREN: all ages welcomed.
DOGS: allowed in 2 cottage bedrooms, not in main hotel.
CREDIT CARDS: all major cards.
PRICES: [2018] per room B&B £200–£405, D,B&B £316–£521. Set lunch £38, à la carte £58, 5-course tasting menu £75. 1-night bookings sometimes refused at weekends.

SEE ALSO SHORTLIST

ST MAWES Cornwall

TRESANTON

Up 137 steps, through 'glorious' gardens, 'one of the most comfortable establishments I've ever stayed in' occupies a higgle piggle of houses with 'extraordinary views' across Falmouth Bay. Olga Polizzi exploits its yachting-clubhouse origins with nautical hues, 'original Cornish art', a Poseidon mosaic. All but two of the 'magnificent bedrooms' face the sea, all have 'bags of charm': deckchair stripes on 'comfortable' bed, coastal prints, 'exceptional cleanliness'. 'The curtains were rich and heavy,' writes one trusted reader, 'and the windows opened (oh joy!). I could hear waves – and very little else.' Apart from the room above: 'slightly better soundproofing would have been even more luxurious.' It wouldn't worry youngsters, exhausted from a day spent in rock pools, the hotel's cinema and playroom. Adventurous guests can sail aboard Pinuccia, the hotel's vintage yacht, while, back on land, chef Paul Wadham's modern, Mediterranean menus include Basque-style monkfish; Porthilly oysters; spicy crab linguine. 'Prettily presented, delicious' breakfasts include 'perfect poached eggs; almost exactly spherical with yolk delightfully soft'. Hotel Endsleigh, Milton Abbot (see entry), is a sister. (Trevor Lockwood, Richard Mitton, and others)

27 Lower Castle Road
St Mawes
TR2 5DR

T: 01326 270055
E: manager@tresanton.com
W: www.tresanton.com

BEDROOMS: 30. In 5 houses.
OPEN: all year.
FACILITIES: 2 lounges, bar, restaurant, cinema, playroom, conference facilities, free Wi-Fi, in-room TV (Freeview), civil wedding licence, terrace, ¼-acre garden, 48-foot yacht, only restaurant wheelchair accessible.
BACKGROUND MUSIC: none.
LOCATION: on seafront, valet parking (car park up hill).
CHILDREN: all ages welcomed.
DOGS: allowed in some bedrooms and in dogs' bar.
CREDIT CARDS: Amex, MasterCard, Visa.
PRICES: [2018] per room B&B from £260. À la carte £44. 1-night bookings refused weekends in high season.

SEE ALSO SHORTLIST

SALCOMBE Devon

SOAR MILL COVE HOTEL

♥ Previous César winner

'We couldn't have enjoyed it more or been more welcome,' write trusted Guide correspondents this year, after dropping by at Keith Makepeace's long-established, family-run hotel overlooking National Trust coastline and sea. 'Excellent in almost every respect,' agreed a Guide regular in 2018. 'The staff were well trained, pleasant and helpful.' Bedrooms ('comfortable and well appointed') look over cove or countryside, with glass doors on to a private furnished patio. 'The setting is gorgeous, and the building well maintained, old-fashioned in the best possible way.' By day, a café offers the likes of crab baguette, Soar Bay lobster. 'The delicious seafood chowder was packed with the freshest shellfish.' By night, in the restaurant, long-standing chef Ian MacDonald creates such dishes as heritage beetroot tarte Tatin; day-boat bream with Provençal mussels, clams, basil oil. Readers had some niggles, however, including the 'high mark-up on wine by the glass'. Breakfast brings Salcombe mackerel smokies, Aune Valley pork sausages, gammon, sauté potatoes – fuel for walking the South West Coastal Path. (Desmond and Jenny Balmer)

Soar Mill Cove
TQ7 3DS

T: 01548 561566
E: info@soarmillcove.co.uk
W: www.soarmillcove.co.uk

BEDROOMS: 22. 21 on ground floor, suitable for disabled.
OPEN: all year, except Jan (open Christmas/New Year).
FACILITIES: lounge, bar, restaurant, coffee shop, free Wi-Fi in reception, in-room TV (Freeview), indoor spring-fed swimming pool (15 by 10 metres), spa, gym, civil wedding licence, 10-acre grounds (tennis, play area), public rooms wheelchair accessible with adapted toilet.
BACKGROUND MUSIC: in public areas.
LOCATION: 3 miles SW of Salcombe.
CHILDREN: all ages welcomed.
DOGS: allowed in all but one bedroom, bar, coffee shop.
CREDIT CARDS: Amex, MasterCard, Visa.
PRICES: [2018] per room B&B £199–£329, D,B&B £269–£409. À la carte £39. 1-night bookings refused holiday weekends.

SEE ALSO SHORTLIST

SANDWICH Kent

Map 2:D5

♔ THE SALUTATION

NEW

César award: romantic hotel of the year

In a gem of a medieval Cinque Port town, this Queen Anne-style house designed by Sir Edwin Lutyens has a new lease of life as an upmarket hotel. Displaying 'evident love for the enterprise', new owners John and Dorothy Fothergill have 'redesigned and refurbished in lavish style', say Guide inspectors. 'The immediate impression is of space and indulgence. Original features abound.' An 'enormous' double-aspect bedroom had a king-size bed with antique carved headboard, a sofa, 'billowing, pale lilac curtains'. Windows overlooked gardens laid out (or at least influenced) by Gertrude Jekyll. In the bar, its walls 'crowded with portraits', a log from the garden burned fragrantly in the grate. 'The personable young barman/maître d'hôtel brought us menus, olives, a dish piled high with caramelised nuts.' The innermost dining room had just 'three long, varnished oak tables'. Behind a glass wall, chef Shane Hughes prepares such dishes as turbot with sweetcorn and watercress, gherkin, potato galette, chicken and butter glaze. Cooking courses will be offered from autumn 2018. At breakfast, choices included omelettes, Belgian waffles, smoked haddock.

Knightrider Street
Sandwich
CT13 9EW

T: 01304 619919
E: enquiries@the-salutation.com
W: www.the-salutation.com

BEDROOMS: 17. 8 in main house, 9 in three cottages.
OPEN: all year.
FACILITIES: drawing room, bar, 3 dining rooms, shop and café, free Wi-Fi, in-room TV (Freeview), civil wedding licence, 3½-acre gardens, unsuitable for disabled.
BACKGROUND MUSIC: in public areas.
LOCATION: town centre, walking distance from train station
CHILDREN: all ages welcomed.
DOGS: allowed in two cottages, gardens and café.
CREDIT CARDS: Amex, MasterCard, Visa.
PRICES: [2018] per room B&B £163–£335, DB&B £250–£425. Tasting menu £70, à la carte £54. Min. 2-night bookings at Christmas.

SEAHAM Co. Durham   Map 4:B4

SEAHAM HALL

Steeped in history, this 'wonderfully civilised' coastal Georgian mansion combines 'style, luxury and high standards'. Just the ticket for a 'sybaritic getaway', say Guide readers this year. Romantic yet boldly modern styling throughout befits the former home of Ada Lovelace (Lord Byron's daughter and the world's first computer programmer). Have someone run your bath – 'staff are helpful above and beyond what one should be able to expect of this level of hotel' – and pick your meal from the pillow menu in the 'large, magnificent' bedroom; one has French doors opening on to a private terrace; another a bathing platform with sea views. Each is equipped with bathrobes, an espresso machine, a card bearing the name of your porter and next day's weather forecast. Eateries include Ozone restaurant, for light, pan-Asian-inspired meals, and Byron's, where chef Damian Broom's daily-changing menu highlights locally sourced ingredients: roasted Whitby sea trout and fennel with saffron mayonnaise. Alongside its Serenity Spa, this is a great base from which to tramp along nearby beaches beneath dramatic cliffs. (David Grant, P and SG)

Lord Byron's Walk
Seaham
SR7 7AG

T: 0191 5161400
E: reservations@seaham-hall.com
W: www.seaham-hall.com

BEDROOMS: 21. 1 suitable for disabled.
OPEN: all year.
FACILITIES: lift, 2 lounges, bar, 2 restaurants, private dining room, conference facilities, in-room TV (Sky, BT), free Wi-Fi, civil wedding licence, spa (treatment rooms, outdoor hot tubs, sun terrace, fitness suite, 20-metre heated swimming pool), 37-acre grounds (terraces, putting green).
BACKGROUND MUSIC: all day in public areas.
LOCATION: 5 miles S of Sunderland.
CHILDREN: all ages welcomed.
DOGS: not allowed.
CREDIT CARDS: Amex, MasterCard, Visa.
PRICES: [2018] per room B&B from £195, D,B&B from £255. Set menu £30, à la carte £50.

SEAHOUSES Northumberland

Map 4:A4

ST AIDAN HOTEL & BISTRO NEW

'Right on the seafront looking out to the Farne
Islands and along the vast beach to Bamburgh
Castle', this 'very comfortable, professionally
run little hotel' enters the guide at the urging
of a trusted reader. Owners Rob and Tegan
Tait and staff are 'very friendly and helpful'.
Spotless bedrooms have been decorated in
seaside shades, 'pale greens and blues', and have
such 'thoughtful extras' as binoculars, to watch
passing ships. Resident Springer-Labrador cross
Moyo welcomes four-legged friends. Downstairs
there is a bar area with an honesty bar. On three
nights a week the breakfast room, with stripped
wooden floor, bespoke furniture and 'stunning
views', is transformed into a bistro popular with
locals ('a number of disappointed people who
hadn't booked were turned away'). Chef James
Ash devises seasonal menus of produce from
local suppliers. Perhaps a signature dish, slow-
cooked beef, red wine, smoked bacon, garlic,
thyme; coq au vin; roast hake fillet, chorizo and
pepper stew. The food is 'well prepared, very
tasty, not gourmet, but it isn't pretending to
be'. Breakfast brings locally smoked fish, free-
range eggs, home-made compote. 'We would
definitely stay again.' (Sarah Tier)

1 St Aidans
Seahouses
NE68 7SR

T: 01665 720355
E: info@staidanhotel.co.uk
W: staidanhotel.co.uk

BEDROOMS: 9. 2 in annexe.
OPEN: all year except 7 days over
Christmas, 2 Jan–2nd weekend Feb,
bistro closed Sun–Wed.
FACILITIES: breakfast room/bistro,
bar area (honesty bar), free Wi-Fi,
in-room TV (Freeview), front
lawn (picnic tables), unsuitable for
disabled.
BACKGROUND MUSIC: chilled acoustic
in public rooms.
LOCATION: 300 yds from harbour,
on north side of village, with views
towards Bamburgh.
CHILDREN: not under 12.
DOGS: allowed in annexe room and 1
area of breakfast room, not in bistro.
CREDIT CARDS: none (debit cards
accepted).
PRICES: [2018] per person B&B
£85–£135. À la carte £28.

SEAHOUSES Northumberland   Map 4:A4

ST CUTHBERT'S HOUSE

✿ Previous César winner

Regular Guide readers laud Jeff and Jill
Sutheran's B&B, forged from a 'delightfully
converted' Presbyterian church, as 'a perfect base
for exploring this beautiful part of the north-east'.
Its former incarnation is recalled by re-integrated
ecclesiastical features including the pulpit and
communion table. The Cuthbert Room, once
the sanctuary, is now the guest lounge with the
original harmonium and wooden pillars joined
by comfy sofas and an honesty bar. Spacious
bedrooms, each named after a saint, have a
devoted following; 'very comfortable with a
stylish shower', 'St Aidan gets lots of morning
light' through the original arched window. All
rooms have a super-king-size bed and Nespresso
machine, alongside fluffy towels, dressing gowns
and Gilchrist & Soames' toiletries. You might
even get live music – the house holds a series
of folk and acoustic concerts. The extensive
locally sourced breakfast includes sausages from
an award-winning Longframlington butcher,
free-range eggs from a nearby farm, oak-smoked
haddock from Seahouses' smokehouse. Jill
supplies home-made marmalade for fresh bread
from Trotter's Bakery. (MG, and others)

25% DISCOUNT VOUCHERS

192 Main Street
Seahouses
NE68 7UB

T: 01665 720456
E: stay@stcuthbertshouse.com
W: www.stcuthbertshouse.com

BEDROOMS: 6. 2 on ground floor,
1 suitable for disabled.
OPEN: all year except 'holiday
periods in winter'.
FACILITIES: lounge, dining area, free
Wi-Fi, in-room TV (Freeview),
public rooms wheelchair accessible.
BACKGROUND MUSIC: instrumental at
breakfast.
LOCATION: under 1 mile from
harbour and village centre.
CHILDREN: not under 12.
DOGS: assistance dogs only.
CREDIT CARDS: MasterCard, Visa.
PRICES: [2018] per room B&B £110–
£130. 1-night bookings occasionally
refused in high season.

SHAFTESBURY Dorset

Map 2:D1

LA FLEUR DE LYS

In a hilltop market town familiar from Ridley Scott's classic Hovis ad (New World Symphony, brass band), this restaurant-with-rooms, launched in 1991, is as good today as it has always been. Since 2003 it has occupied an ivy-clad former girls' boarding school. Owned by 'professional and very helpful' trio, Mary and David Griffin-Shepherd and Marc Preston, it is praised for its 'very friendly' ethos. Bedrooms, named after grape varieties, are pretty and traditional, with a modern bathroom. All have a mini-fridge, fresh coffee, milk, home-made biscuits. Sauvignon was judged 'clean and comfortable but small': if you mean to stay a while, go for a superior room, perhaps with a four-poster. In the kitchen, David and Marc cook such dishes as honey-roasted guineafowl, roast sweet potatoes, broad beans and spring onions in a creamy thyme sauce; sautéed turbot fillet with king prawns on roasted fennel in lobster sauce. There is always a vegetarian option. Wine tastings, cookery demonstrations and music evenings are a regular feature. At breakfast there is 'fresh juice, a good choice of dishes cooked to order'. More reports, please.

25% DISCOUNT VOUCHERS

Bleke Street
Shaftesbury
SP7 8AW

T: 01747 853717
E: info@lafleurdelys.co.uk
W: www.lafleurdelys.co.uk

BEDROOMS: 8. 1, on ground floor, suitable for disabled.
OPEN: all year.
FACILITIES: lounge, bar, dining room, conference room, free Wi-Fi, in-room TV (Freeview), small courtyard garden, restaurant and toilet wheelchair accessible.
BACKGROUND MUSIC: none, but some live music events.
LOCATION: N edge of historic town centre.
CHILDREN: all ages welcomed.
DOGS: not allowed.
CREDIT CARDS: Amex, MasterCard, Visa.
PRICES: [2018] per room B&B single £85–£130, double £100–£170, D,B&B double from £215. Set meals £30–£38, à la carte £40. 1-night bookings sometimes refused at weekends in summer.

SHEFFIELD Yorkshire

Map 4:E4

BROCCO ON THE PARK

✿ Previous César winner

'Effortless charm and warmth' personify Tiina Carr's 'vibrant' hotel, a 'stone's throw' from the Botanical Gardens. Sheffield-inflected hygge, the Scandinavian holistic concept of cosiness, seeps through the Finnish-born owner's elegant parkside Edwardian house, from the 'warm, professional' staff to the 'Scandi-chic' style. Throughout, muted hues, wooden floors and huge windows; a subtle bird theme evokes Picasso, said to have stayed in the building while attending a peace conference. Bedrooms might have a copper bath, or an Arne Jacobsen bubble chair suspended from the ceiling. Each has a 'comfortable' bed, rich lambswool blankets, a little baked treat, an espresso machine and comfy robes. 'Though roadside, I slept soundly.' Down in the restaurant, visitors in 2018 particularly enjoyed chef Leslie Buddington's '"small plates concept" of Nordic-style dishes, which were delivered with great skill'. The vegetarian celeriac steak with pickled apple 'satisfied even the die-hard carnivore'. Breakfast on banana-coconut pancakes, 'beautifully grilled' bacon. A redeveloped terrace opened in the summer. (M and T Sachak-Patwa, Robert Sandham)

92 Brocco Bank
Sheffield
S11 8RS

T: 0114 266 1233
E: hello@brocco.co.uk
W: www.brocco.co.uk

BEDROOMS: 8. 1 suitable for disabled.
OPEN: all year, restaurant closed Sun 6 pm and Christmas Day.
FACILITIES: reception area with sofas, 2 restaurants (1 with bar), free Wi-Fi, in-room smart TV, terrace (barbecue, seating), bicycle hire.
BACKGROUND MUSIC: in restaurant, plus Sunday jazz afternoons.
LOCATION: 1½ miles W of city centre.
CHILDREN: all ages welcomed (under-3s free).
DOGS: allowed only on terrace.
CREDIT CARDS: Amex, MasterCard, Visa.
PRICES: [2018] room only £110–£240. Cooked breakfast from £5, à la carte £40.

SIDLESHAM Sussex

Map 2:E3

THE CRAB & LOBSTER

Facing the 'wide sweep of tidal mudflats' surrounding Pagham Harbour, this whitewashed restaurant-with-rooms stands as a 'tucked-away' beacon of 'delicious food' and 'exceptional hospitality'. Owned by Sam and Janet Bakose, the 350-year-old inn 'has a wonderfully timeless air'. A bright renovation brings a smart rustic-chic style and muted coastal palette to low ceilings and exposed beams. The bar and restaurant with inglenook fireplace, exposed bricks and 'friendly, efficient' staff 'does not disappoint'. Chef Clyde Hollett's seafood-heavy menu features the likes of grilled mackerel fillet with fennel, pepper and citrus salad, orange and tarragon salsa; Selsey crab gratin. The hum of the restaurant may drift up to the room directly above, but 'it's an old building, so not unexpected'. Bedrooms, 'comfortable, with a fine modern bathroom', have the same restful, muted colours and contemporary finish as downstairs. Binoculars are left in rooms that look across the marshland. Adjacent 'roomy, comfortable' Crab Cottage is ideal for self-sufficient groups. At breakfast, 'interesting cooked options' include smoked mackerel with poached eggs and grilled tomatoes. 'Excellently located' for twitchers itching to explore the nearby nature reserve. (Michael Gwinnell, and others)

Mill Lane
Sidlesham
PO20 7NB

T: 01243 641233
E: enquiries@crab-lobster.co.uk
W: www.crab-lobster.co.uk

BEDROOMS: 4. 2 in adjacent self-catering Crab Cottage.
OPEN: all year.
FACILITIES: bar/restaurant, free Wi-Fi, in-room TV (Freeview), terrace, small beer garden, bar and restaurant wheelchair accessible.
BACKGROUND MUSIC: 'quiet' in restaurant and bar.
LOCATION: 6 miles S of Chichester.
CHILDREN: all ages welcomed.
DOGS: allowed in garden area.
CREDIT CARDS: Amex, MasterCard, Visa.
PRICES: [2018] per room B&B single £110–£130, double £185–£310. À la carte £38. 2-night min. stay at weekends.

SIDMOUTH Devon   Map 1:C5

HOTEL RIVIERA

'Old-fashioned in style and lovely for it.'
Returning guests this year were pleased to
discover that Peter Wharton's 'splendid' hotel
overlooking Lyme Bay 'sails gracefully on,
without feeling the need to change things
for the sake of change'. The 'very helpful,
attentive' staff 'maintain all its high standards'.
'Beautifully clean', the public rooms are 'very
comfortable'; 'the decor is in keeping with
the hotel's style (though the red floral carpet
throughout was rather a shock).' 'Our town
room was not so large but fine, with quality
sheets and blankets – what a pleasant change
– and a modern bathroom.' The best rooms
('very grand') have large bay windows offering
'wonderful sea views'. Chef Martin Osedo's
'inviting' menu, including such dishes as steamed
paupiette of lemon sole, salmon mousse, lemon
couscous, fish cream, is 'flawlessly served' in the
dining room, where 'a convivial atmosphere
pervades'. 'It is so special to return to the room
after dinner to find it tidied, curtains drawn and
bed turned down.' Breakfast, served at the table,
is 'extensive': full English, an omelette, kipper,
yogurt, freshly squeezed juices'. (Max Lickfold,
Trevor Lockwood, and others)

The Esplanade
Sidmouth
EX10 8AY

T: 01395 515201
E: enquiries@hotelriviera.co.uk
W: www.hotelriviera.co.uk

BEDROOMS: 26. Some suitable for
disabled.
OPEN: all year.
FACILITIES: lift, lounge, bar,
restaurant, function facilities, free
Wi-Fi, in-room TV (Freeview),
terrace, opposite beach (safe
bathing).
BACKGROUND MUSIC: in bar and
restaurant, occasional live piano
music in bar.
LOCATION: central, on the esplanade.
CHILDREN: all ages welcomed).
DOGS: small dogs allowed in some
bedrooms, not in public rooms
except foyer.
CREDIT CARDS: all major cards.
PRICES: [2018] per person B&B
£121–£198, D,B&B £142–£219. Set
dinner £40–£44, à la carte £44.

SEE ALSO SHORTLIST

SNETTISHAM Norfolk

Map 2:A4

THE ROSE & CROWN

Across from the cricket pitch, Jeannette and Anthony Goodrich's 'delightful' 14th-century whitewashed pub has open fires, low beams, roses round the door. It's very much a village local, child-friendly, studiedly casual. 'No interior designers,' they tell us. If you want somewhere more boutique, perhaps consider sister hotel Bank House, King's Lynn (see entry). The pub bedrooms are, however, individually styled, with desk, comfy armchair, 'decent biscuits', fresh milk in a fridge on the landing. A room with wheelchair access had 'a sizeable wet room, large bed with excellent linen', Designers Guild fabrics – 'everything about it was beautiful'. In one of several dining areas or the walled garden, Jamie Clarke's cooking runs from pub classics (scampi, steak burger) to the likes of slow-cooked shin of beef, burnt leek and Stilton risotto, kale chips; an 'excellent curry special'. Mussels, oysters, lobster, crab are sourced from fishermen at Brancaster and Thornham, game from local estates, meat is traceable from field to table. Breakfast, served until 11 am, brings 'brilliant local sausages and bacon', avocado on sourdough. Snettisham Beach is an RSPB reserve. Sandringham is practically next door. (SP)

Old Church Road
Snettisham
PE31 7LX

T: 01485 541382
E: info@roseandcrownsnettisham.co.uk
W: www.roseandcrownsnettisham.co.uk

BEDROOMS: 16. 2 on ground floor, 1 suitable for disabled.
OPEN: all year.
FACILITIES: 3 bar areas, 2 restaurant rooms, garden room, free Wi-Fi, in-room TV (Freeview), large walled garden (children's play area, climbing frame).
BACKGROUND MUSIC: 'low-key, mainly soft jazz' in dining areas.
LOCATION: in village centre, 5 miles S of Hunstanton.
CHILDREN: all ages welcomed.
DOGS: 'well-behaved dogs' allowed in bedrooms, bars and garden room, not in dining areas.
CREDIT CARDS: Amex, MasterCard, Visa.
PRICES: [2018] per room B&B single £100, double £120, D,B&B (Sun–Thurs) single £125, double £170. À la carte £29..

SOMERTON Somerset

Map 1:C6

THE LYNCH COUNTRY HOUSE

A scattering of jazz memorabilia sets the tone at this Georgian country house B&B on a ridge overlooking the Cary river valley. 'We stayed here for the second year running,' say Guide regulars in 2018. 'It's very comfy.' Owned by musician Roy Copeland, with 'delightful, helpful' Lynne Vincent as manager, it is run with a 'touch of class'. In the 'lovely garden', black swans and ducks mill about on a lake, surrounded by woodland. traditionally decorated bedrooms in the main house and converted coach house are 'very comfortable' and enjoy. Rooms have a country cottage air with pretty florals. However, housekeeping could be better, say some readers. Bathroom fixtures may appear old-fashioned ('they all worked though!'). Lynne has a wealth of local knowledge, with 'superb advice' on where to dine come evening. Top pick: the White Hart (see Shortlist) in the centre of the medieval market town. 'Breakfast is extremely good.' Taken in the orangery, it includes French yogurts, cereals, freshly squeezed orange juice; smoked streaky bacon, toasted muffins, creamy eggs, all cooked to order. Equally tasty is the vista from the belvedere. (Rodney and Mary Milne-Day)

4 Behind Berry
Somerton
TA11 7PD

T: 01458 272316
E: enquiries@thelynchcountry
house.co.uk
W: www.thelynchcountryhouse.
co.uk

BEDROOMS: 9. 4, in coach house, on ground floor.
OPEN: all year, only coach house rooms at Christmas and New Year, no breakfast 25/26 Dec, 1 Jan.
FACILITIES: breakfast room, small sitting area, free Wi-Fi, in-room TV (Freeview), ¾-acre grounds (lake), unsuitable for disabled.
BACKGROUND MUSIC: none.
LOCATION: edge of town.
CHILDREN: all ages welcomed.
DOGS: allowed (not unattended) in 1 coach house room, not in public rooms.
CREDIT CARDS: Amex, MasterCard, Visa.
PRICES: [2018] per room B&B single £70–£95. double £80–£125.,

SEE ALSO SHORTLIST

SOUTH DALTON Yorkshire

Map 4:D5

THE PIPE AND GLASS INN

St Mary's 'stunning spire' rises like Jack's beanstalk – a heavenly marker of the approach to James and Kate Mackenzie's 'sublime' pub-with-rooms. Hidden within the 'enchanting' village's unassuming former coaching inn is a trove of the 'very best hospitality' and 'outstanding food' that 'draws admirers from near and far'. While hand-pulled pints and thick sandwiches are offered in the atmospheric bar, the chef/patron's Michelin-starred restaurant might serve salt-beef hash cake, Yorkshire rhubarb ketchup, crispy pickled onion rings. 'Duck three ways was tender and tasty, the lemon posset good enough for us both to have it three times in four days.' Visitors this year say 'the brilliant staff deserve special mention: all were cheerful, attentive and very efficient'. Ringing a 'beautifully maintained' herb garden are five 'well-appointed' modern bedrooms, bold of pattern and bright of colour. 'Our smart room had a big, comfy bed, spectacular bathroom, large patio, a wood-burning stove and blankets in case it got chilly, plus air conditioning.' Breakfast, pre-ordered, met with 'universal approval': 'Golden' eggs, salty bacon, 'tempting' black pudding, home-baked bread.' (Peter Anderson, and others)

West End
South Dalton
HU17 7PN

T: 01430 810246
E: email@pipeandglass.co.uk
W: www.pipeandglass.co.uk

BEDROOMS: 5. All on ground floor in garden, suitable for disabled.
OPEN: all year, no room reservations Sun and Mon.
FACILITIES: lounge, conservatory, bar, restaurant, private dining room, free Wi-Fi, in-room TV (Freeview), patio (alfresco dining), garden (herbarium, kitchen garden).
BACKGROUND MUSIC: in bar and restaurant.
LOCATION: 7 miles NW of Beverley.
CHILDREN: all ages welcomed ('little people's' menu).
DOGS: not allowed.
CREDIT CARDS: Amex, MasterCard, Visa.
PRICES: [2018] per room B&B £165–£250. À la carte £100.

SOUTH LEIGH Oxfordshire   Map 3:E6

ARTIST RESIDENCE OXFORDSHIRE

NEW

That artful couple Justin and Charlotte Salisbury have transformed a 16th-century, thatched village inn (albeit one that had a helipad) into the newest Residence in their small, quirky boutique hotel chain (see index). Guide inspectors received 'a textbook welcome', before being shown to one of four bedrooms under the eaves, 'a splendid suite with high ceiling, exposed beams, large, high bed, copper bathtub', a 'well-stocked' minibar, an espresso machine, 'upmarket snacks', gowns and slippers, a bathroom with rainfall shower. In the past year, a bedroom and two no-less-splendid suites have been created in outbuildings, or you can opt for the Shepherd's Hut, overlooking the herb garden. 'The public areas have been redecorated in bold, dark colours, William Morris-style wallpaper, heavy wooden furniture, colourful rugs, kilim cushions, neon artwork.' New chef Tim Kewley's 'outstanding' cooking is served in the bar, with its flagstone floors, wood-burner, 'nooks and crannies'. Full marks for 'beautifully presented' 'braised brisket topped with caramelised onions on mash with a delicious rich sauce'. At breakfast, there were freshly squeezed juices, scrambled eggs on a toasted muffin.

The Mason Arms
South Leigh
OX29 6XN

T: 01993 656220
E: oxford@artistresidence.co.uk
W: www.artistresidence.co.uk/
our-hotels/oxford/

BEDROOMS: 9, 1 bedroom and 2 suites in outbuilding, Shepherd's Hut in garden.
OPEN: all year.
FACILITIES: bar, restaurant (2 dining areas, closed Sun eve), free Wi-Fi, in-room TV (Freeview), large beer garden, unsuitable for disabled.
BACKGROUND MUSIC: in pub and restaurant.
LOCATION: countryside, 10 miles from Oxford, 3 miles from Witney centre.
CHILDREN: all ages welcomed.
DOGS: allowed in some rooms and public rooms (£20 per dog per night, dog beds provided).
CREDIT CARDS: Amex, MasterCard, Visa.
PRICES: [2018] Room only £130–£425. À la carte £32. Min. 2-night stay at weekends.

SOUTHAMPTON Hampshire

Map 2:E2

THE PIG IN THE WALL

While smaller than some of its rural siblings, the second of Robin Hutson's Pig hotels, tucked into Southampton's medieval city walls, is certainly not the runt of the litter. It shares the family trait of quirky, informal hospitality. Guests enter through the relaxed hybrid of lounge, bar and reception where 'helpful' staff can check you in and serve a glass of wine with deli-counter fare: perhaps a charcuterie board for lunch, or salmon cakes with pickled cucumber for dinner. For a more 'eventful' meal, take the free Land Rover to The Pig in the Forest, Brockenhurst (see entry). Decor follows the group's shabby-chic style: mismatched armchairs, trophy heads, old artwork, repurposed railway sleeper floorboards. The winning formula also embraces 'modern, well-thought-out and practical' bedrooms, with Nespresso machine, 'efficient blackout system' and well-stocked bedroom 'larder'. Spacious rooms have roll-top bath (most in-room) and 'super-king-size bed with spiralling posts'. 'Some help up with our bags would have been appreciated' to reach a Snug room beneath the roof's timbers. Breakfast is a buffet, or a deli dish, for example, toasted sourdough with spiced avocado and poached egg. (LR, and others)

8 Western Esplanade
Southampton
SO14 2AZ

T: 02380 636900
E: reception@thepiginthewall.com
W: www.thepighotel.com

BEDROOMS: 12. 2 on ground floor.
OPEN: all year.
FACILITIES: open-plan lounge/bar/deli counter, free Wi-Fi, in-room TV (Freeview), public rooms wheelchair accessible.
BACKGROUND MUSIC: in public areas.
LOCATION: on the outskirts of the city.
CHILDREN: all ages welcomed.
DOGS: not allowed.
CREDIT CARDS: Amex, MasterCard, Visa.
PRICES: [2018] room £135–£190. Breakfast £10.

SEE ALSO SHORTLIST

STAMFORD Lincolnshire

THE GEORGE

'As good as ever in all respects,' writes a regular visitor after this year's visit to Lawrence Hoskins's popular hotel, a historic landmark of this Georgian town. 'The reception staff, without exception, were helpful and extremely pleasant.' Past guests including Charles I and William III might have agreed that some rooms are 'quite small', but would surely have appreciated the evening turndown, complimentary morning newspaper, tea or coffee, bathrooms with robes, upmarket toiletries. Larger suites enjoy such features as four-poster or half-tester beds, leather sofa, mullioned windows – a legacy of Lord Burghley's 1597 rebuild of the inn. Public rooms have wood panelling, exposed stone walls, open fires and original signs for London and York, reminders of its days as a stagecoach stop. Daniel Lambert, formerly Britain's heaviest man, whose walking canes decorate the entrance hall, would certainly have enjoyed the food, either the Garden Room's less formal fare, where lobster spaghetti was 'faultless', or the Oak Room, where chef Paul Nicholls's dishes include the likes of roasted rack of lamb, garlic, herb crust, redcurrant, rosemary. Breakfast was 'excellent, cooked to order, plenty of choice'. (Helen Ann Davies, IB, and others)

71 St Martin's
Stamford
PE9 2LB

T: 01780 750750
E: reservations@georgehotelof
   stamford.com
W: www.georgehotelofstamford.
   com

BEDROOMS: 45.
OPEN: all year.
FACILITIES: 2 lounges, 2 bars, 2 restaurants, 2 private dining rooms, business centre, free Wi-Fi, in-room TV (Sky, Freeview), civil wedding licence, 2-acre grounds (courtyard, gardens), public rooms wheelchair accessible, adapted toilet.
BACKGROUND MUSIC: none.
LOCATION: ¼ mile from centre.
CHILDREN: all ages welcomed.
DOGS: allowed, not unattended in bedrooms, only guide dogs in restaurants.
CREDIT CARDS: Amex, Mastercard, Visa.
PRICES: [2018] per room B&B single from £130, double £160–£290. À la carte £65. 1-night bookings refused during Burghley Horse Trials.

SEE ALSO SHORTLIST

STANTON WICK Somerset

Map 1:B6

THE CARPENTERS ARMS

A row of former miners' pantiled cottages combines into a rambling, 'appealing' country inn in a picturesque setting where, regulars report, 'generous portions' and 'generous hospitality' come as standard. Repeat visitors in 2018 found this 'good-value' spot 'excellent as always'. After a busy day they appreciated warm bread, olive oil and balsamic, eaten by the fireside. 'Everyone is so obliging and helpful.' The 'thoroughly attractive' low-beamed bar has a blazing log fire, squashy sofas, hand-pumped ale. Summer sees parasols and blooming flowers open in the beer garden. Varying in size, bedrooms are modern but not voguish. 'Our very comfortable and relaxing room at the rear had dual-aspect windows and a sofa.' A bathroom had a decent shower, 'fluffy towels, an array of toiletries'. In the evening, the 'popular pub' serves new chef Christian Wragg's seasonal menu, perhaps sauté of locally landed monkfish, mussels, prawns, fondant potato, bouillabaisse; West Country rib-eye steak. At breakfast, 'the usual scrum' is avoided thanks to table service: 'very tasty' bacon and sausages, a fruit platter. 'Listing some vegetarian options on the breakfast menu' would be appreciated. (Jeanette Bloor, and others)

Wick Lane
Stanton Wick
BS39 4BX

T: 01761 490202
E: carpenters@buccaneer.co.uk
W: www.the-carpenters-arms.co.uk

BEDROOMS: 13.
OPEN: all year except evenings 25/26 Dec, 1 Jan.
FACILITIES: bar, snug, lounge, 2 restaurants, function room, free Wi-Fi, in-room TV (Freeview), patio, secure parking, public areas accessible for wheelchairs and adapted for disabled.
BACKGROUND MUSIC: none.
LOCATION: 8 miles S of Bristol, 8 miles W of Bath.
CHILDREN: all ages welcomed (under-12s free, children's menu, high chairs, changing facilities available).
DOGS: allowed in bar and outside areas.
CREDIT CARDS: Amex, MasterCard, Visa.
PRICES: [2018] per room B&B single £70–£102, double £100–£170, À la carte £36.50.

STOKE BY NAYLAND Suffolk

Map 2:C5

THE CROWN

NEW

In the Stour valley, close to the Essex border, Richard Sunderland's pub-with-rooms stands in the 'village centre, surrounded by landscaped gardens, with views over lovely countryside'. Accommodation is in a separate, purpose-built block 'designed to match the Suffolk vernacular'. Guide inspectors' ground-floor room had French windows on to a private terrace, 'with a tall hedge, a paved area, shrubs and plants, a garden path right by the window – we were soon on nodding terms with the gardener'. Standard rooms have a walk-in shower, deluxe rooms a bath and separate shower. In the open bar and dining room, 'furnished with rustic-style chairs and tables', there is 'a glass-fronted wine "shop" where bottles can be bought for dinner or to take'. The food receives mixed reviews. Trusted readers enjoyed 'delicious grilled half lobster and dressed crab'. Our inspectors' watercress and asparagus soup, and roasted asparagus with crisp poached egg and hollandaise, were 'very good'; a courgette linguine and an Eton mess were less successful. The wine list was 'a delight, surprisingly reasonable'. Breakfast brings home-made jams and muesli, 'excellent fresh orange juice'. (David Bartley, Michael Gwinnell, and others)

Park Street
Stoke by Nayland
CO6 4SE

T: 01206 262001
E: info@crowninn.net
W: www.crowninn.net

BEDROOMS: 11. In separate annexe, 7 on ground floor, 1 suitable for disabled.
OPEN: all year except 25/26 Dec.
FACILITIES: bar, restaurant, snug area, reception area with seating, terrace, wine shop, free Wi-Fi, in-room TV (BT, Freeview), garden, parking, public rooms wheelchair accessible, adapted toilet.
BACKGROUND MUSIC: none.
LOCATION: village centre.
CHILDREN: all ages welcomed.
DOGS: allowed in parts of restaurant but not in bedrooms.
CREDIT CARDS: Amex, MasterCard, Visa.
PRICES: [2018] per room B&B single £95–£210, double £145–£225, D,B&B double £165–£350. À la carte £35.

STUDLAND Dorset

Map 2:E2

THE PIG ON THE BEACH

♥ Previous César winner

Forged from the coastal villa of an aristocratic MP this 'gloriously Gothic mini-Hogwarts, all gargoyles and turrets' gazes out across the sea to Old Harry Rocks. Though it was 'heaving with young weekend visitors', regular Guide readers found it 'very welcoming, with good interaction between staff and guests'. A friend struggling with the stairs was, without asking, offered an 'equally comfy room lower down. Very touching.' The fourth of Robin Hutson's growing litter, it boasts some 'wonderfully whimsical' rooms; two in thatched dovecotes, one with 'a loo slipped discreetly into a bay window'. All have muted hues, Roberts radio, monsoon shower. In the conservatory dining room – 'shabby chic, informal, no chairs alike' – James Golding and Andy Wright source most ingredients from a 25-mile radius, including the kitchen garden, for dishes including crispy Jurassic Coast gurnard with braised pork cheek; crown of Purbeck partridge. Two gripes, 'Muzak everywhere'; 'food good but menu didn't change over three days'. Lovely grounds include the bunker where Churchill and Eisenhower observed D-Day rehearsals. (Josie and Guy Mayers, IB)

Manor House
Studland
BH19 3AU

T: 01929 450288
E: reservations@thepighotel.com
W: www.thepighotel.com

BEDROOMS: 23. Some on ground floor, 2 Dovecot hideaways, Harry's Hut and Pig Hut in grounds.
OPEN: all year.
FACILITIES: bar, lounge, snug, restaurant, private dining room, free Wi-Fi, in-room TV (Freeview), 2 treatment cabins, garden, unsuitable for disabled.
BACKGROUND MUSIC: all day in public areas.
LOCATION: above Studland beach.
CHILDREN: all ages welcomed.
DOGS: not allowed.
CREDIT CARDS: Amex, MasterCard, Visa.
PRICES: [2018] room only £155–£360. Breakfast £10–£15, à la carte £35. 1-night bookings refused at weekends, Christmas, New Year.

STURMINSTER NEWTON Dorset   Map 2:E1

PLUMBER MANOR

'One for traditionalists,' write trusted Guide readers, of this child-friendly, dog-friendly Jacobean ancestral home in Thomas Hardy country, run by owners Richard and Brian Prideaux-Brune, with Richard's wife, Alison. The welcome is famously warm. Interiors are filled with paintings and antiques. The portrait gallery hosts a grand piano and probably the largest, lumpiest sofa you will ever sit upon. The lovely gardens and house are 'immaculate', and – traditionalists take note – four main-house bedrooms have recently been updated with contemporary Farrow & Ball tones, new carpet, and fresh bathroom with a walk-in shower. 'No avocado bath,' we are told. Our readers stayed in the converted stone barn where rooms still offer a more dated style. Before dinner, guests drink aperitifs by the log fire as Richard Prideaux-Brune makes lively conversation. In the kitchen, brother Brian, with Louis Haskell, cooks a daily-changing menu of such 'good, honest fare' as partridge breast, smoked bacon, apple bubble-and-squeak. Devotees come for the hospitality, the craik, the cooking, the sense of 'true escape', the shooting if that's their bag, the authentic country house experience. (Chris and Erika Savory)

Sturminster Newton
DT10 2AF

T: 01258 472507
E: book@plumbermanor.com
W: www.plumbermanor.com

BEDROOMS: 16. 10 on ground floor in courtyard, 2 suitable for disabled.
OPEN: all year except Feb.
FACILITIES: snug, bar, dining room, gallery, free Wi-Fi, in-room TV (Freeview), 1-acre grounds (garden, tennis, croquet, stream), restaurant, lounge and toilet wheelchair accessible.
BACKGROUND MUSIC: none.
LOCATION: 2½ miles SW of Sturminster Newton.
CHILDREN: all ages welcomed.
DOGS: allowed in 4 courtyard bedrooms, not in public rooms.
CREDIT CARDS: Diners, MasterCard, Visa.
PRICES: [2018] per room B&B single £115–£145, double £160–£240. Set dinner £30–£38.

SWAFFHAM Norfolk

Map 2:B5

STRATTONS

Where does one find sanctuary in the middle of town? At the end of a discreet lane behind the main street. Les and Vanessa Scott's playful, Palladian-style house is all comfort and bonhomie. A pair of preening cats at the door signals that you're in the right place. 'In the sitting area, a wonderfully mad chandelier hangs above arresting, eclectic pieces of art.' The 'cordial, welcoming staff' are managed by Hannah and Dominic Hughes, the Scotts' daughter and her husband. The 'imaginative' bedrooms, spread across the main house and converted outbuildings, are equal parts quirky and practical. One has a Moroccan-style tented ceiling, another a cinema screen and film collection. 'Our comfortable ground-floor suite had an attractive bedroom and sitting room (the walls were amusingly decorated with dog silhouettes), but the deep bathtub in the bathroom was best suited to mountaineers.' In the award-winning basement restaurant, Jules Hetherton whips up modern British dinners based on local, seasonal and ethical produce, while 'tiny, bustling' CoCoes deli serves lunch of 'rightly famous' fishcakes with 'an exceptional fennel slaw'. (MAS, and others)

4 Ash Close
Swaffham
PE37 7NH

T: 01760 723845
E: enquiries@strattonshotel.com
W: www.strattonshotel.com

BEDROOMS: 14. 6 in annexes, 1 on ground floor.
OPEN: all year except 1 week at Christmas.
FACILITIES: drawing room, reading room, restaurant, free Wi-Fi, in-room TV (Freeview), terrace, café/deli, 1-acre garden, café wheelchair accessible.
BACKGROUND MUSIC: all day in public areas.
LOCATION: central, parking.
CHILDREN: all ages welcomed.
DOGS: allowed in some bedrooms (£10 per day), lounges, not in restaurant.
CREDIT CARDS: Amex, MasterCard, Visa.
PRICES: [2018] per room B&B from £99, D,B&B £159–£310. À la carte £30. 1-night bookings refused weekends, 3-night min. bank holidays.

SWALLOWCLIFFE Wiltshire

Map 2:D1

THE ROYAL OAK

♀ Previous César winner

In a 'quiet, wooded valley', this thatched village pub had stood empty and decaying for more than seven years, when three villagers stepped in to rescue it. 'The interiors would not be out of place in the smartest glossies,' say Guide inspectors, who were 'welcomed with charm and warmth'. Past the bar/reception lies 'a succession of drinking and dining areas', with 'well-chosen modern artwork', wooden furniture by local designer Matthew Burt ('I would give my eye teeth for the chairs'). Bedrooms have a cool, contemporary look, proper coffee, fluffy towels. Fonthill, overlooking the garden, had an emperor-size bed, a 'whizzy' shower, 'brilliant lighting from ceiling spots'. Ashcombe, in the eaves, looking into the canopy of the eponymous oak, has a freestanding bath in a stone-walled bathroom, a super-king-size bed – and a beanbag for two. In the oak-beamed conservatory, Michael Smith's inventive dishes might include poached and roasted chicken supreme, parsley root, pea purée, smoked bacon, sauce royale, or a simple rare roast beef sandwich with fries. At breakfast there is home-made granola, smoked salmon, avocado, free-range eggs. 'A remarkable place.' (JM, and others)

Swallowcliffe
SP3 5PA

T: 01747 870211
E: hello@royaloakswallowcliffe.
   com
W: www.royaloakswallowcliffe.
   com

BEDROOMS: 6. 1 suitable for disabled.
OPEN: all year, but no accommodation 25 Dec evening.
FACILITIES: lift, bar, dining room, Oak Room, free Wi-Fi, in-room TV (Freeview), garden with outdoor seating, public rooms wheelchair accessible.
BACKGROUND MUSIC: none.
LOCATION: 2 miles SE of Tisbury.
CHILDREN: all ages welcomed.
DOGS: 'friendly, well-behaved' dogs allowed in 1 bedroom, public rooms except Oak Room (treats, towels provided).
CREDIT CARDS: Amex, MasterCard, Visa.
PRICES: [2018] per room B&B £85–£150. À la carte £33.

TALLAND-BY-LOOE Cornwall

Map 1:D3

TALLAND BAY HOTEL

'The style is one of the unique assets' at Teresa
and Kevin O'Sullivan's cliff-top hotel overlooking
sub-tropical gardens filled with whimsical
sculpture and statuary. 'Taking in all the little
pieces of artwork is entertainment in its own
right.' The welcome is appreciated too. 'The
staff were very kind. Realising my husband's
problem with steps they upgraded us to a ground-
floor room at no extra cost. Comfortable room.
Comfortable bed.' All bedrooms are individually
styled, some with sea and garden views, perhaps
an emperor-size sleigh bed or four-poster, an
egg-shaped bath. In dining room and brasserie
'the food is wonderful'. Chef Nick Hawke's
creative menus use local seafood in such dishes as
macadamia-crusted hake, Cornish crab, saffron
pommes purées, onion fondue, purple sprouting
broccoli, crab bisque. You can eat more simply
from the lounge menu, perhaps Cornish cheeses
or Fowey river mussels. Breakfast has 'everything
you would expect'. And a little more – sausages
for guests' dogs (and chicken for their supper).
'Our dog received treats, bowl and bed. We could
have her with us in the brasserie. This is the most
dog-friendly hotel we know.' (Josie Mayers, BF)

Porthallow
Talland-by-Looe
PL13 2JB

T: 01503 272667
E: info@tallandbayhotel.com
W: www.tallandbayhotel.co.uk

BEDROOMS: 23. 4 in cottages, 6 on
ground floor.
OPEN: all year.
FACILITIES: lounge, bar, restaurant,
brasserie/conservatory, free Wi-Fi,
in-room TV (Freeview), civil
wedding licence, terrace, outside
seating, 2-acre garden, public rooms
wheelchair accessible.
BACKGROUND MUSIC: in bar and
restaurant.
LOCATION: 2½ miles SW of Looe.
CHILDREN: all ages welcomed.
DOGS: welcome by prior
arrangement in bedrooms and
brasserie, not in restaurant (£12.50
per dog per night includes sausage
breakfast, chicken dinner).
CREDIT CARDS: all major cards.
PRICES: [2018] per room B&B
£160–£350, D,B&B £235–£425.
À la carte £44. 1-night bookings
refused weekends in peak season.

TAPLOW Berkshire

Map 2:D3

CLIVEDEN HOUSE

Having hosted everyone from Winston Churchill to Meghan Markle the night before the royal wedding, this 'superbly refurbished' Italianate mansion seduces visitors with the prospect of 'luxurious country house living'. The 17th-century stately home, horseshoeing around the Fountain of Love, is renowned for its 'exceptional hospitality', 'stunning bedrooms' and intriguing aristocratic and political past. Expansive Thames views, 'beautiful grounds' and 'exquisite cuisine' are the finishing touches. 'We had a sublime time,' reports a regular reader, celebrating a special occasion this year. 'Lovely', eclectically styled bedrooms 'lack for nothing', with a 'fetchingly old-fashioned bathroom'; even some smaller rooms have a private terrace with a hot tub. André Garrett's 'outstanding' modern menu (including a solid vegetarian option) is served in the original drawing room overlooking the 19th-century parterre, or in the informal Astor Grill, where classic American and British dishes feature. In warmer weather, champagne cruises and picnics on the Thames can be arranged. Chewton Glen, New Milton (see entry), is under the same ownership. (Matthew Caminer, and others)

Cliveden Road
Taplow
SL6 0JF

T: 01628 668561
E: reservations@clivedenhouse.co.uk
W: www.clivedenhouse.co.uk

BEDROOMS: 48. Some on ground floor, plus 3-bed cottage in grounds, suitable for disabled.
OPEN: all year.
FACILITIES: Great Hall, library, 2 restaurants, private dining rooms, free Wi-Fi, in-room TV (Freeview), civil wedding licence, spa, swimming pools, terrace, tennis, 376-acre National Trust gardens, public areas wheelchair accessible.
BACKGROUND MUSIC: all day in public areas.
LOCATION: 20 mins from Heathrow, 40 mins Central London.
CHILDREN: all ages welcomed.
DOGS: not allowed in restaurants, spa or parts of garden.
CREDIT CARDS: all major cards.
PRICES: [2018] per room B&B £495–£2,175, D,B&B £615–£2,295. Tasting menu £98, à la carte £73. .

TAVISTOCK Devon

Map 1:D4

THE HORN OF PLENTY

'A wonderful place,' writes a trusted reader, of Julie Leivers and Damien Pease's long-established hotel on the Devon/Cornwall border. 'Superb location, spectacular views,' add Guide regulars in 2018. Four bedrooms are in the main building – a Victorian mine captain's house; others are in the original coach house and a purpose-built annexe. Ranging from traditional to contemporary, and from quite cosy to deluxe, all come with a minibar and fresh milk; most have a balcony, full-height window and glass door, with views over the lovely garden and the Tamar valley. 'We had a very comfy room in the annexe, although with a tiny balcony.' A dramatic outlook, too, from the dining room, where chef Ashley Wright's locally sourced seasonal fare includes such 'beautifully prepared and presented' dishes as local lamb, morels, wild garlic, spring onion, heritage carrots. A dessert of lemon posset with strawberries hit the spot. However, other guests were 'rather underwhelmed. The food looked beautiful but was much too fussy: mackerel and crab cancel each other out.' A 'great breakfast' included a 'big bowl of orange and grapefruit segments'. The staff serve with grace and charm. 'We look forward to returning.' (PA, and others)

Gulworthy
Tavistock
PL19 8JD

T: 01822 832528
E: enquiries@thehornofplenty.co.uk
W: www.thehornofplenty.co.uk

BEDROOMS: 16. 12 in old and new coach houses (1–2 mins walk), 7 on ground floor, 1 suitable for disabled.
OPEN: all year.
FACILITIES: lounge/bar, library, drawing room, restaurant, free Wi-Fi, in-room TV (Freeview), civil wedding licence, 5-acre grounds.
BACKGROUND MUSIC: occasional background music in restaurant only, 'when it's quiet'.
LOCATION: 3 miles SW of Tavistock.
CHILDREN: all ages welcomed.
DOGS: allowed in some rooms and library, not in restaurant or drawing room, £10 per dog per night.
CREDIT CARDS: MasterCard, Visa.
PRICES: [2018] per room B&B £120–£155, D, B&B £200–£235. Set dinner £50.

SEE ALSO SHORTLIST

TEFFONT EVIAS Wiltshire

Map 2:D1

HOWARD'S HOUSE

❦ Previous César winner

Thatched cottages and sheep-dotted fields swaddle the single-track roads to this 17th-century mellow-stone Nadder valley house in an 'unspoilt' village. For Guide inspectors in 2018, the 'dreamy bedrooms', 'tranquil garden' and 'sublime dining' are the real draws. In the 'airy sitting room', plush sofas are interspersed with low tables bearing garden-fresh blooms, board games and books. A small snug 'is a fine place to have a drink and read the paper'; the 'beautifully maintained garden' is a tempting alternative. Upstairs, tastefully decorated bedrooms vary in size. 'Our marvellous second-floor room had a huge, cosy bed; spoiling organic toiletries in the sparkling bathroom. A comfy seating area provided plenty of space for our baby boys to roll around. The babbling river was the only sound at night.' Chef Andy Britton's daily-changing menu of locally sourced, seasonal produce (much from the kitchen garden) 'is tremendous'. 'So much effort went into creating an epicurean experience for the whole party. A spinach-lentil crumble, with a burnt-hay-and-oat topping, was heavenly; the wood pigeon breast was an unexpected treat.' Breakfast is 'glorious'.

25% DISCOUNT VOUCHERS

Teffont Evias
SP3 5RJ

T: 01722 716392
E: enq@howardshousehotel.co.uk
W: howardshousehotel.co.uk

BEDROOMS: 9.
OPEN: all year except 23–27 Dec.
FACILITIES: lounge, snug, restaurant, function facilities in coach house, free Wi-Fi, in-room TV (Freeview), 2-acre grounds, restaurant wheelchair accessible.
BACKGROUND MUSIC: in dining room.
LOCATION: 10 miles W of Salisbury.
CHILDREN: all ages welcomed (cot, high chair).
DOGS: allowed (£15 charge) in bedrooms, not in public rooms.
CREDIT CARDS: Amex, MasterCard, Visa.
PRICES: [2018] per room B&B from £150. Tasting menu £80, à la carte £45.

TETBURY Gloucestershire

Map 3:E5

CALCOT MANOR

'A lovely, family-friendly hotel,' was Guide inspectors' verdict on this 16th-century stone manor house with spa in beautiful grounds, 'looking out over rolling hills'. Bedrooms, in main house and converted buildings around a courtyard, some with rustic timbers, are individually styled and chic. Extras include fresh fruit, biscuits, aromatherapy toiletries. A family room had 'books, a jug of water, an espresso machine', modern bathroom with 'very large walk-in shower, an appealing tub'. 'Morning tea and newspaper with no charge – great,' writes a reader this year. The atmosphere is 'cosy and intimate'. Fires burn in 'informal public spaces'. There is gastropub fare in the Gumstool Inn while, in the conservatory, chef Richard Davies's dishes include slow-cooked fillet of Calcot organic beef, salsify, baby leek, shallot mash. Staff are 'young, enthusiastic, happy' – although one guest found the service inattentive, the interpretation of Caesar salad disappointing. Breakfast brings smoothies, kedgeree, 'tasty egg dishes', smoked ham. This is an overtly child-orientated place, but various age limits apply to spa and other facilities. Barnsley House, The Painswick and Lord Crewe Arms have the same owners (see entries).

Tetbury
GL8 8YJ

T: 01666 890391
E: receptionists@calcot.co
W: www.calcot.co

BEDROOMS: 35, 10 (for families) in cottage, 13 around courtyard, on ground floor, some suitable for disabled.
OPEN: all year.
FACILITIES: lounge, 2 bars, 2 restaurants, crèche, free Wi-Fi, in-room TV (Sky, Freeview), civil wedding licence, 220-acre grounds (tennis, heated outdoor 8-metre swimming pool, play area, spa with 16-metre pool), public areas wheelchair accessible, adapted toilet.
BACKGROUND MUSIC: in restaurants.
LOCATION: 3 miles W of Tetbury.
CHILDREN: all ages welcomed.
DOGS: allowed in courtyard bedrooms, not in public rooms.
CREDIT CARDS: Amex, MasterCard, Visa.
PRICES: [2018] per room B&B £229–£374, D,B&B £309–£454. À la carte (Conservatory) £50, (Gumstool Inn) £35.

SEE ALSO SHORTLIST

TETBURY Gloucestershire   Map 3:E5

THE HARE AND HOUNDS

Surrounded by manicured lawns, wild meadow
flowers and woodland, this Cotswold-stone
manor house, a few miles outside Tetbury, has
'exceptional staff, excellent service, delightful
furnishings'. A member of the Cotswold Inns
& Hotels group (see also entry for The Lamb,
Burford), its Victorian mullion windows
and stone fireplaces are enlivened with bold
colours and appealing art, while a woodland
theme (tree wallpaper, a bowl of pine cones)
nods at the nearby National Arboretum. Plush
armchairs, in country tweeds, gather before
open log fires and create nooks in the book- and
curios-filled library and 'well-furnished' sitting
rooms. Varying in size, country house-style
bedrooms are in the main building – those
over the bar may not suit light sleepers – while
rooms in the garden annexes are more modern.
Two (Magnolia, Gamekeeper) have a hot tub
and their own garden. In the buzzy bar, dogs
are given their own menu (braised venison,
liver-and-oat biscuits); fine ales, simple plates
and board games occupy their owners. The
restaurant's 'very good, skilfully prepared
seasonal dishes' include wild mushroom lasagne,
truffle, rocket, goat's cheese. (Mary Coles, MEO)

Westonbirt
Tetbury
GL8 8QL

T: 01666 881000
E: reception@hareandhoundshotel.
   com
W: www.cotswold-inns-hotels.
   co.uk/hare-and-hounds-hotel/

BEDROOMS: 42. 2 suitable for
disabled, 3 in coach house, 5 in
garden cottage, 12 in Silkwood
Court, 1 in gamekeeper's cottage.
OPEN: all year.
FACILITIES: drawing room, lounges,
library, bar, restaurant, private
dining room, free Wi-Fi, in-room
TV (Freeview), civil wedding
licence, gardens, woodland.
BACKGROUND MUSIC: in lounge and
bar.
LOCATION: 3 miles SW of Tetbury.
CHILDREN: all ages welcomed.
DOGS: allowed in some bedrooms,
bar, garden, not in restaurant.
CREDIT CARDS: Amex, MasterCard,
Visa.
PRICES: [2018] per room B&B from
£99, D,B&B from £179. À la carte £35.

SEE ALSO SHORTLIST

THORPE MARKET Norfolk

Map 2:A5

THE GUNTON ARMS   NEW

'A delight not only for art lovers but for all who visit,' say Guide inspectors this year of Ivor Braka's unique pub-with-rooms that upgrades to a full entry. Every corner of the converted country house, that regularly hosted Lily Langtry while Edward VII visited Gunton Hall, has something 'different and interesting', from the fossilised skull of the largest deer ever found to 'fascinating furniture, rugs, vintage artefacts'. The ladies' loo has a Damien Hirst, many Tracey Emins; the men's a David Bailey photograph of the Krays. There are 'two large, comfortable lounges' with books, magazines 'and gorgeous views', a snooker room, a locals' bar. A 'warm, interesting welcome' led to a 'very light, very large room' with Victorian watercolours, a Roberts radio, 'perfect bedside lighting'. The bathroom had a 'stunning' freestanding copper-plated bath, a shower with vintage brass fittings. In the 'bustling' dining room 'with a wonderful arched wooden ceiling' and a huge fireplace for grilling and smoking, Stuart Tattershall's 'beautifully presented, extremely tasty' dishes included 'sea trout with brown shrimps from Cromer, mixed beets with pickled walnuts', vegan and veggie options. Breakfast didn't disappoint.

Cromer Road
Thorpe Market
NR11 8TZ

T: 01263 832010
E: office@theguntonarms.co.uk
W: www.theguntonarms.co.uk

BEDROOMS: 16. 4 in coach house on ground floor, 4 suites in converted barn house, 1 suitable for disabled.
OPEN: all year except Christmas Day, half day on New Year's Eve.
FACILITIES: 3 restaurants, 3 lounges, bar, TV in bar and lounges, free Wi-Fi, set in privately owned 1000-acre game estate, public rooms wheelchair accessible, adapted toilet.
BACKGROUND MUSIC: in bar area.
LOCATION: 5 miles from Cromer, 4 miles from North Walsham.
CHILDREN: all ages welcomed.
DOGS: allowed in 5 dog-friendly bedrooms, public rooms except in Elk dining room.
CREDIT CARDS: Amex, MasterCard, Visa.
PRICES: per room B&B single £85–£310, double £95–£320, single occupancy £85–£310. À la carte from £30. Min. 2-night stays on Sat.

TIMBLE Yorkshire

Map 4:D3

THE TIMBLE INN NEW

'The tranquillity is very appealing' at the Stainsby family's 18th-century coaching inn-turned-gastropub in a hamlet on the slopes of the Washburn valley. Its nominator for a full entry in this year's Guide received a 'friendly welcome' and was checked in at the bar. The mix of traditional and contemporary interiors includes beams, flagstone floors, a brick fireplace alongside ceiling spotlights, gilded mirrors. Quite spacious bedrooms are supplied with upmarket Harrogate toiletries, 'excellent towels and bathrobes'. A first-floor suite had 'a beamed living space' and a bedroom with four-poster, a 'gleaming bathroom with a monsoon shower fitting' over an awkwardly deep bath. 'All the accommodation was obviously very recently and tastefully fitted out.' The mobile phone signal was 'erratic', Internet access proved elusive. The residents' lounge is in the adjoining cottage. Dinner, in the 'intimate' restaurant, served by a 'prompt and professional young waitress', was 'the work of a very competent chef'. Praise for braised, shredded duck leg; pork fillet, braised pig's cheek, celeriac purée, pickled apple, red cabbage. At breakfast, muzak was an irritation, and cooked dishes trumped porridge and fruit salad. (Robert Gower)

Timble
LS21 2NN

T: 01943 880530
E: info@thetimbleinn.co.uk
W: www.thetimbleinn.co.uk

BEDROOMS: 9. 2 in cottages, 4 with own private entrance, 2 on ground floor.
OPEN: all year, restaurant closed Mon/Tues except bank hols lunch.
FACILITIES: bar, restaurant, residents' lounge, free Wi-Fi, in-room TV (Freeview), garden, public rooms wheelchair accessible.
BACKGROUND MUSIC: at meal times in public areas.
LOCATION: centre of village, 10 miles west of Harrogate.
CHILDREN: all ages welcomed.
DOGS: allowed in 2 bedrooms (£20 per dog per night).
CREDIT CARDS: Amex, MasterCard, Visa.
PRICES: [2018] per room B&B £150–£240. À la carte £40.

TISBURY Wiltshire

Map 2:D1

THE BECKFORD ARMS

At an ancient crossroads on the edge of the
Fonthill Estate, Dan Brod and Charlie Luxton's
Georgian pub-with-rooms is a 'popular, good-
value' spot. The 'cosy beamed bar' has all the
traditionally pubby accoutrements yet an 'airy,
modern vibe', with 'comfy sofas' and bright log
fires. Dinners in the pub are 'seriously good',
with 'beautifully cooked, mostly locally sourced'
seasonal dishes, perhaps slow-braised pork belly,
creamed white beans, braised turnips, salsa verde;
salted caramel affogato. In fine weather, the
conservatory restaurant's French doors open on
to the 'charming' terrace and garden. Afterwards,
'country chic-style bedrooms' (above the pub,
or in two lodges 15 minutes' stroll away; some
snug) have 'huge windows', allowing you to
wake to bedside country views; a 'state-of-the-art
shower', fluffy towels and estate-made toiletries.
'The emergency kit bag (toothpaste, deodorant,
feminine supplies) and hospitality tray were
especially appreciated: fresh milk, home-made
biscuits, a cafetière with ground coffee 'receive
full marks'. Walking trails across the estate have
'magnificent views' (ask staff for a map), while
Stonehenge and stately homes are nearby. The
owners' Talbot Inn is in Mells (see entry).

Fonthill Gifford
Tisbury
SP3 6PX

T: 01747 870385
E: info@beckfordarms.com
W: www.beckfordarms.com

BEDROOMS: 10. 2 in lodges on
Fonthill Estate.
OPEN: all year except 25 Dec.
FACILITIES: sitting room (sometimes
Sunday classic-movie nights), bar,
restaurant, private dining room,
free Wi-Fi, in-room TV (Freeview),
function facilities, 1-acre garden,
unsuitable for disabled.
BACKGROUND MUSIC: in public areas
all day.
LOCATION: in village, 1 mile N of
Tisbury.
CHILDREN: all ages welcomed.
DOGS: allowed in 1 bedroom, public
areas.
CREDIT CARDS: MasterCard, Visa.
PRICES: [2018] per room B&B
£95–£195, D,B&B £150–£250.
À la carte £30. 1-night bookings
usually refused weekends.

SEE ALSO SHORTLIST

TITCHWELL Norfolk

BRIARFIELDS

Near the RSPB Titchwell Marsh nature reserve, this dog- and family-friendly hotel is sandwiched between fields and ochre-hued marshland, leading down to the North Sea. Its collection of brick-and-stone farm buildings stands on a coastal road, with paths and coastal trails spiking in all directions. Within the maze of rooms, a cosy snug has a large wood-burner and a guestbook where visiting twitchers leave triumphant notes on which birds they've spotted. The courtyard garden offers a peaceful suntrap on warm days for a Pimm's or pint of Norfolk Brewhouse Moon Gazer ale, while modern bedrooms (various sizes) cluster round a second courtyard. Newer rooms have wooden floor, large mirrors, luxurious shower; some older rooms are more basic. Light bites are served throughout the day in the large, central dining area with its beams and light, airy atmosphere. Freshly caught seafood and produce from local farms feature heavily on the dinner menu, perhaps roast hake, smoked bacon, salsify; seafood meze; butterbean cassoulet, wild mushroom, creamed potato. Vegetarians are well catered for. A solid breakfast puts fuel in the tank for a breezy beach hike. (MC, and others)

Main Road
Titchwell
PE31 8BB

T: 01485 210742
E: info@briarfieldshotelnorfolk.co.uk
W: www.briarfieldshotelnorfolk.co.uk

BEDROOMS: 23. 20 around the courtyard, 1 suitable for disabled.
OPEN: all year.
FACILITIES: bar, dining room, snug, TV lounge (Sky), free Wi-Fi in public areas, in-room TV (Freeview), function facilities, 3-acre garden (play area), public areas and toilets wheelchair accessible.
BACKGROUND MUSIC: all day in bar and restaurant.
LOCATION: off A149 between Burnham Market and Hunstanton.
CHILDREN: all ages welcomed.
DOGS: allowed in some bedrooms, bar.
CREDIT CARDS: MasterCard, Visa.
PRICES: [2018] per room B&B single £80–£125, double £115–£200, D,B&B single £105–£150, double £160–£230. À la carte £30.

TITCHWELL Norfolk

Map 2:A5

TITCHWELL MANOR

Far-reaching, warm, golden marshland provides a striking backdrop to Margaret and Ian Snaith's Victorian farmhouse hotel. Check-in is 'swift and friendly' in the 'mood-lifting' foyer. The 'cosy' lounge has a merry fire, a 'comically long' sofa and plenty of guides, newspapers and hand-drawn walking maps to borrow. The pretty conservatory sees Eric Snaith, the owners' son, and Chris Mann's modern menu, perhaps Norfolk quail, sweet root vegetables. 'We mopped up our deliciously charred, salty mackerel starter; a mango and white chocolate "almost trifle" was a tangy end to the meal.' Most rooms, in the main house or outbuildings, are decorated in the hues of the landscape; each has a large bed, some a reclaimed wooden headboard. 'Our unassuming room, in the handsome annexe, was comfortable, spacious and nicely warm on a drizzly night. From a silent night's sleep, we awoke to birdsong.' A 'sterling' breakfast is 'all about the details': a pat of softened butter; a small ramekin of home-made marmalade. 'A heroic selection of moreish granola and dark yellow scrambled eggs were handily polished off.' 'Great twitching just up the road.' More reports, please.

25% DISCOUNT VOUCHERS

Titchwell
PE31 8BB

T: 01485 210221
E: info@titchwellmanor.com
W: www.titchwellmanor.com

BEDROOMS: 26. 12 in hcrb garden, 4 in converted farm building, 1 in Potting Shed, 2 suitable for disabled.
OPEN: all year.
FACILITIES: lounge, bar, conservatory, restaurant, free Wi-Fi, in-room TV (Freeview), civil wedding licence, in-room treatments, ¼-acre walled garden.
BACKGROUND MUSIC: in restaurant and bar (at mealtimes).
LOCATION: off A149 between Burnham Market and Hunstanton.
CHILDREN: all ages welcomed.
DOGS: allowed in some rooms, bar.
CREDIT CARDS: Amex, MasterCard, Visa.
PRICES: [2018] per room B&B £110–£325, D,B&B £185–£400. À la carte £42. 2-night min. stay at weekends.

TITLEY Herefordshire

Map 3:C4

THE STAGG INN

Previous César winner

'We were made so welcome and were well looked after,' writes a reader, of a stay at this pub-with-rooms at the meeting point of two old drovers' roads. Steve and Nicola Reynolds are in their nineteenth year here, and in 2001 this became the first British pub to be awarded a Michelin star. Accommodation at the inn is snug and can be noisy at weekends. For quiet, choose one of three 'spacious, well-appointed' rooms in the 'beautiful' Georgian vicarage four minutes' walk away, with guest sitting room and lovely garden, where the only sound is the church bell chimes. They are supplied with fresh milk, ground coffee, a minibar; one has an in-room bath and separate shower room. Back in the pub, there are plenty of food options, from a three-cheese ploughman's or home-cured salmon sandwich in the bar, to Steve Reynolds's creative restaurant dishes – maybe venison loin and slow-cooked shoulder, celeriac, chestnuts, kalettes, or one of the appealing vegetarian options. For children there are home-made fish goujons, hand-made sausages with mash. 'The best breakfast ever' includes fresh-baked bread, new-laid, free-range eggs. (KMcM)

25% DISCOUNT VOUCHERS

Titley
HR5 3RL

T: 01544 230221
E: reservations@thestagg.co.uk
W: www.thestagg.co.uk

BEDROOMS: 6. 3 at Old Vicarage (300 yds).
OPEN: all year except 24–26 Dec, 1 Jan, 1 week in Jan/Feb, 27 June–6 July, first 2 weeks Nov, restaurant closed Mon, Tues.
FACILITIES: sitting room (Old Vicarage), bar, dining room, small outside seating area (pub), free Wi-Fi, in-room TV (Freeview), 1½-acre garden (Old Vicarage), unsuitable for disabled.
BACKGROUND MUSIC: none.
LOCATION: on B4355 between Kington and Presteigne.
CHILDREN: all ages welcomed.
DOGS: allowed in pub, some pub bedrooms.
CREDIT CARDS: Amex, MasterCard, Visa.
PRICES: [2018] per room B&B £100–£140. À la carte £35. 1-night bookings occasionally refused at bank holiday weekends.

TRUSHAM Devon

Map 1:D4

THE CRIDFORD INN

Possibly the oldest inn in England, with a medieval wooden window pre-dating glass, this thatched village pub in the Teign valley is 'a gem'. A traditional Devon longhouse, it was a nunnery, property of Buckfast Abbey, when it was listed in the Domesday Book. Today, reached via a single-track road across a brook, it is owned by Sue Burdge, and is a sister to The Nobody Inn at nearby Doddiscombsleigh (see entry). It wins praise for the warm welcome and attentive staff. Among the four inn rooms, Teign has a pretty iron bedstead, a leaded glass casement window. A group or family can book either of two cottages, each equipped with an oven and hob, microwave, toaster; one sleeping five (with a bunk bed), the other, four. While the restaurant's pebble mural dates from 1086, its 'delicious' locally sourced food is far fresher, perhaps Brixham fish pie, tenderstem broccoli; a Sunday roast (booking essential); wild mushroom spelt risotto, spinach, truffle and Grana Pandano; local rib-eye steak, confit tomato, roasted mushroom, chips, watercress salad. All served with rural peace, just a short drive from Exeter. (ET)

Trusham
TQ13 0NR

T: 01626 853694
E: reservations@thecridfordinn.
   co.uk
W: www.thecridfordinn.co.uk

BEDROOMS: 8. 4 in two 2-bed cottages.
OPEN: all year.
FACILITIES: bar, 2 dining areas, free Wi-Fi, in-room TV (Freeview), terrace.
BACKGROUND MUSIC: 'very light' in bar.
LOCATION: 12 miles SW of Exeter.
CHILDREN: not under 8.
DOGS: allowed in 1 bedroom, public rooms.
CREDIT CARDS: MasterCard, Visa.
PRICES: [2018] per room B&B single £85, double £105, cottages per person £43, based on full occupancy, extra bed £25. À la carte £25.

TUDDENHAM Suffolk

Map 2:B5

TUDDENHAM MILL

A recent make-over has turned this 244-year-old
mill into a thoroughly modern restaurant-with-
rooms. Under strapping beams in the main mill,
long-serving chef (and now chef/patron) Lee Bye
serves 'ambitious dinners' ('best undertaken on
an empty stomach') in the restaurant. Dietary
requirements are handled with 'generosity and
graciousness', perhaps Worlington duck egg,
Clem's carrot, oyster mushrooms for vegetarians,
'lamb rump cooked beautifully pink' for
their omnivorous table-mates. 'Afterwards, a
neat bottle of sloe gin left bedside was much
appreciated.' The 'impressive' boutiquey
bedrooms (no twin beds) include a set of 'nooks'
in the meadow, and 'large, well-thought-out
rooms, in a good-looking clapboard building'.
Freshly squeezed orange juice in the mini-fridge
and 'dreamy' views towards the millstream are
pleasing finishing touches. Guide readers this
year say, 'We liked the modern, minimalist
bathroom, but there are flip plugs in the basin
– contact lens wearers beware!' At breakfast
('picture-perfect' French toast, 'deliciously
tart home-made raspberry jam', home-baked
brioche), a window seat overlooking the
millpond and its cadre of swans is a must.

25% DISCOUNT VOUCHERS

High Street
Tuddenham
IP28 6SQ

T: 01638 713552
E: info@tuddenhammill.co.uk
W: www.tuddenhammill.co.uk

BEDROOMS: 20. 17 in 2 separate
buildings, 12 on ground floor, 5 in
'Meadow Nooks' in meadow,
1 suitable for disabled.
OPEN: all year.
FACILITIES: bar, restaurant, function
rooms, free Wi-Fi, in-room TV
(Freeview), civil wedding licence,
treatment room, 12-acre meadow.
BACKGROUND MUSIC: in bar, reception
and restaurant.
LOCATION: in village, 8 miles NE of
Newmarket.
CHILDREN: all ages welcomed.
DOGS: allowed in some bedrooms
(£15 a night), bar.
CREDIT CARDS: Amex, MasterCard,
Visa.
PRICES: [2018] per room B&B £145–
£375, D,B&B £205–£435. À la carte
£39, early dining (Sun–Fri 6.30–7.30
pm) £20, tasting menu £65. 2-night
min. stay at weekends.

TWO BRIDGES Devon

Map 1:D4

PRINCE HALL

'We did 14 miles over the moor today and are now pleasantly weary. It is a great place, very sad and wild,' reads a letter – not from a Guide reader, but from Arthur Conan Doyle, said to have been inspired to write The Hound of the Baskervilles while staying at this 18th-century manor house. Today, it is a 'comfortable, relaxing' hotel, so dog-friendly that even that devilish canine would beg to be admitted. Chris Daly and son Luke provided 'a very friendly welcome, as usual', to a returning visitor. Bedrooms overlook the courtyard, the tree-lined drive or the wild Dartmoor landscape. Some are snug, some spacious. Burrator has a four-poster. All provide good toiletries, 'fresh milk from the landing fridge', the hotel's own spring water. 'Downstairs, a large residents' lounge with plenty of comfortable seating and real fire.' Chef Luke Daly creates such dishes as a West Country rib-eye steak, chunky hand-cut chips, grilled vine tomatoes, herb sauce; pumpkin tortellini with chargrilled vegetables. Some guests found the monthly-changing options a little limited over a four-night stay, but 'enjoyed breakfast's home-made bread toast and Cornish leaf tea'.

Two Bridges
PL20 6SA

T: 01822 890403
E: info@princehall.co.uk
W: www.princehall.co.uk

BEDROOMS: 9.
OPEN: all year.
FACILITIES: lobby, bar, lounge, dining room, free Wi-Fi in some rooms and bar/bistro, in-room TV (Freeview), terrace, 5-acre grounds, public rooms wheelchair accessible.
BACKGROUND MUSIC: none.
LOCATION: 3 miles E of Princetown.
CHILDREN: all ages welcomed.
DOGS: 'very much' allowed (treats; facilities for food storage and dog washing; pet-friendly garden and grounds), not in restaurant, but same menu available in bistro for owners with dogs.
CREDIT CARDS: MasterCard, Visa.
PRICES: [2018] per room B&B single £110, double £176–£209. À la carte £35.

ULLSWATER Cumbria

Map 4: inset C2

HOWTOWN HOTEL

For almost 120 years, the Baldry family have welcomed guests to their ancient farmhouse overlooking Lake Ullswater. 'Wonderfully old-fashioned' or 'lost in time', it's a Marmite sort of hotel (the kind of place where you might indeed expect Marmite along with the butter balls and heather honey, the tomato juice, the Rich Tea biscuits). 'As soon as one steps through the door there is a cosy, comfortable feel.' Small sitting rooms have 'a good fire, china, paintings, fringed lamps'. Bedrooms have no lock or key, 'no TV, no mobile signal or Wi-Fi', just lovely views and quiet. Beds are conventionally dressed, bathrooms supplied with bars of Imperial Leather. Grandfather clocks say 'Time for tea.' A gong summons guests for an 'excellent but never fancy' four-course dinner, perhaps liver and bacon; trifle and ice cream – perfect for hungry fell walkers. 'Chef Colin Akrigg joined from [the legendary] Sharrow Bay, where he worked in its glory years,' says a local devotee. Beds are turned down, electric blankets switched on. 'Everything is done just so,' an inspector relates. 'Tables are beautifully laid. It's so retro it's almost trendy.' (Stephanie Thompson, and others)

Ullswater
CA10 2ND

T: 01768 486514
E: editor@goodhotelguide.com
W: www.howtown-hotel.com

BEDROOMS: 15. 2 in annexe, plus 4 self-catering cottages.
OPEN: end of March–mid-Nov.
FACILITIES: 3 lounges, TV room, 2 bars, dining room, tea room, Wi-Fi in cottages and tea room only, 2-acre grounds, 200 yds from lake (private foreshore, fishing), walking, sailing, climbing, riding, golf nearby, restaurant wheelchair accessible, toilet not adapted.
BACKGROUND MUSIC: none.
LOCATION: 4 miles S of Pooley Bridge, bus from Penrith station 9 miles.
CHILDREN: all ages welcomed.
DOGS: allowed in some bedrooms (£4 per night charge), not in public rooms.
CREDIT CARDS: Mastercard, Visa.
PRICES: [2018] per person B&B £73, D,B&B £108.

UPPER SLAUGHTER Gloucestershire

Map 3:D6

LORDS OF THE MANOR

Ω Previous César winner

A coat of arms and portraits of past owners set the tone at this honey-hued former rectory, recommended by Guide readers for a 'welcoming, comfortable, relaxing' country house experience. The 17th-century building is a 'lovely' rambling hotel with a family crest above the porch, mullion windows, antiques, cosy fireplaces and 'lots of nice touches – board games to play, wellies to borrow'. It is surrounded by several 'beautiful' gardens including a lawn, apparently custom-built for Pimm's and croquet, a walled garden, a wild flower meadow. Inside the elegant dining room, with its beams and original art, chef Charles Smith's 'excellent' seasonal menus might include hand-dived Orkney scallop, green asparagus, squid ink mousseline; fallow deer, buttered hispi cabbage, young beetroots, violet mustard. The 'well-appointed' bedrooms have 'lots of drawers and hangers'; the largest have archetypal Cotswold views, bay windows, colonial four-poster. Management has recently been taken back in-house, although as a reader says: 'Had we not asked, we'd not have known: service was confident and assured. We had a very good time, and hope to return.' (Rosemary Melling, and others)

Upper Slaughter
GL54 2JD

T: 01451 820243
E: reservations@lordsofthemanor.com
W: www.lordsofthemanor.com

BEDROOMS: 26. 16 in converted granary and stables, 1 on ground floor.
OPEN: all year.
FACILITIES: drawing room, lounge bar, restaurant, library, games room, free Wi-Fi, in-room TV (Freeview), civil wedding licence, terrace, 8-acre grounds, some public rooms wheelchair accessible, no adapted toilet.
BACKGROUND MUSIC: in lounge bar and restaurant.
LOCATION: in village, 2 miles N of Bourton-on-the-Water.
CHILDREN: all ages welcomed.
DOGS: allowed in some bedrooms, all public rooms except restaurant.
CREDIT CARDS: Amex, MasterCard, Visa.
PRICES: [2018] per room B&B £150–£510, D,B&B £280–£640. À la carte £73, tasting menu £95. 1-night bookings refused mid-summer Sat.

UPPINGHAM Rutland

LAKE ISLE

The food is the main course at Janine and Richard Burton's restaurant-with-rooms. 'How I wish we had a restaurant anywhere near as good as this where I live now,' writes a visitor this year, after returning to her old Rutland haunt. The 17th-century property, a former shop on the high street of the public school market town, is where chef Stuart Mead creates locally sourced, regularly changing seasonal menus, variously lauded as 'superb', 'very good' and 'cooked to perfection'. A typical dish: cod supreme, Cheddar and mustard seed rarebit, pulled gammon, parsley creamed potato, roasted carrots and leeks, ham crisps. 'To die for' puddings include chocolate and stem ginger délice, burnt honey ice cream, orange-whisky curd. The 'smallish' bedrooms add contemporary flesh to the Grade II listed bones, some with a whirlpool bath, all with tea/coffee-making facilities, home-made biscuits. 'Ours wasn't large but perfectly adequate, the bed extremely comfortable.' Others found their cottage suite bedroom 'very tight'. The 'brilliant' breakfast includes freshly squeezed juices, home-made muesli, grilled salmon and haddock fishcakes – a solid foundation for exploring nearby Rutland Water. (John Bennett, CH)

16 High Street
East Uppingham
LE15 9PZ

T: 01572 822951
E: info@lakeisle.co.uk
W: www.lakeisle.co.uk/

BEDROOMS: 12. 2 in cottages.
OPEN: all year, restaurant closed Sun night, Mon lunch, bank holidays.
FACILITIES: bar, restaurant, free Wi-Fi, in-room TV (Freeview), small car park, unsuitable for disabled.
BACKGROUND MUSIC: in restaurant.
LOCATION: town centre.
CHILDREN: all ages welcomed.
DOGS: allowed in courtyard bedrooms, not in public areas.
CREDIT CARDS: MasterCard, Visa.
PRICES: [2018] per room B&B £70–£120, D,B&B £156–£186. À la carte £35.

VENTNOR Isle of Wight

Map 2:E2

HILLSIDE

'We loved the atmosphere, the decor, the gardens, the quality of service, the freshness of the food.' Unstinting praise this year from trusted readers, for this highly individual small hotel where Gert Bach is an 'excellent, attentive host'. Both he and his 'charming assistant, Andrei, enjoy lingering to chat'. The thatched 19th-century villa perches on wooded south-facing slopes. 'Interiors are mainly white, with exposed floorboards, Nordic-style furniture, colourful abstract oils.' A 'very simple, compact' bedroom had 'fabulous views over the town to the sea, a state-of-the-art shower room, good toiletries, bottled water'. There is no hospitality tray; drinks are served in the conservatory which leads to 'a delightful garden', an enclosure 'populated with goats and happy hens'. Produce from garden, greenhouse and hives appears in 'well cooked and presented dishes'. The 'French with a Scandinavian twist' fare includes pan-fried plaice, shallot beurre noisette, razor clams, wild sea greens, leek and potato gratin. An 'especially good' breakfast provides organic eggs, home-made muesli and preserves, the full English. (Francine and Ian Walsh, Desmond and Jenny Balmer, LR)

25% DISCOUNT VOUCHERS

151 Mitchell Avenue
Ventnor
PO38 1DR

T: 01983 852271
E: mail@hillsideventnor.co.uk
W: www.hillsideventnor.co.uk

BEDROOMS: 12. Plus self-catering apartment.
OPEN: all year.
FACILITIES: restaurant, 2 lounges, conservatory, free Wi-Fi, in-room TV, terrace, 5-acre garden (vegetable garden, sheep, beehives), close to tennis club, golf, unsuitable for disabled.
BACKGROUND MUSIC: in restaurant in evening.
LOCATION: above village centre.
CHILDREN: not under 12.
DOGS: not allowed.
CREDIT CARDS: MasterCard, Visa.
PRICES: [2018] per room B&B single £78–£143, double £156–£196. Set dinner £24–£28, supper Sun/Mon £12–£16. Min. 2-night bookings preferred.

VENTNOR Isle of Wight

THE ROYAL HOTEL

Built in 1832, as Ventnor burgeoned from fishing hamlet to resort for health tourists, the Fisher Hotel became 'royal' thanks to the patronage of Queen Victoria. Today, under the ownership of William Bailey, it's a 'luxurious' place that 'well deserves' its Guide entry, says a trusted reader this year, praising the 'staff consistency, comfort, good food and very personal welcome'. 'WONDERFUL!!' another concurs. 'The reception team are most pleasant and helpful. They booked our ferry both ways, sending us tickets and useful directions.' The traditionally styled bedrooms have fresh fruit, flowers and garden views; family rooms sleep four or five. The 'splendid' Royal Tea is one of the old-fashioned charms, but prudence suggests settling for a slice of Battenberg at cake o'clock, leaving room for new chef Jon-Paul Charlo's inventive cooking. 'Our starter, the Gallybagger cheese soufflé with white onion purée, is amazing! Our favourite pudding is the blood orange panna cotta, candied pistachios, yogurt sorbet, blood orange syrup.' An 'excellent breakfast' has 'many cooked choices'. The sub-tropical gardens and sea bathing are as salubrious today as they were during Victoria's reign. (Mary Coles, Mary Woods).

Belgrave Road
Ventnor
PO38 1JJ

T: 01983 852186
E: enquiries@royalhoteliow.co.uk
W: royalhoteliow.co.uk

BEDROOMS: 51. Some suitable for disabled.
OPEN: all year.
FACILITIES: lift, lounge, bar, 2 restaurants, conservatory, function rooms, free Wi-Fi, in-room TV, civil wedding licence, spa treatment rooms, summer terrace, 2-acre grounds, outdoor heated swimming pool (May–end Sept), rigid inflatable boat for charter.
BACKGROUND MUSIC: in public areas, pianist on peak-season weekends.
LOCATION: short walk from centre.
CHILDREN: all ages welcomed.
DOGS: allowed in some bedrooms for 'a small supplement', not in public areas where food is served.
CREDIT CARDS: Amex, MasterCard, Visa.
PRICES: [2018] per room B&B £195–£305, D,B&B £265–£375. Set dinner £31–£40, tasting menu £50. 2-night min. stay at peak weekends.

VERYAN-IN-ROSELAND Cornwall

❦ THE NARE

César award: seaside hotel of the year

'Old-fashioned in all the best ways', 'a Cornish jewel', 'a real joy – almost a privilege – to stay there'; compliments rain down from trusted readers after recent visits to Toby Ashworth's hotel on the Roseland peninsula. Perched high above Carne Beach in 'stunning gardens', its 'spacious, warm-hued, traditional rooms' – many with balcony and 'divine' views of Gerrans Bay – have fresh flowers, antiques; 'wonderful beds, good linen and expensive toiletries'. Further gold stars: 'sherry by the bedside', shoe cleaning, fresh milk with turn-down, and, 'oh joy, Horlicks'. The 'young but experienced smiling staff' are uniformly praised. 'Many remembered our names. They seem to know instinctively how to look after their guests.' New chef Brett Camborne-Paynter's 'scrumptious dinners', including daily Portloe lobster, are served in a formal silver-service dining room with dress code and dessert trolley. The more casual Quarterdeck offers the likes of Cornish seafood linguine. Breakfast 'keeps the bar high', as does afternoon tea: 'feather-light scones and blackcurrant jam, home-made cakes, proper loose-leaf teas'. 'I wish we could visit more often.' (Tessa Stuart, Peter Govier, IB, and others)

Carne Beach
Veryan-in-Roseland
TR2 5PF

T: 01872 501111
E: stay@narehotel.co.uk
W: www.narehotel.co.uk

BEDROOMS: 37. Some on ground floor, 1 in adjacent cottage, 5 suitable for disabled.
OPEN: all year.
FACILITIES: lift, lounge, drawing room, sun lounge, gallery, study, bar, library, light lunch/supper room, 2 restaurants, conservatory, free Wi-Fi, in-room TV (Sky, Freeview), gym, indoor and outdoor swimming pools, 2-acre grounds, tennis.
BACKGROUND MUSIC: none.
LOCATION: S of Veryan.
CHILDREN: all ages welcomed.
DOGS: allowed in bedrooms, not in public areas (except assistance dogs).
CREDIT CARDS: Amex, MasterCard, Visa.
PRICES: [2018] per room B&B £295–£835, D,B&B £315–£856. Set dinner £50, à la carte £50. Min. 2-night bookings at Christmas, New Year.

WAREHAM Dorset

THE PRIORY

'Definitely one to go back to.' This 'super hotel', housed in a 16th-century priory on the River Frome, continues to gather fans. New visitors give it 'top marks for its very attractive setting and buildings'. They join returning guests in praising the 'excellent service, lovely ambience in its stylish public rooms and delightful gardens'. Afternoon tea is taken in the drawing room or, in clement weather, on the river terrace with commanding views of the Purbeck hills, while the cosy Cloisters bar serves pre-dinner cocktails. 'Comfortable' rooms, in the main house and converted boathouse, are each different, but all have fresh fruit, a minibar, things to read. 'The Boathouse's spacious Kingfisher suite was so comfortable and quiet, with river views from a balcony. The bathroom was sleek and warm.' Two slight niggles, however; no real milk or turn-down. In the new wood-and-glass dining room, Stephan Guinebault's modern French-inspired English dishes were 'well cooked, well presented and amply portioned (although the only vegetarian option didn't change)'. Breakfast is 'great': eggs 'just right', 'delicious' porridge. (Philippa Parker, Max Lickfold, and others)

Church Green
Wareham
BH20 4ND

T: 01929 551666
E: admin@theprioryhotel.co.uk
W: www.theprioryhotel.co.uk

BEDROOMS: 17. Some on ground floor (in courtyard), 4 suites in Boathouse, 1 suitable for disabled.
OPEN: all year.
FACILITIES: sitting room, drawing room, snug bar, 2 dining rooms, free Wi-Fi, in-room TV (Freeview), 4½-acre gardens (croquet, river frontage, moorings, fishing), restaurant wheelchair accessible.
BACKGROUND MUSIC: pianist in drawing room Sat evenings 'and special occasions'.
LOCATION: town centre.
CHILDREN: not under 14.
DOGS: not allowed.
CREDIT CARDS: MasterCard, Visa.
PRICES: [2018] per room B&B single £176–£304, double £220–£380, D,B&B double £265–£430. Set dinner £50. 1-night bookings refused high season, peak weekends.

WELLS Somerset

Map 2:D1

⚜ STOBERRY HOUSE

César award: B&B of the year

'Five stars.' 'Highly recommended.' 'Faultless.'
'Frances, Tim and their lovely staff treat guests
as if they are treasured members of the family.'
This year's Guide received plentiful accolades
for Tim and Frances Meeres Young's B&B in an
18th-century coach house. Wrapped in 25 acres
of parkland with 'magical' views across Wells
Cathedral to Glastonbury Tor, its six-acre garden
displays water features, sculpture and judicious
plantings to maintain year-round interest. Indoors,
where 'every comfort has been thought of', there
is free tea and cake on arrival, a pillow library and
paraben-free, locally made toiletries. The 'utterly
luxurious, beautifully furnished' garden studio
suite, recommended by several readers, offers
'sunset views from the bed, perfect', while the
'lovely, peaceful' Lady Hamilton room sports a
four-poster and 'luxurious touches'. Other rooms
have Mulberry fabrics, a half-tester canopy bed.
A pre-ordered dinner of boeuf bourguignon and
panna cotta was enjoyed, while breakfast, served
in the orangery, with fresh pastries, home-made
jams and multiple cooked options, alongside those
tasty views, is 'to die for'. (Zara Elliott, Alice and
John Sennett, Claire Jaffe-Beer)

Stoberry Park
Wells
BA5 3LD

T: 01749 672906
E: stay@stoberry-park.co.uk
W: www.stoberryhouse.co.uk

BEDROOMS: 7. 1 in studio cottage, 2 in
the gatehouse cottage.
OPEN: all year except 2 weeks over
Christmas and New Year.
FACILITIES: 3 sitting rooms (1 with
pantry), breakfast room, orangery,
free Wi-Fi, in-room TV (Freeview),
6½-acre garden in 25 acres of
parkland.
BACKGROUND MUSIC: none.
LOCATION: outskirts of Wells.
CHILDREN: allowed for parties that
occupy the whole house, if children
are old enough to have their own
room.
DOGS: not allowed.
CREDIT CARDS: Amex, MasterCard,
Visa.
PRICES: [2018] per room B&B
(continental) single £85, double
£95–£157. À la carte £28–£43
(pre-ordered). 1-night bookings
sometimes refused weekends during
high season.

WEST END Surrey

THE INN AT WEST END

Gerry and Ann Price 'set the standard' at their
'well-run' pub/restaurant-with-rooms, where
the 'hands-on owners' foster a hub-of-the-village
atmosphere. It's cemented by locals, who drop
in throughout the day for a hand-pulled pint
or coffee and a chat in the airy, bright, wood-
floored bar with its old wine barrel, cartoons and
prints of hares and pheasants. The like might
show up in the muzak-free restaurant, where
locally caught game features on the 'excellent'
menu. Characteristic dishes: pigeon breasts,
kohlrabi, sprouting broccoli, gin-poached
cherries; haunch of red deer, shoulder croquette,
preserved raspberries, asparagus, chocolate jus; all
accompanied by a 'serious' wine list. Set well back
from road noise, a courtyard garden is edged with
'well-appointed, practical' bedrooms. Named after
something 'personal' in the owners' lives, each is
'bright and modern without being trendy'. 'The
bed was very comfortable, the shower excellent;
we were especially impressed by the thoughtful
design (double power points below the mirror,
good soundproofing, etc).' A leisurely breakfast
(served till 11 am on the weekend) embraces
thickly sliced toast, praiseworthy kedgeree, filter
coffee. Wisley (RHS garden)is close by. (JS, CR)

25% DISCOUNT VOUCHERS

42 Guildford Road
West End
GU24 9PW

T: 01276 485842
E: rooms@the-inn.co.uk
W: www.the-inn.co.uk

BEDROOMS: 12. 1 suitable for
disabled.
OPEN: all year.
FACILITIES: pub/restaurant, free
Wi-Fi, in-room TV (Freeview),
patio, courtyard garden, parking,
bar/restaurant and toilet wheelchair
accessible.
BACKGROUND MUSIC: none.
LOCATION: 6 miles W of Woking.
CHILDREN: welcomed, if old enough
to take their own room.
DOGS: allowed in 2 rooms, bar.
CREDIT CARDS: all major cards.
PRICES: [2018] per room B&B from
£130, D,B&B from £195 ('but ask for
offers'). À la carte £35.

WEST HOATHLY Sussex

Map 2:E4

THE CAT INN

♀ Previous César winner

Popular with locals, ramblers and foodies, this comfortably modernised 16th-century freehouse-with-rooms welcomes visitors with 'big smiles' and a 'warm-hearted atmosphere'. 'Fantastic,' reports a reader in 2018. 'It has comfortable rooms, brilliant food. Wonderfully friendly, relaxed staff.' The pub, all oak beams and inglenook fireplaces, is a haven for real-ale enthusiasts ('proper beer'); its 'high-quality, generously portioned' pub grub and 'efficient' service left guests purring. 'We thoroughly enjoyed the steak, mushroom and ale pie and the almond-crusted whole plaice, not to mention the stand-out gooseberry and apple fool. Even on the busiest night, we weren't kept waiting.' Upstairs, newly redecorated bedrooms enjoy 'little touches': a Nespresso coffee machine, fresh milk, 'decent toiletries', reading material. 'We liked spacious, clean Room 1, with its church view.' Lighter sleepers may need earplugs to block the 'slight' sounds from the bar below. At the 'very good' breakfast, each table is laid with a 'good selection' of muesli, yogurt and fruits. Cooked options follow. 'It's excellent value for money. We will revisit.' (WW, John Gow, and others)

25% DISCOUNT VOUCHERS

North Lane
West Hoathly
RH19 4PP

T: 01342 810369
E: thecatinn@googlemail.com
W: www.catinn.co.uk

BEDROOMS: 4.
OPEN: all year except Christmas, restaurant open New Year's Day for lunch only.
FACILITIES: bar, 3 dining areas, free Wi-Fi, in-room TV (Freeview), terrace (alfresco meals), restaurant wheelchair accessible.
BACKGROUND MUSIC: none.
LOCATION: in village.
CHILDREN: not under 7 (unless 'well-behaved').
DOGS: allowed in bedrooms, bar, specific dining area.
CREDIT CARDS: MasterCard, Visa.
PRICES: [2018] per room B&B single from £90, double from £125.
À la carte £28.

WHASHTON Yorkshire

Map 4:C3

THE HACK & SPADE

'Informal and friendly', Jane Ratcliffe's 'utterly peaceful' B&B stands on a hillside overlooking rolling Yorkshire countryside. Its heritage is writ large across the walls: a double-handed mining spade, hung in an alcove, marking the time when a tiny Georgian ale house was extended into a Victorian pub serving miners from local quarries. Now, the 'comfortable, simply yet tastefully appointed' accommodation includes an 'eye-catching display' of fishing rods, and framed country sports scenes that nod to present attractions. Shooting, fishing and riding can be arranged by the 'very pleasant' Jane, 'whose non-intrusive sociability made it clear why she has regular returning visitors'. The 'comfortable' bedroom offered a 'smart, polished wood-framed bed, bedside tables with brass lamps; a bathroom with spotless fittings, a walk-in monsoon shower'. In the beamed breakfast room with wood-burning stove, Jane's breakfasts use what's fresh, local and available, including 'wonderful blackberries in a fruit salad, perfectly cooked scrambled egg and sumptuous bacon, full of flavour'. A short menu of evening meals, perhaps lamb tagine, or chicken with white wine and tarragon, is available on request. (Robert Gower, and others)

Whashton
DL11 7JL

T: 01748 823721
E: reservations@hackandspade.
   com
W: www.hackandspade.com

BEDROOMS: 5.
OPEN: all year except Christmas/
New Year, last 2 weeks Jan.
FACILITIES: small lounge, breakfast
room, free Wi-Fi, in-room TV
(Freeview), garden, dinner for
guests by prior arrangement,
unsuitable for disabled.
BACKGROUND MUSIC: 'soft' in
restaurant in evening.
LOCATION: 4 miles NW of
Richmond.
CHILDREN: not under 7.
DOGS: not allowed.
CREDIT CARDS: MasterCard, Visa.
PRICES: [2018] per room B&B
£125–£140. À la carte £25.

WHITEWELL Lancashire

Map 4:D3

THE INN AT WHITEWELL

'A lovely place to stay,' writes a reader in 2018, of this popular old inn. On the banks of the River Hodder, it has views to the Forest of Bowland. 'It has a lovely atmosphere,' another reader concurs. Third-generation owner Charles Bowman's taste for antiques and paintings is everywhere evident. One 'very comfortable' main-house bedroom had a 'large four-poster, including canopy'; a coach-house room was 'enormous, with a sofa and chairs, a good bathroom with bath and separate shower' – and when the heating failed, staff went above and beyond duty to resolve the problem. Some rooms have an open fire, perhaps glass doors on to the riverside, an antique bath. There are 'good and reasonably priced' bar meals, while in the restaurant chef Jamie Cadman's menus are big on locally sourced game and meat, perhaps chargrilled beef fillet, roast shallot, flat mushrooms, slow-roasted tomatoes, tarragon butter. At breakfast, some would like more healthy options, 'though I enjoyed my full English'. A ghillie provided for a fishing excursion was 'very professional' and 'made the day enjoyable… I plan to return, and hope next time to catch something.' (Rosemary Melling, Max Lickfold)

nr Clitheroe
Whitewell
BB7 3AT

T: 01200 448222
E: reception@innatwhitewell.com
W: www.innatwhitewell.com

BEDROOMS: 23. 4 in coach house, 150 yds, 2 on ground floor
OPEN: all year.
FACILITIES: 3 bars, restaurant, boardroom, private dining room, in-house wine shop, spa treatments, free Wi-Fi, in-room TV (Freeview), civil wedding licence, 5-acre grounds (wild flower meadow, large river terrace with tables), 7 miles fishing (ghillie available).
BACKGROUND MUSIC: none.
LOCATION: 6 miles NW of Clitheroe.
CHILDREN: all ages welcomed.
DOGS: allowed in bedrooms, not in dining room.
CREDIT CARDS: MasterCard, Visa.
PRICES: [2018] per room B&B single £99–£218, double £137–£270. À la carte £40.

WHITSTABLE Kent

Map 2:D5

THE CRESCENT TURNER HOTEL

Guests enjoy a 'distant view of sea' across fields and houses, from this newly built hotel above a town synonymous with oysters. 'The welcome was friendly, the staff were kind,' says a Guide inspector. 'I was asked if they could use my first name – after that it was "darling".' The decor is contemporary, bold, even slightly brash. A deluxe double ground-floor room was 'very swish, spacious and shiny, with flowery wallpaper, a posh shower room'. Some niggles: no grab handles in the shower; 'unhelpful bedside lights'. Behind net curtains there were doors to the lawn and a small terrace. 'I lunched in the sunshine on a nice terrace, with flower boxes and baskets, a delicious goat's cheese salad.' Scones at teatime were still warm. In the restaurant, 'with big windows looking towards the sea', mainly locally sourced dishes are 'well cooked, not modern or fancy', with fish and seafood, of course. For instance, 'sea bass with crispy skin, crushed potatoes, grilled cherry tomatoes'. For breakfast, a buffet and good cooked choices including the full English, smoked haddock and eggs all ways. (SP, and others)

Wraik Hill
Whitstable
CT5 3BY

T: 01227 263506
E: info@crescentturner.co.uk
W: crescentturner.co.uk

BEDROOMS: 18. 5 on ground floor, 4 suitable for disabled.
OPEN: all year.
FACILITIES: bar/lounge, restaurant, function room, free Wi-Fi, in-room TV (Freeview), civil wedding licence, terrace, 2¼-acre garden, public areas wheelchair accessible, adapted toilet.
BACKGROUND MUSIC: in public areas.
LOCATION: 2 miles SW of town centre.
CHILDREN: all ages welcomed.
DOGS: not allowed.
CREDIT CARDS: MasterCard, Visa.
PRICES: [2018] per room B&B single £75–£135, double £110–£365. À la carte £40–£50.

WILMINGTON Sussex

Map 2:E4

CROSSWAYS HOTEL

Perennial visitors reported 'a warm welcome' from Clive James and David Stott at their restaurant-with-rooms – 'a cherished institution to many Glyndebourne regulars' – at the foot of the South Downs. Fans return for the hosts' 'attention to simple things, like chilling our bottle of wine before we set off for the opera, and their easy (but never intrusive) conversation. It's a cheerful, meticulously informal place.' Individually styled bedrooms, 'clean, comfortable', are supplied with 'well-judged details': fresh milk in the fridge; earplugs to buffer the 'discreet hum' from the nearby road. Each has a new bathroom. In the intimate dining room, local meat and game feature in David Stott's 'seasonal, generous dinners', as well as 'nightly-changing, locally landed fish' from Hastings. Breakfast is 'generous and freshly cooked, though the coffee probably wouldn't keep you awake for long (our only gripe)'. Glyndebourne-goers are well catered for, 'even at short notice', thanks to the hosts' 'finely tuned awareness of the timetable of an evening at the opera'. If opera is off the cards, perhaps a wander in the 'enticing' gardens. 'Excellent value overall.' (Richard Parish, and others)

25% DISCOUNT VOUCHERS

Lewes Road
Wilmington
BN26 5SG

T: 01323 482455
E: stay@crosswayshotel.co.uk
W: www.crosswayshotel.co.uk

BEDROOMS: 7. Plus self-catering cottage and apartment.
OPEN: all year except 21 Dec–late Jan, restaurant closed Sun/Mon.
FACILITIES: breakfast room, restaurant, free Wi-Fi, in-room TV (Freeview), 2-acre grounds (duck pond), unsuitable for disabled.
BACKGROUND MUSIC: occasionally, in dining areas.
LOCATION: 2 miles W of Polegate on A27.
CHILDREN: not under 12.
DOGS: not allowed.
CREDIT CARDS: Amex, MasterCard, Visa.
PRICES: [2018] per room B&B single £85, double £150–£175, D,B&B £220–£240. Set dinner £43.

WINCHESTER Hampshire

Map 2:D2

THE OLD VINE

Built over a subterranean 14th-century tavern, and 'wonderfully situated' a stroll from the cathedral, Ashton Gray's 18th-century pub-with-rooms finds favour with readers again this year. Its 'warm welcome' and 'enthusiastic young staff' are particularly praised. The interiors blend the traditional with smart contemporary, from the bar, with beams and open fires, to bedrooms named after fabric and wallpaper designers. A typically 'delightful' bedroom was 'beautifully decorated' with 'comfy bed and good-quality towels and linen', an espresso machine, a fridge with fresh milk and soft drinks. The Design House Cathedral View Suite, under the eaves, was 'a delight, comfortable, warm and quiet'; a complaint about a rogue shower was promptly addressed. Osborne and Little, overlooking the cathedral green, has Georgian plaster panelling. Seasonal menus range from sandwiches and such pub classics as scampi and chips, to 'agreeable' bistro fare – vegan kedgeree with New Forest mushrooms; braised lamb shank, red wine, redcurrant, rosemary and mint gravy. 'Breakfast service volunteered in room without additional charge was a very charming extra aspect.' (Stephen and Jane Marshall, Keith Salway)

8 Great Minster Street
Winchester
SO23 9HA

T: 01962 854616
E: reservations@oldvinewinchester.com
W: www.oldvinewinchester.com

BEDROOMS: 6. Self-contained 2-bed apartment, with garage, in annexe.
OPEN: all year except Christmas Day.
FACILITIES: bar, restaurant, free Wi-Fi, in-room TV (Freeview), permits supplied for on-street parking, restaurant and bar wheelchair accessible, but not toilets.
BACKGROUND MUSIC: in bar.
LOCATION: town centre, permits supplied for on-street parking.
CHILDREN: all ages welcomed.
DOGS: only in bar.
CREDIT CARDS: Amex, MasterCard, Visa.
PRICES: [2018] per room B&B single £120–£160, double £140–£200. Set menu (2/3 courses) £25 residents only, à la carte £30.

SEE ALSO SHORTLIST

WINDERMERE Cumbria

Map 4: inset C2

CEDAR MANOR

'We arrived hungry and tired, and came away feeling relaxed, recharged and utterly spoiled.' Visitors celebrating a special occasion in 2018 at Caroline and Jonathan Kaye's 'impressive' small hotel 'felt welcome from the moment we walked in'. 'The room was exceptional, the meal superb; the hosts made our stay memorable.' 'Caroline and Jonathan always go the extra mile.' Pleasing touches return their small Lake District hotel to its roots as a Victorian country house retreat, from the locally crafted furniture to replacing used water glasses in the bathrooms ('a dying service'). Local produce feeds long-serving chef Roger Pergl-Wilson's 'imaginative menus', which might include beetroot-and-liquorice-marinated gravlax with kohlrabi-fennel coleslaw; aubergine and chestnut tagine. Each of the 'superbly appointed' bedrooms is different, with a canopy bed here, a four-poster there; some overlook the eponymous Lebanese cedar through ecclesiastical windows. Morning is welcomed by a sturdy Cumbrian grill; locally smoked haddock with hollandaise and a poached egg; American-style pancakes – all cooked to order. (Pauline and Stephen Glover, and others)

Ambleside Road
Windermere
LA23 1AX

T: 015394 43192
E: info@cedarmanor.co.uk
W: www.cedarmanor.co.uk

BEDROOMS: 10. 1 split-level suite in coach house.
OPEN: all year except 17–26 Dec, 3–19 Jan.
FACILITIES: 2 lounges, restaurant, free Wi-Fi, in-room TV (Freeview), patio, ¼-acre garden, unsuitable for disabled.
BACKGROUND MUSIC: 'very quietly', at mealtimes, in lounge and restaurant.
LOCATION: 5-min. walk from town centre.
CHILDREN: not under 10.
DOGS: not allowed.
CREDIT CARDS: MasterCard, Visa.
PRICES: [2018] per room B&B £145–£475, D,B&B £235–£565. Set dinner £35–£45, à la carte £45. 2-night min. stay at weekends preferred.

WINDERMERE Cumbria

Map 4: inset C2

GILPIN HOTEL AND LAKE HOUSE

'They just keep making it better every year,' writes a trusted correspondent, of this luxurious country house hotel in Lakeland countryside. It is 30 years since the Cunliffe family opened what was a modest B&B, and they have never stopped innovating. 'The decor is creative, from the wonderfully restful sitting room to the second restaurant, Gilpin Spice, in three rooms, each with modern Asian style.' Accommodation ranges from bedrooms in the Edwardian main house, to spa lodges with outdoor hot tub, and open-plan garden suites with a lounge, feature fireplace, decked garden and hot tub. Lake House, a satellite operation, is fully staffed, with a residents' lounge, a spa, and chauffeured lifts to home base. Chef Hrishikesh Desai holds a Michelin star for his 'excellent modern British cooking' in HRiSHi restaurant, perhaps roast Cartmel valley venison, glazed dumpling, beetroot Tatin, savoy cabbage, caramelised hazelnuts, blackberry jus. Gilpin Spice serves less expensive, more exotic fare. 'The very different food shows his versatility.' The extensive grounds include a llama paddock. Staff 'could not be nicer'. 'It really is quite exceptional.' (Stephanie Thompson, JC, and others)

Crook Road
Windermere
LA23 3NE

T: 015394 88818
E: hotel@thegilpin.co.uk
W: thegilpin.co.uk

BEDROOMS: 31. 6 in orchard wing, 5 in spa lodges in grounds, 6 in Lake House (½ mile from main house), 1 room suitable for disabled.
OPEN: all year.
FACILITIES: Gilpin Hotel: bar, lounge, 2 restaurants, gardens, 22-acre grounds; Lake House: lounge, conservatory, spa (20-metre heated swimming pool), 100-acre grounds; free Wi-Fi, in-room TV (Sky), civil wedding licence.
BACKGROUND MUSIC: in restaurants.
LOCATION: on B5284, 2 miles SE of Windermere.
CHILDREN: not under 7.
DOGS: allowed in 2 bedrooms, not in public rooms.
CREDIT CARDS: all major cards.
PRICES: [2018] per room B&B from £275, D,B&B from £365. Set dinner £70, tasting menu (HRiSHi) £90.

WOLD NEWTON Yorkshire

Map 4:D5

THE WOLD COTTAGE

'Nothing could have prepared us for the beauty of Wold Cottage, where Katrina welcomed us with warmth and kindness.' A trusted reader echoes our inspectors' endorsement for Katrina and Derek Gray's Georgian manor house B&B in a rural setting outside a small village. Bedrooms, two in a converted barn, are named after former manor residents, and individually designed, some elegant and traditional, some more contemporary. Spacious, west-facing Miss Davy has 'a super-king-size bed with brass headpost, marble fireplace, and full-length, thick gold curtains'. The 'spotless' bathroom had a freestanding bath, walk-in shower and high-quality toiletries including home-made lavender soap. On a chilly spring day a 'roaring log and coal fire made for a homely environment' in the sitting room, its walls hung with 'tasteful original art and prints'. Breakfast brings Filey kippers and smoked haddock, traditional butcher's sausages, free-range eggs, home-made jams, local honey. In a nearby field, on the spot where a meteorite fell in 1795, stands a commemorative column built by Major Edward Topham of Wold Cottage – who in turn is commemorated in a four-poster suite. (Dorothy Latham)

25% DISCOUNT VOUCHERS

Wold Newton
YO25 3HL

T: 01262 470696
E: katrina@woldcottage.com
W: www.woldcottage.com

BEDROOMS: 6. 2 in converted barn, 1 on ground floor, 2 self-catering cottages.
OPEN: all year.
FACILITIES: lounge, dining room, free Wi-Fi, in-room TV (Freeview), 3-acre gardens (croquet) in 240-acre grounds (farmland, woodland), public rooms wheelchair accessible.
BACKGROUND MUSIC: at breakfast in dining room.
LOCATION: just outside village.
CHILDREN: all ages welcomed.
DOGS: not allowed.
CREDIT CARDS: MasterCard, Visa.
PRICES: [2018] per room B&B single £75–£90, double £100–£130, family room £135–£200. 1-night bookings refused at weekends.

WOOTTON COURTENAY Somerset   Map 1:B5

DUNKERY BEACON COUNTRY HOUSE

'Our first visit and not our last to this lovely
welcoming hotel,' writes a trusted reader, of
John and Jane Bradley's Edwardian hunting
lodge, a beacon of excellence in Exmoor national
park. The hosts are 'genuinely caring', writes
another fan, 'Jane front-of-house as wine expert,
John as chef and keen gardener'. Traditionally
styled bedrooms, two with four-poster, have
moorland views, chilled spring water, fresh milk;
luxury rooms have a cafetière, suites an espresso
machine. In the Coleridge restaurant, with views
towards the Coleridge Way, the guests are met,
the feast is set with exemplary punctuality – 'You
may not have time for a pre-dinner drink if
you arrive late!' John Bradley's seasonal menus,
with nightly 'tweaks', are devised around local
and home-grown ingredients. Praise this year
for tempura prawns with coconut; herb-infused
rump of Somerset lamb, smoked garlic, polenta;
'an Exmoor blueberry syllabub I remember
vividly three months later'. At breakfast there is
'an excellent choice of cold and cooked items'.
Sad news: the hotel is on the market, for sale
with much good will and a high reputation.
(Janet Allom, Mary Coles, and others)

25% DISCOUNT VOUCHERS

Wootton Courtenay
TA24 8RH

T: 01643 841241
E: info@dunkerybeacon
accommodation.co.uk
W: www.dunkerybeacon
accommodation.co.uk

BEDROOMS: 8. 1 on ground floor.
OPEN: mid-Feb–27 Dec, restaurant
closed Sun/Mon/Tues.
FACILITIES: lounge, restaurant,
breakfast room, free Wi-Fi in
public areas and some bedrooms,
in-room TV (Freeview), limited
mobile phone reception, ¾-acre
garden (alfresco meals), unsuitable
for disabled.
BACKGROUND MUSIC: in restaurant
in evening.
LOCATION: 4 miles SW of Dunster.
CHILDREN: not under 10.
DOGS: allowed in 2 suites (£5 per
night, max. 2 dogs), not in public
rooms.
CREDIT CARDS: MasterCard, Visa.
PRICES: [2018] per room £85–£170,
D,B&B £147–£232. À la carte £33.
1-night bookings refused Fri/Sat
and on all stays in peak season (but
check for late availability).

YARM Yorkshire

Map 4:C4

JUDGES

♀ Previous César winner

'Wonderful. Ten out of ten,' writes a delighted reader in 2018, of this Victorian retreat and one-time lodgings for circuit judges on the edge of the North Yorkshire moors. Today it is run by Tim Howard for the Downs family owners as an upmarket hotel, with close care for guests' comfort. Light meals and afternoon tea are served in a lounge sporting gilt-framed paintings, antiques and comfy sofas, warmed by an open fire. 'Everything good fun and lovely style,' approves one reader this year. 'Attentive staff,' adds another. 'The service was exceptional.' 'Spacious, luxurious' bedrooms are individually styled, some with a four-poster bed, some with whirlpool bath, all with good fabrics, complimentary sherry, a teddy bear. 'Our room had wonderful views of the beautiful gardens. There was everything you could want, even a television in the bathroom.' Scott Papprill's 'superb' cooking includes such inventive dishes as fillet of wild turbot with vanilla and pancetta butter sauce. A turn-down service, overnight shoeshine and a wake-up call with fresh coffee show attention to detail. (Rosalind and John Coulby, David Dale)

Kirklevington Hall
Yarm
TS15 9LW

T: 01642 789000
E: reception@judgeshotel.co.uk
W: judgeshotel.co.uk

BEDROOMS: 21. Some on ground floor.
OPEN: all year.
FACILITIES: lounge, bar, restaurant, private dining room, free Wi-Fi, in-room TV (Freeview), function facilities, business centre, civil wedding licence, 36-acre grounds (paths, running routes), access to local spa and sports club, unsuitable for disabled.
BACKGROUND MUSIC: Radio 4 at breakfast, classical background music in restaurant.
LOCATION: 1½ miles S of centre.
CHILDREN: all ages welcomed.
DOGS: guide dogs only.
CREDIT CARDS: all major cards.
PRICES: [2018] per room B&B single £99–£205, double £145–£225, D,B&B double £220–£300. Set menu £25, à la carte £56.

YARMOUTH Isle of Wight

Map 2:E2

THE GEORGE

Guests staying at this 17th-century seafront town house are following in illustrious footsteps. Charles II walked on the same stone flags, uneven floors and sweeping staircase when visiting its then resident, Sir Robert Holmes, the island's governor. There has been more contemporary restoration under the present owner, Dame Diane Thompson, former CEO of lottery operators Camelot. The multi-million-pound facelift promises to be a winner. Guide regulars praise its 'very welcoming' staff, 'lovely garden' and 'great position', with a panorama of ferries, yachts and fishermen on the Victorian pier. Inside, the individually designed bedrooms sport a mix of tasteful neutrals, uplifting whites and cool blues. Many overlook the Solent or the harbour. The hotel's two restaurants exploit the natural island bounty, the family-friendly Conservatory serving unfussy brasserie fare alongside garden and sea views, and the fine-dining option offering seasonal dishes including rump and shoulder of lamb, burnt aubergine, yogurt, tomato; chilled gazpacho, scallop tartare. Breakfast is 'good'. The hotel's location makes it an 'advantageous' choice for visitors wanting to leave their car on the mainland. (J and GM)

25% DISCOUNT VOUCHERS

Quay Street
Yarmouth
PO41 0PE

T: 01983 760331
E: info@thegeorge.co.uk
W: www.thegeorge.co.uk

BEDROOMS: 17. 1, on ground floor, suitable for disabled.
OPEN: all year, Isla's restaurant closed Sun–Tues.
FACILITIES: bar, lounge, 2 restaurants, private dining room, free Wi-Fi, in-room TV, civil wedding licence, meeting/function facilities, terrace, garden, public rooms wheelchair accessible, adapted toilet.
BACKGROUND MUSIC: in bar and restaurant, occasional live guitar music in lounge.
LOCATION: town centre, 'leave your car on the mainland and use the island's good bus service'.
CHILDREN: all ages welcomed.
DOGS: allowed in some bedrooms, not in public rooms.
CREDIT CARDS: Amex, MasterCard, Visa.
PRICES: [2018] per room B&B £140–£380. Set menu (Isla's) £55, à la carte (Conservatory) £30.

YORK Yorkshire

Map 4:D4

MIDDLETHORPE HALL & SPA

'Tis a very pritty place,' wrote the diarist and former resident Lady Mary Wortley Montagu. After visiting the National Trust's red brick mansion, Guide readers happily concur: 'stunning exterior', 'wonderful venue', 'an immaculately uniformed staff member waited at the door to uplift luggage to my room'. The twenty-acre grounds 'have many corners to explore', albeit with the background hum of passing traffic. 'Grand' public rooms, with imposing portraits, are 'furnished with antiques, old-fashioned drapes and fabrics'; the lounge has 'intimate groupings of deep sofas and tables, warmed by a roaring fire'. In the wood-panelled, candlelit dining room, chef Ashley Binder's 'very good' seasonal menus exploit produce from the walled kitchen garden, where the 17th-century dovecote is now a wine cellar. A typical dish: skrei cod, broccoli, brown shrimp and preserved lemon. Up the ornate oak staircase, bedrooms in the main house are agreeably traditional to some, 'dated but well coordinated' to others (the spa similarly splits opinion). A bathroom was 'small, but spotless'. Breakfast brings 'excellent molten scrambled egg, freshly squeezed juice, high-quality leaf tea'. (Robert Gower, Paul Abrahams, and others)

Bishopthorpe Road
York
YO23 2GB

T: 01904 641241
E: info@middlethorpe.com
W: www.middlethorpe.com

BEDROOMS: 29. 17 in courtyard, 2 in cottage, 1 suitable for disabled.
OPEN: all year, restaurant closed for lunch Mon, Tues.
FACILITIES: drawing room, sitting rooms, library, bar, restaurant, 2 private dining rooms, free Wi-Fi, in-room TV (Freeview), civil wedding licence, 20-acre grounds, spa (10 by 6 metre indoor swimming pool), public rooms wheelchair accessible, no adapted toilet.
BACKGROUND MUSIC: none.
LOCATION: 1½ miles S of centre.
CHILDREN: not under 6.
DOGS: allowed in garden suites and cottage only, by prior arrangement.
CREDIT CARDS: Amex, MasterCard, Visa.
PRICES: [2018] per room B&B 129–£514, D,B&B from £198. 6-course tasting menu £75, à la carte £59.

SEE ALSO SHORTLIST

ZENNOR Cornwall

Map 1:D1

THE GURNARD'S HEAD

'We cannot praise it too highly,' says a report this year on brothers Charles and Edmund Inkin's dining pub-with-rooms. 'Excellent', another succinctly concurs. As at sister pubs The Felin Fach Griffin and Old Coastguard (see entries), the style is artfully shabby-chic, relaxed, with mix-and-match furniture, rich warm colours, works by local artists. Perfectly placed to tackle the nearby coastal path, it also majors in indolence, perhaps watching the local herd amble past to milking, or curling up fireside with one of the many house paperbacks. Bedrooms have a Roberts radio but no TV, fresh flowers, smart toiletries, Welsh blankets, views of the Atlantic or moors. Chef Max Wilson uses produce from local food producers, purveyors and foragers to devise his menus. 'We want your home-grown fruits and vegetables', reads a chalked sign on the pub wall. You can eat in any of the comfy public rooms, such dishes as ray wing, crushes potatoes, spinach, caper butter; red gurnard, spring onions, ginger, seaweed, cuttlefish; sprouting broccoli, garlic, za'atar, yogurt. The bar, with 'a splendid range of drinks', is a popular local drop-in. (Richard Mitton, CS)

25% DISCOUNT VOUCHERS

Treen
Zennor
TR26 3DE

T: 01736 796928
E: enquiries@gurnardshead.co.uk
W: www.gurnardshead.co.uk

BEDROOMS: 7.
OPEN: all year except 24/25 Dec.
FACILITIES: bar, restaurant, lounge area, free Wi-Fi, 3-acre garden (alfresco dining), public areas wheelchair accessible.
BACKGROUND MUSIC: Radio 4 at breakfast, selected music at other times, in bar and restaurant.
LOCATION: 7 miles SW of St Ives, on B3306.
CHILDREN: all ages welcomed.
DOGS: allowed (water bowls, towels and biscuits provided).
CREDIT CARDS: MasterCard, Visa.
PRICES: [2018] per room B&B single £105–£150, double £125–£190, D,B&B single £133–£178, double £180–£245. Set menus £22–£28, à la carte £28. 1-night bookings refused at weekends occasionally.

SCOTLAND

Dean Village, Edinburgh

ALYTH Perth and Kinross

Map 5:D2

TIGH NA LEIGH **NEW**

Once the local doctor's house, close to the town centre, this 'well-appointed' stone-built Victorian villa is now a modern guest house, enwrapped by 'a pretty, surprisingly large garden'. Returning guests like the hosts: 'Chris and Bettina Black were as welcoming and friendly as ever.' In the 'sizeable' lounges, there are maps and guides to borrow: everything required to plan a day out. The Blacks, founts of local knowledge, can fill in any gaps. Contemporary bedrooms, light and airy, come in different sizes. The single has a brass and iron bed, the most lavish an emperor-size four-poster and a fireplace. 'Our suite had a pleasant sitting room with a sofa, two comfortable chairs, plenty of DVDs, books and magazines. The spacious bathroom had a spa bath.' Ordered in advance, 'good dinners' are served in the modern dining room with striking artwork. Typical dishes: Wagyu beef burger, Scottish Cheddar, smoked bacon; pan-roasted pheasant, pancetta, celeriac and parsnip rösti. 'Vegetarians are served with gusto.' Award-winning breakfasts include the full Scottish, the American (cured ham, free-range eggs any way) and the Canadian with eggy bread, streaky bacon, maple syrup. (John and Elspeth Gibbon)

22–24 Airlie Street,
Alyth
PH11 8AJ

T: 01828 632372
E: book@tighnaleigh.com
W: www.tighnaleigh.com

BEDROOMS: 6. 1 on ground floor, 1 via steep stairs.
OPEN: Feb–Nov.
FACILITIES: lounge, TV room, reading room, conservatory dining room, free Wi-Fi, in-room TV (Freeview), ½-acre landscaped garden with pond, parking, unsuitable for disabled.
BACKGROUND MUSIC: in dining room and main lounge during meal service.
LOCATION: close to town centre.
CHILDREN: not under 12.
DOGS: allowed in bedrooms, in public rooms except dining room.
CREDIT CARDS: all major cards.
PRICES: [2018] per room B&B single £57–£68, double £113–£136. À la carte £26. Min. 2-night stay at weekends.

ARDUAINE Argyll and Bute

LOCH MELFORT HOTEL

'A more beautiful setting than this peaceful bay could hardly be wished for.' Next to the exotic Arduaine Garden, on the 'magical' Argyll coast, Calum and Rachel Ross's dog-friendly country hotel is a 'welcoming, good-value' spot. Sea views are the main feature throughout. Evenings may be spent watching the sun set over the Slate Islands, part of the Inner Hebrides, perhaps with a 'really good' pre-prandial gin and tonic in hand. 'Warm, comfortable' bedrooms are spread across the main house and a 'well-soundproofed' annexe; all rooms enjoy the view. 'Our annexe room (somewhat outdated) had a nice big bed; plenty of storage; lots of hot water in the bathroom.' Fresh towels and treats are provided for canine companions. Five more rooms have been added during an extensive renovation this year, but some things are fine just as they are; a window table in the restaurant lets you watch light change over dinner. New chef Roger Brown may serve Gigha halibut, cassoulet, bacon dust, roast pistachio crust, or perhaps freshly landed langoustines, lobster or crab. In the morning, the 'wee breakfast' is not so wee, but 'well cooked and efficiently served'.

25% DISCOUNT VOUCHERS

Arduaine
PA34 4XG

T: 01852 200233
E: reception@lochmelfort.co.uk
W: www.lochmelfort.co.uk

BEDROOMS: 30. 20 in Sea View Lodge annexe, 10 on ground floor, 1 suitable for disabled, 2 suites, 8 Main House rooms, 1 suitable for disabled.
OPEN: all year except Mon–Wed Nov–Mar, 3 weeks Dec/Jan, open Christmas/New Year.
FACILITIES: sitting room, library, bar/bistro, restaurant, free Wi-Fi, in-room TV (terrestrial), wedding facilities, 17-acre grounds (National Trust for Scotland's Arduaine Garden next door).
BACKGROUND MUSIC: in restaurant and bistro.
LOCATION: 19 miles S of Oban.
CHILDREN: all ages welcomed.
DOGS: allowed in 6 bedrooms (£10 per night), not in public rooms.
CREDIT CARDS: Amex, MasterCard, Visa.
PRICES: [2018] per room B&B £160 £294, D,B&B £232–£366. Set dinner £42.

AUCHENCAIRN Dumfries and Galloway   Map 5:E2

BALCARY BAY HOTEL

'A haven of tranquillity and quiet comfort',
Graeme Lamb's 'well-run' hotel stands in 'a
wonderful setting' on the shore, looking across
the Solway Firth to the Lake District hills. It
is especially loved by retirees for its endearing,
old-fashioned charms. Some return year after
year – if not several times a year – and assure us
standards are maintained. With limited Wi-Fi,
it is not for social-media junkies, but walkers,
birdwatchers and cyclists are in their element.
The wide choice of bedrooms offers views of
the bay or of the landscaped gardens, while both
lounges have an ocean outlook. 'Good lunches
can be taken in the bar', from sandwiches to
Scottish haddock and chips. In the light-filled
conservatory restaurant, at night, chef Craig
McWillliam delivers a daily-changing four-
course menu including such dishes as fillet of
Scottish beef, wild mushrooms, dauphinoise
potatoes, lentil purée, beef jus. 'It is of high
quality.' Add in the location and 'first-class
accommodation' and 'that's why people return,
just as we will'. An 'equally good' breakfast
offers 'a wide choice', including perhaps a
kipper or smoked haddock. (E and JG, and
others)

Shore Road
Auchencairn
DG7 1QZ

T: 01556 640217
E: reservations@balcary-bay-hotel.
co.uk
W: www.balcary-bay-hotel.co.uk

BEDROOMS: 20. 3 on ground floor.
OPEN: 2 Feb–2 Dec.
FACILITIES: 2 lounges, cocktail bar,
conservatory, restaurant, free Wi-Fi
in reception area, in-room TV
(Freeview), 3-acre grounds.
BACKGROUND MUSIC: none.
LOCATION: 2 miles SW of village.
CHILDREN: all ages welcomed.
DOGS: allowed in bedrooms, not in
public rooms (max. 2 small or 1 dog
per room).
CREDIT CARDS: MasterCard, Visa.
PRICES: [2018] per person B&B
£77–£93, D,B&B £92–£127 (min. 2
nights). 1-night bookings usually
refused weekends.

AULDEARN Highland

Map 5:C2

BOATH HOUSE

✪ Previous César winner

'We were looking forward to our stay,' write Guide insiders, on returning to this classical Georgian mansion in 'wonderful grounds', rescued from ruin in the 1990s by Don and Wendy Matheson. It did not disappoint. Indeed, its interiors have recently received a facelift. A basement bedroom sported 'a lovely old sideboard, chairs and round table'. An anteroom had a stone floor, glass ceiling, stairs to the garden. Other rooms have views over lake, woodlands and formal gardens, perhaps an antique four-poster or a half-tester bed. Log fires burn in lounges hung with Scottish art. At dinner, new chef Craig Munro offers a choice of meat, fish and vegetarian dishes using local, home-grown and foraged ingredients. Perhaps halibut, salmon tortellini, sweetcorn, pepper foam; chickpea chilli, cucumber, pickles. One reader, however, felt his wine complaint could have been handled with more grace. Breakfast brings organic duck and hens' eggs, smoked locally caught salmon, woodland mushrooms, home-made jams, honey from the hives. A new café with wood-fired oven serves garden-to-plate fare in the Victorian walled garden. (JT-P, and others)

Boath House
Auldearn
IV12 5TE

T: 01667 454896
E: info@boath-house.com
W: www.boath-house.com

BEDROOMS: 9. 2 in cottages (50 yds), 1 suitable for disabled.
OPEN: all year.
FACILITIES: 2 lounges, whisky bar/library, restaurant, private dining room, free Wi-Fi, in-room TV (Freeview), civil wedding licence, 22-acre grounds (woods, gardens, meadow, streams, trout lake, café), public rooms wheelchair accessible, step up to toilet.
BACKGROUND MUSIC: none.
LOCATION: 2 miles E of Nairn.
CHILDREN: all ages welcomed.
DOGS: allowed in some bedrooms, not in public rooms.
CREDIT CARDS: Amex, MasterCard, Visa.
PRICES: [2018] per room B&B single £190–£260, double £295–£365, D,B&B double £380–£450. Set dinner £45.

BALLANTRAE Ayrshire

Map 5:E1

GLENAPP CASTLE

Mellow sandstone battlements, turrets and
towers are revealed only at the final turn of the
'lengthy' drive through the 'vibrant, meticulously
tended' grounds of Paul and Poppy Szkiler's
19th-century baronial pile. Once unpacked,
further exploration reveals a walled garden with
tea room, 'mature trees and an atmospheric
lake', a croquet lawn, a tennis court. Indoors,
the tone is set by general manager John Orr's
'warm' welcome, and 'refined' details including
'wonderful stucco ceilings, magnificent staircases
with oak banisters, gleaming brass nameplates'.
Rooms are traditional, some with half-tester beds,
fireplaces, chandeliers; in the 'large bathroom',
a Guide insider writes of 'soft towels, robes and
quite a journey from the WC to the bath'. Many
rooms overlook the sea to Ailsa Craig, Arran and,
on a clear day, Northern Ireland. In the dining
room, chef David Alexander's 'high-quality'
food is proudly local: West Coast seafood, game
from surrounding estates, fruit and veg from the
gardens and Victorian greenhouse. A typical dish:
crusted fillet of West Coast halibut, cauliflower
purée, buttered spinach, sherry vinegar and
brown butter reduction. Breakfast included
'home-made muesli, tempting hot dishes'.

Ballantrae
KA26 0NZ

T: 01465 831212
E: info@glenappcastle.com
W: www.glenappcastle.com

BEDROOMS: 17. 7 on ground floor,
some suitable for disabled.
OPEN: all year.
FACILITIES: lift, drawing room,
library, 2 dining rooms, wedding
facilities, free Wi-Fi, in-room TV
(Freeview), 36-acre grounds (walled
gardens, woodland, lake, tennis,
croquet), boat for charter, access to
local spa, public rooms wheelchair
accessible.
BACKGROUND MUSIC: occasional
piano during meals and tea.
LOCATION: 2 miles S of Ballantrae.
CHILDREN: all ages welcomed.
DOGS: allowed in some bedrooms,
not in public rooms.
CREDIT CARDS: Amex, MasterCard,
Visa.
PRICES: [2018] per room B&B
£245–£645, D,B&B £345–£765.
À la carte £69. 1-night bookings
sometimes refused.

BLAIRGOWRIE Perth and Kinross

KINLOCH HOUSE

'So nice to come back here,' writes a trusted reader, on returning to the Allen family's creeper-covered Victorian country house on a hillside above a peaceful valley. 'Faultless in every respect,' adds a Guide regular in 2018, after two 'absolutely magical' days. 'This is how a hotel should be run.' The owners promise 'a home from home', albeit one with oak-panelled hall, grand fireplace and portrait gallery. There is no designer chic, just solid tradition, comfort and a warm welcome with tea on arrival. If there is anything you want, 'just ask at reception and it happens within minutes as though by magic'. Bedrooms, including a four-poster suite, are furnished with antiques and supplied with chocolates, fresh flowers, Arran Aromatics toiletries. Some overlook the gardens, fields grazed by Highland cattle and Marlee Loch. At dinner, Steve MacCallum's 'excellent' daily-changing menus are big on local game, Scottish meat, wild salmon, home-grown fruit and vegetables, perhaps slow-cooked feather blade of beef, creamed leeks, wild mushrooms, fondant potato, roast root vegetables, red wine sauce. 'Breakfast was good, too.' (David Grant, Bill Wood, Ralph Wilson)

Dunkeld Road
Blairgowrie
PH10 6SG

T: 01250 884237
E: reception@kinlochhouse.com
W: www.kinlochhouse.com

BEDROOMS: 15. 4 on ground floor.
OPEN: all year except 2 weeks from mid-Dec, open for New Year.
FACILITIES: bar, lounge, drawing room, conservatory, dining room, private dining room, free Wi-Fi, in-room TV (Freeview), wedding facilities, 28-acre grounds, public areas on ground floor wheelchair accessible.
BACKGROUND MUSIC: none.
LOCATION: 3 miles W of Blairgowrie, on A923.
CHILDREN: all ages welcomed.
DOGS: not allowed.
CREDIT CARDS: Amex, Mastercard, Visa.
PRICES: [2018] per room B&B £185–£340, D,B&B £295–£450. Set dinner £55. 1-night bookings refused at busy periods.

BRIDGEND Argyll and Bute   Map 5:D1

BRIDGEND HOTEL   NEW

Famous distilleries, 'lovely walking trails' and trout-rich lochs are within easy reach of this traditional Scottish country hotel, an Islay fixture for over 150 years. A traditional welcome too. 'Staff could not have been more helpful or positive,' writes a reader in 2018. Morrison tartan – the family owns the Islay Estates, including the hotel – carpets the lounge with its open fire and home-baked treats, while Kate's bar, 'clearly enjoyed by people other than guests', has peaty Islay malts, island ales and The Botanist gin, distilled nearby. In the dining room, its wall hung with coastal landscapes, chef Scott Chance's 'superb, largely locally sourced' food has meat and game from the estate, shellfish from the surrounding ocean. A typical dish: medallions of Islay estate venison, venison faggot, truffle croquet, woodland mushroom, parsnip, woodland berry sauce. More casual bites are available in the bar. The light, bright, bedrooms are individually decorated with touches of tartan and florals, all bathrooms have island toiletries; 'the old, solid walls prevented any noise from other rooms.' Breakfast includes smoked haddock, poached egg, a Loch Fyne kipper. 'We hope to return.'

Bridgend
PA44 7PJ

T: 01496 810212
E: info@bridgend-hotel.com
W: bridgend-hotel.com

BEDROOMS: 11. 1 family room with bunk bed.
OPEN: all year except 19 Dec–3 Jan, restaurant closed Christmas Day, Boxing Day and New Year's Day.
FACILITIES: lounge, bar, restaurant, free Wi-Fi, in-room TV (Freeview), wedding facilities, terrace, garden, drying room, parking.
BACKGROUND MUSIC: in public areas.
LOCATION: centre of small village.
CHILDREN: all ages welcomed.
DOGS: well-behaved dogs allowed in bedrooms, bar.
CREDIT CARDS: all major credit cards.
PRICES: [2018] per room B&B £120–£250, D,B&B £160–£290. À la carte £30. 1-night bookings sometimes refused during Islay Festival end of May.

CALLANDER Perth and Kinross

Map 5:D2

POPPIES HOTEL AND RESTAURANT

On a winding road, past woods, ferns and steel-grey lochs, John and Susan Martin's 'good-value, well-located' small hotel is 'a haven of tranquillity and good food'. The 'affable hosts' and their 'efficient' staff give visitors a 'friendly welcome'. There's no lounge, but a collection of single malts (120 and counting), displayed behind a handsome oak bar, provides enjoyable sampling. Veronika and Csaba Brunner run the 'comfortable' restaurant. Scottish produce is presented in 'some excellent and unusual combinations', perhaps pork terrine, lentil salad, salt-baked beets, wasabi mayo; shakshuka with spinach, potatoes and ciabatta. Afterwards, a 'good night's rest' awaits in 'spotless, tasteful' bedrooms, helped by 'good double glazing for efficient sound insulation'. Some have views across the main road to fields, river and rising hills; others a super-king-size bed and a small sitting area with a sofa; each has a 'modern, stylish' bathroom with plenty of hot water. Breakfast, cooked to order, is 'excellent'. Within 'easy access' of Loch Lomond and the Highlands, 'even for those of us without a car'. 'We enjoyed our stay.' (PB, A and EW, J and EG)

Leny Road
Callander
FK17 8AL

T: 01877 330329
E: info@poppieshotel.com
W: www.poppieshotel.com

BEDROOMS: 9. 1 on ground floor.
OPEN: closed 24 Dec–1 Feb, restaurant usually closed Wed.
FACILITIES: bar, restaurant, free Wi-Fi, in-room TV (Freeview), small front garden, unsuitable for disabled.
BACKGROUND MUSIC: in bar and restaurant.
LOCATION: on A84, ½ mile from town centre.
CHILDREN: all ages welcomed.
DOGS: allowed in 2 bedrooms, not in public rooms.
CREDIT CARDS: Amex, MasterCard, Visa.
PRICES: [2018] per room B&B single £80–£90, double £95–£130, D,B&B £155–£190. À la carte £35.

CHIRNSIDE Scottish Borders   Map 5:E3

CHIRNSIDE HALL

Returning visitors are welcomed 'like old friends' to Christian Korsten's restored 1830s mansion, a short drive from the Lammermuir hills and Berwickshire coast. Built as a holiday home for a wealthy Edinburgh businessman, it sits in verdant Borders countryside, offering 'far-reaching' views to the Cheviots. Its two 'warm, comfortable' and 'grand' lounges sport an open fire, comfy settees and swathes of soft Welsh wool, light modern tartan and tweed. Up the hall's curling late Georgian staircase, past trophy stags' heads (the hotel is popular with shooting parties), bedrooms maintain the country house mood, with 'tasteful' soft furnishings, warm hues and 'modern' bathroom. Some have a contemporary four-poster, original fireplace, sofa and large period windows. Top-floor rooms are snug, with lower ceiling, smaller windows. In the light, elegant dining room, chef Tim Holmes's 'wholesome, well-prepared' daily-changing four-course dinners showcase seasonal, local produce with game from Chirnside's estate, perhaps loin of roe deer, Scottish girolles, celeriac purée, fondant potato, thyme jus; Aberdeen Angus sirloin, peppercorn butter, green beans, sautéed potatoes. Breakfast has a 'good choice of hot and cold options'.

Chirnside
TD11 3LD

T: 01890 818219
E: reception@chirnsidehallhotel.
   com
W: www.chirnsidehallhotel.com

BEDROOMS: 10.
OPEN: all year except Mar.
FACILITIES: 2 lounges, dining room, private dining room/library/conference rooms, free Wi-Fi, in-room TV (Freeview), billiard room, wedding facilities, 1½-acre grounds, lounge and restaurant wheelchair accessible.
BACKGROUND MUSIC: 'easy listening' in public areas.
LOCATION: 1½ miles E of Chirnside, NE of Duns.
CHILDREN: all ages welcomed.
DOGS: allowed in some bedrooms, not in public rooms.
CREDIT CARDS: Amex, MasterCard, Visa.
PRICES: [2018] per room B&B single £100, double £180, D,B&B double £240. À la carte £40.

COLINTRAIVE Argyll and Bute

Map 5:D1

COLINTRAIVE HOTEL

Yachting folk can moor at Patricia Watt's small hotel in a coastal village on the edge of Loch Lomond national park. A former shooting lodge for the Marquis of Bute, it is today the community hub. Next door is the store/post office, also run by the 'welcoming and friendly' Ms Watt. Trusted readers this year had 'a very enjoyable and relaxing stay'. The most expensive of four bedrooms was 'large, with dual-aspect windows and lovely views across the Kyles to Bute'. Named Attenborough in honour of a famous guest, the late Sir Richard, it had period furnishings, an open fireplace, original artwork, home-made biscuits. In the 'homely' bar, a log fire burns on cold days, while in the small dining room, with 'fresh wild flowers on every table', chef David Cumming cooks locally sourced 'very good' food – langoustine, scallops, fish, meat, game. 'The steak-and-Guinness pie was full of tender beef and carrots, and topped with airy puff pastry.' Cooked breakfast lacked smoked haddock or kipper, 'but I probably had only to ask'. Dogs are welcome; come unaccompanied, and black Labrador Caesar will happily take you for walkies. (David Birnic, CE)

Colintraive
PA22 3AS

T: 01700 841207
E: enquiries@colintraivehotel.com
W: www.colintraivehotel.com

BEDROOMS: 4.
OPEN: all year (residents only, 25 Dec).
FACILITIES: lounge, bar, restaurant, free Wi-Fi in reception, in-room TV (Freeview), wedding facilities, small beer garden, yacht moorings.
BACKGROUND MUSIC: in public areas, occasional live music.
LOCATION: in village, 20 miles W of Dunoon.
CHILDREN: all ages welcomed.
DOGS: allowed in bedrooms, public rooms, not in restaurant.
CREDIT CARDS: Diners, MasterCard, Visa.
PRICES: [2018] per room B&B single £85–£140, double £99–£185. À la carte £35.

COLONSAY Argyll and Bute   Map 5:D1

THE COLONSAY

On an island of white-sand beaches and rocky
inlets (human population 135; seals, otters and
eagles unnumbered), Jane and Alex Howard's
18th-century inn sits at the centre of village life,
with quiz nights and live music. Ivan Lisovyy is
the endlessly accommodating manager. Public
rooms have an airy 'seaside feel', with leather
armchairs and tasteful contemporary tones
juxtaposed with old black-and-white island
photographs. Bedrooms are simply furnished
and not huge, but have Designers Guild and
Colefax and Fowler fabrics, along with views
of the hillside, whitewashed church and sea,
across to neighbouring Jura. The atmosphere
is free and easy – eat in the dining room with
wood-burning stove and harbour outlook, in
the bar, or where you will. At lunchtime there
are soups, steak-and-ale pie, organic salad
leaves from the kitchen garden. New chef Salvi
Batalla sources ingredients as locally as possible
for such dishes as casserole of Balnahard beef
and Colonsay ale; pan-seared Colonsay salmon;
spring vegetable risotto with wild garlic pesto.
A children's menu might include local fish with
chips, organic chicken. 'It more than matched
my expectations.' (D and JB)

Colonsay
PA61 7YP

T: 01951 200316
E: hotel@colonsayholidays.co.uk
W: www.colonsayholidays.co.uk

BEDROOMS: 9.
OPEN: mid-Mar–1 Nov, Christmas,
New Year.
FACILITIES: conservatory, 2 lounges,
log room, bar, restaurant, free
Wi-Fi on ground floor, in-room TV
(Sky), 1-acre grounds, ground-floor
public rooms and toilet wheelchair
accessible.
BACKGROUND MUSIC: some in bar.
LOCATION: 400 yds W of harbour.
CHILDREN: all ages welcomed.
DOGS: 1 well-behaved dog allowed
in 2 bedrooms, public rooms except
restaurant.
CREDIT CARDS: MasterCard, Visa.
PRICES: [2018] per room B&B single
from £80, double £110–£160.
Pre-ferry set menus £15–£18 Mon,
Thurs, Fri, Sat, à la carte £28.

CONTIN Highland

Map 5:C2

COUL HOUSE

Approached by a private road, this 'large, rambling but wonderful' late Georgian mansion, in 'magnificent grounds', is owned and cherished by Susannah and Stuart Macpherson. Guide inspectors had 'a real feeling of entering a warm and inviting place', and found Victorian hunting paintings 'very fitting' in public rooms with original fireplaces and ornate plasterwork. A room at the back, with views across the gardens to the hills, had a thistle-patterned fabric pelmet and valance. Concerns over a 'slightly old-fashioned' bathroom have been addressed with a rolling programme of refurbishments – several have been upgraded over the last year. In the octagonal dining room, chef Garry Kenley sources local ingredients for such dishes as fillet steak, shallot purée, sautéed wild mushrooms and a choice of sauces. Not everyone is smitten by the old-fashioned charms ('like stepping back in time', says a detractor, meaning no compliment) and, yes, 'It's not perfect.' But it is in many ways 'a really lovely hotel'. The 'fairy walk' through the rhododendrons is 'magical'. And how many hotels can boast of a Douglas fir planted in 1827 by David Douglas himself?

Contin
IV14 9ES

T: 01997 421487
E: stay@coulhouse.com
W: www.coulhousehotel.com

BEDROOMS: 21. 4 on ground floor, 1 suitable for disabled.
OPEN: all year except 23–26 Dec.
FACILITIES: lounge bar, drawing room, front hall, restaurant, free Wi-Fi, in-room Smart TV, conference/wedding facilities, 8-acre grounds (children's play area, 9-hole pitch and putt).
BACKGROUND MUSIC: in lounge bar and restaurant.
LOCATION: 17 miles NW of Inverness.
CHILDREN: all ages welcomed.
DOGS: allowed in some bedrooms, all public rooms except restaurant (£7.50 per dog per night).
CREDIT CARDS: all major cards.
PRICES: [2018] per room B&B single £75–£110, double £95–£325. À la carte £38.

CRAIGHOUSE Argyll and Bute

JURA HOTEL NEW

In 'a fabulous location on one of the wildest, least-developed of all Scottish islands', the McCallum family's whitewashed pub, restaurant and hotel is the place to eat on Jura. Indeed, it is the only place to eat on Jura, where red deer outnumber the 200 human inhabitants 25 to one. George Orwell loved the mountainous landscape, and stayed in a farmhouse writing Nineteen-Eighty-Four. It was a primitive place compared to this 'comfortable' hotel, where, say the nominators, their premium room had 'a king-size bed, superb modern bathroom, unbelievable view over the Sound of Jura'. None of the bedrooms has TV, but there is much else to watch. 'We saw an otter fishing in the bay, a red deer stag grazing on the grass, a grey seal.' Some rooms are not so spacious, not all enjoy a sea view. Two interconnecting rooms can accommodate a family of four. In the 'cheering, likeable restaurant', 'delicious' dishes include Jura venison in season; locally caught langoustine; Islay crab. Breakfast is 'varied and imaginative; we especially liked the fat pancakes, crispy bacon and maple syrup'. (Alan and Edwina Williams)

Craighouse
Isle of Jura
PA60 7XU

T: 01496 820243
E: hello@jurahotel.co.uk
W: www.jurahotel.co.uk

BEDROOMS: 17. 15 en suite, 2 with private bathroom.
OPEN: all year except 22–28 Dec.
FACILITIES: bar, TV lounge, restaurant, outdoor eating area, free Wi-Fi throughout (residents only), public areas wheelchair accessible, no adapted toilet.
BACKGROUND MUSIC: all day in bar and restaurant.
LOCATION: in village, opposite Small Isles Bay, 300 yds from passenger ferry terminal, 7 miles from car ferry terminal.
CHILDREN: all ages welcomed.
DOGS: allowed in pub only.
CREDIT CARDS: MasterCard, Visa.
PRICES: [2018] B&B per room single £70, double £100–£135. À la carte £27.

THE GOOD HOTEL GUIDE 2019

Use this voucher to claim a 25% discount off the normal price for bed and breakfast at hotels with a 25% DISCOUNT VOUCHERS sign at the end of the entry. You must request a voucher discount at the time of booking and present this voucher on arrival. Further details and conditions overleaf. *Valid to 9th October 2019.*

25% DISCOUNT VOUCHER

THE GOOD HOTEL GUIDE 2019

Use this voucher to claim a 25% discount off the normal price for bed and breakfast at hotels with a 25% DISCOUNT VOUCHERS sign at the end of the entry. You must request a voucher discount at the time of booking and present this voucher on arrival. Further details and conditions overleaf. *Valid to 9th October 2019.*

25% DISCOUNT VOUCHER

THE GOOD HOTEL GUIDE 2019

Use this voucher to claim a 25% discount off the normal price for bed and breakfast at hotels with a 25% DISCOUNT VOUCHERS sign at the end of the entry. You must request a voucher discount at the time of booking and present this voucher on arrival. Further details and conditions overleaf. *Valid to 9th October 2019.*

25% DISCOUNT VOUCHER

THE GOOD HOTEL GUIDE 2019

Use this voucher to claim a 25% discount off the normal price for bed and breakfast at hotels with a 25% DISCOUNT VOUCHERS sign at the end of the entry. You must request a voucher discount at the time of booking and present this voucher on arrival. Further details and conditions overleaf. *Valid to 9th October 2019.*

25% DISCOUNT VOUCHER

THE GOOD HOTEL GUIDE 2019

Use this voucher to claim a 25% discount off the normal price for bed and breakfast at hotels with a 25% DISCOUNT VOUCHERS sign at the end of the entry. You must request a voucher discount at the time of booking and present this voucher on arrival. Further details and conditions overleaf. *Valid to 9th October 2019.*

25% DISCOUNT VOUCHER

THE GOOD HOTEL GUIDE 2019

Use this voucher to claim a 25% discount off the normal price for bed and breakfast at hotels with a 25% DISCOUNT VOUCHERS sign at the end of the entry. You must request a voucher discount at the time of booking and present this voucher on arrival. Further details and conditions overleaf. *Valid to 9th October 2019.*

25% DISCOUNT VOUCHER

CONDITIONS

1. Hotels with a **25% DISCOUNT VOUCHERS** sign have agreed to give readers a discount of 25% off their normal bed-and-breakfast rate.

2. One voucher is good for the first night's stay only, at the discounted rate for yourself alone or for you and a partner sharing a double room.

3. Hotels may decline to accept a voucher reservation if they expect to be fully booked at the full room price.

✂ — — — — — — — — — — — — — — —

CONDITIONS

1. Hotels with a **25% DISCOUNT VOUCHERS** sign have agreed to give readers a discount of 25% off their normal bed-and-breakfast rate.

2. One voucher is good for the first night's stay only, at the discounted rate for yourself alone or for you and a partner sharing a double room.

3. Hotels may decline to accept a voucher reservation if they expect to be fully booked at the full room price.

✂ — — — — — — — — — — — — — — —

CONDITIONS

1. Hotels with a **25% DISCOUNT VOUCHERS** sign have agreed to give readers a discount of 25% off their normal bed-and-breakfast rate.

2. One voucher is good for the first night's stay only, at the discounted rate for yourself alone or for you and a partner sharing a double room.

3. Hotels may decline to accept a voucher reservation if they expect to be fully booked at the full room price.

✂ — — — — — — — — — — — — — — —

CONDITIONS

1. Hotels with a **25% DISCOUNT VOUCHERS** sign have agreed to give readers a discount of 25% off their normal bed-and-breakfast rate.

2. One voucher is good for the first night's stay only, at the discounted rate for yourself alone or for you and a partner sharing a double room.

3. Hotels may decline to accept a voucher reservation if they expect to be fully booked at the full room price.

✂ — — — — — — — — — — — — — — —

CONDITIONS

1. Hotels with a **25% DISCOUNT VOUCHERS** sign have agreed to give readers a discount of 25% off their normal bed-and-breakfast rate.

2. One voucher is good for the first night's stay only, at the discounted rate for yourself alone or for you and a partner sharing a double room.

3. Hotels may decline to accept a voucher reservation if they expect to be fully booked at the full room price.

✂ — — — — — — — — — — — — — — —

CONDITIONS

1. Hotels with a **25% DISCOUNT VOUCHERS** sign have agreed to give readers a discount of 25% off their normal bed-and-breakfast rate.

2. One voucher is good for the first night's stay only, at the discounted rate for yourself alone or for you and a partner sharing a double room.

3. Hotels may decline to accept a voucher reservation if they expect to be fully booked at the full room price.

DUNVEGAN Highland

Map 5:C1

THE THREE CHIMNEYS AND THE HOUSE OVER-BY

'We felt comfortable and well fed,' report readers, following a stay at Shirley and Eddie Spear's remote restaurant-with-rooms overlooking Loch Dunvegan on the Isle of Skye. New arrivals are warmly welcomed. 'We were offered tea and scones, which we enjoyed enormously.' Tastefully neutral, split-level, wood-floored bedrooms in The House Over-By have an espresso machine, comfy seating, double-ended bath with power shower, patio doors on to the garden. A lounge with scenic views hosts breakfast and drinks, with a telescope for viewing wildlife. 'We enjoyed the visiting ducks, who were fed before we enjoyed apertifs.' In the rustic-chic restaurant, chef Scott Davies uses local produce from land and sea to create such dishes as Dunvegan crab, scorched langoustine tails, brown crab ketchup, puffed rice, apple, pickled mussels; Orbost rose beef, heather-smoked potato, charcoal-roasted lettuce, Hebridean Blue, pickled walnut ketchup. Service is 'excellent throughout'. In the morning there are fresh juices, grilled kipper with seaweed butter, and haggis and field mushroom with the full Scottish. 'It was a unique experience to watch a porpoise while having breakfast.' (RO)

Colbost
Dunvegan
IV55 8ZT

T: 01470 511258
E: eatandstay@threechimneys.co.uk
W: www.threechimneys.co.uk

BEDROOMS: 6. All on ground floor (5 split-level) in separate building, 1 suitable for disabled.
OPEN: all year except 17 Dec–17 Jan.
FACILITIES: lounge/breakfast room (House Over-By), restaurant, free Wi-Fi, in-room TV (Freeview), garden on loch, restaurant and lounge wheelchair accessible, adapted toilet.
BACKGROUND MUSIC: in lounge and restaurant, 'for different moods and times of day'.
LOCATION: 5 miles W of Dunvegan.
CHILDREN: all ages welcomed.
DOGS: not allowed.
CREDIT CARDS: Amex, MasterCard, Visa.
PRICES: [2018] per room B&B £360. D,B&B £390. Tasting menu £95, à la carte £68.

EDINBURGH   Map 5:D2

PRESTONFIELD

A tapestry room, a state drawing room, a whisky room, a sitting room lined with gilded Cordoba leather… James Thomson's 17th-century mansion beside Royal Holyrood Park pleases by a fine excess. It is filled with antiques, ancestral portraits, Mortlake tapestries, statuary, swags and drapes. Bathrooms are lined with Venetian glass, mosaic and marble. Suites are named after past visitors. Benjamin Franklin has a silver-leaf sleigh bed, an antique chaise longue, trompe l'oeil drapery, views over gardens and parkland. A former resident, Sir Alexander Dick, is credited with introducing rhubarb to Scotland – hence Rhubarb restaurant, where chef John McMahon's use of local and artisan ingredients is as lavish as everything else. A typical dish: roast roe deer loin, haunch pie and haggis, salt-baked beetroot, red cabbage purée, confit purple potato, semi-dried cherries, pink peppercorn jus. At breakfast, there are freshly squeezed juices, kippers, Finnan haddie. A bar menu is available from noon to night. 'The staff are welcoming, helpful and charming.' In the 'fantastic grounds with peacocks and Highland cattle' there are woodland walks, statues, topiary. Mr Thomson also owns The Witchery by the Castle, Edinburgh (see Shortlist). (JP)

Priestfield Road
Edinburgh
EH16 5UT

T: 0131 225 7800
E: reservations@prestonfield.com
W: www.prestonfield.com

BEDROOMS: 23. 1, on ground floor, suitable for disabled.
OPEN: all year.
FACILITIES: lift, 2 drawing rooms, sitting room, library, whisky bar, restaurant, private dining rooms, free Wi-Fi, in-room TV (Sky), wedding facilities, terraces, tea house, 20-acre grounds (gardens, croquet, putting, paddocks, woodland), public rooms wheelchair accessible, adapted toilet.
BACKGROUND MUSIC: 'when suitable' in public areas.
LOCATION: next to Royal Holyrood Park.
CHILDREN: all ages welcomed.
DOGS: allowed in bedrooms, public rooms and park, not in restaurant (£25 per dog per night).
CREDIT CARDS: all major cards.
PRICES: [2018] per room B&B from £220. Set dinner £40, à la carte £50.

SEE ALSO SHORTLIST

EDINBURGH

THE RAEBURN   **NEW**

Late Georgian elegance meets 21st-century boutique chic in the Maclean family's recently extended hotel overlooking Fettes College and the Edinburgh Academicals rugby ground. Our inspectors' first-floor bedroom had 'superior furniture, bucket chairs, a work table and desk/dressing table, a super-kingsize bed, minibar, espresso machine…', in the bathroom a monsoon shower, Scottish toiletries. Deluxe rooms also have a roll-top bath. The library is the place for 'private conversation and reading', while the buzzy bar and outdoor terrace host casual dining (sharing boards, fish and chips). In the brasserie-style restaurant, chef Daniel Mellor's British fare includes steaks cooked over charcoal. 'Sirloin steak and cider-braised venison haunch were plentiful and appetising', service was 'prompt and courteous'. Breakfast brings 'excellent fruit salad, porridge, sloppy scrambled egg, spicy black pudding'. Options include smoked salmon, chorizo and wild mushroom, the full Scottish or the vegetarian version. 'A cheerful Scottish waitress was well organised, though I did baulk at the phrase "you guys".' 'A quality hotel, centrally sited. The staff could not have been more helpful.'

112 Raeburn Place
Edinburgh
EH4 1HG

T: 0131 332 7000
E: info@theraeburn.com
W: www.theraeburn.com

BEDROOMS: 10. 1 suitable for disabled.
OPEN: all year except 25 Dec.
FACILITIES: bar, restaurant, library/function room, private dining area, conference room, free Wi-Fi, in-room TV (Freeview), beer garden, dining terrace, limited parking, public areas wheelchair accessible, adapted toilet.
BACKGROUND MUSIC: in public areas.
LOCATION: ½ mile from city centre.
CHILDREN: all ages welcomed.
DOGS: allowed in bar, only guide dogs allowed in bedrooms.
CREDIT CARDS: Amex, MasterCard, Visa.
PRICES: [2018] per room B&B £149–£207. À la carte £34.

SEE ALSO SHORTLIST

GAIRLOCH Highland   Map 5:B1

SHIELDAIG LODGE

'Down a long single-track road, flanked by stone
eagles at the gate', Nick and Charlotte Dent's
Victorian hunting lodge enjoys 'a glorious setting'
by Loch Gairloch, 'with enchanting views of
cavorting seals'. From the 'exquisite, oak-panelled
vestibule', to the bar stocking 300 whiskies,
everything impressed our inspectors. 'The first
of two lounges was a pleasingly masculine affair,
with navy-painted walls, deep leather sofas, cloth-
bound books. The other is lighter and more open',
with tall windows on to the water. Bedrooms,
overlooking loch or gardens, are supplied with
fresh milk, shortbread, the occasional amusing
touch. 'Ours had two Harris tweed-covered
armchairs, a long sofa, antique wardrobe, dressing
table and chest of drawers.' The bathroom was
'all wood panelling, long shutters and gleaming
fittings', with 'two sweet rubber Nessies for
company when bathing'. The dining room
serves yet more 'gorgeous panoramas', alongside
seasonal, daily-changing menus embracing
shellfish from the loch, venison and rare breed
lamb and beef from the estate. At breakfast,
creamy porridge and a vegan dish of 'grilled
tomato, succulent grilled mushrooms, baked
beans, potato scone and wilted kale' hit the spot.

Badachro
Gairloch
IV21 2AN

T: 01445 741333
E: reservations@shieldaiglodge.com
W: www.shieldaiglodge.com

BEDROOMS: 12.
OPEN: all year.
FACILITIES: lounge, library, bar,
restaurant, snooker room, free Wi-
Fi, in-room TV (Freeview), garden,
26,000-acre estate (tennis, fishing,
red deer stalking, falconry centre,
motor boat for charter), public areas
wheelchair accessible.
BACKGROUND MUSIC: in lounge, bar
and restaurant.
LOCATION: 4¼ miles S of Gairloch.
CHILDREN: all ages welcomed.
DOGS: not allowed.
CREDIT CARDS: all major credit cards.
PRICES: [2018] per room B&B single
£95–£150, double £130–£350,
D,B&B single £130–£185, double
£199–£419. Set dinner £35.

GLASGOW

Map 5:D2

GRASSHOPPERS

If you're looking for a modestly priced hotel at the heart of the city, this is just the ticket – a modern B&B on the penthouse floor of a handsome, buff stone, 1900s office building, right by Central Station. 'It has a lot going for it,' writes a regular reader this year. 'Handy location for sightseeing, and friendly, helpful staff.' On arrival guests are greeted with tea or coffee and cakes – available at no charge, all day, in 'The Kitchen', the smart if 'cramped' hotel hub. Bedrooms have Caledonian oak floor, king-size bed, power shower and desk, alongside views over the vast Victorian glass station roof. In summer, our reader's room was hot despite a ceiling fan – and opening the window meant letting in street noise. Daily breakfast, and supper from Monday to Thursday, can be taken in Kitchen or bedroom, with ingredients sourced from good local delicatessens – fruit, yogurts, eggs, bacon, cold meats, cheeses, and Scottish porridge, naturally. There are kedgeree days, menus celebrating National and European days. Secure 24-hour parking is available close by but why not let the train take the strain?

6th floor Caledonian Chambers
Glasgow
G1 3TA

T: 0141 222 2666
E: info@grasshoppersglasgow.com
W: www.grasshoppersglasgow.com

BEDROOMS: 29.
OPEN: all year except 4 days Christmas.
FACILITIES: breakfast/supper room, sitting room with small bar, free Wi-Fi, in-room TV (Sky), unsuitable for disabled.
BACKGROUND MUSIC: none.
LOCATION: by Central Station.
CHILDREN: all ages welcomed.
DOGS: allowed.
CREDIT CARDS: Amex, MasterCard, Visa.
PRICES: [2018] per room B&B single £65–£95, double £85–£125, D,B&B double £100–£140. À la carte £17.

SEE ALSO SHORTLIST

GLENELG Highland

THE GLENELG INN

Amid 'some of the most remote and beautiful scenery one can find anywhere in the world', Sheila Condie's traditional Highland inn stands close to the ferry, overlooking the Sound of Sleat. Readers who booked the largest bedroom, on the ground floor, liked the 'comfortable double bed, nice white bedlinen, huge Persian rug covering most of the floor, beautiful, Chinese-style porcelain table lamps', an excellent shower, though they would have preferred a bathroom to an alcove behind a moveable screen. Doors opened on to a sea-view garden where customers sat eating and drinking. Essentially a pub-with-rooms, this is a music venue, so guests should enter into the spirit of fun. There is a cosy bar with log fire, food from a blackboard menu. The 'wonderful young, creative and enthusiastic chef', Verity Hurding, makes creative use of local produce in such dishes as cullen skink; venison with berry jus; duck breast with herbed beans; hand-dived Isle of Skye scallops, samphire, lemon; beer-battered haddock, chips. Sunday roasts are served all day from 12.30. Breakfast brings cranberry and pecan muesli, cold-smoked salmon, kippers. 'Would we stay again? Most definitely yes.'

Glenelg
IV40 8JR

T: 01599 522273
E: info@glenelg-inn.com
W: www.glenelg-inn.com

BEDROOMS: 7. 2, on ground floor, suitable for disabled.
OPEN: all year, but full house bookings only Oct–early Mar.
FACILITIES: bar, restaurant, free Wi-Fi, garden, public rooms wheelchair accessible, adapted toilet.
BACKGROUND MUSIC: in public areas, regular live music events.
LOCATION: 10 miles W of Shiel Bridge over the Mam Rattigan.
CHILDREN: all ages welcomed.
DOGS: allowed in some bedrooms, public rooms (£7 per dog per night).
CREDIT CARDS: MasterCard, Visa.
PRICES: [2018] per room B&B single £85, double £110–£130. À la carte £24.

GLENFINNAN Highland

Map 5:C1

GLENFINNAN HOUSE HOTEL

Built for a veteran of Culloden and remodelled in Victorian times, Jane MacFarlane's stone mansion stands in a breathtaking situation on the shores of Loch Shiel, with views of Ben Nevis and the Glenfinnan Monument. Team Gibson – Manja and Duncan – are long-standing manager and chef. On chilly days, log fires blaze in rooms hung with paintings on a Jacobite theme. Bedrooms have no TV, and no key unless requested, which 'might not suit everyone', but adds to the house-party ambience. All rooms are supplied with cut flowers and a fruit bowl. Many have views of the loch and of the 1814 Glenfinnan Monument, perhaps a four-poster bed, a whirlpool bath. There are reduced rates for children, who will thrill to visit the Glenfinnan Viaduct of Harry Potter fame, while the hotel's classically trained wizard works his magic with Inverawe smoked salmon, Glenfinnan Estate venison, Lochaber lamb, 28-day-aged, chargrilled steaks. You can eat in the restaurant or the bar, where residents rub shoulders with locals, perhaps 'fresh, thick and flaky' fish and chips; vegetarian haggis, turnip and potato clapshot. A great place, at once 'down to earth' and 'very special'.

Glenfinnan
PH37 4LT

T: 01397 722235
E: availability@glenfinnanhouse.com
W: www.glenfinnanhouse.com

BEDROOMS: 14.
OPEN: 23 Mar–31 Oct.
FACILITIES: drawing room, bar/lounge, playroom, restaurant, wedding facilities, free Wi-Fi, 1-acre grounds (play area), unsuitable for disabled.
BACKGROUND MUSIC: Scottish in bar and restaurant.
LOCATION: 15 miles NW of Fort William.
CHILDREN: all ages welcomed.
DOGS: allowed in bedrooms and some public rooms, not in restaurant or drawing room.
CREDIT CARDS: Amex, MasterCard, Visa.
PRICES: [2018] per room B&B single £105–£225, double £125–£245. À la carte £25–£35.

GLENFINNAN Highland

Map 5:C1

THE PRINCE'S HOUSE

'Deserves its entry' is a trusted reader's verdict
on Ina and Kieron Kelly's family-run hotel
in a mountain landscape at the head of Loch
Shiel. Dating in parts from the 1600s, it was
originally a coaching inn, the Stage House,
where travellers could rest on the Road to the
Isles, long before Bonnie Prince Charlie raised
his standard on the loch shore. The cheapest,
standard rooms are 'adequate', with en suite
shower room; some other bedrooms interconnect
to accommodate a family. The most desirable,
Stuart Room, has a Jacobean four-poster and
such extras as a Whisky Mac decanter, fresh
flowers and chocolates. In a wood-panelled
dining room, hung with works by Scottish
and French painters, guests dine on Mr Kelly's
five-course menus, devised around top-notch
local produce from sea, hill, loch and field (the
kitchen cures its herring, bakes its daily bread).
Typical dishes: fillet of turbot, lobster ravioli,
white wine and sweet cicely; breast of Gartmorn
free-range duck, heritage carrot, greens, Tarry
Souchong air. There is simpler food in the Stage
House Bistro, in a 1980s extension overlooking a
nearby burn. Breakfast is 'good'. (RB)

25% DISCOUNT VOUCHERS

Glenfinnan
PH37 4LT

T: 01397 722246
E: princeshouse@glenfinnan.co.uk
W: www.glenfinnan.co.uk

BEDROOMS: 9.
OPEN: mid-Mar–end Oct, 27 Dec–2
Jan, restaurant open Easter–end
Sept.
FACILITIES: restaurant, bistro/bar,
free Wi-Fi, in-room TV (Freeview),
small front lawn, unsuitable for
disabled.
BACKGROUND MUSIC: in restaurant
and bar.
LOCATION: 17 miles NW of Fort
William, 330 yards from Glenfinnan
station.
CHILDREN: all ages welcomed.
DOGS: allowed in bar except during
food service, not in bedrooms.
CREDIT CARDS: Amex, MasterCard,
Visa.
PRICES: [2018] per room B&B single
£80–£95, double £145–£250. Set
menu (in restaurant) 5 courses £55, à
la carte (in bistro) £28.

GRANTOWN ON SPEY Highland

Map 5:C2

CULDEARN HOUSE

'The best hotel break we have ever had.'
William and Sonia Marshall's Victorian villa
received near universal praise from readers this
year. They laud the 'superb hosts'; 'the warm,
friendly' welcome as they got out of their car,
followed by tea and cake in the lounge, the
'bedrooms uniquely decorated with all the
essentials'. Those rooms mix contemporary,
antique and traditional furniture with 'restful'
pastels, florals and stripes; some overlook the
garden and woodlands. Choose carefully:
another reader found a twin room 'very small',
if 'beautifully presented'. At night, guests gather
for canapés, before Mrs Marshall's 'impeccably
presented', 'outstandingly good' locally sourced
dinner. 'I'd never tasted lamb so succulent,
and fillet steak so tender.' 'I believe everything
but the bread was made on the premises.' A
Guide regular was less impressed, however.
In 2018 he was served mushroom risotto with
mashed potato and overcooked cauliflower
and broccoli – 'straight out of the 1970s. Fine
dining it wasn't.' For a nightcap there are many
single malts; at breakfast, 'everything you could
possibly want'. 'We shall definitely be back.'
(Terri Phillips, Norma Curran, and others)

Culdearn House
Grantown-on-Spey
PH26 3JU

T: 01479 872106
E: enquiries@culdearn.com
W: www.culdearn.com

BEDROOMS: 6. 1 on ground floor.
OPEN: all year.
FACILITIES: drawing room, dining
room, free Wi-Fi in bedrooms,
in-room TV (Freeview), ¾-acre
garden, unsuitable for disabled.
BACKGROUND MUSIC: none.
LOCATION: edge of town (within
walking distance).
CHILDREN: not under 10, except by
arrangement.
DOGS: not allowed, except for guide
dogs.
CREDIT CARDS: MasterCard, Visa.
PRICES: [2018] per person B&B
double £80–£90, single occupancy
from £125, D,B&B £100–£170.
À la carte £48.

GRANTOWN-ON-SPEY Highland   Map 5:C2

THE DULAIG   NEW

'There is no finer place to stay to explore the
Highlands,' say fans of Carol and Gordon
Bulloch's 'friendly' B&B, ten minutes' walk from
town, on the edge of the Cairngorms national
park. It receives a full entry this year for 'lovely
amenities', hospitality and attention to detail.
The 'gracious' hosts 'have thought of every
possible personal touch'. The early Edwardian
stone house, designed by Alexander Marshall
Mackenzie (architect of London's Waldorf
Astoria), overlooks 'beautiful gardens', with
summer house, woodland and pond. New arrivals
are welcomed with tea and home-made scones by
the drawing room fire. Each bedrooms is named
after an Arts and Crafts designer and has freshly
baked cakes. Well-equipped bathrooms have
underfloor heating, Scottish toiletries, a choice
of a whirlpool bath, a double-ended slipper bath
with rainfall shower over, or a walk-in shower
with body jets. A breakfast that's 'worth skipping
dinner for' serves porridge with cream, whisky
and heather honey, eggs from the resident free-
range hens, a full Scottish with haggis, local
sausages, black pudding. You can ask for a packed
lunch before hitting the Speyside Malt Whisky
Trail or spending a day fishing. (Nancy Iriye)

Seafield Avenue
Grantown-on-Spey
PH26 3JF

T: 01479 872065
E: enquiries@thedulaig.com
W: www.thedulaig.com

BEDROOMS: 3.
OPEN: all year except Christmas,
New Year.
FACILITIES: drawing room, dining
room, free Wi-Fi, computer
available, in-room TV (Freesat),
1½-acre garden (pond, summer
house), veranda, parking (garage for
motorbikes and bicycles).
BACKGROUND MUSIC: quiet Scottish
music at breakfast 'with guests'
permission'.
LOCATION: 600 yards from
Grantown-on-Spey.
CHILDREN: not under 12.
DOGS: only assistance dogs allowed.
CREDIT CARDS: Amex, MasterCard,
Visa.
PRICES: [2018] per room B&B single
£135–£155, double £175–£195.

INVERKEILOR Angus

GORDON'S

A quiet hamlet, a short hit from the coast, is home to this 'tasteful', family-run restaurant-with-rooms in a 'well-maintained' Victorian terrace house. Visitors this year praise 'friendly, efficient service' from Maria Watson and her son, Garry, the award-winning chef, and his 'excellent food': 'nothing disappoints'. A wood-burning stove in the restaurant 'adds to the character'. The seasonal modern British menus are 'cooked with panache', using 'top-quality produce'. A 'comprehensive wine list' delivers perfect pairings for such dishes as North Sea turbot, chargrilled sweetcorn, crispy chicken wings, mushroom purée, burnt cabbage; pistachio crème brûlée, rhubarb compote, mascarpone sorbet; Scottish cheeses. To go with fine food, fine accommodation. Five individually styled, 'luxurious' bedrooms have bold Scottish flair (thistle-themed wallcovers, punchy tartans), a 'very comfortable bed' and a 'well-appointed bathroom'. 'Our courtyard room was beautifully clean and well furnished.' Breakfast is 'just as good as dinner', with home-baked bread, home-made baked beans. 'The scrambled eggs were the best.' Follow it up with a generous serving of fresh coastal air on the beach at Lunan Bay. (Philip Bright, BW, JG)

Main Street
Inverkeilor
DD11 5RN

T: 01241 830364
E: gordonsrest@aol.com
W: www.gordonsrestaurant.co.uk

BEDROOMS: 5. 1 on ground floor in courtyard annexe.
OPEN: all year except Jan.
FACILITIES: lounge, restaurant, free Wi-Fi in reception, in-room TV (terrestrial), small garden and patio, restaurant wheelchair accessible.
BACKGROUND MUSIC: in restaurant.
LOCATION: in hamlet, 6 miles NE of Arbroath.
CHILDREN: old enough to have own room (no family rooms).
DOGS: not allowed.
CREDIT CARDS: MasterCard, Visa.
PRICES: [2018] per room B&B £110–£165. Set dinner £65.

ISLE OF IONA Argyll and Bute

Map 5:D1

ARGYLL HOTEL

Iona Sound, frescoed with gently bobbing boats, provides a tranquil outlook for the row of crofters' cottages that form this 'amazing little hotel'. Wendy and Rob MacManaway and Katy and Dafydd Russon are its 'warm, informal hosts'. 'This is not some luxury resort – we were delighted with it.' Bedrooms, some 'cosy', might have a sloping ceiling, garden view or wood-burning stove; televisions are eschewed for utter peace and quiet. Wooden benches at the top of the lawned garden that slopes down to the shoreline provide a 'simply heavenly' spot to watch the evening sun with a glass of wine. Chef Richard Shwe makes 'creative' use of locally sourced meat and vegetables (much from the organic kitchen garden) and sustainably landed fish. His 'imaginative' menu doesn't stint vegetarians, perhaps celeriac and apple spelt risotto, mixed brassica, preserved lemon, roast dates; their omnivorous counterparts might dine on braised beef cheek, pastrami tongue, pesto, Parmesan polenta, crispy shallots. At breakfast, organic granola, garden rhubarb and ginger compote, Iona hogget sausages, Mull bacon, and organic eggs supply solid foundation for a day exploring the island's wilds. More reports, please.

25% DISCOUNT VOUCHERS

Isle of Iona
PA76 6SJ

T: 01681 700334
E: reception@argyllhoteliona.co.uk
W: www.argyllhoteliona.co.uk

BEDROOMS: 17. 7 in linked extension.
OPEN: 1 Apr–26 Oct.
FACILITIES: 3 lounges (1 with TV), conservatory, dining room, free Wi-Fi in some public areas, wedding facilities, seafront lawn with benches, organic vegetable garden, lounges/dining room wheelchair accessible, toilet not adapted.
BACKGROUND MUSIC: contemporary Scottish, 'gentle' jazz or country music 'appropriate to the time of day' in dining room.
LOCATION: village centre.
CHILDREN: all ages welcomed (under-4s free (cots), camp beds available for under-12s).
DOGS: up to 2 allowed in bedrooms, not in dining room or sun lounge.
CREDIT CARDS: MasterCard, Visa.
PRICES: [2018] B&B per room £72–£200. À la carte £35. 1-night bookings sometimes refused.

KILBERRY Argyll and Bute

Map 5:D1

KILBERRY INN

♺ **Previous César winner**

Clare Johnson and David Wilson's gloriously remote red-roofed restaurant-with-rooms continues to delight and dazzle. 'It may be my imagination,' wrote a trusted Guide reader on a return visit to the Knapdale peninsula, 'but the sun always seems to shine when we arrive at the Kilberry Inn.' Clare and David set high standards and still attained them for our tenth stay.' Each of the light, unfussy rooms – 'we particularly like the courtyard arrangement' – sports wicker chairs and an upgraded shower room, along with fresh milk and a jar of shortbread. The original cottage makes a cosy snug bar and restaurant, the venue for Clare's 'high-quality' seasonal menu. Local produce flavours dishes including Loch Melfort mussels with shallots, chorizo, thyme and sherry; Gigha halibut, tapenade toasts, blood orange and watercress. Breakfast is equally rewarding, from The Full Kilberry or kippers and smoked salmon from the Isle of Ewe, to Stornoway black pudding. With the Mediterranean garden now maturing, 'it's also very pleasant to sit at one of its many tables, and just chill out'. (GC, J and EG)

Kilberry
PA29 6YD

T: 01880 770223
E: relax@kilberryinn.com
W: www.kilberryinn.com

BEDROOMS: 5. All on ground floor.
OPEN: Tues–Sun, mid-Mar–end Oct; Fri–Sun, Nov–Dec.
FACILITIES: restaurant, snug (wood-burning stove), variable Wi-Fi (Kilberry is a Wi-Fi 'not-spot'), in-room TV (Freeview), small garden, unsuitable for disabled.
BACKGROUND MUSIC: in restaurant at lunch and dinner.
LOCATION: 16 miles NW of Tarbert, on B8024.
CHILDREN: not under 12.
DOGS: allowed by arrangement in 2 bedrooms, not in public rooms.
CREDIT CARDS: MasterCard, Visa.
PRICES: [2018] per room D,B&B £235. À la carte £37. 1-night bookings sometimes refused at weekends.

KILLIECRANKIE Perth and Kinross

Map 5:D2

KILLIECRANKIE HOTEL

♔ Previous César winner

'As excellent as ever.' Regular guests were 'delighted to report' this year that this 'wonderful' 1840s dower house at the gateway to the Highlands 'remains unchanged'. 'It's still personally run by Henrietta Fergusson', with great humour (a sign on the garden gate politely asks visitors to shut the gate to keep out rabbits, adding: 'Notice to rabbits: Keep Out'). An 'excellent team', in tartan skirts and trews, provides 'very able support'. The pleasant lounge has a warming winter fire, helped by an island-hopping whisky menu; on warm days, the 'nicely tended' rhododendron-filled garden is just the place for toothsome afternoon teas. The homely bedrooms come in all shapes and sizes (some are 'rather snug'), but they are 'clean and comfortable'. Each is 'well furnished', with antique pieces, fresh flowers, thick, tartan woollen blankets and a radio with integral phone charger. In the dining room, chef Mark Easton serves a daily-changing menu of 'truly fine food, mixing the best of tradition and expert knowledge', perhaps 'best end' of Perthshire lamb stuffed with red onion mousse; shallot and petit pois tortellini. (P and SG)

Killiecrankie
PH16 5LG

T: 01796 473220
E: enquiries@killiecrankiehotel.
co.uk
W: www.killiecrankiehotel.co.uk

BEDROOMS: 10. 2 on ground floor.
OPEN: 24 Mar–3 Jan.
FACILITIES: sitting room, bar with conservatory, dining room, breakfast conservatory, free Wi-Fi, in-room TV (Freeview), 4½-acre grounds (gardens, woodland), public areas wheelchair accessible.
BACKGROUND MUSIC: none.
LOCATION: hamlet 3 miles W of Pitlochry.
CHILDREN: all ages welcomed.
DOGS: allowed in bar and some bedrooms (not unattended), not in sitting or dining rooms.
CREDIT CARDS: Amex, MasterCard, Visa.
PRICES: [2018] per room B&B £125–£220, D,B&B £160–£340. Set dinner £45. 1-night bookings sometimes refused weekends.

KINCLAVEN Perth and Kinross

Map 5:D2

BALLATHIE HOUSE

In 1922 a young Elizabeth Bowes-Lyon (later Queen Elizabeth, the Queen Mother, as we now think of her) joined a house party at this turreted Victorian country house on the River Tay. No doubt the country sports were a great attraction, then as now, with fishing beats, clay-pigeon shoots. Run by the Milligan family, this 'lovely hotel' stands in extensive grounds roamed by deer, approached by 'a long, attractive drive'. Reception rooms are 'rather grand and comfortable', with roaring fires, antiques, gilt-framed paintings, salmon in glass cases. The main-house bedrooms are individually, traditionally styled, with period features. Further rooms, in a riverside annexe reached by a lit pathway through the garden, have a patio or a balcony – all enjoy Tay views. Yet more, cheaper rooms are found in the Sportsman's Lodge. Light lunches are served in the bar, afternoon tea in the drawing room, while in the restaurant, Scott Scorer gives a modern spin to fine local, seasonal ingredients. Maybe roast venison loin, braised lentils, savoy cabbage, glazed beetroot; roast St Bride's chicken. Breakfast brings kippers, smoked haddock, scrambled eggs; 'excellent ingredients, cooked with care'.

Kinclaven
PH1 4QN

T: 01250 883268
E: email@ballathiehousehotel.com
W: www.ballathiehousehotel.com

BEDROOMS: 50. 16 in riverside building, 12 in Sportsman's Lodge, some on ground floor, 1 suitable for disabled.
OPEN: all year.
FACILITIES: drawing room, bar, restaurant, private dining rooms, free Wi-Fi, in-room TV (Freeview), wedding/function facilities, 900-acre estate (golf, fishing, shooting), public rooms wheelchair accessible, adapted toilet.
BACKGROUND MUSIC: none.
LOCATION: 1½ miles SW of Kinclaven.
CHILDREN: all ages welcomed.
DOGS: allowed in some bedrooms (not unattended), not in public rooms.
CREDIT CARDS: MasterCard, Visa.
PRICES: [2018] per person B&B £82–£127, D,B&B £122–£168. Set dinner £55.

KINGUSSIE Highland

Map 5:C2

THE CROSS AT KINGUSSIE

♀ Previous César winner

'Derek and Celia are just fabulous,' praised
visitors this year. 'Friendly, efficient – and
they've done a magnificent job in maintaining
and enhancing this former tweed mill. We
wish we'd stayed longer.' The Kitchingmans
and their 'enchanting' restaurant-with-rooms
on the River Gynack keep gaining fans. The
'extraordinary food' is well liked too. Chef
David Skiggs presents 'beautiful, high-quality
cooking', using seasonal Scottish produce. A
typical dish: roast halibut, Parmesan gnocchi,
cauliflower, wild mushrooms, samphire, fish
velouté. In the bedrooms, stone walls and rustic
colours lend a soothing feel. 'Our room was
spacious and comfortable, and had plenty of
hot water in the modern bathroom, and good
Wi-Fi. With the windows open, we could hear
the stream gurgling past during the night.' The
'very nice lounge' has lots to entertain, from
a log fire that invites curling up with a good
book, to stacks of board games. Guests can also
play 'spot the red squirrel' – they run along the
woodland edge. Arriving on the sleeper train? A
hearty breakfast awaits, with 'a good choice' of
cooked dishes. (MB, GC, and others)

Tweed Mill Brae
Kingussie
PH21 1LB

T: 01540 661166
E: relax@thecross.co.uk
W: www.thecross.co.uk

BEDROOMS: 8.
OPEN: closed Christmas and Jan,
except Hogmanay.
FACILITIES: 2 lounges (wood-
burning stove), restaurant, free
Wi-Fi, in-room TV (Freeview),
4-acre grounds (terraced garden,
woodland), only restaurant suitable
for disabled.
BACKGROUND MUSIC: none.
LOCATION: 440 yds from village
centre.
CHILDREN: all ages welcomed.
DOGS: not allowed.
CREDIT CARDS: Amex, MasterCard,
Visa.
PRICES: [2018] per room B&B
£100–£200, D,B&B £200–£280.
Set 3-course dinner £55, 6-course
tasting menu £65. À la carte £55.

KIRKBEAN Dumfries and Galloway

Map 5:E2

CAVENS

Merchant Richard Oswald, Cavens's original owner, helped negotiate the 1783 Treaty of Paris – now this 'charmingly run' Georgian manor house attracts modern-day visitors in search of serenity. Angus Fordyce, the 'hospitable, hands-on host', crafts a cosseting, 'restful' atmosphere, helped by 'friendly, smiling staff'. They will pour a tall G&T, allowing you to relax and take in the surroundings. Buffered by acres of landscaped grounds, the 'lovely' antiques, log fires, oriental rugs and oil paintings in public spaces ooze country house character, while squashy sofas and books lend the lounge a genteel intimacy. All of the 'immaculate, comfortable' bedrooms have views of the garden yews and giant rhododendrons, but the best panorama is found in Oswald with its 'wall of windows' (and poem by Rabbie Burns, a previous visitor). Solway has 'a bath for giants'. Resident guests choose any three courses from Angus Fordyce's fuss-free, short market menu, perhaps locally smoked salmon; pan-fried hand-dived scallops, lime, vermouth; strawberry trifle with amaretti biscuits. Wine lovers: a tour of the small private cellar is there for the asking. Breakfast ('particularly good') is fuel for coastal walks, nearby. (BK)

25% DISCOUNT VOUCHERS

Kirkbean
DG2 8AA

T: 01387 880234
E: enquiries@cavens.com
W: www.cavens.com

BEDROOMS: 6. 1 on ground floor.
OPEN: Mar–Nov, exclusive use by groups at New Year.
FACILITIES: 2 sitting rooms, dining room, wine cellar, meeting facilities, free Wi-Fi, in-room TV (Freeview), 10-acre grounds, unsuitable for disabled.
BACKGROUND MUSIC: light classical all day in 1 sitting room, dining room.
LOCATION: in village.
CHILDREN: all ages welcomed.
DOGS: allowed by arrangement, not in public rooms or unattended in bedrooms.
CREDIT CARDS: MasterCard, Visa.
PRICES: [2018] per room D,B&B £200–£300. 1-night bookings refused Easter, bank holidays.

KIRKCUDBRIGHT Dumfries and Galloway   Map 5:E2

GLENHOLME COUNTRY HOUSE

'A wonderful gem of a place,' report delighted readers in 2018 after visiting this Victorian guest house surrounded by 'beautiful gardens'. Owned by artist Jennifer Bristow-Smith and husband, Laurence, a writer and former diplomat, it has an 'idiosyncratic, tasteful' style that includes a wood-panelled hall alive with straw hats, vintage children's books and tall urns of dried flowers. In the book-lined library, comfy chairs, an open fire and old photographs from the time of the Raj, along with objets de curiosité from around the world, reflect the hosts' former globetrotting lives. Each bedroom has a political namesake. Nicolson has a large colonial four-poster bed, an antique Durham quilt; Lansdowne, hand-painted vintage bedheads, a chandelier. All have fluffy towels, luxury toiletries and views. The kitchen garden, alongside spells in Morocco, Asia and Italy, provides inspiration for Laurence Bristow-Smith's 'superb dinners', perhaps filo-wrapped salmon, asparagus, Polish-style mushrooms, followed by chocolate fondant and raspberries. Ask for 'a bit of everything' at breakfast. 'We would recommend anyone to come here – and Kircudbright has a lot more to see than you might think.' (Anne Davies)

Tongland Road
Kirkcudbright
DG6 4UU

T: 01557 339422
E: info@glenholmecountryhouse. com
W: www.glenholmecountryhouse. com

BEDROOMS: 4.
OPEN: all year except Christmas, New Year.
FACILITIES: library, dining room, free Wi-Fi, 2-acre garden (formal gardens, vegetable plot, orchard), unsuitable for disabled.
BACKGROUND MUSIC: none.
LOCATION: 1 mile N of town, an easy walk along the river.
CHILDREN: not under 12.
DOGS: not allowed.
CREDIT CARDS: MasterCard, Visa.
PRICES: [2018] per room B&B single £100–£110, double £120–£135, D,B&B double £200–£215. 3-course menu £40, à la carte £40. 1-night bookings must be fore D,B&B.

KYLESKU Highland

Map 5:B2

KYLESKU HOTEL

Previous César winner

Grey seals loll the day away along an old ferry slipway on the shores of 'wild, beautiful' Loch Glendhu – the 'superb setting' for 'hands-on, energetic' Tanja Lister and Sonia Virechauveix's 'most enjoyable' small hotel. Run with 'informal warmth', the converted former 17th-century coaching inn, recently described as 'wonderful' by Jeremy Clarkson, no less, has a fresh contemporary feel, with wood burners, bleached woods and muted tones that reflect the ever-changing landscape. 'Most of the time there is complete silence.' Smart, individually decorated bedrooms, some compact, are in the main building and a loch-facing extension. The best are in the latter, where spectacular views come with crisp linens, a large bed and smart bathroom with 'a full cohort of good toiletries'. Landed-at-the-door seafood is a speciality, but vegetarians are equally well served in the 'casual, gastropubby restaurant'. Typical dishes: haggis bonbons, red onion marmalade; seared hand-dived scallops, cassoulet, cauliflower purée; a vegetarian burger. A seat by the window ('a rare score') reveals 'a special atmosphere whatever time of day'.
(J and DA, and others)

Kylesku
IV27 4HW

T: 01971 502231
E: info@kyleskuhotel.co.uk
W: www.kyleskuhotel.co.uk

BEDROOMS: 11. 4 in annexe, 1 suitable for disabled.
OPEN: mid-Feb–end Nov.
FACILITIES: lounge, bar, restaurant, free Wi-Fi in bar and lounge, in-room TV (Freeview), small garden (tables for outside eating), area of lounge and dining room wheelchair accessible, toilet not adapted.
BACKGROUND MUSIC: in afternoon and evening, in bar and half the dining area.
LOCATION: 10 miles S of Scourie.
CHILDREN: all ages welcomed.
DOGS: allowed (£10 a night), but not unattended in bedrooms.
CREDIT CARDS: MasterCard, Visa.
PRICES: [2018] per room B&B single £75–£110, double £115–£180. À la carte £45.

LOCHEPORT Western Isles

LANGASS LODGE

Amid the 'drowned landscape' of North Uist, with its tidal strands, lochans and peat bogs, this former shooting lodge overlooking Loch Langass is run as a hotel by Amanda and Niall Leveson Gower. 'It's a lovely location surrounded by wildlife,' say regular readers in 2018. Bedrooms are in the main house and 'a modern extension set into the hillside', reached by a covered walkway. 'Comfortable' and 'stylishly furnished', they are more traditional than chic. An annexe room had 'wooden floors and rugs, French doors on to a little terrace with a lovely outlook'. The inviting bar, with a log-burner, antlers and a fireplace covered in shells, adjoins a conservatory/lounge, 'the nicest room, with big sofas and tables'. Guests can eat here or in the 'bright, airy' dining room, perhaps a seafood platter, Lochmaddy Bay lobster or North Uist venison burger. The staff are 'efficient and helpful'. 'However, some guests in 2018 report 'slow service, inadequate cutlery' and difficulty getting dinner reservations at the time they wanted. Outside the lodge, the island is 'a paradise for wildlife, especially birds'. (PB, and others)

Locheport
HS6 5HA

T: 01876 580285
E: langasslodge@btconnect.com
W: www.langasslodge.co.uk

BEDROOMS: 11. Some in extension, 1 suitable for disabled.
OPEN: Apr–end Oct.
FACILITIES: conservatory, bar, restaurant, free Wi-Fi, in-room TV (Freeview), 11-acre garden in 200-acre grounds, bar and restaurant wheelchair accessible, adapted toilet.
BACKGROUND MUSIC: in public rooms.
LOCATION: 7½ miles SW of Lochmaddy.
CHILDREN: all ages welcomed (2 family rooms, extra beds, children's menu).
DOGS: allowed in bedrooms and public rooms, not in restaurant.
CREDIT CARDS: Amex, MasterCard, Visa.
PRICES: [2018] per room B&B single £80–£115, double £95–£160, family room £120–£175. À la carte £38, bar meals £12.

LOCHINVER Highland

Map 5:B1

THE ALBANNACH

In a wild coastal corner of the Highlands, this white-painted Victorian house gazes out across moorland, croft and sea. Visitors who brave the spindly access road earn broad views and afternoon tea in the cosy conservatory. Bedrooms and suites have a traditional Highland air. 'Our spacious suite, Byre, was comfortable and well furnished; the private terrace with hot tub was a bonus, as was the fresh milk on the hospitality tray (always appreciated).' Once the most northerly Michelin-starred restaurant, it served its last supper in November 2017. Now, come evening, Lesley Crosfield and Colin Craig's acclaimed modern Scottish cooking is served half a mile away in Lochinver in the more informal sister pub, The Caberfeidh. Happily, they are still responsible for the Albannach's breakfast. Served on tableware from a local pottery, 'every element of the cooked breakfast was perfection and full of flavour'. Alongside Greek yogurt, organic honey and muesli, there are free-range croft eggs, wild mushrooms, Lochinver salmon, dry-cured haggis; perfect fuel for exploring nearby mountains and white beaches, or just pottering down to the village. (John and Gillian Charnley, and others)

Baddidarroch
Lochinver
IV27 4LP

T: 01571 844407
E: info@thealbannach.co.uk
W: www.thealbannach.co.uk

BEDROOMS: 5. 1 suite in cottage, 1 suitable for disabled.
OPEN: all year except 18 Nov–20 Dec, 2 Jan–14 Feb, then limited till Easter, closed every Mon year round.
FACILITIES: snug, conservatory, dining room, free Wi-Fi, in-room TV (Freeview), ¾-acre garden in 4 acres of grounds, breakfast room wheelchair accessible.
BACKGROUND MUSIC: none.
LOCATION: ½ mile from village.
CHILDREN: not under 6 (if sharing with parents).
DOGS: not allowed.
CREDIT CARDS: Diners, MasterCard, Visa.
PRICES: [2018] per room B&B (Tues–Sun) £155–£175. 1-night bookings generally refused Sat.

MELROSE Scottish Borders   Map 5:E3

THE TOWNHOUSE

Readers have high praise for the Henderson
family's small hotel, 'right at the centre' of
this Borders town – and right opposite its
sister, or mother, venture, Burts (see Shortlist).
One devotee, who stayed five nights, had
'a beautifully decorated, spotless' bedroom;
another 'a beautiful, large room' and 'utterly
luxurious bathroom'. All rooms are smart and
contemporary. 'If thou wouldst view fair Melrose
aright, Go visit it by the pale moonlight,' advised
Sir Walter Scott, whose house, Abbotsford,
aka 'Conundrum Castle', is five minutes' drive
away. He meant the beautiful Melrose Abbey
ruins as painted by JMW Turner, not Melrose
town, but guests arriving here by moonlight can
dine in the brasserie or more formal restaurant.
The one menu ranges from home-made burger,
Monterey Jack cheese, smoked Virginia bacon,
to such dishes as whole baked plaice with crab
and chive gnocchi, sautéed samphire, confit
cherry tomatoes, crab bisque sauce; 'the most
tender venison'. There are steaks, too, from the
chargrill, and in summer alfresco dining on the
terrace. The staff are 'extremely pleasant and
helpful'. Breakfast brings porridge, kippers, a full
Scottish. (AW, and others)

Market Square
Melrose
TD6 9PQ

T: 01896 822645
E: enquiries@thetownhouse
melrose.co.uk
W: www.thetownhousemelrose.
co.uk

BEDROOMS: 11. 1 on ground floor.
OPEN: all year except Christmas Day,
Boxing Day.
FACILITIES: bar/brasserie, restaurant,
free Wi-Fi, in-room TV (Freeview),
civil wedding licence, decked patio,
parking.
BACKGROUND MUSIC: in brasserie and
restaurant.
LOCATION: town centre.
CHILDREN: all ages welcomed.
DOGS: not allowed.
CREDIT CARDS: Amex, MasterCard,
Visa.
PRICES: [2018] per room B&B single
from £97, double £134–£151, D,B&B
(2-night min. stay) single from £120,
double £186– £202. À la carte £38.

SEE ALSO SHORTLIST

MUIR OF ORD Highland

Map 5:C2

THE DOWER HOUSE

'What a gem!' Robyn and Mena Aitchison, the 'charming' owners, run this 'extremely pleasant small B&B' with 'wonderful hospitality'. Guests are following in esteemed footsteps. The former thatched farmhouse – converted into a romantic cottage for the lady dowager of the Mackenzies of Highfield House – was used as a shooting lodge by Prime Minister Gladstone in the late 19th century. Nowadays it's more peaceful, the 'lovely garden' filled with wild flowers, snowdrops, cherry blossom, native bluebells and rhododendrons, depending on the season. The bedrooms bring the outside indoors, with fresh flowers and garden views, as well as a 'huge' Victorian roll-top bath or a shower. The interior hosts antiques, oriental vases, Persian rugs, groaning bookshelves. Some call it 'a treasure chest', others 'very cluttered, but with mostly interesting objects'. The lounge has a wood-burning stove, board games, while in the dining room, where a baby grand piano sits by the open fire, 'first-rate' breakfasts are served, including eggs from the house's free-range hens. In sum, 'a truly memorable stay' in a spot well positioned for the North Coast 500, top-notch golf, salmon fishing and the Whisky Trail.

Highfield
Muir of Ord
IV6 7XN

T: 01463 870090
E: info@thedowerhouse.co.uk
W: www.thedowerhouse.co.uk

BEDROOMS: 3. All on ground floor, plus small self-contained 2-bed flat.
OPEN: Apr–Oct.
FACILITIES: lounge, dining room, snug/TV room, free Wi-Fi, in-room TV (Freeview), wedding facilities, 5-acre grounds, unsuitable for disabled,
BACKGROUND MUSIC: none.
LOCATION: 14 miles NW of Inverness.
CHILDREN: all ages welcomed.
DOGS: allowed in bedrooms (not on bed or furniture), not in public rooms.
CREDIT CARDS: MasterCard, Visa.
PRICES: [2018] per room B&B single £120–£135, double £145–£165,

MUTHILL Perth and Kinross   Map 5:D2

BARLEY BREE

'It was all excellent.' High praise from visitors
in 2018 for 'attentive but informal' Alison and
Fabrice Bouteloup's red-stone former coaching
inn-cum-restaurant-with-rooms. 'We arrived in
the depths of a grey Scottish winter to a warm,
comfy room and warm, friendly welcome; the
bar and restaurant made cosy with real fires.
The service was superb.' In the 'attractive'
dining room, with its stone, mellow wood
and mantelpiece antlers, everything is soigné.
The Gallic chef/patron's daily-changing menu
'was excellent in taste and presentation'. Local
flavours are given a French twist, perhaps saddle
of Perthshire venison, crispy baby kale, pancetta,
chestnut; a vegetarian lemon and garlic courgette
salad, portobello mushroom, squash purée.
Perfect pairing is made possible with the ready
aid of Alison Bouteloup, a certified Master of
Wine. Bright and modern, the 'spotlessly clean
and inviting' bedrooms are steps away. The
largest overlooks the 11th-century church tower.
All have tea-/coffee-making facilities, a Barley
Bree own-label whisky miniature. At breakfast,
enjoy home-made jam and marmalade on Mr
Bouteloup's acclaimed bread; the cooked dishes
are 'delicious'. (Richard Lumby)

6 Willoughby Street
Muthill
PH5 2AB

T: 01764 681451
E: info@barleybree.com
W: www.barleybree.com

BEDROOMS: 6.
OPEN: all year except 24–26 Dec,
1 week July, restaurant closed Mon,
Tues.
FACILITIES: lounge bar, restaurant,
free Wi-Fi, in-room TV (Freeview),
small terrace and lawn, drying
facilities, restaurant wheelchair
accessible, toilet not adapted.
BACKGROUND MUSIC: in lounge bar
and restaurant.
LOCATION: village centre.
CHILDREN: all ages welcomed.
DOGS: assistance dogs only.
CREDIT CARDS: MasterCard, Visa.
PRICES: [2018] per room B&B
£99–£160. À la carte £43.

OBAN Argyll and Bute

THE MANOR HOUSE

A stone villa built in 1780 for the Duke of Argyll, Leslie and Margaret Crane's small, friendly hotel looks out over Oban Bay to Lismore, the Morvern hills and Mull. Home in the mid-19th century to an evangelising admiral named Otter, it offers deep-water mooring for those arriving by boat. It's 'very handy' for the ferry terminal with regular sailings to the Isles, say readers in 2018, yet 'completely quiet', with 'friendly staff'. Individually styled, 'well-appointed' bedrooms have 'wonderful views', especially those overlooking the harbour (binoculars supplied), some have richly patterned wallpaper, all have Molton Brown toiletries. In the public rooms the decor is 'cosy Scottish', the walls hung with paintings in gilt frames. In the dining room, chef Gerard McCluskey places emphasis on provenance, with local meat, freshly landed fish, organic fruit and vegetables. Typical dishes include West Coast seafood grill, crushed herb potato, tender stem broccoli, fennel; roast saddle of lamb, heritage carrot terrine, spinach and pea mould. Breakfast brings Stornoway black pudding, oak-smoked salmon, kippers from Inverawe Smokehouse. An ideal base for hill walking and exploring the Hebrides. (Christine and Philip Bright)

Gallanach Road
Oban
PA34 4LS

T: 01631 562087
E: info@manorhouseoban.com
W: www.manorhouseoban.com

BEDROOMS: 11. 1 on ground floor.
OPEN: all year except 24–26 Dec.
FACILITIES: lounge, bar, restaurant, free Wi-Fi, in-room TV (Freeview), civil wedding licence, 1½-acre grounds, private car park, access to nearby gym and golf, public areas wheelchair accessible.
BACKGROUND MUSIC: traditional in bar and restaurant.
LOCATION: ½ mile from centre.
CHILDREN: not under 12.
DOGS: allowed in bedroom by arrangement, not unattended, not in public rooms.
CREDIT CARDS: all major cards.
PRICES: [2018] per room B&B £140–£270, D,B&B £225–£360. Set dinner £49, all dishes available à la carte.

SEE ALSO SHORTLIST

PEAT INN Fife

THE PEAT INN

An 18th-century former coaching inn, which gave its name to the village that evolved around it, is run today as a restaurant-with-rooms by chef/proprietor Geoffrey Smeddle and his wife, Katherine. The accommodation is in suites. One is on a single level; seven have steps down to bedroom and bathroom, and up to 'a large lounge area with a settee, table, chairs… all in a nice modern setting with carefully chosen wallpaper'. Here, guests take 'an undoubtedly good continental breakfast'. There is no breakfast room, no full Scottish – but, then, it's not about breakfast. People come to experience Mr Smeddle's modern take on classical cooking, to dine at a leisurely pace, on such dishes as tagine of wood pigeon, couscous, sweetheart cabbage, spiced dried fruits and almonds; seared stone bass, cauliflower cheese, poached lettuce, pink grapefruit and Champagne butter sauce. 'The welcome is warm', with sherry in the room on arrival. The garden is well tended. In the 1980s, under previous owners, the Peat Inn became the first restaurant in Scotland to gain Michelin stardom. It has gone from strength to strength: a gourmet base for visits to the Renaissance splendour of Falkland Palace. (AB, and others)

Peat Inn
KY15 5LH

T: 01334 840206
E: stay@thepeatinn.co.uk
W: www.thepeatinn.co.uk

BEDROOMS: 8. All suites, on ground floor in annexe, 7 split-level, 1 suitable for disabled.
OPEN: all year except 1 week Christmas, 1 week Jan, open from 27 Dec for Hogmanay, restaurant closed Sun/Mon.
FACILITIES: lounge (log fire) in restaurant, free Wi-Fi, in-room TV (terrestrial), ½-acre garden.
BACKGROUND MUSIC: in restaurant.
LOCATION: 6 miles SW of St Andrews.
CHILDREN: all ages welcomed.
DOGS: not allowed.
CREDIT CARDS: Amex, MasterCard, Visa.
PRICES: [2018] per room B&B from £225, D,B&B from £280. Set dinner £55, à la carte £58.

PITLOCHRY Perth and Kinross

Map 5:D2

CRAIGATIN HOUSE AND COURTYARD

Built in the early 1800s, this handsome B&B, a former surgeon's house, stands at the gateway to the Highlands. Andrea and Martin Anderson, its 'warmly welcoming', hands-on owners, are 'very knowledgeable' about nearby dining, with 'great advice' on interesting local sights. Uncluttered rooms, two of them refurbished in 2018, are scattered across the main house and converted stables, each dressed with contemporary pops of colour and equipped with a generous hospitality tray, fluffy towels, quality toiletries, an umbrella for rainy days. Some rooms have a sloping ceiling, a skylight, mountain views; some are nearer the road than others ('although we weren't disturbed by traffic noise'). 'Our comfortable spotlessly clean courtyard suite had a light, bright separate sitting area.' Mornings are greeted in the 'delightful' cedar-and-glass extension with a cosy central wood-burner and views over 'beautifully kept' gardens. It hosts a 'divine' breakfast: Arnold Bennett omelette, pick-your-own-adventure porridge (summer berry compote, made from fruits from the garden; whisky, cream and sugar; Perthshire honey); apple pancakes with grilled bacon. 'Simply superb.' More reports, please.

165 Atholl Road
Pitlochry
PH16 5QL

T: 01796 472478
E: enquiries@craigatinhouse.co.uk
W: www.craigatinhouse.co.uk

BEDROOMS: 14. 7 in courtyard, 2 on ground floor, 1 suitable for disabled.
OPEN: Mar–Dec, closed Christmas, open New Year.
FACILITIES: lounge, 2 breakfast rooms, free Wi-Fi, in-room TV (Freeview), 2-acre garden, lounge/breakfast room wheelchair accessible.
BACKGROUND MUSIC: at breakfast.
LOCATION: central.
CHILDREN: not under 13.
DOGS: not allowed.
CREDIT CARDS: MasterCard, Visa.
PRICES: [2018] per room B&B single £97–£124, double £107–£134. 1-night bookings sometimes refused Sat.

SEE ALSO SHORTLIST

PITLOCHRY Perth and Kinross

Map 5:D2

DALSHIAN HOUSE

Martin and Heather Walls's white-painted Georgian guest house feels 'blissfully remote' – robins and red squirrels in the 'peaceful' surrounding woodland are your only neighbours – but it is within easy distance of bustling Pitlochry. The Wallses are liked for their 'friendly welcome' with visitors invited into the 'comfortable', muzak-free lounge to share their day, or to curl up with a book before the log fire, sip a nip of Edradour whisky and enjoy nibbles from the sideboard. Individually decorated bedrooms mix traditional and modern – 'our family room had everything we needed': self-controlled heating, shortbread on the hospitality tray. Breakfast provides 'a great start to the day' with local honey, fruit (spiced apples, vanilla-scented pears), tattie scones, Dunkeld smoked salmon, French toast with maple syrup ('perhaps with bacon'). Special diets are catered for with a bit of notice. The hosts have ready advice on activities and dining, in town and beyond, and can also provide a packed lunch. Loch shore walks are within driving distance; historic Scone Place and Castle Menzies nearby. Closer to home, the gardens are a boon for birdwatchers. (SM)

25% DISCOUNT VOUCHERS

Old Perth Road
Pitlochry
PH16 5TD

T: 01796 472173
E: dalshian@btconnect.com
W: www.dalshian.co.uk

BEDROOMS: 7.
OPEN: all year except Christmas.
FACILITIES: lounge, dining room, free Wi-Fi, in-room TV (Freeview), 1-acre garden, unsuitable for disabled.
BACKGROUND MUSIC: none.
LOCATION: 1 mile S of centre.
CHILDREN: all ages welcomed.
DOGS: allowed by arrangement, not in public rooms.
CREDIT CARDS: MasterCard, Visa.
PRICES: [2018] per person B&B £37–£45. 1-night bookings refused at New Year.

SEE ALSO SHORTLIST

PITLOCHRY Perth and Kinross

Map 5:D2

THE GREEN PARK

♀ Previous César winner

'From the moment you pull up at this beautiful hotel, you are treated like royalty,' writes a reader on a return visit to this Victorian country house on the shores of Loch Faskally. Two generations of the McMenemie family own and run the place in a spirit of warm hospitality. 'The staff were so helpful,' reports a Guide regular in 2018. 'Nothing was too much trouble – especially when someone was taken ill. Another guest tells us, 'There are so many lovely touches… Tea, coffee and cakes all day, and as much sherry as one likes before dinner.' Public rooms are filled with books, paintings and ornaments. Bedrooms, in the main house and in separate wings, vary in shape, size and style. Each has a fridge. A balcony room with views of the wooded far shore is a prime choice.' Chris Tamblin's 'excellent' modern Scottish with a French accent dishes include roast pork fillet, thyme mousse, chorizo and bean cassoulet. 'The wine list is just amazing' ,with bottles from £14. Breakfast brings 'lots of choice' from buffet and kitchen. In gardens dotted with ironwork sculptures, lawns run down to a waterside terrace. 'We thoroughly recommend it.' (Patrick Gilliat, Jean Taylor)

25% DISCOUNT VOUCHERS

Clunie Bridge Road
Pitlochry
PH16 5JY

T: 01796 473248
E: bookings@thegreenpark.co.uk
W: www.thegreenpark.co.uk

BEDROOMS: 51. 16 on ground floor, 1 suitable for disabled.
OPEN: all year except Christmas.
FACILITIES: 2 lifts, lounge bar, main lounge, sun lounge, free Wi-Fi, in-room TV (BT, Freeview), 3-acre garden, public areas wheelchair accessible.
BACKGROUND MUSIC: none.
LOCATION: ½ mile N of town centre.
CHILDREN: all ages welcomed.
DOGS: allowed in bedrooms, not in public rooms.
CREDIT CARDS: MasterCard, Visa.
PRICES: [2018] per person B&B £85–£95, D,B&B £97–£120. Set dinner £30. No supplement for singles.

SEE ALSO SHORTLIST

PITLOCHRY Perth and Kinross

Map 5:D2

♔KNOCKENDARROCH HOTEL

César award: Scottish hotel of the year
'How refreshing to find a hotel that continues to strive to be the best, and succeed.' Guide readers returned to Struan and Louise Lothian's 'small but pleasing hotel' this year with friends, to find 'the greeting friendly, the room lovely and warm'. Other guests in 2018 praise the 'attentive, good-humoured services. Our stay was a joy.' Downstairs, the lounges mix warming fires, books, wide armchairs and a cabinet full of whiskies. Upstairs, the 'fresh, tasteful' bedrooms continue to be upgraded. All have a modern country-house style, with bright Harris tweeds, but no two are the same. Attic bedrooms have a little balcony, and binoculars to take in the views; colourful suites have a separate sitting area. Rooms at the front have far-reaching views. Graeme Stewart's daily-changing menu might have Scrabster hake, saffron confit potatoes; home-made gnocchi, chargrilled Mediterranean vegetables. 'Our dinners were superb, and so was the wine list; the service was slick and very professional.' Breakfast, including black pudding and haggis, was 'first rate'.
(Ian McKenzie Leighton, Geoff and Cheryl Float, and others)

Higher Oakfield
Pitlochry
PH16 5HT

T: 01796 473473
E: bookings@knockendarroch.co.uk
W: www.knockendarroch.co.uk

BEDROOMS: 14. 2 on ground floor.
OPEN: Feb–20 Dec.
FACILITIES: 2 lounges, restaurant, free Wi-Fi, in-room TV (Freeview), 2-acre wooded garden, bicycle storage, unsuitable for disabled.
BACKGROUND MUSIC: in restaurant in evening.
LOCATION: central.
CHILDREN: not under 10.
DOGS: not allowed.
CREDIT CARDS: Amex, MasterCard, Visa.
PRICES: [2018] per room B&B £150–£295, D,B&B £195–£345. Set dinner £46. 1-night bookings sometimes refused on Sat.

SEE ALSO SHORTLIST

POOLEWE Highland

Map 5:B1

POOL HOUSE

On the shores of Loch Ewe stands a 'deceptively large' 18th-century fishing lodge run as a 'pleasingly eclectic guest house' by the 'very welcoming' Harrison family. An inspector was beguiled. 'The hosts took pains to ensure that every guest's needs were met.' After an informal check-in next to a suit of armour guarding the Jacobean entrance hall, 'we were given a fascinating tour of the house, followed by a delicious spread of leaf tea and cake in the drawing room hung with family photographs nearly a century old'. Individually decorated, suites have 'reaching loch views'. 'We slept soundly on our enormous bed; the Edwardian bathroom was beautiful to behold (though the fittings took a bit of getting used to), with gushing hot water; a peat fire kept our sitting room toasty as we used the hotel's binoculars to chase otters and gaze in envy at Inverewe Garden across the water.' Dinner is an event. Served in the formal dining room, it takes each diner's preferences into account, perhaps 'crisp, flavourful' arancini; 'tasty' chicken breast with Parma ham. Breakfast begins with 'excellent coffee'; 'a delicious full Scottish'.

by Inverewe Garden
Poolewe
IV22 2LD

T: 01445 781272
E: stay@pool-house.co.uk
W: www.pool-house.co.uk

BEDROOMS: 3 suites.
OPEN: Easter–31 Oct, closed Mon except bank holidays, dining room closed Sun (soup and sandwiches available).
FACILITIES: reception room, drawing room/library, dining room, private dining room, billiard/whisky room, free Wi-Fi in public areas, in-room TV (Freeview), ½-acre garden, unsuitable for disabled.
BACKGROUND MUSIC: none.
LOCATION: in village 6 miles NE of Gairloch.
CHILDREN: not under 14.
DOGS: not allowed.
CREDIT CARDS: Amex, MasterCard, Visa.
PRICES: [2018] per room B&B £225–£325. Set menu £48. 1-night bookings refused at weekends.

PORT APPIN Argyll and Bute

THE AIRDS HOTEL

'Highly, highly recommended. We shall return.'
Much praise from a reader for this 'wonderful
little boutique hotel' with 'delightful' views
across Loch Linnhe and the Morvern mountains.
Shaun and Jenny McKivragan are 'engaging'
owners, who run an 'efficient, friendly' place,
with 'great service', including a complementary
prosecco on arrival. The converted ferry inn
has 'sophisticated' but down-to-earth decor:
original artwork, deep sofas, 'a welcoming
coal fire', alongside fresh flowers, shelves of
books, wellies by the door. Chef Chris Stanley's
'top-notch' seasonal menu harvests the West
Coast's bounty for 'among the tastiest food we
have ever consumed': roast rabbit loin, hazelnut
gnocchi, quince; Loch Melfort sea trout, oyster,
sea vegetables, razor clam, hand-rolled linguine.
Readers who noted some of the otherwise 'clean,
comfortable' bedrooms looked a tad 'tired' will
appreciate the hotel's continuous refurbishment.
As well as a good book and a little something
from the whisky bar, there are 'great walks
from right outside the hotel' and bike hire for
two-wheeled exploration. Be warned – the Isle of
Lismore, a short ferry ride away, is 'not as flat as
it might appear'. (Fiona McKirdy, SS, and others)

Port Appin
PA38 4DF

T: 01631 730236
E: airds@airds-hotel.com
W: www.airds-hotel.com

BEDROOMS: 11. 2 on ground floor,
plus 2 self-catering cottages.
OPEN: all year, restaurant closed
Mon/Tues Nov–end Jan (open
Christmas and New Year).
FACILITIES: 2 lounges, conservatory,
whisky bar, restaurant, wedding
facilities, free Wi-Fi, in-room TV
(Freeview), spa treatments, ½-acre
garden (croquet, putting), mountain
bike hire, unsuitable for disabled.
BACKGROUND MUSIC: none.
LOCATION: 20 miles N of Oban.
CHILDREN: all ages welcomed, no
under-8s in dining room in evening
(children's high tea).
DOGS: allowed in bedrooms (not
unattended), not in public rooms
except conservatory.
CREDIT CARDS: MasterCard, Visa.
PRICES: [2018] per room D,B&B
single £225–£495, double £295–£525.

PORT APPIN Argyll and Bute

THE PIERHOUSE

'Log fires were burning in the bar and residents' lounge when we arrived on a miserable day,' write readers this year, of a visit to Nick and Nikki Horne's 'very efficiently run' hotel on the Loch Linnhe shoreline. 'The atmosphere is relaxed,' report Guide regulars in 2018, 'yet the service is attentive and professional. The owner was much in evidence and very approachable.' The 'spacious' bedrooms, contemporary in style, are supplied with a luxury mattress, shortbread, Scottish toiletries. 'In the light and airy restaurant, with a fabulous view towards Lismore and other islands', chef Sergejs Savickis 'has maintained the high standards the hotel is known for. His seafood dishes are impeccable; subtle and intense flavours beautifully balanced. We particularly liked a starter of West Coast scallops and a main of pan-seared rainbow trout.' Breakfast brings freshly baked croissants, Inverawe smoked salmon, home-made jams. 'We will return.' (GC, Andy and Sylvia Aitken)

Port Appin
PA38 4DE

T: 01631 730302
E: reservations@pierhousehotel.co.uk
W: www.pierhousehotel.co.uk

BEDROOMS: 12.
OPEN: all year except 24–26 Dec.
FACILITIES: residents' snug, lounge, bar, restaurant, private dining room, free Wi-Fi, in-room TV (Freeview), wedding facilities, sauna (treatments available), terrace, yacht moorings, unsuitable for disabled.
BACKGROUND MUSIC: in bar and restaurant.
LOCATION: in village, 20 miles N of Oban.
CHILDREN: all ages welcomed (cots, high chairs provided).
DOGS: 'well-behaved, and house-trained dogs' allowed in 3 bedrooms (not unattended), not in public rooms (£15 per night).
CREDIT CARDS: Amex, MasterCard, Visa.
PRICES: [2018] per room B&B £100–£325 (single occupancy of cliff-facing room, Sun–Thurs, Nov–Mar only, £85). À la carte £35–£40.

PORTPATRICK Dumfries and Galloway   Map 5:E1

KNOCKINAAM LODGE

In the lea of the cliffs, overlooking a private beach on the rugged Galloway coast, Sian and David Ibbotson's Victorian hunting lodge offers a great sense of escape. It is easy to imagine Churchill and Eisenhower bunkered here in 1944, just days before the D-Day landings. In the snug panelled bar, stocked with 120 single malts, you can practically catch a whiff of Havana and imagine Winston puffing away. Churchill room has a huge concrete bath, of the type in which he was known to wallow, rehearsing his speeches for the Commons. Other rooms – some double- or triple-aspect – have sea views, perhaps a tester bed. Each is supplied with bathrobes, Scottish toiletries. Morning tea and coffee are delivered to the door. It is all old-fashioned-romantic, and we hear praise, above all, from newly married and honeymoon couples. 'Cosy log fire, good bed, superb food.' 'Tranquil setting, friendliness, attention to detail.' Chef Tony Pierce's modern Scottish cooking is a large part of the appeal. From a dinner menu: roast breast of free-range chicken, wild garlic, parsnip purée, charred tenderstem broccoli, Madeira sauce. 'Recommended without hesitation.'

25% DISCOUNT VOUCHERS

Portpatrick
DG9 9AD

T: 01776 810471
E: reservations@knockinaamlodge.com
W: www.knockinaamlodge.com

BEDROOMS: 10.
OPEN: all year, speciality weekends at Christmas and New Year.
FACILITIES: 2 lounges, bar, restaurant, free Wi-Fi, in-room TV (Freeview), wedding facilities, 20-acre grounds.
BACKGROUND MUSIC: 'easy listening'/ classical in restaurant in evening.
LOCATION: 3 miles S of Portpatrick.
CHILDREN: all ages welcomed, no under-12s in dining room.
DOGS: allowed in some bedrooms, grounds, not in public rooms.
CREDIT CARDS: Amex, MasterCard, Visa.
PRICES: [2018] per person D,B&B single £190–£330, double £155–£230. Set dinner £70. 1-night bookings refused certain weekends, Christmas, New Year.

PORTREE Highland

Map 5:C1

VIEWFIELD HOUSE

'More home than hotel', the Macdonalds'
'fabulous' Victorian country house brims with
family history and aristocratic fixtures. This
year is daughter Iona Macdonald's second solo
season at the wheel. Father, Hugh, has stayed
on to share anecdotes by the fire, and maintain
the house-party feel. Viewfield is popular for its
laid-back air, unstuffy eccentricity and colonial
memorabilia and antiques collected over 150 years
('needs bringing up to date', says one guest). 'All
the staff were friendly and welcoming,' report
regular Guide readers in 2018. In the traditionally
styled bedrooms, vintage touches (a cast iron
bed, a Victorian washstand with a bowl and
jug) and the occasional window seat overlook
mature woodland. 'Our rooms were excellent;
large and comfortable with sea views.' In lieu of
in-room TV, guests are encouraged to mingle
over cocktails, single malt and croquet. Ordered
ahead, dinners consist of fuss-free Scottish fare.
'The parsnip and cumin soup, and the duck
breast in plum sauce were especially good.'
Dietary requests were happily dealt with, 'to the
point of creating a different starter'. Breakfast
includes 'very nice' home-made marmalade.
(Alan and Edwina Williams, and others)

Viewfield Road
Portree
IV51 9EU

T: 01478 612217
E: info@viewfieldhouse.com
W: www.viewfieldhouse.com

BEDROOMS: 11. 1, on ground floor,
suitable for disabled.
OPEN: Apr–Oct.
FACILITIES: drawing room, morning/
TV room, dining room, free Wi-Fi,
20-acre grounds (croquet, swings).
BACKGROUND MUSIC: none.
LOCATION: S side of Portree.
CHILDREN: all ages welcomed.
DOGS: allowed in bedrooms, not in
public rooms.
CREDIT CARDS: MasterCard, Visa.
PRICES: [2018] per person B&B
£73–£100, D,B&B £98–£125. Set
dinner from £25. 1-night bookings
only on application in high season.

SEE ALSO SHORTLIST

RANNOCH STATION Perth and Kinross   Map 5:D2

MOOR OF RANNOCH – RESTAURANT & ROOMS

♙ Previous César winner

The overnight sleeper from London arrives in the middle of nowhere in time for a breakfast of porridge with Drambuie at Scott Meikle and Stephanie Graham's restaurant-with-rooms. Dogs are welcomed by resident canines Wallace and Stanley, and given a cushion by the fire. Humans are greeted by the 'friendly owners', and shown to a small but 'lovely, warm and well-appointed' room with a fridge, binoculars and waterproof map, but no TV, radio, mobile signal or Wi-Fi. In cosy lounges guests read, play Scrabble or pore over a jigsaw puzzle. Packed lunches are supplied to walkers, fuel for exploring the vast swathe of uninhabited moorland and peat bog. 'Everything is delightfully low key, except for the cuisine!' writes an admirer in 2018. Ms Graham's daily-changing menu includes such dishes as slow-cooked beef brisket, roasted neeps, thyme-roasted carrots, horseradish gremolata; also a vegetarian option. 'Young Steph is very, very special in the kitchen... This gem is not a Hilton, nor an InterContinental – those excellent groups can only dream of having a place like this in their collections.' (David Davies, Paul and Jen Hogarth)

Rannoch Station
PH17 2QA

T: 01882 633238
E: info@moorofrannoch.co.uk
W: www.moorofrannoch.co.uk

BEDROOMS: 5.
OPEN: 2nd week Feb–end Oct.
FACILITIES: lounge, bar, conservatory dining room, no Wi-Fi or TV.
BACKGROUND MUSIC: none.
LOCATION: on a single-track, dead-end road, 40 miles W of Pitlochry.
CHILDREN: 'all ages welcomed.
DOGS: welcomed in all areas of the hotel'.
CREDIT CARDS: all major cards.
PRICES: [2018] per room B&B single £125, double £180. Set meals £28–£35.

RATHO Midlothian

Map 5:D2

THE BRIDGE INN AT RATHO

Flanked by the 18th-century stone bridge after which it's named, Graham and Rachel Bucknall's 'characterful' restaurant-with-rooms on the water has much to like. A 'cheerful team', managed by Jackie Fergus, imbues 'an easy, informal air', especially in the 'lively' pub (it's popular with locals, but Guide readers 'didn't notice any noise'). Between the crackling fires and wide range of Scottish ales and whiskies, the 'smart' public rooms have everything needed to keep the cockles cosy. In the 'light-filled' restaurant, freshly picked produce from the walled garden, just up the canal, transforms in chef Ben Watson's 'delicious' dishes, perhaps winter green risotto, blue cheese, pine nut crumble; or roast pinwheel sausage made with the owners' rare breed pigs. At night, the murmur of the canal below filters into each of the tastefully neutral bedrooms. Come morning, there is haggis and tattie scones, the Canadian breakfast, and (collected across the canal) the freshest duck eggs cooked 'to your liking', all part of the 'enormous, very good' breakfast. To burn it off, make the seven-mile yomp along the historic Union Canal's 'pretty' rowpath into Edinburgh. More reports, please.

27 Baird Road
Ratho
EH28 8RU

T: 0131 333 1320
E: info@bridgeinn.com
W: www.bridgeinn.com

BEDROOMS: 4.
OPEN: all year except 24/25 Dec.
FACILITIES: 2 bars, restaurant, free Wi-Fi, in-room TV (Freeview), wedding facilities, terrace (beer garden, boat shed), bar and restaurant wheelchair accessible.
BACKGROUND MUSIC: 'relaxed' all day, monthly live music nights.
LOCATION: in village, 7 miles W of Edinburgh.
CHILDREN: all ages welcomed.
DOGS: allowed in main bar only.
CREDIT CARDS: MasterCard, Visa.
PRICES: [2018] per room B&B £100–£170. À la carte £35.

ST OLA Orkney Islands   Map 5:A3

THE FOVERAN

A passion for all things Orcadian infuses this
'delightful' and 'welcoming' restaurant-with-
rooms overlooking Scapa Flow and the southern
Orkney islands. Guests can sit in a traditional
Orkney chair ('more comfortable than it
looks'), admire a tapestry made by a cousin of
the owners, and enjoy a hint of local whisky
in such dishes as Orkney fillet steak topped
with caramelised onions, a puff pastry lattice
and creamy Highland Park sauce. Brothers
Paul and Hamish Doull and their wives,
Helen and Shirley, are hands-on owners, with
a staff of 'friendly and helpful' young locals.
Bedrooms are small and spruce, with good
toiletries, nothing fancy. But then, this is first
and foremost a restaurant, open for dinner only
which, as a reader observes, 'makes a subtle
difference' – including no check-in before 4.30
pm. There are panoramic, big sky views from
the sea-facing lounge and the popular restaurant
where, along with that fillet steak, Paul Doull's
menus showcase North Ronaldsay mutton, local
lamb, shellfish and seafood. At breakfast there
are free-range eggs, local sausages and black
pudding, home-made bread, bannocks and
preserves. (MM-D)

St Ola
KW15 1SF

T: 01856 872389
E: info@thefoveran.com
W: www.thefoveran.com

BEDROOMS: 8. All on ground floor,
1 single room with bathroom across
the hall.
OPEN: Apr–early Oct, by
arrangement at other times,
restaurant closed variable times in
Apr, Oct.
FACILITIES: lounge, restaurant,
free Wi-Fi, in-room TV, 12-acre
grounds (private rock beach),
restaurant wheelchair accessible.
BACKGROUND MUSIC: local/Scottish
traditional in restaurant.
LOCATION: 3 miles SW of Kirkwall.
CHILDREN: all ages welcomed.
DOGS: not allowed.
CREDIT CARDS: MasterCard, Visa.
PRICES: [2018] per room B&B single
from £85, double from £125,
D,B&B (for dinner up to £30) single
from £112, double from £180.
À la carte £35.

SCARISTA Western Isles

Map 5:B1

SCARISTA HOUSE

♔ Previous César winner

It's worth driving the long road to Scarista House, with its 'well-deserved reputation for excellent feasting' and 'one of Britain's most extraordinary locations'. Owners Neil King, and Tim and Patricia Martin run their small hotel in a 'laid-back but professional manner', helped by 'lovely' local staff. After checking in, a Guide inspector enjoyed 'possibly the best Victoria sponge I've ever tasted'. The library and drawing room have a 'homey atmosphere' and all bedrooms, some in converted outbuildings, offer views of the three-mile-long beach and 'Caribbean-blue' Atlantic. 'At night, the muted sound of the sea; in the mornings, the lowing of cows and cry of seagulls.' 'Good bedside lighting', well-stocked hospitality tray and 'powerful overhead shower' compensated for a soft mattress. The 'delectable' dinner, uses organic, wild and home-made produce in such dishes as fillet of Stornoway-landed turbot, ginger and Monbazillac sauce, wilted pak choi, cumin-roasted potatoes. With notice, 'tricky' diet requests are accommodated: 'vegan scones, with dairy-free spread, really made me feel welcome.' Breakfast delivered 'freshly squeezed orange juice, seriously tasty home-made granola'.

Scarista
HS3 3HX

T: 01859 550238
E: bookings@scaristahouse.com
W: www.scaristahouse.com

BEDROOMS: 6. 3 in annexe.
OPEN: mid-Mar–mid-Oct.
FACILITIES: drawing room, library, 2 dining rooms, free Wi-Fi in most bedrooms and all public areas, wedding facilities, 1-acre garden, unsuitable for disabled.
BACKGROUND MUSIC: none.
LOCATION: 15 miles SW of Tarbert.
CHILDREN: all ages welcomed.
DOGS: allowed in bedrooms and public rooms.
CREDIT CARDS: Amex, MasterCard, Visa.
PRICES: [2018] per room B&B £235. Set dinner £48. Advance 1-night bookings refused.

SLEAT Isle of Skye

✦KINLOCH LODGE

NEW

César award: luxury hotel of the year

'This is not just a good hotel but a very good hotel.' High praise this year from a trusted reader, for every aspect of the hospitality at Lord and Lady Macdonald's historic former hunting lodge on the Isle of Skye. Reached by a long drive, it stands in its own grounds, at the foot of a mountain, overlooking Loch Na Dal. Log fires burn in public rooms hung with ancestral portraits and filled with family memorabilia, including a framed letter from Queen Victoria. Bedrooms are in the original house and a new wing with its own lounge and honesty bar. All are individually styled, with antiques, prints and paintings. Most have a glorious sea view, and even the bathroom of the smallest ('standard') room has a bath and separate walk-in shower. The Macdonalds' 'charming' daughter Isabella is the long-time manager, while chef Marcello Tully has held a Michelin star since 2009 for such seasonal, locally sourced dishes as Shetland cod, caper and pistachio pesto, Drumfearn mussels, cucumber and shallot dressing. There are cookery courses, while 'a lovely ghillie organises fishing, stalking, nature walks and other outdoor experiences'. (Robert Cooper)

Sleat
IV43 8QY

T: 01471 833333
E: reservations@kinloch-lodge.
co.uk
W: www.kinloch-lodge.co.uk

BEDROOMS: 19. 10 in North Lodge, 9 inn South Lodge. 3 on ground floor, 1 suitable for disabled.
OPEN: all year.
FACILITIES: 3 drawing rooms, whisky bar, dining room, in-room TV (Sky), free Wi-Fi, cookery courses, 'huge' grounds on edge of loch, public rooms wheelchair accessible.
BACKGROUND MUSIC: gentle classical in dining room.
LOCATION: on shore of Loch Na Dal on east coast of Skye, not far off A851.
CHILDREN: all ages welcomed.
DOGS: in bedrooms only, and not unattended.
CREDIT CARDS: MasterCard, Visa.
PRICES: [2018] per person, B&B £120–£200, D,B&B £140–£240. Set dinner (5 courses) £80, tasting menu (7 courses) £90.

STRACHUR Argyll and Bute

Map 5:D1

THE CREGGANS INN

In a 'glorious location', this 19th-century
whitewashed inn, perched above Loch Fyne,
is run as a 'terrific' hotel, bar and bistro by Gill
and Archie MacLellan. Prettily styled bedrooms
range from side-facing 'standard' rooms to
loch-view rooms with designer wallpaper and
fabrics. All rooms have good toiletries; superior
loch-view rooms have robes and slippers. 'There
is a nice residents' lounge on the first floor.' The
offer of afternoon tea and cakes on arrival is a
welcome touch, and a dog-lover was taken with
resident canines Hector and Boo. In MacPhunn's
Bistro, Shaun Murray's menu is seasonal, locally
sourced. 'Rack of lamb with herb crust and pea
purée, gratin potatoes with leeks and cream and
bacon was excellent.' Another reader, eating in
the bistro, wondered why the 'lovely restaurant
with fantastic views' was, on that busy night,
unused. Breakfast involves free-range eggs,
potato scones, Loch Fyne kipper, of course. 'The
hotel allowed me to leave my car for a few days
as I was walking the coast, and to change my
clothes on return. They went out of their way to
be helpful.' (GM, CE)

Strachur
PA27 8BX

T: 01369 860279
E: info@creggans-inn.co.uk
W: www.creggans-inn.co.uk

BEDROOMS: 14.
OPEN: all year, except Christmas.
FACILITIES: 2 lounges, bar, dining
room, bistro, free Wi-Fi, in-room
TV (Freeview), function facilities,
2-acre grounds, moorings for guests
arriving by boat.
BACKGROUND MUSIC: all day in bar.
LOCATION: in village.
CHILDREN: all ages welcomed.
DOGS: allowed in bar, bedrooms (not
unattended).
CREDIT CARDS: Amex, MasterCard,
Visa.
PRICES: [2018] per room B&B
£130–£190. À la carte £30.

STRATHTAY Perth and Kinross   Map 5:D2

RIVERWOOD

'Beautiful, beautiful! silvery Tay, Thy scenery
is enchanting on a fine summer day.' The great
McGonagall could have been moved to verse
by the views from Ann and Alf Berry's B&B.
From a conservation village, a driveway leads
to a contemporary house in absolute seclusion,
with its own bluebell wood, on the banks of
that silvery river. Our readers love the 'tranquil
setting', the 'cosy log fire', the 'superb food'.
Interiors are immaculate (no outdoor shoes,
please). The 'comfortable, spacious' bedrooms
and suites, in cool shades (lots of white), have
a river view, espresso machine, mini-fridge, a
bathroom with underfloor heating, Scottish
toiletries. One suite has a private hallway,
lounge, dressing room, a bath and separate walk-
in shower. Some rooms have direct garden access
via glass doors. A 'wonderful' breakfast cooked
by Ann, served by the 'ever-attentive Alf', might
include fruit salad, griddled pancakes, French
toast with crispy bacon, Dunkeld smoked
salmon, rösti. Dinner, available on certain nights,
is worth staying in for. If you're eating out,
Pitlochry, with its theatre and restaurants (see
entries), is a 12-minute drive. Guests can enjoy
fly-fishing, complimentary golf.

25% DISCOUNT VOUCHERS

Strathtay
PH9 0PG

T: 01887 840751
E: info@riverwoodstrathtay.com
W: riverwoodstrathtay.com

BEDROOMS: 7. 4 suites on ground
floor.
OPEN: 6 Feb–20 Dec, 28 Dec–New
Year, dinner available on selected
days (check website).
FACILITIES: lounge/dining room,
library, free Wi-Fi, in-room TV
(Freeview), 4½-acre grounds (lawns,
woodland, fishing), complimentary
access to nearby golf course.
BACKGROUND MUSIC: 'easy listening'
in dining room at mealtimes.
LOCATION: in village, 9½ miles SW
of Pitlochry.
CHILDREN: not under 12.
DOGS: not allowed.
CREDIT CARDS: Diners, MasterCard,
Visa.
PRICES: [2018] per room B&B
£110–£150, D,B&B (on selected
nights) £170–£205. 1-night bookings
sometimes refused in peak season.

STRATHTUMMEL Perth and Kinross   Map 5:D2

THE INN AT LOCH TUMMEL

Having swapped the dark glitz of a Soho nightclub for the big sky splendour of loch and munro, Alice and Jade Calliva are the 'friendly, welcoming' and 'highly motivated' owners of this 18th-century former coaching inn. 'I was immediately struck by the care that had gone into its refurbishment,' writes one reader of the cosy interiors behind the stone facade. A small first-floor library has rich Prussian blue walls, crushed velvet sofas and distressed leather armchairs; on the other side of shelves, the breakfast room gazes across the loch to Schiehallion. Resident pooches Maggie and Mabel slump before the open fire in the tasteful ground-floor snug, while in the bar, with settles, stags' antlers and a wood-burning stove, chef Craig Rushton produces 'outstanding' seasonal dishes, including roulade of Fife pork belly, black pudding, cavolo nero, apple compote, braised Puy lentils, crispy crackling. A new terrace with fire pit offers alfresco dining. The 'comfortable, well-appointed' en suite bedrooms have natural earthy hues, 'free whisky and home-made biscuits'. Breakfast, including the full Scottish, and smoked salmon and scrambled eggs, provides 'excellent' fuel for tackling that next munro. (GM)

Queens View
Strathtummel
PH16 5RP

T: 01882 634317
E: info@theinnatlochtummel.com
W: www.theinnatlochtummel.com

BEDROOMS: 6. 1 on ground floor, 1 suitable for disabled.
OPEN: all year except Christmas, Jan (except New Year's Day), restaurant closed Sun eve, Mon.
FACILITIES: snug, library, bar, breakfast room, free Wi-Fi in communal areas, large garden and patio (alfresco meals and drinks), wedding facilities, public areas wheelchair accessible.
BACKGROUND MUSIC: in bar/restaurant.
LOCATION: 10 miles W of Pitlochry.
CHILDREN: not under 5.
DOGS: allowed.
CREDIT CARDS: MasterCard, Visa.
PRICES: [2018] per room £105–£155. À la carte £27. 1-night bookings refused at peak weekends.

STRONTIAN Highland

Map 5:C1

KILCAMB LODGE

Amid grounds of lawn and woodland, on the shores of Loch Sunart, Sally and David Ruthven-Fox run a welcoming small hotel. 'The staff, in a quiet and efficient way, immediately make you feel comfortable.' The 18th-century house, enlarged by Victorian owners, is traditionally styled, with comfy sofas and log fires. A loch-view bedroom had curtains and bedhead 'like a Victorian children's alphabet book, colourful, interesting, beautifully made'. All bedrooms now have double-glazed windows and a power shower. Since last year, too, the eagle has landed: 'Eddie', a bronze statue, sits at the front to greet new arrivals. Guests can eat in the Driftwood Brasserie (fish and chips, steaks, seafood) or more formally in the dining room. Chef Gary Phillips's dishes are elaborate, for example, loin of Blackface Highland lamb, pistachio and mustard crust, slow-cooked shepherd's pie, carrot and apricot purée, caper and mint butter. 'The Tiree langoustines were served with a delicious and unusual salad with all kinds of seeds.' At breakfast there are kippers, smoked salmon, scrambled eggs on French toast. Overall, 'quite pricey, but well worth it'.

25% DISCOUNT VOUCHERS

Strontian
PH36 4HY

T: 01967 402257
E: enquiries@kilcamblodge.co.uk
W: www.kilcamblodge.co.uk

BEDROOMS: 11.
OPEN: 1 Feb–2 Jan (open New Year).
FACILITIES: drawing room, lounge, bar, restaurant, brasserie, free Wi-Fi, in-room TV (Freeview), wedding facilities, 22-acre grounds, bar, brasserie, restaurant wheelchair accessible, toilet not adapted.
BACKGROUND MUSIC: in restaurant and brasserie in evening.
LOCATION: edge of village.
CHILDREN: all ages welcomed.
DOGS: allowed in 5 bedrooms, not in public rooms, welcome pack (towels, blankets, £12 per dog per night).
CREDIT CARDS: MasterCard, Visa.
PRICES: [2018] per room B&B single £150–£185, double £165–£325, D,B&B double £220–£445. Tasting menu £75 (£17 supplement for D,B&B guests), à la carte £45. 1-night bookings refused Christmas, New Year, Easter.

TARLAND Aberdeenshire

DOUNESIDE HOUSE

'A beautiful location, lovely gardens, good food
and friendly service – and a view from our room
that was probably the best we have ever enjoyed.'
The MacRobert family's 'wonderful' hotel on the
outer reaches of the Cairngorms national park
was much praised by Guide readers this year.
The family home since the 1880s, it has been
'extensively and beautifully' refurbished. The
graceful furnishings and low armchairs by the
grand piano are new; the antiques, silverware,
ceramics and an extensive library are heirlooms.
Open fires keep out the Scottish chill until warm
days, when the terrace doors are flung wide
open, allowing drinks with 'sweeping views' of
the Grampians. Classic bedrooms with natural
tones and the odd bit of tartan look across the
Aberdeenshire countryside from the main house.
On the estate, apartments and cottages (several
recently renovated) have a kitchenette. At lunch
and dinner chef David Butters's 'excellent,
inventive' Scottish menus exploit the walled
garden for such dishes as halibut fillet, braised
oxtail, carrot and anise, baby gem, citrus beurre
blanc. For breakfast, 'smoked haddock, two
poached eggs and a wonderful hollandaise sauce;
good coffee'. (Philip Bright, and others)

Tarland
AB34 4UL

T: 013398 81230
E: manager@dounesidehouse.
co.uk
W: www.dounesidehouse.co.uk

BEDROOMS: 23. 9 in cottages, plus
4 apartments in Casa Memoria,
2 cottages suitable for disabled.
OPEN: all year.
FACILITIES: bar, parlour, library,
restaurant, conservatory, free Wi-Fi,
in-room Smart TV (Freeview),
wedding facilities, health centre
(12.5 metre indoor swimming pool,
all-weather tennis court), 17-acre
grounds, public areas wheelchair
accessible, adapted toilet.
BACKGROUND MUSIC: in bar and
restaurant.
LOCATION: 7 miles NW of Aboyne.
CHILDREN: all ages welcomed.
DOGS: allowed in cottages and
apartments, not in public rooms.
CREDIT CARDS: MasterCard, Visa.
PRICES: [2018] per room B&B from
£154, D,B&B from £230. Set dinner
£35–£45, tasting menu £69.

THORNHILL Dumfries and Galloway
Map 5:E2

TRIGONY HOUSE

In springtime, the drive up to Jan and Adam
Moore's 18th-century former sporting lodge
is 'lined with young trees in blossom, bulbs
everywhere'. Guests arriving with their dog
were greeted by 'a very pleasant, friendly young
woman' (perhaps also by resident retriever Roxy),
and found in their room a welcome pack with a
map of walks. Bedrooms range from 'small but
fine' classics to the Garden Suite, with lobby area
leading to a conservatory and small garden. All
are 'spotless, well cared for', supplied with home-
made shortbread, fresh coffee, organic toiletries.
Views are of hills, woodland or the garden, home
to a Scandinavian sauna and hot tub. You can eat
in the bar (dogs allowed) or dining room. Adam
Moore's evening menus use local and home-grown
produce, Solway scallops, free-range, rare breed
chicken, fruit and vegetables from the organic
kitchen garden (vegetarians happily catered for).
Maybe marjoram-roast chicken breast, pancetta
and Parmesan sauce, crispy leeks; sea bass, white
wine, saffron, lemon balm, tomato concassé. The
morning brings home-made granola, Ayrshire-
cured bacon, award-winning black puddings,
local kippers. 'Our breakfast was lovely.' In sum, a
beautiful setting, 'excellent food, good value'.

25% DISCOUNT VOUCHERS

Closeburn
Thornhill
DG3 5EZ

T: 01848 331211
E: info@trigonyhotel.co.uk
W: www.trigonyhotel.co.uk

BEDROOMS: 9. 1 on ground floor.
OPEN: all year except 25–27, 31 Dec.
FACILITIES: lounge, bar, dining room,
free Wi-Fi, in-room TV (Freeview),
spa treatment room in private
garden (outdoor wood-fired hot
tub, sauna cabin), wedding facilities,
4-acre grounds.
BACKGROUND MUSIC: in bar in
evening.
LOCATION: 1 mile S of Thornhill.
CHILDREN: all ages welcomed.
DOGS: 'well-behaved' dogs 'not
only allowed but welcomed' in
bedrooms, public rooms and
grounds; not in dining room (dog-
sitting, beds, bowls, towels).
CREDIT CARDS: all major cards.
PRICES: [2018] per room B&B single
from £100, double £125–£170,
D,B&B single from £135, double
£195–£240. À la carte £35. 1-night
bookings sometimes refused Sat.

THURSO Highland

Map 5:B2

FORSS HOUSE

Near the mainland's northern tip, Ian and Sabine Richards's Georgian mansion is surrounded by woodland and waterfall on the Forss river, a fishing hotspot. Readers in 2018 'arrived expecting a wonderful country house hotel, and were not disappointed'. Warm hospitality and angling anecdotes are provided by 'delightful' manager Anne Mackenzie. Guests also come for the shooting, deer stalking and many single malts. The main house's grandest bedrooms have a high ceiling, generous en suite bathroom, river views. A Guide regular appreciated a 'huge, really comfortable bed and red sofa, and floral-patterned decor. The bathroom had a vast bath, more like a swimming pool, plenty of hot water, excellent towels.' A 'highlight' was Andrew Manson's 'superb' locally sourced, seasonal food. 'A starter of crab, apple gratings, capers, salmon and Melba toast, and a main of lamb two ways, pea purée, peas and asparagus, were delicious.' 'We rated it the best food of all the very good hotels we visited along the NC500 route.' 'I could have done without the dining room's tacky piped music, but I highly recommend this delightful hotel.' (Chris Elliott, and others)'

25% DISCOUNT VOUCHERS

Forss
Thurso
KW14 7XY

T: 01847 861201
E: relax@forsshousehotel.co.uk
W: www.forsshousehotel.co.uk

BEDROOMS: 14. 3 in main house on ground floor, 6 in 2 neighbouring annexes, 1 in River House suitable for disabled.
OPEN: all year except 23 Dec–4 Jan.
FACILITIES: dining room, breakfast room, lounge, bar, free Wi-Fi, in-room TV (Freeview), meeting room, wedding facilities, 19-acre grounds with river and waterfall.
BACKGROUND MUSIC: in public areas breakfast and evening.
LOCATION: 5 miles W of Thurso.
CHILDREN: all ages welcomed (under-5s free).
DOGS: allowed in Sportsmen's Lodge only.
CREDIT CARDS: all major cards.
PRICES: [2018] per room B&B single £99–£135, double £135–£185, D,B&B single £137–£170, double £205–£260. À la carte £35.

TIRORAN Argyll and Bute

TIRORAN HOUSE

'A gem of a hotel' in 'a beautiful situation, with a view of the loch and the occasional eagle overhead', Laurence and Katie Mackay's Victorian country house delighted readers again this year. 'It is silent (apart from the tumbling burn that runs down through the garden to the loch), the air crisp and clear, no light pollution – who cares if mobile signals are weak and Wi-Fi patchy?' The hosts are praised for their 'warmth, friendliness, local knowledge and enthusiasm'. The Garden bedroom, 'accessed from the side of the house', is spacious, with traditional-style furniture, 'very comfortable bed', posh toiletries, 'everything you could wish for'. The atmosphere is that of a country house party. 'Dinner times were relaxed (just come when you want to) and we enjoyed talking to fellow guests over drinks.' Katie Mackay's menus showcase 'fantastic Scottish ingredients'. 'Think tender Lochbuie rib-eye in a cream and grain mustard sauce, juicy, pink rack of island lamb, poached sea trout, lobster, halibut. All very, very enjoyable.' Breakfast brings 'light, warm croissants', 'amazing smoked haddock', 'soft, juicy poached kippers', 'black pudding to die for'. (Caroline Thomson, David Birnie)

Tiroran
PA69 6ES

T: 01681 705232
E: info@tiroran.com
W: www.tiroran.com

BEDROOMS: 10. 2 on ground floor, 4 in annexes, plus 2 self-catering cottages, 1 suitable for disabled.
OPEN: all year except Nov–Feb, restaurant closed Sun pm, bar food available.
FACILITIES: lounge, breakfast room, dining conservatory, dining/bar area, free Wi-Fi, in-room TV (Freeview), 17½-acre gardens in 56-acre grounds, beach with mooring, wedding facilities, coffee shop, public rooms wheelchair accessible.
BACKGROUND MUSIC: sometimes in bar/dining area.
LOCATION: N side of Loch Scridain.
CHILDREN: all ages welcomed.
DOGS: allowed (not unattended) in annexe bedrooms, not in public rooms.
CREDIT CARDS: MasterCard, Visa.
PRICES: [2018] per room B&B single £125–£190, double £175–£245. À la carte £25–£50.

ULLAPOOL Highland

Map 5:B1

THE CEILIDH PLACE

There's 'a good night's sleep' and more at the
Urquhart family's 'lively' Ceilidh Place – a
popular fusion of cultural hub, bookshop and
small hotel, one street back from the ferry
terminal. Alongside reading matter from its
'excellent, well-stocked' bookshop, and small
library in each bedroom, there is often live
music, and regularly changing art exhibitions
displayed throughout the clutch of whitewashed
cottages. By day, the café serves coffee and cake,
by night it becomes 'a restaurant that is full
every evening', where chef Scott Morrison turns
local and home-grown produce into 'seriously
tasty' dishes. Over four nights a reader 'enjoyed
pork, apricot and pistachio terrine; smoked
haddock chowder; spiced crab in its shell; baked
aubergine with chickpeas, lentils and yogurt
sauce'. There is also a bar with Hebridean
islands' gins and a range of single malts.
Upstairs, the residents' lounge 'overlooks the
village' and has a kitchenette 'fully stocked with
free tea and coffee', and honesty bar. The simple
bedrooms are peaceful: 'Ours was very large
and overlooked the garden; it had a good-sized
bathroom, lots of storage space and two chairs.'
(GC, and others)

12–14 West Argyle Street
Ullapool
IV26 2TY

T: 01854 612103
E: stay@theceilidhplace.com
W: www.theceilidhplace.com

BEDROOMS: 13. 10 with facilities en
suite, plus 11 in Bunkhouse across
road.
OPEN: all year except 2 weeks from
4 Jan.
FACILITIES: bar, lounge, café/
restaurant, bookshop, conference/
function facilities, free Wi-Fi,
wedding facilities, 2-acre garden,
public areas wheelchair accessible.
BACKGROUND MUSIC: 'eclectic' in
public areas.
LOCATION: village centre (large car
park).
CHILDREN: all ages welcomed.
DOGS: allowed.
CREDIT CARDS: MasterCard, Visa.
PRICES: [2018] per room B&B £132–
£170 (rooms in Bunkhouse £24–£32
per person). À la carte £26.

SEE ALSO SHORTLIST

WALKERBURN Scottish Borders

Map 5:E2

WINDLESTRAW

NEW

'A place in the ascendant,' say our inspectors of Sylvia and John Matthews's Edwardian mansion overlooking the Tweed valley. It rises to a full entry this year. Inside the 'imposing front entrance', they ascended a staircase 'its newel posts crowned with griffins and owls', and were shown to 'a small, simply furnished bedroom. There was an espresso machine, a 'large, warm, inviting bathroom with freestanding bath, efficient monsoon shower, underfloor heating'. Most bathrooms have an original Edwardian tub. Public spaces are 'of the highest quality', with 'good art, family memorabilia, open fires'. An oak-panelled dining room opens into a comfortable lounge with views over 'forested slopes, grazing cattle, a wide river'. At dinner, John was on stand-in 'waiting duty', which he accomplished 'with considerable Irish charm and humour'. Chef Stu Waterston sources produce from Borders farmers, kitchen garden and glasshouse. 'Fresh crab with a lemon crust, followed by Scottish salmon, led to a perfectly cooked rack of lamb, four Scottish cheeses in peak condition, a sinfully "moreish" chocolate dessert'. In sum, 'comfort, culinary excellence, beautiful surroundings'.

Galashiels Road
Walkerburn
EH43 6AA

T: 01896 870636
E: stay@windlestraw.co.uk
W: www.windlestraw.co.uk

BEDROOMS: 6.
OPEN: 14 Feb–15 Dec.
FACILITIES: bar, sunroom, lounge/restaurant, free Wi-Fi in reception, in-room TV (Freeview), wedding facilities, 2-acre landscaped garden, parking.
BACKGROUND MUSIC: none.
LOCATION: in Walkerburn, 8 miles east of Peebles.
CHILDREN: all ages welcomed.
DOGS: allowed in bedrooms, public rooms.
CREDIT CARDS: MasterCard, Visa.
PRICES: [2018] per room B&B £200–£280, D,B&B £310–£390. 4-course set menu £55.

WALLS Shetland

BURRASTOW HOUSE

♨ Previous César winner

In 'an extraordinarily beautiful location' on Shetland's wild West coast, 'charming, unobtrusive host' Pierre Dupont runs his guest house on informal lines. The 18th-century property overlooking the Sound of Vaila, extended over the centuries, is cosily furnished, with antiques and paintings. To stay here, says a fan, is to feel like a guest in a private country house. Regular readers this year were greeted by Mr Dupont and given tea in the conservatory with 'a gorgeous piece of cake'. The approach to their loft room felt a little precarious (short, wooden steps, no banister rail). The first-floor Laird's Room, with tester bed, or Vaila, with four-poster, might have been a better bet. Informality cuts both ways. If you want a drink in the lounge, you might have to pop into the kitchen and ask. The dinner menu, decided on the day, is not written but recited. 'On our second night, four of us heard "steak"; it turned out to be skate.' In the dining room, though, the relaxed atmosphere works its magic, people start chatting. 'We all had a great evening.' (A and HB, and others)

Walls
ZE2 9PD

T: 01595 809307
E: info@burrastowhouse.co.uk
W: www.burrastowhouse.co.uk

BEDROOMS: 7. 3 in extension, 2 on ground floor.
OPEN: Apr–Oct.
FACILITIES: sitting room, library, dining room, conservatory, free Wi-Fi in reception and library, in-room TV (Freeview), 'weak mobile phone signal', grounds, wedding facilities, unsuitable for disabled.
BACKGROUND MUSIC: none.
LOCATION: 2 miles from Walls, 27 miles NW of Lerwick.
CHILDREN: all ages welcomed (under-13s half price).
DOGS: not allowed.
CREDIT CARDS: MasterCard, Visa.
PRICES: [2018] per person B&B £50–£60, D,B&B £85–£95. À la carte £35.

WALES

Portmeirion village

ABERAERON Ceredigion   Map 3:C2

HARBOURMASTER HOTEL

'On a sunny evening the effect of the clarity of the light, the pastel-coloured houses and the harbour is reminiscent of Brittany.' The 'lovely setting' of 'hands-on' Glyn and Menna Heulyn's 'popular' former harbourmaster's building on the Georgian quayside causes trusted Guide readers this year to wax poetic. 'Yes, the only place to sit inside is the large bar which by evening is heaving. Yes, its buzzy dining area is noisy. Yes, the stairs are quite steep and there is no lift. But I forgive all that for the joy of sitting outside in the evening sunshine with a drink watching life go by in the harbour.' Upstairs, bedrooms are 'clean, stylish, comfortable; no frills, no cushions piled high on the bed. Lovely toiletries, too,' and a Roberts radio; rooms in the converted warehouse next door are spacious. Chef Ludo Dieumegard's 'superb fresh fish dishes' are served by 'agreeable, motivated staff' in the nautical restaurant. 'The food has always been good but this year it was even better. Our cod with pommes Anna was quite delicious.' The Wales Coastal Path collects walkers from the front door. 'What more could one want?' (Robert Cooper, Frances Thomas, LW)

Pen Cei
Aberaeron
SA46 0BT

T: 01545 570755
E: info@harbour-master.com
W: www.harbour-master.com

BEDROOMS: 13. 2 in cottage, 1 suitable for disabled.
OPEN: all year except 24 (evening)–26 Dec, drinks only on Boxing Day.
FACILITIES: lift, bar, restaurant, free Wi-Fi, in-room TV (Freeview), small terrace, pebble beach (safe bathing nearby), restaurant and bar wheelchair accessible.
BACKGROUND MUSIC: all day in bar.
LOCATION: central, on the harbour.
CHILDREN: not under 5 to stay, must have own room.
DOGS: only guide dogs.
CREDIT CARDS: American Express, MasterCard, Visa.
PRICES: [2018] per room B&B single £110–£255, double £120–£265, D,B&B double £180–£325. Set dinner £27.50–£35, à la carte £35. 1-night bookings refused most weekends, min. 2-night stay for D,B&B rate.

ABERDYFI Gwynedd   Map 3.C3

TREFEDDIAN HOTEL

The Cave family's holiday hotel, in a 'marvellous location' overlooking Cardigan Bay, is 'very much family orientated, and the facilities are excellent – indoor pool, putting green, games room, beach across the road'. For adults there's a library and restful, sea-facing lounges. Devotees return time and again. 'Another delightful visit to this institution of a hotel,' one writes this year. But not everyone wants to stay in an institution. 'Perfectly good, but not perfect for us,' relates another reader, who 'just wanted a base to walk from'. At mealtimes the dining room with ocean views is heaving, and the kitchen in overdrive. Still, 'the waiter had the good sense to ask if we wanted a break before ordering pudding'. Also, 'the food was fine… roast pheasant, chicken, seared swordfish… excellent tropical fruit salad, banoffee pie'. Bedrooms vary. Some have a balcony, some interconnect. 'The top floor suites are worthy of any five-star hotel.' Readers appreciated the hotel 'paying so much attention to standards of service, especially the meticulous housekeeping'. Breakfast brings kippers, home-cooked ham, free-range eggs. (Stephen and Jane Marshall, Peter Anderson, Clive Blackburn, and others)

Tywyn Road
Aberdyfi
LL35 0SB

T: 01654 767213
E: info@trefwales.com
W: www.trefwales.com

BEDROOMS: 59. 1 suitable for disabled.
OPEN: all year except 9 Dec–13 Jan.
FACILITIES: lift, lounge bar, study, family lounge, adult lounge, restaurant, games room (snooker, table tennis, air hockey), free Wi-Fi, in-room TV (Freeview), indoor swimming pool (6 by 12 metres), beauty salon, 15-acre grounds (lawns, sun terrace, tennis, putting green).
BACKGROUND MUSIC: none.
LOCATION: ¼ mile N of Aberdyfi.
CHILDREN: all ages welcomed.
DOGS: allowed in 1 lounge, some bedrooms.
CREDIT CARDS: MasterCard, Visa.
PRICES: [2018] per person B&B £75–£95, D,B&B £100–£140. Set dinner £33. 2-night min. stay preferred (but check for 1-night availability).

ABERGAVENNY Monmouthshire   Map 3:D4

THE ANGEL HOTEL

'Faultless and elegant,' writes a reader after a
visit this year to William Griffiths's 'fine, family-
run hotel', forged from a 19th-century coaching
inn. Its days as a meeting place of the society
dedicated to the Welsh language are long gone,
replaced by 'wonderfully comfortable' bedrooms
speaking the lingua franca of contemporary
hospitality – Villeroy & Boch bathroom fittings,
aromatherapy toiletries, robes, extra fluffy
towels. The 'exceptionally helpful and cheery
staff' are an international lot, too. Original
artwork, selected by the keen eye of Pauline
Griffiths, William's mother and owner of
a local art gallery, decorate the 'excellent
choice of public rooms', including the popular
Foxhunter bar. There is a sense of drama in the
restaurant with its deep burgundy walls, where
a 'first-class' dinner, courtesy of chef Wesley
Hammond, might include grilled prawns and
steak, miso, honey and chilli sauce, coconut rice.
Leave room for the Angel's 'justly renowned'
afternoon tea, and an extensive breakfast,
perhaps involving a Mimosa cocktail of fresh
orange juice and champagne

15 Cross Street
Abergavenny
NP7 5EN

T: 01873 857121
E: info@angelabergavenny.com
W: www.angelabergavenny.com

BEDROOMS: 33. 2 in adjacent mews,
plus two 2-bedroom cottages.
OPEN: all year except 24–27 Dec.
FACILITIES: lift, lounge, bar, tea
room, restaurant, private function
rooms, bakery, free Wi-Fi, in-room
TV (Freeview), civil wedding
licence, courtyard, public rooms
wheelchair accessible.
BACKGROUND MUSIC: in restaurant
and tea room.
LOCATION: town centre.
CHILDREN: all ages welcomed.
DOGS: allowed in the Foxhunter bar
and courtyard.
CREDIT CARDS: Amex, MasterCard,
Visa.
PRICES: [2018] per room B&B
from £109, D,B&B from £169. Set
dinner £30, à la carte £40, breakfast
£15. 1-night bookings sometimes
refused.

ABERGAVENNY Monmouthshire

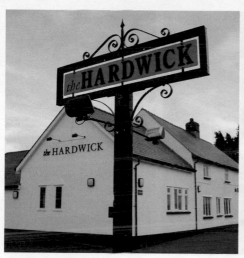

THE HARDWICK

🏆 Previous César winner

'Our third visit.' Readers tempted back this year to celebrity chef Stephen Terry's restaurant-with-rooms – a reinvention of a 'grotty roadside pub'– found everything to their liking. Rooms occupy a timber-clad annexe around a courtyard. 'Ours was fine, modern, well equipped, not very big but perfectly adequate, with welcome air conditioning.' Most have countryside views, a bath with shower, some have a walk-in shower. All have Welsh textiles, a Roberts Radio – but the big attraction is the food. Mr Terry has had a long career in Michelin-starred kitchens, gaining his own first star aged 25, but here the style is simpler, more accessible, with plenty of choice. In the relaxed, spacious restaurant our readers enjoyed a 'sublime' fig and rocket salad; mackerel fillets, deep-fried new potatoes, green beans, lentil, rocket; summer pudding. To 'the buzz of contented diners', another reader adds a murmur of dissent, a tale of a family celebration dinner far short of expectations (when booking, he was not informed Mr Terry was away). However, our happy three-time visitor concludes, 'Staff were good, it's not expensive, we will be back.' (Peter Anderson, and others)

Old Raglan Road
Abergavenny
NP7 9AA

T: 01873 854220
E: info@thehardwick.co.uk
W: www.thehardwick.co.uk

BEDROOMS: 8. 5 on ground floor, 1, with wet room, suitable for disabled.
OPEN: all year except 24–26 Dec.
FACILITIES: bar, restaurant, private dining facilities, free Wi-Fi, in-room TV (Freeview), courtyard (seating 40), small garden, public areas wheelchair accessible.
BACKGROUND MUSIC: 'unintrusive' in public areas.
LOCATION: 2¾ miles S of Abergavenny.
CHILDREN: all ages welcomed.
DOGS: only assistance dogs allowed.
CREDIT CARDS: MasterCard, Visa.
PRICES: [2018] per room B&B single (Mon–Thurs) £115, double £120–£150, D,B&B £199. À la carte £42.

ABERSOCH Gwynedd

Map 3:B2

PORTH TOCYN HOTEL

A Welsh rarebit on the tip of Cardigan Bay,
this 'lovely, wacky' hotel is a family-friendly,
family-run affair. At its heart is the benevolent
host, Nick Fletcher-Brewer ('jolly, jokey,
casual, quirky, a real character'), whose family
has owned the place for 70 years. A ramble
of sitting rooms creates a 'home-away-from-
home' atmosphere, with books, old maps, vases
of tumbling flowers, and help-yourself coffee.
Comfy cushions in front of a log fire in one of
many tucked-away nooks provide relaxation and
warmth after a paddle in the sea (five minutes'
walk away), while a children's snug with games
occupies little ones. Country antiques and
watercolours furnish 'simple, unfussy' bedrooms.
Most have 'amazing' coastal views; several can be
interconnected into a comfortable family suite.
The daily-changing menus, cooked by Louise
Fletcher-Brewer and Darren Shenton-Morris,
'make clever use of ingredients'. Tuck into pan-
fried bacon-wrapped venison, sticky red cabbage
and baby turnips, or perhaps Porth Tocyn fish pie
from the 'Comfort Menu'. Breakfast, including
'tasty' sausages, thick toast, home-made
marmalade and 'delicious local yogurts', lays the
foundations of a classic seaside day. (C and GJ)

Bwlchtocyn
Abersoch
LL53 7BU

T: 01758 713303
E: bookings@porthtocynhotel.co.uk
W: www.porthtocynhotel.co.uk

BEDROOMS: 17. 3 on ground floor.
OPEN: week before Easter–early
Nov.
FACILITIES: sitting rooms, children's
snug, small bar, dining room, free
Wi-Fi, in-room TV (Freeview), 20-
acre grounds (swimming pool, 10
by 6 metres, heated May–end Sept,
tennis), call to discuss wheelchair
access.
BACKGROUND MUSIC: none.
LOCATION: 2 miles outside village.
CHILDREN: all ages welcomed.
DOGS: not allowed in some public
rooms.
CREDIT CARDS: MasterCard, Visa.
PRICES: [2018] per room B&B
£85–£200. À la carte £47. 1-night
bookings occasionally refused.

ABERYSTWYTH Ceredigion

Map 3:C3

GWESTY CYMRU

On the 'upmarket Victorian promenade' of a university town, Huw and Beth Roberts's hotel is 'brightly presented', with 'tables and chairs on a small lawn facing the sea'. The welcoming staff are bilingual, and locally handmade furniture, landscapes by local artists, and displays of Welsh poetry celebrate national identity. Readers liked their bright, light, front-facing bedroom, with its 'large bay window, super-king-size bed, plenty of storage space' and 'a modern en suite with walk-in shower and bath'. There's no residents' lounge but, as a hurricane blew, 'it was pleasant sitting in our armchairs, with a beer, watching the sea crash over the front'. A cheaper, rear-facing room was 'smart, with Welsh oak fittings and splashes of bright colour', say Guide insiders, but it got cooking smells from the kitchen below. In the basement restaurant, 'bistro-style' fare includes such dishes as 'smoked salmon pâté with a mountain of focaccia', and 'good rump of lamb'. 'We enjoyed squash tarte Tatin… Cajun-style chicken strips.' At breakfast there is 'a rather ordinary buffet', but hot dishes had 'high-quality ingredients, and the full Welsh includes laver bread'. (Desmond and Jenny Balmer, GC)

19 Marine Terrace
Aberystwyth
SY23 2AZ

T: 01970 612252
E: info@gwestycymru.co.uk
W: www.gwestycymru.co.uk

BEDROOMS: 8. 2 on ground floor.
OPEN: all year except 22 Dec–4 Jan, restaurant closed for lunch Tues.
FACILITIES: small bar area, restaurant, seafront terrace, free Wi-Fi, in-room TV (Freeview), secure parking (book in advance), unsuitable for disabled.
BACKGROUND MUSIC: 'easy listening' all day in reception and restaurant.
LOCATION: central, on seafront.
CHILDREN: no under-5s, all ages welcomed at lunch.
DOGS: not allowed.
CREDIT CARDS: MasterCard, Visa.
PRICES: [2018] per room B&B single £70–£80, double £90–£155. À la carte £35.

BALA Gwynedd
Map 3:B3

BRYNIAU GOLAU

🜨 Previous César winner

There are 'stunning' views of Bala lake and
Arenig mountain from the bedrooms of this
Victorian house on a hillside in Snowdonia
national park. Visitors this year appreciated the
decor's 'perfect taste'. The comfortable bedrooms
are supplied with cut flowers, home-baked
biscuits, books, magazines. Both Berwyn and
Arenig have an antique four-poster, underfloor
heating in a luxury bathroom with spa bath and
separate shower. Aran is a double-aspect room
with super-king-size bed, a bathroom with a
bath under the window allowing you to soak
while gazing at the lake. Walkers returning
drenched on chilly days find drying facilities,
a fire burning in the sitting room. Breakfast,
served at a long table alongside a grand piano,
includes bread, granola and preserves, home
made by hostess Katrina Le Saux in her kitchen;
the honey is home made by the bees in the
house's hives. There is a full Welsh cooked
breakfast for those who wish, terraces for sitting
out in the landscaped gardens. For a gourmet
meal, Tyddyn Llan in Llandrillo is less than
20 minutes' away by car (see entry). Bodnant
Garden and Portmeirion are an easy drive.

Llangower
Bala
LL23 7BT

T: 01678 521782
E: katrinalesaux@hotmail.co.uk
W: www.bryniau-golau.co.uk

BEDROOMS: 3.
OPEN: Mar–Dec (not Christmas/
New Year).
FACILITIES: sitting room (honesty
bar), dining room, free Wi-Fi,
in-room TV (Freeview), ½-acre
garden (terrace), drying facilities,
canoe/bicycle storage, unsuitable for
disabled.
BACKGROUND MUSIC: dining room
and sitting room linked to Sonos for
guests' own use.
LOCATION: 2 miles SE of Bala.
CHILDREN: babies up to 12 months
and over-10s welcomed.
DOGS: not allowed.
CREDIT CARDS: MasterCard, Visa.
PRICES: [2018] per room B&B single
£90–£110, double £110–£130.
1-night bookings may be refused at
peak times.

SEE ALSO SHORTLIST

BARMOUTH Gwynedd

Map 3:B3

COES FAEN

'The name means "leg of stone",' a Guide inspector tells us – a reference to the rocks on and over which this 'fabulous, ultra-modern' B&B is built. A Victorian lodge with views across the Mawddach estuary has here been dramatically reinvented by owners Sara and Richard Parry-Jones. 'We were amazed at the entrance… an incredible glass staircase… a tunnel, trickling water, which led through to gardens, woods, seats for relaxing and admiring the view.' Mor bedroom had an espresso machine, local spring water, 'a grand marble bathroom with power shower'. Other rooms have, variously, a whirlpool bath, a hot tub on a terrace, an in-room, hand-crafted wooden bathtub, and a cedar and slate steam room. A log-fired biomass boiler supplies underfloor heating throughout. The Parry-Joneses are welcoming hosts, with everyone on first-name terms. Four nights a week, new head chef Wayne Scarlet cooks a Tuscan-inspired dinner in the stone-walled dining room. Perhaps Welsh leek soup with a drizzle of truffle oil; crab and ricotta ravioli. Breakfast brings fruit smoothies, free-range eggs Benedict with crispy pancetta, hot smoked salmon, local sausages, hash browns and much more.

25% DISCOUNT VOUCHERS

Barmouth
LL42 1TE

T: 01341 281632
E: croeso@coesfaen.co.uk
W: coesfaen.co.uk

BEDROOMS: 6. 1, on ground floor, suitable for disabled.
OPEN: all year except Christmas, Jan, restaurant open Wed–Sat for dinner..
FACILITIES: entrance hall, snug with honesty bar, dining room, free Wi-Fi, in-room TV (Freeview), in-room spa treatments, 15-acre grounds (woodland garden), stable for visiting dogs and horses, restaurant and bar wheelchair accessible.
BACKGROUND MUSIC: in public areas.
LOCATION: 1 mile E of town centre.
CHILDREN: not under 18.
DOGS: 'clean, well-behaved, indoor-trained dogs (no puppies)' allowed in 1 bedroom, not in public rooms, dog-sitting service available.
CREDIT CARDS: all major cards.
PRICES: [2018] per room B&B single £115–£220, double £135–£240, D,B&B double £205–£330. Set menus £35–£40, à la carte £40.

BARMOUTH Gwynedd

LLWYNDU FARMHOUSE

It's easy to unwind at 'welcoming' Peter and Paula Thompson's 'super little hotel' overlooking Cardigan Bay and the Lleyn peninsula. Sunset views 'with a bottle of Pouilly Fumé' are 'magical'. The 16th-century farmhouse, surrounded by fields and dry stone walls, offers quirky historic features, including a former latrine turned into a walk-in wardrobe with mullion window; a sink attached to a door; a spiral stone staircase. Some 'comfortable, spotlessly clean' bedrooms in the main house have a four-poster and an inglenook; those in the converted granary offer exposed stone walls and a private entrance. Bathrooms are being updated, but pillows may be 'past their best'. Pre-dinner drinks are served in the 'cosy' lounge with wood-burner. Readers consistently praise the 'delicious' dinners in the candlelit dining room. A member of the Slow Food Movement, Llwyndu embraces local and Welsh ingredients to create a daily-changing menu including such dishes as Cenarth smoked and Hafod cheeses in garlic mayonnaise with spring onions, wrapped in locally cured ham with a Gruyère topping; seared scallops with black pudding and shiitake mushrooms. An 'interesting' wine list oils the wheels.

25% DISCOUNT VOUCHERS

Llanaber
Barmouth
LL42 1RR

T: 01341 280144
E: intouch@llwyndu-farmhouse.co.uk
W: www.llwyndu-farmhouse.co.uk

BEDROOMS: 6. 3 in granary, 1 on ground floor.
OPEN: all year except Christmas, restaurant closed Sun and Wed.
FACILITIES: lounge, restaurant, free Wi-Fi, in-room TV (Freeview), ¼-acre garden in 4-acre grounds.
BACKGROUND MUSIC: 'occasionally and on demand' in dining room.
LOCATION: 2 miles N of Barmouth.
CHILDREN: all ages welcomed.
DOGS: not allowed.
CREDIT CARDS: MasterCard, Visa.
PRICES: [2018] per room B&B £110–£126, D,B&B £135–£155. Set dinner £25–£40. 1-night bookings sometimes refused July/Aug.

BEAUMARIS Anglesey

Map 3:A3

THE BULL BEAUMARIS

Behind the street front of a Georgian coaching inn, in its bones, timbers and staircase, this 'well run' hotel is far older, with a history stretching back to the 1500s. A fire blazes in a jolly bar adorned with knick-knacks and curiosities. Recently refurbished inn bedrooms with original beams have contemporary furnishings; a luxury suite has roll-top bath and walk-in shower. 'Ultra-modern' rooms are located across the road in The Townhouse, a former temperance hotel. Here, an enormous, air-conditioned loft suite can accommodate a family. All rooms – each one's name and interiors based around a colour – have an espresso machine, biscuits, Welsh toiletries. There is choice of where to eat, also. Four nights a week, in the Loft restaurant, chef Andy Tabberner's limited-choice menu offers such 'interesting dishes' as Welsh hogget rump, mint, shallot, liquorice; Harissa-roasted cauliflower, pickled raisin, Tunworth cheese, Welsh truffle. In Coach, a wide selection of brasserie fare includes the likes of beer-battered cod, and boar and chorizo burger. Readers particularly liked their starters: Arbroath smokies, and aubergine dip with tortilla chips, were 'excellent, imaginative, full of flavour'. (A and EW)

Castle Street
Beaumaris
LL58 8AP

T: 01248 810329
E: info@bullsheadinn.co.uk
W: www.bullsheadinn.co.uk

BEDROOMS: 25. 2 on ground floor, 1 in courtyard, 13 in The Townhouse adjacent, 1 suitable for disabled.
OPEN: all year, but limited opening in Christmas period, Loft restaurant opens for dinner Wed–Sat only.
FACILITIES: lift (in The Townhouse), lounge, bar, brasserie, restaurant, free Wi-Fi, in-room TV (Freeview), courtyard (alfresco dining), Coach brasserie wheelchair accessible.
BACKGROUND MUSIC: during all meals in Coach brasserie, at dinner in restaurant.
LOCATION: central.
CHILDREN: all ages welcomed.
DOGS: allowed in 2 bedrooms, bar.
CREDIT CARDS: Amex, MasterCard, Visa.
PRICES: [2018] per room B&B single £100–£115, double £115–£200, D,B&B double £170–£275. Set dinner (restaurant) 5 courses £55, à la carte (brasserie) £29.

BRECHFA Carmarthenshire

Map 3:D2

TY MAWR

♔ Previous César winner

'In a small village in a valley, surrounded by forest walks', Annabel and Stephen Thomas's 16th-century country house is 'ideal for guests wishing to holiday with their four-legged friend'. Inspectors received 'an efficient welcome from Annabel, who signed us in, showed us round and carried our case to our large ground-floor room accessed by a separate outside door'. It was 'beautifully warm' with 'basic, rustic pine furniture, a very comfortable super-king-size bed', a 'rather gloomy' bathroom. The residents' lounge had a wood-burner, while 'a split dining room, divided by a large stone fireplace, is used as a breakfast room at the lower level'. At night, Stephen Thomas creates 'outstanding' locally sourced dishes. 'A Welsh cheese and cauliflower soup, pan-fried duck breast with Cointreau and orange sauce, guineafowl leg and breast with hazelnut stuffing' were all 'consistently appetising', served with 'wonderful moist home-made bread'. The hostess 'works tirelessly to ensure guest satisfaction, providing tea and cake on request'. Breakfast includes free-range eggs, Carmarthen dry-cured ham, local sausages, Wye valley smoked salmon.

25% DISCOUNT VOUCHERS

Brechfa
SA32 7RA

T: 01267 202332
E: info@wales-country-hotel.co.uk
W: www.wales-country-hotel.co.uk

BEDROOMS: 6. 2 on ground floor, 1 with private access.
OPEN: all year.
FACILITIES: sitting room, bar, breakfast room, restaurant, free Wi-Fi, in-room TV (Freeview), 1-acre grounds.
BACKGROUND MUSIC: classical in restaurant during dinner.
LOCATION: village centre.
CHILDREN: not under 10.
DOGS: allowed in bedrooms, sitting room and bar, not in restaurant or breakfast room (no extra charge), biscuits, bowls, and information on local walks provided.
CREDIT CARDS: Amex, MasterCard, Visa.
PRICES: [2018] per room B&B single £80–£100, double £115–£130, D,B&B double £160–£175. Set dinner £25–£30. 1-night bookings occasionally refused on Sat in summer.

CARDIGAN Ceredigion

Map 3:D2

CAEMORGAN MANSION

'Welcoming hosts' David and Beverley Harrison-Wood collect praise for their 'very friendly, well-presented guest house'. The refurbished 19th-century mansion near Cardigan has strong green credentials; in winter months, the 'fantastic' log-burner and biomass underfloor heating are especially welcome. Dinner in the 'elegant' dining room 'was the icing on the cake'. Chefs Abbie Jones and David Harrison-Wood's modern European menus showcase locally sourced produce: roasted monkfish tail, cavolo nero, caramelised onions, beetroot jus; steaks done any way, in an array of sauces (creamy mushroom; Caws Cenarth Blue cheese). The cheesecake (perhaps key lime, perhaps amaretto) 'is not to be missed'. At night, the cosy bedrooms have a 'superb' bed, and sleek modern bathroom with a power shower and eco-friendly toiletries. 'Great extras' include fluffy bathrobes, capsule coffee machine, fresh milk and home-baked biscuits, a library of books. A generous breakfast is 'another delight'. A range of activities is for the taking: good walks and cycling routes along the Coastal Path, just minutes away; dolphin-spotting tours; golf. The tranquil location is within walking distance of Cardigan city centre.

Caemorgan Road
Cardigan
SA43 1QU

T: 01239 613297
E: guest@caemorgan.com
W: www.caemorgan.com

BEDROOMS: 5.
OPEN: all year except Christmas.
FACILITIES: bar, restaurant, free Wi-Fi, in-room TV (Freeview), function facilities, 2-acre gardens, unsuitable for disabled.
BACKGROUND MUSIC: in restaurant only.
LOCATION: ½ mile N of town centre.
CHILDREN: not under 15.
DOGS: assistance dogs only.
CREDIT CARDS: MasterCard, Visa.
PRICES: [2018] per room B&B £94–£130. À la carte £35. 1-night bookings often refused peak weekends.

CRICKHOWELL Powys

GLIFFAES

'Wonderfully located' above the River Usk, this Victorian former vicar's house has a 'timeless quality'. Peta Brabner and Susie and James Suter are, respectively, the second and third generation of the same family to own the hotel. Guests this year were 'enchanted' by the drive through the grounds to the Italianate property's entrance – 'a delightful introduction'. Lazy days are encouraged: the dusky-rose-coloured drawing room filled with flowers, books and sink-into sofas; activities include croquet, afternoon tea on the 'huge terrace looking down into the valley to the river' and fishing on the Usk. The period country house style extends to the bedrooms, some with a Delft-tiled fireplace, canopied four-poster or a balcony. 'Our large, comfortable bed had excellent linen,' reports a Guide regular in 2018. Staff are 'very friendly and efficient'. In the 'first-class' dining room, Karl Cheetham uses seasonal, local and home-grown produce for his 'imaginative' modern Welsh menu. 'Each high-quality dish was a work of art.' Other guests, however, thought it 'too elaborate'. The 'extensive breakfast was presented with all the artistry of a master chef'. (Roy Coates, Max Lickfold, M and PB, and others)

Gliffaes Road
Crickhowell
NP8 1RH

T: 01874 730371
E: calls@gliffaes.com
W: www.gliffaeshotel.com

BEDROOMS: 23. 4 in cottage, 1 on ground floor suitable for disabled.
OPEN: all year except Jan and New Year.
FACILITIES: 2 sitting rooms, conservatory, bar, dining room, free Wi-Fi, in-room TV, civil wedding licence, 33-acre garden (tennis, croquet, private stretch of the River Usk for fly-fishing).
BACKGROUND MUSIC: in bar in evening.
LOCATION: 3 miles W of Crickhowell.
CHILDREN: all ages welcomed.
DOGS: not allowed indoors (free kennels available).
CREDIT CARDS: all major cards.
PRICES: [2018] per room B&B single £135–£173, double £145–£308, D,B&B double £266–£386. À la carte £40. 1-night bookings refused high-season weekends.

DOLFOR Powys

THE OLD VICARAGE

Amid sheep-dotted fields, this red brick Victorian vicarage is run as a 'heart-warming' rural guest house. Owners Helen and Tim Withers are liked for their 'friendly efficiency' and 'dedication to quality'. They are 'equally dedicated' to sustainability, with solar panels, an electric car charging connection, chickens running round the garden and a potager. The cosy bedrooms, named after nearby rivers, have a charming country style, with woollen blankets, a comfortable bed and sweeping views; one might have a fireplace and a roll-top bath, another toile de Jouy wallpaper and sloping ceiling. Travelling with family? Spacious Severn has two comfy rooms. Cold plates and evening meals, served by arrangement, are put together by Tim Withers (special preferences are discussed at booking). This simple, home-cooked fare might include gratin of chicken Savoyarde, crushed potatoes, green beans; home-made ice cream. Breakfast delivers garden-fresh eggs, traditionally cured kippers, organic sausages, Welsh laver bread; a help-yourself buffet of thick yogurt, home-made preserves, cereals. Afterwards, nearby Newtown, dating back to the 13th century, deserves exploration. (JVdB, and others)

Dolfor
SY16 4BN

T: 01686 629051
E: mail@theoldvicaragedolfor.co.uk
W: www.theoldvicaragedolfor.co.uk

BEDROOMS: 4.
OPEN: all year except last 3 weeks Dec, dining room closed Sun.
FACILITIES: drawing room, dining room, free Wi-Fi, in-room TV (Freeview), 1½-acre garden, unsuitable for disabled.
BACKGROUND MUSIC: none.
LOCATION: 3 miles S of Newtown.
CHILDREN: all ages welcomed, under-2s free.
DOGS: not allowed.
CREDIT CARDS: all major cards.
PRICES: [2018] per room B&B single £70–£90, double £95–£120, D,B&B double £145–£170. Set dinner £25. 1-night bookings sometimes refused bank holidays.

DOLGELLAU Gwynedd

Map 3:B3

FFYNNON

'Intimate and eccentric', this one-time cottage hospital on a 'testing' country lane has been converted into a 'stylish' rural guest house at the foot of Cadair Idris. 'Angela and Bernhard Lanz are all-rounders who run the show with aplomb.' An ideal place for walkers, it offers numerous spots to unwind after a day's tramp in surrounding Snowdonia national park: an outdoor hot tub; comfy sofas in the book-strewn lounge with its piano and honesty bar (local beers, snacks). Bedrooms are 'imaginatively themed' (one all pink, another like the set of 'The Mikado'), with views across the valley or landscaped gardens; one spacious bathroom has a spectacular stand-alone bath and separate shower. 'Our bedroom was a joy to loll about in; the comfy bed, pillow menu and utter silence all but guaranteed a good night.' Come dinnertime, Bernhard Lanz's contemporary Welsh food 'modernly presented' is served in a 'handsome' dining room. 'The daily-changing menu (five nights a week) is outstanding – and so is the service.' A typical meal: pan-seared sea bass; honey-glazed banana, chocolate ice cream. Breakfast is 'just as good'. (S and TT)

Love Lane
Dolgellau
LL40 1RR

T: 01341 421774
E: info@ffynnontownhouse.com
W: www.ffynnontownhouse.com

BEDROOMS: 6.
OPEN: all year except Christmas, restaurant closed Tues/Wed in low season.
FACILITIES: sitting room, dining room, study/hall, butler's pantry, free Wi-Fi, in-room TV (Freeview), 'reasonably sized' garden (secluded outdoor hot tub), parking, unsuitable for disabled.
BACKGROUND MUSIC: all day in sitting room and dining room.
LOCATION: town centre.
CHILDREN: all ages welcomed.
DOGS: not allowed.
CREDIT CARDS: MasterCard, Visa.
PRICES: [2018] per room B&B single £110–£160, double £160–£220. Set dinner £30–£50, à la carte £35. 2-night min. stay at weekends and bank holidays.

SEE ALSO SHORTLIST

DOLYDD Gwynedd

Map 3:A3

Y GOEDEN EIRIN

Expect a thoroughly 'warm' 'croeso' at Eluned
Rowlands's B&B on the edge of Snowdonia.
Welsh is the lingua franca of this converted
cowshed, which is imbued with local culture and
heritage. Indeed, the name, Y Goeden Eirin,
meaning The Plum Tree (several grow in the
grounds), was inspired by the writings of friend
and author, John Gwilym Jones. A portrait of
Jones by artist Sir Kyffin Williams hangs in
the dining room, alongside a traditional Welsh
dresser and local slate floors. There's a strong
sustainability ethos too, notes a regular Guide
reader, with in-room recycling instructions,
solar panels, and a kitchen 'committed to local
produce, including vegetables and herbs from
the garden'. An 'extensive' breakfast menu has
freshly squeezed orange juice, and dishes cooked
to order including locally cured bacon, sausages,
black pudding, lamb's kidneys, free-range eggs,
tomato, mushrooms. The bedrooms have views
of Snowdonia or the Menai estuary, 'and prints
of real artistic merit, including some by Henry
Moore'. 'I dreamt of the haunting mountain
views, and of the stars I had seen before drawing
the blind over the large skylight above the bed.'
(S and TT)

Dolydd
LL54 7EF

T: 01286 830942
E: eluned.rowlands@tiscali.co.uk
W: www.ygoedeneirin.co.uk

BEDROOMS: 3. 2 in annexe 3 yds from
house.
OPEN: all year except Christmas/
New Year.
FACILITIES: breakfast room, lounge,
free Wi-Fi, in-room TV (Freeview),
20-acre pastureland, electric car
charging point.
BACKGROUND MUSIC: none.
LOCATION: 3 miles S of Caernarfon.
CHILDREN: not under 12.
DOGS: by prior arrangement only –
ring to discuss.
CREDIT CARDS: none, cash or cheque
payment requested on arrival.
PRICES: [2018] per room B&B single
£65, double £90–£100.

EGLWYSWRW Pembrokeshire   Map 3:D2

AEL Y BRYN

♔ Previous César winner

'Ten gold stars' glitter among a constellation
of guests' praise this year for the 'wonderful'
B&B with its 'aura of tranquillity' and views
over the Preseli hills. Hosts Robert Smith and
Arwel Hughes, 'a well-oiled machine', provide a
'gracious welcome', 'help with luggage' and 'an
interesting tour on arrival' along with 'thoughtful
touches from breakfast menu cards to daily fresh
milk in the room'. Beds are 'divine', bedrooms
'palatial', 'tasteful' and 'comfort personified'; 'our
super, spacious room came with an extra-generous
supply of toiletries and good storage'. Satisfaction
extends to the 'magnificent gardens with
sheltered seating, good plantings, sculptures and
views.' There are 'first-class' breakfasts, 'superb,
well-prepared' evening dishes, perhaps pork
tenderloin with Calvados sauce and hazelnuts,
and 'magnificent masterpiece puddings'. The
unlicensed restaurant doesn't charge for corkage,
either; 'it was like going to a friend's house, such
was the hospitality'. 'We found total peace,'
says one reader, 'only birdsong outside and
gentle classical music within.' (Susan and Colin
Raymond, Dorothy Latham, Margaret Sawyer,
Mabel Tannahill, and many others)

25% DISCOUNT VOUCHERS

Eglwyswrw
SA41 3UL

T: 01239 891411
E: stay@aelybrynpembrokeshire.
co.uk
W: www.aelybrynpembrokeshire.
co.uk

BEDROOMS: 4. All on ground floor.
OPEN: all year except Christmas/
New Year.
FACILITIES: library, music room,
dining room, conservatory
(telescope), free Wi-Fi, in-room
TV (Freeview), courtyard, 2½-acre
garden (wildlife pond, stream,
bowls court).
BACKGROUND MUSIC: occasionally in
music room in evening.
LOCATION: ½ mile N of Eglwyswrw.
CHILDREN: not under 14.
DOGS: not allowed.
CREDIT CARDS: all major cards.
PRICES: [2018] per room B&B
£105–£140. Set dinner £25–£29.

FELIN FACH Powys

Map 3:D4

THE FELIN FACH GRIFFIN

♻ Previous César winner

'Our puppy absolutely loved the place!' writes a reader, of this dining pub in a hamlet between the Brecon Beacons and the Black mountains. One of a trio owned by brothers Charles and Edmund Inkin (see Old Coastguard and Gurnard's Head), it is also popular with pet owners, who describe it as 'truly wonderful' with a 'happy-making atmosphere'. Shabby-chic style runs through the dining areas (the bar, tack room, library and Aga room), but each has its own atmosphere, perhaps a log fire. The welcome extends to locals after a drink, to children, cats and dogs, with resident hounds Max and Lottie usually up for some fun. Bedrooms vary in size but all have a comfortable bed, filter coffee, real milk, shortbread, magazines, flowers, no television (by design) but a Roberts radio, a bathroom with shower. The 'really good' food has a similarly deceptive simplicity, showcasing local ingredients in such dishes as lamb breast, white bean mash, salsa verde, sweetbreads; cod, creamed leeks, crab, cauliflower, Lilliput capers. Breakfast brings soda bread, fruit from the kitchen garden, a 'full Borders'. (Sara Hollowell, Chris Savory)

25% DISCOUNT VOUCHERS

Felin Fach
LD3 0UB

T: 01874 620111
E: enquiries@felinfachgriffin.co.uk
W: www.felinfachgriffin.co.uk

BEDROOMS: 7.
OPEN: all year except 24/25 Dec.
FACILITIES: bar area, dining room, breakfast room, private dining room, free Wi-Fi, limited mobile phone signal, 3-acre garden (stream, kitchen garden, alfresco dining), bar/dining room wheelchair accessible.
BACKGROUND MUSIC: Radio 4 at breakfast, 'selected music' afternoon and evening, in bar and restaurant.
LOCATION: 4 miles NE of Brecon, in village on A470.
CHILDREN: all ages welcomed.
DOGS: allowed in bedrooms (not on bed), in bar and tack room, but not in restaurant (no additional charge), bowls, towels, dog biscuits supplied.
CREDIT CARDS: Diners, MasterCard, Visa.
PRICES: [2018] per room B&B £135–£175, D,B&B £192–£232. À la carte £33, set supper £29.

FISHGUARD Pembrokeshire

Map 3:D1

THE MANOR TOWN HOUSE

The Pembrokeshire Coastal Path runs through the valley below the rear garden terrace of Helen and Chris Sheldon's Georgian town house in this market town between the Preseli hills and the cliffs of Strumble Head. Behind a street front painted a pale pastel blue, two elegant lounges showcase the works of Welsh artists and photographers. The bedrooms – four with sea view, two with town view, some with original fireplace – are individually styled. Comfortable beds are king-size or super-king-size – except, in the 'single' room, which has a double. Guests can take afternoon tea with home-baked cakes by a log fire – or alfresco when the sun shines, gazing out over Cardigan Bay. Those fancying something stronger can choose from the wine list, or help themselves to a beer or spirits from the honesty bar. At breakfast there are organic free-range eggs, free-range bacon, locally made bread and pastries, a cooked daily special. Packed lunches to order, a laundry service and drying facilities are provided. Bike hire can be arranged, and the owners will advise on where to eat out. More reports, please.

11 Main Street
Fishguard
SA65 9HG

T: 01348 873260
E: info@manortownhouse.com
W: www.manortownhouse.com

BEDROOMS: 6.
OPEN: all year except 23–28 Dec.
FACILITIES: 2 lounges, breakfast room, free Wi-Fi, in-room TV (Freeview), small walled garden, unsuitable for disabled.
BACKGROUND MUSIC: classical in breakfast room.
LOCATION: town centre.
CHILDREN: all ages welcomed.
DOGS: not allowed.
CREDIT CARDS: MasterCard, Visa.
PRICES: [2018] per room B&B single £75–£95, double £85–£130. 1-night bookings sometimes refused peak weekends.

GLYNARTHEN Ceredigion

PENBONTBREN

♦ Previous César winner

Surrounded by rolling countryside, yet just a hill away from the sea, this 'first-rate' former Victorian farm B&B 'is a very special place set in beautiful grounds'. Returning Guide readers this year found everything 'just as wonderful as before'. 'Enthusiastic' Richard Morgan-Price and Huw Thomas are 'charming hosts'. A series of converted outbuildings houses 'magnificently equipped' suites. Each different, they have a homely separate sitting area, Welsh woollens, fresh daily milk and Welsh cakes on the hospitality tray, extra reading lamps. 'It was so relaxing sitting on our private patio with a glass of wine, enjoying the delightful views.' A new garden room, slightly smaller than the suites, has its own pergola. The hosts have 'excellent' dining recommendations (and 'Richard is always keen to hear' reports afterwards), but readers found 'the splendid farm shop at the end of the lane, and the well-stocked kitchen had everything we needed – and staff looked after the washing-up next morning'. Richard Morgan-Price's 'plentiful, freshly cooked breakfast is served by very friendly staff with fresh linen on the tables and beautiful chinaware'. (Janet Allom, and others)

Glynarthen
SA44 6PE

T: 01239 810248
E: contact@penbontbren.com
W: www.penbontbren.com

BEDROOMS: 6. 5 in annexe, 1 in garden, 3 on ground floor, 1 family suite, 1 suitable for disabled.
OPEN: all year except Christmas.
FACILITIES: breakfast room (wheelchair accessible), free Wi-Fi, in-room TV (Freeview), 7-acre grounds.
BACKGROUND MUSIC: none.
LOCATION: 5 miles N of Newcastle Emlyn.
CHILDREN: all ages welcomed.
DOGS: allowed in some bedrooms, not in breakfast room.
CREDIT CARDS: MasterCard, Visa.
PRICES: [2018] per room B&B £95–£130. 1-night bookings sometimes refused weekends.

HARLECH Gwynedd

CASTLE COTTAGE

On 'one of the steepest, narrowest streets' in a 'town of sudden vistas', just above the castle, this restaurant-with-rooms has been run by chef/patron Glyn Roberts and his wife, Jacqueline, since 1989. Guide inspectors were this year 'warmly greeted' by Mr Roberts, who carried their bags up to a bedroom with 'comfort as well as charm'. There was fresh milk, 'an imaginative hospitality tray', all manner of teas, good biscuits. 'The bed was large and comfortable; in the bathroom was everything we needed.' Most rooms, in the 400-year-old main building and its next-door contemporary (a former inn), have a low ceiling, exposed beams. All have modern furnishings, some a view of sea or mountains. The food is the highlight, however; fortunately, the bar's 'intrusive background music' was more muted in the restaurant. A regularly changing, locally sourced menu features such dishes as roasted rack of Welsh lamb with herb crust, rosemary and garlic mash, buttered carrots, red wine jus. A wild mushroom risotto, and sea bass with prawns, were 'subtly delicious'. A breakfast of 'home-mixed muesli and Manx kippers' was equally 'outstanding'. Be aware that check-out is by 10.30 am.

25% DISCOUNT VOUCHERS

Y Llech
Harlech
LL46 2YL

T: 01766 780479
E: glyn@castlecottageharlech.co.uk
W: www.castlecottageharlech.co.uk

BEDROOMS: 7. 4 in annexe, 2 on ground floor.
OPEN: all year except 3 weeks Nov, Christmas and New Year, restaurant closed Sun–Wed in winter months, Sun–Tues in summer.
FACILITIES: bar/lounge, restaurant, free Wi-Fi, in-room TV (Freeview), unsuitable for disabled.
BACKGROUND MUSIC: in bar and restaurant at mealtimes.
LOCATION: town centre.
CHILDREN: all ages welcomed.
DOGS: not allowed.
CREDIT CARDS: MasterCard, Visa.
PRICES: [2018] per room B&B single £85–£125, double £130–£175. Set menus £39–£42, tasting menu £45.

LAMPETER Ceredigion

THE FALCONDALE

Surrounded by 'handsome' gardens bursting with rhododendrons, this 'striking' Italianate villa is a peaceful spot in an idyllic setting. 'Top-notch hosts' Chris and Lisa Sutton give visitors – and their dogs – 'such a nice welcome'. Some guests this year were 'delighted by this small hotel' where 'classically styled' bedrooms, varying in size, overlook the garden, valley or woodland; the best have a Juliet balcony. Other regular readers, however, found the 'room facilities basic', particularly the bathroom, 'though the lovely grounds and friendly staff fully lived up to our expectations'. The 'spacious, traditional' public rooms have log fires; the conservatory a cosy spot for dogs to curl up after long walks. In the restaurant, where tables by tall windows enjoy widescreen views across the Teifi valley, new chef Tony Schum showcases seasonal Ceredigion produce, perhaps duck, braised red cabbage, fondant potato, confit carrot. At breakfast, 'interesting' cooked options include bacon, cockles, laver bread or mushroom fricassée, poached egg on toast, a full Welsh: all solid foundations for a day exploring the grounds and riverside market town, just a mile away. (LL, and others)

25% DISCOUNT VOUCHERS

Falcondale Drive
Lampeter
SA48 7RX

T: 01570 422910
E: info@thefalcondale.co.uk
W: www.thefalcondale.co.uk

BEDROOMS: 17.
OPEN: all year.
FACILITIES: lift (does not access all bedrooms), bar, 3 lounges, conservatory, restaurant, free Wi-Fi, in-room TV (Freeview), civil wedding licence, beauty treatment room, terrace, 14-acre grounds (lawns, woodland), restaurant and ground floor wheelchair accessible with adapted toilet.
BACKGROUND MUSIC: in restaurant and lounges.
LOCATION: 1 mile N of Lampeter.
CHILDREN: all ages welcomed.
DOGS: allowed (£10 per night), not in main dining room.
CREDIT CARDS: MasterCard, Visa.
PRICES: [2018] per room B&B £100–£205, D,B&B (min. 2 nights) £170–£295. À la carte £45.

LLANDRILLO Denbighshire   Map 3:B4

TYDDYN LLAN

'One comes for the food, and it doesn't disappoint,' reports a trusted Guide reader after a 2018 visit to Susan and Bryan Webb's Michelin-starred restaurant-with-rooms in a 'peaceful, rural location'. The 'main event' is served in dining rooms 'where an air of quiet calm prevails' with Bryan Webb's menus exploiting seasonal Welsh produce, perhaps loin of venison with goat's cheese gnocchi, port and elderberry sauce. 'We had two excellent meals. Nothing complicated or pretentious. Turbot on leek risotto with red wine sauce was delicious and, at £55 for two courses, the meal was not overpriced.' Service is 'professional, friendly'. The other part of Tyddyn Llan's formula is its 'tastefully decorated, well-furnished, comfortable rooms' with 'uplifting' contemporary hues and a 'decent bathroom', slightly let down by 'captive coat hangers' and 'poor bedside lights'. Small niggles, however. Tyddyn Llan is run with aplomb by Susan Webb. 'Madame is constantly watchful, ensuring everything is as it should be while giving guests her undivided attention. This is the French model, and a very good one.' Breakfast with 'decent' coffee and 'everything freshly cooked' is 'fine'. (David Hampshire, and others)

Llandrillo
LL21 0ST

T: 01490 440264
E: info@tyddynllan.co.uk
W: www.tyddynllan.co.uk

BEDROOMS: 13. 3 with separate entrance, 1, on ground floor (garden suite), suitable for disabled.
OPEN: all year except Mon, Tues and last 2 weeks Jan, restaurant closed Wed/Thurs lunch.
FACILITIES: 2 lounges, bar, 2 dining rooms, free Wi-Fi, in-room TV (Freeview), civil wedding licence, 3-acre garden.
BACKGROUND MUSIC: none.
LOCATION: 5 miles SW of Corwen.
CHILDREN: all ages welcomed.
DOGS: allowed in some bedrooms (£10 per night), not in public rooms.
CREDIT CARDS: Amex, MasterCard, Visa.
PRICES: [2018] per room B&B £180–£250, D,B&B £320–£430. Set dinner £65, tasting menus £75–£90 (plus optional 10% service on food and drink charges). 1-night bookings refused at Christmas.

LLANDUDNO Conwy

Map 3:A3

BODYSGALLEN HALL AND SPA

'Without exception the house and its antique contents are fabulous; it's an absolute gem,' wrote a long-term Guide reader after visiting the National Trust hotel overlooking Snowdonia. The Grade I listed mansion 'is furnished in suitably grand style', reports another, 'with staff in plaid waistcoats carrying your bags and bringing the tea'. Grand indeed. The panelled drawing room has two fireplaces, the 13th-century tower a spiral staircase, the magnificent grounds an acclaimed 17th-century parterre. 'Our huge suite had a very comfortable bed, high-quality linen, good, unobtrusive lighting, and leaded windows that opened easily. Everything was done with style and taste.' No tea-making facilities here; 'A gentleman delivers a proper brew when you require it.' Staff are widely praised – 'one feels welcome' – particularly the waitresses and 'charming, helpful' maître d', a hotel veteran of 37 years. Dining produced less unanimity, however. One reader found the food 'excellent', particularly a specially requested dover sole Véronique; another thought Chef John Williams's modern classics too fussy, 'a misguided desire to show creativity'. Breakfast was 'passable'. Overall, 'we'd return, it's a lovely place to stay'. (David Hampshire, Ralph Wilson)

The Royal Welsh Way
Llandudno
LL30 1RS

T: 01492 584466
E: info@bodysgallen.com
W: www.bodysgallen.com

BEDROOMS: 31. 16 in cottages, 1 suitable for disabled.
OPEN: all year, restaurant closed Mon and Tues lunch.
FACILITIES: hall, drawing room, library, bar, dining room, free Wi-Fi, in-room TV (Sky, Freeview), civil wedding licence, 220-acre park (gardens, tennis, croquet), spa (16-metre swimming pool).
BACKGROUND MUSIC: none.
LOCATION: 2 miles S of Llandudno and Conwy.
CHILDREN: no under-6s in hotel, or under-8s in spa.
DOGS: not allowed.
CREDIT CARDS: Amex, MasterCard, Visa.
PRICES: [2018] per room B&B single £170–£410, double £190–£470, D,B&B double £354–£634. À la carte £60. 1-night bookings sometimes refused.

SEE ALSO SHORTLIST

LLANDUDNO Conwy

OSBORNE HOUSE

Blond sofas, fluted pillars, chandeliers, paintings, oriental rugs, gilded mirrors… Opulence abounds in this bay-fronted Victorian former gentleman's residence on the prom. Owned by the Maddocks and Waddy families, it displays the high style of the 1850s, when the resort first boomed. The 'rooms' are suites, no less, with a separate sitting room, lavishly appointed and so reasonably priced. They have, variously, a four-poster bed with diaphanous drapes, antiques, original working gas fireplace and marble fire surround. Each room has a marble bathroom with a cast iron bath and walk-in shower. 'Beautifully furnished,' say our readers, and 'very atmospheric'. There is no lift, so the fourth-floor attic room is not for everyone. Second-floor rooms have the best views. Food is served all day in the bistro, from the continental breakfast, through brunch (maybe omelette and hash browns; eggs Benedict with smoked salmon), to lobster roll with sweet-potato fries, burgers, steaks, cod and chips and more. There are unchanging specials – Thursday, navarin of lamb, Friday, fish crumble… As a bonus, guests have the use of the spa at big-sister hotel the Empire, round the corner.

17 North Parade
Llandudno
LL30 2LP

T: 01492 860330
E: sales@osbornehouse.com
W: www.osbornehouse.co.uk

BEDROOMS: 7.
OPEN: all year, except 16–28 Dec.
FACILITIES: sitting room, bar, café/bistro, small patio, in-room TV (terrestrial), free Wi-Fi, unsuitable for disabled.
BACKGROUND MUSIC: in public rooms.
LOCATION: on promenade.
CHILDREN: not under 14.
DOGS: not allowed (except guide dogs, 'welcome in suites and café').
CREDIT CARDS: Amex, MasterCard, Visa.
PRICES: [2018] per room B&B £135–£185, D,B&B £160–£215. À la carte £25. 1-night bookings refused weekends.

SEE ALSO SHORTLIST

LLANGAMMARCH WELLS Powys   Map 3:D3

THE LAKE

Cocooned in 'lovely, peaceful grounds in glorious countryside', Jean-Pierre Mifsud's 'welcoming' Victorian country house hotel continues to offer an enjoyable bucolic break. In 2018, readers highlighted the 'pleasant service, and staff who could not have been more friendly and enthusiastic', although a 'little more professionalism wouldn't go amiss' (no help was offered with luggage, turn-down missed). Rooms with 'typical country house furnishings' were 'spacious and attractively decorated', with 'lovely views and large fluffy towels'; less popular was the 'disappointing polyester duvet'. The spa was 'very good with a large pool' and, should you venture outside in your robe, the extra health dividend of a sometimes bracing stroll to its door. New chef Mike Evans's contemporary Celtic cuisine, served among gilt-framed portraits and sash curtains, includes such dishes as rump of Welsh lamb, dauphinoise potatoes, creamed leeks, carrots and jus. 'It's good, accurately cooked fish and meat', if sometimes a little 'overcomplicated'. Breakfast could have laid deeper foundations 'but at least we had plenty of tea'. Northcote Manor, Burrington, Devon (see Shortlist), is under the same ownership. (David Hampshire, and others)

Llangammarch Wells
LD4 4BS

T: 01591 620202
E: info@lakecountryhouse.co.uk
W: www.lakecountryhouse.co.uk

BEDROOMS: 32. 12 suites in adjacent lodge, 7 on ground floor, 1 suitable for disabled.
OPEN: all year except 24–26 Dec.
FACILITIES: lounge, bar, restaurant, breakfast room, free Wi-Fi, in-room TV (Freeview), spa (15-metre swimming pool, restricted hours for under-16s, no under-8s), civil wedding licence, 50-acre grounds (tennis, trout lake, 9-hole, par-3 golf course).
BACKGROUND MUSIC: none.
LOCATION: 8 miles SW of Builth Wells.
CHILDREN: all ages welcomed, no under-8s in spa.
DOGS: allowed (£15 charge per dog), not in main lounge or dining room.
CREDIT CARDS: Amex, MasterCard, Visa.
PRICES: per room B&B £205–£260, D,B&B (min. 2 nights) £245–£340. Set dinner £45.

LLANTHONY Monmouthshire   Map 3:D4

LLANTHONY PRIORY HOTEL

Ecclesiastical historians rejoice! In the 'romantic' setting of a vertiginous valley beneath the Black mountains, this 'atmospheric' small hotel partly occupies an ivy-clad medieval tower. It is one of four Grade 1 listed buildings in the ruined priory's precincts. Until recently, the rooms that housed 12th-century Augustinian monks remained a 'fairly hairshirt' prospect. 'Dark and cold, with rickety furniture wobbling on uneven floors.' Now, thank heavens, a decent facelift. 'Bedrooms have been refurbished in a tasteful and restful way. They are minimal, not minimalist, in a style appropriate to the ancient buildings; they have a comfortable bed and good bedding, a chair, dressing table, good bedside lights and little else. No knick-knacks.' Tower shower rooms still require an ascent or descent of the spiral staircase. Dinner, served in the vaulted crypt by the log fire, is for trenchermen not gourmands, perhaps Abbot's Casserole – beef in wine, tomato and chestnut sauce; Brother James Pork – tenderloin simmered in apple, cider and cranberry. Numerous opportunities to walk it off include nearby Offa's Dyke, and the opposite hillside from where JMW Turner once painted the skeletal ruins. (AT, IB)

Llanthony
NP7 7NN

T: 01873 890487
E: llanthonypriory@btconnect.
   com
W: www.llanthonyprioryhotel.
   co.uk

BEDROOMS: 7. All with shared showers/bathrooms.
OPEN: Fri–Sun (Nov–Mar), Tues–Sun (Apr–Oct), 27 Dec–1 Jan, closed Mon except bank holidays.
FACILITIES: lounge, bar, dining room, no Wi-Fi or TV, extensive grounds (including priory ruins), unsuitable for disabled.
BACKGROUND MUSIC: none.
LOCATION: 10 miles N of Abergavenny.
CHILDREN: not under 5.
DOGS: not allowed.
CREDIT CARDS: Mastercard, Visa.
PRICES: [2018] per room B&B single £75–£80, double £95–£100.

LLYSWEN Powys

Map 3:D4

LLANGOED HALL

A romantic Jacobean mansion, first opened as a hotel in 1990 by the late Sir Bernard Ashley, remains home to his 'fabulous collection of paintings, sculptures and antiques'. The Hall was remodelled by Clough Williams Ellis for a London bowler-hat maker in around 1913, and has the feel of a 'luxurious' Edwardian country house, with 'open fires, squashy sofas, fresh flowers'; in the bedrooms a decanter of sherry, bowl of fruit, mineral water. Manager Calum Milne oversees the 'impeccable' staff. 'Everyone addressed us by name.' Even the most affordable rooms are large, well equipped and furnished, with bath and separate shower. Some of the more expensive have a four-poster. Wake-up calls, if requested, come with tea or coffee and newspaper. Chef Nick Brodie uses produce from the organic kitchen garden, greenhouse and smokehouse, eggs from the ducks, hens and quail. His fixed-price, daily-changing dinner menu includes such dishes as Welsh lamb loin, parmesan risotto, roast baby onion, chanterelles – and always a vegetarian option. Acclaimed afternoon teas include the Laura Ashley with elderflower champagne. The 'tranquil' grounds, leading to the River Wye, are 'filled with birdsong'.

Llyswen
LD3 0YP

T: 01874 754525
E: reception@llangoedhall.com
W: www.llangoedhall.com

BEDROOMS: 23.
OPEN: all year.
FACILITIES: great hall, morning room, library, bar/lounge, restaurant, billiard room, function rooms, free Wi-Fi, in-room TV (Freeview), civil wedding licence, 17-acre gardens and parkland, unsuitable for disabled.
BACKGROUND MUSIC: during functions. Pianist on special occasions.
LOCATION: 12 miles NE of Brecon.
CHILDREN: all ages welcomed.
DOGS: allowed in bedrooms with £120 professional allergy clean, not in public rooms, heated kennels (no charge) available.
CREDIT CARDS: Amex, MasterCard, Visa.
PRICES: [2018] per room B&B £150–£450. D,B&B £250–£550. Three-course dinner £55, eight-course tasting menu £110 (two weeks' notice required).

NARBERTH Pembrokeshire

Map 3:D2

THE GROVE

♧ Previous César winner

Behind mature trees in 26 acres of gardens and meadows overlooking the Preseli hills, this whitewashed 18th-century mansion offers a 'bucolic setting with that "away from it all" feeling', reports a reader after this year's visit. Rooms, some in the main house, others in nearby cottages, range from contemporary rustic – stand-alone baths, tastefully neutral hues – to warmly traditional. 'Everything was harmonious and pleasing to the eye, the bedroom restful and well appointed.' It was also slightly overheated: 'If staying longer I'd have requested a lighter duvet or sheet and blanket.' Neil and Zoë Kedward's hotel is about eating as well as sleeping. Chef Allister Barsby's 'accomplished food showed flashes of imagination with unusual but successful flavour combinations' – perhaps salt cod, braised lettuce, tomato, tempura anchovy, shallot and bacon sauce. The wine list is 'strong if somewhat pricey'. Afternoon tea is served in one of the handsome lounges, cocktails are in the candlelit bar. Breakfast was 'wonderful and varied'. 'I had some of the best eggs Benedict I can recall; the sourdough pancakes with blueberries were a delight.' (Sara Hollowell, PJ)

25% DISCOUNT VOUCHERS

Molleston
Narberth
SA67 8BX

T: 01834 860915
E: reservations@grovenarberth.co.uk
W: www.thegrove-narberth.co.uk

BEDROOMS: 26. 12 in cottages in the grounds, some on ground floor, 1 suitable for disabled.
OPEN: all year.
FACILITIES: 3 lounges, bar, 3 restaurant rooms, free Wi-Fi, in-room TV (Sky), in-room spa treatments, civil wedding licence, 26-acre grounds, boules, croquet, ground floor wheelchair accessible.
BACKGROUND MUSIC: in public areas.
LOCATION: 1 mile S of Narberth.
CHILDREN: all ages welcomed.
DOGS: allowed in some bedrooms and lounge, towels, blankets, treats.
CREDIT CARDS: Amex, MasterCard, Visa.
PRICES: [2018] per room B&B £240–£650, D,B&B £368–£778. Tasting menu £94, à la carte £69. 1-night bookings refused during festive season.

SEE ALSO SHORTLIST

NEWPORT Pembrokeshire

Map 3:D1

CNAPAN

Friendly and welcoming as ever, this B&B is
run by second-generation owners Michael and
Judith Cooper, and their son, Oliver. Launched
in 1984 with Judith's late parents, Cnapan has
featured in the Guide for more than 30 years.
The pretty, Grade II late Georgian house in
a conservation area is a great base for those
wanting to explore the Preseli hills, to walk the
Pembrokeshire Coastal Path, to spend a day
on nearby sandy beaches, or simply to browse
this small seaside town's shops and galleries.
Bedrooms, some with views of mountain
and Norman castle, are contemporary, 'not
luxurious', 'not huge', but 'fresh and bright',
with original artwork, good toiletries, a
'sparkling bathroom', and wool blankets to go
with a super-king-size bed. While the family
no longer serve dinner, there are good places to
eat out, including Llys Meddyg up the road (see
next entry), pubs, cafés, a seafood restaurant –
the Coopers will happily advise. The feeling is
that of a family home. Guests can also take tea in
the flower-filled garden, while breakfast brings
local produce cooked to order, home-made
marmalade. More reports, please.

East Street
Newport
SA42 0SY

T: 01239 820575
E: enquiry@cnapan.co.uk
W: www.cnapan.co.uk

BEDROOMS: 5. Plus self-catering
cottage.
OPEN: all year except a few days over
Christmas and Feb.
FACILITIES: sitting room, bar,
restaurant (for parties of 20 or
more), free Wi-Fi, in-room TV
(Freeview), small garden, restaurant
wheelchair accessible.
BACKGROUND MUSIC: none.
LOCATION: town centre.
CHILDREN: all ages welcomed.
DOGS: not allowed.
CREDIT CARDS: MasterCard, Visa.
PRICES: [2018] per room B&B single
£75, double £98. 1-night bookings
sometimes refused at peak times.

NEWPORT Pembrokeshire   Map 3:D1

LLYS MEDDYG

♛ Previous César winner

'The best of its kind.' Standing in an 'appealing' village is Edward and Louise Sykes's small, 'equally professional and personable' Georgian restaurant-with-rooms. It is founded on 'a strong ethos and natural hospitality'. Hot drinks, a crackling fire and easy conversation are hallmarks of the downstairs lounge. The cellar bar and rustic dining room are 'obvious local gathering places', especially at weekends. 'The food was excellent'; 'What punchy flavours, and what well-assembled dishes – pretty without being precious.' Highlighting Welsh produce, Stuart Wills's modern menus pair foraged razor clams with black pudding, home-smoked salmon with pickled sea greens; a 'sweet–tart rhubarb and custard was a prom dress of a dessert'. Later, a cosy night beckons in 'well-organised, comfortable' bedrooms supplied with fresh milk and biscuits 'thick with dark chocolate chips'. (One small niggle: a low bed, 'just inches from the floor'.) A breakfast of 'frothy, freshly squeezed orange juice, cafetière coffee, home-made blueberry jam, a fine crêpe and rich yogurt' sets you up for exploring Pembrokeshire's Coastal Path. (Chris Savory, and others)

25% DISCOUNT VOUCHERS

East Street
Newport
SA42 0SY

T: 01239 820008
E: info@llysmeddyg.com
W: www.llysmeddyg.com

BEDROOMS: 8. 1 on ground floor, 3 in mews annexe, plus a cottage.
OPEN: all year.
FACILITIES: bar, lounge, restaurant, kitchen garden dining area (open in summer holidays), free Wi-Fi, in-room TV (Freeview), civil wedding licence, garden, unsuitable for disabled.
BACKGROUND MUSIC: in bar and dining room.
LOCATION: central.
CHILDREN: all ages welcomed.
DOGS: allowed in 3 annexe bedrooms, bar.
CREDIT CARDS: MasterCard, Visa.
PRICES: [2018] per room B&B single £80–£145, double £100–£160, D,B&B double £150–£220.
À la carte £33.

PENARTH Vale of Glamorgan

Map 3:E4

♔RESTAURANT JAMES SOMMERIN

César award: Welsh restaurant-with-rooms of the year

With a Michelin star and 'spectacular' views of the Severn estuary and famous pier from a prime spot on Penarth's late Victorian esplanade, James Sommerin's family-run restaurant-with-rooms is 'a very pleasant place to stay'. The glass-fronted dining room offers clean contemporary design, with light turquoise leather seating nodding to the sea, and a head-height window allowing glimpses of the kitchen where the acclaimed chef works alongside his daughter, Georgia (James's wife, Louise, runs front-of-house). The locally sourced food is 'terrific', writes a regular reader. 'A fantastic dining experience,' writes another. Dishes garnering praise include wild sea bass, langoustine, ginger, artichoke; partridge, mushroom, vanilla, onion; 32-day-aged sirloin, oxtail, shallot, red wine jus. Upstairs are 'beautifully appointed, very modern' bedrooms; 'extremely comfortable' beds and top-class toiletries. Five rooms have a queen-size bed and 'wonderful views' through floor-to-ceiling windows, although one guest considered them 'slightly basic'. Breakfast includes home-made granola, coffee, eggs all ways. Service was 'excellent and discreet'. 'Wonderful in every aspect.' (Peter Kettell, Catrin Treadwell)

The Esplanade
Penarth
CF64 3AU

T: 02920 706559
E: info@jamessommerinrestaurant.co.uk
W: www.jamessommerinrestaurant.co.uk

BEDROOMS: 9. 1 suitable for disabled.
OPEN: all year except Mon, 24–26 Dec, 1 Jan, restaurant closed 26 Dec, 1 Jan.
FACILITIES: bar, restaurant, private dining room, free Wi-Fi, in-room Smart TV, restaurant and bar wheelchair accessible, adapted toilet.
BACKGROUND MUSIC: in bar and restaurant.
LOCATION: on the esplanade.
CHILDREN: all ages welcomed.
DOGS: not allowed.
CREDIT CARDS: Amex, MasterCard, Visa.
PRICES: [2018] per room B&B £150–£170, D,B&B £240–£260. Tasting menu £65–£95, à la carte £40.

SEE ALSO SHORTLIST

PWLLHELI Gwynedd   Map 3:B2

THE OLD RECTORY

The leafy, flower-lined drive is a colourful welcome to Gary and Lindsay Ashcroft's part-Georgian rectory on the Llyn peninsula. The 'friendly' hosts are especially praised for their 'outstanding attention to detail'. Visitors are greeted with tea in the sitting room, and a crisply burning fire in cold weather; 'special treats' (sherry, chocolate) in the bedrooms; and a menu of aromatherapy massages and beauty treatments that can be arranged. 'They have thought of everything when it comes to visitors' comfort.' In the lounge, antiques, artwork and deep leather sofas invite lazy afternoons, while bedrooms are homely, with broad views across the gardens. The bright dining room, whose elegant period windows catch the morning sun, is the venue for breakfast at a communal table, starting with an 'abundance' of cereals and fresh fruits. Generous cooked dishes are prepared using locally sourced fish and meat, and eggs from free-range hens, served alongside home-made bread and preserves. The well-informed Ashcrofts will 'helpfully' supply a list of nearby restaurants, beaches and myriad local attractions, from golf clubs to boat trips and heritage railway rides. Picnics are a request away.

25% DISCOUNT VOUCHERS

Boduan
Pwllheli
LL53 6DT

T: 01758 721519
E: theashcrofts@theoldrectory.net
W: www.theoldrectory.net

BEDROOMS: 4. Plus a self-catering cottage and lodge.
OPEN: all year except Christmas and New Year.
FACILITIES: drawing room, breakfast/dining room, free Wi-Fi, in-room TV (Freeview), 3-acre grounds, beach hut in season, unsuitable for disabled.
BACKGROUND MUSIC: none.
LOCATION: 4 miles NW of Pwllheli.
CHILDREN: all ages welcomed.
DOGS: only assistance dogs allowed in house (kennel and run available).
CREDIT CARDS: MasterCard, Visa.
PRICES: [2018] per room B&B £100–£120. 1-night bookings refused some weekends, high season and bank holidays.

PWLLHELI Gwynedd

Map 3:B2

PLAS BODEGROES

In a sylvan setting on the remote Lleyn peninsula, Gunna and Chris Chown's Georgian country house has enchanted guests for over 30 years. In 'beautiful, well-maintained gardens', more than 100 varieties of old roses grow, some climbing the iron veranda pillars (romantically, Plas Bodegroes means Rosehip Hall). Bedrooms come in varied shapes, sizes and hues, but all have fresh milk, home-baked biscuits and Egyptian cotton bedlinen, with the option of sheets and blankets or duvet. One in the courtyard annexe was 'large, with king-size bed, coffee table, armchairs', plenty of storage space, and a 'smallish but perfectly formed' bathroom. In a dining room hung with artwork, Hugh Bracegirdle's menus showcase the best of Welsh produce, from Black beef and lamb, from mountain and salt marsh, to free-range pork and chicken, to fruit, vegetables and herbs from the kitchen garden. It's 'verging on fine dining, without the fuss', says one reader. 'We particularly enjoyed pumpkin and sunflower-seed tagliatelle, lemon sole and crab paupiette, shellfish sauce; roast loin of lamb with cutlet mint bonbon.' Mr Chown cooks a 'good breakfast with a wide choice of quality ingredients'. (GC)

Nefyn Road
Pwllheli
LL53 5TH

T: 01758 612363
E: info@bodegroes.co.uk
W: www.bodegroes.co.uk

BEDROOMS: 10. 2 in courtyard cottage.
OPEN: all year except Christmas, 3 Jan–6 Feb, restaurant closed for dinner Sun and Mon.
FACILITIES: lounge, bar, breakfast room, restaurant, free Wi-Fi, in-room TV (Freeview), 5-acre grounds (courtyard garden), unsuitable for disabled.
BACKGROUND MUSIC: none.
LOCATION: 1 mile W of Pwllheli.
CHILDREN: all ages welcomed.
DOGS: allowed in some bedrooms for 'a nominal charge', not in public rooms.
CREDIT CARDS: MasterCard, Visa.
PRICES: [2018] per room B&B single £90–£130, double £110–£150, DB&B double £200–£240. Set dinner £45. 1-night bookings sometimes refused bank holidays.

ST DAVID'S Pembrokeshire

TWR Y FELIN HOTEL   **NEW**

Around a working windmill built in 1806,
a former temperance hotel has had a multi-
million-pound facelift, becoming 'Wales's first
contemporary art hotel'. The architect owner
has lavished 'loving care and attention to detail'
on the redesign, says its nominator this year.
The bedrooms, decorated in shades of chocolate
and white, have a safe, a mini-fridge and
espresso machine, along with robes and slippers,
aromatherapy toiletries. Rooms in the Oriel wing
at ground-floor level have a terrace; those above
have a Juliet balcony. A suite in the windmill
tower has a spiral staircase from the lounge to
the old observatory, with panoramic views of
the St David's peninsula. Overall the style is
'smart city type' with lots of dark wood, perhaps
'slightly incongruous' in Britain's smallest city.
Art, as ever, is personal. The paintings – many
especially created by street artists – were 'not to
my taste'. The entire property is hypoallergenic,
hence a no-dogs policy. In the dining room, chef
Simon Coe's menus showcase local ingredients in
such dishes as lemon sole, cod tortellini, lobster
emulsion, broad bean and samphire. 'Dinner was
excellent, as was breakfast.' (Robert Cooper)

Caerfai Road
St David's
SA62 6QT

T: 01437 725 555
E: stay@twryfelinhotel.com
W: www.twryfelinhotel.com

BEDROOMS: 21. Some on ground
floor, some in separate wing, 1
suitable for disabled.
OPEN: all year.
FACILITIES: bar, restaurant, lounge,
free Wi-Fi, in-room TV (Sky),
landscaped grounds, civil wedding
licence, public areas wheelchair
accessible.
BACKGROUND MUSIC: in public areas.
LOCATION: a few hundred metres
from centre of St David's.
CHILDREN: not under 12.
DOGS: not allowed.
CREDIT CARDS: Amex, MasterCard,
Visa.
PRICES: [2018] per room B&B
£200–£370, D,B&B £270–£430. À la
carte £35. Normally 2-night min.
stay Fri and Sat, but check for one-
night availability.

SEE ALSO SHORTLIST

SAUNDERSFOOT Pembrokeshire

Map 3:D2

ST BRIDES SPA HOTEL

'The physical ambience and sea coast views are wonderful,' write trusted readers, of this spa hotel overlooking bay and village on the Pembrokeshire coast. It is the reinvention of an older hotel, by owners Lindsey and Andrew Evans, with a holiday, leisure vibe, albeit slightly 'impersonal'. From private balcony, restaurant, bar and spa, guests can gaze out over the sands. 'Very stylish' bedrooms have handmade furniture, artwork, a woven throw. 'Fresh milk in a fridge was a nice touch,' another reader notes, advising that a 'better' (medium) room was 'smallish, although with a high-quality bathroom'; 'best' would have been better yet. A note from management warned of a £75 charge if robes and slippers went AWOL. At dinner in the Cliff restaurant, Michael Mathieson's menus showcase local, seasonal produce in such dishes as Atlantic cod poached in olive oil, braised and crispy wild black rice, samphire, Normandy sauce. The wine list is 'extensive and modern'. Breakfast brings 'delicious' sautéed mushroom and laver bread on a toasted muffin; pancakes; smoked haddock, free-range eggs. Staff are 'mostly friendly, efficient' and legion. 'We would return.' (P and SG)

St Brides Hill
Saundersfoot
SA69 9NH

T: 01834 812304
E: reservations@stbridesspahotel.com
W: stbridesspahotel.com

BEDROOMS: 34. 1 suitable for disabled. Plus six 2-bed apartments in grounds, and self-catering apartments in village.
OPEN: all year.
FACILITIES: lift, lounge, bar, restaurant, Gallery dining area, meeting/function rooms, free Wi-Fi, in-room TV (Freeview), civil wedding licence, terraces, art gallery, spa (treatment room, infinity hydro pool).
BACKGROUND MUSIC: all day in public spaces.
LOCATION: 3 mins' walk to village.
CHILDREN: all ages welcomed.
DOGS: allowed in some ground-floor apartments, not in hotel.
CREDIT CARDS: Amex, MasterCard, Visa.
PRICES: [2018] per room B&B £170–£320, D,B&B £200–£340 (at limited times of the year). À la carte £35.

SKENFRITH Monmouthshire   Map 3:D4

THE BELL AT SKENFRITH

'A great base for exploring', Richard Ireton and Sarah Hudson's 'pleasing, white-painted coaching inn' stands overlooking an old stone bridge across the River Monmow, while 'behind it, green hills gently rise'. Popular with walkers and their dogs, it accepts orders for picnic lunches. 'When my friend said she'd have to leave before breakfast, they offered to pack her a smoked salmon sandwich,' a Guide insider reports. A 'large, handsome' top-floor bedroom under the eaves, 'decorated in tranquil shades', had a seating area with sofa and table, 'biscuits, ground coffee, milk in a vacuum flask'. Pricier rooms have, variously, a four-poster, a bath and walk-in shower, a separate sitting room. At night, all are 'countryside silent'. In the dining room, Mr Ireton, 'every inch the jolly innkeeper, toured the tables to chat', as diners addressed themselves to chef Joseph Colman's 'very good, very satisfying' cooking. A typical dish: Brecon lamb rump, olive mash, peas, fine green beans, minted jus. At breakfast there were local yogurts, smoked salmon, 'three kinds of ham', home-made bread (from the inn's new bakery, recently opened) and jam, hot food cooked to order.

Skenfrith
NP7 8UH

T: 01600 750235
E: enquiries@skenfrith.co.uk
W: thebellatskenfrith.co.uk

BEDROOMS: 11.
OPEN: all year.
FACILITIES: bar/sitting room, bar, restaurant, Wine Room (for reading, relaxing, private dining), function facilities, free Wi-Fi, in-room TV (BT, Freeview), 2-acre grounds (terrace, garden), restaurant, bar and terrace wheelchair accessible.
BACKGROUND MUSIC: 'intermittently' in bar and restaurant.
LOCATION: 9 miles W of Ross-on-Wye.
CHILDREN: all ages welcomed.
DOGS: 'well-behaved dogs' allowed in bedrooms and Dog and Boot bar, biscuits, washing facilities, towels.
CREDIT CARDS: MasterCard, Visa.
PRICES: [2018] per room B&B £150–£230, D,B&B £190–£270. À la carte £36. 1-night bookings refused Sat.

TYWYN Gwynedd

Map 3:B3

DOLFFANOG FAWR

With Tal-y-llyn lake practically in the back garden, Cadair Idris behind, and 'some of the finest walks in any national park', Alex Yorke and Lorraine Hinkins's Snowdonia B&B wins praise again this year. The original 18th-century farmhouse has four immaculate guest bedrooms, decorated in contemporary style, with Welsh blankets, L'Occitane toiletries, a shower or a bath with shower over. One dual-aspect room has views towards the lake at the back, and the Dyfi hills to the fore. 'Our well-appointed bedroom had an excellent en suite.' A log-burner blazes in a lounge with squashy leather sofas, maps, books and guides (for anyone devising their own routes, 'Alex's knowledge is invaluable'). On four nights a week, Lorraine cooks a 'four-course, superb-value set dinner' using local produce, perhaps Welsh Black beef, salt marsh lamb, wild sea trout – 'a delight not to be missed'. It is served communally, sociably, round an oak table. Let them know of any special dietary requirements. Breakfast provides 'freshly squeezed orange juice, fresh fruit, home-made granola and preserves, the option of fish if you do not want the traditional Welsh breakfast'. (Bob and Jean Henry)

Tal-y-llyn
Tywyn
LL36 9AJ

T: 01654 761247
E: info@dolffanogfawr.co.uk
W: dolffanogfawr.co.uk

BEDROOMS: 4.
OPEN: Mar–Oct, dinner served Wed–Sat.
FACILITIES: lounge, dining room, free Wi-Fi, in-room TV (Freeview), 1-acre garden (hot tub), unsuitable for disabled.
BACKGROUND MUSIC: none.
LOCATION: by lake, 10 miles E of Tywyn.
CHILDREN: not under 10.
DOGS: allowed by arrangement, in bedrooms (not unattended) and lounge 'if other guests don't mind', not in dining room.
CREDIT CARDS: MasterCard, Visa.
PRICES: [2018] per room B&B single from £90, double £110–£120. À la carte £28 (2% surcharge if paying by credit card). 1-night bookings often refused.

WHITEBROOK Monmouthshire   Map 3:D4

THE WHITEBROOK

Embedded firmly in the Wye valley, Chris and
Kirsty Harrod's Michelin-starred restaurant-
with-rooms again delighted readers' taste buds
in 2018. Once located – 'above a hamlet's single
track road, only signed once you're there' – it
offers guests a fine welcome: 'Lazarus and
his Salvador Dalí moustache greeted us with
enthusiasm, showed us our room and returned
with warm, meltingly delicious Welsh cake.'
'Well-equipped' contemporary bedrooms are
'functional rather than overtly luxurious', with
'good-quality bedding, enormous bath and
walk-in shower, organic toiletries and very good
tea from a Cornish estate'. Chris's cooking,
however, is the true star. The veteran of Le
Manoir aux Quat'Saisons exploits the verdant
locale to forage for ingredients, combining them
with local produce to spectacular effect, perhaps
Huntsham Farm sucking pig, caramelised
celeriac, pear, lamb's sorrel. 'The food is
absolutely delicious, the concepts brilliant. My
wife declared the poached pear with buttermilk,
maritime pine yogurt crumble to be the finest
dessert she'd tasted.' Good food comes with
'knowledgeable, efficient and very entertaining
service: a great meal'. (David Hampshire)

Whitebrook
NP25 4TX

T: 01600 860254
E: info@thewhitebrook.co.uk
W: www.thewhitebrook.co.uk

BEDROOMS: 8.
OPEN: all year, except 24–26 Dec,
1–16 Jan, restaurant closed Mon,
and Tues lunch.
FACILITIES: lounge/bar, restaurant,
business facilities, free Wi-Fi, in-
room TV (Freeview), terrace, 2-acre
garden, River Wye 2 miles (fishing),
restaurant and women's toilet
wheelchair accessible.
BACKGROUND MUSIC: 'chill-out' in
restaurant and lounge.
LOCATION: 6 miles S of Monmouth.
CHILDREN: all ages welcomed, not to
be left unattended in rooms, over-8
only in restaurants on weekdays,
over-16 only at weekends.
DOGS: only guide dogs allowed.
CREDIT CARDS: Amex, MasterCard,
Visa.
PRICES: [2018] per room B&B £130-
£235, D,B&B £240-£399. 7-course
dinner £82, set lunch £39-£59.

CHANNEL ISLANDS

La Corbière lighthouse, Jersey

HERM

THE WHITE HOUSE

Visitors are not spoilt for choice of places to stay on this tiny, car-free island – they're just spoilt at the island's best and only hotel. You let them know the time of your ferry, and they collect your bags by tractor: 'The portage of luggage works well.' The public rooms are well kept and comfortable, with 'cheerful' coal fires lit on cold days. Bedrooms overlook the garden or Channel, or both: 'Ours had large windows, great views of the garden, the pool and the sea to Guernsey.' The young staff are 'excellent, friendly, helpful and well trained'. Complimentary tea and coffee are provided in the lounges, and there is plenty of outdoor seating in sun and shade. Brasserie fare is served in the Ship Inn, while in the Conservatory fine-dining restaurant, there are uninterrupted sea views to complement chef David Hook's imaginative, locally sourced dishes including salt Atlantic cod, scallop mousse, squid ink pasta, hazelnut granola; braised pig's cheeks, pan-fried monkfish, carrot and cardamom mash, star anise jus. Children love the freedom of the island, the bunk beds, the cafés on Shell Beach and Belvoir Bay.

Herm
GY1 3HR

T: 01481 750075
E: hotel@herm.com
W: www.herm.com

BEDROOMS: 40. 23 in cottages, some on ground floor.
OPEN: late Apr–early Nov.
FACILITIES: 3 lounges, 2 bars, 2 restaurants, conference room, free Wi-Fi, 1-acre gardens (tennis, croquet, 7-metre solar-heated swimming pool, beach 200 yds, Herm only reached by boat, 'a challenge' for disabled.
BACKGROUND MUSIC: in the Ship Inn (live music and speakers) and Sunday afternoon tea (harpist).
LOCATION: by harbour, ferry from Guernsey (20 mins).
CHILDREN: all ages welcomed.
DOGS: allowed in 2 bedrooms (£20 per dog per night), reception lounge, garden bars, subject to restrictions.
CREDIT CARDS: MasterCard, Visa.
PRICES: [2018] per person B&B £72–£117, D,B&B £107–£162. Set dinner £35, à la carte £26.

LITTLE SARK Sark

Map 1: inset E6

LA SABLONNERIE

A horse-drawn carriage brings guests to this rose-covered, 16th-century farmhouse on a car-free island. Regular readers described it as 'paradise', following an 'umpteenth visit' this year. The hotel 'turns on the personality of its owner', Elizabeth Perrée, says one who knows it well. 'Elizabeth is as charming and helpful as ever,' says another. By its own admission the hotel occupies 'a time warp of simplicity'. 'Delightful' bedrooms, in main house and surrounding cottages, are quaintly, individually styled. 'The chef continues to delight us with excellent food,' served in the old-fashioned dining room, or alfresco. Typical dishes: roasted scallops with garlic butter; veal with Madeira sauce and wild mushrooms; lobster thermidor. With no TV and limited Wi-Fi, people come to read (and write), to watch the cormorants and puffins, to take sightseeing and fishing boat trips. There is no swimming pool – but no swimming pool could compare with a dip in the Venus rock pool. On a rainy day, 'the staff were very helpful… Not only did they dry our things but also washed and ironed them as appropriate.' (John Barnes, RC)

Little Sark
Sark, via Guernsey
GY10 1SD

T: 01481 832061
E: reservations@sablonneriesark.com
W: www.sablonneriesark.com

BEDROOMS: 22. Some in nearby cottages.
OPEN: mid-Apr–Oct.
FACILITIES: 3 lounges, 2 bars, restaurant, Wi-Fi by arrangement, civil wedding licence, 1-acre garden (tea garden/bar, croquet).
BACKGROUND MUSIC: classical/piano in bar.
LOCATION: Little Sark, via boat from Guernsey (guests will be met at the harbour on arrival).
CHILDREN: all ages welcomed.
DOGS: allowed at hotel's discretion in some bedrooms, not in public rooms.
CREDIT CARDS: MasterCard, Visa.
PRICES: [2018] per person B&B £97–£165, D,B&B £136–£195. Set menus £30, à la carte £50.

ST BRELADE Jersey   Map 1: inset E6

THE ATLANTIC HOTEL

With 'spectacular' views over landscaped
gardens to St Ouen's Bay, Patrick Burke's
upmarket hotel is 'just about perfect for a restful
break'. Founded by Patrick's father, Henry, in
1970, it stands in six acres of grounds beside La
Moye golf course, with five miles of sandy beach
below. The sea-facing bedrooms have Channel
views from full-height windows and balconies,
a marble bathroom, smart contemporary
furnishings and decor. Golf-view rooms,
although similarly 'beautifully appointed', lack
the wow factor of a sea vista. Snacks are served
all day in the lounge and on the terrace while,
in the Ocean restaurant, new chef Will Holland
(who gained a Michelin star in his twenties)
cooks a daily-changing market menu alongside
the à la carte. Typical dishes: pan-fried sea bass,
crab risotto, locally foraged sea vegetables, crispy
shallots, onion oil; roast beef fillet and braised
cheek, bone marrow crust, parsnip purée,
smoked bacon, red wine sauce. A seven-course
gourmet menu, showcasing Jersey produce, is
available in the Tasting Room, opened this year.
'The staff are the hotel's greatest asset,' says a
reader. 'This is what a good hotel should be.'

Le Mont de la Pulente
St Brelade
JE3 8HE

T: 01534 744101
E: info@theatlantichotel.com
W: www.theatlantichotel.com

BEDROOMS: 50. Some on ground
floor.
OPEN: 2 Feb–2 Jan.
FACILITIES: lift, lounge, library,
cocktail bar, restaurant, private
dining room, fitness centre
(swimming pool, sauna, mini-gym),
free Wi-Fi, in-room TV (Sky), civil
wedding licence, 6-acre garden
(tennis, indoor and outdoor heated
swimming pools, 10 by 5 metres),
unsuitable for disabled.
BACKGROUND MUSIC: in restaurant,
lounge and cocktail bar in evenings.
LOCATION: 5 miles W of St Helier.
CHILDREN: all ages welcomed.
DOGS: only assistance dogs allowed.
CREDIT CARDS: all major cards.
PRICES: [2018] per room B&B single
£120–£440, double £140–£460. Set
dinner £50, tasting menu £80, à la
carte £65.

SEE ALSO SHORTLIST

ST PETER Jersey

Map 1: inset E6

GREENHILLS COUNTRY HOTEL & RESTAURANT

Narrow, leafy lanes lead to this 17th-century, pink granite country house, a relatively recent addition to the Seymour Hotels group, a family business approaching its centenary. 'Clearly, a lot of money has been spent on it,' writes a reader, who could find nothing to fault ('which is rare'). The rural setting, the pool, the planters brimming with flowers create a pleasing first impression. It continues in the striking bar with its copper lights, mellow beams and stone walls, and in the cosy lounge with its vintage prints. Resident manager Carmelita Fernandes and her 'personable, attentive' staff are warmly welcoming. Bedrooms, refurbished in contemporary style, have home-baked biscuits, mineral water, bathrobes, good toiletries. Superior rooms, with French doors opening to garden and pool, offer a seating area, espresso machine, bath and walk-in shower. In the restaurant, chef Lukasz Pietrasz showcases local produce from hand-dived scallops to those peerless kidney-shaped potatoes. A typical dish: hake fillet, crushed Jersey Royals, spinach, lemon and caper butter. A crab sandwich with chilled wine, or a Jersey cream tea alfresco, is a particular treat.

Mont de l'école
St Peter
JE3 7EL

T: 0845 800 5555
E: reservations@seymourhotels.com
W: www.seymourhotels.com/green hills-hotel/

BEDROOMS: 31. 10 on ground floor, 1 suitable for disabled.
OPEN: all year except 22 Dec–mid-Feb.
FACILITIES: 2 lounges, bar, restaurant, garden, terrace (alfresco meals), free Wi-Fi, in-room TV, civil wedding licence, outdoor heated swimming pool, complimentary access to leisure club at sister hotel, The Merton, public rooms wheelchair accessible, adapted toilet.
BACKGROUND MUSIC: in public areas.
LOCATION: 8 miles NW of St Helier.
CHILDREN: all ages welcomed.
DOGS: allowed in 4 ground-floor bedrooms by arrangement (£10 per dog per night), no puppies, but assistance dogs 'always welcome'.
CREDIT CARDS: all major cards.
PRICES: [2018] per room B&B £87–£218. Set dinner £28–£35, à la carte £50.

ST PETER PORT Guernsey

Map 1: inset E5

LA FREGATE

'Well worth the walk up from the middle of town,' say visitors to this extended 18th-century town house spectacularly set high above St Peter Port's harbour. The hotel's bright, uncluttered bedrooms, many with balcony or terrace, some recently refurbished, offer widescreen panoramas of ocean and neighbouring Sark, Herm and Brecqhou. The interiors, tasteful in neutral beige, aqua and peach hues, don't attempt to distract from the outside drama (although one room in the original house has a wooden four-poster and antiques). All rooms have fluffy robes, quality bedding, seating area and turn-down. In the unfussy, wood-floored dining room, which exploits the hotel's cliff-top perch with acres of glass, new chef Tony Leck's seasonal menu showcases local seafood, with the likes of local skate wing, crushed new potatoes, prawn, Lilliput caper and asparagus butter. On fine days, the terrace, with its old granite walls, is the sun-soaked spot for consuming Herm island oysters or hand-picked Guernsey chancre crab. 'We worked our way through the set, the à la carte and the vegetarian menus. Interesting breads accompanied.' Breakfast brings a 'large range' of cooked dishes. (J and MB)

Beauregard Lane
St Peter Port
GY1 1UT

T: 01481 724624
E: enquiries@lafregatehotel.com
W: www.lafregatehotel.com

BEDROOMS: 22.
OPEN: all year.
FACILITIES: lounge/bar, restaurant, lift, private dining/function rooms, free Wi-Fi, in-room TV (Freeview), terrace (alfresco dining), ½-acre terraced garden, unsuitable for disabled.
BACKGROUND MUSIC: in bar.
LOCATION: hilltop, 5 mins' walk from centre.
CHILDREN: all ages welcomed.
DOGS: guide dogs only.
CREDIT CARDS: Amex, MasterCard, Visa.
PRICES: [2018] per room B&B single £100, double £205–£450. Set dinner £39, à la carte £50.

SEE ALSO SHORTLIST

ST SAVIOUR Jersey

Map 1: inset E6

LONGUEVILLE MANOR

'The best on the island', 'the most spectacular and sumptuous', this luxurious, family-friendly manor house hotel (Relais & Châteaux) 'just gets better'. Third-generation owners Malcolm and Patricia Lewis have introduced a spa, a luxury yacht, and now a wine cellar/museum. Behind the grand 16th-century stone facade, a far older house, much altered over centuries, has every modern comfort. Bedrooms blend creams, neutrals and harmonious hues with contemporary furnishings, perhaps a freestanding bath and walk-in shower. Some have garden access, outdoor seating; all provide bathrobes, slippers, smart toiletries. You can dine in the 15th-century Oak Room (the original panelling augmented with broken-up oak chests by an enterprising former resident, a Victorian vicar named Bateman), or in the 'larger, lighter' Garden Room. Chef Andrew Baird makes creative use of local produce, including ingredients from the 19th-century kitchen garden and glasshouses. For instance, line-caught cod, cannellini beans, garden kale, piquillo pepper, chorizo. Children are kept amused with nature trails, treasure hunts, cookery lessons and a swimming pool in gardens landscaped by the Revd Bateman, with woodland walks.

Longueville Road
St Saviour
JE2 7WF

T: 01534 725501
E: info@longuevillemanor.com
W: www.longuevillemanor.com

BEDROOMS: 30. 8 on ground floor. Suite of 2 in cottage.
OPEN: all year except 3–31 Jan.
FACILITIES: lift, 2 lounges, cocktail bar, 2 dining rooms, free Wi-Fi, in-room Smart TV, function/conference facilities, civil wedding licence, spa (treatments, mini-gym, spa pool, terrace), 18-acre grounds (croquet, tennis, outdoor heated swimming pool, woodland), most public areas wheelchair accessible, no adapted toilet.
BACKGROUND MUSIC: in bar and restaurant.
LOCATION: 1½ miles E of St Helier.
CHILDREN: all ages welcomed.
DOGS: allowed, not in dining rooms.
CREDIT CARDS: all major cards.
PRICES: [2018] per room B&B £195–£375, D,B&B £315–£485. Set dinner £45, 'discovery' menu £85, à la carte £65. 1-night bookings refused weekends, bank holidays.

IRELAND

Irish landscape

BAGENALSTOWN Co. Carlow

Map 6:C6

LORUM OLD RECTORY

♔ Previous César winner

Afternoon tea is taken by a turf fire in the drawing room of this 'beautiful' 19th-century granite rectory at the foot of the Blackstairs mountains. Interiors are filled with books, paintings, photographs, family mementos, fresh-cut flowers. An 18th-century grandfather clock chimes in the hall. The 'friendly' owner, Bobbie Smith, is the life and soul of the place, our readers tell us: 'She and her daughter made us so welcome in their wonderful home.' The 'cosy, comfortable and spotless' bedrooms have period furniture and immense charm, perhaps a four-poster, an original fireplace. All come with home-baked biscuits. Candlelit dinner is served at the mahogany table in the warmly red dining room, where silverware gleams in the firelight. The chef hostess is a member of Euro-Toques, which celebrates the best food grown, raised, fished in Ireland. She uses local, mainly organic ingredients to create a daily four-course dinner, and hearty breakfasts with home-made bread and jams. The gardens are surrounded by pastureland and Christmas tree crops. People come to walk, cycle and play golf, but most of all to relax and be spoilt. (AM)

25% DISCOUNT VOUCHERS

Kilgreaney
Bagenalstown
R21 RD45

T: 00 353 59 977 5282
E: bobbie@lorum.com
W: www.lorum.com

BEDROOMS: 4.
OPEN: Feb–end Nov.
FACILITIES: drawing room, study, dining room, snug, free Wi-Fi, 1-acre garden (croquet) in 18-acre grounds, wedding facilities, unsuitable for disabled.
BACKGROUND MUSIC: none.
LOCATION: 4 miles S of Bagenalstown on R705 to Borris.
CHILDREN: all ages welcomed.
DOGS: by arrangement, not in public rooms.
CREDIT CARDS: MasterCard, Visa.
PRICES: [2018] per room B&B single €110–€120, double €170–€190, D,B&B double €270–€290. Set dinner €50

BALLINGARRY Co. Limerick

Map 6:D5

THE MUSTARD SEED
AT ECHO LODGE

'Tranquil air of relaxed calm', 'Good for the soul', 'An oasis of peace'. We hear perennial praise for John Edward Joyce's country house hotel. Built in 1885 by the parish priest – and for a long time home to the Mercy order of nuns – it stands in lovely grounds 'full of colour', with orchard and kitchen garden. In 2016 it passed seamlessly into the ownership of long-serving manager Mr Joyce, and everything is as it ever was. Bedrooms are traditional, furnished with antiques (perhaps a four-poster), and have luxury toiletries, mineral water, tea and coffee facilities on request ('but we'd rather make it for you,' they say). A deluxe suite opens on to the garden (ideal for dog owners). On arrival, 'a great, friendly welcome, tea and home-baked biscuits'. In the evening, chef Angel Pirev's four-course menus include such dishes as Ballinwillinn farm beef loin, fillet, kale, parsley root, apple wedge, jus. 'Meal delightful, service a little stiff at first but readily became relaxed,' a reader writes. In the morning, in the sunny breakfast room, there is soda bread, eggs from the hotel's hens, 'lovely cooked items'. (John Hood, HS)

Ballingarry

T: 00 353 69 68508
E: mustard@indigo.ie
W: www.mustardseed.ie

BEDROOMS: 16. 1, on ground floor, suitable for disabled.
OPEN: all year except 24–26 Dec.
FACILITIES: library, restaurant, entrance hall, sunroom, free Wi-Fi, in-room TV (terrestrial), wedding facilities, 12-acre grounds, restaurant and public rooms wheelchair accessible.
BACKGROUND MUSIC: in restaurant.
LOCATION: in village, 18 miles SW of Limerick.
CHILDREN: all ages welcomed.
DOGS: 'well-behaved' pets welcome, in designated bedrooms (not unattended), not in public rooms.
CREDIT CARDS: Amex, MasterCard, Visa.
PRICES: [2018] per person B&B €90–€160, D,B&B €129–€195. Set menus €48–€62.

BALLYCASTLE Co. Mayo

Map 6:B4

STELLA MARIS

Guests can 'watch the dolphins frolicking in the bay' from the extensive conservatory of Frances Kelly-McSweeney's hotel in a 'dramatically beautiful' setting on the Wild Atlantic Way. Overlooking Bunatrahir Bay, it originated as a coastguard headquarters in the 1800s, before a stint hosting the Sisters of Mercy, eventually re-emerging as a hotel in the 1960s. For Frances Kelly it was a place of girlhood memories, and when it came up for sale in 2000, she and her American husband, the late Terence McSweeney, bought it and embarked on two years of renovation. Most of the 'comfortable, individually furnished' bedrooms have a sea view. Plus points for 'bedlinen changed every second night; linen napkins at dinner and breakfast'. Fires burn in an enfilade of cosy public rooms painted in warm shades of rose and peach. The dining room was created from four small, separate rooms, with a central fireplace. The hostess, with her chef's hat on, devises short daily menus based on fresh local produce – typically soup, pasta, steaks, grilled prawns. This is wonderful walking country, with spectacular golf courses a 40-minute drive away.

Ballycastle

T: 00 353 96 43322
E: info@stellamarisireland.com
W: www.stellamarisireland.com

BEDROOMS: 11. 1, on ground floor, suitable for disabled.
OPEN: 1 May–30 Sept, restaurant closed Mon evening.
FACILITIES: lounge, bar, restaurant, conservatory, free Wi-Fi ('most dependable in public areas'), in-room TV (Freeview), 2-acre grounds, public rooms wheelchair accessible.
BACKGROUND MUSIC: none.
LOCATION: 1½ miles W of Ballycastle.
CHILDREN: not under 5.
DOGS: not allowed.
CREDIT CARDS: MasterCard, Visa.
PRICES: [2018] per room B&B single €85, double €150–€190. À la carte €35.

BALLYMOTE Co. Sligo

Map 6.B5

TEMPLE HOUSE

Sheep crop the grasses in the parkland around Roderick and Helena Perceval's classical Georgian mansion overlooking a lake and a ruined 13th-century castle – a working private estate rather than romantic Grand Tour fantasy. Guests follow a half-mile drive before entering a vestibule with 'a stag's head, a large fossil and shell collection gathered by an antecedent'. After a 'warm handshake' they are shown to their bedroom, ascending a grand staircase beneath ancestors in gilt frames. All rooms have park views, antiques, hunting prints and the like. Showers have 'excellent water pressure' (a selling point). Evening drinks are served in the morning room, where estate logs burn on cold days. Annual refurbishment keeps things quite smart, but there remains a 'lived-in feel' to public rooms. Diners sit down together at a mahogany table laid with silverware, and choose from a short, locally sourced seasonal menu, perhaps thick onion tart and greenhouse rocket; lemon chicken; braised Temple House lamb with rosemary jus. At breakfast, a buffet is set out on the sideboard (stewed rhubarb, fruit compote, home-made muesli, bread and marmalade), while the hosts cook a decent full Irish.

Ballinacarrow
Ballymote
F56 NN50

T: 00 353 87 997 6045
E: stay@templehouse.ie
W: www.templehouse.ie

BEDROOMS: 6.
OPEN: Apr–mid-Nov.
FACILITIES: morning room, dining room, vestibule, table tennis room, free Wi-Fi, wedding facilities, 1½-acre garden on 1,000-acre estate, water sports on site.
BACKGROUND MUSIC: none.
LOCATION: 12 miles S of Sligo.
CHILDREN: all ages welcomed.
DOGS: not allowed.
CREDIT CARDS: Mastercard, Visa.
PRICES: [2018] per room B&B single €110–€145, double €170–€210. Set dinner €55.

BALLYVAUGHAN Co. Clare

Map 6:C4

❦GREGANS CASTLE HOTEL

César award: Irish hotel of the year

On the Wild Atlantic Way, with views across the Burren to Galway Bay, 'delightful' Gregans Castle is 'the epitome of understated country-house hotel luxury', writes a Guide regular this year. Owned by Simon Haden and Frederieke McMurray, its mid-18th century interiors have been given an elegant contemporary spin with monogrammed carpets and charcoal-grey walls in the bar and dining room. The 'big and individually decorated' bedrooms, with uplifting splashes of colour, are filled with books and antique furniture from around the world. The staff are 'unfailingly friendly and helpful', and 'little touches, including candles being lit in public spaces at dusk, exude style and comfort'. Chef Robbie McCauley took over the kitchen reins in 2018, offering such dishes as roasted Kilshanny lamb, wild garlic, morel, asparagus, Madeira jus. 'The cooking is first rate: imaginative and elegant without being pretentious. I enjoyed smoked eel mousse and ceviche of scallops; and the grouse.' Breakfast, showcasing local suppliers, includes grilled bacon and sausage with wild boar puddings and free-range eggs; fuel to walk across the Burren or cruise under the Cliffs of Moher. (Richard Parish)

Gragan
East Ballyvaughan
H91 CF60

T: 00 353 65 707 7005
E: stay@gregans.ie
W: www.gregans.ie

BEDROOMS: 21. 7 on ground floor, 1 suitable for disabled.
OPEN: mid-Feb–early Dec.
FACILITIES: drawing room, bar, dining room, free Wi-Fi (not in restaurant), 15-acre grounds (ornamental pool, croquet), wedding facilities, safe sandy beach 4½ miles, golf, riding, hill walking nearby.
BACKGROUND MUSIC: all day in bar, during meals in dining room.
LOCATION: 3½ miles SW of Ballyvaughan.
CHILDREN: all ages welcomed.
DOGS: allowed in some ground-floor bedrooms, not in public rooms.
CREDIT CARDS: all major cards.
PRICES: [2018] per room B&B €280–€485. Set menu and à la carte €75. 1-night bookings sometimes refused Sat.

CASTLEHILL. Co. Mayo

Map 6:B4

ENNISCOE HOUSE

'As the owners claim, this is neither B&B nor hotel, but a family home that welcomes guests,' writes a Guide insider, of this 'classic Georgian manor house, deep in the countryside' beneath Mount Nephin. 'A combination of relaxed hospitality and able efficiency set the pace for our two-night stay.' Susan Kellett and her son, DJ, are welcoming hosts. The interiors are 'a fair chaos of antiques, paintings and period furnishings', stuffed animals, family portraits. There are two 'enormous' sitting rooms, one with a 'decidedly aristocratic air', the other less formal, where tea was served by a peat fire. Approached by a 'grand staircase', the lofty Major's Room had a bed with a quarter canopy, blankets rather than a duvet, no cups or kettle – just ask and a tea tray is delivered. A 'glorious' bathroom had 'a deep, Victorian bathtub with amazing views', separate shower, 'good toiletries'. Guests gather for drinks in the former library, before dinner cooked by Susan with locally produced, fished, foraged and home-grown ingredients. Breakfast, too, is 'just wonderful', with creamy porridge, home-made bread, the full Irish.

25% DISCOUNT VOUCHERS

Castlehill
F26 EA34

T: 00 353 96 31112
E: mail@enniscoe.com
W: www.enniscoe.com

BEDROOMS: 6. Plus self-catering units behind house.
OPEN: Apr–end Oct, New Year.
FACILITIES: 2 sitting rooms, dining room, free Wi-Fi (in public rooms, some bedrooms), wedding facilities, 160-acre estate (3-acre garden, tea room, farm, heritage centre, forge, fishing, woodland walks), unsuitable for disabled.
BACKGROUND MUSIC: occasionally in public areas.
LOCATION: 2 miles S of Crossmolina, 12 miles SW of Ballina.
CHILDREN: all ages welcomed.
DOGS: allowed in bedrooms, not in public rooms.
CREDIT CARDS: MasterCard, Visa.
PRICES: [2018] per person B&B €90–€130, D,B&B €130–€170. Set menus €50.

CASTLELYONS Co. Cork

BALLYVOLANE HOUSE

A mildly bohemian air filters through the Green family's wisteria-hung Georgian country house hotel, bordered by bluebell woods. Jenny and Justin Green are the 'wonderfully relaxed, informal hosts; they welcome guests as though they are a favourite relative'. The 'magnificently furnished' public rooms display 'judicious good taste, yet it is clearly the family's home'. There is an appealing mix of antiques and retro furniture, stacks of ('mostly Irish') books and squashy chaises longues; children's music sits on the grand piano. A well-stocked honesty bar includes 'wonderfully fragrant' Bertha's Revenge Gin from the house's own distillery. Each bedroom is individually styled, though all have thoughtful comforts: home-made fruit cordial, freshly baked cookies, an espresso machine. 'Our spacious room' had a large bed; a 'noble bathroom, with mounting steps up to a very deep bath'. New chef Steven Mercer continues the farm-to-fork ethos, serving perhaps nettle soup with Pernod; roast marinated butterflied leg of McGrath's lamb, green sauce, wild garlic mash; home-made pistachio ice cream. Breakfast (served till noon) is a 'splendid' start to a day filled with tractor rides and exploring woodland trails.

Castlelyons
P61 FP70

T: 00 353 25 36349
E: info@ballyvolanehouse.ie
W: www.ballyvolanehouse.ie

BEDROOMS: 6. Plus 'glamping' tents May–Sept.
OPEN: all year except Christmas/ New Year (self-catering only).
FACILITIES: hall, drawing room, honesty bar, dining room, free Wi-Fi, wedding facilities, 80-acre grounds (15-acre garden, croquet, tennis, 3 trout lakes, woodland, fields), unsuitable for disabled.
BACKGROUND MUSIC: none.
LOCATION: 22 miles NE of Cork.
CHILDREN: all ages welcomed (tree house, farm animals, games, high tea).
DOGS: allowed, but kept on lead during shooting season July–Jan.
CREDIT CARDS: MasterCard, Visa.
PRICES: [2018] per room B&B from €198, D,B&B from €258. Set dinner €60.

CLIFDEN Co. Galway

THE QUAY HOUSE

'It is impossible not to like Julia and Paddy
Foyle', the 'delightful hosts' of this 'sybaritic'
harbourside B&B on the fringes of the Wild
Atlantic Way. 'They have a genuine interest
in seeing everyone who passes through their
doors happy,' writes a Guide inspector. It is not
unusual to see guests pad into the 'light-filled
main sitting room' to sit before the fire in their
slippers. The ramble of interlinking properties,
including a 19th-century harbourmaster's house,
is stuffed with antiques and curios – the hosts
are itinerant auction hoppers – 'yet the melee
of styles and periods works'. Each individually
fashioned bedroom has a terrace or balcony. 'We
spread ourselves out in a roomy, well-equipped
triple with squashy seating and large bathroom.
We slept like tops on very comfortable beds.'
Breakfast, 'cheerfully served in the pleasant
conservatory', starts with a buffet of fresh fruit
salad, Irish cheeses and cold cuts, a tempting
'breakfast cake'. 'Freshly squeezed orange
juice and excellent coffee arrived at the table,
followed by perfectly poached eggs, piping hot
potato pancakes.' The hosts provide driving and
walking routes: 'Julia transformed our itinerary.'

Beach Road
Clifden
H71 XF76

T: 00 353 95 21369
E: thequay@iol.ie
W: www.thequayhouse.com

BEDROOMS: 16. 3 on ground floor,
1 suitable for disabled, 7 studios (6
with kitchenette) in annexe.
OPEN: end Mar–end Oct.
FACILITIES: 2 sitting rooms, breakfast
conservatory, free Wi-Fi, in-room
TV (Freeview), small garden,
fishing, sailing, golf, riding nearby,
breakfast room and public areas
wheelchair accessible.
BACKGROUND MUSIC: none,
LOCATION: on harbour, 8 mins' walk
from centre.
CHILDREN: all ages welcomed.
DOGS: not allowed.
CREDIT CARDS: MasterCard, Visa.
PRICES: [2018] per room B&B single
€95–€120, double €155–€175.
1-night bookings refused bank
holiday Sat.

SEE ALSO SHORTLIST

CLIFDEN Co. Galway

SEA MIST HOUSE

A knock at the cherry-red door to this 'characterful' B&B is answered by 'warm, inherently hospitable' Sheila Griffin. The Georgian house has been the 'well-cared-for' family home for nearly a century. The 'wonderfully relaxed', recently updated sitting rooms are full of old pictures, books, DVDs and 'comfortable, sink-into' sofas; each has a 'warming' fire in the evening. 'A reading nook under a window has a well-lit, fat little armchair and occasional table to put a drink on; an excellent use of space with a great library.' Traditionally styled bedrooms have a comfortable bed, a 'well-stocked' tea/coffee tray. 'Our large room had a spotless shower room with a narrow walk-in shower and plentiful hot water. A lovely window seat overlooked the street; thick curtains kept out any ambient light or noise overnight. We slept very well.' The bright breakfast room is overlooked by the colourful grounds, which slope up the side of the house towards beehives, a chicken run and kitchen garden at the rear. 'Marvellous' breakfast might have fruit-studded scones, Connemara smoked salmon, 'Ireland's best cup of coffee': fuel to explore nearby Twelve Bens.

Seaview
Clifden
H71 NV63

T: 00 353 95 21441
E: sheila@seamisthouse.com
W: www.seamisthouse.com

BEDROOMS: 4.
OPEN: mid-Mar–end Oct.
FACILITIES: 2 sitting rooms, conservatory dining room, mini-library, free Wi-Fi, ¾-acre garden, unsuitable for disabled.
BACKGROUND MUSIC: none.
LOCATION: just down from the main square, on the edge of town.
CHILDREN: not under 4.
DOGS: not allowed.
CREDIT CARDS: Amex, MasterCard, Visa.
PRICES: [2018] per person B&B €40–€55.

SEE ALSO SHORTLIST

CLONES Co. Monaghan

Map 6:B6

HILTON PARK

It is easy to see why this 18th-century Italianate country house is known locally as The Castle. 'Grand iron gates surmounted by eagles' guard the estate entrance, before a mile-long drive through 'inspirational' grounds – the stage for golf, fishing, shooting, cycling and wild swimming. It has been in the family for ten generations, and the current 'enthusiastic, committed' owners, Fred and Joanna Madden, extend a 'very warm welcome'. Guests 'enjoy unfettered access to a house filled with flowers, antiques, 'stacks of books, family portraits and photos'. Its bedrooms also sport 'an abundance of period furniture and reading material'. 'Ours had an extremely comfortable super-king-size bed, and a view of amazingly symmetrical topiary and lush greenery sloping towards the mirror-like lake.' The 'excellent' menus, cooked by Fred, a trained chef with a slow food ethos (his mother Lucy is an acclaimed food writer), are sourced from the estate and the four-acre walled garden. Dinner, served in the 'intimate' candlelit dining room, includes such dishes as rack of spring lamb, herb crust, quince, mint jelly. An 'excellent' breakfast offers Fermanagh black pudding, organic smoked salmon.

Clones
H23 C582

T: 00 353 47 56007
E: mail@hiltonpark.ie
W: www.hiltonpark.ie

BEDROOMS: 6.
OPEN: Mar–mid-Dec, groups only at Christmas/New Year.
FACILITIES: 3 drawing rooms, study, breakfast room, dining room, games room, billiard room, free Wi-Fi (in public areas), wedding facilities, 600-acre grounds (3 lakes for fishing and wild swimming, golf course, croquet).
BACKGROUND MUSIC: occasionally in dining room.
LOCATION: 4 miles S of Clones.
CHILDREN: all ages welcomed.
DOGS: not allowed.
CREDIT CARDS: Diners, MasterCard, Visa.
PRICES: [2018] per room B&B from €189, D,B&B from €309. Set dinner €60.

DRINAGH Co. Wexford

Map 6:D6

KILLIANE CASTLE COUNTRY HOUSE & FARM

'A beautiful place with great hosts.' Guide readers 'highly recommend' this well-located former 15th-century castle-turned-farmhouse-turned-country guest house in Ireland's Ancient East. Surrounded by a working dairy farm, it is owned by Kathleen and Jack Mernagh, whose father acquired the property in 1920. 'We were warmly welcomed by Kathleen, who showed us around before inviting us to have a cup of tea and home-made biscuits in a lovely snug.' Traditional interiors include gilt-framed mirrors, a grandfather clock and country-style bedrooms reached by an elegant 17th-century staircase. 'Our room was beautifully decorated, in keeping with the house's history. We slept soundly on a huge, comfortable bed. The tasteful, well-equipped bathroom had a great tub.' In summer months, Patrycja Mernagh cooks modern Irish dinners, while 'tasty breakfasts' are served every day. Using the farm's produce and home-baked bread, the cooking 'is especially good'. 'Baked eggs with chorizo and mushroom, and the Full Irish, were to die for.' Ask the hosts for sightseeing tips: 'The Mernaghs added a few gems to our itinerary.' Rosslare ferry terminal is eight miles away. (RF)

Drinagh
Y35 E1NC

T: 00 353 53 915 8885
E: info@killianecastle.com
W: www.killianecastle.com

BEDROOMS: 10, 2 in former stable block.
OPEN: mid-Feb–mid-Dec.
FACILITIES: reception, lounge (honesty bar), snug, dining room, free Wi-Fi, in-room TV (Freeview), garden, large grounds (nature trail, tennis, croquet, pitch and putt, 300-metre driving range) in 230-acre dairy farm, unsuitable for disabled.
BACKGROUND MUSIC: in dining room and reception.
LOCATION: 1½ miles S of Drinagh.
CHILDREN: all ages welcomed.
DOGS: allowed in grounds, not indoors.
CREDIT CARDS: MasterCard, Visa.
PRICES: [2018] per room B&B single €85–€95, double €120–€155, D,B&B double €190–€225. À la carte €35.

GLASLOUGH Co. Monaghan

CASTLE LESLIE

Scottish Baronial meets Italian Renaissance in Samantha Leslie's Victorian pile on one of the last great Irish castle estates still owned by the founding family. The Leslies can trace their colourful history back to Attila the Hun, but there are few hotels more civilised than this one. Interiors are replete with antiques, portraits, miniatures. Castle bedrooms come with 'old-world eccentricity', a vivid personal story, perhaps lake views, a four-poster, a bath in a curtained alcove, a bathroom with double-ended spa bath and murals washed by changing light effects. Rooms in the stone-built lodge are 'well lit and designed, very smart, a decent size, with good bathroom, bath and walk-in shower'. Afternoon tea is served in the drawing room, 'country home cooking' in Conor's bar, while in Snaffles restaurant (they're big on horses here) executive head chef Philip Brazil's fine-dining menus include such dishes as breast of Silverhill duck, garlic and nutmeg potato mousseline, marinated carrot strip, blackberry jus. At breakfast, a huge choice includes maple-cured bacon, organic eggs, black-and-white artisan puddings; cream cheese and hand-smoked salmon bagel. 'The whole place smacks of being well run.'

Glaslough
H18 FY04

T: 00 353 47 88100
E: info@castleleslie.com
W: www.castleleslie.com

BEDROOMS: 49 bedrooms. 29 in Lodge (some suitable for disabled).
OPEN: all year except 17–27 Dec.
FACILITIES: drawing rooms, bar, breakfast room, restaurant, conservatory, billiard room, library, cinema, free Wi-Fi, in-room TV, wedding/conference facilities, spa, 14-acre gardens on 1,000-acre estate (equestrian centre, tennis, wildlife, lakes, boating, fishing), public areas wheelchair accessible.
BACKGROUND MUSIC: all day in public areas of Lodge.
LOCATION: 7 miles NE of Monaghan.
CHILDREN: all ages welcomed.
DOGS: allowed on estate, in Old Stable Mews rooms, otherwise overnight in stables.
CREDIT CARDS: Amex, MasterCard, Visa.
PRICES: [2018] per room B&B from €130, D,B&B from €230. Set dinner €65. 1-night bookings sometimes refused.

GOREY Co. Wexford   Map 6:D6

MARLFIELD HOUSE

Lavish, 'prompt and very attentive' hospitality
is the order of the day at this 'distinguished'
family-run hotel in an 'imposing' Regency house
surrounded by 36 acres of grounds. The approach
winds past 'extensive, well-kept gardens with
gravel paths and tended topiary', woodland, a
lake and manicured lawns. The large entrance
hall's grand piano adds to the 'highest-quality
stylish ambience'. Antiques, low-slung armchairs
and fresh flowers fill two lounges. Upstairs,
passing 'an impressive triple chandelier', Guide
inspectors considered their bedroom 'a very
pleasant environment, with lined cream curtains,
a super-king-size bed, firm mattress and soft
pillows adding up to a most restful sleep'. More
sockets and a full-length mirror would have been
even better. Chef Ruadhan Furlong's 'tempting'
menu in the fine-dining Conservatory restaurant
was 'division one without quite being top of the
league', with such dishes as guineafowl, chicory,
prune, polenta and red cabbage. Breakfast was
thought 'excellent'. Marlfield House's garden-to-
table ethos also shines through in the Duck, where
the casual, modern fusion menu includes haddock
tempura; lamb kofta kebabs on rosemary skewers,
served in recently renovated courtyard buildings.

25% DISCOUNT VOUCHERS

Courtown Road R742
Gorey
Y25 DK23

T: 00 353 53 942 1124
E: info@marlfieldhouse.ie
W: www.marlfieldhouse.com

BEDROOMS: 19. 8 on ground floor.
OPEN: Feb–New Year, Conservatory
restaurant closed Mon/Tues every
week, plus Wed night/Thurs night/
Sun night from 1 Feb–mid-May, 1
Oct–31 Dec, Duck restaurant closed
for 2 weeks in Jan, Mon/Tues Jan–
Apr, Oct–Dec.
FACILITIES: reception hall, drawing
room, library/bar, 2 restaurants, free
Wi-Fi, in-room TV (Freeview),
wedding facilities, 36-acre grounds
(gardens, tennis, croquet, wildfowl
reserve, lake).
BACKGROUND MUSIC: in library/bar.
LOCATION: 1 mile E of Gorey.
CHILDREN: all ages welcomed.
DOGS: allowed ('always on a lead')
by prior arrangement, not in public
rooms.
CREDIT CARDS: all major cards.
PRICES: [2018] per room B&B
€230–€670, D,B&B €350–€790. Set
dinner €66.

KENMARE Co. Kerry

Map 6:D4

BROOK LANE HOTEL

In a small town well placed for tours of the Ring of Kerry, and the Wild Atlantic Way, Una and Dermot Brennan's hotel is family-run, with a lot of heart and luxury boutique aspirations. Beyond the car park a 'warm, very friendly, helpful' welcome awaits. Stylish seating alcoves off the corridor have 'leather sofas, designer lighting, tied-back curtains, space-enhancing mirrors, good modern art'. Bedrooms are smart, contemporary, with 'comfortable bed', a range of facilities (a whirlpool bath, maybe), robes, slippers, good toiletries, 'wonderful underfloor heating', room service. Food is served all day in the popular Casey's bar, where a fixed-price dinner menu might include rare-breed pork belly duo from the owners' farm, confit cabbage, hazelnuts, cider glaze, pork jus. There is more choice at sister restaurant No. 35, a 15-minute walk away. Breakfast is served until late in a room next to the bar, where the 'delightful, articulate' Una was presiding when our inspector called. Organic eggs are from their 'happy hens'. The situation is not bucolic, but the hotel wins approval for good accommodation, 'good value and a genuine sense of hospitality'. (JM, and others)

Sneem Road
Kenmare
V93 T289

T: 00 353 64 664 2077
E: info@brooklanehotel.com
W: www.brooklanehotel.com

BEDROOMS: 22. 9 on ground floor, 1 suitable for disabled.
OPEN: all year except 24–26 Dec.
FACILITIES: lift, bar/restaurant, library, reception area (seating, open fire), free Wi-Fi, in-room TV (terrestrial), wedding facilities, public areas wheelchairs accessible with adapted toilet.
BACKGROUND MUSIC: in public areas.
LOCATION: 5-min. walk from town centre.
CHILDREN: all ages welcomed, cots, roll-away beds, children's menus.
DOGS: not allowed.
CREDIT CARDS: Diners, MasterCard, Visa.
PRICES: [2018] per room B&B single from €83, double from €99, D,B&B double from €170. Set menus €35 (Casey's bar) , à la carte €40 (No. 35 Restaurant, 15 mins' walk away).

SEE ALSO SHORTLIST

KINSALE Co. Cork

Map 6:D5

THE OLD PRESBYTERY

Built by a Spanish merchant in 1750 and, as you
would guess, once home to the parish priest,
this smart town-centre B&B has been run for
more than 20 years by 'likeable' hosts Philip
and Noreen McEvoy. 'Charming and quirky',
with a 'steep, narrow staircase', it has interiors
filled with family possessions, antiques, lamps,
ornaments, in the manner of a private home.
Two of the traditional bedrooms – iron and
brass beds, wooden chests, neutral yet warm
hues – have a balcony, one a roof garden,
another a four-poster, some a whirlpool bath.
The split-level, two-room penthouse suite
with kitchenette has a claw-footed bath and
spiral metal staircase. 'Guests have the use of
a small but comfortable sheltered patio.' A
reader enjoyed the 'novel touch' of the offer of
cheese and wine in the late afternoon. Water
is heated by solar panels, cleaning products
are eco-friendly, all food and drink is organic
and Fairtrade. An 'excellent' breakfast with a
changing menu, cooked by Philip McEvoy, a
professional chef, includes farmhouse cheeses,
free-range eggs, the full Irish, a daily fish
special, perhaps a hot, fruit-filled crêpe with
maple syrup.

43 Cork Street
Kinsale
P17 AE80

T: 00 353 21 477 2027
E: info@oldpres.com
W: www.oldpres.com

BEDROOMS: 9. 3 in adjacent annexe.
OPEN: Mar–Oct.
FACILITIES: sitting room, dining
room, free Wi-Fi, in-room TV
(Freeview), patio with seating,
secure parking, unsuitable for
disabled.
BACKGROUND MUSIC: in dining room
at breakfast.
LOCATION: town centre.
CHILDREN: all ages welcomed.
DOGS: not allowed.
CREDIT CARDS: MasterCard, Visa.
PRICES: [2018] per room B&B €100–
€200. 1-night bookings sometimes
refused May–Sept.

LETTERFRACK Co. Galway

Map 6:C4

ROSLEAGUE MANOR

♥ Previous César winner

'It doesn't seem to change,' says a reader who first stayed some 30 years ago at this pink-washed Georgian country house 'in a glorious setting', with gardens bordering Ballinakill Bay. Many others return year after year. Built in 1820, it has been run as a hotel by the Foyle family for more than 50 years. The 'very special' ambience owes much to third-generation owner Mark Foyle's 'endless enthusiasm' and 'easy-going hospitality'. Turf fires burn in public rooms filled with antiques and family possessions. Bedrooms are in the original house and a newer wing, some with a sea view against a mountain backdrop. Each is unique: 'Nothing is standard… the eclectic style is one of the attractions.' One room might have a half-tester bed or four-poster, another a slipper bath and walk-in shower, another patio seating. In the dining room, chef Emmanuel Neu's daily-changing menus harness local and home-grown produce for such dishes as Irish Hereford beef fillet, caramelised baby onions, pepper sauce; steamed turbot fillet, courgette spaghetti, saffron beurre blanc. Breakfast brings everything you'd expect, plus, perhaps, devilled kidneys, fresh mackerel. (EC, and others)

Letterfrack

T: 00 353 95 41101
E: info@rosleague.com
W: www.rosleague.com

BEDROOMS: 21. 2 on ground floor.
OPEN: mid-Mar–mid-Nov.
FACILITIES: 2 drawing rooms, conservatory/bar, dining room, free Wi-Fi, in-room TV (Freeview), wedding facilities, 25-acre grounds (tennis).
BACKGROUND MUSIC: none.
LOCATION: 7 miles NE of Clifden.
CHILDREN: all ages welcomed.
DOGS: 'well-behaved' dogs allowed.
CREDIT CARDS: MasterCard, Visa.
PRICES: [2018] per room B&B single from €100, double €150–€230, D,B&B double from €190. Set dinner €36–€50, à la carte €42. Min. 2-night stay at bank holiday weekends.

LIMERICK Co. Limerick

Map 6:D5

NO. 1 PERY SQUARE

A grand little handful of Georgian terraces combines into Patricia Roberts's lovingly restored, 'elegant' town house hotel. Painted boxes of books, tubs of flowers and a dappling of mirrors line the public spaces. An open fire in the bar and soft candlelight in the vaulted basement spa create a restful atmosphere. Bedrooms vary in size and style. Up the house's original staircase are 'elegant, spacious' period-style rooms, all heritage colours, handmade beds and lofty sash windows. 'Ours had a big bathroom with roll-topped bath, and overlooked the attractive Pery Square.' Down the corridor, Club Rooms are smaller and more modern, with courtyard or rooftop views. Chef Tim Harris's 'excellent' cooking highlights seasonal fare in the 'very pleasant' bistro restaurant, perhaps wild garlic risotto, broad bean, mascarpone; or pork belly, Medjool date stuffing. Breakfast includes 'fine' Limerick ham and artisan bacon and sausages, 'served by very jolly staff'; 'the fresh fruit salad could have been fresher, but it was replaced immediately'. Guests this year enjoyed complimentary tickets provided for a local theatre/arts festival: 'A nice touch.' (David Britton)

Georgian Quarter
Limerick

T: 00 353 61 402402
E: info@oneperysquare.com
W: www.oneperysquare.com

BEDROOMS: 20. 3 suitable for disabled.
OPEN: all year except 24–27 Dec.
FACILITIES: lift, lounge, drawing room, restaurant, private dining room, free Wi-Fi, in-room TV (Freeview), wedding facilities, small kitchen garden, terrace, basement spa, deli/wine shop.
BACKGROUND MUSIC: in restaurant and lounge.
LOCATION: central.
CHILDREN: all ages welcomed.
DOGS: not allowed.
CREDIT CARDS: Amex, MasterCard, Visa.
PRICES: [2018] per room B&B from €195, D,B&B from €295. Set dinner €25–€45, à la carte €49.

LISDOONVARNA Co. Clare

Map 6:C4

SHEEDY'S

Expertly tended rose gardens front this
'wonderfully well-run small hotel', gazing out
towards the windswept Burren countryside. The
'inimitable' Martina and John Sheedy are the
fourth generation at the helm. 'The pair are gifted
hosts through and through,' say Guide inspectors
in 2018, 'and they expect nothing less from their
well-trained staff.' Bedrooms are 'cocooning':
'There was no noise; we slept so well on twin
beds with crisp white bedlinen and sink-into
pillows. The blissful bath had plenty of spaces for
a wine glass.' Each room has many thoughtful
extras (home-made biscuits, a proper repair kit,
bathrobes, fine toiletries). Diners eat by firelight
in the atmospheric bar or restaurant. The chef/
patron has long supported a sustainable, go-local
ethos. ('We stopped by the local smokehouse
after discovering it supplied my delicious smoked
salmon starter.') His French-inflected Irish dishes
included 'delicious crab risotto, a succulent vegan
chickpea-roast vegetable ragout; divine, creamy
coconut sorbet'. Breakfast has all the standards
(porridge, a full Irish, 'lovely sausages and
mushrooms'), plus 'something a little different',
perhaps fluffy pancakes, bagels with St Tola
goat's cheese.

Lisdoonvarna

T: 00 353 65 707 4026
E: info@sheedys.com
W: www.sheedys.com

BEDROOMS: 11. Some on ground
floor.
OPEN: Easter–Sept, closed Mon/
Tues in Apr, restaurant closed Sun
evening July–Sept.
FACILITIES: sitting room/library, sun
lounge, bar, restaurant, free Wi-Fi,
in-room TV (Freeview), ½-acre
garden, restaurant wheelchair
accessible, adapted toilet.
BACKGROUND MUSIC: 'easy listening'
at breakfast, light jazz at dinner.
LOCATION: 20 miles SW of Galway.
CHILDREN: over-11s welcomed.
DOGS: not allowed.
CREDIT CARDS: MasterCard, Visa.
PRICES: [2018] per room B&B
€139–€180, D,B&B €220–€280. À la
carte €48. 1-night bookings refused
weekends in Sept.

LONGFORD Co. Longford

Map 6:C5

VIEWMOUNT HOUSE

♔ Previous César winner

A long drive through parkland brings guests to this Georgian mansion beside the golf course on the edge of town, where Beryl and James Kearney are the 'warm and friendly' hosts. They are 'richly deserving' of the numerous awards they hold, say Guide inspectors, who were checked in by Mr Kearney ('all relaxed geniality') before he carried their cases and printed out their boarding passes for next day's flight. One of two ground-floor rooms, 'each on two levels' with a pine staircase leading up to a galleried sitting room, it 'exuded good judgement and taste'. It had an original fireplace, a 'robust' wooden bed, rugs on wood flooring, underfloor bathroom heating and a spa bath. All rooms have antiques, fresh flowers, handmade toiletries. In VM restaurant in the converted stables, new chef Robert Groot Koerkamp creates such dishes as salt-fried John Stone sirloin steak, saffron potato, shallot, porcini; monkfish, Jerusalem artichoke, kale, pickle, fish sauce. Breakfast brought freshly squeezed clementine juice, stewed rhubarb, eggs scrambled to order. 'Well-maintained, inter-linked small gardens include a Japanese themed area, complete with pagoda, bridges and pond.'

25% DISCOUNT VOUCHERS

Dublin Road
Longford
N39 N2X6

T: 00 353 43 334 1919
E: info@viewmounthouse.com
W: www.viewmounthouse.com

BEDROOMS: 12. 7 in modern extension, some on ground floor, 1 suitable for disabled.
OPEN: all year except 28 Oct–7 Nov, restaurant open Wed–Sat for dinner, Sun lunch, closed 25–27 Dec.
FACILITIES: reception room, library, sitting room, breakfast room, restaurant, free Wi-Fi, in-room TV, wedding facilities, 4-acre grounds (pond, orchard, herb garden, Japanese garden), breakfast room and restaurant wheelchair accessible.
BACKGROUND MUSIC: none.
LOCATION: 1 mile E of town centre.
CHILDREN: all ages welcomed.
DOGS: not allowed.
CREDIT CARDS: Amex, MasterCard, Visa.
PRICES: per room B&B from €160. Set dinner €65 (early bird dinner €38), Sun lunch €38.

MAGHERALIN Co. Armagh

Map 6:B6

NEWFORGE HOUSE

✿ Previous César winner

A Georgian house in extensive grounds by the
Lagan river, John and Louise Mathers's 'first-
rate' guest house is an 'outstanding' place to stay.
There's an orchard, a vegetable garden and wild
flower meadow, but it's the hosts' 'considerable
people skills' that really impress: 'All guests are
greeted unflinchingly by their first name – quite
a feat.' The property displays antique furnishings
collected by the six generations of Matherses
who have called it home – their names adorn
the 'tasteful', individually decorated bedrooms.
Beaumont has tweed, suede and floor-to-ceiling
windows; Spence a roll-top bath and relaxing
shades of green; Hanna has a four-poster, and the
original fireplace in the bathroom. All overlook
the courtyard or grounds. In the dining room
with white linen and sprays of flowers, John's
seasonal, locally sourced menu might include roast
pale-smoked hake, mustard and parsley cream;
dry-aged County Down lamb rump, rosemary
and garlic pan juices. Breakfast, again cooked by
John, who 'seeks to do simple things well – there
is no doubting his success', includes fresh orange
juice and 'wonderfully yellow' scrambled eggs
from Newforge's chickens. (RG)

58 Newforge Road
Magheralin
BT67 0QL

T: 028 9261 1255
E: enquiries@newforgehouse.com
W: www.newforgehouse.com

BEDROOMS: 6.
OPEN: Feb–19 Dec, restaurant closed
Sun/Mon evenings.
FACILITIES: drawing room, dining
room, free Wi-Fi, in-room TV
(Freeview), wedding facilities,
2-acre gardens (vegetable
garden, wild flower meadow,
orchard, woodland) in 50 acres of
pastureland, unsuitable for disabled.
BACKGROUND MUSIC: in dining room.
LOCATION: edge of village, 20 miles
SW of Belfast.
CHILDREN: over-10s welcomed.
DOGS: not allowed.
CREDIT CARDS: Diners, MasterCard,
Visa.
PRICES: [2018] per room B&B single
€89–€135, double €129–€199,
D,B&B double €219–€289. À la
carte €45.

MOUNTRATH Co. Laois

Map 6:C5

ROUNDWOOD HOUSE   `NEW`

Infused with warmth, Paddy and Hannah Flynn's
Georgian mansion beneath the Slieve Bloom
mountains, regains a full entry this year. It may
be a little lived in, but few hotels can match its
character. Trusted readers give a flavour: 'We
sat by the log fire in the drawing room drinking
wine and talking with Hannah and Paddy until
well into the night.' Public spaces have original
decorative features, period furnishings. Hannah's
childhood home, the house has a library devoted
to the evolution of civilisation, assembled by her
father. Bedrooms have antiques, books, artwork,
comfortable bed (niggles, a 'minute' bathroom,
a cracked basin). Four rooms are in the even
older Yellow House. A communal no-choice
dinner is cooked by Paddy. Vegetarian readers
enjoyed a 'beautifully presented' parsnip and
cashew nut terrine, curried carrot soup, sesame
ginger vegetable stack, 'perfect cheeses'. Meat-
eaters devoured lamb loin medallions, blueberry
reduction, squash purée, green beans almondine,
mint sauce, garlic and lemon cubed potatoes.
'We've enjoyed Paddy's cooking before but it's
now on a different level.' Breakfast, served until
11 am, brings home-made bread, yoghurt, muesli,
fruit compote, a full Irish. (Jeanette Bloor)

25% DISCOUNT VOUCHERS

Mountrath
R32 TK79

T: 00 353 57 873 2120
E: info@roundwoodhouse.com
W: www.roundwoodhouse.com

BEDROOMS: 10. 4 in garden building.
OPEN: all year except 24–26 Dec.
FACILITIES: drawing room, dining
room, study, library, free Wi-Fi,
wedding facilities, 18-acre grounds,
parking, unsuitable for disabled.
BACKGROUND MUSIC: none.
LOCATION: 3 miles N of village.
CHILDREN: all ages welcomed,
under-5s sharing with parents free,
travel cots, children's supper.
DOGS: not allowed.
CREDIT CARDS: all major cards.
PRICES: [2018] per room B&B single
€105, double €160–€210, D,B&B
double €205–€220. Set dinner (3
courses, Sun–Thurs) €45, (5 courses,
all week) €60, children's supper
€12.50.

MULTYFARNHAM Co. Westmeath

Map 6:C5

MORNINGTON HOUSE

'In rolling countryside with views of mountains
and hills', Anne and Warwick O'Hara run their
18th-century mansion-turned-guest house with
a commitment and enthusiasm that delighted
our inspectors. After 'a warm and friendly
greeting', tea and cakes were served by the fire
in a lounge with tall, dual-aspect windows,
'pretty flower arrangements, original wallpaper
from 1896'. Upstairs, a short corridor led to a
private bathroom, then to a country house-style
bedroom with 'a smallish brass-framed double
bed, white shutters, a simple, tiled fireplace'.
All bedrooms have antiques, a comfy armchair,
fresh flowers. Before a set dinner cooked by
Anne and served at 8 pm, guests gather and
help themselves to gin or sherry. The candlelit
dining room has a rich, red carpet and curtains,
1930s wallpaper. The night's menu might
typically be soup, braised beef, frangipane tart
with strawberry ice cream. Plentiful vegetables
are from the kitchen garden. In the morning
Warwick dons the apron to prepare and serve
breakfast, cooking dishes to order including
'tasty and appetising poached eggs and black
pudding'. The entire stay proved 'a unique
experience, one to be seized on and cherished'.

25% DISCOUNT VOUCHERS

Multyfarnham
N91 NX92

T: 00 353 44 937 2191
E: stay@mornington.ie
W: www.mornington.ie

BEDROOMS: 4.
OPEN: 19 Apr–31 Oct (and for
groups in Nov).
FACILITIES: drawing room, dining
room, free Wi-Fi in reception and
some bedrooms, 50-acre grounds
(¾-acre garden, croquet, bicycle
hire), unsuitable for disabled.
BACKGROUND MUSIC: none.
LOCATION: 9 miles NW of
Mullingar.
CHILDREN: welcomed by
arrangement only.
DOGS: not allowed.
CREDIT CARDS: all major cards.
PRICES: [2018] per person B&B single
€95, double €150. Set dinner €45.

OUGHTERARD Co. Galway

Map 6:C4

CURRAREVAGH HOUSE

Reputedly Ireland's longest running hotel under one family's ownership: its 'true country house' atmosphere and easy access to rural pursuits draw back guests year after year. 'We met a gentleman who first came half a century ago.' The early Victorian manor house forgoes TVs, cutting-edge technology, slick bathrooms or even keys in its spacious, homely bedrooms, some with period furniture and shutters. Instead, there are books, big windows with 'wonderful views' of Lough Corrib, and 'easy-going, warm hospitality' from fifth-generation owners Henry and Lucy Hodgson. 'The hotel is unapologetically what it is,' says one regular visitor this year. 'Reassuring, cosy, undemanding.' Guests can fish with local ghillies, walk through acres of parkland, or choose from six nearby golf courses. Indoors, unfussy country house dinners, cooked by Prue Leith-trained Lucy Hodgson, reliably deliver main courses of 'lamb, beef, venison, hake or cod, plated in a modest quantity, with seconds offered – a perfect compromise'. After dessert, there are Irish cheeses; 'a very happy formula'. As for the breakfasts, 'the Irish formula is always available, but so is scrambled egg and smoked salmon'. (Richard Parish, PH)

25% DISCOUNT VOUCHERS

Oughterard

T: 00 353 91 552312
E: mail@currarevagh.com
W: www.currarevagh.com

BEDROOMS: 12.
OPEN: 15 Mar–31 Oct.
FACILITIES: sitting room/library, drawing room, dining room, free Wi-Fi, 180-acre grounds (lakeshore, fishing, ghillies available, boating, tennis, croquet), golf, riding nearby, unsuitable for disabled.
BACKGROUND MUSIC: none.
LOCATION: 4 miles NW of Oughterard.
CHILDREN: all ages welcomed.
DOGS: allowed in 1 bedroom, not in public rooms.
CREDIT CARDS: Diners, MasterCard, Visa.
PRICES: [2018] per person B&B €75–€110, D,B&B €110–€135. Set dinner €50.

RATHMULLAN Co. Donegal

Map 6:B5

RATHMULLAN HOUSE

Lawns run down to a sandy beach on the shores of Lough Swilly from this engaging country house, built for a bishop in 1760 and enlarged by serial extensions. It has been in the Wheeler family since 1962, and Mark and Mary are the second generation to run it. In lounges and library there are deep armchairs, paintings, antiques, ticking clocks, blazing turf fires. The Raja Room recalls colonial India. The older bedrooms are large, even huge, lovingly put together, idiosyncratic. Some have lough views; some interconnect. Those in the Regency wing, added in 2004, are more contemporary, with balcony or patio. In the Cook & Gardener restaurant, fruit and vegetables from the kitchen garden, and locally landed fish, feature in such dishes as seafood chowder; hand-picked Burtonport crab linguine; roast breast of free-range Glin Valley chicken, champ, garden leaves and shallot purée. Guide readers love the 'totally relaxed feeling', the 'charming staff', the 'incredible walled garden', and the 'delectable wood-fired pizzas' and Italian ice cream in the subterranean Tap Room. A breakfast buffet of 'delightful surprises' is also appreciated. Golf courses abound. (L and PS)

Rathmullan
F92 YA0F

T: 00 353 74 915 8188
E: reception@rathmullanhouse.com
W: www.rathmullanhouse.com

BEDROOMS: 34. Some on ground floor, 1 suitable for disabled.
OPEN: all year, except midweek during first 3 weeks of December, 24-28 December, 2–31 January. Only open weekends in February, March until Easter.
FACILITIES: 4 sitting rooms, library, TV room, playroom, cellar bar/pizza parlour, restaurant, free Wi-Fi, in-room TV (terrestrial), wedding facilities, 15-metre heated indoor swimming pool, 7-acre grounds (tennis, croquet).
BACKGROUND MUSIC: none.
LOCATION: ½ mile N of village.
CHILDREN: all ages welcomed.
DOGS: allowed in bedrooms, not in public rooms.
CREDIT CARDS: Amex, MasterCard, Visa.
PRICES: [2018] per person B&B €80–€145. D,B&B €115–€190. À la carte €45. 1-night bookings sometimes refused.

RIVERSTOWN Co. Sligo

Map 6:B5

COOPERSHILL

An ostentation of peacocks and formal gardens greets visitors to the O'Hara's otherwise laid-back and informal Georgian mansion. Simon and Christina O'Hara, the seventh generation of the family to live within its robust walls, have a welcoming buzz as the 'gracious' hosts. They invite guests 'to feel that they are visiting old friends'. Bursting with fresh flowers from the award-winning gardens, the large, antique-filled rooms have the peaceful air that comes with being sheltered by a vast patchwork of wood and pastureland. Bedrooms eschew TV and radio, in favour of newspapers and a small library of novels to be enjoyed from a chaise longue and high old bed, or while luxuriating in the 1900s canopied bath and green-tiled grotto found in one of the rooms. Irish country dinners, served under the watchful eye of 18th-century family portraits, have limited choice but the freshest ingredients. Most of the produce is grown and reared within 200 yards of the dining room: the ultimate farm-to-fork. At breakfast, home-baked potato bread and fresh eggs from the neighbour's hens are ideal high-grade fuel for exploring Yeats country. (CG, and others)

Riverstown
F52 EC52

T: 00 353 71 916 5108
E: reservations@coopershill.com
W: www.coopershill.com

BEDROOMS: 7.
OPEN: Apr–Oct, off-season house parties by arrangement.
FACILITIES: front hall, drawing room, dining room, snooker room, free Wi-Fi, wedding facilities, 500-acre estate (garden, tennis, croquet, woods, farmland, river with trout fishing), unsuitable for disabled.
BACKGROUND MUSIC: none.
LOCATION: 11 miles SE of Sligo.
CHILDREN: all ages welcomed.
DOGS: not allowed.
CREDIT CARDS: MasterCard, Visa.
PRICES: [2018] per person B&B €101–€125, D,B&B €157–€181. Set dinner €56.

SHANAGARRY Co. Cork

Map 6:D5

BALLYMALOE HOUSE

'Remains a flagship in its idiom,' writes a trusted reader, of this legendary enterprise, centred on a wisteria-draped Georgian house grafted on to the remains of a Norman castle. When farmer's wife Myrtle Allen, who sadly died in June 2018, opened a restaurant here in 1964, it was with all the values of localism, freshness and seasonality we espouse today. Since then Ballymaloe has acquired a shop, café, cookery school and heated swimming pool, but traditions prevail. 'The welcome was warm, hospitality first class.' Afternoon tea is served by the drawing room's crackling fire. Bedrooms are supplied daily with fresh-cut flowers (sweet peas, old roses), and offer 'utter comfort'. Some are on the ground floor, with courtyard access. In the restaurant, chef Jason Fahey works with seasonal ingredients from the walled garden and home farm, to create his 'superb', daily-changing menus. Sample dishes: escalope of Ballycotton John Dory, garden herb relish, pak choi; roast East Cork beef with red wine sauce, salsa verde, horseradish cream and garden green onions. Overall, Ballymaloe is 'excellent', run by 'kind people'. The breakfast is 'everything you would wish'. (Richard Parish, and others)

Shanagarry
P25 Y070

T: 00 353 21 465 2531
E: res@ballymaloe.ie
W: www.ballymaloe.ie

BEDROOMS: 29. 9 in adjacent building, 3 on ground floor suitable for disabled.
OPEN: all year, except 24–26 Dec, 7 Jan–3 Feb.
FACILITIES: drawing room, bar, 2 small sitting/TV rooms, conservatory, restaurant, private dining rooms, free Wi-Fi, wedding/event facilities, 6-acre gardens, 300-acre farm, tennis, 9-hole golf course, outdoor heated swimming pool (10 by 4 metres, summer), cookery school, café/kitchen shop, restaurant wheelchair accessible.
BACKGROUND MUSIC: none.
LOCATION: 20 miles E of Cork.
CHILDREN: all ages welcomed.
DOGS: not allowed.
CREDIT CARDS: Amex, MasterCard, Visa.
PRICES: [2018] per room B&B single €200–€205, double €215–€315, D,B&B double €350–€465. Set dinner (5 courses) €75.

SHORTLIST

The Shortlist complements our main section by
including potential but untested new entries
and appropriate places in areas where we have
limited choice. It also has some hotels that have
had a full entry in the Guide, but have not
attracted feedback from our readers.

Headlam Hall, Darlington, Co. Durham

LONDON

Map 2:D4

THE ALMA, 499 Old York Road, Wandsworth, SW18 1TF. Tel 020 8870 2537, www.almawandsworth. com. Off the tourist trail, this brick-and-tile Victorian pub (Young & Co's Brewery), in a gentrified slice of South London, is popular with locals. Beyond the bar's hubbub, spacious accommodation is found in a quiet coaching house courtyard. The stylish bedrooms have hand-printed wallpaper, bespoke furnishings, a capsule coffee machine; some rooms can accommodate a fold-out bed for a child. Among the more spacious, a garden suite has a private terrace and outdoor seating. The light, modern dining room serves decent gastropub fare, perhaps Young's ale-battered cod, thick cut chips, mushy peas. Weekends have a leisurely start: breakfast is served until 11 am. (Opposite Wandsworth Town railway station; 15 mins to Waterloo) BEDROOMS 23, 2 on ground floor suitable for disabled. OPEN all year. FACILITIES bar, restaurant, function room, free Wi-Fi, in-room TV (Sky, Freeview), civil wedding licence, complimentary use of spa and gym nearby. BACKGROUND MUSIC in bar and restaurant. LOCATION by Wandsworth Town railway station. CHILDREN all ages welcomed. DOGS allowed. CREDIT CARDS Amex, MasterCard, Visa. PRICES per room B&B from £139. À la carte £35.

THE AMPERSAND, 10 Harrington Road, SW7 3ER. Tel 020 7589 5895, www.ampersandhotel.com. A trove of museums and galleries are a stone's throw from this characterful Victorian hotel. Its modern incarnation draws inspiration from local landmarks with the high-ceilinged bedrooms following different themes linked to nearby museums: astronomy, botany, geometry, music and ornithology. Varying in size (some allow smoking), each has plush fabrics, a smart bathroom with upmarket toiletries, bright hues, free soft drinks in the minibar. Suites have floor-to-ceiling windows and a balcony. Down the filigree period staircase, the basement restaurant serves cocktails and Mediterranean dishes under the cellar arches. Light meals and afternoon tea are available in the drawing room with its deep sofas and armchairs. (Underground: South Kensington) BEDROOMS 111, some suitable for disabled. OPEN all year. FACILITIES lifts, bar, restaurant, private dining room, drawing rooms, business centre, games room, gym, free Wi-Fi, in-room TV, public parking nearby. BACKGROUND MUSIC in public areas. LOCATION South Kensington. CHILDREN all ages welcomed. DOGS allowed. CREDIT CARDS Amex, MasterCard, Visa. PRICES per room from £192. Buffet breakfast £16, à la carte £32.

THE ARCH LONDON, 50 Great Cumberland Place, Marble Arch, W1H 7FD. Tel 020 7724 4700, www. thearchlondon.com. The Bejerano family's distinctive hotel close to Marble Arch and Hyde Park retains a bijou feel, despite sprawling across seven Georgian town houses and two mews homes. It is liked for its cosseting details and accommodating staff. Artworks by rising British artists line the corridors. Comprehensively equipped bedrooms mix original features with unflinching colour. All provide state-of-the-art technology, Nespresso machine, a complimentary overnight shoe shine and a bathroom with upmarket toiletries. A bubbly cream tea is served in the champagne lounge, while the brasserie gives British classics a modern twist, perhaps grilled bavette steak, caramelised shallots, grain mustard dressing, rocket salad. Breakfast (charged separately) has comprehensive cooked options. (Underground: Marble Arch) BEDROOMS 82, 2 suitable for disabled. OPEN all year. FACILITIES 2 bars, brasserie, library, gym, free Wi-Fi, in-room TV (Sky), valet parking. BACKGROUND MUSIC in public spaces. LOCATION near Marble Arch Underground. CHILDREN all ages welcomed. DOGS allowed (in bedrooms, some public rooms). CREDIT CARDS Amex, MasterCard, Visa. PRICES per room from £264. Breakfast (continental) £19. Set menus £35–£45.

BATTY LANGLEY'S, 12 Folgate Street, Spitalfields, E1 6BX. Tel 020 7377 4390, www.battylangleys.com. Georgian 'Grand Taste' and sybaritic comforts are the trademarks of Peter McKay and Douglas Blain's eccentric hotel in gentrified Spitalfields. Two 18th-century buildings have been artfully restored with an air of playful opulence. The wood-panelled sitting room, with its plush sofas, cosy nooks and a well-stocked honesty bar, offers a tranquil escape from nearby bustling Brick Lane and the City. In the bedrooms, crushed velvet bedspreads and goose down-filled pillows sit comfortably with modern comforts and quirky details – bathrooms might have a loo behind a bookcase, or a 'bathing machine'. Breakfast, delivered to the room, has yogurt, fruit, granola, fresh pastries, bagels. (Underground: Liverpool Street; Overground: Shoreditch High Street) BEDROOMS 29, 1 suitable for disabled. OPEN all year. FACILITIES lift, library, parlour, lounge, meeting rooms, free Wi-Fi, in-room TV, small courtyard. BACKGROUND MUSIC none. LOCATION 5 mins' walk from Liverpool Street station. CHILDREN all ages welcomed (under-12s free of charge, by arrangement). DOGS assistance dogs only. CREDIT CARDS Amex, MasterCard, Visa. PRICES per room from £212. Breakfast £11.95.

BERMONDSEY SQUARE HOTEL, 9 Bermondsey Square, Tower Bridge Road, Bermondsey, SE1 3UN. Tel 020 7378 2450, www.bermondseysquarehotel.co.uk. Galleries, antiques and arthouse cinema – oh my! Buzzy Bermondsey is home to trendsetting London culture and this youthful, privately owned hotel. Snappy bedrooms offer good-value, comfortable accommodation in a bright, modern setting. Spacious top-floor suites have expansive views stretching to Big Ben, and private terraces, one with a large hot tub; on lower levels, some rooms share a terrace. The book-lined lounge/restaurant serves an all-day British menu; a lively patio on the square opens for dining in fine weather. The hotel is alcohol free, but glasses are provided for guests who bring their own, to have in their bedroom. Breakfast has smoothies and breakfast burrito. (Underground: Bermondsey, London Bridge) BEDROOMS 90. 4 suitable for disabled. OPEN all year. FACILITIES lift, open-plan lounge/restaurant/co-working space, free Wi-Fi, in-room TV (Freeview), meeting rooms, terrace. BACKGROUND MUSIC in public spaces. LOCATION near

Bermondsey Station, London Bridge Station. **CHILDREN** all ages welcomed. **DOGS** allowed (boutique dog beds). **CREDIT CARDS** Amex, MasterCard, Visa. **PRICES** per room B&B from £129.

THE BULL & THE HIDE, 4 Devonshire Row, Bishopsgate, EC2M 4RH. Tel 020 7655 4805, www.thebullandthehide. com. Inside the Square Mile, good food and sharp accommodation are found at this popular tavern with a contentious history – two of its former owners were reputedly the 'true' authors of certain Shakespearean plays. Part of Hush Heath Estate, its guests check in at the copper-fronted bar, also the place to enjoy a locally distilled gin. Upstairs, well-designed bedrooms have good lighting; underfloor heating in the bathroom. A shared pantry is available to guests in superior rooms. Alongside the Hide restaurant's seasonal menu, quality pub grub, sourced from nearby markets, is served all day in the bar. Breakfast has avocado on toast, various omelettes. Some ambient noise can be expected. (Underground: Liverpool Street) **BEDROOMS** 7. **OPEN** all year, except Christmas. **FACILITIES** bar, restaurant (closed Sat lunch, Sun), private dining room, free Wi-Fi and local telephone calls, in-room TV (Sky). **BACKGROUND MUSIC** in bar and restaurant. **LOCATION** Shoreditch. **CHILDREN** all ages welcomed. **DOGS** assistance dogs allowed. **CREDIT CARDS** All major cards. **PRICES** per room from £150. Breakfast £10, à la carte £38.

CHARLOTTE STREET HOTEL, 15–17 Charlotte Street, Bloomsbury, W1T 1RJ. Tel 020 7806 2000, www.firmdalehotels. com. A hop, skip and jump from Soho and the West End theatres, the zesty embrace of art and colour characterise this hotel as one of Tim and Kit Kemp's Firmdale group. Public spaces are light, with cosy log-burning fires and modern British art (the hotel's design was inspired by the Bloomsbury set); a well-stocked honesty bar is tempting. Bedrooms are light, bright and bold; varying in size, some can be connected to accommodate a group. Younger guests are warmly welcomed with a gift, a mini-bathrobe, milk and cookies at bedtime. The lively restaurant serves chef Bradd Johns's modern British classics. (Underground: Goodge Street, Tottenham Court Road) **BEDROOMS** 52, 1 suitable for disabled. **OPEN** all year, restaurant closed Sun noon–5 pm. **FACILITIES** bar/restaurant, drawing room, library, free Wi-Fi, in-room TV (Freeview), civil wedding licence, cinema, gym. **BACKGROUND MUSIC** yes. **LOCATION** 1 min N of Soho. **CHILDREN** all ages welcomed. **DOGS** not allowed. **CREDIT CARDS** Amex, MasterCard, Visa. **PRICES** per room B&B from £260. Set menu £25, à la carte £40.

CITIZENM BANKSIDE, 20 Lavington Street, Southwark, SE1 0NZ. Tel 020 3519 1680, www.citizenm.com/ destinations/london/london-bankside-hotel. Style-conscious, budget-friendly and well located – a winning combination for this 'excellent-value' hotel within easy reach of London's financial and cultural quarters. Part of a chain for 'mobile citizens', it has a cool, international atmosphere and gets the basics right: sleep, shower, Wi-Fi, breakfast, a welcoming public space. Guests check themselves in and show themselves to their room, but 'friendly and helpful' staff are there if required. Highlights of the bright, modular bedrooms: a huge bed, blackout blinds, cutting-edge technologies (a touch-screen tablet controls lighting, room temperature, window blinds and on-demand TV). Breakfast brings 'divine' freshly squeezed clementine juice; 'truly excellent' coffee. See CitizenM Tower of London, next entry. (Underground: London Bridge, Southwark) BEDROOMS 19, 12 suitable for disabled. OPEN all year. FACILITIES lift, open-plan lobby/bar/deli, work stations, meeting rooms, free Wi-Fi, in-room TV. BACKGROUND MUSIC in public spaces. LOCATION Bankside, close to Tate Modern. CHILDREN all ages welcomed. DOGS not allowed. CREDIT CARDS All major cards. PRICES per room from £189. Breakfast from £13.95. Registered 'Citizens' receive the best available rate and a complimentary drink on arrival.

CITIZENM TOWER OF LONDON, 40 Trinity Square, City of London, EC 3N 4DJ. Tel 020 3519 4830, www.citizenm.com. Breathtaking views, a super-cool interior, a tech-lover's dream, this Dutch-owned modern hotel delivers good-value accommodation with bundles of style. Check yourself in (multilingual staff are on hand when needed). In the buzzy living room-cum-lobby: jaunty furnishings, iMac-adorned work stations, a library of design, fashion and travel books. The open-kitchen canteen serves breakfasts, light lunches and simple dinners. Snug, state-of-the-art bedrooms have a large bed, a free minibar; a touch-screen tablet to control lighting, temperature and the TV. Some have a picture-window facing straight on to the Tower of London. On the top floor, a residents-only bar gazes across the capital old and new.

(Underground: Tower Hill) BEDROOMS 370, some suitable for disabled. OPEN all year. FACILITIES lift, residents' bar, open-plan lobby/canteen/workspace, meeting rooms, free Wi-Fi, in-room TV. BACKGROUND MUSIC in public areas. LOCATION by Tower Hill Underground station. CHILDREN all ages welcomed. DOGS not allowed. CREDIT CARDS Amex, MasterCard, Visa. PRICES room from £179. Breakfast £13.95. Registered 'Citizens' receive the best available rate.

COUNTY HALL PREMIER INN, Belvedere Road, Southbank, SE1 7PB. Tel 0871 527 8648, www.premierinn.com/gb/en/home. For good-value accommodation in the heart of the action, it's hard to beat this historic Portland stone-built former county hall, now part of the Premier Inn hotel chain. The rooms are 'simply furnished' (most have a king-size bed, however), and breakfast can be busy, but the riverside location – under the gaze of the London Eye – is splendid. Plus decent double glazing and thick blackout curtains minimise street noise. Self-service check-in booths are in the lobby; down the hall, the restaurant serves steaks, burgers, salads. The Sea Life London Aquarium is within the same building; the Royal Festival Hall and Hayward Gallery are five minutes' walk away. (Underground: Waterloo, Westminster) BEDROOMS 314, some suitable for disabled. OPEN all year. FACILITIES lift, lobby, bar, restaurant, free Wi-Fi, in-room TV (Freeview), conference facilities. BACKGROUND MUSIC in public areas. LOCATION South Bank. CHILDREN all ages welcomed. DOGS not allowed. CREDIT CARDS Amex, MasterCard, Visa. PRICES per room from £104. Meal deal (dinner and breakfast) from £23.99.

COVENT GARDEN HOTEL, 10 Monmouth Street, Covent Garden, WC2H 9HB. Tel 020 7806 1000, www.firmdalehotels. com. West End experiences of every kind are on the doorstep of this well-heeled hotel in ever-buzzing Theatreland. The wood-panelled drawing room and characterful bedrooms display co-owner Kit Kemp's signature modern English style: all sassy wallpapers, elegantly mismatched furnishings and vintage prints. Bedrooms are utterly individual, with theatrical bursts of colour; most have views across the city; some have a deep bathtub in a granite-and-oak bathroom. Connecting rooms are ideal for families and groups. A modern menu, available in Brasserie Max or in the rooms, includes such dishes as roast leg of lamb, aubergine, parsley, tabbouleh, tahini. Breakfast (charged extra) includes vegan and vegetarian options. (Underground: Covent Garden, Leicester Square) **BEDROOMS** 58. **OPEN** all year. **FACILITIES** drawing room, library, restaurant, meeting room, free Wi-Fi, in-room TV (Freeview), cinema, spa room, gym. **BACKGROUND MUSIC** in public areas. **LOCATION** in Covent Garden. **CHILDREN** all ages welcomed (amenities, treats, activities). **DOGS** small dogs allowed, by arrangement. **CREDIT CARDS** Amex, MasterCard, Visa. **PRICES** per room from £426. Breakfast £15.50–£28.50, à la carte £42.

DORSET SQUARE HOTEL, 39–40 Dorset Square, Marylebone, NW1 6QN. Tel 020 7723 7874, www.firmdalehotels. com. The quiet Regency garden square, home to this discreet town house hotel, was the original site of Thomas Lord's cricket ground. That history is imaginatively captured throughout the stylish property thanks to the experienced hands of the Firmdale Hotel group. Bold patterns and prints eddy pleasingly in the high-ceilinged drawing room with its honesty bar and open fire, and in the individually decorated bedrooms. While varying in size, most have views of a leafy private garden. Children are welcomed with special toiletries and a creative afternoon tea. At mealtimes, the Potting Shed restaurant serves Mediterranean-inspired English brasserie dishes such as confit chicken leg, roasted garlic mash, Swiss chard. (Underground: Marylebone) **BEDROOMS** 38, 1 suitable for disabled. **OPEN** all year. **FACILITIES** lift, drawing room, bar, restaurant, free Wi-Fi, in-room TV (Freeview), room service. **BACKGROUND MUSIC** live guitar evenings in bar and restaurant Tues and Thurs. **LOCATION** in Marylebone. **CHILDREN** all ages welcomed (changing facilities, cots, babysitting). **DOGS** allowed by arrangement. **CREDIT CARDS** Amex, MasterCard, Visa. **PRICES** per room from £240. Continental breakfast buffet £12.50, set menu £23.50, à la carte £33.

ECCLESTON SQUARE HOTEL, 37 Eccleston Square, Belgravia, SW1V 1PB. Tel 020 3503 0691, www.ecclestonsquarehotel. com. Be 'wowed' by Olivia Byrne's sophisticated Pimlico hotel, where 'domesticated heaven' meets high-spec technology. The 'super-friendly staff' at the Georgian building maintain an 'impeccable' standard. The 'comfortable rooms' (some small, some with a balcony) have a monochrome palette and high-tech-but-intuitive features: a 'digital concierge' on an iPad; smart-glass shower walls; an adjustable bed with massage settings. Rooms have a do-it-yourself capsule coffee machine, and genteel pots of tea are delivered on request. Guests are also given a smartphone loaded with local information and free mobile Internet. Neighbourhood eateries abound, but there are also simple dishes in the cocktail lounge, perhaps a lobster roll or grilled salmon. (Underground: Victoria) **BEDROOMS** 39. **OPEN** all year. **FACILITIES** drawing room, cocktail lounge, free Wi-Fi, in-room TV (Sky), parking discounts. **BACKGROUND MUSIC** in public areas. **LOCATION** 5 mins' walk from Victoria train and tube station. **CHILDREN** over-13s welcomed. **DOGS** not allowed. **CREDIT CARDS** all major cards. **PRICES** per room B&B from £220. 25% DISCOUNT VOUCHERS

THE FIELDING, 4 Broad Court, off Bow Street, Covent Garden, WC2B 5QZ. Tel 020 7836 8305, www.thefieldinghotel.co.uk. 'Simple, well located and representing good value', this small hotel with a pretty, flower-decked Georgian exterior is 'remarkably quiet' considering its prime position in bustling Covent Garden. Henry Fielding, the novelist and one-time local magistrate, lends his name. Audience and cast members of the nearby Royal Opera House like it for its well-turned-out but modest bedrooms and reliable staff. Each room has a comfortable bed, clean, well-equipped bathroom (only two have a bath), 'excellent lighting', tea- and coffee-making facilities, slippers and an eye mask. There's no breakfast, but there's plenty of choice in the surrounding neighbourhood – ask the 'helpful staff' at reception for recommendations. (Underground: Covent Garden) **BEDROOMS** 25, some on ground floor. **OPEN** all year. **FACILITIES** free Wi-Fi, in-room TV (Freeview),

free access to nearby spa and fitness centre. **BACKGROUND MUSIC** none. **LOCATION** Covent Garden. **CHILDREN** all ages welcomed (travel cots). **DOGS** not allowed. **CREDIT CARDS** all major cards. **PRICES** per room single from £108, double from £168.

41, 41 Buckingham Palace Road, Victoria, SW1W 0PS. Tel 020 7300 0041, www.41hotel.com. Front-facing rooms peep into the royal mews from the fifth floor of this historic building, overlooking Buckingham Palace. Discreet, luxurious, this Red Carnation group hotel gets to know its guests before arrival, the better to anticipate their whims: a questionnaire safeguards personal preferences (pillow firmness, a humidifier, yoga mat, etc.) in the distinctive black-and-white bedrooms; home-made treats and season-specific bathrobes are among the thoughtful extras. Jeeves and Wooster-style pampering is bolstered by a personal butler and an invitation to 'plunder the pantry'. Sister hotel The Rubens (within the same building) takes care of lunch and dinner. On Sundays, a leisurely start: breakfast is served until 1 pm. (Underground: Victoria) **BEDROOMS** 30, some suitable for disabled if requested. **OPEN** all year. **FACILITIES** lounge, free Wi-Fi, in-room TV (Sky), room service, butler and chauffeur service, free access to nearby spa and gym. **BACKGROUND MUSIC** in public areas. **LOCATION** near Victoria station. **CHILDREN** all ages welcomed. **DOGS** allowed (concierge, welcome hamper, bed). **CREDIT CARDS** all major cards. **PRICES** per room B&B from £365.

GOOD HOTEL, Royal Victoria Dock, Western Gateway, London Docklands,

E16 1FA. Tel 020 3637 7401, www.
goodhotellondon.com. A short gangway
over the Thames accesses this 'young,
trendy looking' floating hotel 'with a
cause'. The social business, moored
in Royal Victoria Docks, invests in
charitable initiatives, including on-the-
job training for long-term-unemployed
locals. A guest this year found its staff
'very good', but felt housekeeping let the
side down. The 'great, spacious' open-
plan industrial-style living room has
freelancers and budding entrepreneurs
in mind (communal tables, work
stations), balanced by cosy, cushion-filled
nooks. All-day breakfast and light bites
are served in the living room, and on the
Astroturfed rooftop garden. Minimalist
bedrooms have original artwork and
tea-making facilities; picture windows
look across the water to the city. (DLR:
Royal Victoria) BEDROOMS 148. OPEN
all year. FACILITIES bar, lounge, library,
restaurant, meeting rooms, free Wi-Fi,
lift, terrace, 24-hour concierge service,
bicycle hire. BACKGROUND MUSIC in
public areas. LOCATION near City
Airport. CHILDREN all ages welcomed
(cots, extra beds). DOGS assistance dogs
only in bedrooms, other dogs on lead
in public areas. CREDIT CARDS Amex,
MasterCard, Visa. PRICES per room B&B
from £95. À la carte: £29.

GREAT NORTHERN HOTEL, Pancras
Road, King's Cross, N1C 4TB. Tel 020
3388 0800, www.gnhlondon.com. This
revamped north London landmark-
turned-luxury hotel is the jewel of
regentrified King's Cross. The red brick
railway stopover, designed by Lewis
Cubitt in 1851, opens on to the western
concourse of King's Cross station.
Travellers en route to the Continent
like its convenience for St Pancras

International terminus, next door. The
bedrooms' handsome fittings and decor
evoke the elegance of vintage sleeper
carriages. A help-yourself pantry on
each floor has teas, good coffee, biscuits,
cakes; the lively Plum + Spilt Milk
restaurant, named after the livery of the
Flying Scotsman's dining cars, serves
'excellent' modern dishes including
lamb rack, shallot and wild garlic purée,
spring vegetables. (Underground: King's
Cross St Pancras, Euston) BEDROOMS 91,
some suitable for disabled. OPEN all year.
FACILITIES lift, 3 bars, restaurant, Kiosk
food stall, free Wi-Fi, in-room TV
(Sky), room service. BACKGROUND MUSIC
in bars and restaurant. LOCATION King's
Cross. CHILDREN all ages welcomed.
DOGS not allowed. CREDIT CARDS All
major cards. PRICES per room B&B from
£219. À la carte £45.

HAM YARD HOTEL, One Ham Yard,
Soho, W1D 7DT. Tel 020 3642 2000,
www.firmdalehotels.com. Guests are
bowled over by this tranquil Soho hotel.
While it shares the well-considered
design of its Firmdale Hotels group
siblings, the original 1950s bowling alley
is all its own. A Tony Cragg sculpture
greets visitors in the courtyard entrance,
a hint of the coolly tasteful interiors
awaiting within: vibrant fabrics,
quirky furniture and the latest from
an international roster of artists. The
elegant bedrooms have city or courtyard
views through floor-to-ceiling windows.
There's top-to-bottom appeal from a
beehive-lined residents' roof terrace
to a neon lady diver overlooking the
basement bar; in between, the well-
stocked library and the vast restaurant
serve quick teas and leisurely meals.
(Underground: Piccadilly Circus)
BEDROOMS 91, 6 suitable for disabled.

OPEN all year. FACILITIES lift, bar, restaurant, drawing room, library, meeting rooms, spa, gym, free Wi-Fi, in-room TV (Freeview), civil wedding licence, rooftop terrace and garden, valet parking (charge). BACKGROUND MUSIC in bar. LOCATION Soho. CHILDREN all ages welcomed. DOGS allowed 'on a case by case basis'. CREDIT CARDS Amex, MasterCard, Visa. PRICES per room from £426. Breakfast from £18. À la carte £42.

HAYMARKET HOTEL, 1 Suffolk Place, West End, SW1Y 4HX. Tel 020 7470 4000, www.firmdalehotels.com. A gleeful mix of vintage furnishings and striking artworks mark this 'beautiful, very quiet hotel' as a Firmdale mainstay, ideally situated for Theatreland. Guests in 2018 were 'delighted' by the staff: 'The service is excellent.' The vibrant library and the buzzy conservatory are made for relaxation; in the 'stunning heated indoor pool', a pewter bar rustles up made-to-order cocktails. The 'lovely, characterful' bedrooms have 'a very comfortable bed', a granite-and-oak bathroom. Brumus restaurant serves modern bistro dishes – taken on the terrace when the weather's fine. 'Breakfast is top-quality': huevos rancheros, 'wonderful granola' and 'fresh-pressed apple and watermelon juice' are highlights. (Underground: Green Park, Piccadilly) BEDROOMS 50, plus 5-bed town house, some suitable for disabled. OPEN all year. FACILITIES lift, lobby, library, conservatory, bar, restaurant, free Wi-Fi, in-room TV, civil wedding licence, indoor swimming pool, gym. BACKGROUND MUSIC in bar and restaurant. LOCATION in the heart of London's theatre district. CHILDREN all ages welcomed. DOGS allowed 'on a case by case basis'. CREDIT CARDS Amex,

MasterCard, Visa. PRICES per room B&B from £324. Breakfast from £18.

HENRIETTA HOTEL, 14–15 Henrietta Street, WC2E 8QH. www. henriettahotel.com. A Gallic oasis created by four Parisians (Experimental group), this small hotel occupies a couple of red-brick Victorian town houses with a literary past as the offices of Victor Gollancz, off busy Covent Garden Piazza. Soft curves in the chic bedrooms soften strong colours and marble skirtings, while beds sport a signature multi-layered headboard; one room at the top has views across to the London Eye from a petite balcony. The long, quirkily designed restaurant and bar has a mezzanine floor for intimate dining. The bistro is run by chef Sylvain Roucayrol, whose south-west France and Basque dishes include Galician octopus with herb relish. (Underground: Covent Garden) BEDROOMS 18. OPEN all year. FACILITIES bar, restaurant, free Wi-Fi, in-room TV, lift. BACKGROUND MUSIC none. LOCATION Covent Garden. CHILDREN all ages welcomed. DOGS assistance dogs allowed. CREDIT CARDS Amex, MasterCard, Visa. PRICES per room B&B from £250. Breakfast £15.

THE HOXTON HOLBORN, 199–206 High Holborn, WC1V 7BD. Tel 020 7661 3000, thehoxton.com. Attracting bright young things, 'budget' is far from 'boring' at this former office-block-turned-cool hotel. The cavernous lobby is the antithesis of a dull office, with communal tables, conveniently placed sockets and complimentary newspapers encouraging casual meetings between entrepreneurial types. Stylish bedrooms have smart features (under-bed storage, a flip-lid desk) and thoughtful touches (blackout curtains, a Roberts radio, a map of local hotspots). Eateries abound: all-day Brooklyn-style Hubbard & Bell; light bites, coffees and cocktails at Holborn Grind; spit-roasted birds at the Chicken Shop. Breakfast bags left on the door handle at night are, by morning, filled with a granola pot, fruit and a bottle of orange juice. Magic. (Underground: Holborn) BEDROOMS 174, some suitable for disabled. OPEN all year. FACILITIES lift, open-plan lobby/lounge/co-working space, café/bar, 2 restaurants, free Wi-Fi, meeting/function rooms. BACKGROUND MUSIC live DJ nights. LOCATION Holborn. CHILDREN all ages welcomed. DOGS assistance dogs only. CREDIT CARDS all major cards. PRICES per room B&B from £99.

THE HOXTON SHOREDITCH, 81 Great Eastern Street, Shoreditch, EC2A 3HU. Tel 020 7550 1000, thehoxton.com. 'Intensely stylish', this good-value hotel welcomes visitors with a playful blend of slick architecture and arcade-game nostalgia. Design aficionados appreciate the industrially chic lobby/lounge, and the shrewd use of space in the bedrooms, which pack in a huge circular mirror, desk, comfortable bed; 'splendid' bathrooms have a powerful shower. Larger, eclectically styled Concept rooms (requested at booking) are individually designed by local artists. Standard for all guests: a neighbourhood guidebook; an hour of free international calls. The busy Hoxton Grill with its exposed brick walls serves American-style grub all day. Mornings, a breakfast bag is delivered to the door (fruit, granola, bottled orange juice). (Underground: Old Street) BEDROOMS 210, 11 suitable for disabled. OPEN all year. FACILITIES lift, lounge,

shop, free Wi-Fi, courtyard, meeting rooms. BACKGROUND MUSIC in public areas. LOCATION Shoreditch. CHILDREN all ages welcomed. DOGS assistance dogs allowed. CREDIT CARDS all major cards. PRICES per room B&B from £99.

H10 LONDON WATERLOO, 284–302 Waterloo Road, ES1 8RQ. Tel 020 7928 4062, www.h10hotels.com/en/london-hotels/h10-london-waterloo. There is plenty to toast at this good-value hotel within walking distance of the National Theatre and the South Bank. A complimentary glass of cava – a nod to the chain hotel's Spanish origins – welcomes guests. Newspapers and magazines are available in the lounge. Floor-to-ceiling windows in the understated modern bedrooms (some small) have 'good double glazing' to protect from outside noises; some offer panoramas of the city. The very best views – and cocktails – are in the eighth-floor Waterloo Sky bar. 'Excellent cooked dishes' and a 'considerable breakfast buffet' kickstart the day, while the first-floor restaurant serves Mediterranean fare with a Spanish flourish. (Underground: Waterloo) BEDROOMS 177, some suitable for disabled. OPEN all year. FACILITIES 2 bars, restaurant, free Wi-Fi, in-room TV. BACKGROUND MUSIC in public areas. CHILDREN all ages welcomed. DOGS assistance dogs allowed. CREDIT CARDS all major cards. PRICES per room B&B from £119, D,B&B from £141. À la carte £30.

INDIGO, 16 London Street, Paddington, W2 1HL. Tel 020 7706 4444, www.ihg.com/hotelindigo/hotels/gb/en/reservation. Ideally located for guests travelling onward, this modern hotel is within easy reach of Paddington station and express trains to Heathrow. Part of the InterContinental Hotels group, it stands in a collection of converted 18th-century town houses. A specially commissioned glass staircase leads to well-designed bedrooms, brightened by colourful accents and a photographic mural of nearby Hyde Park or Little Venice; attic rooms (small) have great character, sloping ceilings. The essentials are in each: a capsule coffee machine, complimentary soft drinks, earplugs; a spa-inspired shower. Contemporary takes on British classics are served in the London Street brasserie. Breakfast (good choice) arrives with views over leafy Norfolk Square. (Underground: Paddington) BEDROOMS 64, 2 suitable for disabled. OPEN all year. FACILITIES lounge/lobby, bar, brasserie, free Wi-Fi, in-room TV, terrace. BACKGROUND MUSIC in public areas. LOCATION Paddington. CHILDREN all ages welcomed. DOGS assistance dogs allowed. PRICES per room B&B from £177.

THE KENSINGTON, 109–113 Queen's Gate, Kensington, SW7 5LR. Tel 020 7589 6300, www.doylecollection.com/hotels/the-kensington-hotel. Walking distance from the attractions of South Kensington, this 'elegant yet hip, fun' hotel is 'conveniently located' for museum-hoppers and shop-till-you-droppers. The genial Victorian town house hotel (Doyle Collection) is run by 'such pleasant, helpful, accommodating staff'. 'The rooms are clean and cosy', with a marble bathroom with underfloor heating, spoiling bath products, and a capsule coffee machine as standard; sizes vary. Afternoon tea (gluten-free options available) in the 'uncluttered drawing room' is a civilised

affair; cleansing juices and smoothies are a healthy alternative. Chef Steve Gibbs's seasonal, modern menus, served in the 'lovely restaurant' or the wood-panelled bar, include the likes of crab tagliatelle, sauce Americaine. (Underground: South Kensington) BEDROOMS 150, 5 suitable for disabled. OPEN all year. FACILITIES 3 drawing rooms, bar, restaurant, free Wi-Fi, in-room TV, meeting rooms. BACKGROUND MUSIC none. CHILDREN all ages welcomed. DOGS assistance dogs allowed. CREDIT CARDS Amex, MasterCard, Visa. PRICES per room from £210. Continental breakfast £17.

KNIGHTSBRIDGE HOTEL, 10 Beaufort Gardens, Knightsbridge, SW3 1PT. Tel 020 7584 6300, www.firmdalehotels.com. All is serene at this handsome 1860s town house hotel (Firmdale group) just minutes from Hyde Park. Co-owner Kit Kemp combines statement pieces, antique prints and earthy tones in its cosy sitting rooms. A striking oversized headboard and good bedside lighting feature in the bright, spacious bedrooms. Each has a powerful shower; front rooms overlook verdant Beaufort Gardens. A short all-day room-service menu stands in lieu of a restaurant, offering the likes of crab and chilli spaghetti, while Princes and Princesses are spoiling for children (jellies, milkshakes). Museums proliferate in nearby South Kensington, but those exhausted by crowds and culture can recover with cocktails and in-room beauty treatments. (Underground: Knightsbridge) BEDROOMS 44. OPEN all year. FACILITIES drawing room, library, bar, free Wi-Fi, in-room TV (Freeview), civil wedding licence, room service. BACKGROUND MUSIC in public spaces. LOCATION Knightsbridge. CHILDREN all ages welcomed. DOGS small dogs allowed by arrangement. CREDIT CARDS Amex, MasterCard, Visa. PRICES per room from £306. Breakfast £18.

THE LASLETT, 8 Pembridge Gardens, Notting Hill, W2 4DU. Tel 020 7792 6688, www.living-rooms.co.uk. Celebrating its eclectic locality, this vibrant hotel occupies a row of five white stucco Victorian houses. One of Tracy Lowy's Living Rooms collection, it draws inspiration and energy from Notting Hill – in fact, it's named after Rhaune Laslett, a community activist who co-founded the area's annual carnival. The public spaces (part art gallery, part coffee house, part drinking hole) offer the relaxed vibe of a popular neighbourhood-hangout. Penguin classics, original artwork and vintage curios are found in the chic bedrooms; all are air conditioned, with well-equipped bathroom providing bathrobes and high-end toiletries. Eat brunch till 4 pm; all-day small plates, large plates, sweets and nibbles. (Underground: Notting Hill Gate) BEDROOMS 51, 2 are mezzanine, 5 suitable for disabled. OPEN all year. FACILITIES bar/restaurant, lift, front terrace, free Wi-Fi, in-room TV (Sky), room service, complimentary passes to local gym, discounts at nearby restaurants. BACKGROUND MUSIC all day in public areas. LOCATION next to Notting Hill Gate tube station. CHILDREN all ages welcomed. DOGS small dogs allowed by arrangement. CREDIT CARDS Amex, MasterCard, Visa. PRICES per room single from £180, double from £220. Breakfast £21. À la carte £42.

LIME TREE HOTEL, 135–137 Ebury Street, SW1W 9QU. Tel 020 7730 8191, www.limetreehotel.co.uk. Bright modernity filters through this smart, surprisingly affordable Belgravia B&B run by Charlotte and Matt Goodsall. Staff are always on hand to help carry luggage up the many flights of stairs across the two Georgian town houses. Uncluttered bedrooms have their original high ceiling, cornicing and fireplace, sash windows and the occasional creaky floorboard. They vary in size (those in the eaves are smallest), but all have the necessary basics – tea- and coffee-making facilities, a bathroom with good toiletries, a safe, a wide-screen TV. A small sitting room has guidebooks and magazines; the neat rear garden is scented with roses in the summer. (Underground: Victoria) BEDROOMS 25. OPEN all year. FACILITIES sitting room, breakfast room, free Wi-Fi, in-room TV (Freeview), meeting facilities, garden. BACKGROUND MUSIC none. CHILDREN over-5s welcomed. DOGS not allowed. CREDIT CARDS MasterCard, Visa. PRICES per room B&B £130–£250.

THE MAIN HOUSE, 6 Colville Road, Notting Hill, W11 2BP. Tel 020 7221 9691, themainhouse.co.uk. In chic yet quirky Notting Hill, visitors can live like a local at Caroline Main's eclectic Victorian guest house. Each spacious, uncluttered suite occupies an entire floor and has a tasteful mix of mellow wood, white walls and harmonious prints and artworks. Independent travellers are well supplied with the essentials for city exploration (guidebooks and maps, water, an umbrella), plus everything they might have forgotten (books, a hair dryer). The day starts with tea or coffee brought to the room, then breakfast at the nearby deli or artisan bakery (discounts available). Guests can also entertain visitors – a special doorbell is just for that purpose. (Underground: Notting Hill Gate) BEDROOMS 4. OPEN all year. FACILITIES free Wi-Fi, in-room TV (Sky), roof terrace, airport chauffeur service, DVD library. BACKGROUND MUSIC none. LOCATION 1 mile W of London's West End. CHILDREN well-behaved children of all ages welcomed. DOGS not allowed. CREDIT CARDS MasterCard, Visa. PRICES per room £130–£150 (3-night min. stay).

THE MONTAGUE ON THE GARDENS, 15 Montague Street, Bloomsbury, WC1B 5BJ. Tel 020 7637 1001, www.montaguehotel.com. Like its neighbour, the British Museum, this Bloomsbury town house hotel displays impressive antiques and curios, along with historical links to the rascally duke of Montagu – but it also has comfortable beds and excellent service. The plush property (Red Carnation Hotels group), managed by long-serving Dirk Crokaert, backs on to a leafy private garden and brims with gilded mirrors, original artworks and tapestried fabrics. Individually styled bedrooms balance high-spec technology, including on-demand films, with lavish furnishings and extras such as a bathrobe and slippers for a child. At dinner, the bistro's seasonal British cuisine includes rack of lamb with herb crust, horseradish croquettes, broad beans, carrot purée. (Underground: Russell Square) BEDROOMS 100, 1 suitable for disabled. OPEN all year. FACILITIES lounge, bar, bistro, 2 conservatories, free Wi-Fi, in-room TV (Sky), civil wedding licence, meeting/function rooms, garden terrace, cigar terrace. BACKGROUND MUSIC classical/contemporary in public areas, live jazz in bar. LOCATION Bloomsbury. CHILDREN all ages welcomed. DOGS

allowed. CREDIT CARDS all major cards. PRICES per room B&B single from £250, double from £270.

THE NADLER KENSINGTON, 25 Courtfield Gardens SW5 0PG 020 7244 2255, www.nadlerhotels.com/the-nadler-kensington. One of the Nadler Hotels group, this modernised Edwardian property attracts travellers seeking a stylish stay without breaking the bank. Minimalist rooms (some small) have neutral tones, light wood and everything one might need: a well-equipped mini-kitchen, a capsule coffee machine, Fairtrade teas; independently controlled heating and air conditioning; a choice of pillows. Comfy family rooms sleep four. Neighbourhood eateries take the place of a restaurant, and many of them offer discounts for guests. A continental breakfast may be delivered to the bedroom. South Kensington's museums are within easy reach, while a sister hotel is found in Liverpool – see Shortlist entry. (Underground: Earl's Court, Gloucester Road) BEDROOMS 65, some with bunk bed, 1 suitable for disabled. OPEN all year. FACILITIES lobby, free Wi-Fi, in-room TV, access to local gym, bicycle hire. BACKGROUND MUSIC in public areas. LOCATION South Kensington. CHILDREN all ages welcomed. DOGS assistance dogs allowed. CREDIT CARDS all major cards. PRICES per room from £179. Breakfast £9.50.

THE PILGRM, 25 London Street, W2 1HH. Tel 020 7667 6000, thepilgrm. com. A ticket toss from the station, three meticulously restored Victorian town houses in a Paddington side street have been reinvented as 'an affordable boutique hotel'. Check-in is by laptop in the coffee shop lobby (open to everyone).

A digital key system accesses rooms 'on the small side' but uncluttered, with 'all the essentials': a safe under the bed, hanging space for clothes, natural toiletries. A 'compact spotless' bathroom had a 'large shower head, amazing water pressure'. Room service is ordered by text and breakfast is served until 3 pm in the stylishly updated first-floor lounge. After that, chef Sara Lewis cooks a mix of global flavours including lentil dahl with grilled mackerel. (Underground: Paddington) BEDROOMS 73. OPEN all year. FACILITIES coffee shop, lounge, free-Wi-Fi, in-room TV, lift. BACKGROUND MUSIC in public areas. LOCATION Paddington. CHILDREN all ages welcomed (cots). DOGS not allowed. CREDIT CARDS MasterCard, Visa. PRICES per room B&B £110–£220.

THE PILOT, 68 River Way, Greenwich, SE10 0BE. Tel 020 8858 5910, www. pilotgreenwich.co.uk. Old meets new at this Georgian inn, built to serve local coal workers, that now overlooks the stark modernity of Canary Wharf. Run by Fuller's, it is probably the oldest surviving building on the Greenwich peninsula, with maps, globes and naval references creating the feel of a coastal tavern. Real ales are on tap in the traditional bar, while seasonal gastropub fare, perhaps harissa lamb chops, aubergine, feta, mint, pomegranate, roasted garlic, is served in the dining areas or the well-shaded garden. The nautical theme runs through most of the neat bedrooms; others are quirkily decked out in record covers, clocks, sunglasses. The O2 arena is nearby. (Underground: North Greenwich) BEDROOMS 10. OPEN all year. FACILITIES bar, restaurant, free Wi-Fi, in-room TV (Freeview), function facilities, garden, roof terrace, parking. BACKGROUND MUSIC in public areas. LOCATION 12 mins' walk from O2 centre. CHILDREN all ages welcomed. DOGS assistance dogs allowed. CREDIT CARDS MasterCard, Visa. PRICES per room B&B from £160.

QBIC HOTEL, 42 Adler Street, Whitechapel, E1 1EE. Tel 020 3021 3300, qbichotels.com/london-city. The daily grind has been banished from this youthful, budget-friendly hotel in a former East London office block. In its place, a buzzy, hospitable atmosphere and off-beat style. Guests join locals at work or relaxation in the Scandinavian-style lobby – bright rugs, wooden floors, mismatched furniture – over coffee and tea (complimentary for residents). Futuristic bedrooms have good basics (comfortable bed, compact shower room), plus clever touches including a Skype-ready television, free digital newspapers and magazines. No restaurant perhaps, but plentiful curry houses and bagel shops in nearby Brick Lane. (Vending machines cater for those in a rush.) Breakfast 'grab bags' contain juice, fruit, a cereal bar. (Underground: Aldgate East, Whitechapel). BEDROOMS 183, some suitable for disabled. OPEN all year. FACILITIES lift, lounge, bar, free Wi-Fi, in-room TV (Freeview), meeting facilities. BACKGROUND MUSIC in public spaces. LOCATION Whitechapel. CHILDREN all ages welcomed. DOGS allowed in some bedrooms (not in bar or restaurant). CREDIT CARDS Amex, MasterCard, Visa. PRICES per room B&B from £73. Breakfast buffet £10.

ROSEATE HOUSE, 3 Westbourne Terrace, Paddington, W2 3UL. Tel 020 7479 6600, www.roseatehouselondon. com. 'Extremely nice staff' create a 'comfortable, homely atmosphere' at this elegant town house hotel on the way to Hyde Park. Public spaces are decorated with period furnishings and oil paintings; traditionally styled bedrooms look on to the tree-lined street or a private mews. The rooms vary in size – a four-poster suite has its own sitting room – but all have an antique desk, an easy chair; a well-supplied limestone shower or bathroom with bathrobes, slippers, high-end toiletries. In the bar: cocktails and small plates, maybe line-caught cod and lemon orzo; spinach and ricotta ravioli. Breakfast can be taken in the bedroom. (Underground: Paddington, Lancaster Gate) BEDROOMS 48. OPEN all year. FACILITIES lift, bar, restaurant, free Wi-Fi, in-room TV, business/function facilities, terrace, garden, parking. BACKGROUND MUSIC in reception, bar and restaurant during the day. LOCATION Hyde Park. CHILDREN all ages welcomed. DOGS allowed in bedrooms only. CREDIT CARDS Amex, MasterCard, Visa. PRICES per room B&B from £179. Breakfast £15.

ST JAMES'S HOTEL AND CLUB, 7–8 Park Place, St James's, SW1A 1LS. Tel 020 7316 1600, www.stjameshotelandclub. com. A quiet country house atmosphere lingers at this plush former diplomats' club close to Green Park. The Mayfair spot mixes sybaritic interiors with handsome attention to detail; swish bedrooms have hand-printed wallpaper, a Murano glass chandelier, slick technology (including free international calls from provided smart phones), spoiling toiletries; two have sweeping London views from a private terrace. In the Michelin-starred kitchen, chef William Drabble's French-inspired menu caters for pre- and post-theatre supper crowds. Harkening back to the Victorian ritual, the 1840 Afternoon Tea staunches 'that sinking feeling', with rediscovered recipes (including palace favourite: the sherry-soaked 'tipsy' cake) and cups worthy of Queen Victoria herself. (Underground: Green Park) BEDROOMS 60, 2 on ground floor. OPEN all year. FACILITIES lounge, bar, bistro, restaurant (closed Sun, Mon), 4 private dining rooms, free Wi-Fi, in-room TV, civil wedding licence, function rooms. BACKGROUND MUSIC in public areas. LOCATION near Mayfair, Buckingham Palace and St James's Palace. CHILDREN all ages welcomed. DOGS not allowed. CREDIT CARDS all major cards. PRICES per room B&B from £340, D,B&B from £449. À la carte £75

ST PAUL'S HOTEL, 153 Hammersmith Road, Hammersmith, W14 0QL. Tel 020 8846 9119, www.stpaulhotel.co.uk. Uncluttered modern bedrooms plus a good location make easy sums at this august former boys' school, now a smart hotel near the Olympia conference centre. Impressive architectural details mark it as a design by architect Alfred Waterhouse; the well-maintained Romanesque style, arches, terracotta brickwork nodding to his more famous Natural History Museum. Trim bedrooms share tastefully muted contemporary hues with the period features; some have an original fireplace; each has a marble bathroom, a minibar, tea and coffee facilities. Afternoon tea is a bubbly affair; unfussy European dishes feature in the light-filled restaurant, perhaps roast hake with clam chowder; zingy vegetable risotto. (Underground: Hammersmith, Kensington Olympia, Barons Court) BEDROOMS 35, 1 suitable for disabled. OPEN all year. FACILITIES lift, bar, restaurant, free Wi-Fi, in-room TV, wedding/business facilities, garden, limited parking. BACKGROUND MUSIC in public areas. LOCATION Hammersmith. CHILDREN all ages welcomed. DOGS not allowed. CREDIT CARDS MasterCard, Visa. PRICES per room B&B from £160. Continental breakfast £10, à la carte £35.

SLOANE SQUARE HOTEL, 7–12 Sloane Square, Chelsea, SW1W 8EG. Tel 020 7896 9988, www.sloanesquarehotel. co.uk. Once a Beatles haunt, where the Fab Four would come together, this 'ideally located hotel' enjoys a pleasing atmosphere in a 'charming neighbourhood'. 'Wonderfully efficient staff' carry luggage up to 'comfortable, well-designed bedrooms' where golden slumbers await; there's capsule coffee, a well-stocked minibar and blackout curtains. Front rooms gaze across the 'buzzy square', while at the rear, quieter rooms overlook the Arts and Crafts architecture of Holy Trinity church. Interconnecting rooms suit a family. The 'bustling' Côte brasserie next door is convenient for dinner; dishes are also 'promptly delivered' to the room. Breakfast has 'good cooked options', fuel for a retail expedition to the shops of King's Road. (Underground: Sloane Square) BEDROOMS 102. OPEN all year. FACILITIES lift, bar, meeting rooms, free Wi-Fi, in-room TV, room service, parking (extra charge). BACKGROUND MUSIC in public areas. CHILDREN all ages welcomed. DOGS not allowed. CREDIT CARDS MasterCard, Visa. PRICES per room B&B from £206. Cooked breakfast £19.

SOFITEL LONDON ST JAMES, 6 Waterloo Place, St James's, SW1Y 4AN. Tel 020 7747 2200, sofitelstjames.com.

A continental air drifts through this well-located neoclassical hotel (part of the French chain), off Pall Mall. Bright, spacious bedrooms, in a choice of shape and size, have a refined black-and-white palette and classic portraits of London; a comfortable bed, a minibar, a capsule coffee machine, plush bathrobes are standard. An elegant spiral staircase sweeps down into the theatrical Balcon brasserie, where vintage cocktails and classic French cuisine are available all day. In the rose-filled lounge, afternoon tea and delicate pastries are served to gentle, live harp music. Breakfast sets guests up to explore nearby West End and royal landmarks. (Underground: Charing Cross, Piccadilly Circus) BEDROOMS 183, 1 suitable for disabled. OPEN all year. FACILITIES lounge, bar, restaurant, free Wi-Fi, in-room TV, business facilities, spa, gym, valet parking. BACKGROUND MUSIC in public areas. LOCATION city centre. CHILDREN all ages welcomed. DOGS assistance dogs allowed. CREDIT CARDS all major cards. PRICES room only from £305. Breakfast £25.

THE SOHO HOTEL, 4 Richmond Mews, off Dean Street, Soho, W1D 3DH. Tel 020 7559 3000, www.firmdalehotels. com. Sculptor Fernando Botero's ten-foot high bronze cat cheekily pokes its tongue out at guests in the lobby of this buzzy Firmdale hotel. Surrounded by some of the capital's most vibrant nightlife, it has the witty flourishes and cool contemporary design typical of co-owner Kit Kemp. Throughout are zingy colour schemes, bold artworks and masses of fresh flowers. Delightfully individual bedrooms have a flamboyant padded headboard, huge warehouse-style windows, a modern bath- or shower room. Interconnecting suites are ideal for a family; younger guests are showered with books, board games, a mini-bathrobe, bedtime milk and cookies. Refuel restaurant caters for every taste, from vegan to omnivorous. (Underground: Leicester Square) BEDROOMS 96, 4 suitable for disabled, plus 4 apartments. OPEN all year. FACILITIES lift, drawing room, library, bar, restaurant, 4 private dining rooms, free Wi-Fi, in-room TV (Freeview), civil wedding licence. BACKGROUND MUSIC in public spaces. LOCATION between Dean and Wardour Streets. CHILDREN all ages welcomed. DOGS small dogs allowed by arrangement. CREDIT CARDS Amex, MasterCard, Visa. PRICES per room only from £294. Breakfast £26, set dinner £23–£25, à la carte £36.

SOUTH PLACE HOTEL, 3 South Place, Bishopsgate, EC2M 2AF. Tel 020 3503 0000, southplacehotel.com. 'Distinctly cool' European luxury combines with 'exceptionally good value' in this City hotel designed by Terence Conran. A favourite after-work haunt of financial types, it's liked for its 'friendly staff', 'beautiful rooms' and 'tasty breakfasts'. A wide choice offers something different for every meal: cocktails and snacks on the roof-top terrace; updated British classics in the Chop House; sophisticated seafood in the Michelin-starred Angler restaurant (closed Sat lunch, Sun). 'Truly relaxing, quiet rooms' have original artwork, bespoke furniture, and a well-equipped bathroom, either with a deep tub, or a walk-in slate shower. A morning paper arrives with breakfast, perhaps pastries, fruit compote and cooked dishes. 'Recommended 100%.' (Underground: Liverpool Street, Moorgate) BEDROOMS

80, 4 suitable for disabled. OPEN all year. FACILITIES lift, 4 bars, 2 restaurants, residents' lounge room, gym, spa, free Wi-Fi, in-room TV (Sky, Freeview), meeting rooms, garden, civil wedding licence. BACKGROUND MUSIC in public areas, live DJ weekends in bars. CHILDREN all ages welcomed. DOGS small/medium-size dogs allowed. CREDIT CARDS all major cards. PRICES per room B&B from £220. Tasting menus (Angler restaurant) £60–£90, set dinner (Chop House) £22.50–£27.50.

THE STAFFORD, 16–18 St James's Place, St James's, SW1A 1NJ. Tel 020 7493 0111, www.thestaffordlondon. com. Sanctuary has long been sought (and found) at this calm, comfortable town house hotel. In the 17th century, underground tunnels provided a safe link between its 380-year-old wine cellars and St James's Palace. More recently, the subterranean labyrinth provided shelter during WW2 bombing raids, while servicemen found solace in the famous American bar that still displays many wartime mementoes. Plush rooms in the main house retain a period feel, while those in mews and carriage houses have more contemporary comforts. In the Game Bird restaurant, chef James Durrant creates such dishes as roasted wild turbot, smoked aubergine purée, mussel broth. Breakfasts, including waffles and maple syrup, are indulgent. (Underground: Green Park) BEDROOMS 107, some suitable for disabled. OPEN all year. FACILITIES lift, lounge, bar, restaurant, free wi-fi, in-room TV, civil wedding licence, function facilities, courtyard, parking. BACKGROUND MUSIC in public areas. CHILDREN all ages welcomed. DOGS not allowed. CREDIT

CARDS all major cards. PRICES per room B&B from £355. Breakfast £32.

TEN MANCHESTER STREET, 10 Manchester Street, Marylebone, W1U 4DG. 20 7323 3333, www. tenmanchesterstreethotel.com. The air of a cool London club permeates this inconspicuous Marylebone bolthole, an easy stroll from Regent's Park. The discreet tone is set in the black-marbled reception where attentive staff welcome arrivals. Cigar aficionados are in luck: on-site is a walk-in humidor, sampling room, and all-weather smoking terrace. Individually designed, comfortable bedrooms sport muted colours, rich velvet and plush comforts (electronic curtains, a rain shower); there's space to spread out in four courtyard rooms that open on to a private terrace with seating, music and heaters. Modern Italian cuisine tempts all day in the restaurant. The Wallace Collection in Manchester Square is close by. (Underground: Baker Street, Bond Street, Marylebone) BEDROOMS 44, some suitable for disabled. OPEN all year. FACILITIES bar, cigar lounge and terrace, free Wi-Fi, in-room TV (Sky). BACKGROUND MUSIC in public areas. LOCATION on a quiet street in Marylebone. CHILDREN all ages welcomed. DOGS assistance dogs allowed. CREDIT CARDS Amex, MasterCard, Visa. PRICES per room B&B £185–£515.

TOWN HALL HOTEL & APARTMENTS, Patriot Square, Bethnal Green, E2 9NF. Tel 020 7871 0460, www.townhallhotel. com. As trendsetters move ever eastwards, this Edwardian former town hall in Bethnal Green is increasingly in the thick of it. The well-designed hotel showcases splendid architecture (the grand entrance's marble floors

and stately staircases: a studio-style suite with a triple-height ceiling). Everywhere one-off vintage pieces, bright fittings, modern accessories. In the spacious bedrooms: a sheepskin rug by the comfortable bed, a barista-quality coffee machine, cleverly positioned glass walls. The Corner Room attracts the hip and happening for casual meals, while the Typing Room serves chef Lee Westcott's acclaimed modern fare including Aylesbury duck, turnip, black garlic. Mornings bring a generous breakfast buffet and free shuttle bus to the City. (Underground: Bethnal Green) BEDROOMS 98, 4 suitable for disabled. OPEN all year. FACILITIES lift, cocktail bar, 2 restaurants, indoor swimming pool, gym, free Wi-Fi, in-room TV, civil wedding licence, function facilities, limited street parking. BACKGROUND MUSIC in public areas. LOCATION East End. CHILDREN all ages welcomed. DOGS assistance dogs allowed. CREDIT CARDS MasterCard, Visa. PRICES per room from £162. Breakfast from £15.

THE VICTORIA INN, 77–79 Choumert Road, Peckham, SE15 4AR. Tel 020 7639 5052, www.victoriainnpeckham. com. This transformed former Victorian public house has been part of the landscape since 1878. Local history is captured in old photographs and modern art. Behind the handsomely restored bar: Victorian tiling and traditional mirroring; in front: locals and residents, dark leather banquettes, mismatched tables and chairs. Craft beers and artisan spirits are served alongside inspired gastropub dishes including IPA beer battered haddock, pea puree, tartare sauce. Mid-century modern dominates the well-kitted-out bedrooms upstairs. Each has a large bed; a capsule coffee machine; useful technology including independently controlled air conditioning. Breakfast is as hearty as you like. (Overground railway station: Peckham Rye) BEDROOMS 15. OPEN all year. FACILITIES bar, dining room, private function room, free Wi-Fi, in-room TV (Freeview), small beer garden. BACKGROUND MUSIC in public areas. LOCATION Peckham, 15 mins by train to central London. CHILDREN all ages welcomed. DOGS not in bedrooms or restaurant. CREDIT CARDS Amex, MasterCard, Visa. PRICES per person B&B £80-£175. À la carte £35.

VICTORY HOUSE, 14 Leicester Place, WC2H 7BZ. Tel 020 3909 4100, www. victoryhouselondon.com. On frenetic Leicester Square, a majestic terracotta building – once a popular Parisian style brasserie designed by Walter Emden – is now a modern Art Deco-inspired hotel. Part of the MGallery by Sofitel boutique collection, it has a discreet entrance leading to light-filled spaces sporting soft hues, brass and wood fittings, and a cinematic theme with portraits of movie icons and silent films screened near each floor's lift. Sparsely furnished bedrooms (some small) have a tidy palette with geometric flooring and metro-tiled bathrooms. The bistro below serves classic French dishes, with heaters and blankets protecting diners on the covered terrace. Breakfast brings freshly squeezed juices, smoothies, pancakes with fruit purée. (Underground: Leicester Square) BEDROOMS 86, 4 suitable for disabled. OPEN all year. FACILITIES lift, restaurant/ bar, free Wi-Fi, in-room TV (Freeview), complimentary access to local gym, business facilities. BACKGROUND MUSIC in public areas. LOCATION in Leicester Square. CHILDREN all ages welcomed (under-18s must be accompanied by an adult). DOGS assistance dogs only. CREDIT CARDS Amex, MasterCard, Visa. PRICES per room B&B £179–£388. À la carte £30.

ENGLAND

ALFRISTON Sussex
Map 2:E4
DEANS PLACE, Seaford Road, BN26
5TW. Tel 01323 870248, www.
deansplacehotel.co.uk. On the outskirts
of a picturesque Sussex village stands
this 'handsome, extensively enlarged'
old farmhouse, run by 'friendly,
attentive staff'. 'Clean, comfortable
bedrooms' can be 'a bit small' but
nevertheless feel expansive, thanks
to 'splendid views of the ornamental
gardens'. The outdoor spaces deserve
exploration, with a meandering brook,
a croquet lawn and a putting green.
Terraces have 'plenty of seating'.
Mealtimes feature a 'small but well-
balanced menu' of modern British
dishes; puddings are 'perfection on a
plate'. 'We enjoyed excellent light plates
in the relaxing, quiet bar.' Breakfast on
'good traditional stuff', in 'enormous'
portions. BEDROOMS 36, 1 suitable for
disabled. OPEN all year. FACILITIES
bar, restaurant, function rooms, free
Wi-Fi, in-room TV (Freeview), civil
wedding licence, terrace, 4-acre garden,
outdoor swimming pool (May–Sept).
BACKGROUND MUSIC in dining room,
occasional live jazz at Sunday lunch.
LOCATION Alfriston village, 3 miles from
the coast and walking distance of South
Downs. CHILDREN all ages welcomed.
DOGS allowed in some bedrooms. CREDIT
CARDS Amex, MasterCard, Visa. PRICES
per room B&B from £75, D,B&B from
£170. À la carte meal £38.
25% DISCOUNT VOUCHERS

WINGROVE HOUSE, High Street,
BN26 5TD. Tel 01323 870276, www.
wingrovehousealfriston.com. A colonial-
style veranda wraps around this refined
19th-century restaurant-with-rooms in a
picturesque village. Friendly staff create
an 'immediately relaxing' atmosphere,
helped by a cosy lounge with an open
fire, and the house's heated, all-weather
terraces. Bright, chic bedrooms, some
newly created in an ancient malt house,
mix neutral hues, tweed and dark wood;
most have verdant views; one large
room expands under exposed beams
in the eaves. Chef Mathew Comben's
'top-quality' modern European dishes,
served in the bright, spacious restaurant,
showcase the local and the seasonal,
perhaps fried fillet of beef, onion rings,
hand cut chips, watercress, garlic and
rosemary butter. A plentiful breakfast
starts the day. Driving to Glyndebourne
takes 20 minutes. BEDROOMS 12, 3 on
ground floor. OPEN all year. FACILITIES
lounge/bar, restaurant, free Wi-Fi,
in-room TV (Freeview), terrace,
walled garden. BACKGROUND MUSIC in
public areas. LOCATION at the end of
the village High Street. CHILDREN all
ages welcomed (no family rooms). DOGS
'well behaved dogs are welcome on the
terrace'. CREDIT CARDS MasterCard, Visa.
PRICES per room B&B £110–£195. Set
dinner £35.

ALKHAM Kent
Map 2:D5
THE MARQUIS AT ALKHAM, Alkham
Valley Road, CT15 7DF. Tel 01304
873410, www.themarquisatalkham.
co.uk. Well located for continental
travellers, this white-painted restaurant-
with-rooms on the road to Dover is a
destination in itself with rural views,
an interesting history and 'excellent
food'. The stylishly updated 200-year-
old former pub (recently acquired
by GSE group) has restful bedrooms

upstairs and in nearby cottages, each with a large bed and underfloor heating. Cricket fans can request a room overlooking the village cricket ground; rooms at the back are best for light sleepers. In the smart dining room, chef/manager Stephen Piddock builds his menus (including one for vegetarians) around locally sourced produce, perhaps pan-roasted Hythe sea bass; Romney Marsh lamb. A generous breakfast might include grilled kippers, Kentish ham. BEDROOMS 10, 1 suitable for disabled, 3 rooms in 2 cottages, 3 mins' drive away. OPEN all year. FACILITIES lounge/bar, restaurant (closed Mon lunch), free Wi-Fi, in-room TV (Freeview), civil wedding licence, small garden. BACKGROUND MUSIC in restaurant. LOCATION 4 miles W of Dover. CHILDREN all ages welcomed (over-8s only in restaurant in evening). DOGS not allowed. CREDIT CARDS Amex, MasterCard, Visa. PRICES per room B&B from £99, D,B&B from £189. Tasting menu £35–£65, à la carte £40.
25% DISCOUNT VOUCHERS

ALLERFORD Somerset
Map 1:B5

CROSS LANE HOUSE, TA24 8HW. Tel 01643 863276, crosslanehouse.com. Medieval meets modern at this 'very well-adapted' 15th-century farmhouse on a National Trust estate. Bedrooms mix tasteful natural hues and fabrics with quirky original features. 'Our good-sized room overlooked the road, but was peaceful. It had a comfy bed, plenty of storage, many complimentary treats – biscuits, fruit, sweets; the bathroom was smallish but fine.' 'Fine, not outstanding' daily-changing modern menus (Thurs–Sat only) showcase produce from Exmoor and surrounds including salmon, spinach risotto; 'excellent' summer pudding. Afternoon tea is 'a treat: sandwiches, fruit scones, chocolate mousse, a small mountain of very good cakes'. At breakfast: freshly pressed apple juice, bacon from pigs reared just down the road. BEDROOMS 4. OPEN all year, closed Christmas and New Year, restaurant closed Sun–Wed FACILITIES lounge/bar, restaurant, free Wi-Fi, in-room TV (Freeview), 1-acre garden (alfresco dining), unsuitable for disabled. BACKGROUND MUSIC in lounge and dining room, late afternoon and evening. LOCATION 4¼ miles W of Minehead. CHILDREN not under 16. DOGS allowed in bedroom (£8 per night), not in public rooms. CREDIT CARDS Amex, MasterCard, Visa. PRICES per room B&B £150. À la carte £37.
25% DISCOUNT VOUCHERS

ALNWICK Northumberland
Map 4:A4

THE COOKIE JAR, 12 Bailiffgate, NE66 1LU. Tel 01665 510465, www.cookiejaralnwick.com. A former convent opposite Alnwick Castle has received a heavenly makeover into a luxurious boutique hotel. Owned by Debbie Cook, the striking sandstone property is washed with natural light, highlighting Wedgwood-blue hues and quirky original features. Handsome bedrooms (six with castle views) have comfy seating, well-chosen coffee and teas, home-made biscuits from the cookie jar. A dramatic suite in the former chapel retains a high ceiling, stained-glass windows. Afternoon tea and 'small plates' (weekdays) and scrummy dinners (Friday and Saturday) including Northumbrian lamb, hot Greek salad, olive oil jus, are served in the bistro. Shooting parties and their dogs are welcome. The hidden garden cigar shack is a place of sanctuary. BEDROOMS 11, some suitable for disabled. OPEN all year. FACILITIES lounge, bistro, drying room, secure gun room, terrace with fire pit, garden, free Wi-Fi, in-room TV (Freeview). BACKGROUND MUSIC in public areas. LOCATION opposite castle. CHILDREN all ages welcomed. DOGS in some bedrooms, not in public areas, 5 kennels for gun dogs. CREDIT CARDS MasterCard, Visa. PRICES per room £160–£295. Set 3-course dinner £39.50.

AMBLESIDE Cumbria
Map 4: inset C2

NANNY BROW, Nanny Brow, LA22 9NF. Tel 01539 433232, www. nannybrow.co.uk. Homely character, tumbling views and relaxed efficiency – the key elements of Sue and Peter Robinson's Arts and Crafts house. The 'sympathetically restored' Lakeland stone property, built in 1904, overlooks walkers' paradise Brathay valley. A nod to its architect, Francis Whitwell, in the decor: architectural drawings, photographs and paintings. Varying in size, the individually styled bedrooms are a well-chosen mishmash of antiques and contemporary pieces, although guests report that housekeeping could sharpen its act. At night, staff don't stay on-site, but are a mobile phone-call away. Breakfast ('good cafetière coffee; good black pudding'), served in the original dining room, has a 20-mile-radius farm-to-plate ethos, and a 'reasonable buffet'. BEDROOMS 14, 2 in annexe, sharing a lounge. OPEN all year. FACILITIES lounge, bar, breakfast room, free Wi-Fi, in-room TV (Freeview), civil wedding licence, 6-acre grounds, unsuitable for disabled. BACKGROUND MUSIC 'at low volume' in breakfast room and bar. LOCATION 1½ miles W of Ambleside. CHILDREN over-12s welcomed. DOGS not allowed. CREDIT CARDS Amex, MasterCard, Visa. PRICES per room B&B £130–£280. 1-night bookings refused weekends.

APPLEDORE Devon
Map 1:B4

THE SEAGATE, The Quay, EX39 1QS. Tel 01237 472589, theseagate.co.uk. A relaxed atmosphere wafts through this white-painted 17th-century inn overlooking Torridge estuary, where dogs and muddy boots are welcomed. The airy, simply decorated bedrooms combine nautical hues and artworks with shutters, pale wood. Some have original beams; each has tea- and coffee-making facilities, a flat-screen TV. A family room has a bunk bed for the children. Chef Ben Niell's seasonal menus feature estuary-caught seafood, with daily-changing fish specials; weekend barbecues in summer months are a major draw – as are the terraces with peachy sunset views. Breakfast brings tasty cooked dishes, local yogurts, fresh fruit – a solid foundation for exploring the narrow cobbled streets of Appledore. BEDROOMS 17, 2 suitable for disabled. OPEN closed Christmas night only. FACILITIES open-plan restaurant/ bar, free Wi-Fi, in-room TV (Freeview), 2 terraces, walled garden. BACKGROUND MUSIC in public areas. LOCATION 2 miles from Bideford. CHILDREN all ages welcomed (travel cot, bunk beds, high chairs). DOGS allowed. CREDIT CARDS Amex, MasterCard, Visa. PRICES per room B&B single £70, double from £99. À la carte £24. 2-night min. stay at weekends preferred.
25% DISCOUNT VOUCHERS

ARMSCOTE Warwickshire
Map 3:D6

FUZZY DUCK, Ilmington Road, CV37 8DD. Tel 01608 682635, www. fuzzyduckarmscote.com. The Slater siblings have country comfort down to a fine art at their stylish 18th-century coaching inn – a local hotspot for real ales, signature cocktails and zesty pub classics. Typical fare: chicken, leek and pancetta pie, champ mash. Above the restaurant, heritage-style bedrooms, each named after a type of duck – some found on local lakes – combine Art Deco flourishes with large beds, high-quality linens, and bathrooms supplied with robes and complimentary goodies from the owners' beauty company, Baylis & Harding. Some rooms are ideal for a family, having a loft bed tucked in above the bathroom, and a dress-up box for younger guests. Guidebooks and wellies can be borrowed for a countryside ramble. BEDROOMS 4. OPEN all year. FACILITIES bar, restaurant, snug, free Wi-Fi, in-room smart TV (Freeview), 1-acre garden. BACKGROUND MUSIC in public areas. LOCATION 7 miles from Stratford-upon-Avon. CHILDREN all ages welcomed. DOGS allowed (welcome pack, home-made dog biscuits and snacks in the bar). CREDIT CARDS Amex, MasterCard, Visa. PRICES per room B&B from £110. À la carte £32.

ARNSIDE Cumbria
Map 4: inset C2

NUMBER 43, 43 The Promenade, LA5 0AA. Tel 01524 762119, www.no43. org.uk. Lesley Hornsby's modern B&B in a tall Victorian house gazes across the Kent estuary to the Lakeland fells – and provides binoculars to take it all in. The bay window of the bright, airy art-hung sitting room is a tranquil spot to savour the view, along with a tipple from the dining room's honesty bar. Pretty bedrooms provide homely comforts: biscuits, posh teas and freshly ground coffee; milk in the mini-fridge; spoiling toiletries. Suite Two has a sofa, atmospheric landscape photographs, a wide-screen panorama. At breakfast, a feast: home-made compotes, home-roasted maple syrup granola, locally caught and smoked haddock. A light supper platter includes smoked fish, local cheeses, pâtés. BEDROOMS 5. OPEN all year. FACILITIES lounge, dining room, free Wi-Fi, in-room TV (Freeview), terrace. BACKGROUND MUSIC at breakfast. LOCATION village centre, on the Promenade. CHILDREN over-5s welcomed. DOGS not allowed. CREDIT CARDS MasterCard, Visa. PRICES per room B&B £125–£185. 2-night min. stay at weekends.

ASTHALL Oxfordshire
Map 2:C2

THE MAYTIME INN, OX18 4HW. Tel 01993 822068, www.themaytime. com. A 'delightful, friendly place', this 'extraordinarily good-value' 17th-century mellow stone coaching inn has an authentic country air. In its popular bar, exposed 17th-century stonework, old timbers and a 'good selection of gins', ales and ciders, along with many locals. The kitchen sends a hearty roast to the table on Sundays; 'delicious local and seasonal' dishes, pub classics on other days, perhaps lamb rump, parmesan risotto, spinach, roasted shallots, wild mushrooms. 'Comfortable, beautifully converted' bedrooms, in the main building and around the courtyard, have mellow wood, light decor, and a serenade of the burbling Windrush stream. Two rooms have a stand-alone bath and walk-in shower. Breakfast is 'imaginative, top notch'. BEDROOMS 6, all on ground floor. OPEN all year. FACILITIES bar, restaurant, free Wi-Fi, in-room TV (Freeview), large terrace and garden. BACKGROUND MUSIC in bar and restaurant areas. LOCATION 2 miles from Burford. CHILDREN all ages welcomed (under-18s must be accompanied by an adult). DOGS allowed in public areas, not in bedrooms. CREDIT CARDS Diners Club, MasterCard, Visa. PRICES per room B&B £95–£160, D,B&B £135–£200. À la carte £30.

AYSGARTH Yorkshire
Map 4:C3
STOW HOUSE, Leyburn, DL8 3SR. Tel 01969 663635, www.stowhouse. co.uk. At this playful, welcoming B&B in a solidly Victorian former rectory, owners Phil and Sarah Bucknall claim to 'eschew chintz, embrace eclecticism'. They have filled their house with contemporary art, books and the crackling fire of several wood-burners. Cheeky touches in the bedrooms include a wall-mounted kangaroo; a burnished-orange chaise longue; a papier mâché badger overlooking a claw-footed bath. There are pieces of period furniture, exposed timbers and fabulous views of Wensleydale. The hostess's made-to-order cocktails are the perfect pick-me-up after hiking – Bolton Castle is a four-mile yomp from the front door. At breakfast, local produce is transformed into hearty fare, including home-made sausages from the local butcher. BEDROOMS 7, 1 on ground floor. OPEN all year, except 23–28 Dec. FACILITIES sitting room, snug, dining room, free Wi-Fi, in-room TV (Freeview). BACKGROUND MUSIC none. LOCATION 7 miles from the Leyburn, 9 miles from Hawes.

CHILDREN all ages welcomed. DOGS well-behaved dogs allowed in 5 bedrooms. CREDIT CARDS MasterCard, Visa. PRICES per room B&B £110–£175. 2-night min. stay at weekends May–Sept.
25% DISCOUNT VOUCHERS

BAINBRIDGE Yorkshire
Map 4:C3
YOREBRIDGE HOUSE, Leyburn, DL8 3EE. Tel 01969 652060, www. yorebridgehouse.co.uk. International joie de vivre is found in well-travelled Charlotte and David Reilly's revamped former Victorian school and headmaster's house. In a pretty Dales village on the River Ure, it has lofty, characterful bedrooms, perhaps with a bedhead fashioned from an antique Moroccan window; Caribbean seashells; a private terrace with a hot tub worthy of California, alongside contemporary earth tones and exposed timbers. All rooms have fabulous views, posh smellies, fluffy robes. Afternoon tea is worth the trip to the Master's Room, while in the shamelessly romantic dining room Chef Dan Shotton's seasonal, locally sourced fare includes duck, beetroot and chicory; halibut, butternut squash, smoked eel. BEDROOMS 12, some on ground floor suitable for disabled, 4 in schoolhouse, plus The Barn suite in village, 5 mins' walk. OPEN all year. FACILITIES lounge, bar, garden room, restaurant, free Wi-Fi in public areas, in-room TV (Sky), civil wedding licence, 2-acre grounds. BACKGROUND MUSIC all day in public areas. LOCATION outskirts of Bainbridge. CHILDREN all ages welcomed. DOGS allowed (in 2 rooms, by arrangement). CREDIT CARDS MasterCard, Visa. PRICES per room B&B from £220, D,B&B from £340. À la carte £60.

BAINTON East Yorkshire
Map 4:D5

WOLDS VILLAGE, Manor Farm, YO25 9EF. Tel 01377 217698, www.woldsvillage.co.uk. Guests enjoy an imaginative take on traditional Yorkshire Wolds accommodation at this Georgian farmstead. Sally and Chris Brealey, along with Maureen Holmes, Sally's mother, have created an intriguing destination, where rooms and restaurant are joined by a tea shop, gift shops and an art gallery – and where the surrounding woods contain several bear sculptures, part of a whimsical art collection along a meandering forest trail. A barn, traditionally built using reclaimed materials, houses comfortable, soundproofed bedrooms. Decor in each heralds a different historic period, from Tudor to Art Deco; tea- and coffee-making facilities are provided. The restaurant and tea room serve locally sourced country classics (ploughman's salads, pies, vegetarian options). BEDROOMS 7, 3 on ground floor, 1 suitable for disabled. OPEN all year, except 2 weeks from 28 Dec. FACILITIES lounge, bar, restaurant, free Wi-Fi, in-room TV (Freeview), art gallery, 6-acre grounds. BACKGROUND MUSIC in restaurant. LOCATION 6 miles W of Driffield. CHILDREN all ages welcomed. DOGS allowed in outside courtyard. CREDIT CARDS all major cards. PRICES per room B&B single from £70, double from £100, D,B&B double from £140. À la carte £25.
25% DISCOUNT VOUCHERS

BARNSLEY Gloucestershire
Map 3:E6

THE VILLAGE PUB, GL7 5EF. Tel 01285 740421, www.thevillagepub.co.uk. The hub of a pretty Cotswolds village, this mellow-stoned pub-with-rooms (Calcot Hotels) is liked for its stylish rooms and relaxed nature. Ranging from snug to capacious, spruce bedrooms (separate entrance) might have a high four-poster bed, a claw-footed bath, exposed beams. Some visitors suggest that light sleepers request a room away from the road. In the pub (principally a restaurant) chef Francesco Volgo offers seasonal farmhouse classics including roasted pork belly, fondant potato, poached rhubarb, sprouting broccoli. Breakfast brings apple juice; home-made jam, home-baked bread; scrambled Burford Brown eggs. Guests receive complimentary access to the nearby grounds of sister hotel Barnsley House (see main entry), designed by gardening doyenne, Rosemary Verey. BEDROOMS 6. OPEN all year. FACILITIES bar, restaurant, free Wi-Fi, in-room TV (Freeview). BACKGROUND MUSIC in bar and restaurant. LOCATION on the B4425 Cirencester to Bibury road, 4 miles NE of Cirencester town. CHILDREN all ages welcomed. DOGS allowed. CREDIT CARDS Amex, MasterCard, Visa. PRICES per room B&B from £109, D,B&B from £169. À la carte £30.

BARNSTAPLE Devon
Map 1:B4

BROOMHILL ART HOTEL, Muddiford Road, EX31 4EX. Tel 01271 850262, www.broomhillart.co.uk. Weird, wonderful, full of colour: Rinus and Aniet van de Sande's well-liked, 'quirky', late-Victorian hotel receives praise for its confluence of art, culture and hospitality. Ringed by woodland, it stands amid a well-curated contemporary sculpture garden – one of the South West's largest permanent collections. The 'interesting' display continues in the large ground-floor art gallery and spacious, tasteful, contemporary bedrooms. In some rooms the comfortable bed offers views of the alfresco sculptures; bathrooms are smallish but smart. Mediterranean 'slow food' and tapas take centre stage in the award-winning Terra Madre restaurant, with such dishes as linguine, garlic mushrooms, grated Haloumi, Turkish pepper; Spanish salad, Cecina, Iberico sausage, fennel, sweet potato. BEDROOMS 6. OPEN all year, except 21 Dec–8 Jan. Restaurant closed Sun evening. FACILITIES bar, restaurant, library, lounge, art gallery, free Wi-Fi, in-room TV, civil wedding licence, 10-acre grounds including terrace. BACKGROUND MUSIC none. LOCATION 4 miles N of Barnstaple. CHILDREN all ages welcomed. DOGS allowed in garden by arrangement. CREDIT CARDS MasterCard, Visa. PRICES per room B&B single from £75, double £85–£145, D,B&B double (Wed–Sat) £145–£185.

BATH Somerset
Map 2:D1

ABBEY HOTEL, 1–3 North Parade, BA1 1LF. Tel 01225 461603, abbeyhotelbath. co.uk. Three art-filled Georgian town houses combine into this 'quirky, modern hotel', now part of the KE Hotels portfolio. It is liked for its 'super-friendly staff', 'attractive bedrooms' and 'all kinds of interesting art'. Well-equipped bedrooms, recently refurbished, 'have everything you need and more'; they vary in size and accessibility (some have easier lift access); some offer far-reaching views. Light sleepers might request a 'blissfully quiet' room at the rear. Some bathrooms sport unusual features, a bath beneath graffiti-covered tiles; a period fireplace.

In the unstuffy, scarlet-hued restaurant, chef Rupert Taylor's 'beautifully presented' modern dishes include pan-fried salmon, pink fir potatoes, tomato, shallot and herb salsa. The 'exemplary' breakfast has 'all the classics'. BEDROOMS 62. OPEN all year. FACILITIES lift, bar, restaurant, function facilities, free Wi-Fi, in-room TV (Freeview), front terrace. BACKGROUND MUSIC all day in bar. LOCATION central. CHILDREN all ages welcomed. DOGS allowed in bedrooms and bar, not in restaurant. CREDIT CARDS all major cards. PRICES per room B&B from £135, D,B&B from £185. À la carte £30. 1-night bookings sometimes refused.

DORIAN HOUSE, 1 Upper Oldfield Park, BA2 3JX. Tel 01225 426336, www. dorianhouse.co.uk. Strands of music and romance mingle on the southern residential slopes of the city at this Victorian villa B&B owned by cellist Timothy Hugh and his wife, Kathryn. Only a ten-minute stroll from the bustling centre, it has complimentary parking (a bonus in Bath) and is a quiet, reflective spot, with plenty of garden seats for contemplation. Modern bedrooms, named after the Hughs' favourite composers, mix period features, bold artworks and Asian antiques. Some rooms offer 'fabulous Royal Crescent views', others overlook the secluded hillside garden. Modern marble bathrooms have fluffy towels, robes, high-pressure shower, French herbal toiletries. The tasty breakfast has fruit, freshly baked croissants, the full English. BEDROOMS 13, 1 on ground floor. OPEN all year. FACILITIES lounge, conservatory breakfast room/ music library, free Wi-Fi, in-room TV (Freeview), small garden, parking.

BACKGROUND MUSIC classical in breakfast room and lounge. LOCATION 10-min. walk to the centre of town. CHILDREN all ages welcomed. DOGS not allowed. CREDIT CARDS MasterCard, Visa. PRICES per room B&B £65–£195.

GRAYS, 9 Upper Oldfield Park, BA2 3JX. Tel 01225 403020, www.graysbath. co.uk. A tranquil atmosphere and glorious city skyline views are offered at this freshly modern B&B in a Victorian villa with manicured gardens. Inside, soft colours rest against crisp whites; framed Audubon-reminiscent prints, pastoral fabrics, fresh flowers and Provençal-style furniture induce a serene atmosphere. Bright bedrooms are individually styled: one has a triple-aspect window gazing across to the Royal Crescent; a blue-hued attic room has a breezy vibe. Most of the bathrooms have a deep tub; all offer natural toiletries, towelling robes. Breakfast, served in the conservatory, has a help-yourself spread (cereals, yogurts, compotes, preserves); meaty and vegetarian options cooked to order. On-site parking is a major perk in Bath. BEDROOMS 12, 4 on ground floor. OPEN all year except 3 days over Christmas. FACILITIES lounge, breakfast room, free Wi-Fi, in-room TV (Freeview), small garden, parking. BACKGROUND MUSIC none. CHILDREN over-12s welcomed. DOGS not allowed. CREDIT CARDS Amex. PRICES per room B&B £110–£245. 2-night min. stay at weekends preferred.

GROVE LODGE, 11 Lambridge, BA1 6BJ. Tel 01225 310860, www. grovelodgebath.co.uk. Flamboyantly colourful, Mary and Giovanni Baiano's Georgian villa interweaves old-world charm, expert interior design and high-spec technology. There are crystal chandeliers, velvet sofas, and whimsical wallpaper including chinoiserie. Spacious suites, spread over the first and second floors, have an original fireplace, moulded covings, a Bose speaker, capsule coffee machine, home-made biscotti and fudge; each has a private drawing room where breakfast (granola; yogurt; potato cakes; the full English) arrives on a polished tray. Large windows overlook the verdant front garden and countryside. The hospitable Anglo-Italian owners offer a complimentary pick-up service (by arrangement) for guests arriving by train or bus. A scenic 20-minute walk along the canal reaches the city centre. BEDROOMS 3 suites. OPEN Feb–Dec. FACILITIES free Wi-Fi, in-room TV (Freeview), large front garden. BACKGROUND MUSIC none. LOCATION 1.7 miles from Bath Spa station. CHILDREN 12 and over. DOGS not allowed. CREDIT CARDS Amex, MasterCard, Visa. PRICES per room B&B from £110. 1-night bookings sometimes refused at weekends.
25% DISCOUNT VOUCHERS

HARINGTON'S HOTEL, 8–10 Queen Street, BA1 1HE. Tel 01225 461728, www.haringtonshotel.co.uk. Through a classical arch, on a narrow central lane, this boutique city hotel has bags of character and a genial atmosphere. Well-equipped bedrooms are spread across the three upper floors – no lift, but friendly staff help with luggage. Each room, some compact, all with vividly patterned wallpaper, has great basics (tea- and coffee-making facilities; oversized towels, a power shower), plus quirky touches (stag-head wall hook, a Bakelite telephone). Light meals, hot drinks are served in the lounge; in the bar, Bath ales and hand-mixed cocktails. Breakfast has bacon butties, pancakes, leaf teas. The secluded courtyard offers a contemporary take on the thermal baths – a private hot tub (extra charge). BEDROOMS 13, plus self-catering town house and apartments. OPEN all year, except 25, 26 Dec. FACILITIES lounge, breakfast room, café/bar, free Wi-Fi, in-room TV (Freeview), conference room, small courtyard, secure parking nearby (cost extra). BACKGROUND MUSIC in public areas. LOCATION city centre. CHILDREN all ages welcomed. DOGS not allowed. CREDIT CARDS Amex, MasterCard, Visa. PRICES per room B&B £100–£190. 2-night min. stay on some weekends.

PARADISE HOUSE, 86–88 Holloway, BA2 4PX. Tel 01225 317723, www.paradise-house.co.uk. A 'good-value option at a good address': a slim stretch of the River Avon separates the city from David and Annie Lanz's peaceful B&B, set in a half-acre walled garden. It receives praise for its 'top-notch breakfasts', 'most comfortable' bedrooms and 'willing, laid-back staff'. The elegant Georgian drawing room has floor-to-ceiling windows, an open fire, fine city views – the perfect spot for afternoon tea or a preprandial drink. A choice of period- or modern-styled bedrooms: each has 'an excellent bed', 'a powerful shower' in a handsome bathroom 'could perhaps do with more storage space'. Breakfast has an 'extensive' menu with good vegetarian options. BEDROOMS 12, 4 on ground floor, 3 in annexe. OPEN all year, except 25, 26 Dec. FACILITIES drawing room, breakfast room, free Wi-Fi, in-room TV (Freeview), ½-acre garden, parking. BACKGROUND MUSIC in public areas ('Classic FM'). LOCATION

15 mins' downhill walk to the centre. CHILDREN all ages welcomed. DOGS not allowed. CREDIT CARDS Amex, MasterCard, Visa. PRICES per room B&B £150–£260. 2-night min. stay at weekends.

THE ROSEATE VILLA, Henrietta Road, BA2 6LX. Tel 01225 466329, www. roseatevillabath.com. This 'nearly faultless B&B', standing in 'pretty gardens', is in a leafy neighbourhood 'within walking distance of everything' – but guests might not want to leave. On arrival at the villa, formed from two converted Victorian houses, visitors receive 'a friendly welcome' from 'delightful' managers Caroline Browning and Jean-Luc Bouchereau (and dog, Muttley), along with 'a generous tea' including home-baked cakes. All around, well-chosen antiques and interesting prints. The individually decorated bedrooms have a Nespresso machine, an in-room tablet; home-made shortbread and fresh milk. Breakfast brings a complimentary Buck's Fizz, paired with, perhaps, yogurt compotes, croissants, 'proper kippers'. The hosts offer informed dinner recommendations in Bath centre. BEDROOMS 21. 2-room suite on lower ground floor. OPEN all year. FACILITIES breakfast room, free Wi-Fi, in-room TV, small garden, terrace, parking. BACKGROUND MUSIC 'soft' radio in breakfast room. LOCATION 3 mins' walk from the city centre, by Henrietta Park. CHILDREN all ages welcomed. DOGS allowed. CREDIT CARDS Amex, MasterCard, Visa. PRICES per room B&B £180–£200.

TASBURGH HOUSE, Warminster Road, BA2 6SH. Tel 01225 425096, tasburghhouse.co.uk. 'Lovely views'

over the city extend from Susan Keeling's hilltop red-brick Victorian house, where 'luxurious-feeling bedrooms', 'lovely location' and the staff's 'helpful local knowledge' are much liked. Emma Moon is the new manager. 'Well-equipped, comfortable bedrooms' (some 'a little tight') have large sash windows; good toiletries and bath towels; a well-stocked hospitality tray with tea, coffee, biscuits. Three have French doors leading to the garden terrace. In the 'pretty conservatory', breakfast options include smoked trout; French toast with bacon, maple syrup; porridge with honey from the house's hives; afternoon cream teas are served on request. The canal towpath, at the bottom of the garden, provides a 20-minute walk into town. BEDROOMS 15, 3 accessed from garden terrace. OPEN all year except Christmas. FACILITIES bar, dining room, conservatory, free Wi-Fi, in-room TV (Freeview), 7-acre garden, suitable for limited mobility. BACKGROUND MUSIC all day in bar, dining room and conservatory. LOCATION ½ mile E of city centre. CHILDREN over-6s welcomed. DOGS not allowed. CREDIT CARDS MasterCard, Visa. PRICES per room B&B (continental) from £115, D,B&B from £246.

THREE ABBEY GREEN, 3 Abbey Green, BA1 1NW. Tel 01225 428558, threeabbeygreen.com. Central Bath is on the doorstep of Nici and Alan Jones's good-value B&B on a cobbled Georgian square, a toga toss from the Abbey and Roman baths. Accommodation sprawls comfortably across two well-restored town houses with parts dating back to 1689. Each room has its own extra feature, perhaps clever eaves storage, a fireplace in the bathroom, a huge four-poster bed and enormous windows overlooking the leafy square. Pale hues and a springy mattress in the Jane Austen wing, up narrow, winding stairs, would be familiar to her heroines. Breakfast has plentiful cooked options, home-made preserves. Any queries about the locale are readily answered by the friendly hosts. BEDROOMS 10, 3 in adjoining building, 2 on ground floor suitable for disabled, plus 1-bedroom apartment. OPEN all year except 24–26 Dec. FACILITIES dining room, free Wi-Fi, in-room TV (Freeview). BACKGROUND MUSIC in breakfast room. LOCATION city centre. CHILDREN all ages welcomed. DOGS not allowed. CREDIT CARDS MasterCard, Visa. PRICES per room B&B £90–£240. 2-night min. stay at weekends.

BELPER Derbyshire
Map 2:A2

DANNAH FARM, Bowmans Lane, Shottle, DE56 2DR. Tel 01773 550273, www.dannah.co.uk. On a 150-acre working farm, clucking hens are the only neighbours at Joan and Martin Slack's 'charming, welcoming' B&B in the Derbyshire Dales. Bedrooms, decked out 'with all the luxury trimmings', are 'spacious and beautifully clean'; some have a baronial-style bed forged from old timbers, or a four-poster. Split-level suites have a deck and hot tub, as does a contemporary cabin in its own walled garden. Supper platters (meats, cheeses, fish, salads, home-made bread and puddings) can be arranged; the hosts can recommend local eateries too (and will arrange transport if needed). The 'plentiful' breakfast is a 'delicious' start to the day, including just-plucked farmyard eggs, thickly cut home-made bread.

BEDROOMS 8, 4 in adjoining converted barn, 3 on ground floor. OPEN all year except Christmas. FACILITIES 2 sitting rooms, dining room, meeting room, free Wi-Fi, in-room TV (Freeview), large walled garden, parking. BACKGROUND MUSIC none. LOCATION 2 miles from Belper. CHILDREN all ages welcomed. DOGS allowed (in certain rooms). CREDIT CARDS MasterCard, Visa. PRICES per room B&B £145–£295. Supper platter £18.95. 2-night min. stay on Fri, Sat. 25% DISCOUNT VOUCHERS

BEXHILL-ON-SEA Sussex
Map 2:E4

COAST, 58 Sea Road, TN40 1JP. Tel 01424 225260, www.coastbexhill.co.uk. Piero and Lucia Mazzoni bring 'warm' Italian hospitality to the British seaside at their 'impeccably decorated' B&B. A new take on the old world wafts through the Edwardian villa: dusky wood floors, a minimalist grey and white palette, against which there are occasional colour pops: red wingback chairs, clusters of yellow flowers. Genteel, recently refurbished bedrooms (some compact) have little luxuries: biscuits and a capsule coffee machine; a cascade shower; fluffy towels on a heated rail; underfloor heating in the bathroom; high-end toiletries. The best room has a whirlpool bath on its own balcony with sea views. Breakfast includes pancakes with crème fraîche and maple syrup, fresh fruit, home-baked bread. BEDROOMS 5. OPEN all year. FACILITIES lounge, breakfast room, free Wi-Fi, in-room TV (Freeview, Sky), secure bicycle storage. BACKGROUND MUSIC in breakfast room. LOCATION town centre, 100 m from the seafront. CHILDREN over-4s welcomed. DOGS not allowed. CREDIT CARDS Amex, MasterCard, Visa. PRICES per room B&B single from £80, double from £90. 1-night bookings sometimes refused.

BIBURY Gloucestershire
Map 3:E6

THE SWAN, The Swan Hotel, GL7 5NW. Tel 01285 740695, www.cotswold-inns-hotels.co.uk/the-swan-hotel. Visitors flock to the peaceful banks of the River Coln – home to swans and to this busy 17th-century former coaching inn (Cotswold Inns and Hotels). William Morris famously called Bibury the most beautiful English village, and rolling meadow views pour into well-equipped bedrooms, decorated in a light country style, and supplied with high-quality toiletries and a capsule coffee machine. The pretty garden's cottage suites are ideal for larger groups. There's decent gastropub fare served in the bar and courtyard, and modern European cooking in the brasserie, perhaps the hotel speciality: poached Bibury trout, prawn ravioli, fennel, baby spinach, bisque. Breakfast brings freshly squeezed juice, home-made Drambuie marmalade, local organic preserves. BEDROOMS 22, some on ground floor, 4 in garden cottages. OPEN all year. FACILITIES lift, lounge, bar (wood-burning stove), brasserie, free Wi-Fi, in-room TV (Freeview), ½-acre garden, civil wedding licence, functions. BACKGROUND MUSIC in public spaces ('subtle'). LOCATION village centre. CHILDREN all ages welcomed. DOGS well-behaved dogs allowed (in bar, lounge, garden, some bedrooms). CREDIT CARDS Amex, MasterCard, Visa. PRICES per room B&B from £110. À la carte (brasserie) £35.
25% DISCOUNT VOUCHERS

BIRMINGHAM Warwickshire
Map 3:C6
THE HIGH FIELD TOWN HOUSE,
23 Highfield Road, Edgbaston,
B15 3DP. Tel 01216 476466, www.
highfieldtownhouse.co.uk. Run in
conjunction with The High Field
gastropub next door, this white-fronted
Victorian villa in upmarket Edgbaston
has received a fashionable facelift.
With the feel of a 'boutique country
house', its welcoming sitting room
sets a homely scene with vases of fresh
flowers, complimentary newspapers and
a capsule coffee machine. Something a
little stronger is found in the honesty bar
or in the gastropub, alongside seasonal
British fare including Cornish lamb
cutlets, braised belly, minted gnocchi,
baby gem, peas. Well-chosen antiques
and retro furnishings fill the creative
bedrooms (some large enough to suit a
family). Interesting breakfast choices
include pulled bacon and cheddar
potato cake, poached egg; free-range
sausage bloomer roll. BEDROOMS 12.
Some suitable for disabled. OPEN all
year, except 24–25 Dec. FACILITIES
sitting room, bar, restaurant in adjacent
building, free Wi-Fi, in-room TV
(Freeview), private dining, terrace,
garden, parking. BACKGROUND MUSIC
in sitting room. LOCATION 5 mins from
city centre. CHILDREN all ages welcomed.
DOGS allowed. CREDIT CARDS Amex,
MasterCard, Visa. PRICES per room B&B
£120–£160. Fixed price menu £13.75.
À la carte £35.

BISHOP'S TACHBROOK
Warwickshire
Map 2:B2
MALLORY COURT, Harbury Lane, CV33
9QB. Tel 01926 330214, www.mallory.
co.uk. A classic English country escape

is offered at this 'beautifully situated'
Lutyens-style house with a long-
standing reputation for 'magnificent
hospitality' and 'pleasingly professional
staff'. The main building and 'modern'
annexes stand in ten acres of 'well-
manicured gardens' complete with
a zigzagging mini-maze. Laurels
are never rested upon: the 'constant
facelifts' include refurbished rooms,
a garden-view spa. 'Well-equipped'
bedrooms, some with bold striped
wallpaper, others more conservative,
are in the main house and the Knights
Suite annexe; all have a comfortable
bed, bathrobes, fine toiletries. There
is an 'excellent' daily-changing menu
of locally-sourced seasonal dishes
(including kitchen garden produce)
in the oak-panelled restaurant, and
'perfectly cooked' informal fare in the
'light, stylish' brasserie. BEDROOMS 43,
11 in Knight's Suite, 12 in Orchard
House, some suitable for disabled. OPEN
all year. FACILITIES 2 lounges, brasserie
(Thurs jazz nights, closed Sun eve),
restaurant, lift, free Wi-Fi, in-room TV,
civil wedding licence, function facilities,
fitness suite, spa, garden, terrace.
BACKGROUND MUSIC in public rooms.
CHILDREN all ages welcomed. DOGS
not allowed. CREDIT CARDS all major
cards. PRICES per room B&B from £193.
À la carte £45.

BISHOPSTONE Wiltshire
Map 3:E6
HELEN BROWNING'S ROYAL OAK, Cues
Lane, SN6 8PP. Tel 01793 790481,
helenbrowningsorganic.co.uk. On a
working organic farm on the edge of the
Wiltshire Downs, this quirky, affable
pub-with-rooms reflects the vision of
food ethics pioneer Helen Browning.
The well-established pub (Arkell's

Brewery) is loved for the real ales, organic wines and generous organic meals (meat from the farm, produce from local villagers). Set around a sunny courtyard – another long-closed village pub – appealingly rustic bedrooms have woollen throws, a comfortable bed. Each is named after a field on her farm (immortalized in a giant photo on one wall). The residents' lounge, with books, hot drinks, a record player (and Helen's partner Tim's old LPs) is made for 'wallowing in'. BEDROOMS 12. All in annexe, 100 metres from pub. OPEN all year. FACILITIES lounge, pub, meeting/function room, free Wi-Fi, in-room TV (Freeview), ½-acre garden (rope swing, Wendy house, 'flighty hens'), parking. BACKGROUND MUSIC in public areas. LOCATION on an organic farm, in village, 7 miles E of Swindon, 10 miles from Marlborough. CHILDREN all ages welcomed. DOGS allowed in 2 bedrooms, public rooms. CREDIT CARDS MasterCard, Visa. PRICES per room B&B from £85. À la carte £29.

BLACKBURN Lancashire
Map 4:D3

MILLSTONE AT MELLOR, Church Lane, Mellor, BB2 7JR. Tel 01254 813333, www.thwaites.co.uk/hotels-and-inns/inns/millstone-at-mellor. A home-away-from-home mood permeates this 'lively, friendly' stone-built pub-with-rooms in a Ribble valley village. One of Thwaites Inns of Character, it focuses on providing country-style accommodation, 'confident, well-prepared' cooking, and decent cask ales. The restaurant, 'clearly the pub's main attraction', celebrates local produce (Lancashire meats and cheese, especially) in dishes such as roasted pork belly, cauliflower purée, garlic mash, apple soup, crispy

crackling, sage jus. Upstairs, each of the well-appointed bedrooms is styled differently, but thoughtful extras (fresh milk, tea- and coffee-making facilities, home-made biscuits, 'fleecy bathrobes') come as standard. Some rooms, facing the road, may not suit light sleepers. Leisurely starts at weekends: breakfast is served till 10 am. BEDROOMS 23, some suitable for disabled. OPEN all year. FACILITIES residents' lounge, bar, restaurant, free Wi-Fi, in-room TV (Sky, Freeview), terrace, parking. BACKGROUND MUSIC radio at breakfast. LOCATION in village. CHILDREN all ages welcomed. DOGS allowed (in bar area only). CREDIT CARDS Amex, MasterCard, Visa. PRICES per room B&B £80–£130. À la carte £30.

BLACKPOOL Lancashire
Map 4:D2

NUMBER ONE ST LUKE'S, 1 St Lukes Road, FY4 2EL. Tel 01253 343901, www.numberoneblackpool.com. A three-minute amble from the famous promenade and Pleasure Beach, Mark and Claire Smith's South Shore B&B offers comfy, good-value, contemporary accommodation. Spotless bedrooms, decorated in a fresh, modern style, have a king-size bed and make-yourself-at-home extras (including a large TV screen and a games console for nights in); cosseting bathrooms have a power shower, a spa bath, plus wall-mounted TV and a music system. Breakfast specials include a 'full Blackpool'. A large conservatory overlooks the garden. A universal electric car charging point is available for guests' use. (See also sister hotel Number One South Beach, next Shortlist entry.) BEDROOMS 3. OPEN all year. FACILITIES dining room, conservatory, free Wi-Fi, in-room

TV (Freeview), garden, parking. BACKGROUND MUSIC none. LOCATION 2 miles S of town centre. CHILDREN over-4s welcomed. DOGS not allowed. CREDIT CARDS Amex, MasterCard, Visa. PRICES per room B&B from £110.

NUMBER ONE SOUTH BEACH, 4 Harrowside West FY4 1NW. Tel 01253 343900, www.numberonesouthbeach. com. Modern, personal accommodation is found minutes from Blackpool's Pleasure Beach at this cheery hotel by the sea. Janet and Graham Oxley, and Claire and Mark Smith, are the enthusiastic owners (see Number One St Luke's, previous entry). Individually decorated bedrooms, many with a bright, mood-lifting palate, enjoy rolling refurbishing tweaks and smart technological touches: remote-controlled lighting, a waterproof TV by the spa bath; the best have a balcony with sea views; some a contemporary four-poster, all have a king-size bed. The games room has an indoor golf simulator for wet days. Dinner, perhaps grilled sea bass, tarragon, white wine sauce, requires advance notice. Breakfast, featuring all the favourites, uses local produce. BEDROOMS 14, some suitable for disabled. OPEN all year except 26–31 Dec. FACILITIES lounge, bar, restaurant, games room, lift, free Wi-Fi, in-room TV (Freeview), meeting/conference facilities, parking. BACKGROUND MUSIC quiet classical music in bar and lounge. LOCATION 2½ miles S of Blackpool town centre. CHILDREN over-4s welcomed. DOGS assistance dogs only. CREDIT CARDS Amex, MasterCard, Visa. PRICES per room B&B £139–£175. À la carte £28. 2-night min. stay at weekends in high season.
25% DISCOUNT VOUCHERS

BOURNEMOUTH Dorset
Map 2:E2
THE GREEN HOUSE, 4 Grove Road, BH1 3AX. Tel 01202 498900, www. thegreenhousehotel.com. Sustainability is the new black at this handsome Victorian villa with pristine green credentials. The garden is eco-aware, the roof sports solar panels and beehives – fuelling breakfast in more ways than one. In the smart bedrooms, some snug, there are, of course, harmonious earth tones and eco prints. Organic bedlinen and natural materials are cossetingly cool and contemporary. The best rooms have a reclaimed Victorian tub, but all receive the morning-fresh biscuits. In the Arbor restaurant chef Andy Hilton's unfussy, modern menus use organic, Fairtrade and locally sourced ingredients in such dishes as Creedy Carver duck breast, confit leg suet pudding, garlic mashed potatoes. Breakfast keeps the bar high and green. BEDROOMS 32, 1 suitable for disabled. OPEN all year. FACILITIES bar, restaurant, lift, free Wi-Fi, in-room TV (Freeview), civil wedding licence, 1-acre garden, terrace, parking. BACKGROUND MUSIC in public areas. LOCATION short walks to town centre and to beach. CHILDREN all ages welcomed. DOGS not allowed. CREDIT CARDS Amex, MasterCard, Visa. PRICES per room B&B from £119, D,B&B from £179. À la carte £35. One-night bookings refused Sat at peak times.

URBAN BEACH, 23 Argyll Road, BH5 1EB. Tel 01202 301509, www. urbanbeach.co.uk. In a buzzy spot near Boscombe beach, Mark Cribb's quirky hotel has a happy, laid-back atmosphere. Its easy-going interiors include driftwood lamps, and surf boards hanging on the walls, but the well-stocked bar, particularly its extensive cocktail menu, is a serious business. Bedrooms mix ochres, earth tones and neutrals; one has a contemporary four-poster, another a painted Japanese headboard; a spacious triple-aspect room suits a family. All rooms have a powerful shower, crisp bedlinens, cafetière coffee. Essentials left at home (umbrellas, wellies, even phone chargers) can be borrowed. Food is served till late in the bistro/bar. Breakfast is just as relaxed: smoothies, eggs all ways, Fairtrade coffee, available until 11.30 am. BEDROOMS 12. OPEN all year. FACILITIES bar/bistro, free Wi-Fi, in-room TV, heated covered deck, limited on-site parking, free street parking. BACKGROUND MUSIC in public areas, occasional live guitar music. LOCATION 1 mile E of the town centre. CHILDREN all ages welcomed. DOGS allowed (in public areas). CREDIT CARDS MasterCard, Visa. PRICES per room B&B single from £58, double from £80. À la carte £32. 2-night min. stay at weekends.

BOWNESS-ON-WINDERMERE
Cumbria
Map 4: inset C2
LINDETH HOWE, Lindeth Drive, LA23 3JF. Tel 015394 45759, www.lindeth-howe.co.uk. The verdant surrounds of this hillside Victorian country house have moved visitors since the late 19th century. It was then that sixteen-year-old Beatrice Potter, holidaying in this house, discovered the inspiration for her 'little books'. The well-appointed country-style bedrooms (tweeds, vintage photographs, floral curtains) overlook the sweeping gardens and fells; three ground-floor rooms have direct garden access. The morning room has books and board games for

inclement days, although the brave will tramp out from the front door, rain or shine. In the dining room, with its huge panoramic windows, chef Chris Davies serves innovative British dishes including pot-roasted Cumbrian chicken, pheasant chipolatas, sprouts, fondant potato, cauliflower purée. BEDROOMS 35, 3 suitable for disabled. OPEN all year. FACILITIES morning room, lounge, bar, restaurant, free Wi-Fi, in-room TV (Freeview), civil wedding licence, sun terrace, 6-acre grounds, indoor swimming pool, spa facilities, electric car charging point, electric bicycles for hire. BACKGROUND MUSIC in bar and restaurant. LOCATION 1 mile from Bowness Pier. CHILDREN all ages welcomed. DOGS allowed (in some bedrooms, not in public rooms). CREDIT CARDS Amex, MasterCard, Visa. PRICES per room B&B from £210, D,B&B from £284. À la carte £48. 1-night bookings sometimes refused.

THE RYEBECK, Lyth Valley Road, LA23 3JP. Tel 015394 88195, www.ryebeck.com. An unpretentious, gabled Arts and Crafts country house has 'tantalising' views of Lake Windermere and Coniston Fells. Some of the bright, spacious bedrooms take in the lake from a private patio or Juliet balcony; home-made biscuits, tea and coffee from a local merchant, Cumbria-made toiletries are found in all. Chef Cameron Smith's 'reasonably priced', 'inventive, well-presented' dishes, using Lakeland produce, are served in the modern, glass-walled restaurant. OS maps for fell walks from the door are available to borrow – the less rugged might prefer a leisurely stroll through the grounds. Sister hotels Hipping Hall, Cowan Bridge, and Forest Side, Grasmere (see main entries), are well liked by Guide readers. BEDROOMS 26. OPEN all year. FACILITIES bar, lounge, restaurant, free Wi-Fi, in-room TV (Freeview), civil wedding licence, 5-acre grounds, bicycle storage, parking, BACKGROUND MUSIC in bar, restaurant. LOCATION on the Lyth Valley Road, 10-min. walk from Bowness-on-Windermere centre. CHILDREN all ages welcomed. DOGS allowed (in garden-access bedrooms, public rooms; guests may dine with their pets in the lounge by prior arrangement). CREDIT CARDS Amex, MasterCard, Visa. PRICES per room B&B £159–£279, D,B&B £229–£329. À la carte £37.

25% DISCOUNT VOUCHERS

BRADFORD-ON-AVON Wiltshire
Map 2:D1

TIMBRELL'S YARD, 49 Saint Margaret's Street, BA15 1DE. Tel 01225 869492, timbrellsyard.com. By the footpath skirting the Avon, this popular bar/restaurant-with-rooms occupies a Grade II listed building in a 'delightful little town'. Owned by the Stay Original Company, its 'excellent' bar has a 'great selection' of craft spirits, local ales, West Country ciders. 'Interesting' dishes are plied in the industrial-style dining areas although one Guide insider found the quality variable. Outdoor seating in the courtyard 'is a plus'. Along a maze of stairs and corridors, voguish bedrooms (many facing the river) have modern textiles ranged across reclaimed furniture, timber cladding and wonky floors: split-level suites ('steep, polished steps') have deep window seats. See also The Swan, Wedmore, and The White Hart, Somerton (Shortlist entries). BEDROOMS 17. OPEN all year. FACILITIES bar, restaurant, private dining room, free Wi-Fi, in-room TV (Freeview), river-facing terrace. BACKGROUND MUSIC in public areas 'to suit time and ambience'. LOCATION centre of Bradford-on-Avon. 3-min. walk from railway station. CHILDREN all ages welcomed. DOGS allowed in all rooms (£10 per dog per stay). CREDIT CARDS MasterCard, Visa. PRICES per room B&B from £95, D,B&B from £135. À la carte £30.

BREEDON ON THE HILL
Derbyshire
Map 2:A2

BREEDON HALL, Nr Derby, DE73 8AN. Tel 01332 864935, www.breedonhall. co.uk. A charming stopover not far from the M1, Charles and Charlotte Meynell's B&B in a listed Georgian manor house has bags of style and a splendid walled garden. The welcoming red brick family home has a grand entrance and a country house atmosphere; in the fire-warmed drawing room guests are offered tea and biscuits, or can help themselves to a drink from the honesty bar. Some of the spacious bedrooms, each named after a local hunt, have elegant sash windows, others have exposed timbers; all have oodles of character. Plentiful breakfasts include fresh fruit, home-made granola and eggs from the Meynells' hens. Local pub grub is as near as the end of the drive. BEDROOMS 5, plus 3 self-catering cottages. OPEN closed Sundays, Christmas and New Year. FACILITIES drawing room, dining room, snug, free Wi-Fi, in-room TV (Freeview), 1-acre grounds, civil partnership licence, parking. BACKGROUND MUSIC none. LOCATION Calke Abbey, Staunton Harold Church, Donington Park Race Track and National Forest are close by. CHILDREN all ages welcomed. DOGS well-

behaved dogs allowed (resident dog).
CREDIT CARDS MasterCard, Visa. PRICES
per room B&B from £80. À la carte £45.

BRIGHTON Sussex
Map 2:E4
FIVE, 5 New Steine, BN2 1PB. Tel
01273 686547, www.fivehotel.com. A
pebble's throw from the beach, Caroline
and Simon Heath's stylish Georgian
B&B offers cosy accommodation and
hearty breakfasts. Dazzling sea views
pour in through many of the bedrooms'
handsome sash windows; the well-
equipped rooms, some compact, have
good toiletries, fresh flowers, regal
purple accents, and colourful splashes of
art. Breakfast hampers arrive at the door
at a time to suit: muffins, cereal, yogurts,
fruit and juice; perhaps champagne and
breakfast cakes too, if a special occasion
is being celebrated. A handsome
'launching point', the town house is
ideally located for exploring Brighton;
as proud locals, the Heaths have
extensive neighbourhood knowledge
to mould the day's itinerary. BEDROOMS
9. OPEN all year. FACILITIES free Wi-
Fi, in-room TV (Freeview), DVD
library, bicycle storage. BACKGROUND
MUSIC none. LOCATION seafront central
location. CHILDREN over-5s welcomed.
DOGS not allowed. CREDIT CARDS
Amex, MasterCard, Visa. PRICES per
person B&B £45–£70. 2-night min.
stay at weekends.

PASKINS, 18–19 Charlotte Street, BN2
1AG. Tel 01273 601203, www.paskins.
co.uk. Ahead of the curve, Susan and
Roger Marlowe's characterful B&B
within the East Cliff conservation area
has long been a bastion of sustainable
practices and high-quality, locally
sourced organic food. Forged from twin

19th-century stucco houses in Kemp
Town, it has an Art Nouveau reception,
and an Art Deco theme in the rest of
the property. Upstairs, 'comfortable'
bedrooms, their bathroom stocked
with certified cruelty-free toiletries,
are colourful and eclectic. A creative,
international flair takes over breakfast,
with organic porridge with ice gold
whisky (for those who prove Scottish
heritage); Cajun vegan sausages; warm
croissants; 'Pavilion' rarebit; just-landed
fishy specials. BEDROOMS 19. OPEN from
mid-Feb, closed 24–26 December.
FACILITIES dining room, free Wi-Fi, in-
room TV (Freeview), parking vouchers
(£10 for 24 hours). BACKGROUND MUSIC
none. LOCATION 10 mins' walk from
centre. CHILDREN all ages welcomed.
DOGS allowed (not unattended) in some
bedrooms, by arrangement. CREDIT
CARDS Amex, MasterCard, Visa. PRICES
per room B&B £60–£190. Discounts for
Vegetarian Society, Vegan Society and
Amnesty International members.

A ROOM WITH A VIEW, 41 Marine
Parade, BN2 1PE. Tel 01273 682885,
www.aroomwithaviewbrighton.com.
Steps from the beach in arty Kemp
Town, Stephen Bull's 'immaculately
presented' Regency house is a 'small
but so comfortable' B&B. The 'cheerful,
friendly' spot has an appealing, unfussy
decor, with pictures of the town by local
artists. Bedrooms, each 'light, airy and
clean', have their own style; a 'comfy
bed', 'thoughtful' comforts (ear plugs
in the bedside drawer, biscuits and a
capsule coffee machine, 'fluffy towels
and dressing gowns'), perhaps a walk-in
wet room or a freestanding tub in the
bathroom. Almost all look over the sea
and down to Palace Pier. The highlight
is the 'excellent' breakfast: blueberry

pancakes, 'highly recommended double eggs Benedict'. A bonus: on-site parking. BEDROOMS 9. OPEN all year. FACILITIES lounge, breakfast room, free Wi-Fi, in-room TV, parking. BACKGROUND MUSIC 'Gentle' in breakfast room. LOCATION in Kemp Town. CHILDREN over-11s welcomed. DOGS not allowed. CREDIT CARDS all major credit cards. PRICES per room B&B single from £79, double £114.

BROADWAY Worcestershire
Map 3:D6

THE OLIVE BRANCH, The Olive Branch, WR12 7AJ. Tel 01386 853440, www. theolivebranch-broadway.com. 'Helpful owners' Pam and David Talboys run their 'beautifully appointed' B&B in a Grade II listed late 16th-century building overlooking a Cotswold high street of mellow stone houses. The country cottage-style bedrooms are well equipped with 'a comfy bed, beautiful linen and towels, decent storage space, a small but lavishly provisioned bathroom'. The enclosed rear garden is a serene spot to enjoy a tipple from the honesty bar in the homely sitting room. 'First-rate breakfasts', taken in the front parlour with its original stone flags, are stocked with home-made breads, jams, cakes and smoothies. The couple speak Spanish, some Afrikaans; the breakfast menu is available in Japanese. BEDROOMS 7, some on ground floor, 1 suitable for disabled. OPEN all year. FACILITIES lounge, breakfast room, free Wi-Fi, in-room TV, ¼-acre garden, 'easy parking'. BACKGROUND MUSIC in lounge, breakfast room. LOCATION in village centre. CHILDREN all ages welcomed. DOGS not allowed. CREDIT CARDS MasterCard, Visa. PRICES per room B&B single £80–£105, double £122–£139.

BROCKENHURST Hampshire
Map 2:E2

DAISYBANK COTTAGE, Sway Road, The New Forest, SO42 7SG. Tel 01590 622086, www.bedandbreakfast-newforest.co.uk. Leafy trails through the New Forest lead to a gingerbread Arts and Crafts house, home to 'perfect hosts' Ciaran and Cheryl Maher's B&B. Home-made cupcakes appear on guests' arrival, perhaps with a pick-me-up from the well-stocked honesty bar. 'Spacious, beautifully decorated' bedrooms are scattered across the main house and a prettily converted garden cottage; each has a wide bed, plantation shutters and a well-appointed bathroom or wet room; a Nespresso machine; hand-made chocolates; high-quality toiletries. Some cottage suites have their own patio with garden access; the shepherd's hut has a wood burner. Breakfast orders, placed in the flowerpot outside the room at night, are transformed into 'fantastic' Aga-fresh fare. BEDROOMS 8. All on ground floor, plus 1-bed shepherd's hut available Apr–Sept, some suitable for disabled but not fully adapted. OPEN all year, except 1 week over Christmas. FACILITIES 2 sitting rooms, breakfast room, free Wi-Fi, in-room TV (Freeview), ½-acre garden, parking. BACKGROUND MUSIC in breakfast area. LOCATION ⅔ mile S of Brockenhurst village. CHILDREN over-8s welcomed. DOGS not allowed. CREDIT CARDS Diners Club, MasterCard, Visa. PRICES per room B&B £110–£160. 2-night min. stay preferred.
25% DISCOUNT VOUCHERS

BROOK Hampshire
Map 2:E2

THE BELL INN, Roger Penny Way, nr Lyndhurst, SO43 7HE. Tel 023 8081 2214, www.bellinn-newforest.co.uk.

Flanked by two golf courses, this 18th-century coaching inn, in a quiet New Forest hamlet, is 'a great option for a relaxed weekend away'. Updated in modern country style, the red-brick building has been in the Eyre family since 1782. 'Simple, pleasant bedrooms', distinct in character, may have a lounge area, beams or a sloping ceiling. The cosy bar serves hearty British favourites (and a splendid range of gins), while 'more gourmet dishes' are found in the farmhouse-style dining room, perhaps chargrilled Swallowfield farm bacon chops, pineapple chutney, crushed peas, creamy mash, grilled tomatoes. A 'good choice' at breakfast includes eggs all ways, kippers. Dogs receive a plethora of treats. BEDROOMS 28, some interconnecting, 8 on ground floor. OPEN all year. FACILITIES bar, lounge, 3 dining areas, free Wi-Fi, in-room TV (Freeview), civil wedding licence, beer garden, patio, parking. BACKGROUND MUSIC in public areas. LOCATION 1 mile from J1 of the M27, on the edge of the New Forest. CHILDREN all ages welcomed. DOGS allowed in some ground-floor bedrooms, bar, not in dining room. CREDIT CARDS MasterCard, Visa. PRICES per room B&B single from £84, double £109–£199, D,B&B double £159–£249. À la carte £30. 2-night min. stay on Fridays/Saturdays.

BUCKDEN Cambridgeshire
Map 2:B4

THE GEORGE, High Street, PE19 5XA. Tel 01480 812300, www. thegeorgebuckden.com. In a 'quaint village' just off the Great North Road, Anne and Richard Furbank's 19th-century coaching inn is done up with a dash of good-humour. Each of the bedrooms is named after a famous (or infamous) George – Eliot, Orwell, Best, etc; their style is perhaps 'a little old-fashioned', but all have a 'clean, modern bathroom', with a drench shower, spoiling toiletries. 'Dedicated young staff' extend a 'warm welcome'. Downstairs, in the 'popular, family-friendly restaurant', chef El Akil Benaissa's 'truly excellent' modern British dishes include Cumbrian lamb chop and kofta, garlic mash, green beans, pancetta, lemon and thyme jus. Breakfast brings 'perfectly poached eggs' and 'excellent' coffee. BEDROOMS 12, 3 suitable for disabled. OPEN all year except 25–26 Dec evenings, 1 Jan. FACILITIES lift, bar, lounge, restaurant, private dining rooms, free Wi-Fi, in-room TV (Freeview), civil wedding licence, courtyard. BACKGROUND MUSIC in public areas. LOCATION ¼ mile from centre. CHILDREN all ages welcomed. DOGS allowed, not unattended in bedrooms, only guide dogs in restaurants. CREDIT CARDS all major cards. PRICES per room B&B £95–£150, D,B&B £155–£210. À la carte £50.

BUCKFASTLEIGH Devon
Map 1:D4

KILBURY MANOR, Colston Road, TQ11 0LN. Tel 01364 644079, www. kilburymanor.co.uk. Julia and Martin Blundell's peaceful countryside B&B occupies a characterful Devonshire longhouse dating back to the 17th century, just up from the River Dart. Homely bedrooms, spread across the main house and converted barn, have oodles of character; the loft room has a vaulted beamed ceiling; all have a generous hospitality tray, aromatic toiletries. Served in the pretty dining room with wood-burning stove, breakfast brings home-made preserves and compotes, devilled tomatoes on granary toast, English muffin with locally smoked salmon. Dietary requirements are catered for with advance notice. The hosts have dining recommendations in the evening. Great walks virtually from the door: Dartmoor national park's open moorland and wooded gorges await nearby. BEDROOMS 4, 2 in converted stone barn across the courtyard, plus a 1-bedroom cottage. OPEN all year. FACILITIES breakfast room, free Wi-Fi, in-room TV (Freeview), 4-acre garden, courtyard, bicycle and canoe storage. BACKGROUND MUSIC none. LOCATION 1 mile from Buckfastleigh centre. CHILDREN over-8s welcomed. DOGS not allowed. CREDIT CARDS none accepted. PRICES per room B&B single from £65, double £80–£99. 2-night min. Apr–Sept.

BURFORD Oxfordshire
Map 3:D6
BAY TREE HOTEL, Sheep Street, OX18 4LW. Tel 01993 822791, www.cotswold-inns-hotels.co.uk/the-bay-tree-hotel. A wisteria-festooned arch frames the entry to this prettily refurbished hotel, in a hilly Cotswold town. Forged from a row of 17th-century honey-stone houses, the hotel (Cotswold Inns and Hotels) has flagstone floors, ancient beams, a galleried staircase and huge open fireplaces. The country-contemporary bedrooms (some compact) have their own style, with a mix of florals, checks, tweeds, hunting themed fabrics. All have fluffy robes, upmarket toiletries, a Nespresso machine. For canine travellers, there are garden rooms with direct outdoor access. In the bar, board games, local ales, ciders, and light meals; in the restaurant, well-crafted modern British cuisine including barramundi,

seafood chowder, baby leeks, Persian potato, samphire. BEDROOMS 21, 2 adjoining garden rooms on ground floor. OPEN all year. FACILITIES library, bar, restaurant, free Wi-Fi, in-room TV (Freeview), civil wedding licence, function facilities, patio, walled garden. BACKGROUND MUSIC in public areas ('subtle'). LOCATION 5 mins' walk from Burford High Street. CHILDREN all ages welcomed. DOGS well-behaved dogs allowed in some bedrooms and in public rooms. CREDIT CARDS Amex, MasterCard, Visa. PRICES per room B&B from £110, D,B&B from £186. Set menu 2 courses £36, 3 courses £38.
25% DISCOUNT VOUCHERS

BURRINGTON Devon
Map 1:C4
NORTHCOTE MANOR, Northcote Manor Hotel, EX37 9LZ. Tel 01769 560501, www.northcotemanor.co.uk. Deep in the Taw valley, Jean-Pierre Mifsud's wisteria-hung 18th-century manor house is a characterful 'high standard' hideaway, surrounded by orchards and woodlands. 'All the staff were attentive, helpful and polite.' The lounge ('very comfortable') is 'tastefully furnished'; stacks of books to borrow line the 'great log stove'. A series of staircases ('designed perhaps by Escher') lead to the bedrooms. Snug or spacious, traditional or modern, with terrace or garden views, they have 'all the necessities'. 'Housekeeping was excellent', as were Chef Richie Herkes's menus: 'a good choice, well cooked'. The tasting menu is 'unmissable'. Breakfast maintained standards, with good vegan options. See also sister hotel The Lake, Llangammarch Wells (main entry). BEDROOMS 16, 5 in extension, 1 suitable for disabled. OPEN all year.

FACILITIES 2 lounges, bar, 2 restaurants, free Wi-Fi, in-room TV (Freeview), civil wedding licence, 20-acre grounds. BACKGROUND MUSIC classical in public areas after midday. LOCATION 3 miles S of Umberleigh. CHILDREN all ages welcomed. DOGS allowed in some bedrooms, not in 1 lounge or restaurant. CREDIT CARDS Amex, MasterCard, Visa. PRICES per room B&B £170–£280, D,B&B £260–£340. À la carte £45.

BURY ST EDMUNDS Suffolk
Map 2:B5

THE NORTHGATE, Northgate Street, IP33 1HP. Tel 01284 339604, www. thenorthgate.com. A revitalising make-over has turned this large, red brick Victorian hotel into a smart spot on one of the arteries leading into the heart of the historic town. Owned by the small Chestnut Inns group, it has spacious, well-decorated bedrooms with a muted palette, Provençal furniture, modern bathroom with stylishly retro fittings. Some have a fireplace, an in-room bath; those facing the garden are quietest. Cocktails, ordered from a vast selection in the slick, contemporary bar, have a preprandial zing before inventive dishes in the handsome restaurant. Perhaps pan-fried hake, curried chickpeas, clams and spinach. Breakfast brings grilled avocado on sourdough; eggs many ways; the full Suffolk. The sister Packhorse Inn is in Newmarket (see main entry). BEDROOMS 10. OPEN all year. FACILITIES bar/lounge, restaurant, private function room, free Wi-Fi, in-room TV (Freeview), garden, terrace, parking. BACKGROUND MUSIC in public areas. LOCATION 6-min. walk into town. CHILDREN all ages welcomed. DOGS allowed in 1 bedroom, in public rooms except chef's table. CREDIT CARDS Amex,

MasterCard, Visa. PRICES per person B&B single £115–£140, double £140–£280. À la carte £35.

CAMBRIDGE Cambridgeshire
Map 2:B4

GONVILLE HOTEL, Gonville Place, CB1 1LY. Tel 01223 366611, www. gonvillehotel.co.uk. Overlooking verdant Parker's Piece, this large, family-owned hotel is a short walk to colleges, shops and cafés. It is liked for its 'delightful, helpful staff'. 'They enthusiastically recommended the wonderful Fitzwilliam Museum.' A cheerful air floats throughout the dapper public spaces. The modern bedrooms (quietest at the rear) 'lack a bit of character, but not comfort or equipment', with a decent hospitality tray, all-natural toiletries; an evening turn-down and a virtual valet service (using the provided iPad). 'Tasty' snacks and meals are served in the Atrium brasserie; fine dining, courtesy of chef Hans Schweitzer, in Cotto restaurant. A 'good, not excellent' breakfast had an 'enormous buffet', made-to-order cooked dishes. BEDROOMS 84, some on ground floor. OPEN all year. FACILITIES bar, lounge, 2 restaurants, free Wi-Fi, in-room TV (Freeview), parking (£15 council charge), bicycles to borrow. BACKGROUND MUSIC in public areas. LOCATION in centre. CHILDREN all ages welcomed (under-12s free). DOGS allowed in reception area, some bedrooms. CREDIT CARDS Amex, MasterCard, Visa. PRICES per room B&B from £177. Set dinner (Cotto) £70–£75, à la carte (Atrium brasserie) £50.

QUY MILL HOTEL & SPA, Church Road, Stow-cum-Quy, CB25 9AF. Tel 01223 293383, www.cambridgequymill.co.uk.

Standing in well-maintained gardens, a 19th-century water mill is now a modern spa hotel. Stylish rooms in the original building have long views over the grounds or river, some have a four-poster, a fireplace; larger rooms (some with private patio, exposed timbers) are in converted barns across the courtyard. Served in the garden-facing Mill House restaurant, or on the patio, chef Gavin Murphy's modern British and European dishes use locally sourced ingredients. All-day light bites are served in the lounge/bar. The hardest decision is picking from over 50 malt whiskies for a nightcap. The spa has a sauna, treatment rooms, a mud chamber and indoor pool. BEDROOMS 51, some in converted barns across courtyard, 1 suitable for disabled. OPEN all year, no food served on Christmas Day. FACILITIES bar/lounge, restaurant, free Wi-Fi, in-room TV (Freeview), civil wedding licence, conference facilities, leisure centre, 2-acre grounds, parking. BACKGROUND MUSIC in public areas. LOCATION 5 miles NE of Cambridge city centre. CHILDREN all ages welcomed. DOGS not allowed. CREDIT CARDS Amex, MasterCard, Visa. PRICES per room B&B £100–£300, D,B&B £170–£400. À la carte £45.

THE VARSITY HOTEL & SPA, 24 Thompson's Lane, off Bridge Street, CB5 8AQ. Tel 01223 306030, www.thevarsityhotel.co.uk. 'Helpful staff' and a 'very convenient location' on the River Cam win top marks for this modern hotel. It embraces gown: a bowler-hatted doorman is a retired college porter; different colleges lend their names for room categories; campus memorabilia line the corridors. Up on the roof terrace, 'wonderful views' of Jesus Green and nearby campuses can be enjoyed over cocktails. Cool, contemporary bedrooms are each their own; some have an inspiring outlook; others a large four-poster bed or extra seating. River bar serves a classic surf and turf menu by the waterside; on the sixth floor, brasserie-style fare is available all day. 'Really good breakfasts' have much choice. BEDROOMS 48, 3 suitable for disabled. OPEN all year except Christmas. FACILITIES lift, bar, 2 restaurants, roof terrace, health club and spa, free Wi-Fi, in-room TV, civil wedding licence, conference facilities, valet parking service (charge). BACKGROUND MUSIC in restaurants. LOCATION by Cam, in centre. CHILDREN all ages welcomed. DOGS not allowed. CREDIT CARDS Amex, MasterCard, Visa. PRICES per room B&B from £255.

CANTERBURY Kent
Map 2:D5

CANTERBURY CATHEDRAL LODGE, The Precincts, CT1 2EH. Tel 01227 865350, www.canterburycathedrallodge.org. Housed within an architect-designed complex, this contemporary hotel enjoys a 'prime position' in the 'serene grounds' of the UNESCO-designated World Heritage site. Despite the age difference the solid stone and woodwork building 'fits in well' with the medieval cathedral and its ecclesiastical surroundings. Run by 'cheerful staff', it offers special after-hours access into the precincts – 'a singular privilege'. 'Comfortable' bedrooms are simple, uncluttered linear, with a good shower room. Cathedral-facing options have 'blissful' views. At breakfast in the busy refectory or on the terrace, a 'small buffet' and 'well-served' hot dishes lay heavenly foundations for the day. Guests have discounts at local restaurants, 'many within easy walking distance'. BEDROOMS 35, 1 suitable for disabled. OPEN all year. FACILITIES lift, sitting room, breakfast room, free Wi-Fi, in-room TV (Freeview), Campanile garden, meeting/function facilities, limited parking (pre-booking required). BACKGROUND MUSIC none. CHILDREN all ages welcomed. DOGS not allowed. CREDIT CARDS all major cards. PRICES per room B&B single £95, double £99–£195.

CHATTON Northumberland
Map 4:A3

CHATTON PARK HOUSE, New Road, nr Alnwick, NE66 5RA. Tel 01668 215507, www.chattonpark.com. Well-manicured lawns stretch away from Paul and Michelle Mattinson's 'most welcoming' Georgian house where tranquillity is part of the package. A child-free spot, it has plenty of space to recharge. The large, airy sitting room has cosy armchairs for reading a borrowed book or a newspaper; the manicured grounds are ideal for restful strolls; a weak mobile signal allows guests to properly disconnect. The well-equipped, capacious bedrooms, all garden-facing, have thoughtful extras (tea/coffee-making facilities, a mini-fridge, fluffy bathrobes, good toiletries); two have a separate lounge. Ordered in advance, breakfasts are generous (oak-smoked local kippers, locally made jams). The Mattinsons have much knowledgeable advice about the area. BEDROOMS 4, plus 2-bed self-catering lodge with private garden. OPEN Mar–Nov. FACILITIES sitting room, breakfast room, free Wi-Fi, in-room TV (Freeview), 4-acre grounds, parking. BACKGROUND MUSIC none. LOCATION ½ mile from Chatton. CHILDREN not allowed. DOGS not allowed. CREDIT CARDS MasterCard, Visa. PRICES per

room B&B £130–£249. 1-night bookings sometimes refused.

CHELTENHAM Gloucestershire
Map 3:D5

BEAUMONT HOUSE, 56 Shurdington Road, GL53 0JE. Tel 01242 223311, www.bhhotel.co.uk. Close to the centre of this Regency town, Fan and Alan Bishop's white-painted Victorian villa B&B is a good base during festivals, races and all things in between. The fetching bedrooms (some snug) are individually designed. Spacious suites, including one with an Africa theme, another Asia, have a spa bath in the bathroom, high-end toiletries. In all rooms: tea- and coffee-making facilities, bottled water, biscuits. The neat lawn and well-maintained garden are worth a visit with a little something from the honesty bar. Breakfast options include Cotswold herb sausage; smoked haddock, poached eggs. The Bishops, self-identifying foodies, have recommendations for eating in the buzzy Montpellier quarter. BEDROOMS 16. OPEN all year. FACILITIES lounge, breakfast room, free Wi-Fi, in-room TV (Sky, Freeview), garden, parking. BACKGROUND MUSIC in breakfast room. LOCATION 1 mile S of town centre. CHILDREN all ages welcomed. DOGS not allowed. CREDIT CARDS Amex, MasterCard, Visa. PRICES per room B&B £75–£220. 2-night min. stay on Sat night, and during festivals and Cheltenham Gold Cup.

BUTLERS, Western Road, GL50 3RN. Tel 01242 570771, www.butlers-hotel. co.uk. A discreet buttling theme permeates Paul Smyth and Shaun Bailey's 'enjoyable, quirky' B&B in a former 19th-century gentleman's residence. Its 'exceptional service and good value' are nothing less than might be expected. Alongside Edwardian paraphernalia and curios, the lounge's bookshelves make it 'a tempting place to lose time in'. 'Elegant, capacious bedrooms' each bear the name of a famous butler (Jeeves, Hudson, Brabinger, etc.); inside, a 'very comfortable bed, pleasing antiques; a gleaming bathroom' with a powerful shower; some rooms offer views of the distant Malvern hills. Breakfast's cooked dishes, which can be taken on the roof terrace, are 'perfectly tasty'. The 'quiet, well-located spot' is 'an easy walk' from the centre. BEDROOMS 8. OPEN all year except Christmas. FACILITIES drawing room, breakfast room, free Wi-Fi, in-room TV (Freeview), ¼-acre garden, parking. BACKGROUND MUSIC quiet radio in the morning. LOCATION 10 mins' stroll to the promenade or Montpellier. CHILDREN over-9s welcomed. DOGS not allowed. CREDIT CARDS MasterCard, Visa. PRICES per room B&B single from £80, double from £99. 2-night min. stay during weekends and festivals.

THE CHELTENHAM TOWNHOUSE, 12–14 Pittville Lawn, GL52 2BD. Tel 01242 221922, www.cheltenhamtownhouse. com. On a tree-lined street, Adam and Jayne Lillywhite's restful B&B, in a town house designed by Victorian architect John Forbes, has rooms to suit most budgets. A neutral palette, fresh flowers and an open fire create a soothing atmosphere in the lounge, helped by newspapers, a library of books and a well-stocked honesty bar. The light, harmoniously decorated bedrooms can be snug or sizeable (particularly the family room, which can sleep

five); luxury rooms have a towering ceiling, an extra sofa bed, perhaps an original fireplace. All rooms are well equipped with tea/coffee-making facilities, biscuits, good toiletries. Manager/chef Nathaniel Leitch cooks a varied breakfast. No need for a car: two bicycles and helmets are available to borrow. BEDROOMS 26, 5 studio apartments, 4 in separate building. OPEN all year, room only rate for 4 days around Christmas. FACILITIES lift, lounge, breakfast room, free Wi-Fi, in-room TV (Freeview), sun deck, limited on-site parking (permits supplied for street). BACKGROUND MUSIC none. LOCATION Cheltenham, 5 mins' walk from the town centre. CHILDREN all ages welcomed. DOGS not allowed. CREDIT CARDS Amex, MasterCard, Visa. PRICES per room B&B £78–£140.

No. 131, 131 The Promenade, GL50 1NW. Tel 01242 822939, theluckyonion. com/property/no-131. With an eye on the Imperial Gardens across the road, this well-restored Georgian villa has a bijou, grown-up atmosphere. It's one of Sam and Georgie Pearman's Lucky Onion group (see next entry). Relaxed lounges have squashy sofas, tables groaning with magazines, striking modern art. Scattered across voguish bedrooms (some snug) with well-integrated original features, more works from the likes of David Hockney and Banksy, a 'great bed'; a decadent bathroom, sometimes accessed by steps, with a hook on the deep tub for a wine glass. Nespresso machines, locally made minibar snacks are standard. The bar has inspired cocktails; equally creative: the restaurant's locally sourced dishes and serious steaks. Breakfast is also excellent. BEDROOMS 11. OPEN all year.

FACILITIES drawing room, lounge, bar, restaurant, private dining rooms, games room, free Wi-Fi, in-room Apple TV (Sky), terrace, parking. BACKGROUND MUSIC all day in public areas. LOCATION in town centre. CHILDREN all ages welcomed. DOGS not allowed. CREDIT CARDS Amex, MasterCard, Visa. PRICES per room B&B from £180, D,B&B from £240. À la carte £35.

NO. 38 THE PARK, 38 Evesham Road, GL52 2AH. Tel 01242 822929, theluckyonion.com/property/no-38-the-park. Easy-going cool seeps through this rustically chic Georgian town house B&B (owned by Sam and Georgie Pearman, see previous Shortlist entry), overlooking elegant Pittville Park. The Pearmans' love of modern art is very much in evidence: Hockneys and Blakes hang above vases of fresh flowers and shelves of art books. The walk-in honesty bar is seriously impressive. Modish bedrooms (some snug) have their own style, a claw-footed bath here, a vividly coloured mohair blanket or original fireplace there. All have king-size beds, decent robes, good toiletries, Nespresso machines. For dinner, sister restaurant The Tavern, ten minutes' walk away, is an easy option. A help-yourself buffet is set up in the beamed breakfast room. BEDROOMS 13, 1, on ground floor, suitable for disabled. OPEN all year. FACILITIES sitting room, open-plan dining area, private dining room, free Wi-Fi, in-room Apple TV (Sky), small courtyard garden, limited parking. BACKGROUND MUSIC all day in public areas. LOCATION 10 mins' walk from Cheltenham town centre. CHILDREN all ages welcomed. DOGS allowed in bedrooms and public rooms. CREDIT CARDS Amex,

MasterCard, Visa. PRICES per room B&B £110-£400.

CHESTER Cheshire
Map 3:A4

THE CHESTER GROSVENOR, Eastgate, CH1 1LT. Tel 01244 324024, www.chestergrosvenor.com. Grand from every direction, this 'very smart' Grade II listed hotel (Bespoke Hotels) is 'a very good place to stay, peopled with polite, cheerful staff'. Bedrooms are up 'the wide staircase, past the huge, dramatic chandelier'. Some are modern, some traditional; all have a comfortable bed and 'every amenity' (air conditioning, double glazing, a marble bathroom with 'piping hot water'). In the light-filled brasserie, classic modern dishes; in chef Simon Radley's Michelin-starred restaurant, 'splendid service' and 'superb food, in an entirely different class', perhaps maple roast pigeon, sweet cabbage heart, Alsace sausage, red lentil. A wide choice at breakfast ('ample, excellent'). Centrally located, the hotel is ideal for exploring the city. BEDROOMS 80, 1 suitable for disabled. OPEN all year except Christmas. FACILITIES lift, drawing room, lounge, bar, brasserie, restaurant, meeting/private dining rooms, free Wi-Fi, in-room TV (Sky, Freeview), civil wedding licence, function facilities, spa, parking. BACKGROUND MUSIC in public areas. LOCATION in city centre. CHILDREN all ages welcomed (over-11s only in restaurant). DOGS not allowed. CREDIT CARDS all major cards. PRICES [2018] per room B&B from £155. Tasting menu (restaurant) £69 or £99, à la carte (brasserie) £45.

ODDFELLOWS, 20 Lower Bridge Street, CH1 1RS. Tel 01244 345454, www.oddfellowschester.com. The former meeting spot of an altruistic society of misfits and artists (the Odd Fellows), so rumour has it, this 'great' neoclassical hotel redefines 'quirky' yet keeps high standards every which way. Wickerwork bunnies box; typewriters chase up the walls; Mad Hatter-esque style bounds through the restaurant, a nod to Cheshire. The bedrooms, in the main house and a modern annexe, are just as comfortably eccentric: perhaps a circular bed, Randolph Caldecott illustrations. Tempting cocktails and imaginative, uncomplicated dishes are served in the 'secret garden', the flamboyant lounge bar and the mural-decorated restaurant. Come morning, awake to a bagged breakfast (croissant, natural yogurt, fresh orange juice, fruit). BEDROOMS 18, 14 in annexe, 1 suitable for disabled. OPEN all year except Christmas Day. FACILITIES lobby, bar, restaurant, private dining room, free Wi-Fi, in-room TV, civil wedding licence, terrace, garden. BACKGROUND MUSIC in public areas. LOCATION in city centre. CHILDREN all ages welcomed. DOGS not allowed. CREDIT CARDS all major cards. PRICES per room B&B from £169.

CHICHESTER Sussex
Map 2:E3

CHICHESTER HARBOUR HOTEL, North Street, PO19 1NH. Tel 01243 778000, www.harbourhotels.co.uk/hotels/chichester. Priory Park, where WG Grace once wore whites, is a cricket ball throw away from this Georgian hotel inside the city's Roman walls. Within the Grade II* listed building, a cheery design melds with well-maintained original features (grand staircase, marble fireplaces, large sash windows). Colourful bedrooms are individually done, with an oversized headboard,

velvet cushions, bold wallpaper and leafy or cathedral views. The marble-topped bar with its Art Deco vibe attracts locals for pre-dinner drinks and cocktail master-classes, before settling in the Jetty restaurant for brasserie dishes (seafood, grills and salads). Underneath, the subterranean spa has a hydro pool and many treatments, available to hotel guests (small extra charge). BEDROOMS 36, plus 1-bedroom cottage. OPEN all year. FACILITIES bar, restaurant, orangery, private dining room, free Wi-Fi, in-room TV, lift, terrace, spa, gym, civil wedding licence, business facilities, limited parking. BACKGROUND MUSIC in public areas. LOCATION within the city walls. CHILDREN all ages welcomed (cots, extra beds, over-3s £25). DOGS not allowed. CREDIT CARDS Amex, MasterCard, Visa. PRICES per room B&B from £155, D,B&B from £205. Set dinner £12.75, à la carte £30. 2-night min. stay preferred.

CHIDDINGFOLD Surrey
Map 2:D3

THE CROWN INN, The Green, Petworth Road, GU8 4TX. Tel 01428 682255, thecrownchiddingfold.com. In the 13th century, a hostelry on this spot provided sleep and sustenance for monks on pilgrimage to Canterbury. These days, Daniel and Hannah Hall continue the tradition of hospitality in their 'lovely' 16th-century country inn. The timber-framed building is full of 'traditional character'; in the popular bar, local tipples are served amid medieval carvings, 'massive beams' and inglenook fireplaces. In the oak-panelled restaurant, 'delicious pub grub is attentively served to well-scrubbed tables'. Characterful well-appointed bedrooms, all sloping floors and antique furnishings, have chic toiletries, a digital radio. Across the courtyard, two rooms have French doors on to a private garden. Breakfast has freshly squeezed juices, morning baked pastries, good cooked choices. BEDROOMS 8. OPEN all year. FACILITIES bar, snug, restaurant, free Wi-Fi, in-room TV (Sky, Freeview), 2 small courtyard gardens, large terrace, parking, public rooms wheelchair accessible. BACKGROUND MUSIC in public areas. LOCATION 20 mins from Guildford. CHILDREN all ages welcomed. DOGS allowed in bar and lounge, not in bedrooms. CREDIT CARDS Amex, MasterCard, Visa. PRICES per room B&B £95–£210, D,B&B £175–£200.

CHILGROVE Sussex
Map 2:E3

THE WHITE HORSE, 1 High Street, PO18 9HX. Tel 01243 519444, www. thewhitehorse.co.uk. Chic and rustic, this 'simply lovely' spot, in the foothills of the South Downs, is a countryside inn through and through. In the bar, mellow old wood, vintage pictures, the odd fox's head; in the restaurant, chef Rob Armstrong's 'simple but satisfying meals' exploiting local produce, including foraged fare, freshly caught trout from nearby rivers; pigeon and rabbit from local estates. Expansive views of the South Downs pour in through the large picture windows of the 'comfortable' courtyard bedrooms, where a cosy country style is complete with woolly blankets, sheepskin rugs and exposed beams; some rooms have a private patio, and an outdoor hot tub. BEDROOMS 15. All on ground floor, 13 in rear annexe. OPEN all year. FACILITIES bar, restaurant, private dining room, free Wi-Fi, in-room TV, function facilities, 2 patios, garden, croquet,

parking, helipad. BACKGROUND MUSIC 'Soft' in public areas, live jazz on Sun afternoons. LOCATION 6 miles from Chichester. CHILDREN all ages welcomed. DOGS allowed (£15 per night). CREDIT CARDS all major cards. PRICES per room B&B from £99. À la carte £30.

CHURCH STRETTON Shropshire
Map 3:C4

VICTORIA HOUSE, 48 High Street, SY6 6BX. Tel 01694 723823, www. victoriahouse-shropshire.co.uk. 'Splendid all round', Diane Chadwick offers 'well-priced, comfortable and convenient accommodation, with superb breakfasts' at her town-centre B&B. The 'wonderfully energetic, helpful' hostess has a careful eye for detail, much appreciated by guests. The homely bedrooms are 'tastefully done', with a comfortable bed, original artwork and a well-supplied hospitality tray (biscuits, hot chocolate, complimentary sherry). In a pretty room overlooking the garden, the breakfast buffet is chock full of fruit compotes, organic yogurt, and organic muesli from a nearby farm; hot dishes include egg and soldiers, bacon from locally reared pigs. The trails of the Shropshire hills are within walking distance; treats in café and tea room, nearer still. BEDROOMS 6. OPEN all year. FACILITIES seating area, breakfast room, café/tea room, free Wi-Fi, in-room TV (Freeview), walled garden, pay-and-display parking (deducted from hotel bill or permits supplied). BACKGROUND MUSIC in breakfast room. LOCATION in town centre. CHILDREN all ages welcomed. DOGS allowed in some bedrooms and in the café. CREDIT CARDS Amex, MasterCard, Visa. PRICES per room B&B £60–£96.
25% DISCOUNT VOUCHERS

CLEY-NEXT-THE-SEA Norfolk
Map 2:A5

CLEY WINDMILL, The Quay, NR25 7RP.
Tel 01263 740209, www.cleywindmill.
co.uk. Anyone braving the climb to
the top of Julian and Carolyn Godlee's
characterful B&B and restaurant is
well rewarded. Accessed by a ladder,
the top-floor Wheel Room yields
breathtaking views over salt marsh
and sea, which peel away from the
19th-century grinding mill on the
north Norfolk coast. Other rooms,
decorated in muted hues, overlook
the reed beds or the charming village,
from the former store rooms and
outbuildings. Eaten communally,
a daily-changing set supper menu
showcases Norfolk produce (Cromer
crab; Norfolk lamb), and can be tailored
with advance notice to suit special diets.
Binoculars, field guides and regular
events at the next-door bird sanctuary
are perfect for twitchers. BEDROOMS 9.
3 in converted boathouse and granary,
some ground floor rooms suitable for
disabled, but bathrooms not adapted.
OPEN all year, self-catering only over
Christmas and New Year. FACILITIES 2
lounges, restaurant, Wi-Fi, in-room TV
(Freeview), civil wedding licence, ¼-acre
gardens. BACKGROUND MUSIC in dining
room at dinner. LOCATION Northerly
Village next to the River Glaven and
1 km from the sea. CHILDREN all ages
welcomed. DOGS not allowed. CREDIT
CARDS MasterCard, Visa. PRICES per
room B&B £159–£225, D,B&B £224–
£290. Set menu £32.50. 2-night min. stay
on Fri and Sat nights.

COLEFORD Gloucestershire
Map 3:D4

FOREST HOUSE, Cinder Hill GL16 8HQ.
Tel 01594 832424, forest-house.co.uk.
Barbara and Simon Andersen 'get
almost everything right' at their small
hotel in a market town in the Wye
valley, a friendly, affordable base for
exploring the Forest of Dean. Dating
back to the 1790s, the former home of
pioneering metallurgist David Mushet,
has been extended and modernised
over the years. Immaculate bedrooms
have pine furniture, armchairs, 'good
lighting', tea, coffee and biscuits;
bathrooms have a power shower,
good-quality toiletries. The bar's coffee
machine provides complimentary
fill-ups. The restaurant specialises in
slow-cooked meat dishes including
braised beef brisket, horseradish mash,
Madeira gravy, steamed vegetables, but
has wide-ranging options. 'Both our
dinners were delicious.' Breakfast brings
smoked haddock; eggs all ways; a Forest
House full English. BEDROOMS 8. OPEN
22 Dec–8 Jan. FACILITIES bar/lounge,
restaurant, small dining room, lawned
front garden, rear car park, secure
bicycle storage, free Wi-Fi, in-room
TV (Freeview), restaurant wheelchair
accessible. BACKGROUND MUSIC in bar and
restaurant. LOCATION in town centre.
CHILDREN all ages welcomed. DOGS not
allowed. CREDIT CARDS all major cards.
PRICES per room B&B single £75–£85,
double £90–£120. À la carte £27.

COLWALL Worcestershire
Map 3:D5

COLWALL PARK HOTEL, Walwyn
Road, WR13 6QG. Tel 01684 540000,
colwall.co.uk. A tranquil, dog-friendly
Edwardian country house offers a
restful change of pace to guests of
all breeds and most budgets. The
'charming hotel' has well-appointed
bedrooms (some snug), including suites
to suit a larger group. In each: spoiling

toiletries, home-made biscuits, a dog treat, lovely views of the Malvern hills. The latter rise from the bottom of the verdant lawned garden, with walking trails from the gate. Packed lunches and maps are readily provided by the 'helpful, efficient staff'. In the restaurant, 'excellent' modern British meals; in the bar, a log fire, local real ales, Herefordshire cider. Seasonal Vale of Evesham produce features in all meals, including the 'diverse' breakfast. BEDROOMS 22. OPEN all year. FACILITIES 2 lounges, library, bar, restaurant, free Wi-Fi, in-room TV (Freeview), 2-acre garden, civil wedding licence, conference facilities. BACKGROUND MUSIC none. LOCATION halfway between Malvern and Ledbury on B4218. 50 yds from Colwall train station with direct links to London Paddington. CHILDREN all ages welcomed (extra bed £35 per night). DOGS allowed in bedrooms, bar and garden. CREDIT CARDS MasterCard, Visa. PRICES per room B&B from £95, D,B&B from £145.

CONSTANTINE Cornwall
Map 1:E2
TRENGILLY WARTHA INN, TR11 5RP Tel 01326 340332, www.trengilly. co.uk. Surrounded by gardens thick with enormous ferns and tiny orchids, Will and Lisa Lea's family-friendly pub-with-rooms is a lively destination in a secluded wooded valley. Locals flock to the bar, with its piano, settles, wood-burner and beams covered in beer mats, for its real ales and ciders, occasional folk music evenings and classic farmhouse cooking. Chef Nick Tyler's award-winning, locally sourced fare may also be eaten in the bistro or conservatory. Many of the country cottage-style bedrooms have

uninterrupted valley or garden views; one might have a hand-crafted bedhead, another its own private, covered deck area. Unique accommodation is also offered in two 'tree-top' safari tents. A full Cornish breakfast fuels the day. BEDROOMS 12, 2 in garden annexe. OPEN all year except Christmas. FACILITIES bar, restaurant, conservatory, private dining room, games room, free Wi-Fi, in-room TV (Freeview), terrace, 6-acre garden, public rooms wheelchair accessible. BACKGROUND MUSIC live music in bar 'now and again'. LOCATION 15 mins' drive from Falmouth. CHILDREN all ages welcomed. DOGS allowed. CREDIT CARDS Amex, MasterCard, Visa. PRICES per room B&B single from £77, double from £84. À la carte £25.

CORNWORTHY Devon
Map 1:D4
KERSWELL FARMHOUSE, Kerswell Farm, TQ9 7HH. Tel 01803 732013, www. kerswellfarmhouse.co.uk. Taking its name from the wells and cress beds found in the grounds fed by nearby springs, Nichola and Graham Hawkins's B&B is enwrapped by their small working farm. Throughout the well-renovated 400-year-old longhouse, antiques blend with farmhouse furnishings, fresh-cut flowers spill from vases, and myriad contemporary artworks hang on walls and decorate crannies. The old milking parlour, as well as housing the honesty bar, exhibits the work of contemporary ceramicists, glassmakers, painters and photographers. The comfortable bedrooms have all the essentials, plus thoughtful extras (teas and ground coffee, fluffy bathrobes, novels and magazines). At breakfast, farm-fresh produce appears on the plate: sausages

from home reared pigs; eggs from free-range hens. BEDROOMS 5, 1 in adjacent barn, 1 on ground floor. OPEN April–Oct. FACILITIES 2 dining rooms, sitting room, art gallery, free Wi-Fi, in-room TV (Freeview), 14-acre grounds, parking. BACKGROUND MUSIC none. LOCATION 4 miles S of Totnes, 4 miles N of Dartmouth. CHILDREN over-12s welcomed. DOGS not allowed. CREDIT CARDS none accepted. PRICES [2018] per room B&B single £90–£125, double £115–£150. 2-night min. stay preferred.

CORSHAM Wiltshire
Map 2:D1

THE METHUEN ARMS, 2 High Street, SN13 0HB. Tel 01249 717060, www.themethuenarms.com. Handsome and historic, this buzzy pub-with-rooms (owned by Butcombe Brewery) has character to spare. The conscientiously restored Georgian coaching inn, down the High Street from stately Corsham Court of Poldark fame, has been given a voguish makeover, with tweed cushions, heritage hues and botanical prints hanging above plush sofas. Alongside craft brews, guests find chef Leigh Evans's acclaimed Italian-influenced British dishes, perhaps game and suet pudding, parsnips, mash. Bedrooms are neatly designed (some snug), each with tall Georgian windows, a deep armchair, mini-fridge and tea- and coffee-making facilities; Bramley toiletries; a Roberts radio. Some have a four-poster. At breakfast, interesting cooked options, plus freshly baked pastries and home-made granola. BEDROOMS 14, 1 in annexe. OPEN all year. FACILITIES bar, restaurant, private dining rooms, free Wi-Fi, in-room TV (Freeview), garden, courtyard, parking. BACKGROUND MUSIC in private dining areas and bar.

LOCATION 8 miles NE of Bath. CHILDREN all ages welcomed. DOGS allowed in some bedrooms, bars, courtyard (£15 per night). CREDIT CARDS Amex, MasterCard, Visa. PRICES per room B&B £140–£240. À la carte £35.
25% DISCOUNT VOUCHERS

COVENTRY Warwickshire
Map 3:C6

BARNACLE HALL, Barnacle Hall Farm, CV7 9LH. Tel 02476 612629, www.barnaclehall.co.uk. Beyond the old oak door of this 16th-century farmhouse is a tranquil escape – three miles from the M6, a 20-minute drive from Coventry, and a world away from both. The characterful house stands within lush gardens swaddled by surrounding fields. Its low doorways, nooks and crannies, and steps of varying heights betray its age, but the spacious, traditionally decorated bedrooms have all the modern essentials: a flat-screen TV, a radio alarm, individually controlled central heating. They also come with a generous hospitality tray and fresh flowers. Breakfast caters for all, with advance notice, with fresh fruit and cereal, as well as hot dishes cooked to order. BEDROOMS 3. OPEN all year except Christmas. FACILITIES sitting room, dining room, free Wi-Fi, in-room TV (Freeview), patio, garden. BACKGROUND MUSIC none. LOCATION 20 mins NE of Coventry, SE of Nuneaton. CHILDREN all ages welcomed. DOGS assistance dogs accepted. CREDIT CARDS none accepted. PRICES B&B single £45–£55, double £75–£85.

COOMBE ABBEY, Brinklow Road, Binley, CV3 2AB. Tel 02476 450450, www.coombeabbey.com. Traces of a past life as a 12th-century Cistercian abbey filter through this atmospheric, historic hotel, which combines 'character, eccentricity and individuality at its best'. It stands amid a 'well-maintained' country park and 'superb' formal gardens. The 'stunning' building's grand interiors include the carved stone pulpit, antique armchairs and series of confessional booths in the high-vaulted lobby. Glorious 'bed chambers' may have a canopy bed, original moulding or mullion windows, while the well-designed bathrooms sport such features as a Victorian bath or a richly tiled waterfall shower; some may even be hidden behind a bookcase. In the evening, a modern take on British cooking is served in the candlelit conservatory. BEDROOMS 119. OPEN all year. FACILITIES bar, restaurant, private dining rooms, free Wi-Fi, in-room TV, wedding/conference facilities, terrace, 500-acre grounds, parking (£5 per day). BACKGROUND MUSIC in public areas. CHILDREN all ages welcomed. CREDIT CARDS Amex, MasterCard, Visa. PRICES per room B&B from £150, D,B&B from £225.

COVERACK Cornwall
Map 1:E2
THE BAY HOTEL, North Corner, nr Helston, TR12 6TF. Tel 01326 280464, thebayhotel.co.uk. Stepped lawns, then buckets and spades in the sand are all that separates this 'welcoming, relaxed hotel' from the sea. Following severe flood damage last year, Victoria and Nicholas Sanders have redecorated the entire place top to toe. Coastal cool has been restored to each bedroom (some snug), with Cornish colours, tongue-and-groove panelling and a powerful new shower in the bathroom. Huge windows give nearly all the bedrooms

horizon views; the best have a balcony, or a private terrace, accessed through pretty French doors. Bay-landed lobster and chefs Ric House and Chris Conboye's 'excellent' daily-changing menus are served in the candlelit restaurant. Full Cornish breakfasts. A dog-friendly beach awaits just outside. BEDROOMS 15, 1, on ground floor, suitable for disabled. OPEN end Mar–end Oct. FACILITIES lounge, bar/restaurant, conservatory, free Wi-Fi, in-room TV (Freeview), 2 tiered gardens, large sun terrace, parking. BACKGROUND MUSIC quiet classical music or blues in bar and restaurant. LOCATION village centre, 9 miles SE of Helston. CHILDREN all ages welcomed ('we are not suitable for babies or very young children'). DOGS allowed in bedrooms and on lead in grounds, not in public rooms. CREDIT CARDS MasterCard, Visa. PRICES per room B&B from £150, D,B&B from £170. Set dinner £35. 1-night bookings sometimes refused.

COWLEY Gloucestershire
Map 3:D5
COWLEY MANOR, GL53 9NL. Tel 01242 870900, www.cowleymanor.com. Zesty by design, laid-back by nature, this family-welcoming country house hotel and spa sprawls across a fine Italianate building. All around: 'beautiful, natural' parkland, Victorian cascades (wellies provided) and unusual Grade II listed gardens. Bright, spacious bedrooms, in the main house and converted stable block, are all bold prints, and handmade furniture and fabrics by British designers; each is well equipped with a coffee machine, natural bath products, a wireless sound system. Wood-panelled Malt restaurant brings together modern informality and 'fabulous' seasonal

English dishes; the bar and sitting room serve all-day light bites. Sunk into the hillside, the 'great' glass-fronted C-Side spa has an indoor and an outdoor pool, both heated all year round. BEDROOMS 30, 15 in converted stables. OPEN all year. FACILITIES bar, sitting room, billiard room, restaurant, private sitting room, garden room, dining room, free Wi-Fi, in-room TV (Sky), 55-acre grounds, civil wedding licence, spa. BACKGROUND MUSIC in public areas. LOCATION 10 mins' drive S of Cheltenham. CHILDREN all ages welcomed. DOGS allowed in 2 bedrooms, some public rooms. CREDIT CARDS Amex, MasterCard, Visa. PRICES per room B&B from £185–£675, D,B&B from £255–£705. À la carte £45. 1-night bookings sometimes refused.

CRAYKE Yorkshire
Map 4:D4

THE DURHAM OX, Westway, YO61 4TE. Tel 01347 821506, thedurhamox.com. Michael and Sasha Ibbotson's village pub-with-rooms has stone flags, wood panelling and log fires – the legacy of three centuries of hosting visitors following an ancient Celtic trail to York. The popular bar offers well-pulled pints and an 'interesting, varied' blackboard menu of 'excellent' pub classics and daily specials (including vegetarian and gluten-free options), perhaps grilled Yorkshire pork chop, bubble and squeak, seasonal greens, apple sauce. The old outbuildings are now roomy country-style bedrooms. In each: a large bed, a spot to sit with a cuppa from the hospitality tray, good toiletries. On clear days, panoramic views stretch all the way to York Minster. Walks from the door; walking guides available. BEDROOMS 6, 1 suite accessed via external stairs, plus 3-bed self-catering cottage

in village. OPEN all year. FACILITIES 3 bars, restaurant, private dining room, free Wi-Fi, in-room TV (Freeview), function facilities, 2-acre grounds, parking. BACKGROUND MUSIC in pub and restaurant. LOCATION 3 miles E of Easingwold town centre. CHILDREN all ages welcomed. DOGS allowed in public areas, some bedrooms. CREDIT CARDS Amex, MasterCard, Visa. PRICES per room B&B from £120, D,B&B from £165. À la carte £30.

DARLINGTON Co. Durham
Map 4:C4

HEADLAM HALL, nr Gainford, DL2 3HA. Tel 01325 730238, www. headlamhall.co.uk. When the only aim is to relax, the Robinson family's cosseting Jacobean manor house is happy to oblige. Ringed by walled gardens, with farmland sprawling beyond, the stately property has an intimate, 'country house feel' running through its smart, contemporary public spaces. The panelled sitting room is scattered with squashy seating, its walls hung with serene pastoral scenes. Uncluttered chic-rustic bedrooms (in the main house, converted outbuildings and mews cottages) have harmonious heathery and pale hues; some have lovely views over the grounds. Fresh fruit and vegetables from the garden are used in the locally sourced, seasonal modern menus. Along with spa treatments, bicycles and classic cars (extra charge) are available to borrow. BEDROOMS 38, 9 in coach house, 6 in mews, 7 in spa, 2 suitable for disabled. OPEN all year except 24–27 Dec. FACILITIES lift, bar, brasserie, lounge, drawing room, library, private dining rooms, free Wi-Fi, in-room TV (Freeview), civil wedding

licence/function facilities, 4-acre garden, spa, tennis, 9-hole golf course. BACKGROUND MUSIC all day in lounge, bar and restaurant. LOCATION 8 miles W of Darlington. CHILDREN all ages welcomed. DOGS allowed in bedrooms and public rooms. CREDIT CARDS Amex, MasterCard, Visa. PRICES per room B&B single £115–£205, double £145–£235, D,B&B double £215–£305. À la carte £35.
25% DISCOUNT VOUCHERS

HOUNDGATE TOWNHOUSE, 11 Houndgate, DL1 5RF. Tel 01325 486011, www.houndgatetownhouse.com. Natalie Hambleton's guest house and restaurant offer bags of style, nicely droll touches and a convenient location, close to the town's iconic clock tower. A felt moose head greets visitors walking into the restored 18th-century town house. Throughout, a stylish mix of arresting wallpaper and bespoke furniture complements original features including an elegant curved staircase, original fireplaces, magnificent Georgian windows. In each voguish bedroom, heritage colours and charming prints; the best have a huge four-poster bed and a free-standing bath. The cool café/bar serves all-day light bites and classic dishes till 8 pm; three nights a week, cocktails precede a bistro-style menu. A leisurely breakfast (served until noon) has much choice. BEDROOMS 8, 1 suitable for disabled. OPEN all year except Sun, 25–26 Dec, 1 Jan. FACILITIES lift, lounge, bar, restaurant, free Wi-Fi, in-room TV (Freeview), terrace, complimentary use of local pool. BACKGROUND MUSIC in reception, bar and restaurant. LOCATION town centre. CHILDREN all ages welcomed. DOGS not allowed. CREDIT CARDS all major cards. PRICES

per room B&B single £90–£140, double £100–£150, D,B&B double £139–£189. À la carte £28.
25% DISCOUNT VOUCHERS

DARTMOUTH Devon
Map 1:D4

STRETE BARTON HOUSE, Totnes Road, Strete, TQ6 0RU. Tel 01803 770364, www.stretebarton.co.uk. The Far East meets the South-West at Stuart Litster and Kevin Hooper's inviting B&B in a South Hams coastal village. Uncluttered, contemporary bedrooms in their Jacobean manor house have silks, tassels, Buddha sculptures and Chinese calligraphy, to go with the fresh flowers, magazines, biscuits and a beverage tray. With three large sofas, there is generous space in the cosy lounge to enjoy the hosts' good cheer and slice of welcome cake – and enjoy the widescreen views across Start Bay. Fresh fruit, local yogurts, Devon sausages at breakfast. With the Coastal Path directly outside, there are good walks from the front door; advice and guide books are readily available. BEDROOMS 6, 1 in cottage annexe. OPEN all year. FACILITIES sitting room, breakfast room, free Wi-Fi, in-room TV (Freeview), ⅓-acre garden. BACKGROUND MUSIC none. LOCATION 5 miles W of Dartmouth. CHILDREN over-8s welcomed. DOGS allowed in cottage suite. CREDIT CARDS Amex, MasterCard, Visa. PRICES per person B&B from £55. 1-night bookings sometimes refused.
25% DISCOUNT VOUCHERS

DELPH Lancashire
Map 4:E3

THE OLD BELL INN, Huddersfield Road, nr Oldham, OL3 5EG. Tel 01457 870130, www.theoldbellinn.co.uk. In a scenic village outside Manchester, Philip

Whiteman's 'well-kept, traditional' inn occupies an 18th-century coaching house. The popular bar is 'all polished brass, shiny bottles and hard-working staff'. The gin emporium stocks over 600 varieties, a Guinness World Record. 'Excellent meals, freshly prepared, full of flavour' are served in the informal brasserie, including mature cheddar and Wigmore cheese, roasted red onion in home-made shortcrust pastry. The cosy restaurant is popular for its imaginative menus, daily specials and prime steaks. 'Clean, workaday bedrooms' are well equipped (quieter ones at the rear). To escape the bar crowds, overnight guests may use a first-floor conservatory lounge. At breakfast: hearty cooked options, freshly squeezed orange juice, pastries. BEDROOMS 18. OPEN all year. FACILITIES bar, lounge, brasserie, restaurant, free Wi-Fi, in-room TV, function facilities, terrace, parking. BACKGROUND MUSIC in public areas. LOCATION 5 miles from Oldham. CHILDREN all ages welcomed. DOGS not allowed. CREDIT CARDS Amex, Mastercard, Visa. PRICES per room B&B single £62.50–£75, double £105–£135. À la carte £32.

DERBY Derbyshire
Map 2:A2

THE COACH HOUSE, 185A Duffield Road, DE22 1JB. Tel 01332 554423, coachhousederby.com. Vibrantly colourful inside, Rob and Roberta Aitken's handsome Victorian B&B occupies a historic mill village near Darley Abbey. Help-yourself home-made brownies and books galore add allure to plush seating in the vivid blue snug; all around, something to catch the eye: playful animal-themed curios, a large tiled fireplace, a wood bar.

B&B guests stay in simple, grey-toned bedrooms or in spacious, design-led rooms (feature wallpaper, bright cushions, soft fabrics) in the stable annexe; one has a Juliet balcony, another access to the charming garden. 'Rustic' breakfast, in a calming green-hued room, includes fresh juice, 'creamy yogurt, delicious warmed red berry coulis'. In sum, 'Plenty of style, a very useful place for Derby.' BEDROOMS 7, 3 in annexe. OPEN all year. FACILITIES snug, restaurant, free Wi-Fi, in-room TV (Freeview), small garden. BACKGROUND MUSIC in snug. LOCATION 2 miles from Derby station. CHILDREN all ages welcomed. DOGS allowed, except in 1 room. CREDIT CARDS Amex, MasterCard, Visa. PRICES per room B&B £47–£186

DITTISHAM Devon
Map 1:D4

FINGALS, Old Coombe Manor Farm, TQ6 0JA. Tel 01803 722398, www.fingals.co.uk. 'To call it a hotel is to miss the point.' In a peaceful valley, Richard Johnston's quirky B&B is 'a blend of rural escape and aristocratic eccentricity'. The dog- and family-friendly 17th-century manor house has been 'artistically extended'. The casual approach may not be for everyone. There is 'a slightly haphazard grandeur' to bedrooms, 'but the mattresses and linens are top notch'. Each room is different: one has a wild brook running past, another a tall four-poster bed. Telephoning ahead to discuss options is a good idea. The lounge, bar and the greenhouse pool are mingling points. The host cooks an organic, three-course dinner, perhaps twice a week. BEDROOMS 3. OPEN Easter–New Year, self-catering only at Christmas, restaurant closed mid-week unless by arrangement. FACILITIES dining room, honesty bar, sitting room, games room, free Wi-Fi, in-room TV (Freeview), indoor swimming pool, 2-acre garden, tennis court, unsuitable for disabled. BACKGROUND MUSIC classical in bar and breakfast room. LOCATION in hamlet, 7 miles N of Dartmouth. CHILDREN all ages welcomed. DOGS allowed in bedrooms, not in public rooms. CREDIT CARDS Amex, MasterCard, Visa. PRICES per room B&B £110–£235. Set dinner £36.

DONNINGTON Sussex
Map 2:E3
THE BLACKSMITHS, Selsey Road, nr Chichester, PO20 7PR. Tel 01243 785578, the-blacksmiths.co.uk. Steeped with Scandinavian cool, Mariella and William Fleming's renovated village pub-with-rooms is a stylishly relaxed spot near the Chichester canal towpath. A blazing fire entices visitors into the bar, as does the strong list of local ales and organic wines, including bubbly from the nearby Tinwood Estate. Chic, minimalist bedrooms have a large bed, plump armchairs and country views; two have an original fireplace, a roll-top bathtub; shared is the small seating area (books, hospitality tray, a bright orange fridge for guests' use). Pub classics and more modern dishes are served in the snug, elegant dining room or the walled terrace. The chicken flock supplies breakfast. BEDROOMS 3. OPEN all year except Christmas, New Year's Eve. FACILITIES bar, restaurant, free Wi-Fi, in-room TV (Freeview), patio garden, parking. BACKGROUND MUSIC in public areas, occasional live music events. CHILDREN all ages welcomed. DOGS allowed. CREDIT CARDS MasterCard, Visa. PRICES per room B&B £120–£150.

DULVERTON Somerset
Map 1:B5
THREE ACRES COUNTRY HOUSE, Ellersdown Lane, Brushford, TA22 9AR. Tel 01398 323730, www. threeacresexmoor.co.uk. Attention to detail, peaceful surroundings and cheerful hospitality make Julie and Edward Christian's 'beautifully furnished' B&B 'a special place'. At the end of a curving tree-lined lane, the 1930s house overlooks Exmoor national park from secluded grounds. Light suppers (home-made soups, sandwiches), ordered in advance, may be taken in the traditional bar/lounge. Thoughtful extras in the individually decorated bedrooms include ground coffee, fresh milk, Exmoor spring water, a silent-tick alarm clock). Mornings begin with a birdsong serenade for a decent breakfast, perhaps home-made fruit compote with Exmoor honey; smoked Exe valley trout; home-made veggie sausage. The hosts know the best local picnicking spots; guests need but ask. Hampers, packed lunches available. BEDROOMS 6, 1 on ground floor, 1 family suite in small annexe. OPEN all year. FACILITIES bar, lounge, breakfast room, free Wi-Fi, in-room TV (Freeview), sun terrace, 2-acre grounds. BACKGROUND MUSIC none. LOCATION outskirts of village. CHILDREN all ages welcomed. DOGS not allowed in the house. CREDIT CARDS Amex, MasterCard, Visa. PRICES per person B&B £45–£75. 2-night min. stay preferred.
25% DISCOUNT VOUCHERS

DUNWICH Suffolk
Map 2:B6
THE SHIP AT DUNWICH, St James Street, IP17 3DT. Tel 01728 648219, www. shipatdunwich.co.uk. 'Unpretentious

and friendly', the creeper-covered red-brick building has been a good base for outdoorsy types since the Tudors' reign. Once a smugglers' haunt, it now attracts birders and their dogs. The inn (part of Agellus hotels) is close to the beach and the RSPB reserves at Dingle Marshes and Minsmere. The cosy bar with wood-burner is popular for its real ales; the wood-floored restaurant for 'generous portions' of such dishes as home-made rabbit and venison pie. The sheltered courtyard and 'lovely garden' are ideal sun traps. Inside, traditionally decorated bedrooms are each different (some snug); the best have expansive marsh views; others, in converted outbuildings, are 'perfect for dogs'. Breakfast has 'excellent choice'. BEDROOMS 16, 4 on ground floor in converted stables, 1 suitable for disabled. OPEN all year. FACILITIES restaurant, bar, courtyard, free Wi-Fi, in-room TV (Freeview, smart TV in family rooms), garden. BACKGROUND MUSIC none. LOCATION a few hundred yards from Dunwich beach. CHILDREN all ages welcomed. DOGS 'warmly welcomed inside and out.' CREDIT CARDS MasterCard, Visa. PRICES per room B&B £120–£140. À la carte £25.

DURHAM Co. Durham
Map 4:B4
FORTY WINKS GUEST HOUSE & RESIDENCE, 40 South Street, DH1 4QP. Tel 0191 386 8217, www. fortywinksdurham.co.uk. Brimful with curiosities, Debbie and Nigel Gadd's opulent Edwardian house is on a quiet cobbled street a short walk from the town centre and castle. Spread over four floors, its 'entertaining if slightly overcrowded' public rooms display wall trophies, a diving helmet, a penny

farthing, life-size giraffe, taxidermy specimens wearing a hat. The up-to-date bedrooms have 'excellent lighting, instant hot water, and extremely comfortable beds; a clever use of space'. Rooms at the front gaze across woods and the river to the cathedral and castle; churchyard views at the back. 'Breakfast was all one could wish for. The eggs were absolutely fresh, a rich orange, the fruit bowl was ample, the coffee excellent.' BEDROOMS 8. OPEN all year, except 24–27 Dec. FACILITIES dining room, study, free Wi-Fi, in-room TV (Freeview), courtyard, public parking (charge). BACKGROUND MUSIC 'classical music' at breakfast. LOCATION a short walk from the city centre. CHILDREN over-16s welcomed. DOGS not allowed. CREDIT CARDS Amex. MasterCard, Visa. PRICES per room B&B £110–£195.

EAST WITTON Yorkshire
Map 4:C4
THE BLUE LION, nr Leyburn, DL8 4SN. Tel 01969 624273, www.thebluelion. co.uk. Across a cobbled driveway, Paul and Helen Klein's 'lovely, good-value' 18th-century inn is an 'utterly authentic' slice of rural Wensleydale hospitality. The former coaching house is liked for its 'good atmosphere' and 'outstanding service'. Within, crackling log fires, settles, 'pleasant, knowledgeable staff', and many locals (a bowl of water is put out for their dogs) enjoying hand-pumped ales. In the bar and the candlelit restaurant, the 'well-executed British comfort food' includes slow-cooked belly pork, pig's cheek, black pudding Scotch egg. Provençal-style bedrooms, 'spotlessly clean and comfortable', occupy the main building and converted outbuildings, just outside. Breakfast will see you through to

lunch: 'fresh orange juice, good strong coffee', smoked haddock, poached eggs. BEDROOMS 15, 9 in courtyard annexe. OPEN all year. FACILITIES 2 bars, 2 dining areas, private dining room, free Wi-Fi, in-room TV (Freeview), 1-acre garden, parking, restaurant, bar wheelchair accessible. BACKGROUND MUSIC none. LOCATION in village. CHILDREN all ages welcomed (under-2s free). DOGS allowed in bar, some bedrooms. CREDIT CARDS MasterCard, Visa. PRICES per room B&B £99–£155, D,B&B £145–£195. À la carte £31.95.

EASTON GREY Wiltshire
Map 3:E5

WHATLEY MANOR, SN16 0RB. Tel 01666 822 888, www.whatleymanor. com. 'Such a treat.' Surrounded by 'gorgeous' grounds, this revitalised 18th-century luxury hotel and amenity-packed spa girds the eastern Cotswolds. The gardens' design, based on the 1920s blueprint, incorporates secluded arbours, woodland trails and wild flower meadows. Inside, original artworks of horses and a rich palette. Up the wide original staircase, even the smallest bedroom is roomy; many have garden views. A choice of meals: chef Niall Keating's Michelin-starred tasting menus (including vegetarian) in the restaurant; soul food in the informal brasserie, perhaps seared sea bream, butternut squash risotto, citrus kale chimichurri; a chef's table in The Green Room, for up to twelve diners. A 'very good' buffet at breakfast. BEDROOMS 23, some on ground floor, 1 suitable for disabled. OPEN all year, restaurant closed Mon, Tues. FACILITIES 3 lounges, 2 bars, brasserie, restaurant, cinema, gym, spa, free Wi-Fi, in-room TV (Sky, Freeview), civil wedding

licence, conference facilities, 12-acre garden. BACKGROUND MUSIC in public areas. LOCATION 6½ miles from Tetbury. CHILDREN over-11s welcomed. DOGS allowed in some rooms (treats and toys, £30 per night). CREDIT CARDS Amex, MasterCard, Visa. PRICES per room B&B from £260. Tasting menu £120, à la carte £35.

EBRINGTON Gloucestershire
Map 3:D6

THE EBRINGTON ARMS, The Ebrington Arms, GL55 6NH. Tel 01386 593223, www.theebringtonarms.co.uk. The community hub of a classic Cotswold village of tiny lanes and stone cottages, this 17th-century tavern (with Victorian additions) has been renovated by Jim and Claire Alexander with tasteful, pared-back simplicity. In the friendly bar and restaurant, there are low beams, exposed stone walls, worn flagstone floors and settles bearing check-patterned cushions. Locals, visitors and real-ale enthusiasts mingle over the pub's own craft beers, or devour tasty variations on pub classics, perhaps chicken breast, stuffed leg, pancetta, charred leek, potato terrine. Upstairs, cottage-style bedrooms are simply decorated with substantial oak furniture and woollen throws; a decanter of sherry and home-made biscuits are homely touches. The enclosed garden offers splendid countryside views. BEDROOMS 5. OPEN all year, except Christmas. FACILITIES bar, restaurant, free Wi-Fi, in-room TV (Freeview), beer garden. restaurant wheelchair accessible. BACKGROUND MUSIC none. LOCATION in village; close to Snowshill Manor, Hidcote Gardens, Chipping Campden. CHILDREN over-16s welcomed. DOGS allowed in beer garden and bar. CREDIT

CARDS MasterCard, Visa. PRICES per room B&B £139–£169. 2-night min. stay at weekends.

EDENBRIDGE Kent
Map 2:D4

HEVER CASTLE B&B, Hever, TN8 7NG. Tel 01732 861800, www.hevercastle. co.uk. Double-moated 13th-century Hever Castle, the childhood home of Anne Boleyn, is now home to a sumptuous B&B. Bedrooms are in two Tudor-style Edwardian additions, the Aster and Anne Boleyn wings. Each room blends Tudor-inspired features and comforts fit for a queen: a gold-coloured chaise longue, a four-poster, a glimpse of the castle through mullion windows; spoiling toiletries in a decadent bathroom of limestone or marble. Moulded ceilings, grand chimney pieces and rich tapestries heighten the grandeur. Breakfast, a lavish affair, is served in each wing's own dining room. Residents are granted complimentary open-hours access to the castle and grounds and, after hours, to the peaceful gardens. BEDROOMS 28, some on ground floor, some suitable for disabled, plus self-catering Medley Court cottage. OPEN all year except 25 and 31 Dec. FACILITIES lounge, billiards room, free Wi-Fi, in-room TV (Sky, Freeview), 680-acre grounds, parking. BACKGROUND MUSIC none. LOCATION 1½ miles from Hever station. CHILDREN all ages welcomed. DOGS not allowed. CREDIT CARDS all major cards. PRICES per room B&B £170–£265.

EDINGTON Wiltshire
Map 2:D1

THE THREE DAGGERS, 47 Westbury Road, nr Westbury, BA13 4PG. Tel 01380 830940, www.threedaggers.co.uk.

The hub of the village, within trotting distance of the iconic white horse, this 'impressive' pub-with-rooms has much going on. A buzzy on-site microbrewery calls to craft-beer lovers; the well-stocked farm shop and 'well-populated' dining room entice epicures; a take-one-leave-one library beguiles bookworms. 'Splendid' bedrooms have fresh flowers, fluffy towels and a cool, rustic flair. In the kitchen, seasonal food exploits ingredients from the pub's own Priory Farm, nearby; in the garden, pizzas arrive courtesy of the wood-fired oven. Away from it all, the comfy residents' lounge has a generous stash of tea, coffee and biscuits – and, befitting the many muddy trails from the door, there are wellies to borrow. BEDROOMS 3. OPEN all year except 25, 26, 31 Dec. FACILITIES bar, dining area, private dining room, free Wi-Fi, in-room TV (Freeview), civil wedding licence, garden, microbrewery, farm shop. BACKGROUND MUSIC in public areas. LOCATION 10 mins' drive from Westbury. CHILDREN all ages welcomed. DOGS welcomed. CREDIT CARDS Amex, MasterCard, Visa. PRICES per person B&B from £99. À la carte £25.

EGHAM Surrey
Map 2:D3

THE RUNNYMEDE ON THAMES HOTEL AND SPA, Windsor Road, TW20 0AG. Tel 01784 220946, www. runnymedehotel.com. An idyllic spot on and off the water, this Thames-side hotel and spa is 'so very relaxing'. 'When not enjoying spa treatments, I could spend hours watching the boats go through the lock.' The uninspiring 1970s building belies the attractive interiors and myriad quirky touches (retro decor, oversized deckchairs, toy ducks in the lounge). Modern clean-lined bedrooms have 'every amenity' (feather bedding, air-conditioning, bathrobes, slippers); those facing the river have 'spectacular' views. Quieter rooms are away from the road. Choose to eat buffet-style overlooking the water, or sample 'excellent' traditional dishes in The Lock Bar & Kitchen, all light wood, pale hues and monochrome photographs.'The made-to-order breakfast is spectacular.' BEDROOMS 180, some suitable for disabled. OPEN all year. FACILITIES lounge, 2 restaurants, free Wi-Di, in-room TV (Freeview), civil wedding licence, indoor and outdoor pools, 12-acre grounds, parking. BACKGROUND MUSIC in public areas. LOCATION close to Windsor Castle, Windsor Great Park and Legoland. CHILDREN all ages welcomed. DOGS allowed in some bedrooms, by prior arrangement, not in public areas. CREDIT CARDS all major cards. PRICES per room B&B £145–£380. D,B&B £165–£430. Set menus £24–£29; à la carte £32.

ELTERWATER Cumbria
Map 4: inset C2

THE ELTERMERE INN, Elterwater, LA22 9HY. Tel 015394 37207, www.eltermere. co.uk. In verdant surrounds, this 'clearly popular' 18th-century country house has 'stunning views' across to the Langdale Pikes. Trusted Guide readers in 2018 praised the new management: 'They know how to hire good staff; everything was in excellent shape.' Bedrooms are spread along short corridors, up steep steps – 'but worth the effort'. Each is different; there are modern bathrooms and showers. 'We particularly like the top-floor room with a roll-top bath and long views.' Served on white-clothed tables in the bright restaurant, chef Derek Peart's 'very well presented',

modern menu includes lamb rump, parmesan mash; venison croquet. Many walks start and end at the cosy bar. BEDROOMS 12. OPEN all year except 24–27 Dec. FACILITIES 2 lounges, bar, restaurant, free Wi-Fi (in public areas), 3-acre garden, terrace, complimentary passes for Langdale Hotel spa. BACKGROUND MUSIC contemporary in public areas. LOCATION 4½ miles from Ambleside. CHILDREN all ages welcomed. DOGS allowed in 3 bedrooms, bar and garden. CREDIT CARDS all major cards. PRICES per room B&B £149–£295. À la carte £30. 2-night min. stay at weekends.

ELTON Cambridgeshire
Map 2:B4

THE CROWN INN, 8 Duck Street, PE8 6RQ. Tel 01832 280232, www. crowninnelton.co.uk. Paths through open countryside lead to the shady horse chestnut tree that guards this pretty, thatch-roofed country inn. Most guests prefer to arrive by car, but whatever their means, nearly all roll up here for chef/patron Marcus Lamb's hearty Sunday roasts and pub classics, perhaps cider-glazed ham, free-range eggs, hand-cut chunky chips. The 'well-equipped', modern bedrooms, each named after a neighbouring village or landmark, are supplied with bottled water, fresh milk, tea and coffee tray. Across the courtyard, two have a private garden accessed via French windows. Overheated walkers can refresh in the relaxing beer garden. Packed lunches are available for jaunts into the wild. BEDROOMS 8, 2 on ground floor. OPEN all year except 1–7 Jan. FACILITIES bar, snug, restaurant, free Wi-Fi, in-room TV (Freeview), parking. BACKGROUND MUSIC in bar and restaurant. LOCATION in village 5 miles off the A1 and 8 miles from central Peterborough. It is nestled in the heart of a rural village in walking distance to the River Nene. CHILDREN all ages welcomed. DOGS allowed in bar. CREDIT CARDS Amex, MasterCard, Visa. PRICES per room B&B single from £80, double from £140, D,B&B single from £105, double from £200. À la carte £28.

EXETER Devon
Map 1.C5

THE CITY GATE, Iron Bridge, Lower North Street, EX4 3RB. Tel 01392 495811, www.citygatehotel. com. Abutting the Roman city walls, this style-savvy red-brick old coaching inn (Young's Brewery) has a lively atmosphere. Inside, a host of interesting curios including a vintage sewing machine, a ship's masthead, and splashes of colour lend a quirky yet unpretentious vibe. 'Boutiquey' bedrooms are themed (water, wool, cotton); all are supplied with a capsule coffee machine, various teas, complimentary port and Devon fudge with little 'Eat Me Drink Me' signs (and who are we to resist?); a glossy metro-tiled bathroom. Microbrewed drinks and traditional pub classics are served all day in the buzzy restaurant (half-panelled walls, mismatched chairs). In balmy weather, diners spill on to the large beer garden. BEDROOMS 15. OPEN all year. FACILITIES 2 bars, snug, restaurant, conservatory, free Wi-Fi, in-room TV (Sky), function facilities, large beer garden, limited parking, bar and garden wheelchair accessible. BACKGROUND MUSIC in public areas. LOCATION central. CHILDREN all ages welcomed. DOGS allowed in public areas. CREDIT CARDS all major cards. PRICES per person B&B £99–£150. À la carte £30.

SOUTHERNHAY HOUSE, 38 Southernhay East, EX1 1NX. Tel 01392 439000, southernhayhouse.com. Minutes from the cathedral quarter, Deborah Clark and Anthony Orchard combine heritage and urban cool at their luxury town house hotel. The Grade II* listed Georgian mansion has a growing reputation for its lively cocktail bar and small restaurant; the all-day seasonal menu, including such dishes as star anise pork fillet, aubergine, shallots, pear, can be taken on the ironwork garden veranda. Individually decorated with prints and antiques, bedrooms have a handmade bed, top-notch entertainment (large TV, radio, an iPod docking station); two have a free-standing in-room roll-top bath. For breakfast: creamy porridge, fruit compotes, freshly baked pastries; a stack of pancakes with streaky bacon and maple syrup. BEDROOMS 10. OPEN all year. FACILITIES bar, restaurant, private dining, free Wi-Fi, in-room TV (Freeview), small lawn, veranda, terrace, civil wedding licence. BACKGROUND MUSIC in public areas. LOCATION central Exeter. CHILDREN over-11s welcomed. DOGS bar, terrace only. CREDIT CARDS MasterCard, Visa. PRICES per room B&B from £150. À la carte £30

FAIRFORD Gloucestershire
Map 3:E6

THE BULL HOTEL, Market Place, GL7 4AA. Tel 01285 712535, thebullhotelfairford.co.uk. Facing the market square, a stone-built 15th-century building – which has variously hosted a monks' chanting-house, a post office and a coaching inn – has been overhauled by Sebastian and Lana Snow (see also main entry for The Plough at Kelmscott). Its cosy bar has exposed stonework and an impressively horned bull's head over the crackling fire, while the multi-level dining areas are given depth and style with deep colours, timber features and burnished metal artefacts. The Mediterranean-influenced menus highlight Italian regional cuisines. Serene, pale-walled bedrooms have been filled with well-chosen vintage finds and pure wool throws; bathrooms have locally made toiletries. Fishing enthusiasts will appreciate the hotel's private stretch of the River Coln. BEDROOMS 21. OPEN all year. FACILITIES bar, lounge, morning room, function room, 3 dining rooms, free Wi-Fi, in-room TV (Freeview), terraces, private fishing rights. BACKGROUND MUSIC in bar, dining rooms. LOCATION in village centre. CHILDREN all ages welcomed (cots, z-beds). DOGS in 1 bedroom and bar. CREDIT CARDS Amex, MasterCard, Visa. PRICES per person B&B £75–£220, D,B&B £90–£220. À la carte £30.

FALMOUTH Cornwall
Map 1:E2

HIGHCLIFFE, 22 Melvill Road, TR11 4AR. Tel 01326 314466, www. highcliffefalmouth.com. 'Beautifully decorated, a little quirky, scrupulously clean', Vanessa and Simon Clark's 'highly recommended' Victorian town house lies between the town and the seafront. Inside, the B&B brims with interesting features and lively colours. High-ceilinged, imaginatively designed bedrooms share a hip, 'boutiquey' look, and thoughtful amenities; some offer sweeping views of the sun rising over the harbour and estuary. In the breakfast room with its multi-coloured chairs, guests enjoy freshly squeezed juices; many daily specials (wilted spinach and garlic mushrooms on organic bread; home-made rösti with a

poached egg, dry-cured streaky bacon and seaweed). 'Superb hosts', the Clarks offer helpful advice on where to eat, drink and visit. BEDROOMS 8. OPEN all year, except 27 Nov–11 Jan. FACILITIES lounge, breakfast room, free Wi-Fi, in-room TV (Freeview), parking. BACKGROUND MUSIC occasionally in dining room. LOCATION centrally located. CHILDREN over-7s welcomed. DOGS not allowed. CREDIT CARDS MasterCard, Visa. PRICES per room B&B single £45–£63, double £72-£115. 1-night bookings sometimes refused.

THE ROSEMARY, 22 Gyllyngvase Terrace, TR11 4DL. Tel 01326 314669, www. therosemary.co.uk. The whole of Falmouth Bay stretches away from Lynda and Malcolm Cook's 'delightful' B&B, just two minutes from the beach. The 'agreeable' hosts welcome guests with a drink and lemon drizzle cake. 'Clean, comfortable' bedrooms in the Edwardian town house are well supplied (everything needed for hot drinks, filtered water, biscuits, spoiling toiletries, fluffy bathrobes); the best have 'fantastic views'. The same panorama is enjoyed in the lounge over a Cornish cream tea. Guests wanting to explore might ask for a picnic hamper with home-baked cake, before embarking on a coastal ramble. Breakfasts has 'first class' choices: home-made preserves, Cornish honey, fresh fruit (all diets catered for). 'What a pleasure.' BEDROOMS 8. OPEN generally Feb–end Oct, 'but call for winter availability'. FACILITIES lounge, bar, dining room, free Wi-Fi, in-room TV (Freeview), garden, sun deck. BACKGROUND MUSIC none. LOCATION beach and seafront are 200m away, town 10 mins' walk. CHILDREN all ages welcomed. DOGS allowed in some bedrooms by arrangement (not unattended). CREDIT CARDS MasterCard, Visa. PRICES per room B&B single £50–£75, double £79–£162. 2-night min. stay preferred.

THE ROYAL DUCHY HOTEL, Cliff Road, TR11 4NX. Tel 01326 313042, royalduchy.co.uk. From a quiet seafront road, this festively updated turn-of-the-century edifice has spectacular views over the azure bay. The family-friendly hotel fuses traditional service ('attentive, competent, friendly') with modern style. There are 'comfortable, well-equipped' bedrooms, 'excellent' public spaces, a cocktail bar, and an 'elegant' restaurant serving British cuisine with international influences, including such dishes as pan-fried bream, scallop, olive crushed potatoes, ratatouille, sauce vierge. Lighter meals, in the lounge, or alfresco on the terrace, are served with wide-screen views. Afternoons are made for lazing on the lawn, spa therapies, a dip in the indoor pool – or the English Channel. Part of the Brend group, its sister hotel is the Victoria Hotel, Sidmouth (see Shortlist). BEDROOMS 45. OPEN all year. FACILITIES bar, restaurant, terraces, snooker room, free Wi-Fi, in-room TV, lift, spa, indoor pool, garden, parking. BACKGROUND MUSIC in public areas. LOCATION on seafront, a short walk into town. CHILDREN all ages welcomed. DOGS not allowed. CREDIT CARDS MasterCard, Visa. PRICES [2018] per room B&B from £218. Set dinner £39.

FAR SAWREY Cumbria
Map 4: inset C2
CUCKOO BROW INN, LA22 0LQ. Tel 015394 43425, www.cuckoobrow. co.uk. In a pretty village where once trod Beatrix Potter, between Lake Windermere and Hawkshead, a characterful 18th-century inn offers fuss-free country hospitality. Muddy dogs and walkers join the throng in the convivial bar (wood-burning stove, garlands of hops) and dining room, for local ales and traditional pub fare including steak and Kendal creamy cheese pie, home-cured ham with duck eggs. Most of the modern, simply decorated bedrooms are in an annexe attached to the main building; family rooms have a screened-off area for children; superior rooms have a roll-top bath in a smartly refurbished bathroom. Come evening, the old stables' squashy sofas, games and log-burning stove create a cosy retreat. BEDROOMS 14, some on ground floor. OPEN all year. FACILITIES bar, lobby, dining room, lounge/games room, free Wi-Fi, in-room TV (Freeview), terrace, small garden. BACKGROUND MUSIC in bar, lounge, games room. LOCATION in the centre of a small village. CHILDREN all ages welcomed. DOGS in bedrooms and public rooms (£10 per night). CREDIT CARDS MasterCard, Visa. PRICES per room B&B from £130, D,B&B from £170.

FERRENSBY Yorkshire
Map 4:D4
THE GENERAL TARLETON, Boroughbridge Road, HG5 0PZ. Tel 01423 340284, www.generaltarleton. co.uk. Not far from the road to Scotland, Chef/patron John Topham and his wife, Claire's, restaurant-with-rooms 'is great at what it does: provide fantastic service, excellent food and comfortable rooms'. It also represents 'great value for money'. It's 'just the place to break up trips across the

border'. After a drink by the fire in the comfortable cocktail lounge, 'first-rate' dishes are served in the stone-walled restaurant; perhaps twice-baked ewes' milk soufflé; char-grilled haunch of venison dauphinoise potato, chervil root, celeriac, beetroot, kale, blackberries. Modern bedrooms have warm, rich hues, home-made biscuits and luxury smellies. Harrogate, York and the Dales are within an easy drive. BEDROOMS 13. OPEN all year, no accommodation 24–26 Dec, 1 Jan. FACILITIES bar, cocktail lounge, atrium, restaurant, private dining room, free Wi-Fi, in-room TV (Freeview), parking. BACKGROUND MUSIC in public areas. LOCATION 4 miles from Knaresborough. CHILDREN all ages welcomed. DOGS not allowed. CREDIT CARDS MasterCard, Visa. PRICES per room B&B single from £75, double from £129. À la carte £35.

FOLKESTONE Kent
Map 2:E5

ROCKSALT, 4–5 Fish Market, CT19 6AA. Tel 01303 212070, www. rocksaltfolkestone.co.uk. Assertive and stylish, this dark-timber-and-glass, purpose-built restaurant-with-rooms cantilevers over the harbour, the better to soak up views stretching to the Channel. Owned by Mark Sargeant (a Gordon Ramsey alumnus) and Josh de Haanare, its 'imaginative', wide-ranging menu uses fish caught off the south-east coast, served to the long leather banquette, or on the deck on balmy days. What to expect: seaweed butter poached Dover sole; baked mussels, smoked bacon, Kentish cider. Two minutes away, above a sister restaurant, bedrooms look out at the water (binoculars provided); stripped-back brick walls, antique beds and a

Provençal palette prove a chic formula. Come morning, a continental breakfast hamper is delivered to the room. BEDROOMS 4. OPEN all year. FACILITIES bar, restaurant, terrace, free Wi-Fi, in-room TV (BT), on-street parking. BACKGROUND MUSIC in restaurant. CHILDREN all ages welcomed. DOGS not allowed. CREDIT CARDS Amex, MasterCard, Visa. PRICES per room B&B £85–£120. À la carte £40.

FONTMELL MAGNA Dorset
Map 2:E1

THE FONTMELL, SP7 0PA. Tel 01747 811441, www.thefontmell.co.uk. Carefully restored, with an abundance of quirky details – a stream separates the dining room from bar – this well-designed roadside inn is a social media hit. Upstairs, appealing, eclectic bedrooms might have exposed beams, a bay-window reading nook, a squashy sofa, a roll-top bath on a wooden dais. Downstairs, the appealing bar lures in (and rewards) locals with craft beers and weekly-changing guest ales. In the bookshelf-lined dining room, chef/patron Tom Shaw uses locally sourced produce, including the pub's own rare-breed pigs, in such dishes as aromatic pulled pork shoulder, pancakes, spring onion, chilli apple sauce, cucumber, hoisin. On weekend summer evenings the garden's wood-fired oven delivers fresh pizza. BEDROOMS 6. OPEN all year. FACILITIES bar, restaurant, free Wi-Fi, in-room TV (Freeview), large garden, DVD library. BACKGROUND MUSIC in public areas. LOCATION Shaftesbury. CHILDREN all ages welcomed. DOGS allowed in 1 bedroom. CREDIT CARDS all major cards. PRICES per room B&B £85–£145. À la carte £30.

FOWEY Cornwall
Map 1:D3

THE OLD QUAY HOUSE, 28 Fore Street, PL23 1AQ. Tel 01726 833302, theoldquayhouse.com. Once the refuge of seamen, this 'marvellously situated' Victorian building has transformed into a stylish quayside hotel with dazzling estuary views. Public spaces, overseen by 'exceptionally friendly, helpful' staff, have been 'tastefully rejuvenated'. Classic French fare with a Cornish twist, perhaps local pollock, roast cauliflower, confit potato, shellfish bisque, is served in the informal restaurant or out on the 'beautiful terrace'. Thoughtful touches abound in the 'clean, fresh, contemporary' bedrooms: biscuits and bottled water, books and DVDs, local guides, umbrellas and raincoats. A fridge on the landing has little jugs of fresh milk. Expect a wake-up call of seagulls and lapping sea. Breakfast is in the sun-drenched restaurant. BEDROOMS 11. OPEN all year. FACILITIES open-plan lounge, bar, restaurant, free Wi-Fi, in-room TV, civil wedding licence, terrace, parking permits supplied. BACKGROUND MUSIC 'relaxed' at mealtimes. LOCATION central location within the town of Fowey. CHILDREN over-11s welcomed. DOGS not allowed. CREDIT CARDS Amex, MasterCard, Visa. PRICES per room B&B from £145. Set dinner £30–£37.50.

GATWICK Sussex
Map 2:D4

LANGSHOTT MANOR, Ladbroke Road, Langshott, Horley, RH6 9LN. Tel 01293 786680, www.alexanderhotels.co.uk/langshott-manor. Modern flourishes blend with history and tradition at this 'wonderfully atmospheric' old building. The well-maintained Elizabethan manor house (Alexander Hotels) has low, beamed ceilings, thick oak doors, open fireplaces. Each room has jaunty colours and fabrics, a contemporary bathroom, great basics (tea-/coffee-making facilities, bathrobes, slippers); suites may have an antique bathtub, a four-poster, a separate living area. Bickering ducks on the small lake sometimes provide a natural wake-up call. Guests this year reported inter-room noise ('the lack of soundproofing due to the building's age, I suspect'); light sleepers might discuss rooms at booking. Chef Phil Dixon's modern European menu uses ingredients from the kitchen garden. Imaginative breakfasts. Convenient for Gatwick airport. BEDROOMS 22, 15 in mews. OPEN all year. FACILITIES 3 lounges, bar, restaurant, private dining room, free Wi-Fi, in-room TV (Freeview), civil wedding licence, conference facilities, terrace, 3-acre garden. BACKGROUND MUSIC in lounges and restaurant. LOCATION 8 mins' drive from Horley, 10 mins' drive from Gatwick airport. CHILDREN all ages welcomed. DOGS allowed in 2 rooms, by arrangement. CREDIT CARDS Amex, MasterCard, Visa. PRICES [2018] per room B&B from £119, D,B&B from £219. À la carte £49.50, tasting menu £70. 2-night min. stay preferred.

GILSLAND Cumbria
Map 4:B3

THE HILL ON THE WALL, Brampton, CA8 7DA. Tel 01697 747214, www.hillonthewall.co.uk. Protected from the border's lawless raiders by a 16th-century 'bastle', Elaine Packer's 'superb' Georgian farmhouse overlooking Hadrian's Wall is full of 'every comfort'. Proper tea and home-made cake, taken by the drawing room fire or in the 'beautiful' walled garden, welcome arriving guests. Shutters at the windows promise a sound night in the traditionally decorated bedrooms; 'sumptuously styled', each is well supplied with glossy magazines, cafetière coffee, a biscuit barrel and chocolates. 'So peaceful.' Ordered the night before, breakfast features 'delicious' home-cooked Northumbrian fare; the 'gigantic portions' are just the thing for hikers and bikers setting off for the day. Packed lunches available (£6). BEDROOMS 3, 1 on ground floor. OPEN Mar–Oct. FACILITIES lounge, breakfast room, free Wi-Fi, in-room TV (Freeview), 1-acre garden, terrace, parking, secure bicycle storage. BACKGROUND MUSIC none. LOCATION 1 mile W of Gilsland on the B6318. CHILDREN over-10s welcomed. DOGS not allowed. CREDIT CARDS MasterCard, Visa. PRICES per person B&B from £40.

WILLOWFORD FARM, Willowford, CA8 7AA. Tel 01697 747962, willowford. co.uk. Roman history doesn't get much closer than at Liam McNulty and Lauren Harrison's rustic B&B. The longest unbroken stretch of Hadrian's Wall cuts through the yard of their organic sheep and cattle farm. Cosy bedrooms, in the converted byre, gaze upon the remains of a bridge and two turrets. Spacious, clutter-free and full of character, they have exposed wood beams, antique furniture, a heated floor of local Westmorland slate; each is supplied with Fairtrade tea and coffee, and is energy-efficient to boot. The nearby Samson Inn, under the same management (lifts cheerfully offered), uses the farm's produce. Breakfast options include porridge, pastries, smoked trout with scrambled eggs.

Packed lunches available (£6). BEDROOMS 5, all on ground floor, 1 suitable for disabled. OPEN Mar–Nov. FACILITIES lounge/breakfast room, free Wi-Fi, in-room TV (Freeview). BACKGROUND MUSIC none. LOCATION ½ mile W of Gilsland, between Gilsland village and Birdoswald Roman fort. CHILDREN all ages welcomed. DOGS well-behaved dogs allowed by arrangement in bedrooms, not in public rooms (£5 charge, chickens and sheep on farm). CREDIT CARDS MasterCard, Visa. PRICES per room B&B single £68–£75, double £95–£100.

GOATHLAND Yorkshire
Map 4:C5

FAIRHAVEN COUNTRY GUEST HOUSE, The Common, YO22 5AN. Tel 01947 896361, www. fairhavencountryguesthouse.co.uk. Head straight out on to beautiful moorland from the doorstep of Peter and Sarah Garnett's Edwardian guest house in a scenic village within the North York Moors national park. Return by steam locomotive to Goathland station – a stand-in for Hogsmeade in the Harry Potter films. The hosts provide a welcoming pot of tea and home-made cake in the large, comfortable lounge with its open fire, games, books and TV. Traditionally furnished bedrooms have fine views, seating, well-stocked trays; fresh milk and filtered water awaits in the dining room fridge. An extensive, locally sourced breakfast includes baked spiced plums with home-made granola, Greek yogurt; a Whitby kipper. There is a lawned back garden and a front terrace to catch the sunset. BEDROOMS 9, one with separate private bathroom. OPEN all year except 1 week Christmas, 3-day only package deals at New Year.

FACILITIES lounge, dining room, front terrace, in-room TV (Freeview), free Wi-Fi, large garden, parking, secure bicycle storage. Dinner available on certain evenings, winter; all year for parties of 6 or more. BACKGROUND MUSIC during breakfast. LOCATION close to the North Yorkshire Moors Steam Railway, 8 miles from Whitby. CHILDREN all ages welcomed. DOGS not allowed. CREDIT CARDS MasterCard, Visa. PRICES per room B&B single £47–£79, double £98–£110.

GRANGE-OVER-SANDS Cumbria
Map 4: inset C2

CLARE HOUSE, Park Road, LA11 7HQ. Tel 01539 533026, www.clarehousehotel.co.uk. 'Wonderfully old-fashioned', the Read family's traditional hotel 'continues to tick all the right boxes'. 'Cheerful and helpful staff, nice views, excellent food' impressed Guide readers this year. The comfortably furnished Victorian house has log fires in the sitting rooms. 'Our clean, well-appointed room had an equally good bathroom; we slept well on a firm, comfortable bed.' Morning coffee and afternoon tea can be enjoyed in the lounges or the 'well-tended' garden. Andrew Read and Mark Johnston's 'interesting menu' has 'beautifully presented' English and French dishes, perhaps brisket slow-cooked in beer, celeriac cream, rosemary roast potatoes, seared broccoli, rich gravy. 'An innovative and plentiful breakfast, served at table, exceeded expectations'. BEDROOMS 18, 1 on ground floor suitable for disabled. OPEN mid-Mar–mid-Dec. FACILITIES 2 lounges, dining room, free Wi-Fi, in-room TV, ¾-acre grounds, parking. BACKGROUND MUSIC none. LOCATION in village. CHILDREN all ages welcomed. DOGS assistance dogs accepted. CREDIT CARDS MasterCard, Visa. PRICES per person B&B £78–£87, D,B&B £98–£107. À la carte £40. 25% DISCOUNT VOUCHERS

GRASMERE Cumbria
Map 4: inset C2

THE GRASMERE HOTEL, Broadgate, LA22 9TA. Tel 015394 35277, www.grasmerehotel.co.uk. 'An ideal base to explore Wainwright's favourite fells or absorb the poetic delights of Wordsworth', Kevin and Nicki Winsland's small country hotel has reaching views across to the River Rothay. Linked lounges in the Victorian house have 'comfy armchairs and sofas' clustering around low tables and a fire. Named after local luminaries, 'modern, spotless bedrooms' are clad in soothing pales and neutrals. 'Our road-facing rooms was restful.' Whether the mid-week four-course dinners, or the mixed platter served when the restaurant (overlooking the verdant garden) is closed, the 'splendid dishes' are praised. Packed lunch, plus routes for easy rambles (and more challenging hikes) are a request away. BEDROOMS 11. OPEN all year except 31 Dec–26 Jan. FACILITIES lounge, restaurant, free Wi-Fi, in-room TV (Freeview), ½-acre garden, unsuitable for disabled. BACKGROUND MUSIC in lounge and restaurant during mealtimes. LOCATION in village. CHILDREN over-9s welcomed. DOGS 1 small to medium dog allowed, by arrangement, in some bedrooms, not in public rooms. CREDIT CARDS MasterCard, Visa. PRICES per room B&B single £67–£97, double £122–£154, D,B&B single £92–£122, double £172–£204. 4-course dinner £25 (for residents). 2-night min. stay normally required (check for 1-night availability), Sat and bank holiday Sun night reservations must include dinner.

GRASSINGTON Yorkshire
Map 4:D3

GRASSINGTON HOUSE, 5 The Square, BD23 5AQ. Tel 01756 752406, www. grassingtonhouse.co.uk. For over 100 years, visitors have crossed the cobbled square of a Dales village in search of sustenance and safe harbour at this striking limestone house. Today, chef/patron John Rudden and his wife, Sue, have added many glamorous touches to the Grade II listed Georgian restaurant-with-rooms, including cascading chandeliers, bold brass sculptures, ornate fireplaces. In the individually decorated bedrooms, perhaps a balcony or window seat; each has tea and coffee, home-made flapjacks, waffle bathrobes, organic toiletries. The hosts have also updated the sustenance. Their rare-breed pigs feature on the 'excellent' menu in the smart restaurant and fireside bar, with such dishes as chicken breast, pea ravioli, pancetta, spring cabbage. BEDROOMS 9. OPEN all year except Christmas Day. FACILITIES lounge, bar, restaurant, free Wi-Fi, in-room TV, civil wedding licence, function facilities, terrace, cookery classes, parking. BACKGROUND MUSIC in public areas. LOCATION in village square, 16 mins' drive from Skipton. CHILDREN all ages welcomed. DOGS not allowed. CREDIT CARDS MasterCard, Visa. PRICES per room B&B £135–£155, D,B&B £225–£245 (Sat only). Set dinner £40.

GREAT LANGDALE Cumbria
Map 4: inset C2

THE OLD DUNGEON GHYLL, LA22 9JY. Tel 01539 437272, www.odg.co.uk. Fell walkers, climbers – including some of Britain's greatest mountaineers – and sleepy travellers have sought this unpretentious, dog-friendly inn, in a 'glorious setting', for more than 300 years. Standing at the head of the Great Langdale valley, the inn is managed for the National Trust by Jane and Neil Walmsley. Visitors like the 'willing, helpful staff' and 'reasonably priced accommodation'. Home-baked treats are an indulgent addition to morning coffee or afternoon tea, served in the residents' lounge. Most of the 'quite basic', 'country-style' rooms have dramatic, uninterrupted views of the surrounding fells. The popular Hikers' bar (one-time cow stalls) dishes up 'straightforward pub food'. Just ask about walking routes and packed lunches. BEDROOMS 12. OPEN all year except 24–26 Dec. FACILITIES residents' bar and lounge, dining room, bar, free Wi-Fi in public areas and some bedrooms, 1-acre garden, drying room, parking. BACKGROUND MUSIC none, live music on first Wed of every month. LOCATION 5 miles from Hawkshead. CHILDREN all ages welcomed. DOGS allowed (£5 per night). CREDIT CARDS MasterCard, Visa. PRICES per room B&B from £58. À la carte £25. 2-night min. stay at weekends.

HALIFAX Yorkshire
Map 4:D3

SHIBDEN MILL INN, Shibden Mill Fold, HX3 7UL. Tel 01422 365840, shibdenmillinn.com. Opposite Red Beck, the stream that once powered its machinery, this former mill draws visitors to the wooded Shibden valley. Simon and Caitlin Heaton's refurbished 17th-century inn might run on different fuel, but it's still packed with original features including the oak beams and fireplace in the bustling bar, where guests sample Shibden Mill's own brew. Jolly bedrooms are individually styled, a soaring ceiling in one; a stone archway in another, leading to a free-standing bath. All are supplied with teas and coffees, towelling robes, a DVD-player. The traditional menu has a few surprises: Yorkshire steaks grilled, as one might expect, but also interesting vegan options, such as artichoke and chicory buckwheat pizza. BEDROOMS 11. OPEN all year except 25–26 Dec, 1 Jan. FACILITIES bar, restaurant, private dining room, free Wi-Fi, in-room TV (Freeview), small conference facilities, patio, parking, complimentary access to local health club. BACKGROUND MUSIC in main bar and restaurant. LOCATION 2 miles from Halifax town centre. CHILDREN all ages welcomed. DOGS allowed in bar. CREDIT CARDS Amex, MasterCard, Visa. PRICES per room B&B £95–£238, D,B&B £188–£259. À la carte £35.

HARROGATE Yorkshire
Map 4:D4

THE WEST PARK HOTEL, 19 West Park, HG1 1BJ. Tel 01423 524471, www.thewestparkhotel.com. Facing the leafy Stray's open parkland, this alluring town-centre hotel is in a seamlessly converted Victorian coach house. Nathan George manages for Provenance Inns & Hotels. Seasonal menus of fresh fish and seafood, sharing platters and grills are served in the buzzy brasserie (zinc-topped bar, sea-green leather banquettes, designer lighting); in clement weather, the courtyard opens for alfresco dining. Well-appointed bedrooms (quieter ones at the back) have a large bed, a coffee machine and tasty nibbles; in the bathrooms, spoiling toiletries, underfloor heating and speakers. Two penthouse duplexes have room to stretch out: a lounge and dining area, plus access to a roof terrace. BEDROOMS 25, some suitable for disabled. OPEN all year. FACILITIES bar, brasserie, meeting/private dining rooms, free Wi-Fi, in-room TV (Freeview), large walled terrace, adjacent NCP car park, pay and display street parking. BACKGROUND MUSIC in public areas. LOCATION town centre. CHILDREN all ages welcomed. DOGS well-behaved dogs allowed in some bedrooms, bar. CREDIT CARDS all major cards. PRICES per room B&B £225–£375, D,B&B £285–£435. À la carte £30.

HEACHAM Norfolk
Map 2:A4

HEACHAM HOUSE, 18 Staithe Road, PE31 7ED. Tel 01485 579529, www.heachamhouse.com. North Norfolk's wide sands and salt marshes are within a flat, short-ish walk of Rebecca and Robert Bradley's fine B&B. While the red-brick Victorian house casts an eye over a duck-filled pond, twitchers may be more interested in the RSPB sites at nearby Snettisham and Titchwell. Tea and home-made cake are a tasty welcome to the lounge with its toasty fire. Bedrooms might be individually decorated, but in common are the fresh flowers, home-baked biscuits; bathrobes, fluffy towels, face cloths. A generous start to the day: home-baked bread, home-made preserves, award-winning sausages. Walking and cycling routes from the door. A drying room is much appreciated on inclement days. BEDROOMS 3. OPEN all year. FACILITIES sitting room, breakfast room, free

Wi-Fi, in-room TV (Freeview), garden, parking, bicycle storage. BACKGROUND MUSIC none. LOCATION centre of village overlooking large duck pond, 3 miles from Hunstanton. CHILDREN over-14s welcomed. DOGS not allowed. CREDIT CARDS none accepted. PRICES per room B&B single £70–90, double £95–£105.

HERTFORD Hertfordshire
Map 2:C4
NUMBER ONE PORT HILL, 1 Port Hill, SG14 1PJ. Tel 01992 587350, www. numberoneporthill.co.uk. In a pleasant market town, Annie Rowley's artful Georgian B&B is an Aladdin's cave of vintage glassware, sculptures and 'an unbelievable collection' of objects. The town house, featured in Pevsner's guide to Hertfordshire, has 'immaculately kept' rooms; two are cosy, one large, with French gilt bed, a bathroom with a raised boat bath. Plentiful extras include Belgian hot chocolate, snacks, bathrobes, 'eclectic' reading material. Traffic noise is muted by 'very good' double glazing, though some noise travels between rooms. Come morning, a 'superb' breakfast, with freshly ground coffee and home-made preserves, is taken communally, or in the shade of the walled garden's ancient wisteria. Monthly pop-up supper club. BEDROOMS 3. OPEN all year except Christmas. FACILITIES drawing room, free Wi-Fi, in-room TV (Sky, Freeview), gardens, limited street parking. BACKGROUND MUSIC at breakfast (radio). LOCATION 5 mins' walk from town centre. CHILDREN over-12s welcomed ('though exemptions may be made, if discussed, for younger children'). CREDIT CARDS Diners Club, MasterCard, Visa. PRICES per room B&B £130–£160.

HEXHAM Northumberland
Map 4:B3
THE HERMITAGE, Swinburne, NE48 4DG. Tel 01434 681248. Three miles from Hadrian's Wall, among rolling Northumbrian countryside, Catherine Stewart's 'just lovely' B&B is surrounded by a lawned, walled garden. Inside the 'beautiful house', built with the same variety of stone found in the ancient fortification, visitors are welcomed with a pot of tea and home-baked cake. The large, comfortable lounge is made homely by antiques, old artworks, a crackling fire and a small library of books. The suntrap garden's blooms appear in the peaceful, traditional and 'very comfortable' bedrooms, alongside period furniture, a bathroom with a roll-top bath. The hostess is a font of local knowledge, from nearby eateries to easily accessible circular walks. 'Excellent' communal breakfasts. BEDROOMS 3. OPEN all year. FACILITIES drawing room, breakfast room, free Wi-Fi, 2-acre grounds, terrace, tennis court. BACKGROUND MUSIC none. LOCATION 7 miles from nearest town. CHILDREN babes in arms, and over-7s welcomed. DOGS not allowed. CREDIT CARDS None accepted. PRICES per room B&B £55–£90.

HITCHIN Hertfordshire
Map 2:C4
THE FARMHOUSE AT REDCOATS, Redcoats Green SG4 7JR. Tel 01438 729500, farmhouseatredcoats.co.uk. With views across gently undulating Hertfordshire countryside, this sprawling old building, with its outlying stables and barns, dates back to the 15th century. Now extensively restored as a hotel and restaurant, it is the latest addition to the Nye family's Anglian Country Inns. They have retained many original

features, with comfortable sitting areas and warming fires in myriad nooks and crannies. In the main house, bedrooms are classically furnished; simpler annexe rooms have stable partitions, original floors and tiling. Farm-to-table produce (some from the kitchen garden), alongside seasonal game, are served in the large conservatory restaurant, perhaps oven-roasted guinea fowl supreme, slow-braised leg sausage roll, purple potato, spring cabbage, farmhouse brown sauce. There is a hearty breakfast. BEDROOMS 27, 23 in converted stables and barns. Some on ground floor. OPEN all year. FACILITIES lounge, conservatory restaurant, private dining, free Wi-Fi, in-room TV (Freeview), civil wedding licence, 4-acre grounds, parking. Unsuitable for disabled. BACKGROUND MUSIC 'subtle' in public areas. LOCATION 9 mins' drive from Stevenage. CHILDREN all ages welcomed. DOGS allowed in stable rooms (charge). CREDIT CARDS all major cards. PRICES per room B&B £115–£145. À la carte £40.

HOLT Norfolk
Map 2:A5

BYFORDS, 1–3 Shirehall Plain, NR25 6BG. Tel 01263 711400, www.byfords.org.uk. At the centre of a 'bustling' Georgian market town, this all-day café, store and 'posh' B&B 'creates a busy holiday atmosphere'. Guests this year liked the 'friendly staff, who made the stay enjoyable'. A winding staircase at the back of the deli leads up to bedrooms bursting with character, with stripped wood flooring and vintage furnishings. While each is different, all have home-made biscuits, a fridge containing fresh milk and water. 'Our light, airy room, overlooking the square,

was very comfortable.' The 'rustic' restaurant serves a 'good if a little formulaic' seasonal menu. Breakfast sees hot dishes from the café menu. Picnic items, and more, are available in the deli. BEDROOMS 16, plus self-catering apartment. OPEN all year. FACILITIES café, deli, free Wi-Fi, in-room TV (Sky), terrace, private secure parking. BACKGROUND MUSIC in café. LOCATION central. CHILDREN all ages welcomed. DOGS not allowed. CREDIT CARDS Amex, MasterCard, Visa. PRICES per room B&B £165–£215, D,B&B £205–£255.

HOOK Hampshire
Map 2:D3

TYLNEY HALL, Ridge Lane, Rotherwick, RG27 9AZ. Tel 01256 745532, www.tylneyhall.co.uk. Far-reaching views of 'peaceful' countryside roll away from this luxurious, 'very grand' Victorian mansion; Gertrude Jekyll designed the 'spectacular' surrounding gardens. 'Numerous, always helpful' staff are on hand to give a warm welcome: a sweet welcome pack for young travellers, plus bowls, a bed and 'high-quality dog food' for Fido. 'Our second-floor room was spotlessly clean, well equipped and comfortable (52 steps, no lift)'; 'swift' golf carts transport guests between the main house and nearby cottage rooms; ground-floor garden rooms allow owners to easily let out the dog. In the wood-panelled restaurant, menus with a flourish; those in the lounge or on the garden-facing terrace are more informal. Can be busy with weddings. BEDROOMS 112, some in cottages in the grounds, some on ground floor, 1 suitable for disabled. OPEN all year. FACILITIES 2 lounges, bar, restaurant, private dining rooms, free Wi-Fi, in-room TV (Freeview),

civil wedding licence, conference/
function facilities, spa, 66-acre grounds,
public rooms wheelchair accessible.
BACKGROUND MUSIC occasionally
piano in the restaurant or jazz in the
Tylney Suite. LOCATION 14 mins' drive
from Basingstoke. CHILDREN all ages
welcomed. DOGS allowed in some rooms
(£25 per night). CREDIT CARDS Amex,
MasterCard, Visa. PRICES per room B&B
from £250. À la carte £45.

HUDDERSFIELD Yorkshire
Map 4:E3

THE THREE ACRES INN & RESTAURANT,
Roydhouse, HD8 8LR. Tel 01484
602606, www.3acres.com. 'High on the
hills' near Huddersfield, this 'friendly'
roadside drovers' inn has 'detour-
worthy food'; 'tremendous views to
all sides' are nearly as impressive. The
pub-with-rooms came on to the scene
40-odd years ago; today, Brian Orme
and Neil Truelove are still at the helm,
along with Neil's son, Tom. Bedrooms,
spread across the main building and
garden cottages, are 'comfortable,
clean and functional, with an agreeable
bed'; lighter sleepers might bring ear
plugs (some guests noticed noise from
a neighbouring room). Locals join
residents in the 'civilised' dining room
for the 'high-quality' modern British
menu. The day starts well: home-
made muesli, local bacon and sausage,
porridge with cream and golden syrup.
BEDROOMS 17, 1 suitable for disabled, 8
in adjacent cottages. OPEN all year except
evenings 25–26 Dec, midday 31 Dec,
evening 1 Jan. FACILITIES bar, restaurant,
free Wi-Fi, in-room TV (Freeview),
civil wedding licence, small function/
private dining facilities, terraced garden.
BACKGROUND MUSIC in bar, restaurant.
LOCATION 6 miles from Huddersfield

town centre. CHILDREN well-behaved
children welcomed. DOGS not allowed.
CREDIT CARDS Amex, MasterCard, Visa.
PRICES per room B&B single £50–£100,
double £80. À la carte £45.

HURLEY Berkshire
Map 2:D3

HURLEY HOUSE, Henley Road, SL6
5LH. Tel 01628 568500, hurleyhouse.
co.uk. Rebuilt and reinvented by
Bassam Shlewet, this small hotel brings
'great service', chic style and impressive
cuisine to a picturesque stretch of the
Thames Path. The smartly rustic bar
has a cosy wood-burning stove, exposed
brickwork, wooden beams. Award-
winning chef Michael Chapman draws
in diners from near and far for his
'excellent' British menus, 'promptly
served by charming waiters' in the
restaurant, where a huge window
lets you observe the working kitchen.
Understated bedrooms in creams and
greys have urbane comforts (large bed,
luxury bedlinen and towels, coffee
machine, air conditioning, underfloor
heating, a 'strong shower'); calls to UK
landlines are free. Efficient insulation
subdues noise from the adjacent busy
road. BEDROOMS 10, some suitable for
disabled. OPEN all year. FACILITIES bar,
snug, restaurant, private dining room,
free Wi-Fi, in-room TV (Freeview),
function facilities, civil wedding licence,
spa treatments, terrace, lawn, parking.
BACKGROUND MUSIC in public areas until
11 pm. LOCATION 3 miles from Marlow,
5 miles from Henley on Thames, 5
miles from Maidenhead, 10 miles from
Windsor. CHILDREN all ages welcomed.
DOGS allowed. CREDIT CARDS Amex,
MasterCard. PRICES per room B&B from
£170. À la carte £45.
25% DISCOUNT VOUCHERS

IRONBRIDGE Shropshire
Map 3:C5

THE LIBRARY HOUSE, 11 Severn
Bank, TF8 7AN. Tel 01952 432299,
www.libraryhouse.com. 'Beautifully
decorated' and properly bookish, this
Grade II listed village library has been
converted into a cheerful B&B near the
River Severn. Run by Sarah and Tim
Davis, the book-lined sitting room
of the Georgian building retains the
original library shelves; it's a cosy spot,
especially in chilly weather when the
log burner blazes. Writers lend their
names to the well-equipped bedrooms.
Chaucer opens on to a private garden
terrace; Eliot is all lofty ceiling and
long views towards the river. In each:
waffle dressing gowns, fresh milk, a
hot-water bottle. Convenient for visiting
the UNESCO World Heritage site of
Ironbridge Gorge and the open-air
museum at Blists Hill. BEDROOMS 3.
OPEN all year. FACILITIES sitting room,
breakfast room, free Wi-Fi, in-room TV
(Freeview), courtyard, mature garden,
passes for local car parks. BACKGROUND
MUSIC none. LOCATION town centre.
CHILDREN over-13s welcomed. DOGS not
allowed. CREDIT CARDS MasterCard,
Visa. PRICES per room B&B single
£75–£95, double £100–£125.

KESWICK Cumbria
Map 4: inset C2

DALEGARTH HOUSE, Portinscale, CA12
5RQ. Tel 017687 72817, dalegarth-
house.co.uk. A mile outside Keswick,
surrounded by splendid scenery, stands
Craig and Clare Dalton's welcoming,
good-value Edwardian guest house.
The pick of Cumbria is within easy
reach. Visitors receive a warm greeting,
starting outside with the riot of
colourful potted plants leading up to
the cherry red front door. After a day
of outdoor activity, you can head for
the bar with its grandfather clock, and
the peaceful bedrooms. Each simply
furnished room has a hospitality tray
and flat-screen TV; nearly every room
has memorable views of Derwent Water
and the surrounding fells. The locally
sourced breakfast, served in the dining
room, is hearty fuel before another day
of fresh air. BEDROOMS 10, 2 on ground
floor in annexe. OPEN Mar–mid-Dec.
FACILITIES lounge, bar, dining room, free
Wi-Fi, in-room TV (Freeview), garden,
parking, bicycle storage. BACKGROUND
MUSIC occasional radio at breakfast.
LOCATION 1½ miles W of Keswick.
CHILDREN over-11s welcomed. DOGS not
allowed. CREDIT CARDS MasterCard,
Visa. PRICES per person B&B £45–£57.
2-night min. stay preferred.

LYZZICK HALL, Underskiddaw, CA12
4PY. Tel 01768 772277, lyzzickhall.
co.uk. 'Glorious fell views', 'excellent
food' and 'capable, obliging staff' are
found at this family-friendly spot at the
foot of Skiddaw. The early Victorian
hotel has been owned by the Fernandez
family, now co-owners with the Lake
family, for 25 years. The 'stunning
scenery' can be enjoyed from most of the
'well-equipped' bedrooms; all overlook
the landscaped gardens, and have
contemporary bathrooms with good
toiletries. The lounge has a warming
fire; the indoor swimming pool suits
those unwilling to brave nearby
Derwent Water. There are 'excellent'
British dishes, 'divine desserts' and
'whatever the children fancy'. Breakfast
has no buffet, but 'plenty of choice'.
Many walks from the door. BEDROOMS
30, 1 on ground floor. OPEN Feb–Dec
except 24–26 Dec. FACILITIES 2 lounges,

bar, orangery, restaurant, free Wi-Fi, in-room TV (Freeview), heated indoor swimming pool, spa facilities, 4-acre grounds. BACKGROUND MUSIC in public areas. LOCATION 2 miles N of Keswick. CHILDREN all ages welcomed. DOGS allowed in 1 bedroom, if supervised at all times. CREDIT CARDS MasterCard, Visa. PRICES per room B&B £168–£260, D,B&B £220–£312. À la carte £42.

KINGSBRIDGE Devon
Map 1:D4

THURLESTONE HOTEL, Thurlestone, TQ7 3NN. Tel 01548 560382, www. thurlestone.co.uk. For 120 years the Grose family have looked after this 'family-friendly' hotel approached by lanes 'resplendent with wild flowers'. 'Stunning' widescreen views of the sub-tropical gardens and the coastline are found in most of the well-equipped bedrooms; family rooms have a bunk bed, or extra space for a cot/additional bed. Guests this year found it 'decidedly old-fashioned in many respects'. Real ales and fresh seafood are found in the 16th-century village inn or the terrace bistro, while in the smart Trevilder restaurant the food was 'good classic stuff', the service disorganised. Rock pools are five minutes away; a plethora of on-site diversions includes croquet, tennis, a spa; a children's club during the school holidays. BEDROOMS 65, 2 suitable for disabled. OPEN all year. FACILITIES lift, lounges, bar, restaurant, bistro, village pub, free Wi-Fi, in-room TV (Sky), civil wedding licence, function facilities, terrace, spa, outdoor heated swimming pool, tennis, 9-hole golf course. BACKGROUND MUSIC none. LOCATION 4 miles SW of Kingsbridge. CHILDREN all ages welcomed. DOGS allowed in some bedrooms, not in public rooms. CREDIT

CARDS Amex, MasterCard, Visa. PRICES [2018] per room B&B from £180. À la carte £40. 2-night min. stay.

KINGSWEAR Devon
Map 1:D4

KAYWANA HALL, Higher Contour Road, TQ6 0AY. Tel 01803 752200, www. kaywanahall.co.uk. Across the estuary from Dartmouth, in its own hillside woodland, stands Tony Pithers and Gordon Craig's ultra-modern 1960s house (one of four like it in Devon). It has a curving staircase, a zinc roof and glass walls. An adults-only B&B, it is intimate and discreet. Light-filled bedrooms each have their own entrance and private deck reached via steep steps. Abstract art dots the sleek, well-designed interiors; each room is well appointed, with plenty of extras (a mini-fridge, an iPod docking station, espresso machine, fudge, home-made biscuits). Breakfast, in the open-plan dining room/kitchen overlooking the swimming pool, might start with freshly squeezed juices, locally baked bread, fruit compote, seasonal berries; plenty of cooked options. BEDROOMS 4. OPEN Apr–Sept. FACILITIES breakfast room, free Wi-Fi in bedrooms, in-room TV (Freeview), 12-acre grounds, 9-metre heated outdoor swimming pool, parking. BACKGROUND MUSIC none. LOCATION 5 mins from Dartmouth via ferry. CHILDREN not accepted. DOGS assistance dogs allowed. CREDIT CARDS MasterCard, Visa. PRICES per room B&B £165–£210.

KIRKBY LONSDALE Cumbria
Map 4: inset C2

SUN INN, 6 Market Street, LA6 2AU. Tel 015242 71965, www.sun-inn.info. The sun and moon make their haste, but this 400-year-old inn near the River Lune remains a dependably restful spot for locals, travellers, hikers and their dogs. Iain and Jenny Black maintain a 'friendly atmosphere'. The bar is popular for its real ales and log fires; wonky beams add to the ambience. Well-regarded modern country cooking features in the restaurant (dogs can also look forward to a treat after long walkies on the fells). Country-style bedrooms have a comfortable Cumbrian-made bed, Swaledale wool carpets, a host of extras: fresh milk, local biscuits, bottled water. Come morning, a tasty breakfast of home-made granola, pastries, fresh and poached fruit on the buffet. BEDROOMS 11. OPEN all year. FACILITIES bar, restaurant, free Wi-Fi, in-room TV (Freeview), parking (permits supplied), bar and restaurant wheelchair accessible. BACKGROUND MUSIC in bar. LOCATION town centre. CHILDREN all ages welcomed. DOGS allowed in bedrooms, public rooms (separate dog-friendly area in restaurant). CREDIT CARDS MasterCard, Visa. PRICES per room B&B £117–£169, D,B&B £177–£229. À la carte £34. 25% DISCOUNT VOUCHERS

KNARESBOROUGH Yorkshire
Map 4:D4

NEWTON HOUSE, 5–7 York Place, HG5 0AD. Tel 01423 863539, newtonhouseyorkshire.com. A warm welcome awaits at Denise Carter's 'enjoyable, good-value' B&B at the centre of a 'lovely' market town. 'Spacious, well-appointed' bedrooms in the 'fascinating' 18th-century house are traditionally decorated; each has a comfortable bed, its own little library, a hospitality tray. Local beers, spirits and soft drinks are kept in the well-stocked honesty bar. In the evenings,

light bites (perhaps soup, an omelette, a sandwich) might be 'rustled up'; the hostess can recommend nearby eateries for more substantial fare. Home-baked sourdough bread and Aga-made jams and compotes are a worthy start to 'excellent organic, "slow" breakfasts'; accompanying cooked options include locally sourced eggs, smoked fish, bacon and sausages. A bonus: on-site parking. BEDROOMS 12, 2 on ground floor suitable for disabled, 2 in converted stables. OPEN all year. FACILITIES sitting room, dining room, conservatory, free Wi-Fi, in-room TV (Freeview), courtyard garden, parking. BACKGROUND MUSIC Classic FM at breakfast. LOCATION town centre, 4 miles from Harrogate. CHILDREN all ages welcomed. DOGS allowed in 2 stable block rooms with outside access (home-made treats). CREDIT CARDS Amex, MasterCard, Visa. PRICES per room B&B single £60–£100, double £85–£125.

LANCASTER Lancashire
Map 4:D2

GREENBANK FARMHOUSE, Abbeystead Road, LA2 9BA. Tel 07512 520229, www.greenbankfarmhouse.co.uk. A former cheese-making farm, where Sally and Simon Tait 'warmly welcome' visitors to their 'well-appointed', 'very affordable' B&B, offers 'wonderful views of the moorlands'. 'A good centre for exploring the area.' Twitchers can take their field book into the conservatory lounge, from where many bird species can be spotted flitting about in the gardens. The 'spacious', country-style bedrooms have 'ample storage', 'adequate lighting'; 'even the loo' has sweeping views of the surrounding fells. Freshly cooked breakfasts, ordered the night before, are 'excellent': farm-fresh eggs, home-made bread, loose-leaf tea, local bacon and sausages. The hosts are a wealth of local information, including dining hotspots in neighbouring Dolphinholme. BEDROOMS 4, 1 on ground floor. OPEN all year. FACILITIES conservatory breakfast room/sitting area, free Wi-Fi, in-room TV (Freeview), 6-acre grounds (some working farmland), parking. BACKGROUND MUSIC none. LOCATION 20 mins from centre of Lancaster (own transport essential). CHILDREN over-12s welcomed. DOGS not allowed. CREDIT CARDS all major cards. PRICES per person B&B single £55, double £65.

LANCHESTER Co. Durham
Map 4:B4

BURNHOPESIDE HALL, Durham Road, lDH7 0TL. Tel 01207520222, www.burnhopeside-hall.co.uk. Well placed for visits to Durham, Christine Hewitt's Grade II* listed home is surrounded by extensive gardens among acres of rolling farmland and forest. Inside, timeless elegance fuses with hospitable informality. Cosseting rooms include spacious, traditional bedrooms in the house or farmhouse, and cottage suites. Some have gorgeous period windows, an open fireplace, a sleigh bed, exposed timbers. Home-made, home-reared, home-grown fare features at breakfast; dinner may be requested in advance. A fantastic spot for cyclists, walkers and riders: trails lead to the river and the Lanchester Valley Railway Path. The house has cleaning facilities for muddy paws and boots; a drying room; stabling for guests' horses. BEDROOMS 12, 5 in The Farmhouse, 3 in cottage in the grounds. OPEN all year. FACILITIES sitting room, dining room, library, billiard room, free Wi-Fi, in-room TV (Freeview), 475-acre grounds. BACKGROUND

MUSIC none. LOCATION 5 miles NW of Durham. CHILDREN all ages welcomed. DOGS welcomed (resident dogs). CREDIT CARDS Amex, MasterCard, Visa. PRICES per room B&B single £70–£85, double £100–£120. Dinner, by arrangement, £30. 25% DISCOUNT VOUCHERS

LAVENHAM Suffolk
Map 2:C5

THE SWAN AT LAVENHAM HOTEL & SPA, High Street, CO10 9QA. Tel 01787 247477, theswanatlavenham.co.uk. 'So cosy and welcoming', this swish hotel (TA Hotel Collection, see also The Crown, Woodbridge, Shortlist) is formed from three timber-framed 15th-century buildings in a medieval village. With a 'lovely' lobby and interlinked areas separated by open wood-beamed partitions, there is plenty of seating. Along twisty corridors, the country house-style bedrooms each have an oversized headboard, bathrobes, laptop, safe, iron and board. Characterful suites have a separate lounge, inglenook fireplace, mullioned windows. Dining options abound: light bites in the Airmen's bar; re-thought British favourites in the 'bright, modern' brasserie overlooking the garden; refined dishes in the Gallery restaurant. A regular reader found the service rather abrupt. If you need to revitalise, the Weavers' House Spa awaits. BEDROOMS 45, 1 suitable for disabled. OPEN all year. FACILITIES lounges, bar, brasserie, restaurant, free Wi-Fi, in-room TV (Freeview), civil wedding licence, private dining/function facilities, spa (treatment rooms, sauna, steam room, outdoor hydrotherapy pool), terrace, garden, parking. BACKGROUND MUSIC occasional, in public areas. LOCATION in village. CHILDREN all ages welcomed. DOGS in some rooms (£12 per dog per night). CREDIT CARDS all major cards. PRICES per room B&B £100-£315, D,B&B £170-£385.

LEATHERHEAD Surrey
Map 2:D4

BEAVERBROOK, Reigate Road, KT22 8QX. Tel 01372 227670, beaverbrook. co.uk. Famous politicians and luminaries have pow-wowed and partied in this country pile, once the rural retreat of press baron Lord Beaverbrook. A large white building on a Surrey hillside, it has been transmuted into a lavish modern hotel. Its illustrious past is celebrated with bedrooms named after famous visitors ranging from Winston Churchill to Elizabeth Taylor. It has a well-stocked library, glamorous Roaring Twenties-style bar and Art Deco screening room. A grand staircase flows up to floral-patterned bedrooms with an original fireplace, a luxury bathroom; large windows or a balcony look over the downs. Garden House rooms are funkier, with woodland views. Dine on beautifully presented Japanese cuisine or seasonal, Italian-inspired dishes. A state-of-the art spa opens in late 2018. BEDROOMS 29, in main house and garden. OPEN all year. FACILITIES bar, lounge, 2 restaurants (The Dining Room closed Sun night, all day Monday), library, cinema, free Wi-Fi, in-room TV, 400-acre grounds, walled garden, woodlands, lake, parking. Cookery school. BACKGROUND MUSIC in restaurant and bar. LOCATION on a 400-acre estate in the Surrey hills. CHILDREN all ages welcomed, (cots, extra beds, special menus). DOGS welcomed in Garden House rooms. CREDIT CARDS Amex, Mastercard, Visa. PRICES per room from £215. Breakfast: continental £15, full £18. Dinner set menus £60, £90 (The Dining Room), £54 (Garden House).

LECHLADE Gloucestershire
Map 3:E6

THE FIVE ALLS, Filkins, GL7 3JQ. Tel 01367 860875, thefiveallsfilkins.co.uk. Quirky and sophisticated: Lana and Sebastian Snow twist expectations at their 18th-century Cotswold dining pub-with-rooms. Flagged floors, stone walls and a huge fireplace are offset by colourful textiles, Bill Brandt prints and playful wallpapers; a pleasing concession to tradition is the leather chesterfield sofas by the log fire. The popular bar and dining area are comfortably informal. On sunny days, European influenced 'turf-to-table' dishes, whipped up by Sebastian Snow — perhaps game pie, caramelised root vegetables, mashed potato — are served on the garden's picnic tables. Soft colours, neutral hues and cosy comforts turn the upstairs bedrooms into a calming retreat. The Snows also own The Plough, Kelmscott (see main entry) and the Bull Hotel, Fairford (see Shortlist), nearby. BEDROOMS 9, 5 in annexe. OPEN all year. FACILITIES snug, bar, restaurant, free Wi-Fi, in-room TV (Freeview), garden, parking. BACKGROUND MUSIC in public areas. LOCATION in scenic village of Filkins, 10 mins' drive from Lechlade. CHILDREN all ages welcomed. DOGS allowed in public rooms, not in bedrooms. CREDIT CARDS Amex, MasterCard, Visa. PRICES per room B&B £115–£160. À la carte £30.

LEDBURY Herefordshire
Map 3:D5

THE FEATHERS, High Street, HR8 1DS. Tel 01531 635266, www.feathersledbury. co.uk. Hosting travellers since 1564,

this famous black-and-white-timbered Tudor pile is now a spa hotel. Owned by the Coaching Inn group, it has many original features: a wonky staircase, leaded windows, a ghostly apparition. 'It would benefit from a little refurbishment,' say readers this year. The 'spacious' bedrooms are well supplied (bottled water, fruit, chocolates, robes). Coaching rooms have Tudor beams; high-ceilinged Dancing rooms are in the Victorian ballroom. In Quills restaurant, diners sit down to Suzie Isaacs's 'very good' modern British dishes, perhaps hake fillet with crayfish thermidor. Fuggles brasserie is a laid-back alternative. Breakfast brings a 'good choice of cold and cooked options – the full English was particularly appreciated'. BEDROOMS 22, 1 suite in cottage, also self-catering apartments. OPEN all year. FACILITIES lounge, bar, brasserie, restaurant, free Wi-Fi, in-room TV (Sky, Freeview), function facilities, spa, indoor swimming pool, gym), civil wedding licence, terraced garden, parking, restaurant suitable for disabled. BACKGROUND MUSIC none. LOCATION town centre. CHILDREN all ages welcomed. DOGS allowed in bedrooms and bar, only guide dogs in restaurant and brasserie. CREDIT CARDS Amex, MasterCard, Visa. PRICES per room B&B £90–£240, D,B&B £150–£320. À la carte £30.
25% DISCOUNT VOUCHERS

LEVENS Cumbria
Map 4: inset C2
HARE AND HOUNDS, LA8 8PN. Tel 015395 60004, www.hareandhoundslevens.co.uk. In the Lyth valley, Becky and Ash Dewar's 16th-century hostelry is a village pub 'with a modern twist'. Visitors mingle with regulars in the lively, slate-floored, beamed bar, where hand-drawn cask ales, craft beers and cocktails made with locally produced spirits are a big draw. Upstairs, distinctive bedrooms have duck-egg blue panelling, soft contemporary hues. Most offer a long view, all enjoy homely extras: home-made brownies, freshly ground coffee, fresh milk, a digital radio, Cumbrian-made toiletries. Home-made comfort food (seafood pot; 'unusual burgers') is served in the light-filled dining room. Breakfast starts with fruit, cereals and yogurt, and works up to a range of cooked fare. Muddy boots and dogs are welcomed. BEDROOMS 4. OPEN all year, no accommodation 24–25 Dec. FACILITIES pub, lounge, restaurant, free Wi-Fi, beer garden, parking. BACKGROUND MUSIC in pub and restaurant. LOCATION in village. CHILDREN all ages welcomed. DOGS allowed in pub and garden. CREDIT CARDS Amex, MasterCard, Visa. PRICES per room B&B single £75–£135, double £85–£145. À la carte £50 for 2 people. 2-night min. stay for weekends booked 1 month in advance.

LEWANNICK Cornwall
Map 1:D3
COOMBESHEAD FARM, PL15 7QQ. Tel 01566 782 009, www.coombesheadfarm.co.uk. Attracting foodies from near and far, this hybrid of informal guesthouse and restaurant occupies a 16th-century farmhouse, among acres of meadows and woodland. Run by chef Tom Adams, it has 'delightful, enthusiastic young staff'. A youngish clientele ('it all felt very hipster') enjoys 'stupendous dishes', rustled up in an open kitchen in the 'feasting barn', using home-smoked, -cured and -pickled ingredients, Cornish organic produce

and locally foraged wild food. Many of the wines come from Tom's brother's French vineyard. Handsomely rustic bedrooms are countryside fresh, with views stretching across to Dartmoor. Breakfast, naturally, is a feast: home-made yogurts, home-baked breads, freshly milled oats and grains. Bread workshops are taught by the in-house baker, one Sunday a month. BEDROOMS 5, 1 with adjoining bunk-bedroom. OPEN all year except Jan, restaurant Thurs–Sun. FACILITIES living room, library, dining room, kitchen, bakery, free Wi-Fi, 66-acre grounds, parking. BACKGROUND MUSIC in evening in living room, dining room and kitchen. LOCATION in village, 3 miles from A30, 6 miles from Launceston. CHILDREN over-15s welcomed. DOGS allowed in bedrooms, public rooms. CREDIT CARDS Amex, MasterCard, Visa. PRICES per room B&B from £130. Set dinner menu £65.

LICHFIELD Staffordshire
Map 2:A2

SWINFEN HALL, Swinfen, WS14 9RE. Tel 01543 481494, swinfenhallhotel. co.uk. 'Such excellent attention to detail.' Approached through 'well-maintained grounds', entered under a balustraded minstrel's gallery, the Wiser family's 'superb' Georgian manor is a 'very grand' affair. Grand but not stuffy. The 'friendly staff' create a 'relaxing experience'. Each spacious, individually decorated bedroom has good technology (iPod docking station, DVD-player), and views over formal gardens or parkland. Cocktails are sipped in the clubby lounge, or the 'lovely' Edwardian bar, with 'lots of wood panelling, and stained glass'. The bar offers lighter bites, perhaps fish and chips; Scotch eggs and tomato salad, while, in the award-winning restaurant, chef Ryan Shilton cooks estate-reared venison and lamb, alongside produce from the Victorian walled garden and orchard. BEDROOMS 17. OPEN all year except Christmas Day evening, Boxing Day. FACILITIES bar, lounge, cocktail lounge, restaurant, function/private dining rooms, free Wi-Fi, in-room TV (Sky), civil wedding licence, 100-acre grounds, parking, restaurant wheelchair accessible. BACKGROUND MUSIC 'as appropriate' in cocktail lounge, bar, restaurant. LOCATION 2 miles S of Lichfield just off the A38. CHILDREN all ages welcomed. DOGS not allowed. CREDIT CARDS Amex, MasterCard, Visa. PRICES per room B&B single £125–£330, double £155–£350. À la carte £50, tasting menus £50–£80.

LINCOLN Lincolnshire
Map 4:E5

BRIDLEWAY BED & BREAKFAST, Riseholme Gorse, LN2 2LY. Tel 01522 545693, www.bridlewaybandb.co.uk. A smart trot up the bridleway stands artist Jane Haigh's rural B&B. Always on hand, the hostess provides a welcoming tea (homemade scones, clotted cream) on arrival; advice on local restaurants; even a lift into Lincoln, nearby. Country-cosy rooms in converted stables, all exposed brickwork, contemporary grey and pale hues, mellow wood, have their own entrance, bathrobes, underfloor heating; a coffee machine and baked treats. Breakfast, in the conservatory, brings fresh fruit salad, Aga-cooked porridge, and a wide range of hot dishes, using eggs from Jane's hens; a continental option can be delivered to the room. Wellies and the family dogs can be borrowed for muddy walks. Stabling provided. BEDROOMS 4, all in converted outbuildings. OPEN 1

Jan–9 Dec. FACILITIES conservatory, free Wi-Fi, in-room TV (Freeview), ½-acre grounds leading to bridleway, 2 stables, manège, paddock for guests' horses. BACKGROUND MUSIC in conservatory at breakfast. LOCATION 3½ miles from Lincoln. CHILDREN over-15s welcomed. DOGS not allowed. CREDIT CARDS all major cards. PRICES per room B&B single £83-£110, double £93–£125.
25% DISCOUNT VOUCHERS

THE CASTLE HOTEL, Westgate, LN1 3AS. Tel 01522 538801, castlehotel. net. Opposite the castle walls, on the site of the Roman Forum, this sleek Bailgate area hotel is primely located for exploring the city's history. It's primely run too, by a personable, efficient staff. 'Comfortable', compact bedrooms in the main building, modishly decorated in earthy hues, have views of the castle walls or the medieval cathedral. Courtyard rooms in the peaceful, 250-year-old coach house, are conveniently all on the ground floor, with parking just outside. The hungry flock to consume 'beautifully presented' modern European dishes, perhaps salt and caramel belly pork, glazed apple, hips cabbage, smoked butter mash, washed down with interesting English or Israeli wines. The elegant bar has lighter, bistro-style options. BEDROOMS 18, 1 suitable for disabled, plus 1 apartment, and 2-bed Castle Mews (available for self-catering). OPEN all year except 24–26 Dec. FACILITIES 2 small lounges, bar, restaurant, free Wi-Fi, in-room TV, wedding/function facilities, spa treatments, parking. BACKGROUND MUSIC in public areas. CHILDREN all ages welcomed. DOGS not allowed. CREDIT CARDS MasterCard, Visa. PRICES per room B&B single £90–£140, double £90–£150, D,B&B £120–£220. Set menus £30–£35, à la carte £35.

LITTLE ECCLESTON Lancashire
Map 4:D2
THE CARTFORD INN Cartford Lane, PR3 0YP. Tel 01995 670166, www. thecartfordinn.co.uk. Buzzy design and imaginative French-inflected cooking attract visitors from near and far to Julie and Patrick Beaumé's 17th-century coaching inn. A bright makeover brings a light touch to the banks of the River Wyre. The eco-minded pair chose reclaimed, upcycled or locally crafted fittings and furnishings, including light fittings by a local glassblower, for the bedrooms and the two treehouse-style 'pods'. In the highly regarded kitchen, Lancastrian produce is given a Gallic tweak; in the convivial bar, regional cask ales and a house brew take centre stage. From all parts: a panorama of the Bowland Fells. Delicacies from the deli, TOTI, can be picked up for the journey home. BEDROOMS 17, some in riverside annexe, 1 suitable for disabled, 2 lodges in grounds. OPEN all year except 24–28 Dec. FACILITIES bar, restaurant, delicatessen, free Wi-Fi, in-room TV (Freeview), riverside terrace, garden, parking. BACKGROUND MUSIC in public areas. LOCATION near Blackpool, Cleveleys, Rossall and Garstang. Easily reached from the M6 and the M55. CHILDREN all ages welcomed. DOGS not allowed. CREDIT CARDS all major cards. PRICES per room B&B single from £80, double from £130. À la carte £33.

LIVERPOOL Merseyside
Map 4:E2
HARD DAYS NIGHT, Central Buildings, North John Street, L2 6RR. Tel 01512 361964, www.harddaysnighthotel.com.

Fans of the Fab Four will want to say 'Hello!' to this Beatles-themed hotel, close to the famous Cavern Club. Brimming with personality, the grand Victorian building cleverly displays original art, photographs and references to the Liverpool band against well-maintained original features. Help is a shout away with 'friendly staff' on hand. The individually decorated bedrooms promise comfortable nights. In each, a large bed, 'good fittings', a well-equipped bathroom; some rooms have a private balcony with panoramic views; the quietest rooms overlook the rear. Sleek Bar Four serves fab cocktails. Traditional British dishes, given a contemporary twist, shake it up in the pop art-filled restaurant, eight days a week. BEDROOMS 110, 5 suitable for disabled. OPEN all year. FACILITIES lift, lounge/bar, cocktail bar, restaurant, free Wi-Fi, in-room TV (Sky), civil wedding licence, function facilities, parking discounts. BACKGROUND MUSIC all day in public areas, live music on Fri and Sat nights in bar. LOCATION city centre. CHILDREN all ages welcomed. DOGS assistance dogs allowed. CREDIT CARDS all major cards. PRICES per room B&B from £126, D,B&B from £154. À la carte £25.
25% DISCOUNT VOUCHERS

HOPE STREET HOTEL, 40 Hope Street, L1 9DA. Tel 0151 709 3000, www.hopestreethotel.co.uk. In the buzzing heart of the city, opposite the Philharmonic Hall, a Venetian palazzo facade conceals this contemporary hotel, 'ideally placed' for discovering the wonderful history and architecture. The former carriage works' 'airy, modern' public spaces have a stripped-back style, all exposed brick walls, vintage metal supports and old beams. Varying in size, Scandi-minimalist bedrooms (white walls, uncovered wood floors); some, at the top, have 'wonderful views' of the river or city landmarks. The restaurant is the place for 'delicious' modern British dishes using regional produce; in the bar: informal fare and made-to-order cocktails. The cooked dishes, at breakfast, 'are generous' (the continental selection, perhaps, less so). BEDROOMS 89, some interconnecting, 2 suitable for disabled. OPEN all year. FACILITIES lift, lounge, bar, restaurant, private dining rooms, free Wi-Fi, in-room TV (Sky, Freeview), civil wedding licence, functions, leisure facilities, limited parking nearby (£10 charge). BACKGROUND MUSIC in public areas. LOCATION city centre, in Hope Street, the main artery through Liverpool's Georgian neighbourhood, bookended majestically by the city's two cathedrals. CHILDREN all ages welcomed. DOGS allowed (£15 per night). CREDIT CARDS Amex, MasterCard, Visa. PRICES per room B&B from £89, D,B&B from £163. À la carte £40.

THE NADLER LIVERPOOL, 29 Seel Street, L1 4AU. 0151 705 2626, www.nadlerhotels.com/the-nadler-liverpool. Practical, 'affordably luxurious' accommodation is on offer in an impressively restored former printworks near the Albert Dock. This 'efficient' hotel has well-designed, air-conditioned bedrooms to suit all needs, from a snug double to a two-level suite with a private courtyard. Triple-glazed windows and a compact kitchen (a microwave, a small sink, a fridge, crockery, cutlery) come as standard. In lieu of a restaurant or bar, guests are given exclusive discounts at selected eateries in the characterful surrounding Ropewalk area. A continental breakfast (ordered in advance) is taken in the lounge. Sister hotels within the small chain include the Nadler Kensington, London (see Shortlist). BEDROOMS 106, some suitable for disabled. OPEN all year. FACILITIES lift, lounge, meeting room, free Wi-Fi, in-room TV, 30 mins of free national landline calls per day, parking discounts. BACKGROUND MUSIC in public areas. LOCATION in Ropewalk area. CHILDREN all ages welcomed. DOGS assistance dogs allowed. CREDIT CARDS all major cards. PRICES per room B&B from £76. Breakfast £12.

LOOE Cornwall
Map 1:D3

THE BEACH HOUSE, Marine Drive, Hannafore, PL13 2DH. Tel 01503 262598, www.thebeachhouselooe.co.uk. 'A spoiling welcome' from hosts Rosie and David Reeve sets the tone at their 'ideally located' seafront B&B. Superb coastal views are shared across the comfortable garden room (where tea and home-made cake greet arriving visitors) and homely bedrooms. The latter are 'spotlessly clean' and stocked with teas, fresh coffee, a fridge with fresh milk, 'regularly replenished' bottles of Cornish water. Three rooms face the sea; two access the garden. Come morning, a help-yourself spread (fresh fruit, home-made muffins, yogurt) is followed by tasty cooked-to-order hot dishes. Steps away: coastal trails, rock pools and sandy beaches; only a bit further: fishing villages. The hosts have ready local knowledge. BEDROOMS 5. OPEN all year except Christmas. FACILITIES garden room, breakfast room, free Wi-Fi, terrace, ½-acre garden, beach opposite, spa treatments. BACKGROUND MUSIC in breakfast room. LOCATION ½ mile from centre. CHILDREN over-15s welcomed. DOGS not allowed. CREDIT CARDS MasterCard, Visa. PRICES per room B&B £85–£135. 2-night bookings preferred.

LUDLOW Shropshire
Map 3:C4

THE CLIVE, Bromfield, SY8 2JR. Tel 01584 856565, www.theclive.co.uk. A regular visitor to this 'old favourite' in 2018 found The Clive to be 'as good as ever', with plenty to satisfy epicures. The 18th-century farmhouse sits on the Earl of Plymouth's Oakley Park estate, within walking distance of the Ludlow Food Centre – both of which provide produce for the restaurant. A generous sea bass fillet with samphire, spinach, a vermouth cream sauce 'had excellent flavour'. 'A special mention for the passionfruit coulis. I would have had it every night!' Another guest found the service 'pleasant enough but a bit laid back'. The 'crisply modern' bedrooms, with exposed timbers and high ceiling, are 'stylish, spacious and efficiently equipped'; 'big, comfy bed' and 'nice, big bathroom', but 'very little hanging space' and 'some road noise'. Still, this remains a decent, 'very good value' spot. BEDROOMS 14, all in adjoining annexes, some on ground floor, 1 suitable for disabled. OPEN all year except 26 Dec. FACILITIES bar, café, restaurant, free Wi-Fi, in-room TV (Freeview), conference room, courtyard. BACKGROUND MUSIC in public areas. LOCATION 4 miles NW of Ludlow. CHILDREN all ages welcomed. DOGS allowed in 1 bedroom, bar, not in restaurant. CREDIT CARDS all major cards. PRICES per room B&B £115–£175, D,B&B £165–£220. À la carte £28–£40. 25% DISCOUNT VOUCHERS

LUPTON Cumbria
Map 4: inset C2

THE PLOUGH, Cow Brow, LA6 1PJ.
Tel 01539 567700, theploughatlupton.
co.uk. Ideally placed for exploring the
Lake District and the Yorshire dales,
Paul Spencer's laid-back inn sprawls
comfortably on the road to Lupton.
The 18th-century hostelry has been
refurbished with a modern rustic look:
wide wooden tables and mismatched
chairs, a wood-burning stove,
sheepskin-covered bar stools under oak
beams. Diners come for well-considered
British cooking, with good vegetarian
options such as hay-baked celeriac,
toasted quinoa, roasted baby onions,
onion jus. Graceful country bedrooms
(some snug) have pale furniture, perhaps
a brass bed, squashy armchairs, a vast
beamed bathroom with slipper bath.
Many rooms have glorious views over
Farleton Knott. Rooms away from
the road are quietest. BEDROOMS 6. OPEN
all year, no accommodation 24–25
Dec. FACILITIES lounge, bar, restaurant,
free Wi-Fi (signal variable), in-room
TV (Freeview), civil wedding licence,
terrace, garden, restaurant suitable for
wheelchairs, parking. BACKGROUND MUSIC
in reception, bar and restaurant. LOCATION
1 mile off junction 36, M6. 4 miles from
Kirkby Lonsdale. CHILDREN all ages
welcomed. DOGS allowed in bar, all but 1
bedroom. CREDIT CARDS MasterCard, Visa.
PRICES per room B&B from £85. D,B&B
from £115. À la carte £30.
25% DISCOUNT VOUCHERS

LURGASHALL Sussex
Map 2:D3

THE BARN AT ROUNDHURST, Lower
Roundhurst Farm, GU27 3BY. Tel
01428 642535, thebarnatroundhurst.
com. A 'stunningly restored' 17th-
century threshing barn in the South
Downs national park is the heart of
Moya and Richard Connell's rural
B&B and working organic farm. The
barn is dramatic: lofty, open-plan, with
huge oak beams, modern artwork,
vintage leather seating and rough-
hewn wooden pieces, a contemporary
wood-burner. A striking staircase curls
up to a small glass-fronted library and
honesty bar. In a ring of converted
outbuildings, 'spacious, comfortable'
bedrooms, some with exposed timbers,
have all the usual amenities, plus a few
21st-century necessities (wine glasses,
a corkscrew, a yoga mat). The farm's
produce is showcased in the 'superb'
breakfast's sausages, eggs and home-
made jam. BEDROOMS 6. OPEN all year.
FACILITIES open-plan lounge/dining area,
library/bar, free Wi-Fi, in-room TV
(Freeview), meeting/function facilities,
small garden on 250-acre farm, barn
wheelchair accessible. BACKGROUND
MUSIC mixed in lounge. LOCATION 2
miles S of Haslemere. CHILDREN over-
12s welcomed. DOGS not allowed. CREDIT
CARDS MasterCard, Visa. PRICES per
room B&B from £128. Set menu £40.

LYME REGIS Dorset
Map 1:C6

ALEXANDRA HOTEL, Pound Street,
DT7 3HZ. Tel 01297 442010, www.
hotelalexandra.co.uk. With thrilling
views over Lyme Bay, the Jurassic Coast
and the Cobb, Kathryn Haskins's luxury
hotel and restaurant is surrounded by
lush clifftop gardens. Owned by her
family for decades, the 'beautifully'
renovated 18th-century house displays
prints by the ornithologist John Gould,
whose father was the head gardener.
Traditionally styled bedrooms,
furnished with plush fabrics and

antiques, vary in size and shape; most have sea views; bathrooms are glossy. Two serviced courtyard apartments are ideal for a family. Seasonal, locally sourced meals are served in the soothing restaurant or the new orangery. The garden terrace is a scenic spot for an alfresco meal. The hotel's aromatherapy treatments use hand-made Devonshire essential oils. BEDROOMS 23, plus 2 apartments in courtyard. OPEN all year, except 30 Dec-31 Jan. FACILITIES bar, sitting room restaurant, orangery, free Wi-Fi, in-room TV (Freeview), treatment room, civil wedding licence, private functions, limited parking. BACKGROUND MUSIC in public areas at meal times. LOCATION close to the beach and harbour. CHILDREN all ages welcomed. DOGS allowed in bar, sitting room, garden. CREDIT CARDS MasterCard, Visa. PRICES per room B&B single from £95, double £180–£350, À la carte £35.

DORSET HOUSE, Dorset House, DT7 3HX. Tel 01297 442055, www. dorsethouselyme.com. The eye-catching interior of Lyn and Jason Martin's refurbished Regency B&B is bested only by the coastal views from its lofty sash windows. The fire-warmed snug is tailor-made for absorbing a newspaper or book, while everything and anything can be toasted with locally produced Castlewood bubbly from the honesty bar. Freshly styled bedrooms have clean lines, splashes of blue and mustard; many enjoy sea views. Each is provided with thoughtful extras: thick bathrobes, natural toiletries, artisan teas, home-made brownies. Breakfast treats, Aga-fresh and made with organic or local produce, include apple and rhubarb juice, home-made granola, cake of the day (you're on holiday), seasonal fruit, the full Dorset. BEDROOMS 5. OPEN all year except Christmas. FACILITIES snug, breakfast room, reception, free Wi-Fi, in-room TV (Freeview), veranda, paid parking nearby. BACKGROUND MUSIC in breakfast room. LOCATION 300m from town centre. CHILDREN all ages welcomed. DOGS not allowed. CREDIT CARDS Amex, MasterCard, Visa. PRICES per room B&B single £85–£165, double £95–£175. 2-night min. stay.

LYTHAM Lancashire
Map 4:D2

THE ROOMS, 35 Church Road, FY8 5LL. Tel 01253 736000, www. theroomslytham.co.uk. Renewed into a comfortably cool B&B, Andy Baker's Victorian house on the Fylde coast is a rejuvenating spot that takes good design seriously. Sleek and contemporary, the well-fitted bedrooms make a feature of a sloping ceiling, a skylight, a staircase leading to the bathroom; all have good technology, plus underfloor heating and a rain shower in the stylish bathroom. The morning meal (perhaps taken in the walled garden) highlights fresh local produce: a custom-blended smoothie, some locally baked bread, perhaps a Buck's Fizz; cooked dishes include smoked haddock, waffles and pancakes. Top tip: the helpful host is a fount of knowledge; the best pizza-and-jazz hotspots, a speciality. BEDROOMS 5 ('lots of stairs'), plus 2-bed serviced apartment. OPEN all year. FACILITIES breakfast room, free Wi-Fi, in-room TV (Freeview), meeting facilities, decked garden. BACKGROUND MUSIC in breakfast room. LOCATION ¼ mile W of town centre. CHILDREN all ages welcomed. DOGS assistance dogs allowed. CREDIT CARDS Amex, MasterCard, Visa. PRICES

per room B&B single £90–£110, double
£110–£140.
25% DISCOUNT VOUCHERS

MALVERN WELLS Worcestershire
Map 3:D5

THE COTTAGE IN THE WOOD, Holywell
Road, WR14 4LG. Tel 01684 588860,
www.cottageinthewood.co.uk. In a
'stunning setting' that inspired CS
Lewis, Julia and Nick Davies's 18th-
century dower house stands high in the
Malvern hills. A 'modern makeover'
has added a few 'tastefully flamboyant
touches'; Wedgwood blues, hardwood
floors. Long-serving staff are liked for
their 'friendly attentiveness'. The stylish
restaurant and bar have 'excellent food
and drink'. Bedrooms (some snug), each
with its own character, might have
extensive views. A torch is recommended
for those in the grounds; continuing
refurbishment is planned. On the
'delicious, novel breakfast menu':
avocado, poached eggs and bacon;
assorted wild mushrooms on toast;
home-made baked beans. Minor gripes
from readers this year: paper breakfast
napkins, bar muzak. Overall, 'very
good'. BEDROOMS 30, 4 in Beech Cottage,
19 in Coach House, 10 on ground floor,
1 suitable for disabled. OPEN all year.
FACILITIES bar, restaurant, meeting room,
free Wi-Fi, in-room TV (Freeview),
8-acre grounds, parking, public rooms
wheelchair accessible, adapted toilet.
BACKGROUND MUSIC 'quiet, relaxing
music' in restaurant and bar. LOCATION 4
miles from Malvern Wells. CHILDREN all
ages welcomed. DOGS allowed in some
bedrooms (£10 per night), not in public
rooms. CREDIT CARDS all major cards.
PRICES per person B&B single £89–£129,
double £90–£199, D,B&B double £155.
À la carte £40.

MANCHESTER Greater Manchester
Map 4:E3

THE COW HOLLOW HOTEL, 57 Newton
Street (corner of Bradleys Court),
M1 1ET. Tel 0161 228 7277, www.
cowhollow.co.uk. In the hip northern
quarter, Mujtaba and Amelia Ranahas
have alchemised a Victorian textile
warehouse into a glamorous hotel with
a cool cocktail bar. The industrial design
(brick walls, a metal stairway, beds
made out of railway sleepers) comes
with softer touches (a chandelier of
laced tree branches), high technology
and 'just-fussy-enough' staff. Tempting
complimentary treats include bubbles
and nibbles from the evening Prosecco
cart; milk and cookies later. Come
morning, a light continental breakfast-
in-a-bag (granola, yogurt, toast, OJ,
croissants, fruit) is brought up to chic,
space-efficient bedrooms. Useful media
include Netflix access, a smart TV.
The Aviary café offers guests free hot
drinks day and night. No restaurant,
but discounts at local eateries. BEDROOMS
16. OPEN all year except 25–26 Dec.
FACILITIES cocktail bar, free Wi-Fi,
in-room TV (Netflix). BACKGROUND
MUSIC in cocktail bar. LOCATION in
Manchester's Northern Quarter.
CHILDREN all ages welcomed (sharing
with one adult, max. room occupancy
of two). DOGS not allowed. CREDIT CARDS
all major cards. PRICES per room B&B
£89–£199.

DIDSBURY HOUSE, Didsbury Park,
Didsbury Village, M20 5LJ. Tel 0161
448 2200, www.eclectichotels.co.uk/
didsbury-house. The prevailing winds
of a home-away-from-home breeze
through this Victorian villa in a leafy
urban village. One of the Eclectic Hotels
group (see Eleven Didsbury Park, next

Shortlist entry), the voguish B&B was designed with a boutique mindset: vintage prints and statement wallpaper, tempered by fresh flowers, many books, open fires and sink-into sofas. The bedrooms, each its own, have original features (high windows, delicate cornices), perhaps a freestanding roll-top bath. Inviting afternoon teas are followed by light bites and aperitifs in one of the relaxed loungers or on the walled terrace. Leisurely weekends are de rigueur: breakfast is served until noon. BEDROOMS 27, some suitable for disabled. OPEN all year. FACILITIES 2 lounges, bar, breakfast room, free Wi-Fi, in-room TV (Sky), civil wedding licence, meeting room, walled terrace. BACKGROUND MUSIC 'chill-out' music in public areas. LOCATION The city centre and airport are a quick train (or taxi) ride away. .CHILDREN all ages welcomed. DOGS not allowed. CREDIT CARDS all major cards. PRICES per room £120–£300. Breakfast £16. À la carte £25.

ELEVEN DIDSBURY PARK, 11 Didsbury Park, Didsbury Village, M20 5LH. Tel 0161 448 7711, www.eclectichotels. co.uk/eleven-didsbury-park. 'My first choice in Manchester,' says a regular Guide reader this year. Sun loungers recline and hammocks swing in the walled garden of this peaceful suburban Victorian town house (Eclectic Hotels group, see Didsbury House, previous entry). Elsewhere, the relaxed vibe spreads to the sitting room's squashy sofas, cosy nooks and open fire; the high-ceilinged reception with its hand-crafted wood bar. Comfortable, snug bedrooms are spread over three floors; they have a private balcony, a roll-top bath. In all, spa-worthy toiletries, a minibar, a butler tray with

fresh milk. Breakfast arrives in the bright conservatory. The city centre and airport are a short train-ride or drive away. BEDROOMS 20, 1 on ground floor, suitable for disabled. OPEN all year. FACILITIES 2 lounge/bars, free Wi-Fi, in-room TV (Sky), veranda, walled garden, wedding/conference facilities, parking. BACKGROUND MUSIC all day in public areas. LOCATION Didsbury, Manchester. CHILDREN all ages welcomed. DOGS not allowed. CREDIT CARDS all major cards. PRICES per room from £150. Breakfast £16. À la carte menu £28.

MARAZION Cornwall
Map 1:E1
GODOLPHIN ARMS, West End, TR17 0EN. Tel 01736 888510, www. godolphinarms.co.uk. 'Superbly located in a beautiful setting.' Guide readers in 2018 were thrilled by this 'fabulous (and fabulously dog friendly)' seaside spot. Across the causeway from St Michael's Mount, James and Mary St Levan's 'unpretentious' inn wins praise for its 'excellent accommodation', 'super food' and 'attentive, professional staff'. Uplifting coastal colours and local artwork brighten the bedrooms; many have superb views; in all are bathrobes, good toiletries. Some are accessed via 'steep stairs' (discuss room choice when booking). 'Our well-kitted-out room had a larger-than-normal bathroom.' Caught-that-day seafood is a highlight of the 'fresh, tasty' menu in the light-filled restaurant with its breezy Scandinavian vibe (and spectacular terrace) where an extensive breakfast includes smoked salmon; buttermilk pancakes, the full Cornish. BEDROOMS 10, some suitable for disabled. OPEN all year. FACILITIES 2 bars, split-level dining area, free Wi-Fi, in-room TV

(Freeview), wedding/function facilities, 2 terraces, parking, dining room wheelchair accessible. BACKGROUND MUSIC in public areas, occasional live acoustic music. LOCATION 3.8 miles E of Penzance. CHILDREN all ages welcomed. DOGS allowed in 2 bedrooms, designated dining area, on terrace. CREDIT CARDS MasterCard, Visa. PRICES per room B&B from £100. À la carte £28.

MOUNT HAVEN HOTEL & RESTAURANT, Turnpike Road, TR17 0DQ. Tel 01736 719937, www.mounthaven.co.uk. 'We had unobstructed views across Mount's Bay, and enjoyed two glorious sunsets and a harvest moon.' Praise in 2018 for this hotel with vistas of St Michael's Mount, fully exploited by floor-to-ceiling windows, and sliding glass doors leading into its lounge. Staff were 'friendly, helpful' although, our inspector felt they were over-stretched. Contemporary bedrooms are generously supplied with 'all the essentials needed' including a Nespresso machine; the best views are from rooms at the top (although many stairs, no lift). Chef Ross Sloan uses daily-picked, local ingredients in his 'excellent' menus. Breakfast brings a 'really good cooked platter'. A range of holistic treatments is available. Sister hotel to Godolphin Arms, Marazion (see Shortlist, previous entry). BEDROOMS 19, some on ground floor. OPEN all year, except Christmas/ New Year (ring to check exact dates). FACILITIES bar, restaurant, free Wi-Fi, in-room TV (Freeview), spa treatments, sun terrace, ½-acre grounds. BACKGROUND MUSIC in bar and restaurant. LOCATION 4 miles E of Penzance. CHILDREN all ages welcomed. DOGS allowed in some rooms (£15 per night; bowl, bed, treats provided, not allowed in restaurant).

CREDIT CARDS MasterCard, Visa. PRICES per room B&B £170–£280, D,B&B £220–£330. Set menu £20–£25.

MARCHAM Oxfordshire
Map 2:C2

B&B RAFTERS, Abingdon Road, OX13 6NU. Tel 01865 391298, bnb-rafters. co.uk. Sigrid Grawert is the warm hostess of this inviting B&B on the edge of a pretty Oxfordshire village. High praise this year from a reader after a long holiday in five-star hotels: 'It's every bit as good as any of them.' The stylish, modern bedrooms have delicate accents, leafy plants and upscale technology; some have a freestanding bath and a private balcony; a water bed. The fluffy robes, welcoming drinks tray, power shower and clever bathroom storage are standard. The relaxing suntrap garden now has an outdoor seating area. Breakfasts are communal gatherings over freshly squeezed orange juice, home-baked bread, home-made jams, a superb porridge menu. Vegetarian and special diets are catered for. BEDROOMS 4. OPEN all year except Christmas, New Year. FACILITIES lounge, breakfast room, free Wi-Fi, in-room TV (Freeview), garden, parking. BACKGROUND MUSIC none. LOCATION 3 miles W of Abingdon, 8 miles S of Oxford CHILDREN over-11s welcomed. DOGS not allowed. CREDIT CARDS MasterCard, Visa. PRICES per room B&B £67–£139. 2-night min. stay on bank holiday weekends. 25% DISCOUNT VOUCHERS

MARGATE Kent
Map 2:D5

THE READING ROOMS, 31 Hawley Square, CT9 1PH. Tel 01843 225166, www.thereadingroomsmargate.co.uk.

When Louise Oldfield and Liam Nabb restored their B&B on a Georgian square, they struck a careful balance between the preservation of a 200-year history and a thoroughly 21st-century makeover. In each bright, airy bedroom, occupying an entire floor, technological flourishes (underfloor heating, flat-screen TV, etc) work with stripped wooden floors, enormous sash windows, original shutters and vintage plasterwork. Each design is different, but in common are the large Provençal-style bed, neutral hues, fresh flowers, vintage books; a 'cavernous' bathroom with a freestanding roll-top bath. Breakfast is a leisurely spread (fresh pressed juice, freshly baked sourdough bread, cooked options) at a bedroom table overlooking the square, 'beautifully served' at a time of your choosing. BEDROOMS 3. OPEN all year. FACILITIES free Wi-Fi, in-room TV (Freeview), parking vouchers available. BACKGROUND MUSIC none. LOCATION 4 mins' walk from the seafront and Old Town. CHILDREN not allowed. DOGS not allowed. CREDIT CARDS Amex, MasterCard, Visa. PRICES per room B&B £170. 2-night min. stay at weekends and bank holidays.

MATLOCK Derbyshire
Map 3:A6
THE MANOR FARMHOUSE, Manor Farm, Dethick, DE4 5GG. Tel 01629 534302, www.manorfarmdethick. co.uk. Approached along winding lanes, past dry stone walls, Gilly and Simon Groom's 'wonderfully quiet' Elizabethan stone house is surrounded by a working sheep farm. The 'excellent, very comfortable' B&B was once the home of Anthony Babington, executed for his plot to put Mary, Queen of Scots on the throne. Bedrooms, large and traditionally furnished, may be found in a beamed hayloft; or in the main house, with doors to the garden. Guests gather in the listed property's original Elizabethan kitchen to breakfast around the large refectory table. Ordered the night before, the morning meal caters for all diets, and is made with fresh local and organic ingredients, including home-grown produce. BEDROOMS 4, 1 suitable for disabled. OPEN all year. FACILITIES sitting rooms, breakfast room, free Wi-Fi, in-room TV, 1-acre grounds, drying facilities, bicycle/motorcycle storage. BACKGROUND MUSIC none. LOCATION 4 miles SE of Matlock. CHILDREN babes in arms and over-4s welcomed. DOGS not allowed. CREDIT CARDS Mastercard, Visa. PRICES per room B&B £85–£99. 2-night min. stay on Sat, Apr–Oct.

MATLOCK BATH Derbyshire
Map 3:B6
HODGKINSON'S HOTEL, 150 South Parade, nr Matlock, DE4 3NR. Tel 01629 582170, www.hodgkinsons-hotel.co.uk. With 'superb views' of spectacular limestone cliffs, Chris and Zoe Hipwell's Georgian town house hotel is 'a very special spot' near the River Derwent. Most of the listed property's carefully restored Victorian features (tiled entrance hall, ornate glasswork, the original wood-and-glass bar) originate from the ownership of wine merchant Job Hodgkinson, and have been carefully restored. Some of the traditionally furnished bedrooms have river views; in one, a four-poster bed; in each, a handsome walnut-trimmed bathroom has a roll-top bath or walk-in shower. Leigh Matthews's 'excellent' modern British menus are

served in the restaurant; breakfast options include an omelette, kedgeree or a full vegetarian. 'Excellent walks, some challenging', straight from the door. BEDROOMS 8. OPEN all year except Christmas week. FACILITIES sitting room, bar, restaurant, free Wi-Fi, in-room TV, terraced garden, limited on-site parking (additional parking nearby). BACKGROUND MUSIC radio (daytime), 'mix of lounge and easy listening' (evening) in bar and restaurant. LOCATION centrally located in Matlock Bath village and approx. 1 mile from Matlock and Cromford. CHILDREN all ages welcomed. DOGS allowed in lounge, some bedrooms (£10 per night), not in bar or restaurant. CREDIT CARDS Amex, MasterCard, Visa. PRICES per room B&B single £77–£125, double £95–£155. D,B&B £149–£209. Set dinner £27–£30. 2-night min. stay on Sat.

MAWNAN SMITH Cornwall
Map 1:E2

BUDOCK VEAN, nr Helford Passage, TR11 5LG. Tel 01326 252100, www. budockvean.co.uk. Hidden within wooded acres on the Helford river, this 18th-century manor house was recently revamped, acquiring 'a fresh feel'. Guide readers admire the 'beautiful location and excellent food', although this year some felt the service didn't match the standards elsewhere. Many of the well-equipped bedrooms are newly refurbished. 'Our room, overlooking the golf course, was very well done, with particularly good lighting.' Days might be spent on the golf course, by the swimming pool, on the tennis courts or kayaking up nearby Frenchman's Creek. Whatever the pursuit, the smart restaurant is worth the visit for chef Darren Kelly's locally influenced menus including Cornish turbot, hake and venison. A separate vegetarian menu is 'excellent'. BEDROOMS 57, plus 4 self-catering cottages, some suitable for disabled. OPEN all year except 2–25 Jan. FACILITIES lift, 2 lounges, cocktail bar, conservatory, bar, restaurant, free Wi-Fi, in-room TV (Freeview), civil wedding licence, 65-acre grounds, spa. BACKGROUND MUSIC 'gentle' live piano or guitar music in evening in restaurant. LOCATION 6 miles SW of Falmouth. CHILDREN all ages welcomed. DOGS allowed in most bedrooms, not in public rooms. CREDIT CARDS MasterCard, Visa PRICES per person B&B £73–£144, D,B&B £97–£168. Set dinner £44. 25% DISCOUNT VOUCHERS

MIDHURST Sussex
Map 2:E3

THE CHURCH HOUSE, Church Hill, GU29 9NX. Tel 01730 812990, www. churchhousemidhurst.com. Visitors to Fina Jurado's genteel B&B, in a medieval market town, are in for a surprise: a string of four 13th-century cottages has been knocked through to create a 'wonderful' open space. Guests are welcomed with tea and home-baked cake in one of the elegant sitting rooms and eating areas, each with polished oak floors, oriental carpets, period features and vintage finds. Most bedrooms are up the curving staircase. Stylishly rustic, one has a dramatic, high-beamed ceiling, super king-size bed, stained glass window and in-room roll-top bathtub; another has a velvet chaise-longue, and makes full use of centuries-old timbers to create a mezzanine. Communal breakfasts bring organic yogurts, home-made preserves,

locally sourced eggs and sausages.
BEDROOMS 5, 1 on ground floor suitable
for disabled. OPEN all year except
Christmas. FACILITIES sitting room/
dining room, conservatory, free Wi-Fi,
in-room TV (Sky, Freeview), garden.
BACKGROUND MUSIC none. LOCATION
town centre. CHILDREN all ages
welcomed. DOGS not allowed. CREDIT
CARDS MasterCard, Visa. PRICES per
room B&B £140–£165.

MILLOM Cumbria
Map 4: inset C2
BROADGATE HOUSE, Broadgate,
Thwaites, LA18 5JZ. Tel 01229 716295,
www.broadgate-house.co.uk. Visitors
to Diana Lewthwaite's country house in
Beatrix Potter country are guaranteed
a colourful welcome – its grounds,
designed into 'garden rooms', provide
blooms across all seasons. With a
dramatic backdrop of the Lakeland
fells, the white-painted Georgian house
has been home to the owner's family
for almost 200 years. Flowery guest
bedrooms have pretty country character
and garden views. Bathrooms are
shared (but only ever with members
of the same party), and have a throne
loo, freestanding bath. Handsome
public spaces have antique furniture,
ancestral portraits, plush fabrics, and an
original fireplace or two. Keen birders
should carry binoculars: snow buntings,
flycatchers and other sorts have graced
the gardens. BEDROOMS 5. OPEN all year
except 1–23 Dec. FACILITIES sitting room,
dining room, breakfast room, free Wi-
Fi, 2-acre garden. BACKGROUND MUSIC
none. CHILDREN over-10s welcomed.
DOGS not allowed in the house. CREDIT
CARDS none accepted. PRICES per room
B&B single £55, double £95. Dinner (by
arrangement) £30.

MISTLEY Essex
Map 2:C5
THE MISTLEY THORN, High Street,
CO11 1HE. Tel 01206 392821, www.
mistleythorn.co.uk. Constable country
reaches to the doorstep of this affable,
historic restaurant-with-rooms
in a coastal village known for its
swans. Transformed by chef Sherri
Singleton and her husband, David
McKay, the former 18th-century
coaching inn, on the site where Essex
witches were tried, is a welcoming
space. The 'unpretentious' menus
specialise in well-prepared Mersea
oysters and locally landed seafood,
as well as interesting vegetarian
options, all served in the relaxed,
beamed drinking and dining areas
(smart tongue-and-groove panelling,
a wood-burning stove). Bedrooms
are soothingly decorated, and have
nice extras (dressing gowns, luxury
toiletries, home-made biscuits); four
have views down the Stour estuary.
Rooms at the back are quietest. An
extensive breakfast includes smoked
Lowestoft haddock, an omelette
Arnold Bennett. BEDROOMS 12, 3
with separate entrance, 1 suite in
Little Thorn Cottage. OPEN all year
except Christmas Day. FACILITIES
bar, restaurant, free Wi-Fi, in-room
TV (Freeview), outdoor seating,
cookery workshops (special room
rates for attendees). BACKGROUND
MUSIC in restaurant during mealtimes.
LOCATION village centre, 9 miles
W of Harwich. CHILDREN all ages
welcomed. DOGS small/medium dogs
allowed in some rooms and in 'quiet
part' of restaurant. CREDIT CARDS
Amex, MasterCard, Visa. PRICES per
room B&B (Tues–Sat) £105–£170,
D,B&B £120–£220.

MORECAMBE Lancashire
Map 4:D2

THE MIDLAND, Marine Road West,
LA4 4BU. Tel 01524 424000, englishlakes.
co.uk. In a 'superb position on the
marine parade', this 'Art Deco wonder'
was restored to its former glory by
the small English Lakes group. The
architecture, a backdrop for the
Poirot series, 'adds a touch of historic
enchantment', writes a Guide regular in
2018. Every table has a sea view through
floor-to-ceiling windows in the 'lovely'
Sun Terrace restaurant, which follows
the curve of the building. 'The food
was excellent, the wine list extensive,
both enhanced by the extraordinary bay
views.' Reached up a 'charming' spiral
staircase (or by a small lift), curved
corridors, quirky bedrooms. 'Our
spacious room had an excellent bed, a
neat arrangement of cupboards; a fridge
with milk.' Morning brings 'a good
breakfast'. Ideal for the midday Isle
of Man ferry. BEDROOMS 44, 2 suitable
for disabled. OPEN all year. FACILITIES
lift, lounge, bar/café, restaurant,
free Wi-Fi, in-room TV, function
rooms, civil wedding licence, beauty
treatments, parking. BACKGROUND MUSIC
'1930s/1950s music' in bar, restaurant.
LOCATION overlooking Morecambe
Bay. CHILDREN all ages welcomed. DOGS
welcomed (not in restaurant). CREDIT
CARDS Amex, MasterCard, Visa. PRICES
per room B&B £125–£400. D,B&B
£181–£456.

MORETON-IN-MARSH
Gloucestershire
Map 3:D6

THE OLD SCHOOL, Little Compton,,
GL56 0SL 07831 098271, www.
theoldschoolbedandbreakfast.com.
Epicurean delights and country
comforts add up to a top-notch B&B
in a Cotswolds village. Food writer and
stylist Wendy Vale welcomes visitors
to her Victorian schoolhouse B&B
with a relaxing cuppa and home-made
cake in the vast old school hall, now a
downstairs dining room and vaulted
upstairs living room with wood-burner
and sofas. Fresh blooms add to the cheer
of the cosy bedrooms, each supplied
with a super king-sized bed, fluffy
bathrobes, complimentary refreshments
and thick towels. The day starts with
freshly ground coffee, tasty granola, WI
jams and jellies, and 'eggs in all guises',
cooked by the hostess. Gold-star dinners
(BYOB) and even picnic hampers ('rugs
and brollies included') can be arranged.
BEDROOMS 4, 1 on ground floor. OPEN all
year. FACILITIES 2 sitting rooms, dining
room, free Wi-Fi (computer available),
in-room TV (BT, Freeview), 1-acre
garden, parking. BACKGROUND MUSIC
none. LOCATION 3 miles E of Moreton-
in-Marsh. CHILDREN over-12s welcomed.
DOGS not allowed. CREDIT CARDS Amex,
MasterCard, Visa. PRICES per room B&B
single £120–£135, double £135–£160.
2-night min. stay at weekends. 4-course
dinner (for 4 or more guests staying 2 or
more nights) £32.

MULLION Cornwall
Map 1:E2

POLURRIAN BAY HOTEL, Polurrian Road,
TR12 7EN. Tel 01326 240421, www.
polurrianhotel.com. Bird's-eye views
of the Lizard peninsula, little luxuries
and an relaxed air turn this clifftop
hotel (Luxury Family Hotels) into a
stress-busting retreat for the whole
family. Parents relax while children's
activities abound: rock-pool hopping, a
film club, art and cookery classes; there's
even an Ofsted-accredited crèche for

babies. The stunning coast views extend into the well-appointed bedrooms; in many, space for an extra bed or cot; some interconnect to accommodate a larger family. Informal, all-day menus are served in the lounge (or the terrace on balmy days); after the children's bedtime, more sophisticated meals are taken in the restaurant, perhaps macadamia crusted cod fillet, orzo, salsa verde. BEDROOMS 41, some on ground floor, 1 suitable for disabled. OPEN all year. FACILITIES lift, lounge, snug, dining room, cinema, nursery, games room, spa, 9-metre pool, free Wi-Fi, in-room TV, civil wedding licence, function facilities, 12-acre grounds, terrace. BACKGROUND MUSIC in dining areas. LOCATION in Mullion village. CHILDREN all ages welcomed. DOGS allowed in some bedrooms, not in restaurant or part of lounge. CREDIT CARDS Amex, MasterCard, Visa. PRICES per room B&B from £120, D,B&B from £190. À la carte £38. 2-night min. stay in peak season.

NETLEY MARSH Hampshire
Map 2:E2
SPOT IN THE WOODS, 174 Woodlands Road, SO40 7GL. Tel 02380 293784, www.spotinthewoods.co.uk. A metamorphosis is underway on the edge of the New Forest: formerly TerraVina, this comfortable Victorian villa has a new name and a revamped style. 'It still has the same happy service and high standards,' report Guide inspectors in 2018. Nina and Gérard Basset continue to run the show, if a little more in the background. 'We slept really well in our well-equipped bedroom (a little seating area, a capsule coffee machine, good lighting); the sparkling clean bathroom had a claw-footed bath, organic toiletries and generous towels.'

Three rooms have a patio garden, three a roof terrace. No need to rush: an all-day menu, including breakfast, is served in the large airy kitchen café, even after check-out. BEDROOMS 11. 3 on ground floor, 1 suitable for disabled. OPEN all year. FACILITIES café, free Wi-Fi, in-room TV (Sky, Freeview), 1½-acre grounds, bicycle storage. BACKGROUND MUSIC none. LOCATION 8 miles W of Southampton, 4 miles N of Lyndhurst. CHILDREN all ages welcomed. DOGS allowed in some bedrooms, all public areas. CREDIT CARDS Amex, MasterCard, Visa. PRICES per room B&B single £75–£145, double £85–£155. 2-night bookings preferred at weekends.

NEWBY BRIDGE Cumbria
Map 4: inset C2
THE SWAN HOTEL & SPA, The Colonnade, LA12 8NB. Tel 015395 31681, www.swanhotel.com. Surrounded by gardens that sweep down to the River Leven, the Bardsley family's 'good-value', child-friendly former 17th-century coaching house is a lively, welcoming spot. Guide inspectors in 2018 liked the 'affable, efficient staff', and the restaurant's 'brasserie atmosphere'. There's a playful vibe in the public areas (parrot-print wallpaper, up-to-date florals, pompom-fringed lampshades); the spa is cool-contemporary. A spectrum of bedrooms: from top-floor adult-only suites, to interconnecting family rooms. 'Ours was a good size with cheery furnishings; spoiling toiletries and vast towels in the well-equipped bathroom.' 'Excellent' food in the restaurant and 'clearly popular bar' was 'fresh-tasting, well-cooked'; 'the lemon posset and brioche bread-and-butter pudding were especially liked'. A

'truly outstanding' breakfast included home-made jams, 'fabulous hand-cut ham'. BEDROOMS 54, some suitable for disabled, plus 5 self-catering cottages. OPEN all year. FACILITIES sitting room, library, Swan Inn, restaurant, juice bar, free Wi-Fi, in-room TV (Sky), civil wedding licence, function facilities, spa (treatments), indoor pool, gym, terrace, 10-acre grounds, parking, mooring. BACKGROUND MUSIC in public areas. LOCATION 9 miles from Ulverston, Grange-over-Sands and Bowness-on-Windermere. CHILDREN all ages welcomed. DOGS allowed in pub only. CREDIT CARDS MasterCard, Visa. PRICES B&B £110–£450. À la carte £30. 2-night min. stay on bank holiday weekends.

NEWMARKET Suffolk
Map 2:B4

BEDFORD LODGE, Bury Road, CB8 7BX. Tel 01638 663175, bedfordlodgehotel.co.uk. Amid acres of 'lovely' rose gardens and landscaped lawns, this family-run hotel combines old-fashioned comfort and modern flourishes with 'superb service'. The town's racing heritage gallops through the former Georgian hunting lodge; racing silks and original artworks sit 'delightfully' against the regal palette and dark leather armchairs. In many of the 'well-maintained' bedrooms (some compact), guests awake to the sight of prize-winning steeds being put through their paces on the training gallops next door; the best room has a pretty balcony. In the restaurant, the menu has plenty of healthy options (no doubt appreciated by guests using the hotel's spa), as well as tempting indulgences (cakes, a champagne list). 'Excellent breakfasts.' BEDROOMS 77, some suitable for disabled. OPEN all year. FACILITIES bar, sitting room, library, restaurant, private dining room, free Wi-Fi, in-room TV (Sky, Freeview), civil wedding licence, function facilities, 3-acre grounds, spa facilities, gym. indoor pool, parking. BACKGROUND MUSIC in public areas. LOCATION in heart of city, close to A14 and all motorways. CHILDREN all ages welcomed. DOGS allowed on the terrace only. CREDIT CARDS Amex, MasterCard, Visa. PRICES per room B&B from £180. 2-night min. stay on bank holiday weekends.

NEWQUAY Cornwall
Map 1:D2

THE HEADLAND HOTEL, Headland Road, TR7 1EW. Tel 01637 872211, www.headlandhotel.co.uk. A Victorian pile almost as impressive as the Atlantic swell outside, the Armstrong family's child- and dog-friendly hotel overlooks one of Cornwall's surfing hotspots. It has its own surf academy teaching guests how to hang ten. Service may not always match the location. 'After a warm welcome we felt staff appeared indifferent to the guests,' wrote one reader, who also complained of a geriatric mattress. Most of the modern bedrooms have spectacular views stretching towards Fistral beach. Buckets and spades are available for the beach; games, books and DVDs suit rainy days; as do sessions at the cool, contemporary spa. Wild seascapes are an epic side dish to dining on the laid-back Terrace, or in sophisticated, white-tablecloth Samphire. BEDROOMS 95, 1 suitable for disabled, plus 39 self-catering cottages in the grounds. OPEN all year. FACILITIES lounges, bar, 2 restaurants, free Wi-Fi, in-room TV, civil wedding licence, conference/event facilities, 10-acre grounds, indoor and outdoor heated swimming pools, spa, gym, tennis. BACKGROUND MUSIC in restaurant. LOCATION on a rugged headland overlooking Fistral Beach. CHILDREN all ages welcomed. DOGS allowed in bedrooms and public spaces (£24 per night). CREDIT CARDS Amex, MasterCard, Visa. PRICES per room B&B single £70–£425, double £120–£475, D,B&B £180–£535. À la carte £36.

LEWINNICK LODGE, Pentire headland, TR7 1QD. Tel 01637 878117, lewinnicklodge.co.uk. Given the rugged setting and exhilarating Atlantic views, you might feel you were on the edge of the world. Turn inside, however, and this cliff-edge hotel is sleek and stylish, with a laid-back vibe. Most of the minimalist bedrooms watch over a vista that stretches towards Towan Head and pristine Fistral beach. A handful of ocean-view bedrooms, opened this year by owners Pete and Jacqui Fair, enjoy the same features: a comfy bed, home-made biscuits, binoculars; organic toiletries, a slipper bath. An 'uncomplicated, tasty' Cornish menu showcases the freshest seafood, with monthly-changing specials. Diners can sit by floor-to-ceiling windows in the 'busy, informal' restaurant and bar, or outside on the spectacular decked terrace. Good walks from the door. BEDROOMS 17, some suitable for disabled. OPEN all year. FACILITIES lift, bar, restaurant, free Wi-Fi, in-room TV, in-room spa treatments, parking. BACKGROUND MUSIC in public areas. LOCATION Pentire Headland, Newquay. CHILDREN all ages welcomed. DOGS allowed in some bedrooms and bar only. CREDIT CARDS Diners Club, MasterCard, Visa. PRICES per room B&B £155–£260. À la carte £28.

NORTHALLERTON Yorkshire
Map 4:C4

CLEVELAND TONTINE, Staddlebridge, DL6 3JB. Tel 01609 882671, www. theclevelandtontine.com. Travellers heading between London and Sunderland have long stopped at this Georgian hostelry which skirts the North York moors. Today, the former coaching inn (part of the Provenance Inns group) is much liked; a 'splendid' hotel where 'delicious food' is only one of the draws. The welcome is warm, the atmosphere homely. The drama of the 'wonderful, light-filled' drawing room is as much about its 'quirky' original features (plasterwork starfish, elephants, vines) as its bold styling. Equally dramatic are the well-appointed, individually designed bedrooms, some with a four-poster, a stand alone bath, designer wallpaper. Efficient sound insulation is appreciated. Candlelit dinners are cooked 'with flair'; a generous locally sourced breakfast includes 'proper, thick toast'. The Carpenters Arms, Felixkirk (see main entry) is a sister hotel. BEDROOMS 7. OPEN all year. FACILITIES lounge, bar, bistro, free Wi-Fi, in-room TV (Freeview), room service, function facilities, garden, parking. BACKGROUND MUSIC in public areas. LOCATION 8 miles NE of Northallerton. CHILDREN all ages welcomed. DOGS allowed in bar and lounge. CREDIT CARDS Amex, MasterCard, Visa. PRICES per room B&B £130–£170, D,B&B £200–£240. Set menu from £22, à la carte £35.

NORWICH Norfolk
Map 2:B5

NORFOLK MEAD, Church Loke, Coltishall, NR12 7DN. Tel 01603 737531, www.norfolkmead.co.uk.

'Perfect peace and quiet' drifts across 'lush grounds', from the River Bure up to James Holliday and Anna Duttson's 'splendid', wisteria-hung Georgian house. The relaxed atmosphere is in part thanks to 'informal, attentive' staff; spa treatments and plenty of cosy nooks do the rest. 'Well-equipped, individually decorated bedrooms', some snug, some spacious, have light uplifting decor. Some have a fireplace, others a four-poster, an in-room egg bath. Lighter sleepers might enquire about which rooms are quietest at booking. The cottage and summer houses in the grounds suit groups. The 'pleasant' dining room serves 'satisfactorily cooked, elaborately presented' modern British dishes. Come morning, breakfast is 'so good': home-made cereals, 'perfect scrambled eggs'. BEDROOMS 15, 2 in cottage, 3 in summer houses. OPEN all year. FACILITIES lounge, bar, snug, restaurant, private dining, 2 beauty treatment rooms, free Wi-Fi, in-room TV (Freeview), civil wedding licence, walled garden, fishing lake. BACKGROUND MUSIC in public areas. LOCATION approx. 20 mins' drive from Norwich. CHILDREN all ages welcomed. DOGS allowed in some rooms in grounds (£20 per night). CREDIT CARDS MasterCard, Visa. PRICES per room B&B from £135, D,B&B from £170. Set menus £31–£39.

OLD COLWALL Herefordshire
Map 3:D5
THE BULL SHED, The Barn, Park Farm, WR13 6HE. Tel 01684 541262, www. bullshedbarn.com. On a former dairy farm, Amanda and Lee Jay invite guests to 'rest, graze and roam' in their strikingly transformed 150-year-old barn. Vast glass doors open into a dramatic beamed space. 'Rest' begins on the oversized sofas by a roaring wood burner in the sitting room, and continues in the bedrooms above (some interconnecting). Rooms have a wide bed, fluffy bathrobes, a smart bathroom with luxury toiletries; the best gaze out at the Malvern hills. 'Graze' starts with the breakfast: the hostess, a MasterChef quarter-finalist, might whip up home-made granola, poached eggs on avocado, a Full Bull. Walking boots are a must: great 'roaming' from the door. A cooking school is planned. BEDROOMS 5. OPEN all year except Christmas, New Year. FACILITIES 2 lounge/dining areas, in-room TV (Freeview), free Wi-Fi, 8-acre grounds, parking. BACKGROUND MUSIC in guest lounges (requests taken). LOCATION 1 mile from village. CHILDREN over-7s welcomed. DOGS assistance dogs allowed. CREDIT CARDS Amex, MasterCard, Visa. PRICES per room B&B £135–£265. 2-night min. stay at weekends preferred. Exclusive use bookings available.

OUNDLE Northamptonshire
Map 2:B3
LOWER FARM, Main Street, Barnwell, PE8 5PU. Tel 01832 273220, www. lower-farm.co.uk. A series of disused outbuildings on the Marriott family's small arable farm has been converted into homely B&B rooms. Surrounded by fields and fresh air, it's a wholesome setting. Robert Marriott and his brother, John, run the farm; Caroline Marriott is the 'friendly, accommodating' hostess. Simple, attractive bedrooms, arranged around a central courtyard, occupy the converted milking parlour and stables; several may be connected to suit a family. The hearty farmhouse breakfast might include porridge with

fresh cream, a farmer's butty, steak and eggs (a speciality); ideal fuel for tackling walking and cycling tracks from the door, including the Nene Way footpath which runs through the farm. BEDROOMS 10, all on ground floor, 1 suitable for disabled. OPEN all year. FACILITIES breakfast room, free Wi-Fi, in-room TV (Freeview), courtyard garden, parking. BACKGROUND MUSIC radio 'if guests wish' in breakfast room. LOCATION 3 miles from Oundle. CHILDREN all ages welcomed. DOGS allowed in 2 bedrooms, not in public rooms. CREDIT CARDS Amex, MasterCard, Visa. PRICES per person B&B £50–£90.
25% DISCOUNT VOUCHERS

OXFORD Oxfordshire
Map 2:C2
THE BELL AT HAMPTON POYLE,
11 Oxford Road, Hampton Poyle, OX5 2QD. Tel 01865 376242, www.thebelloxford.co.uk. Owner George Dailey revitalised this honey-stone roadside pub, north of Oxford, from a tired boozer into a popular village hub. Guests in 2018 were impressed by the welcoming atmosphere and 'very good evening meal, even after the Bell's exceptionally busy lunch'. Steaks, wood-fired pizzas, pub classics and British dishes with an out-of-the-box twist have locals flocking for the food. In the pub, flagstone floors and 18th-century beams have been preserved; deep leather chairs are set around a large log fire. Bedrooms, 'very comfortable and very clean', are well stocked with tea- and coffee-making facilities and posh toiletries; a bath or a monsoon shower. Blenheim Palace is not far away. BEDROOMS 9, 1 on ground floor. OPEN all year. FACILITIES 2 bars, library, restaurant, free Wi-Fi, in-room TV (Freeview), function facilities, terrace, parking. BACKGROUND MUSIC in bar. LOCATION 10 miles from Oxford, Bicester Village and Woodstock. CHILDREN all ages welcomed (no extra beds or facilities). DOGS allowed in bar, not in bedrooms. CREDIT CARDS Amex, MasterCard, Visa. PRICES per room B&B single £95–£150, double £120–£175. À la carte £30 (£15 3-course set menu Mon–Thurs, 6 pm–7.30 pm).

BURLINGTON HOUSE, 374 Banbury Road, OX2 7PP. Tel 01865 513513, www.burlington-hotel-oxford.co.uk. The scent of freshly baked bread wafts through this affable B&B in a leafy suburb, gently hailing the start of a new day. It's part of breakfast's minor feast: a help-yourself spread also ladened with freshly squeezed orange juice and freshly ground coffee, home-made granola and yogurt. Cooked to order, hot dishes include field mushrooms on toast, and there's an impressive omelette menu (perhaps filled with gruyère cheese or marmalade). Set about the main house and around the courtyard, the dapper bedrooms (some snug) all have a comprehensive refreshment tray with fruit teas and home-made biscuits. Frequent buses into the city; the bus stop is a minute down the road. BEDROOMS 12, 4 on ground floor, 2 in courtyard. OPEN all year except Christmas, New Year. FACILITIES sitting room, breakfast room, free Wi-Fi, in-room TV, small garden, limited parking. BACKGROUND MUSIC none. CHILDREN over-11s welcomed. DOGS allowed in bedrooms, public spaces. CREDIT CARDS Amex, MasterCard, Visa. PRICES per room B&B from £80. 1-night bookings sometimes refused at weekends.

VANBRUGH HOUSE HOTEL, 20–24 St Michael's Street, OX1 2EB. Tel 01865 244622, www.vanbrughhousehotel. co.uk. Conveniently located near the Oxford Union, this Cotswold-stone town house once held council offices; today it banishes the workaday as a 'friendly,' boutique hotel with 'very pleasant staff'. Within the thoughtfully restored conjoined 17th- and 18th-century buildings, designed by Sir John Vanbrugh (Blenheim Palace), elegant original fireplaces and handsome wood panelling complement bright design (rococo mirrors, vivid patterns, bespoke furnishings). The heritage-hued bedrooms (some small) are well equipped, with comfortable seating, a Nespresso machine, a daily-restocked refreshments tray ('a nice touch'); some bathrooms are 'small-ish'. Breakfasts include home-made jams; Cumberland or veggie sausages; 'nicely cooked eggs Benedict'. Light lunches are available; 'at dinner, the pick of Oxford's eateries is at the door'. BEDROOMS 22, 1 suitable for disabled. OPEN all year. FACILITIES breakfast room, free Wi-Fi, in-room TV (Freeview), small terrace, park-and-ride recommended. BACKGROUND MUSIC 'Soft classical in reception, easy-listening in the restaurant.' LOCATION Oxford town centre. CHILDREN all ages welcomed. DOGS not allowed. CREDIT CARDS Amex, MasterCard, Visa. PRICES per room B&B £176–£379. 2-night min. stay at weekends.

PENRITH Cumbria
Map 4: inset C2

THE HOUSE AT TEMPLE SOWERBY, Temple Sowerby, CA10 1RZ. Tel 017683 61578, www.templesowerby. com. In a Knights Templar village with a backdrop of imposing Cross Fell mountain, a Georgian mansion and converted coach house are home to a personable small hotel. Alison and Andi Sambrook took over as owners in January 2018. 'We were very impressed. They have an informal, friendly approach but maintain a high standard of service.' Elegant, country-style lounges have open fires and beams. Freshly redecorated bedrooms can be compact 'but they're comfortable'. Some might have a dressing area; a spa bath and separate shower. Road-facing rooms are reputedly quiet, but light sleepers might discuss options. Birdwatching is 'a perennial pursuit' in the verdant walled garden ('the engaging ducks' perhaps the easiest to spot). In the restaurant, chef Jack Bradley's 'interesting' seasonal modern menus are 'a real treat'. Walking boots won't be wasted. BEDROOMS 12, 2 on ground floor, 4 in coach house. OPEN all year. FACILITIES 2 lounges, bar, restaurant, conference/function facilities, free Wi-Fi, in-room TV (Freeview), civil wedding licence, 1½-acre garden; unsuitable for disabled. BACKGROUND MUSIC 'carefully chosen' music in restaurant in the evening. LOCATION village centre. CHILDREN over-12s welcomed. DOGS allowed in coach house rooms only (not unattended). CREDIT CARDS Amex, MasterCard, Visa. PRICES per room B&B £110–£170, D,B&B £150–£250. Set dinner £35–£45. 1-night bookings occasionally refused. 25% DISCOUNT VOUCHERS

PENZANCE Cornwall
Map 1:E1

ARTIST RESIDENCE CORNWALL, 20 Chapel Street, TR18 4AW. Tel 01736 365664, www.artistresidence.co.uk/ our-hotels/cornwall. Tucked into streets behind the harbour, this 'achingly cool' 17th-century house has 'lovely staff', 'well-appointed bedrooms' and 'tasty breakfasts'. Typical of Justin and Charlotte Salisbury's eclectic collection (see main entries for Artist Residence in London and in Brighton), it brims with 'intriguing artworks' and vintage flourishes. Bedrooms, mildly eccentric, are all different: one is small; another has expansive views; a third, a hand-painted mural soaring up the walls and across the ceiling. Whatever their angle, each is 'clean, comfortable', and has a Roberts radio, Nespresso machine, mini-fridge of local goodies, organic Bramley toiletries. Informal meals draw diners to the 'quirky' Cornish Barn restaurant/bar/smokehouse, perhaps 'truly stupendous beer-can-smoked chicken'. Breakfast is 'first-rate'. BEDROOMS 22 bedrooms, 1 suite, plus a 3-bedroom cottage. OPEN all year except Christmas Day. FACILITIES bar, restaurant, garden, free Wi-Fi, in-room TV (Freeview). BACKGROUND MUSIC in public areas. LOCATION town centre. CHILDREN all ages welcomed. DOGS allowed in some rooms and in the restaurant. CREDIT CARDS Amex, MasterCard, Visa. PRICES per room from £85–£440. 1-night stay sometimes refused at weekends.

VENTON VEAN, Trewithen Road, TR18 4LS. Tel 01736 351294, ventonvean. co.uk. A frisbee fling from the waterfront, Philippa McKnight and David Hoyes's intimate B&B is a soothing place to be beside the seaside. Striking colours, vintage furnishings and artistic flourishes complement rather than compete with the house's original Victorian stained-glass panels and fireplaces. There's a fabulously lush garden; an airy sitting room with plenty of books. The spacious bedrooms,

all elegant contemporary hues, some with painted floorboards, have a king-size bed and thoughtful extras (a refreshments tray, bathrobes, eco-friendly toiletries); one has an antique chandelier, hanging hooks reclaimed from the Savoy's cloakroom in London. Breakfasts keep food-miles low and creativity high: perhaps Mexican tortillas with hot salsa and fried eggs. BEDROOMS 5, 1 with adjoining single room, suitable for a family. OPEN all year except 25–26 Dec. FACILITIES sitting room, dining room, free Wi-Fi, in-room smart TV, garden. BACKGROUND MUSIC at breakfast in dining room. LOCATION 7 mins' walk from the centre of Penzance and Penzance seafront. CHILDREN over-4s welcomed. DOGS not allowed. CREDIT CARDS MasterCard, Visa. PRICES per room B&B single £72–£90, double £82–£100.

PRESTON Lancashire
Map 4:D2
BARTON GRANGE HOTEL, 746–768 Garstang Road, Barton, PR3 5AA. Tel 01772 862551, www.bartongrangehotel. com. 'An enjoyable menu' and 'enthusiastic, helpful staff' are highlights at the Topping family's large, 'very pleasant' hotel. The former country pile of a cotton mill owner, it offers easy access to the M6, making it 'an excellent stop-over spot'. Some of the well-appointed bedrooms are compact, but have been 'well designed to maximise space'; each has received a recent makeover. Time spent enjoying the residents-only spa facilities, including a swimming pool and new treatment rooms, rejuvenates before dinner. Served in the Walled Garden restaurant, the locally sourced 'beautifully cooked' dishes include Fleetwood hake fillet,

saffron potatoes, artichoke purée, baby leeks, crayfish tail, hazelnut burnt butter. Unhurried mornings call for the breakfast buffet; a 'grab-and-go' breakfast bag speeds things up. BEDROOMS 5, 8 in Garden House in the grounds, 1 suitable for disabled. OPEN all year. FACILITIES lift, lounge, snug, bistro/wine bar, meeting/private dining room, free Wi-Fi, in-room TV (Sky), civil wedding licence, leisure centre, parking. BACKGROUND MUSIC none. LOCATION 6 miles from Preston city centre. CHILDREN all ages welcomed. DOGS not allowed. CREDIT CARDS Amex, MasterCard, Visa. PRICES per room B&B from £69.

RAMSGATE Kent
Map 2:D6

THE FALSTAFF, 16–18 Addington Street, CT11 9JJ. Tel 01843 482600, www.thefalstaframsgate.com. Two 'tastefully refurbished' Regency town houses near the harbour combine into this 'buzzy, friendly' pub-with-rooms. Trusted readers in 2018 found the service 'efficient and personable, if a bit inconsistent'. Guests can take a real ale by the wood-burning stove, or have coffee with 'a slice of obviously home-made cake'. Sometimes there's live piano music. 'It's all a bit pleasantly unpredictable.' Heritage shades, vintage furnishings, oriental rugs and fine prints characterise the well-liked bar and the neatly done bedrooms. Each room is stylistically different and has 'a terrific bathroom'. 'Really pleasing breakfasts with good coffee and full English, not a cornflake packet in sight'; four nights a week, 'an interesting dinner menu'. BEDROOMS 8, plus 2 self-catering apartments. OPEN all year. FACILITIES bar, restaurant, deli, free Wi-Fi, in-room TV (Freeview), garden, parking, bicycle storage. BACKGROUND MUSIC in restaurant. LOCATION in town, a minute's walk to the seafront. CHILDREN all ages welcomed. DOGS allowed in 1 bedroom (garden access). CREDIT CARDS Amex, MasterCard, Visa. PRICES per room B&B £89–£139.

REETH Yorkshire
Map 4:C3

CAMBRIDGE HOUSE, Arkengarthdale Road, DL11 6QX. Tel 01748 884633, www.cambridgehousereeth.co.uk. An ideal base for exploring James Herriot country, Robert and Sheila Mitchell's 'relaxing, welcoming' B&B offers great walking and cycling routes, straight from the door – and 'splendid' facilities for wet or muddy kit. The owners 'are genuinely caring', writes a nominator in 2018; they provide a drying room, a boot-cleaning service and bicycle storage. Comfortable bedrooms with 'superb views' over Swaledale have fresh milk, biscuits, chocolates (all except the single have a bath and shower). Afternoons bring tea and home-made cake to the conservatory; the lounge has deep armchairs, a log fire in winter. 'Breakfast is a gastronomic adventure; every taste catered for. One can indulge in anything from a trout to speciality crumpets to a full Yorkshire.' BEDROOMS 5. OPEN all year, except 21 Dec–8 Feb. FACILITIES lounge, dining room, conservatory, free Wi-Fi, in-room TV (Freeview), small garden, terrace, parking. BACKGROUND MUSIC at breakfast. LOCATION 9 miles from Leyburn. CHILDREN over-11s welcomed. DOGS well-behaved dogs allowed by arrangement, in bedroom and conservatory only (not unattended, £5 per night). CREDIT CARDS MasterCard, Visa. PRICES per room B&B single £80–£100, double £95–£110.

RICHMOND Yorkshire
Map 4:C3

EASBY HALL, Easby, DL10 7EU. Tel 01748 826066, www.easbyhall.com. Overlooked by the ruins of Easby Abbey, Karen and John Clarke provide luxurious B&B accommodation in a rustic country house setting. Afternoon tea in the drawing room is a relaxed affair. Spacious suites, in a separate wing from the Georgian house, are sumptuous: a huge bed dressed with a velvet coverlet, throws and piles of cushions; a log-burner or open fire – a champagne fridge in each adds to the ambience. The dreamy gardens are fringed by woodland walks, an orchard, a paddock. Breakfast, at a time to suit the guest, has home-made preserves with fruit from the kitchen garden (anyone for gooseberry and elderflower?); poached pears from the orchard; local bacon; eggs from resident hens. BEDROOMS 3, 1 suitable for disabled, plus 2-bed self-catering cottage. OPEN all year. FACILITIES drawing room, dining room, free Wi-Fi, in-room TV (Freeview), gardens, paddocks, loose boxes and stables for horses. BACKGROUND MUSIC none. LOCATION less than 2 miles E of Richmond. CHILDREN all ages welcomed. DOGS 'Obedient, house-trained dogs allowed'. CREDIT CARDS none accepted. PRICES per room B&B single from £180, double from £216.
25% DISCOUNT VOUCHERS

RIPLEY Surrey
Map 2:D3

BROADWAY BARN, High Street, GU23 6AQ. Tel 01483 223200, www.broadwaybarn.com. Horticulture and history rub shoulders at Mindi McLean's B&B – her refurbished 200-year-old barn is just a few minutes' drive from RHS Wisley. Little luxuries fill the creatively decorated bedrooms: fresh flowers, dressing gowns, slippers, chocolates and home-made shortbread. Bathrooms, with underfloor heating, are stocked with complimentary toiletries; one has a raised slipper bath set against walls of artfully-illuminated exposed brick. Taken in the light-filled conservatory, breakfast has plenty of choice. Tables, overlooking the walled garden, are laden with fresh fruit, home-baked bread, home-made granola and preserves, village honey; daily specials might include a healthy eggs Benedict. In the evening, perhaps a foray to the Michelin-starred Clock House restaurant in the village High Street. BEDROOMS 4, plus self-catering flat and cottages. OPEN all year. FACILITIES conservatory sitting room/breakfast room, free Wi-Fi, in-room TV (Freeview), small garden. BACKGROUND MUSIC soft music during breakfast. LOCATION centre of small historic village. CHILDREN over-11s welcomed. DOGS not allowed. CREDIT CARDS Amex, MasterCard, Visa. PRICES per room B&B £120.

ROMSEY Hampshire
Map 2:E2

THE WHITE HORSE HOTEL & BRASSERIE, 19 Market Place, SO51 8ZJ. Tel 01794 512431, www.thewhitehorseromsey.co.uk. 'We enjoyed it greatly.' For centuries a focal point in this prosperous market town, this ever-evolving inn has been a hospitable spot. 'Smartly refurbished' with modern additions, it is run by 'friendly, professional staff', report readers this year. Individually decorated bedrooms retain characterful features such as exposed beams, sloping ceiling; loft apartments, over two floors, have a sitting area and solid oak flooring. In the clapboard coach house opposite, two large suites blend old with new (classic decor; a TV over the bath). Throughout the day, breakfasters, brunchers, lunchers and diners pile on to the leather seating and stripy banquettes in the sophisticated brasserie for 'excellent' meals. BEDROOMS 29, 3 in coach house opposite. OPEN all year. FACILITIES bar, 2 lounges, restaurant, 2 function rooms, free Wi Fi, in-room TV (Freeview), courtyard. BACKGROUND MUSIC in bar, brasserie. LOCATION town centre. CHILDREN all ages welcomed. DOGS allowed in bedrooms (£10 per night), not brasserie. CREDIT CARDS Amex, MasterCard, Visa. PRICES per room B&B £105–£295. A la carte £35.

RYE Sussex
Map 2:E5

THE HOPE ANCHOR, Watchbell Street, TN31 7HA. Tel 01797 222216, www. thehopeanchor.co.uk. The shipbuilders, boozy sailors and notorious Tenterden smuggling gang that once formed the clientele of this 18th-century watering hole, have been replaced by peace-seeking travellers bent on finding a decent meal. Guests of John Sankey's hotel, at the end of a cobbled street, stay in rooms that have old-fashioned tendencies but are 'warm and comfortable', and supplied with good essentials: a hospitality tray, a clock radio, slippers. Some rooms have a four- poster bed; many offer long views across the quayside, the Romney Marshes and Camber Castle. Traditional English dishes dominate the menu; daily fish specials showcase catch of the day, straight from Rye Bay. BEDROOMS 16, 3 in cottage and apartments, 10 yds away,

1 on ground floor with patio. OPEN all year. FACILITIES lounge, bar, restaurant, private dining room, free Wi-Fi, in-room TV (Freeview), wedding facilities, parking permits supplied. BACKGROUND MUSIC in public areas. LOCATION in the citadel of a medieval town. CHILDREN all ages welcomed. DOGS allowed in some bedrooms, not in restaurant. CREDIT CARDS Amex, MasterCard, Visa. PRICES per room B&B £95–£185, D,B&B £140–£200.

ST ALBANS Hertfordshire
Map 2:C3

SOPWELL HOUSE HOTEL, Cottonmill Lane, AL1 2HQ. Tel 01727 864477, sopwellhouse.co.uk. A country retreat just outside St Albans occupies an extended 300-year-old manor house, once the home of Lord Louis Mountbatten. The hotel is 'professional and well run', say inspectors in 2018. It has plush seating in the cosy cocktail lounge and an 'airy, pretty conservatory'. A choice for diners: the 'bustling brasserie' for classic bistro dishes, or the restaurant's sophisticated dining. 'Modern, clean lines' abound in the 'practical, neat, if slightly characterless' bedrooms, which have 'an excellent shower'; in the stable block are stylish 'more tasteful' mews suites. A gallery of signed football shirts reflects the hotel's popularity with top teams (Barcelona stayed here). There is a popular spa; several walled gardens are within the extensive grounds. Breakfast was 'plentiful, nicely served with freshly squeezed orange juice'. BEDROOMS 128, 16 mews suites. OPEN all year. FACILITIES cocktail lounge, bar, 2 restaurants, meeting and conference facilities, free Wi-Fi, in-room TV (Sky, BT), civil wedding licence, spa, indoor pool, gym,

12-acre grounds. BACKGROUND MUSIC in cocktail lounge. LOCATION 1.6 miles from the city centre and rail station. CHILDREN over-11s welcomed. DOGS not allowed. CREDIT CARDS Amex, MasterCard, Visa. PRICES per room £154–£459, D,B&B £204–£509. 3-course set dinner menu £31.50 (brasserie), £39.50 (restaurant).

ST AUSTELL Cornwall
Map 1:D2

LOWER BARNS, Lower Barn, PL26 6ET. Tel 01726 844881, lowerbarnswedding. co.uk. A faintly bohemian B&B on the Roseland peninsula throws riotous colour and eye-catching features together in joyful combinations. Each well-equipped, spacious, sybaritic bedroom in Janie and Mike Cooksley's Cornish abode (and in several quirky buildings accessed through the garden) has its own style. One has a stone-built sauna; another a gypsy caravan parked outside its front door; some have a chandelier, perhaps a modern four-poster. Informal dinners, arranged in advance, are served in the 'party shed' in the wild flower garden. Guests in three garden suites have breakfast delivered to the room; the rest gather in the conservatory for fresh fruit compotes, home-baked muffins, locally smoked fish, farm sausages, eggs all ways. BEDROOMS 8, 4 in the grounds, 1 suitable for disabled. OPEN all year. FACILITIES conservatory breakfast room, dining room, free Wi-Fi, in-room TV (BT), civil wedding licence, small function facilities, garden, gym, spa treatments, outdoor hot tub, parking. BACKGROUND MUSIC equipment 'so guests can play their own music' in one dining room. LOCATION 7 miles SW of St Austell, 1 mile past The Lost Gardens of Heligan. CHILDREN all ages welcomed. DOGS

allowed in 2 suites, with own bedding. CREDIT CARDS MasterCard, Visa. PRICES per room B&B £130–£180, D,B&B £230–£280. Set dinner £50. 2-night min. stay at weekends.

ST IVES Cornwall
Map 1:D1

HEADLAND HOUSE, Headland Road, Carbis Bay, TR26 2NS. Tel 01736 796647, www.headlandhousehotel. co.uk. A tranquil retreat from the bustle of nearby St Ives, Mark and Fenella Thomas's chic Edwardian house stands above Carbis Bay. Characterful, well-equipped bedrooms share marine and pale hues, but are otherwise individual; a garden room has loungers on a private deck; in another, beach views are best admired from a broad window seat; some rooms have a stand-alone bath near exposed stone walls. Afternoons bring home-made cake to the room, while a garden hammock is a relaxed spot to tackle a book from the lounge's collection, or a complimentary evening drink. Cornish breakfasts, hearty and organic, kickstart the day with a view across the water. BEDROOMS 9, 3 off the courtyard garden. OPEN mid-Mar–Oct. FACILITIES snug lounge, conservatory breakfast room, free Wi-Fi, in-room TV (Freeview), large front garden, terrace, parking. BACKGROUND MUSIC none. LOCATION 1½ from St. Ives centre, 5 mins from Carbis Bay beach. CHILDREN over-15s welcomed. DOGS allowed. CREDIT CARDS MasterCard, Visa. PRICES per room B&B from £169. 2-night min. stay preferred.

TREVOSE HARBOUR HOUSE, 22 The Warren, TR26 2EA. Tel 01736 793267, www.trevosehouse.co.uk. 'A great deal of effort has been put in by the owners and it shows.'; praise for Angela and Olivier Noverraz's 'delightful small B&B' by Guide readers this year. The 'beautifully appointed' 1850s mid-terrace house has bags of style. Tip-top tech mingles with vintage furnishings; coastal hues wash over the design-conscious decor. The cosy lounge has deep-cushioned chairs to sink into, books to borrow and cocktails to mix in the honesty bar. Individually styled bedrooms each have a large bed and organic toiletries; most overlook the harbour and the bay. Breakfast (outside or in the bright breakfast room) has home-made preserves, 'smoothie shots', good veggie-friendly cooked choices including sautéed mushroom cassette, crumbled goat's cheese on sourdough. BEDROOMS 6, 1 in rear annexe. OPEN mid-Apr–Dec. FACILITIES Snug, breakfast room, free Wi-Fi, in-room TV (BT), in-room treatments, terrace, limited parking close by. BACKGROUND MUSIC in snug. LOCATION town centre. CHILDREN over-11s welcomed. DOGS not allowed. CREDIT CARDS Amex, MasterCard, Visa. PRICES per room B&B £160–£275.

ST LEONARDS-ON-SEA Sussex
Map 2:E4

ZANZIBAR INTERNATIONAL HOTEL, 9 Eversfield Place, TN37 6BY. Tel 01424 460109, zanzibarhotel.co.uk. Brimming with an 'interesting collection' of curios from far-flung lands, Max O'Rourke's characterful seafront hotel is both 'splendidly quirky' and 'utterly relaxed'. While guests enjoy a welcome drink, 'efficient staff' take care of luggage. The distinctive bedrooms are set over several floors. Decorated to reflect different destinations, they have a 'huge variety': Antarctica is dazzlingly white, with a faux polar bear throw, floor-to-ceiling windows and 'wonderful sea views'; Manhattan is a loft with jukebox and aquarium coffee table. 'The busy road in front quietens at night.' A beachy bar offers cocktails and water views. Breakfast comes with a side dish of the day's newspapers, plus suggestions for outings and eateries. BEDROOMS 8, 1 on ground floor. OPEN all year. FACILITIES bar, breakfast room, free Wi-Fi, in-room TV (Freeview), garden. BACKGROUND MUSIC 'quiet' in bar. LOCATION seafront, 650 yds W of Hastings pier. CHILDREN over-5s welcomed. DOGS allowed in bedrooms (£30 per night). CREDIT CARDS Amex, MasterCard, Visa. PRICES per room B&B from £115. À la carte £35.

ST MARY'S Isles of Scilly
Map 1: inset C1

ST MARY'S HALL HOTEL, Church Street, Hugh Town, TR21 0JR. Tel 01720 422316, www.stmaryshallhotel. co.uk. Just beyond Hugh Town, this 'consistently good' hotel is minutes from two sandy beaches, and across from the Victorian church that shares its name. 'Very well run' by the 'knowledgeable, helpful' manager Roger Page, it has 'unfailingly friendly, efficient' staff. A wide staircase leads to bright, comfortable bedrooms with a large bed, luxury toiletries, home-made biscuits on a well-stocked tray; fresh milk, delivered daily in an insulated flask. Most rooms overlook the garden's sub-tropical plants and palm trees; one has spectacular views over the harbour to neighbouring islands. Chef Ben Hingston's 'delicious' dishes exploit fresh local seafood, meat from the owners' rare breeds farm. Breakfast brings freshly squeezed juice, smoked Devon trout with scrambled eggs. BEDROOMS 27. OPEN 16 Mar–16 Oct.

FACILITIES bar, 2 lounges, restaurant, free Wi-Fi, in-room TV (Freeview). BACKGROUND MUSIC in public areas. LOCATION 5-min. walk to the town centre, 10-min. walk to quay. CHILDREN all ages welcomed. DOGS allowed in ground-floor suites, public rooms. CREDIT CARDS MasterCard, Visa. PRICES per room single £84–£206, double £168–£306, D,B&B double £208–£346, À la carte £45.

ST MAWES Cornwall
Map 1:E2

THE ST MAWES HOTEL, 2 Marine Parade, TR2 5DW. Tel 01326 270 170, www.stmaweshotel.com. Gazing across to the harbour to St Anthony's Head, David and Karen Richards's casual, quayside spot is liked for its seaside charm and 'very good situation'. No residents' lounge, rather 'a large, open-plan ground-floor area'; interiors are 'beautifully done' with cheerily striped seating, local art, seafaring paraphernalia. Cocktails, nibbles and locals' salty tales are served in the lively bar; great plates, perhaps roast cod, shellfish bisque, peas, lettuce, in the Upper Deck restaurant, where 'provenance is important'. 'Very comfortable' bedrooms sport marine stripes; underfloor heating in the bathroom is welcome. Some suit a family. A decent breakfast includes toasted brioche with seared banana, peanut butter, Cornish honey. Big-sister hotel Idle Rocks is up the street (see main entry). BEDROOMS 7, 4 in annexe around the corner. OPEN all year. FACILITIES bar, lounge, restaurant, function/private dining room, free Wi-Fi, in-room TV (Freeview). BACKGROUND MUSIC all day in public areas, occasional live music in bar.

LOCATION village centre. CHILDREN all ages welcomed. DOGS allowed in bar, 2 bedrooms (bed, towel, bowl, treats, maps of local walks, £30 per stay). CREDIT CARDS all major cards. PRICES per room B&B from £190. 2-night min. stay at weekends.

ST MELLION Cornwall
Map 1:D3

PENTILLIE CASTLE, Paynters Cross, PL12 6QD. Tel 01579 350044, www. pentillie.co.uk. Historic grounds tumble away from this 'magnificent, lovingly restored' castellated mansion on the banks of the Tamar river. The grand country B&B is steeped in history. The Coryton family home for nearly 300 years, it has stately sitting rooms filled with antiques, old mirrors and original artwork; the open fires are ideal spots for afternoon tea or pre-dinner libation. On sunny days, the terrace takes over. Glorious views pour into the spacious bedrooms, each named after a family character. The morning meal hinges on estate-produced jams, honey, apple juice and eggs. Come evening, a three-course dinner every Thursday; on others, a 'DIY' Aga-warmed supper – a selection includes Looe Bay fish pie; slow-cooked beef shin lasagne (order in advance). BEDROOMS 9, 1 on ground floor, suitable for disabled. OPEN all year, exclusive use Christmas and New Year. FACILITIES morning room, drawing room, dining room, guest kitchen, free Wi-Fi, in-room TV (Freeview), civil wedding licence, 55-acre grounds, terrace, heated outdoor swimming pool. BACKGROUND MUSIC none. LOCATION near St Mellion, 20 mins' drive from Plymouth city centre. CHILDREN all ages welcomed. DOGS allowed in heated boot room, on lead in garden. CREDIT CARDS Amex,

MasterCard, Visa. PRICES per room B&B £155-£230. Set menu £35.
25% DISCOUNT VOUCHERS

SALCOMBE Devon
Map 1:E4

SALCOMBE HARBOUR HOTEL, Cliff Road, TQ8 8JH. Tel 01548 844444, www.harbourhotels.co.uk/hotels/salcombe. 'It was not only the view that made our stay, but the whole ambience,' writes a Guide regular this year, of this Victorian hotel and spa on the Salcombe estuary. Most of the soothingly yachtie bedrooms have a balcony, huge windows, and binoculars to exploit the 'stupendous' panorama. Inside, maritime stripes and shades of blue mix with porthole mirrors and the occasional lifebelt. Ice and lemon slices are delivered to the bedroom each evening, to complement gin or sherry from the decanters. Devon produce and the day's catch are served in Jetty restaurant and on the sunny terraces. While 'expensive', the final bill was 'a pleasant surprise'. The Chichester Harbour Hotel and Southampton Harbour Hotel (see Shortlist entries) are sisters. BEDROOMS 50, some suitable for disabled. OPEN all year. FACILITIES bar/lounge, Jetty restaurant, free Wi-Fi, in-room TV (Freeview), civil wedding licence, spa, private moorings. BACKGROUND MUSIC in public areas. LOCATION town centre. CHILDREN all ages welcomed. DOGS allowed in some bedrooms, not in public rooms. CREDIT CARDS Amex, MasterCard, Visa. PRICES per room B&B £175–£600, D,B&B £225–£650. À la carte £50. 1-night bookings sometimes refused.

SOUTH SANDS, Bolt Head, TQ8 8LL. Tel 01548 845 900, www.southsands.com. This lively hotel, in a sheltered cove, is surrounded by a wide terrace which faces the beach. The 'informal' lounge and, breezy bedrooms are styled in coastal colours. Rooms, each named after a sailing boat, and including suites large enough for a family, have seaside touches (seascape paintings; a seagull sculpture); those at the front have sea views. Preprandials out on the terrace might be followed by fresh-as-can-be seafood and other locally sourced fare, perhaps pan-fried monkfish, savoy cabbage, caramelised cabbage purée, pickled vegetables. Breakfast is extensive. Coastal paths start from the back door; a beautiful National Trust garden, Overbeck's, is up the hill. For pedestrians, the most fun way to reach the lively town centre is by taking the sea tractor, then the small ferryboat. BEDROOMS 27, 1 room suitable for disabled. OPEN all year. FACILITIES bar, restaurant, free Wi-Fi, in-room TV (Freeview), civil wedding licence, terrace. BACKGROUND MUSIC in restaurant and bar area. LOCATION on South Sands Beach just outside Salcombe town centre (a little bit more than a mile). CHILDREN all ages welcomed. DOGS allowed in some bedrooms. CREDIT CARDS MasterCard, Visa. PRICES per room B&B £75–£218. À la carte £45. 1-night bookings refused weekends in peak season.
25% DISCOUNT VOUCHERS

SALISBURY Wiltshire
Map 2:D2

LEENA'S GUEST HOUSE, 50 Castle Road, SP10 3RL Tel 07814 897907, www.leenasguesthouse.co.uk. A 15-minute walk from the cathedral, the Street family's 'first-rate guest house' provides good-value B&B accommodation. The 'informative, very helpful', multilingual hosts enjoy practising their French, German and Suomi with guests. The Edwardian house is modest and traditionally styled, but 'well decorated, comfortably appointed'. 'Immaculate' bedrooms have 'a comfortable bed, a choice of pillows, interesting toiletries'; the hospitality tray is supplied with chocolates and biscuits; some road noise might be expected. Served on pretty blue-and-white crockery, the 'imaginative' breakfast has 'good granola, delicious cooked salmon with scrambled eggs'; in season, berries from the garden. A nearby riverside footpath leads to the city centre. BEDROOMS 6, 1 on ground floor. OPEN Apr–Dec. FACILITIES lounge, breakfast room, free Wi-Fi, in-room TV (Freeview), garden, parking. BACKGROUND MUSIC ambient from kitchen. LOCATION 12 mins' walk via pretty riverside footpaths to town centre and Salisbury cathedral. CHILDREN all ages welcomed. DOGS not allowed. CREDIT CARDS none accepted. PRICES [2018] per room B&B £90–£150.

SCARBOROUGH Yorkshire
Map 4:C5

PHOENIX COURT 8–9 Rutland Terrace, Queens Parade, YO12 7JB. Tel 01723 501150, www.phoenixcourt.co.uk. Overlooking the surf-licked sands of North Bay, Donna and Mike Buttery's unassuming guest house is liked for its 'good central position' and the 'warm welcome' of the hosts. Spacious, no-nonsense bedrooms are kept spic-and-span; many have superb sea views, all have a hospitality tray, toiletries. 'We slept well.' There's a new honesty bar. Come morning, in the dining room, recently refreshed with contemporary grey and pale hues, a 'great breakfast': a Yorkshire smoked kipper, Wensleydale

cheese and fruit bread, a full English (Mike's big breakfast), and vegetarian version thereof. Walkers and cyclists welcomed; a packed lunch can be ordered. The private car park is a bonus. BEDROOMS 13, 1 on ground floor. OPEN New Year, Feb–Nov. FACILITIES lounge (bar area), breakfast room, free Wi-Fi, in-room TV (Freeview), drying facilities, parking. BACKGROUND MUSIC local radio in breakfast room. LOCATION 10 mins' walk from the town centre and South Bay. CHILDREN all ages welcomed. DOGS not allowed. CREDIT CARDS MasterCard, Visa. PRICES per room B&B £40–£85.

SEDBERGH Cumbria
Map 4:C3

THE MALABAR, Garths, Marthwaite, LA10 5ED. Tel 015396 20200, www. themalabar.co.uk. Surrounded by walking country, Graham and Fiona Lappin's B&B at the foot of the Howgill fells in the far western Dales is a welcome sight for hikers and tea connoisseurs. Home-baked treats, plus a choice of 12 different teas, welcome arriving guests. The restored 18th-century cattle barn now houses chic, spacious accommodation with original stone walls and oak beams; warm colours and block-print fabrics reflect the owners' time spent in India and southeast Asia – as does the freshly made lassi at breakfast. Taken at a communal table or in the garden (at a time to suit), it also offers home-baked bread, seasonal juices and local specials, perhaps wild boar bacon or venison sausages. Simple suppers may be pre-booked. BEDROOMS 6, 1 family suite with private entrance. OPEN all year. FACILITIES bar, sitting room, dining room, free Wi-Fi, in-room

TV (Freeview), ⅓ acre garden, parking. BACKGROUND MUSIC in public areas at meal times. CHILDREN all ages welcomed. DOGS allowed in 1 suite. CREDIT CARDS MasterCard, Visa. PRICES per room single £140–£220, double £160–£240.

SEDGEFORD Norfolk
Map 2:A5

MAGAZINE WOOD, Peddars Way, nr Hunstanton, PE36 5LW. Tel 01485 750740, www.magazinewood.co.uk. The wild Norfolk coast is minutes away from the rustic luxury of Pip and Jonathan Barber's chic B&B in the countryside. Suites are all self-contained; each luxurious room has light, contemporary hues, harmonious prints and artworks, its own entrance and terrace. Boutique styling supplies each with a large bed, mood lighting; in the bathroom, a deep bath and separate shower. Thoughtful extras add to the cocoon: books, DVDs, binoculars; a tablet computer serves as online concierge, to summon breakfast, download a newspaper, create a bespoke itinerary. The day begins 'anytime': a well-stocked cupboard contains muesli, cereals, fruits and croissants; milk, organic yogurts are in the fridge. Cooked breakfasts are ordered the night before (charged extra). BEDROOMS 3, all on ground floor, 2 in converted barn. OPEN all year except Christmas. FACILITIES free Wi-Fi, in-room TV (on-demand movies), 3-acre grounds, parking. BACKGROUND MUSIC none. LOCATION 5 miles from Hunstanton. CHILDREN infants welcomed. DOGS allowed (not unattended) in 1 bedroom. CREDIT CARDS MasterCard, Visa. PRICES per room B&B £115–£144. Cooked breakfast £5–£7. 2-night min. stay most weekends.

SHANKLIN Isle of Wight
Map 2:E2

RYLSTONE MANOR, Rylstone Gardens, Popham Road, PO37 6RG. Tel 01983 862806, www.rylstonemanor.co.uk. Atop the cliffs of Sandown Bay, Mike and Carole Hailston's 'delightfully relaxing' island hotel enjoys a 'lovely' setting: it stands within the perimeter of public gardens with steps leading down to the sands. There is plenty of space inside the 19th-century gentleman's residence, where sitting rooms and bar sport rich hues, period furnishings and leaded windows. Some of the traditionally styled bedrooms offer tantalising glimpses of the sea through leafy trees. A daily-changing menu of modern and classic dishes is served in the chandelier-lit dining room, perhaps herb-crusted sea bass fillet, Pernod and thyme jus. The secluded private garden surroundiong the house is 'a pleasant place to sip wine'. The Hailstons are founts of Isle of Wight information. BEDROOMS 9. OPEN 8 Feb–2 Nov. FACILITIES drawing room, bar/lounge, dining room, free Wi-Fi, in-room TV (Freeview), terrace, ¼-acre garden in 4-acre public gardens. BACKGROUND MUSIC none. LOCATION Shanklin old village. CHILDREN over-16s welcomed. DOGS assistance dogs allowed. CREDIT CARDS MasterCard, Visa. PRICES per room B&B single £110–£125, double £135–£165, D,B&B double £193–£223. 2-night min. stay in peak season. **25% DISCOUNT VOUCHERS**

SHEFFORD WOODLANDS
Berkshire
Map 3:E6

THE PHEASANT INN, Ermin Street, RG17 7AA. Tel 01488 648284, www. thepheasant-inn.co.uk. Popular with the racing fraternity and couples in search of a weekend escape, this old sheep drover's inn is on the village outskirts, with wide views over the Berkshire Downs. Its modern rural revamp from owner Jack Greenall has given the cosy, traditional snug a rich colour scheme. The old settle and deep armchair by an open fire are ideal to sink into with a good book – and there are plenty to borrow. Fresh, comfortable bedrooms have well-chosen fabrics, wallpaper and artwork, along with a Roberts radio, Bramley toiletries, plush robes. Chef Andy Watts's elevated pub food (locally sourced where possible) is served in the large, light-filled restaurant. Breakfast is an occasion worth rising for. BEDROOMS 11. OPEN all year. FACILITIES bar, restaurant, private dining room, free Wi-Fi, in-room TV (Sky), courtyard, garden, parking. BACKGROUND MUSIC in public areas. LOCATION 15 mins from Newbury. CHILDREN all ages welcomed. DOGS allowed, by arrangement. CREDIT CARDS Amex, MasterCard, Visa. PRICES per person B&B £115–£135. À la carte £28.

SHERBORNE Dorset
Map 2:E1

THE EASTBURY HOTEL, Long Street, DT9 3BY. Tel 01935 813131, www. theeastburyhotel.co.uk. The 'lovely' walled garden surrounding this small hotel gives it a country house vibe in the middle of this historic market town. The 'pleasant retreat', taken over in 2018 by Peter and Lana de Savary, has been restored to its Edwardian splendour. Bedrooms are 'comfortable, well furnished', all different. Some have a private garden. The bar and lounge serve afternoon teas and light bites, also available on the terrace in

good weather. Come evening, the restaurant offers 'tasty' seasonal menus with such dishes as venison loin, salt baked swede, kale, toasted oats, crispy sage. Plans are afoot for a spa and new garden suites. Sherborne Abbey is close by. BEDROOMS 23, 3 with external access, 1 suitable for disabled. OPEN all year. FACILITIES drawing room, lounge, bar, library, conservatory restaurant, private dining room, free Wi-Fi, in-room TV (Freeview), wedding/function facilities, terrace, 1-acre walled garden. BACKGROUND MUSIC in bar and restaurant. LOCATION town centre. CHILDREN all ages welcomed. DOGS allowed in bedrooms and lounge only (£20 per night). CREDIT CARDS Amex, MasterCard, Visa. PRICES per room B&B single £110–£130, £170–£295, D,B&B single £149–£169, double £248–£373. Tasting menu £45.

THE KINGS ARMS, North Street, Charlton Horethorne, DT9 4NL. Tel 01963 220281, www.thekingsarms. co.uk. Hands-on chef/patron Sarah Lethbridge and her husband, Anthony, have entertained guests at their restored stone-walled country pub for ten years. Colourful, individually styled bedrooms overlook the pretty village (four miles outside Sherborne) or the croquet lawn; in each, towelling bathrobes and a good refreshments tray. Though roadside, 'I wasn't aware of any noise.' The day's newspapers are stacked in the snug, which is warmed by a wood-burning stove. Public rooms have myriad artworks (all for sale). 'Very friendly bar staff serve local ales and ciders in the modern country-style bar. Innovative takes on classic pub grub in the restaurant include roast lamb rump, pommes

Anna, pea, lettuce, mint fricassee, redcurrant jus. BEDROOMS 10, 1 suitable for disabled. OPEN all year, limited service over Christmas, New Year. FACILITIES lift, snug, bar, restaurant, free Wi-Fi, in-room TV (Freeview), terrace, garden, free use of local sports centre, discounts at Sherborne Golf Club, parking. BACKGROUND MUSIC none. LOCATION in village 4 miles NE of Sherborne. CHILDREN all ages welcomed. DOGS allowed in bar. CREDIT CARDS MasterCard, Visa. PRICES per room B&B from £145. À la carte £30–£35.

SHREWSBURY Shropshire
Map 3:B4

CHATFORD HOUSE, Chatford, Bayston Hill, SY3 0AY. Tel 01743 718301, www.chatfordhouse.co.uk. 'All-round first-class hosts', Christine and Rupert Farmer offer guests a slice of the good life at their B&B on a small organic farm – and greet them with a piece of home-baked cake. Close to the Shropshire Way, the 18th-century farmhouse has cottage-style bedrooms full of spoiling touches: fresh flowers, magazines, and a regularly topped-up hospitality tray. In each, views of the pretty garden or towards the Wrekin. Come morning, Aga-cooked breakfasts use the owners' produce; home-made jams and local honey sweeten the feast. Great walks from the garden gate, beginning with the orchard and a visit to the farm animals. Not much further afield is Lyth Hill. BEDROOMS 3. OPEN all year, limited service over Christmas, New Year. FACILITIES sitting room, breakfast room, free Wi-Fi, in-room TV, garden, orchard, parking. BACKGROUND MUSIC none. LOCATION 4 miles S of Shrewsbury. CHILDREN all ages welcomed. DOGS assistance dogs allowed, all others allowed by prior arrangement only. CREDIT CARDS none accepted. PRICES per room B&B single £60, double £75–£85.

GROVE FARM HOUSE, Condover, SY5 7BH. Tel 01743 718544, www.grovefarmhouse.com. Just outside a village near Shrewsbury stands this idyllic Georgian house where Liz Farrow's guests are spoiled by cosseting hospitality. The third-generation owner of the peaceful B&B welcomes all with tea and cake. The country cottage-style bedrooms, on the first and second floors, are provided with home-made shortbread and garden blooms, fluffy bathrobes and lush toiletries. A DVD-player and library mean that cosy nights in are on the cards. Come morning, the hostess's home-baked bread and muffins, and home-made granola, underpin a generous buffet; dishes cooked to order use eggs from the garden hens, meats from nearby farms. Local walks and eateries abound; Liz has ready advice to tailor the day's plans. BEDROOMS 4, plus 2 self-catering suites. OPEN all year except Christmas, New Year. FACILITIES lounge, dining room, free Wi-Fi, in-room TV (Freeview), ½-acre garden, parking. BACKGROUND MUSIC none. LOCATION ¾ miles from Condover. 5½ miles S of Shrewsbury town centre. CHILDREN all ages welcomed. DOGS not allowed. CREDIT CARDS MasterCard, Visa. PRICES per room B&B single from £75, double from £100. 2-night min. stay Apr–Sept.

LION AND PHEASANT, 49–50 Wyle Cop, SY1 1XJ. Tel 01743 770345, www.lionandpheasant.co.uk. Original character and voguish style combine at this centrally located 16th-century coaching inn 'with easy access to all parts of the city'. Much liked are the 'friendly staff' and 'well-cooked modern dishes'. In the buzzy bar, regional real ales, flagstone floors, exposed beams and open fireplaces. 'The upper floor of the split-level restaurant is the nicer place to eat', perhaps braised lamb shoulder, pommel purée, great onion, shallot and wild garlic. 'We were well satisfied.' Upstairs, the bedrooms display minimalist design; in some, river views; a contemporary four-poster; a magnificent array of exposed loft timber; in all, 'a comfortable bed; a good shower'. Rooms at the rear are quietest. Breakfast is varied and plentiful. BEDROOMS 22. OPEN all year except 25–26 Dec. FACILITIES 2 bars, restaurant, function room, free Wi-Fi, in-room TV (Freeview), garden terrace, parking (narrow entrance). BACKGROUND MUSIC in public areas, occasional live music in bar. LOCATION central, near English Bridge. CHILDREN all ages welcomed. DOGS allowed on garden terrace only. CREDIT CARDS MasterCard, Visa. PRICES per room B&B single from £99, doubles from £115. À la carte £38.

SIDMOUTH Devon
Map 1:D5

VICTORIA HOTEL, The Esplanade, EX10 8RY. Tel 01395 512651, victoriahotel. co.uk. 'Blissfully old-fashioned', this large, traditional hotel is steps from the sheltered bay that has attracted visitors since Victorian times. Its regular crowd returns for the 'sumptuous bedrooms', 'delightful gardens' and 'unfailingly helpful staff'; Saturday-night dinner-dances are the icing on the cake. 'Wonderful' esplanade views pour in through bay windows in the sun lounge, and into most of the comfortably conservative bedrooms (some have a private balcony). Come evening, a chocolate is left on the pillow during the 'immaculate' turn-down. Diners eat to live music in the Jubilee restaurant; and enjoy chef Stuart White's modern, French-inflected menu in the informal White Room restaurant. The garden has restful benches among the flowerbeds. BEDROOMS 61, 3 poolside suites. OPEN all year except 25–26 Dec. FACILITIES sun lounge, lounge bar, 2 restaurants, free Wi-Fi, in-room TV (Sky, Freeview), spa, garden, outdoor and indoor swimming pools, tennis court, putting, parking. BACKGROUND MUSIC in public areas. CHILDREN all ages welcomed. DOGS not allowed. CREDIT CARDS MasterCard, Visa. PRICES per room B&B from £254. Set dinner £42, à la carte £48. 2-night min. stay.

SISSINGHURST Kent
Map 2:D5

THE MILK HOUSE, The Street, TN17 2JG. Tel 01580 720200, themilkhouse. co.uk. Guests to Dane and Sarah Allchorne's 'enjoyable' pub-with-rooms may well feel like the cats that got the cream. The 16th-century hall house blends a buzzy, village-hub feel with a jocund dairy theme. Bedrooms with such names as Byre, Buttery, Churn, are unfussily voguish, decorated in creamy palette, and with a 'very comfortable bed', and fresh flowers in milk pails. Rear rooms are quietest. Proper pub food, cask ales and local beers are served alongside wood-fired pizza under the bar's timber beams. The Tudor fireplace is lit on cold days. More creative, modern plates are served in the rustic dining room, perhaps chargrilled pork chop, champ mash, spring leeks, sage butter. Breakfast is a feast. BEDROOMS 4. OPEN all year. FACILITIES bar, restaurant, private dining room, free Wi-Fi, in-room TV (Freeview), sun terrace, large garden, parking. BACKGROUND MUSIC in bar and restaurant. LOCATION in village. CHILDREN all ages welcomed. DOGS allowed in bar and garden only. CREDIT CARDS Amex, MasterCard, Visa. PRICES per room B&B from £80. 2-night min. stay at weekends.

SISSINGHURST CASTLE FARMHOUSE,
nr Cranbrook, TN17 2AB. Tel 01580 720992, www. sissinghurstcastlefarmhouse.com. Sue and Frazer Thompson's serene Victorian farmhouse B&B draws garden-lovers on pilgrimage, and history buffs – and everyone in between. It is sheltered by a National Trust estate of ancient woodland, farmland (guests have out-of-hours access) and Vita Sackville-West's acclaimed gardens. The peaceful, country-style bedrooms mix contemporary and period furniture; mullioned windows look out at the estate or towards Sissinghurst Castle's Elizabethan tower (where imprisoned French naval officers received more robust hospitality during the Seven Years' War). Served in the sitting room or on the south-facing lawn, guests are welcomed with tea and home-baked cake. Breakfast brings a spread of Kentish orchard fruits, locally smoked bacon and salmon, hearty sausages. Picnic lunches can be arranged. BEDROOMS 7, 1 suitable for disabled. OPEN Mar–Nov. FACILITIES lift, sitting room, dining room, free Wi-Fi, in-room TV, small functions, ¾-acre garden. BACKGROUND MUSIC none. LOCATION on the National Trust estate known as Sissinghurst Castle, a mile from the centre of Sissinghurst village. CHILDREN all ages welcomed. DOGS allowed in bar and garden only. CREDIT CARDS MasterCard, Visa. PRICES per room

B&B £150–£200. 2-night min. stay at weekends, Easter–Sept.

SOMERTON Somerset
Map 1:C6
THE WHITE HART, Market Place, TA11 7LX. Tel 01458 272273, whitehartsomerton.com. A foodie destination skirting the Somerset Levels, this rustic-chic pub-with-rooms gathers praise for its 'superb meals' and quirky, well-appointed bedrooms. Its menu of British pub classics, interspersed with more innovative fare, is 'top notch'. Hungry guests flock to the cosy bar with its wood-burning stove, and the conservatory dining room; on clement days, outdoor picnic benches are laden. Careful details (Moorish tiles, a listing Pink Panther clinging to a lampshade) bring a whimsical air to the well-equipped bedrooms; each has a large bed, deep-pile towels, natural toiletries. A leisurely breakfast (served till 11 am) includes such dishes as smashed avocado on malted toast, chilli sauce, slow-roasted tomatoes. Part of the small Stay Original Company; see also Timbrell's Yard, Bradford-on-Avon (Shortlist). BEDROOMS 8. OPEN all year (except 1 day at end of July). FACILITIES bar, restaurant, free Wi-Fi, in-room smart TV, large courtyard garden, bicycle storage. BACKGROUND MUSIC in bar. LOCATION in town centre. CHILDREN all ages welcomed. DOGS allowed in bedrooms (£10 per dog per stay). CREDIT CARDS Diners Club, MasterCard, Visa. PRICES per room B&B from £85, D,B&B from £100. À la carte £27.

SOUTH ALKHAM Kent
Map 2:D5
ALKHAM COURT, Meggett Lane, nr Dover, CT15 7DG. Tel 01303 892056, www.alkhamcourt.co.uk. 'Simply the very best,' wrote one reader this year.

From on high, Wendy and Neil Burrows's farmhouse enjoys stunning sunsets over the Alkham valley. B&B guests are offered 'delicious' home-made cake on arrival, a picnic for walks on the Kent Downs; an evening bowl of soup; the chance to unwind in the the sauna. 'I felt truly looked after,' another reader enthuses. 'Wendy and Neil are warm, attentive hosts.' Discreet bedrooms each have a private entrance; within the country-style rooms: fresh flowers, robe and slippers, coffee machine, mini-fridge, biscuits and complimentary sherry; expansive rustic views. An oak-framed shepherd's hut in the garden has a log-burner. An 'outstanding' breakfast brings home-baked muffins, local pressed apple juice, garden-fresh eggs. 'I wish we could have stayed for weeks.' BEDROOMS 4, plus shepherd's hut, 1 suitable for disabled. OPEN all year except 24–25 Dec. FACILITIES sitting/breakfast room, free Wi-Fi, in-room TV (Freeview), spa barn, large garden within 60-acre grounds, parking. BACKGROUND MUSIC none. LOCATION in a rural location near Dover; 20 mins' drive from Canterbury. 5 mins from M20, 10 mins from Eurotunnel and Port of Dover. CHILDREN all ages welcomed. DOGS allowed in Garden Room, in Sun Room; must be on lead at all times outside because of livestock (£10 per night). CREDIT CARDS MasterCard, Visa. PRICES per room B&B single £80–£100, double £140–£170; 2-bedroom family suite £240. 2-night min. stay on bank holiday weekends and in high season.
25% DISCOUNT VOUCHERS

SOUTH BRENT Devon
Map 1:D4
GLAZEBROOK HOUSE, Glazebrook, TQ10 9JE. Tel 01364 73322, www. glazebrookhouse.com. 'Full of surprises': curiosities and vintage pieces burst through Fran and Pieter Hamman's 19th-century manor house on the edge of Dartmoor national park. The 'zany' styling is inspired by Alice in Wonderland. Drums, hats and old street signs adorn the walls; chandeliers and a stuffed flamingo decorate the hall. 'Large, bright' bedrooms continue the theme: Mad Hatter has a display of antique plates; Tweedle Deez has twin four-poster beds. Amenities are luxurious: a smartly tiled, Escher-esque bathroom; abundant extras, including chocolates, mini-bottles of wine. The glamorous bar has local beers, custom cocktails; the 'pleasant, airy' dining room serves chef Ben Palmer's imaginative dishes, perhaps pan-fried market fish, shellfish orzo, crispy soft shell crab. Guided walking tours are available on Dartmoor. BEDROOMS 9, 1 on ground floor, 1 suitable for disabled. OPEN all year. FACILITIES bar, drawing room, library, restaurant, Chef's Kitchen patio, free Wi-Fi, in-room TV (Freeview), civil wedding licence, 3½-acre mature garden, parking. BACKGROUND MUSIC in public areas, except library and tasting room. LOCATION 1 mile SW of town center CHILDREN over-15s welcomed. DOGS not allowed. CREDIT CARDS all major cards. PRICES per room B&B £199–£324. À la carte £45.
25% DISCOUNT VOUCHERS

SOUTHAMPTON Hampshire
Map 2:E2
SOUTHAMPTON HARBOUR HOTEL, Ocean Village, SO14 3QT. Tel 0238 110 3456, www.harbourhotels.co.uk/ hotels/southampton. A taste of life at sea is creating waves at this large, contemporary hotel jutting out over

Ocean Village Marina. It is managed by Simon Maguire for Harbour Hotels. Ship-shape inside, it is bright, with colourful fabrics; porthole-shaped mirrors, vintage glass fish floats, a giant lobster, adding nautical fun. A chunky white stairway leads up from the wood-floored lobby. Bedrooms have pale-toned walls, retro furnishing and marble bathroom. A bathrobe, slippers, coffee machine and complimentary grog (decanters of gin and sherry) are supplied. For cocktails and light bites, the buzzing sixth-floor HarBar has wonderful (if also industrial) harbour views. An abundance of sea-sourced dishes features in the award-winning Jetty restaurant. BEDROOMS 85, 6 apartments, some suitable for disabled. OPEN all year. FACILITIES bar, restaurant, café, free Wi-Fi, in-room TV (Freeview), indoor swimming pools, gym, valet parking. BACKGROUND MUSIC in public areas. LOCATION on marina. CHILDREN all ages welcomed. DOGS assistance dogs only. CREDIT CARDS Amex, MasterCard, Visa. PRICES per room B&B £165–£650, D,B&B £220–£705. Set menu £30. À la carte £25.95. 2-night min. stay during Southampton Boat Show and Cowes Week.

WOODLANDS LODGE HOTEL, Bartley Road, SO40 7GN. 02380 292257, www. woodlands-lodge.co.uk. Touring dogs and their discerning owners are warmly welcomed at Imogene and Robert Anglaret's 'perfect little dog-friendly hotel' which has walkies straight into the surrounding New Forest. Seven spacious bedrooms in the former hunting lodge (two with direct garden access) are set aside for man's best friend, who receives a treat, a blanket and a towel on arrival; the owner will perhaps be more pleased by the smart, modern, country design, and the wide garden and woodland views. Dogs may accompany owners eating in the bar and lounge; Hunters restaurant serves all-day light bites, while the Cattle Grid offers more substantial fare using locally sourced and grown ingredients. BEDROOMS 17, 2 with garden access, 1 suitable for disabled. OPEN all year. FACILITIES lounge, bar, conservatory, restaurant, free Wi-Fi in public areas, in-room TV (Freeview), civil wedding licence, business facilities, 3-acre garden. BACKGROUND MUSIC radio or 'easy listening' in bar and restaurant. LOCATION 4 miles outside Lyndhurst, approx 1 mile from Ashurst train station, 15 mins' drive from Southampton. CHILDREN all ages welcomed. DOGS allowed in some bedrooms, bar, lounge. CREDIT CARDS MasterCard, Visa. PRICES per room B&B from £69, D,B&B from £129.

SOUTHWOLD Suffolk
Map 2:B6

SUTHERLAND HOUSE, 56 High Street, IP18 6DN. Tel 01502 724 544, www. sutherlandhouse.co.uk. In a handsome 15th-century building on the High Street, Andy and Kinga Rudd's restaurant-with-rooms casts modern fabrics, and contemporary and vintage furnishings against aged beams, elm floorboards and medieval windows. It is rich with history: the Duke of York (later James II) was a frequent visitor when commanding the English navy during the Anglo-Dutch war. Upstairs are characterful bedrooms, each different: one has a double-ended slipper bath on a platform before an original fireplace; in another, French doors open on to the walled garden;

another has a sleigh bed under a sublime 17th-century pargeted ceiling (an architectural feature also found in the bar/dining area). The buzzy restaurant specialises in seasonal dishes, especially just-caught harbour-fresh fish. BEDROOMS 5, 1 suitable for disabled. OPEN all year. Restaurant closed every Mon, and 25 Dec. FACILITIES bar, restaurant, free Wi-Fi, in-room TV (Freeview), garden. BACKGROUND MUSIC in public areas. LOCATION town centre. CHILDREN not allowed. DOGS not allowed. CREDIT CARDS MasterCard, Visa. PRICES per room £100–£200. À la carte £25. 2-night min. stay on Sat.

STAMFORD Lincolnshire
Map 2:B3

THE BULL AND SWAN AT BURGHLEY, High Street, St Martins, PE9 2LJ. Tel 01780 766412, www.hillbrookehotels. co.uk/the-bull-and-swan. In the late 17th century, the Honourable Order of Little Bedlam (an aristocratic drinking club) rampaged through this sympathetically refurbished coaching inn – today an altogether more honourable crowd crosses its mellow stone threshold. They come for the modern pub grub served in the lively dining areas, and the garden's new 'pizza potting shed' (open on warm-weather weekends). Characterful bedrooms, each named after the pseudonym of a Bedlam member, mix vintage furnishings and modern conveniences. Some have exposed stones or feature wallpaper, perhaps an original fireplace, mullioned window. Extras include fancy tea, 'proper coffee', biscuits, a mini-bottle of organic vodka. Burghley House is nearby. One of the small Hillbrooke Hotels group (see The Master Builder's, Beaulieu, main

entry). BEDROOMS 9. OPEN all year. FACILITIES bar, 3 dining areas, private dining/meeting room, free Wi-Fi, in-room TV (Freeview), terrace, parking. BACKGROUND MUSIC in bar. LOCATION 5-min. walk into town centre. CHILDREN all ages welcomed. DOGS allowed (in 3 rooms; dog bed, bowls, special treats, room-service menu, £20) CREDIT CARDS Amex, MasterCard, Visa. PRICES per room B&B £85–£180, D,B&B £135–£220. À la carte £30.

STOWMARKET Suffolk
Map 2:C5

BAYS FARM, Forward Green, Earl Stonham, IP14 5HU, 01449 711286, www.baysfarmsuffolk.co.uk. Waving wild flowers, part of Stephanie and Richard Challinor's award-winning gardens, greet visitors to a pretty B&B, surrounded by rolling fields. An appealing country feels pervades their restored 17th-century farmhouse. Simple, refined bedrooms have pleasing views over the landscaped garden; in each, organic toiletries for the oversized shower, a DVD library. A quirky shepherd's hut in the wild-flower garden, all pale blues and cream, is well equipped, with a traditional wood burner plus all the extras. Served in the former dairy (the oldest part of the house), a hearty breakfast has home-made bread, marmalade and jams; dry-cured Suffolk bacon. Simple suppers (fish pie; pâté and Suffolk chutney) can be arranged. BEDROOMS 5. OPEN all year. FACILITIES reception hall, drawing room, dining room, free Wi-Fi, in-room TV (Freeview), 4-acre garden. BACKGROUND MUSIC in drawing room and dining room, 'we will turn it off if asked'. LOCATION 4 miles E of Stowmarket. CHILDREN over-11s welcomed. DOGS not allowed. CREDIT CARDS all major cards. PRICES per room B&B £90–£140. À la carte £30.

STRATFORD-UPON-AVON
Warwickshire
Map 3:D6

WHITE SAILS, 85 Evesham Road, CV37 9BE. Tel 01789 550469, www.white-sails.co.uk. The Bard is within easy reach of Denise Perkin's restful B&B – the RSC theatres are just a 20-minute stroll from the suburban house with its distinctive blue entrance pillars. Help-yourself extras in the lounge (complimentary sherry, espresso coffee, home-made treats) create a home-from-home atmosphere. 'Clean and comfy' bedrooms in pretty colours, including one containing a four-poster, are well supplied with bathrobes, a digital radio/iPod docking station, home-baked cake; chilled water and fresh milk are left in a silent fridge. Breakfast is a feast of home-made granola, bread and cakes; cooked-to-order dishes, include eggs Benedict or smoked haddock with poached eggs. Anne Hathaway's cottage and Stratford racecourse are nearby. BEDROOMS 4. OPEN all year except Christmas and New Year's Day. FACILITIES lounge, dining room, free Wi-Fi, in-room TV (Freeview), garden. BACKGROUND MUSIC yes. LOCATION 1 mile W of centre. CHILDREN over-11s welcomed. DOGS not allowed. CREDIT CARDS Amex, MasterCard, Visa. PRICES per room B&B single £90–£115, double £105–£132, 1-night bookings sometimes refused weekends.

SWINBROOK Oxfordshire
Map 3:D6

THE SWAN INN, OX18 4DY. Tel 01993 823339, www.theswanswinbrook.co.uk.

'Swooning views of the Windrush valley' lead the way to this 'informal inn' hung with wisteria, where Guide inspectors were welcomed by 'a charming family of resident fluffy-legged bantams'. Small wonder that David Cameron brought France's president here to see a classic rural pub. Rustic yet chic bedrooms, in converted stables, have 'a large, comfortable bed with crisp bedlinens'. 'Rooms in the cottage by the river are especially good.' There could perhaps be more storage, greater attention to detail: 'The coffee mugs didn't fit in the capsule coffee machine.' 'Sophisticated' dishes are served in the labyrinthine pub, amid folksy touches and black-and-white photographs of the Mitford clan (the late Dowager Duchess of Devonshire spent her childhood in the village). BEDROOMS 11, 7 on ground floor, 5 in riverside cottage, some suitable for disabled. OPEN all year except Christmas/New Year. FACILITIES bar, restaurant, free Wi-Fi, in-room TV (Freeview), garden, orchard, unsuitable for disabled. BACKGROUND MUSIC in bar and restaurant. LOCATION 2 miles E of Burford. CHILDREN all ages welcomed. DOGS not allowed. CREDIT CARDS Diners, MasterCard, Visa. PRICES per room B&B from £125, D,B&B from £185. À la carte £30. 1-night bookings sometimes refused.

TAUNTON Somerset
Map 1:C5

THE CASTLE AT TAUNTON, Castle Green, TA1 1NF. Tel 01823 272671, www.the-castle-hotel.com. In the town centre, a 'beautifully furnished, traditional, very comfortable and cheerfully run' hotel stands inside a wisteria-festooned medieval castle. Extended and rebuilt over centuries, it has character and

history to spare – and is as good as ever, say several readers in 2018. The buzzy brasserie has 'delicious' food with inventive flavours and textures, perhaps pan-fried gurnard, wild mushroom, cauliflower, potato purée, white wine cream. The 'charming' Castle Bow restaurant has a more sedate ambience for chef Liam Finnegan's à la carte and tasting menus. 'Individual and comfortable', 'airy' bedrooms have high-quality bedlinen; a turn-down service at night. But lighting may be 'rather dim'. 'Excellent' breakfasts include an extensive buffet with home-made bread and jams, muesli and 'piping hot' cooked dishes. BEDROOMS 44, 2 suitable for disabled. OPEN all year. FACILITIES lounge/bar, 2 restaurants, private dining/meeting rooms, free Wi-Fi, in-room TV (Freeview), lift, ramps, civil wedding licence, ¼-acre garden. public rooms wheelchair accessible, adapted toilet. BACKGROUND MUSIC 'easy listening' in bar, restaurant, brasserie. LOCATION town centre. CHILDREN all ages welcomed. DOGS allowed in bedrooms (£15 a night), BRAZZ bar. CREDIT CARDS all major cards. PRICES B&B £165–£255, D,B&B £209–£299. À la carte Castle Bow £40, BRAZZ £30.
25% DISCOUNT VOUCHERS

TAVISTOCK Devon
Map 1:D4

TAVISTOCK HOUSE HOTEL, 50 Plymouth Road, PL19 8BU. Tel 01822 481 627, www.tavistockhousehotel.co.uk. Pristine throughout, Brad and Gill Walker's small hotel is a harmonious mix of spruce amenities and well-maintained original features. The house, built by the Duke of Bedford in 1850, is five minutes' walk from the town square. Chic bedrooms (some snug),

with grey and white hues and the odd splash of colour, are well appointed, with luxurious bedlinen, a capsule coffee machine, smart TV, a tablet computer to access free online newspapers; bath- and shower rooms have underfloor heating. Hearty breakfasts and all-day light bites are served in a serene room with marble fireplace, half-panelled walls and contemporary art, plus a well-stocked honesty bar. The large front garden has outdoor seating. The neighbourhood's eateries are nearby. BEDROOMS 6. OPEN all year except 25–26 Dec, 31 Dec, 1 Jan. FACILITIES breakfast room/lounge with honesty bar, free Wi-Fi, in-room TV (Freeview, Netflix), front garden. BACKGROUND MUSIC in public areas. LOCATION in town centre. CHILDREN over-9s welcomed. DOGS not allowed. CREDIT CARDS Diner's Club, MasterCard, Visa. PRICES per room B&B £104–£144.

TENBURY WELLS Worcestershire
Map 3:C5

THE TALBOT INN, Newnham Bridge, WR15 8JF. Tel 01584 781941, www.talbotinnnewnhambridge.co.uk. 'A useful stopover', this revamped roadside Victorian coaching inn 'is liked by locals for its much-praised food and good value'. Barnaby Williams is the 'hard-working, ever-present' owner. Inside is 'an open and contemporary rustic space (a wood burner, a hops-hung ceiling, black-and-white photographs of its history), with a cosy little sitting room off the main area; it has a very pleasant atmosphere'. Chef Jacob Vaughan's imaginative pub grub, much of it cooked in the Josper charcoal oven, is served on scrubbed pine tables; perhaps partridge breast, confit legs, Puy lentils, poached pear, parsnip crisps. 'Bright and immaculately kept' bedrooms have

a modern style that takes advantage of their generous proportions. BEDROOMS 7. OPEN all year. FACILITIES bar, snug, 2 dining areas, free Wi-Fi, in-room TV (Freeview), garden, parking. BACKGROUND MUSIC in dining areas 'but we can turn it off if asked'. LOCATION 4 miles from Tenbury Wells, 12 miles from Ludlow. CHILDREN all ages welcomed. DOGS allowed in 3 bedrooms, bar. CREDIT CARDS Amex, MasterCard, Visa. PRICES per room B&B from £90. À la carte £30. 2-night min. stay preferred at weekends May–Sept.
25% DISCOUNT VOUCHERS

TETBURY Gloucestershire
Map 3:E5

THE ROYAL OAK, 1 Cirencester Road, GL8 8EY. Tel 01666 500021 theroyaloaktetbury.co.uk. In a cluster of Cotswold stone buildings, Chris York and Kate Lewis run their all-round inviting pub with-rooms with great community spirit. The dog-friendly, family-friendly spot has welcomed travellers since the 18th century. The buzzy bar, its counter built from wood panels salvaged from a church, has real ales, and real tunes from a reconditioned jukebox. At mealtimes, 'high-quality' seasonal produce transforms into tasty pub grub, including a singular vegan menu. Summertime, a vintage Airstream trailer serves Tex Mex classics outside. Rustic bedrooms, across the courtyard, have a mix of Arts & Crafts-style pieces, vegan chocolates, bottled filtered water. Top-floor rooms gaze across the valley; a spacious mezzanine suite suits a family. At breakfast, a long buffet, plus cooked options. BEDROOMS 6, 1 suitable for disabled. OPEN all year except 1 week Jan. FACILITIES bar, restaurant, private dining/

meeting room, free Wi-Fi, in-room TV (Freeview), large garden, parking, bicycle storage. Bar, garden wheelchair accessible, adapted toilet. BACKGROUND MUSIC in bar and restaurant, monthly live music sessions. LOCATION a few mins' walk up the hill from the town centre. CHILDREN all ages welcomed. DOGS allowed in ground-floor rooms, bar and garden, not in restaurant. CREDIT CARDS Amex, MasterCard, Visa. PRICES per room B&B £85–£180. À la carte £35. 2-night min. bookings preferred.
25% DISCOUNT VOUCHERS

THORNHAM Norfolk
Map 2:A5

THE LIFEBOAT INN, Ship Lane, PE36 6LT. Tel 01485 512236, www.lifeboatinnthornham.com. Overlooking salt marsh and sea, this atmospheric 16th-century inn has rescued travellers from storms and hunger for over 500 years. These days, its stunning coastal location also draws twitchers and ramblers. Its oak-beamed bar has warming fires, settles and exposed stone walls hung with vintage agricultural equipment. Fresh seasonal dishes, daily specials and a good selection of vegetarian/vegan options are served in the restaurant and under the conservatory's 200-year-old vine. Good weather draws diners on to the terrace. Most of the cosy bedrooms, each named after a crew member of a famous Hunstanton lifeboat, look out to the North Sea. At breakfast, even Fido gets a sausage. An Agellus Hotel (see also The Ship at Dunwich, Shortlist). BEDROOMS 13, 1 on ground floor, in cottage. OPEN all year. FACILITIES bar, 2 lounge areas, conservatory, restaurant, meeting room, private dining room, free

Wi-Fi, in-room smart TV (Freeview), terrace, garden, parking. BACKGROUND MUSIC all day in public areas. LOCATION in a small coastal village 14 miles NE of Hunstanton. CHILDREN all ages welcomed. DOGS allowed in bedrooms, public rooms (£10 per stay). CREDIT CARDS MasterCard, Visa. PRICES per room B&B £130–£225. À la carte £28. 2-night min. stay preferred.
25% DISCOUNT VOUCHERS

THORNTON HOUGH Merseyside
Map 4:E2
MERE BROOK HOUSE, Thornton Common Road, Wirral, CH63 0LU. Tel 07713 189949, www.merebrookhouse. co.uk. Rising up from a dell of mature trees, this Edwardian country house provides relaxed B&B accommodation to visitors to the Wirral peninsula. Lorna Tyson and her husband, Donald, a farmer, have a laid-back approach – 'no notices/rules anywhere!' Unfussy yet pretty bedrooms occupy the original building and a converted coach house; individually decorated, they overlook the garden or countryside. Both buildings have their own lounge and a residents' kitchen stocked with complimentary home-made cakes, snacks and hot drinks (home-made ready meals are available for re-heating). Come morning, the conservatory provides a breakfast of super-local ingredients including honey from the garden beehives; milk from the Tysons' dairy cows; apple juice from orchard fruit. BEDROOMS 8, 4 in main house on first floor, 4 in coach house (3 on ground floor). OPEN all year, limited availability over Christmas, New Year. FACILITIES 3 lounges, conservatory, dining room, guest kitchens, free Wi-Fi, in-room TV (Freeview), wedding/function facilities, 1-acre garden in 4-acre grounds. BACKGROUND MUSIC none. LOCATION centre of Wirral peninsula, 20 mins' drive from Chester and Liverpool. CHILDREN all ages welcomed. DOGS assistance dogs only. CREDIT CARDS MasterCard, Visa. PRICES per room B&B £75–£130.
25% DISCOUNT VOUCHERS

THURNHAM Kent
Map 2:D5
THURNHAM KEEP, Castle Hill, nr Maidstone, ME14 3LE. Tel 01622 734149, www.thurnhamkeep.co.uk. A long drive through landscaped gardens reveals this 'simply wonderful' Edwardian B&B where visitors are rewarded by a sweet welcome from 'charming host', Amanda Lane: 'The best shortbread ever.' Built from the ruins of Thurnham Castle, the 'magnificent place' stands on the crest of the North Downs. Up an oak staircase, each traditionally furnished bedroom has its own elegant personality; in two, a huge, original Edwardian bath in the bathroom; in all, soft pastels, splendid period furniture. A family might opt for a spacious self-contained suite in newly converted stables. A communal breakfasts brings home-made jams, garden hive-gathered honey, fresh-from-the-coop eggs. Supper might be arranged in advance; plenty of nearby pubs, too. 'We'd love to return.' BEDROOMS 3, plus self-contained suite in grounds. OPEN Mar–mid-Dec. FACILITIES sitting room, dining room, conservatory, billiard room, free Wi-Fi, in-room TV (Freeview), 7-acre terraced garden, terrace, heated outdoor swimming pool, tennis, parking. BACKGROUND MUSIC none. LOCATION 3 miles from Maidstone. CHILDREN over-9s welcomed. DOGS not

allowed. CREDIT CARDS all major cards.
PRICES per room B&B £145–£160.

TILLINGTON Sussex
Map 2:E3

THE HORSE GUARDS INN, Upperton
Road, nr Petworth, GU28 9AF. Tel
01798 342332, www.thehorseguardsinn.
co.uk. Walk across Petworth Park
to this 350-year-old, quintessentially
English village inn, once a regular
stopover for the Household Cavalry,
who would rest their horses en route
to Portsmouth. The rambling, updated
interiors have stripped floorboards,
scrubbed pine tables, eye-catching
curiosities and log fires. Pretty florals
add country charm to simply decorated
bedrooms, some snug, some with
low beams. A short daily-changing
menu is ultra-seasonal, with the inn's
own vegetables, or locally foraged
ingredients. A Guide regular this year
enjoyed 'interesting starters', followed
by a 'richly flavoured' duck leg goulash.
Breakfast was 'tasty, well cooked'. Staff
were 'invariably friendly and obliging'.
The suntrap garden is strewn with
hammocks, deckchairs and straw-bale
seats. BEDROOMS 3, 1 in cottage. OPEN all
year, limited availability over Christmas,
New Year. FACILITIES bar, restaurant,
free Wi-Fi, in-room TV (Freeview),
garden, secure bicycle storage.
BACKGROUND MUSIC none. LOCATION in
village, close to Petworth House and
Park. CHILDREN all ages welcomed. DOGS
well-behaved dogs allowed. CREDIT
CARDS MasterCard, Visa. PRICES per
room B&B from £110.

TISBURY Wiltshire
Map 2:D1

THE COMPASSES INN, Lower Chicksgrove,
nr Salisbury, SP3 6NB. Tel 01722 714318,
thecompassesinn.com. A local hotspot
'in the middle of nowhere', this thatch-
roofed 14th-century inn is worth the
trip down a winding country lane in the
Nadder valley. Inside are cosy nooks
and crannies; owner Ben Maschler
has retained the pub's flagstone floors
and ancient beams, and the inglenook
fireplace that keeps things warm. The
sophisticated pubby menu changes
daily, using seasonal and local produce;
cocktails, local ales and European wines
make good accompaniment. Airy and
simply furnished bedrooms, above
the pub, have a cheerful cottagey feel,
updated with Anglepoise lamps, a
Roberts radio and a stack of Penguin
Classics. The footpaths and sheep trails
of the Nadder valley start from the
door. BEDROOMS 4, plus 2-bed self-
catering cottage. OPEN all year except
25 Dec. FACILITIES bar, restaurant, free
Wi-Fi, in-room TV (Freeview), ¼-acre
garden. BACKGROUND MUSIC none,
occasional live music events. LOCATION
2 miles E of Tisbury. CHILDREN all ages
welcomed. DOGS allowed. CREDIT CARDS
MasterCard, Visa. PRICES per room
B&B from £110. À la carte £26. 2-night
min. stay on summer and bank holiday
weekends.

TIVERTON Devon
Map 1:C5

HARTNOLL HOTEL, Bolham, EX16 7RA.
Tel 01884 252777, www.hartnollhotel.
co.uk. Restored and refurbished by
its owner, Claire Carter, this 'lovely'
country house has a 'luxurious,
contemporary' style and 'friendly,
welcoming staff who really make the
place'. 'It is consistently good,' writes
a Guide regular this year. Modern
bedrooms may vary in size, but all
have a 'cosy, country-chic feel and all

the necessary conveniences', including crisp bedlinens, fluffy bathrobes; a marble bathroom (the glass bathroom door might make it too intimate for some). One splendid stay was marred by the hotel's over-zealous heating of bedrooms. Local ales are served in the bar; Devon produce in the 'excellent' conservatory restaurant. 'A perfect dinner. My dessert was to die for.' The 'completely beautiful' grounds have quirky sculptures and water features. BEDROOMS 25, 5 in Gatehouse. OPEN all year. FACILITIES bar, 2 sitting rooms, conservatory restaurant, free Wi-Fi, in-room TV (Freeview), civil wedding licence, garden, parking. BACKGROUND MUSIC in reception, bar and sitting room. LOCATION 2 miles from Tiverton town centre and 10 mins from Jct 25, M5. CHILDREN all ages welcomed. DOGS allowed in some bedrooms and public rooms, not in conservatory (£10 per night). CREDIT CARDS Amex, MasterCard, Visa. PRICES per room B&B single £115–£165, double £140–£190. À la carte £37.

TOLLARD ROYAL Wiltshire
Map 2:E1

KING JOHN INN, SP5 5PS. Tel 01725 516207, www.kingjohninn.co.uk. Sophisticated yet unpretentious, this ivy-wrapped pub-with-rooms in the depths of Thomas Hardy country 'entices' with classic British grub and rustic chic bedrooms. The 'simply set' dining room, with its monochrome photos of country life, has a 'good atmosphere'; it's a genial spot to dine on gastropubby dishes, made with a farm-to-fork ethos – or sea-to-plate for the likes of fillet of john dory, new potatoes, purple sprouting broccoli, wild garlic pesto. Warm weather brings

diners outside into the Victorian tiered garden. Bedrooms (some up 'steep, narrow stairs') have a 'pleasing, restful' feel, all pale colours, antiques, home-made shortbread, books to read; thoughtful extras include Bramley toiletries, fancy teas, an espresso machine. BEDROOMS 8, some on ground floor, 3 in coach house. OPEN all year. FACILITIES lounge, bar, restaurant, free Wi-Fi, in-room TV, garden, parking. BACKGROUND MUSIC none. LOCATION 6 miles W of Shaftesbury. CHILDREN all ages welcomed. DOGS allowed by prior arrangement. CREDIT CARDS MasterCard, Visa. PRICES per room B&B from £90. À la carte £35.

TOPSHAM Devon
Map 1:C5

THE SALUTATION INN, 68 Fore Street, EX3 0HL. Tel 01392 873060, www. salutationtopsham.co.uk. A stone's throw from the River Exe, this characterful property with a rich history has welcomed the weary since the 1720s. Now sleekly updated with a nod to its maritime past, the inn is owned and run by the Williams-Hawkes family. It has hosted some dashing events in its time, from inaugural hot-air balloon trips, to a horse-leaping stunt over a dining room table. Today's excitement is more genteel and gastronomic: afternoon teas, lunches in the atrium café, and weekly-changing tasting menus, expertly executed by Tom Williams-Hawkes. Restrained, modern bedrooms share a galley kitchen for help-yourself hot drinks, toast, fruit and home-made biscuits. The RSPB Bowling Green Marsh nature reserve is nearby. BEDROOMS 6, 2 suites. OPEN all year except 25 Dec evening, 26 Dec, 1 Jan. FACILITIES 2 lounges, restaurant, café, meeting/function room, free Wi-Fi, in-room TV (Freeview), walled seating area, parking, restaurant wheelchair accessible, adapted toilet. BACKGROUND MUSIC in public areas. LOCATION town centre. CHILDREN all ages welcomed. DOGS allowed. CREDIT CARDS MasterCard, Visa. PRICES per room B&B £135–£225, D,B&B £200–£295. Set menu £43. 2-night min. stay at weekends May–Oct.

TORQUAY Devon
Map 1:D5

MEADFOOT BAY, Meadfoot Sea Road, TQ1 2LQ. Tel 01803 294722, www.meadfoot.com. Close to the beach, Phil Hartnett and Vicki Osborne's recently refurbished B&B makes a tranquil 'home from home'. Run by manager Jody Miller and a friendly team, the Victorian villa has generous windows that let light flood into comfortable sitting areas, painted in calming colours and with plush seating, mirrors, chandeliers. Individually designed bedrooms, each named after a South Devon cove, have clean lines, contemporary hues, a smart bathroom, along with fresh milk in the fridge, complimentary sherry, plenty of storage; three have a private terrace. Breakfast brings a wide choice of cooked dishes; muesli, granola, compotes and preserves are home made. Guests wishing to avoid the short trip in to town, can order sharing platters and light bites in the evening. BEDROOMS 15. OPEN all year, except Dec–Feb. FACILITIES lounge, bar, dining room, library, in-room free Wi-Fi. TV (Freeview), terrace, parking. BACKGROUND MUSIC in public areas. LOCATION 3 mins' walk behind Meadfoot beach, 15 mins' walk from Torquay harbour. CHILDREN over-13s welcomed.

DOGS allowed in 1 room, not inside the hotel. CREDIT CARDS Amex, MasterCard, Visa. PRICES per room B&B £75–£220. 2-night min. stay in high season and bank holidays.

ORESTONE MANOR, Rockhouse Lane, Maidencombe, TQ1 4SX. Tel 01803 897511, www.orestonemanor.com. In sub-tropical gardens with views over Lyme Bay, the D'Allen family's hotel occupies a grand Georgian manor house, once home to John Callcott Horsley, designer of the first Christmas card. Its greetings now extend far beyond Yuletide. In the public rooms, comfortable leather settees join an 'eclectic assortment of artefacts', from colourful Persian-style carpets to Victorian artworks, sculpted elephants and rabbits, a classical Greek statue. Some ornate, some capacious, each bedroom has a 'state-of-the-art bathroom packed with goodies'. Most have sea views, some an outdoor hot tub. In the restaurant, Devonshire produce prevails: Exmoor lamb, Teign River mussels, Torbay scallops; fruit and vegetables from the kitchen gardens. Breakfast includes freshly squeezed juice, kippers, West Country ham with poached eggs. BEDROOMS 14, 3 in grounds. OPEN all year except Jan. FACILITIES bar, 2 lounges, 2 dining rooms, free Wi-Fi, in-room TV (Sky), patio, 2-acre grounds, parking. BACKGROUND MUSIC in public areas. LOCATION 4½ miles N of Torquay. CHILDREN all ages welcomed, over-9s only in main restaurant at dinner. DOGS not allowed in bedrooms. CREDIT CARDS Amex, MasterCard, Visa. PRICES per room B&B single £95–£335, double £110–£350, D,B&B double £164–£404. Table d'hôte menus £27, à la carte £40.

THE 25 BOUTIQUE B&B, 25 Avenue Road, TQ2 5LB. Tel 01803 297517, www.the25.uk. Gleeful design and a zesty touch fill 'charming, personable hosts' Andy and Julian Banner-Price's 'meticulously maintained', award-winning Edwardian B&B near Torre Abbey. The decor has a playful air (a zebra in sunglasses here, a psychedelic colour scheme there) – 'edgy but comfortably short of giddy'. A refreshing drink and slice of cake welcome arriving visitors. Bedrooms, each utterly different, have 'plenty of storage space and proper hangers', a hi-tech shower room with mood lighting; 'lavish amenities including fresh-baked treats'. Breakfast brings a fruit smoothie, followed by fruit salad, home-made yogurt and granola, and a choice of hot dishes. Garden paths lead towards the seafront, and the main harbour's shops, restaurants and bars. BEDROOMS 6. OPEN Feb–Oct. FACILITIES drawing room, dining room, free Wi-Fi, in-room smart TV (movies on demand), patio, parking. BACKGROUND MUSIC at breakfast. LOCATION 5 mins' walk from the sea, 20 mins' walk from town. CHILDREN not allowed. DOGS not allowed. CREDIT CARDS all major cards. PRICES per room B&B single £99-£159, double £120–£175.
25% DISCOUNT VOUCHERS

TRESCO Isles of Scilly
Map 1: inset C1
THE NEW INN, New Grimsby, TR24 0QG. Tel 01720 422849, www.tresco. co.uk/staying-on-tresco/the-new-inn. 'Deliberately unchanged', the only pub on Robert Dorrien-Smith's private, car-free island is a 'relaxed', characterful gathering place. With a fabulous setting, just back from the beach, it has 'lovely accommodation', and Michelin-rated menus showcasing bountiful Scillonian produce. Surf and turf with Bryher lobster and chargrilled Tresco beef steak; pesto rosti is among the good veggie dishes, many of them sourced from the Tresco Abbey gardens. By the 'well-stocked bar', a wood-burning stove is a welcome harbour on chilly days. In good weather, move into the 'very pretty', canopied garden. Recently updated bedrooms are simply done with a beachy palette; welcoming treats include freshly ground coffee, home-made biscuits, high-end toiletries. Those in the modern annexe are more spacious. BEDROOMS 16, some on ground floor. OPEN all year. FACILITIES bar, residents' lounge, restaurant, free Wi-Fi, in-room TV (Freeview), patio, garden, pavilion, heated outdoor swimming pool. BACKGROUND MUSIC in pub and restaurant, occasional live music events. LOCATION near New Grimsby harbour. CHILDREN all ages welcomed. DOGS allowed in public bar and beer garden, assistance dogs allowed in bedrooms. CREDIT CARDS MasterCard, Visa. PRICES per person B&B £65–£115, D,B&B £100–£165. À la carte £35.

TROUTBECK Cumbria
Map 4: inset C2
BROADOAKS, Bridge Lane, LA23 1LA. Tel 01539 445566, www. broadoakscountryhouse.co.uk. On a wonderfully scenic perch above Windermere, Tracey Robinson and Joanna Harbottle's 19th-century stone-and-slate country house is a 'very welcoming' retreat. Set in seven acres of landscaped grounds, it has 'helpful, charming staff'. The 'gorgeous bedrooms' have bold wallpaper, antique furnishings; perhaps a roll-top bath

or a sunken spa bath in the bathroom. One suite lets a family spread out over two bedrooms and a lounge; another has a Victorian four-poster, its own log fire and views of the Langdale pikes. The panelled sitting room serves pre-dinner canapés, before Sharon Elders's 'excellent' French-accented Cumbrian fare in the Oaks brasserie, including daily-changing vegan and vegetarian dishes. Plentiful choice at breakfast: freshly baked muffins, griddled pancakes, beech-smoked Cartmel valley kippers. BEDROOMS 20, some on ground floor, 5 in coach house, 3 detached garden suites. OPEN all year except Jan. FACILITIES sitting room, bar, restaurant, orangery, free Wi-Fi, in-room TV (Freeview), civil wedding licence, 8-acre grounds, complimentary access to nearby spa. BACKGROUND MUSIC 'on low volume' in public areas. LOCATION 2 miles N of Bowness-on-Windermere CHILDREN over-4s welcomed. DOGS allowed in some bedrooms, on lead in garden, bar and lounge. CREDIT CARDS Diners Club, MasterCard, Visa. PRICES per room B&B £155–£335, D,B&B £185–£375. Set menu £47.50. 25% DISCOUNT VOUCHERS

TUNBRIDGE WELLS Kent
Map 2:D4

THE MOUNT EDGCUMBE, The Common, TN4 8BX. Tel 01892 618854, www. themountedgcumbe.com. With a leafy garden overlooking the common, Robert and Sally Hogben's nattily refurbished Georgian building is an appealing spot for an alfresco rendezvous. Families, dog-owners and real ale connoisseurs gather at picnic tables under parasols, while cooler months signal a retreat to the cosy bar's log fire and remarkable snug, with leather sofas in a 6th-century sandstone cave. On two floors, the informal restaurant offers a broad, seasonally changing menu of sharing platters, healthy options and classic pub dishes. At the top, six uniquely decorated bedrooms have harmonious hues, antiques, plantation shutters and colourful cushions patterned with wildlife. Various extras include an in-room roll-top bath, views of the common or Edgcumbe rocks. BEDROOMS 6. OPEN all year, closed for accommodation 24, 25 and 31 Dec. FACILITIES bar, restaurant, free Wi-Fi, in-room TV (Freeview), garden. BACKGROUND MUSIC in bar, restaurant. LOCATION ½ mile from station. CHILDREN all ages welcomed (cot). DOGS in bar, restaurant, garden, not in rooms. CREDIT CARDS Amex, MasterCard, Visa. PRICES per room B&B single from £95, double from £110. À la carte £30.

ULVERSTON Cumbria
Map 4: inset C2

THE BAY HORSE, Canal Foot, LA12 9EL. Tel 01229 583972, thebayhorsehotel.co.uk. Right at the water's edge, Robert Lyons and Lesley Wheeler's pub-with-rooms is 'an amiable, comfortable place' that draws regular returnees year after year. 'The friendly staff even welcomed our dogs.' Afternoon tea in one of the cosy sitting areas is enjoyed. The traditionally furnished bedrooms each have many board games, books and magazines. Guests this year felt the decor was a bit 'tired', but 'the view was wonderful'; six rooms have French doors to a terrace. Robert Lyons's candlelit dinners (no longer one sitting, but at times between 7 pm and 8.15 pm) are popular with residents and locals; reservations may be needed. 'Everything was beautifully done; we especially enjoyed the excellent fish dishes.' The breakfasts are 'exceptional'. BEDROOMS 9. OPEN all year. FACILITIES bar/lounge, restaurant, free Wi-Fi, in-room TV (Freeview), picnic area, parking, bar and restaurant suitable for wheelchair users. BACKGROUND MUSIC in bar and restaurant. LOCATION 1½ miles from town centre. CHILDREN over-8s welcomed. DOGS allowed in bedroom (2 dogs max.), not in restaurant. CREDIT CARDS all major cards. PRICES per room B&B £95–£115, D,B&B £165–£185. À la carte £40. 2-night min. stay preferred.

UPTON MAGNA Shropshire
Map 3:B5

THE HAUGHMOND, Pelham Road, nr Shrewsbury, SY4 4TZ. Tel 01743 709918, www.thehaughmond.co.uk. Hungry locals, ramblers and cyclists refuel on food and sleep at Mel and Martin Board's swish 17th-century village inn. Top-notch country fare (whipped up by the host, a self-taught cook) is served in the bustling restaurant. A dessert of warm chocolate moelleux, mint ice cream, chocolate tulip was 'particularly good'. Above the bar, cottage-style bedrooms, all solid oak and crisp bedlinen, have a well-supplied refreshments tray, a smart TV with on-demand movies; one, in the eaves, has a Juliet balcony overlooking the fields. Staff were 'very pleasant and easy to talk to', according to a reader this year, but 'unfortunately, there was a lack of attention to detail'. The deli/farm shop has picnic hampers, takeaway lunches. BEDROOMS 7, 2 in annexe. OPEN all year except Christmas Day, New Year's Day. FACILITIES bar/brasserie, breakfast room, conservatory, free

Wi-Fi, in-room smart TV, terrace, ½-acre garden, parking. BACKGROUND MUSIC 'on low volume' in public areas. LOCATION 4 miles from Shrewsbury. CHILDREN all ages welcomed. DOGS allowed (not unattended) in bedrooms, on lead in public areas (£10 per night, own bed required). CREDIT CARDS MasterCard, Visa. PRICES per room B&B £90–£120. À la carte £30.
25% DISCOUNT VOUCHERS

WADDESDON Buckinghamshire
Map 2:C3

THE FIVE ARROWS, High Street, HP18 0JE. Tel 01296 651727, fivearrowshotel. co.uk. A Victorian inn, originally built to house architects and craftsmen constructing nearby Waddesdon Manor, is now a 'comfortable' hotel run by the Rothschild family trust and the National Trust. Hotel guests receive complimentary entry to the manor house. The half-timbered, ornately patterned Grade II listed building retains wrought ironwork and Elizabethan chimneys; recent refurbishment has resulted in pleasing bedrooms with contemporary natural hues, some with original timbers. Light sleepers may hear traffic noise from the 'busy' road (some guests report barely noticing it). The 'spruced-up' restaurant produces 'excellent, flavoursome cooking', perhaps plaice, cauliflower, raisins, cauliflower carpaccio, cumin oil, alongside wines from the family's vineyard. Breakfast choices include oak-smoked salmon, grilled kippers, a three-egg omelette. BEDROOMS 16, 5 in Old Coach House, 3 on ground floor in courtyard. OPEN all year. FACILITIES bar, restaurant, free Wi-Fi, in-room smart TV (Freeview), civil wedding licence, 1-acre garden. BACKGROUND MUSIC in

restaurant. LOCATION in Waddesdon
village near the gates of Waddesdon
Manor. CHILDREN all ages welcomed.
DOGS allowed in some bedrooms, not in
food service areas. CREDIT CARDS Amex,
MasterCard, Visa. PRICES per room B&B
single from £95, double from £145,
D,B&B single from £125, double from
£205. À la carte £29.

WADEBRIDGE Cornwall
Map 1:D2
TREWORNAN MANOR, Trewornan
Bridge, PL27 6EX. Tel 01208 812359,
www.trewornanmanor.co.uk. Near the
mouth of the Camel estuary, Paul and
Lesley Stapleton have transformed their
listed early 13th-century manor house
into a lovingly restored B&B. Through
the granite pillared gateway, eight acres
of mature gardens contain an idyllic
spot for a complimentary cream tea.
The log-warmed lounge has a well-
stocked honesty bar. Spacious bedrooms
have emperor-size bed, a hospitality
tray with home-made treats, views of
the courtyard and/or gardens. Some
bathrooms have a free-standing bath and
walk-in shower. Hospitable owners, the
Stapletons provide late-arriving B&B
guests with a small snack menu. Hearty
Cornish breakfasts, which include home-
made blueberry pancakes with clotted
cream, can be walked off on the footpath
to the village. Mountain bikes can be
borrowed. BEDROOMS 7, 2 in annexe, 1
on ground floor. OPEN all year. FACILITIES
lounge, snug, dining room, free Wi-Fi,
in-room TV (Freeview), civil wedding
licence, 8-acre gardens. BACKGROUND
MUSIC in dining room, lounge. LOCATION
1 mile N of Wadebridge. CHILDREN over-
13s welcomed. DOGS not allowed. CREDIT
CARDS MasterCard, Visa. PRICES per room
B&B £120–£210.

WARKWORTH Northumberland
Map 4:A4
WARKWORTH HOUSE HOTEL, 16 Bridge
Street, NE65 0XB. Tel 01665 711276,
www.warkworthhousehotel.co.uk.
On a loop of the River Coquet, Sandra
Thomas's hotel is a welcoming spot for
travelling dogs and their two-legged
friends. In the centre of a Georgian
village dominated by a medieval castle,
the 18th-century coaching inn retains its
fine staircase and traditional lounge. Its
convivial atmosphere is helped by staff
who 'deserve a medal' for their cheerful,
efficient service. Many of the bright
bedrooms have a touch of French style,
some with bright splashes of colour,
and overlook manicured gardens.
'Great', generous dishes, perhaps ham
hock, chicken and stilton crumble, leek
cream sauce and mash, are served in
the bar and lounge, or in the informal
bistro next door. Beaches, gardens, golf
courses are all close by. BEDROOMS 14, 2
on ground floor. OPEN all year. FACILITIES
bar, lounge, restaurant, free Wi-Fi, in-
room TV, parking. BACKGROUND MUSIC
none. LOCATION 15 mins' walk from
a beach. CHILDREN all ages welcomed
(rooms cannot accommodate extra beds).
DOGS allowed in 1st-floor rooms (£10 per
stay). CREDIT CARDS MasterCard, Visa.
PRICES per room B&B from £129. 2-night
min. stay on Fri and Sat.

WARTLING Sussex
Map 2:E4
WARTLING PLACE, Herstmonceux,
nr Hailsham, BN27 1RY. Tel 01323
832590, www.wartlingplace.co.uk.
The 'beautiful gardens', 'wonderful
atmosphere' and 'pleasant rooms' were
highlighted by guests this year, who
praised this 'delightful' B&B, 'very
convenient for Glyndebourne and the

coast'. The hosts, Rowena and Barry Gittoes, 'always make things easy for everybody'. Their Grade II listed Georgian former rectory, in three acres of gardens with rural views towards the South Downs, has tidy public spaces brimming with interesting prints, and cosy nooks. Well-appointed bedrooms have 'real coffee', Fairtrade teas; a DVD library; two have an antique four-poster. Leisurely breakfast, taken in the bedroom or in the spacious dining room, has fresh fruit, cereals, honey from local bees; smoked salmon from Hastings, local meats, herbs from the garden: 'Delicious.' Picnic hampers can be arranged. BEDROOMS 4, plus 2-bed self-catering cottage suitable for disabled. OPEN all year. FACILITIES drawing room, dining room, free Wi-Fi, in-room TV (Freeview), 3-acre garden, parking. BACKGROUND MUSIC none. LOCATION 5 miles E of Hailsham. CHILDREN all ages welcomed. DOGS not allowed. CREDIT CARDS Amex, MasterCard, Visa. PRICES per room B&B single £100–£115, double £130–£160.

WARWICK Warwickshire
Map 3:C6

PARK COTTAGE, 113 West Street, CV34 6AH. Tel 01926 410319, www.parkcottagewarwick.co.uk. Hanging baskets of colourful blooms, and wonderfully wonky timbers front Janet and Stuart Baldry's 'warm, good-value' 15th-century B&B. A guest in 2018 marvelled at the Baldrys' 'true colours': 'Trapped by a snowstorm, they turned their reception into a crisis centre, cheerfully helping their guests to battle the elements.' Across sloping floors and up a steep staircase, the 'comfortable bedrooms' are all different – one has an antique four-poster bed, another

a king-size spa bath; a third, access to the pretty patio garden. 'Splendid breakfasts, expertly cooked by Stuart Baldry', are served to tables set on the original sandstone floor of the former castle dairy. BEDROOMS 7, 2 on ground floor. OPEN all year except Christmas, New Year. FACILITIES reception/sitting area, breakfast room, free Wi-Fi, in-room TV (Freeview), small garden, parking. BACKGROUND MUSIC none. LOCATION Warwick town centre. CHILDREN all ages welcomed. DOGS allowed (not unattended) in bedrooms, on lead in public areas (£10 per night, own bed required). CREDIT CARDS Amex, MasterCard, Visa. PRICES per room B&B single from £79, double from £92. 1-night bookings sometimes refused.

WATCHET Somerset
Map 1:B5

SWAIN HOUSE, 48 Swain Street, TA23 0AG. Tel 01984 631038, www.swain-house.com. Watched over by a 150-year-old lighthouse, the coastal spot that inspired Coleridge bears the statue of the ancient mariner; but, just up from the famous harbour, Jason Robinson's bijou B&B has more youthful appeal. The 18th-century town house and shop has a stylish verve, with an inviting mix of slate floors, soft velvet and warm wood. In each of the chic bedrooms, a king-size bed stands under a mural of an Old Master painting; thoughtful extras abound: waffle bathrobes, fluffy towels, chic toiletries; a roll-top slipper bath and separate walk-in shower in the bathroom. Breakfast has a range of home-cooked dishes, including a full veggie option. Evenings, a light charcuterie supper can be arranged. BEDROOMS 4. OPEN all year except Christmas, New Year. FACILITIES lounge, dining room, free Wi-Fi, in-room TV (Freeview). BACKGROUND MUSIC none. LOCATION 100 metres from harbour marina. CHILDREN over-11s welcomed. DOGS not allowed. CREDIT CARDS Amex, MasterCard, Visa. PRICES per room B&B £135.

WATERGATE BAY Cornwall
Map 1:D2

WATERGATE BAY, On the beach, TR8 4AA. Tel 01637 860543, www.watergatebay.co.uk. Whether testing the surf for the first time, or paddle boarding like an old pro, there's a pursuit to suit at Will Ashworth's 'great' beachside hotel. The modern building stands on a stretch of sandy beach, where the on-site Extreme Academy hosts adrenalin-driven activities (kitesurfing, wave skiing). Off the sands, the sleek Swim Club has every facility for deep relaxation; the Kids Zone gives children three areas to play. At mealtimes, choose between: American-style classics at Zacry's; seasonal grub in the Living Space; fresh seafood at the Beach Hut, Italian-inspired dishes at Jamie Oliver's Fifteen, inspiring young Cornish chefs. Finally, a quiet night beckons from the 'super-clean' bedrooms, each with a coastal vibe (many with views to match). BEDROOMS 71, 2 suitable for disabled. OPEN all year. FACILITIES lounge/bar, 3 restaurants, free Wi-Fi, in-room TV (Freeview), civil wedding licence, terrace, sun deck, indoor/outdoor swimming pool, spa treatments. BACKGROUND MUSIC all day in public areas. LOCATION 5 miles N of Newquay. CHILDREN all ages welcomed. DOGS allowed in some bedrooms, 2 restaurants (£15 per night, dog-friendly beach). CREDIT CARDS Diners Club, MasterCard, Visa. PRICES per room B&B £185 £365, D,B&B £240 420. À la carte (Zacry's restaurant) £40.

WEDMORE Somerset
Map 1:B6

THE SWAN, Cheddar Road, BS28 4EQ. Tel 01934 710337, www.theswanwedmore.com. 'Simple, almost basic but what great value,' writes a delighted regular reader this year, about this pleasingly updated 18th-century beer house. A 'friendly' pub-with-rooms, it has a 'lovely, informal atmosphere' with real ales, comfy seating, stripped wooden floors. Come summer, locals and residents decant on to the cheery terrace. Upstairs, 'smart' modern bedrooms (well stocked with ground coffee, old-fashioned sweets, 'super toiletries') have much personality: a pink-painted claw-foot bath; Beatles LP covers on a wall. Chef Tom Blake's unpretentious gastropub menu exploits local produce for such dishes as Gloucester Old Spot pork belly, basil, apple, spring bubble and squeak, heritage carrots. 'Breakfast is a real treat.' Part of the Stay Original Company, like Timbrell's Yard, Bradford-on-Avon (see Shortlist). BEDROOMS 7. OPEN all year. FACILITIES bar, restaurant, free Wi-Fi, in-room TV, function facilities, terrace, garden, parking. BACKGROUND MUSIC in bar. LOCATION village centre. CHILDREN all ages welcomed. DOGS allowed (£10 per dog per stay). CREDIT CARDS Diners Club, MasterCard, Visa. PRICES per room B&B from £75, D,B&B from £100.

WELLS-NEXT-THE-SEA Norfolk
Map 2:A5

THE GLOBE INN, The Butlands, NR23 1EU. Tel 01328 710206, www.theglobeatwells.co.uk. Facing an expansive green ringed by lime trees in this quaint seaside town, Stephen and Antonia Bournes have refashioned a plain, old inn into a contemporary hotel and restaurant. A coastal theme in the cheery dining room (wood flooring, exposed brickwork, maritime artwork) extends to spruce new bedrooms and apartments in the coach house. Seasonal menus 'with a French influence' might include game pie or locally harvested moules frites cooked three ways. In the courtyard: a wood-fired pizza oven and fish smoker for alfresco dining. Residents have use of a private sun trap roof terrace with waitress service. The hotel's beach hut can be hired by the day (buckets, spades, deckchairs, picnic blankets provided). BEDROOMS 19, 12 in coach house, 1 suitable for disabled. OPEN all year. FACILITIES bar, restaurant, orangery, free Wi-Fi, in-room TV (Freeview), residents-only private roof terrace, courtyard. BACKGROUND MUSIC in bar, restaurant. LOCATION town centre. CHILDREN all ages welcomed. DOGS allowed in 6 courtyard rooms, part of restaurant. CREDIT CARDS MasterCard, Visa. PRICES per person B&B £110–£190, D,B&B £140–£220. À la carte £27.

WESTBROOK Herefordshire
Map 3:D4

WESTBROOK COURT B&B, nr Hay-on-Wye, HR3 5SY. Tel 01497 831752, www.westbrookcourtbandb.co.uk. On a winding road in cider country, tucked behind a rambling 17th-century farmhouse, a timber-clad stable is home to five voguish B&B suites. Kari and Chris Morgan have transformed the space into something sleek and unexpected. Bold colour and some quirky flourishes (a bird-cage lampshade; trompe l'oeil book-lined wallpaper) are splashed about the spacious, light-filled rooms. Each has its own lounge area and a private sun-trap deck; in four, a mezzanine bedroom yields views of Merbach hill. At weekends, the Morgans invite guests to share home-baked, garden-reared breakfast in the farmhouse kitchen; weekdays, pastries, smoked salmon, fruit and yogurt are brought to the door first thing. 'Speedy suppers' can be arranged. BEDROOMS 5, 1 suitable for disabled. OPEN all year. FACILITIES breakfast room/kitchen, free Wi-Fi, in-room TV (Freeview), 5-acre grounds, terrace, cycle and kayak storage. BACKGROUND MUSIC classical in breakfast room. LOCATION 3 miles E of Hay-on-Wye. 2 minutes drive to Dorstone Village. CHILDREN all ages welcomed. DOGS allowed in bedrooms (not in breakfast room). CREDIT CARDS MasterCard, Visa. PRICES per room B&B from £95.

WESTGATE Co. Durham
Map 4:B3

WESTGATE MANOR, Westgate, DL13 1JT. Tel 01388 517371, www.westgatemanor.co.uk. 'Just perfect,' say readers this year of Kathryn and Stuart Dobson's large Victorian manor house in the heart of Weardale. 'The owners made us welcome the moment we arrived.' Decorated in fine style, its red front door opens on to chandelier-lit rooms filled with antique furniture and displays of fresh flowers. In the sitting room, a log-burner; comfy sofas under huge windows gazing across sheep-speckled hillsides. All the traditional 'high standard' country-house bedrooms have exposed beams and beautiful views; a splendid bathroom with underfloor heating; some have a four-poster or half-tester bed. The orangery is an inviting dining spot any time; pre-booking may be necessary for 'superb' evening meals including minted lamb shank, seasonal vegetables, creamy mash. BEDROOMS 5, 1 suitable for a family. OPEN all year. FACILITIES lounge, dining room, orangery, garden room, in-room TV (Freeview), free Wi-Fi, patio, secure bike storage, parking. BACKGROUND MUSIC in reception, dining room. LOCATION 40 mins' drive from Durham. CHILDREN all ages welcomed. DOGS not allowed. CREDIT CARDS Amex, MasterCard, Visa. PRICES per room B&B £129–£145, À la carte £27.

WESTLETON Suffolk
Map 2:B6

THE WESTLETON CROWN, The Street, nr Southwold, IP17 3AD. Tel 01728 648777, www.westletoncrown.co.uk. Visitors answering the call of the wild birds at the RSPB nature reserve at Minsmere convene with locals at this 12th-century coaching inn, much-liked for its dog-friendly atmosphere. 'Hearty yet sophisticated dishes', perhaps grilled seabass fillet, ratatouille, new potatoes, basil pesto, are served before the fire in the cosy parlour, or in the airy Garden Room; on fine days, dining heads into the terraced garden. A separate menu and colouring book for children. Country-style bedrooms have local magazines, ground coffee, home-made biscuits. Visiting dogs are welcomed with biscuits, a blanket and breakfast sausage. Breakfast brings many choices including eggs Benedict with Suffolk ham; Lowestoft smoked haddock with poached eggs. A sister hotel to The Lifeboat Inn, Thornham (see Shortlist). BEDROOMS 34, some in cottages and converted stables in grounds, 1 suitable for disabled. OPEN all year. FACILITIES bar, snug, lounge, conservatory, 2 dining areas, free Wi-Fi, in-room TV (Freeview), civil wedding licence, terraced garden. BACKGROUND MUSIC all day in dining areas. LOCATION in countryside, 3 miles from Dunwich beach. CHILDREN all ages welcomed. DOGS allowed in bedrooms and public rooms (£7.50 per night, outdoor dog wash). CREDIT CARDS Amex, MasterCard, Visa. PRICES per room B&B £110–£215. À la carte £30.
25% DISCOUNT VOUCHERS

WHEATHILL Shropshire
Map 3:C5

THE OLD RECTORY, nr Ludlow, WV16 6QT. Tel 01746 787209, www.theoldrectorywheathill.com. A cheerful welcome awaits horses, hikers and hounds at Izzy Barnard's wild flower-filled Georgian house in prime Shropshire hacking and walking country. A blazing fire in the drawing room and piles of books help guests wind down; the soothing sauna completes the job. A candlelit four-course dinner may be served (by arrangement); or perhaps simple home-made soup and a sandwich. The country-style bedrooms have home-away-from-home comforts, with a large bed, antique furnishings and biscuits to nibble (horses and dogs have their own accommodation). At breakfast, home-made bread and jams, home-cured bacon; knitted cosies keep warm eggs from the resident ducks. Guides and route cards detailing nearby bridleways are available. BEDROOMS 3. OPEN all year except Christmas, Jan. FACILITIES drawing room, dining room, sauna, free Wi-Fi, in-room TV (Freeview), 7-acre gardens, boot room, tack room, loose boxes for horses. BACKGROUND MUSIC none. LOCATION 7 miles from Ludlow. CHILDREN all ages welcomed, by arrangement. DOGS allowed (£10 per night in boot room). CREDIT CARDS MasterCard, Visa. PRICES per room B&B single £80–£120, double £95–£135. Set dinner £35, supper tray £10. 2-night min. stay preferred.

WINCHESTER Hampshire
Map 2:D2

HANNAH'S, 16a Parchment Street, SO23 8AZ. Tel 01962 840623, hannahsbedandbreakfast.co.uk. A 19th-century former dancehall and livery stable in the city centre has been transformed into a lofty B&B packed with personal touches. Hannah McIntyre home-bakes a help-yourself afternoon spread of sweet treats for guests. Squashy sofas sit next to a log burner in the book-lined library; a grand piano stands on a raised platform in the beamed breakfast room. Voguishly designed mezzanine bedrooms have wooden floors, a huge bed; ladder-style stairs lead to a bath and fig-and-vanilla-scented toiletries hand-made by the hostess. Breakfast, too, is a home-made treat of granola and berries, seed loaves, plus custom blended teas and coffees; a weekend special (perhaps piles of sausages, scrambled eggs, roast tomatoes, mushrooms). BEDROOMS 3. OPEN Feb–mid-Dec, closed Mon–Wed (self-catering rooms in cottage opposite open all days). FACILITIES breakfast room, library, free Wi-Fi, in-room TV (Freeview), terrace. BACKGROUND MUSIC in communal areas. LOCATION 2 mins' walk from the town centre. CHILDREN over-11s welcomed. DOGS allowed. CREDIT CARDS Amex, MasterCard, Visa. PRICES per room B&B from £155.

THE WYKEHAM ARMS, 75 Kingsgate Street, SO23 9PE. Tel 01962 853834, www.wykehamarmswinchester.co.uk. A 'top-rate pub-with-rooms', this 18th-century coaching inn (Fuller's Hotels and Inns) near the cathedral bursts with character. Under a different name, the pub hosted Lord Nelson on his way to Portsmouth. Jon Howard manages the establishment with 'helpful, friendly staff'. The cosy bar has real ales (five are usually on tap), a log fire, school-desk tables and walls crammed with pictures and breweriana. Fresh pub classics are served in the wood-panelled dining room. Some of the individually decorated bedrooms are up a narrow staircase; all are well-equipped with a Nespresso machine, a free-of-charge minibar, high-quality toiletries. Pub chatter ('perfectly bearable') stops around 11 pm; light (and early) sleepers may wish to discuss room options. Breakfast is 'excellent', with 'outstanding' local black pudding. BEDROOMS 14, 7 in adjacent building. OPEN all year. FACILITIES bar, 2 restaurants, 2 function rooms, free Wi-Fi, in-room TV (Freeview), small patio, parking. BACKGROUND MUSIC none. LOCATION central. CHILDREN over-11s welcomed. DOGS allowed in 2 bedrooms and bar, not in restaurant (£7.50 per night). CREDIT CARDS Amex, MasterCard, Visa. PRICES per room B&B single from £69, double from £109. À la carte £32.

WOLTERTON Norfolk
Map 2:A5

THE SARACEN'S HEAD, Wall Road, NR11 7LZ. Tel 01263 768909, www.saracenshead-norfolk.co.uk. With the Norfolk countryside stretching away on all sides, Tim and Janie Elwes's ivy-covered Georgian inn enjoys 'a beautifully rural setting'. The Elweses have refurbished the farmhouse (designed in 1806 to mimic a Tuscan farmhouse) from top to bottom, following water damage from winter deluges. The result is as cosy as ever. Bright public spaces have a zingy, contemporary feel; wood-burners keep the place homely. The bedrooms are cheery, with splashes of colour amid simple, country furnishings. In the restaurant, Norfolk plates include local North Sea mussels, Brancaster smoked salmon, Cromer crab. The comfy first-floor sitting area has piles of books and maps about the area, perfect for planning jaunts to the Broads or the nearby coast. BEDROOMS 6. OPEN all year except 24–27 Dec, 2 weeks late Feb/early Mar, restaurant closed Sun evening, Mon lunch Nov–Apr. FACILITIES lounge, bar, restaurant, free Wi-Fi, in-room TV (Freeview), courtyard, 1-acre garden, restaurant and bar wheelchair accessible, no adapted toilet. BACKGROUND MUSIC in bar and dining rooms. LOCATION 5 miles N of Aylsham. CHILDREN all ages welcomed. DOGS allowed in bedrooms, back bar, not in restaurant. CREDIT CARDS MasterCard, Visa. PRICES per room B&B single £75, double £110–£120, D,B&B double £175. À la carte £36.

WOODBRIDGE Suffolk
Map 2:C5

THE CROWN, The Thoroughfare, IP12 1AD. Tel 01394 384242, www. thecrownatwoodbridge.co.uk. A 'comfortable, welcoming' spot in a market town close to the Suffolk coast, this popular 16th-century coaching inn now offers 'cool', modern interiors alongside traditional hospitality. The wooden sailing skiff suspended above the bar is a nod to the area's nautical heritage. 'Excellent food', served in the restaurant, makes the most of Suffolk's seasonal larder with such dishes as tuna marinated in rosemary and garlic, tomato ragout, rosemary roast potatoes; diners spill out on to the large terrace in warmer weather. Upstairs, 'relaxing bedrooms' are swathed in soothing, natural tones; in each, goose-down pillows, underfloor heating, top-quality toiletries. Biscuits, piles of books and local magazines, are a nice touch. 'Particularly good service.' BEDROOMS 10. OPEN all year. FACILITIES restaurant, bar, private dining room, free Wi-Fi, in-room TV (Sky), terrace, parking, restaurant and bar wheelchair accessible. BACKGROUND MUSIC in public areas, plus regular live music. LOCATION town centre. CHILDREN all ages welcomed. DOGS allowed in bar. CREDIT CARDS Amex, MasterCard, Visa. PRICES per room B&B £100–£210, D,B&B £150–£260. À la carte £34. 1-night bookings refused Sat.

WOODSTOCK Oxfordshire
Map 2:C2

THE FEATHERS, 16–20 Market Street, OX20 1SX. Tel 01993 812291, www. feathers.co.uk. 'The best of old-world charm and modern facilities', this child-friendly hotel in a Cotswolds market town near Blenheim Palace has bags of personality. The cosy bar (popular with locals) is 'just the place to unwind', perhaps with one of its collection of more than 400 gins – a Guinness world record). Up the winding staircases, 'spotless' bedrooms have a comfortable bed, 'playful decor', bright splashes of colour, quirky touches (a jar of Jelly Babies, a sloping wooden floor). In the busy restaurant, with its wood panels and vibrant statement carpet, head chef 'Wolf' Chodurski serves innovative country-style dishes, perhaps lasagne of wild rabbit, foraged mushrooms, chervil. 'Perfect on all levels.' Sister hotel Lords of the Manor is in Upper Slaughter (see main entry). BEDROOMS 21, 1 suitable for disabled, 5 in adjacent town house. OPEN all year. FACILITIES study, bar, restaurant, free Wi-Fi, in-room TV (Freeview), courtyard. BACKGROUND MUSIC none. LOCATION town centre. CHILDREN all ages welcomed. DOGS allowed in some bedrooms, public rooms, not in restaurant. CREDIT CARDS all major cards. PRICES per room B&B from £99, D,B&B from £149. À la carte £40.

WOOLACOMBE Devon
Map 1:B4

WATERSMEET, EX34 7EB. Tel 01271 870333, www.watersmeethotel.co.uk. 'Beautifully located' on the South West Coastal Path, this former Edwardian gentleman's retreat has clifftop views of the three-mile-long beach. Nowadays, the 'comfortable, relaxed' hotel is owned by Amanda James, and run with 'friendly, helpful staff'. All but three bedrooms look out to Woolacombe Bay: 'Ours had beautiful views of a small cove with golden sand, rocks and waves.' Ask for one of the recently refurbished bedrooms – a couple this year felt their accommodation was a little tired. Chef John Prince's British dishes, served in the informal bistro and candlelit restaurant, are of an 'excellent standard'. Breakfast is 'good and plentiful'. Great walks through National Trust land and a beach are on the doorstep. 'We hope to return.' BEDROOMS 29, 3 on ground floor,

1 suitable for disabled. OPEN all year. FACILITIES lift, lounge, snug, bar, restaurant, bistro, free Wi-Fi, in-room TV (Freeview), terrace, civil wedding licence, function facilities, ½-acre garden, heated outdoor swimming pool, treatment room, restaurant wheelchair accessible. BACKGROUND MUSIC in public areas. LOCATION behind beach, slightly to N of village centre. CHILDREN all ages welcomed (children's tea). DOGS not allowed. CREDIT CARDS MasterCard, Visa. PRICES per room B&B from £120, D,B&B from £210. À la carte £50.

WORCESTER Worcestershire
Map 3:C5

THE MANOR COACH HOUSE, Hindlip Lane, WR3 8SJ. Tel 01905456457, www.manorcoachhouse.co.uk. In 'a lovely rural location' yet within easy reach of the town centre and Worcester cathedral, Chrissie Mitchell's 'spotless' and 'very reasonable' B&B is 'surrounded by delight'. The converted outbuildings are set around a courtyard; there are old cart wheels and farm paraphernalia in front, a lush garden behind. Arriving guests are offered tea, cake and helpful local information. 'Comfortable and immaculate' bedrooms (one a duplex family suite with a kitchenette) have 'excellent lighting', small fridge, bathrobes, fresh milk available on request. 'The newly installed walk-in shower was first class,' reported a Guide regular this year. There is a 'good' breakfast, although it is perhaps 'not the high point it once was'. Local pubs are within walking distance. BEDROOMS 5, all double, in converted outbuildings, 3 on ground floor. OPEN all year except Christmas. FACILITIES breakfast room, free Wi-Fi,

in-room TV (Freeview), 1-acre garden.
BACKGROUND MUSIC none. LOCATION 2
miles from city centre. CHILDREN all ages
welcomed. DOGS not allowed. CREDIT
CARDS MasterCard, Visa. PRICES per
room B&B single from £59, double from
£85, D,B&B from £89.

YELVERTON Devon
Map 1:D4

CIDER HOUSE, Buckland Abbey,
PL20 6EZ. Tel 01822 259062, www.
cider-house.co.uk. In the former brew
house, Bertie and Bryony Hancock's
sophisticated B&B is surrounded by the
National Trust's Buckland Abbey estate.
Impeccably designed in contemporary
country house style, the elegant drawing
room has an open fire, fresh flowers;
maps and guide books. Mullioned
windows in the light, airy and pretty
first-floor bedrooms reveal glorious
views; bathrooms are glamorous, with
a free-standing roll-top bath. Breakfast
includes eggs from the owners' rare
breed chickens, meat from their
saddleback pigs, and groat's pudding,
a Devon speciality. Residents receive
complimentary passes for the abbey, the
one-time home of Sir Francis Drake,
and access to its gardens. For romantics,
luxury shepherd's cabins have a glass
ceiling above the bed; a wood-burner;
DIY provisions in the galley kitchen.
BEDROOMS 4, plus 2 adult only self-
catering shepherd's huts. OPEN Mar–Oct.
FACILITIES drawing room, free Wi-Fi,
in-room TV (Freeview), civil wedding
licence, terrace, garden, 700-acre
grounds, parking. BACKGROUND MUSIC
none. LOCATION 1 mile from village, 4
miles N of Plymouth. CHILDREN over-
11s welcomed. DOGS not allowed. CREDIT
CARDS MasterCard, Visa. PRICES per
room B&B £140–£190.

YORK Yorkshire
Map 4:D4

BAR CONVENT, 17 Blossom Street, YO24
1AQ. Tel 01904 643238, www.bar-
convent.org.uk.Peace, quiet and a slap-
up breakfast are to be found at a B&B in
England's oldest active convent, next to
the city's medieval walls. Lesley Baines
manages the Grade I listed building,
which still houses a community of
sisters who share their garden, domed
chapel and antique religious texts with
guests. Simple, immaculate bedrooms
(some designed by Olga Polizzi) have a
'wickedly comfortable' bed and a well-
equipped refreshment tray. Breakfast
is served in the café, in a Victorian
atrium. There's a communal kitchen
for DIY dinners; the pick of York's
eateries are on the doorstep. Guests
enjoy a discounted entrance to the
on-site living Heritage Centre and the
convent, founded in 1686. BEDROOMS
20, 4 with shared bathrooms. OPEN all
year except some days over Christmas.
FACILITIES lift (to 1st and 2nd floors),
sitting room, kitchen, licensed café,
meeting rooms, free Wi-Fi, in-room TV
(Freeview), ¼-acre garden, museum,
shop, chapel. BACKGROUND MUSIC none.
LOCATION 5 mins' walk from the railway
station. CHILDREN all ages welcomed.
DOGS assistance dogs only. CREDIT CARDS
MasterCard, Visa. PRICES per room B&B
from £45–£120.

SCOTLAND

ABERDEEN Aberdeenshire
Map 5:C3

ATHOLL HOTEL, 54 King's Gate, AB15
4YN. Tel 01224 323505, atholl-aberdeen.
co.uk. The spires of this granite
Victorian Gothic Revival building
soar skyward, an easy-to-spot beacon
for this traditional hotel within reach
of the city centre. Convenient for the
airport, it's a popular spot with business
travellers. Fuss-free bedrooms have
cheery tartan bedcovers and cushions;
an array of necessary amenities includes
a tea and coffee tray, hair-dryer, iron
and ironing board. Spacious suites
suit a family. The restaurant, bar and
lounge serve generously portioned,
straightforward locally sourced dishes,
perhaps grilled peppered hake, linguine
with spring onion, tomato, sugar snap
peas. At breakfast, try tattie scones or
the smoked Finnan haddie. Golf courses
are close to gloved hand. BEDROOMS 34,
2 suitable for disabled. OPEN Mar–Oct,
shepherd's huts all year except Feb.
FACILITIES lift (to 1st floor), lounge,
bar, restaurant, patio, free Wi-Fi,
in-room TV (Sky Sports), weddings,
functions, parking. BACKGROUND MUSIC
in restaurant. LOCATION 1½ miles W of
city centre. CHILDREN all ages welcomed
(special menu, £10 per night). DOGS not
allowed. CREDIT CARDS all major cards.
PRICES per room B&B single £65–£75,
double £80–£99. À la carte £30.

ALLANTON Scottish Borders
Map 5:E3

ALLANTON INN, nr Duns, TD11 3JZ.
Tel 01890 818260, www.allantoninn.
co.uk. Guide readers this year 'enjoyed
the warm welcome' from 'helpful hosts'
Katrina and William Reynolds at their
'good-value' 18th-century restaurant-
with-rooms in a Borders village. 'They
showed a real interest in our holiday
plans.' The former coaching house has
'a happy blend of modern furnishings,
contemporary artwork, and the feel of
a traditional country pub'. 'Cheerfully'
served in the informal restaurant,
locally sourced dishes dominate chef
Lee Cessford's menu; 'good puddings'.
The bar has a 'spectacular' gin menu.
'Our smart bedroom was immaculately
clean; the small bathroom had all we
needed.' 'Very good breakfasts' start
the day with 'a generous choice of fruit
compotes; good-quality sausages, bacon
and haggis'. Day permits for trout and
salmon fishing are available. BEDROOMS
6. OPEN all year except 25–26 Dec.
FACILITIES bar, 2 restaurant areas, free
Wi-Fi, in-room TV (Freeview), large
garden, parking. BACKGROUND MUSIC
in bar and restaurant. LOCATION village
centre. CHILDREN all ages welcomed.
DOGS not allowed. CREDIT CARDS Amex,
MasterCard, Visa. PRICES per room B&B
£80–£105, D,B&B £120–£150.

APPLECROSS Highland
Map 5:C1

APPLECROSS INN, Shore Street, IV54
8LR. Tel 01520 744262, www.applecross.
uk.com. In rounding the final bend of
an 11-mile stretch of winding single-
track road, visitors might breathe a sign
of relief at the sight of Judith Fish's
white-painted hostelry. The small
dining room takes full advantage of
its isolated setting on the Applecross
peninsula, serving feasts of ocean-fresh
seafood, perhaps dressed prawns or
king scallops straight from the bay.
In the buzzy bar, Scottish gins, single
malts and local ales are served before

the log fire. In spring and summer, a retro food truck sells ice-creams, cakes and coffees on the seashore. Superlative views across the Inner Sound of Raasay extend from the clean, comfortable bedrooms; there may be some pub noise. Cyclists, walkers, kayakers and campers are welcomed. BEDROOMS 7, 1 on ground floor. OPEN all year, no accommodation for 2 weeks over Christmas, New Year. FACILITIES bar, dining room, free Wi-Fi, beer garden, bicycle storage, bar, dining room wheelchair accessible, adapted toilet. BACKGROUND MUSIC in bar. LOCATION 85 miles W of Inverness, opposite the Isle of Skye, approx. 2 hours' drive. CHILDREN all ages welcomed, not in bar after 8.30 pm. DOGS allowed in 2 bedrooms, on lead in bar (£15 per stay). CREDIT CARDS MasterCard, Visa. PRICES per person B&B £70. À la carte £35.

ARINAGOUR Argyll and Bute
Map 5:C1

COLL HOTEL, Isle of Coll, PA78 6SZ. Tel 01879 230334, collhotel.com. The buzzy hub of this Inner Hebridean island, this small hotel has been run by three generations of the Oliphant family since the 1960s. It offers sublime sea views from Coll's only village. Bedrooms have an understated style and plentiful homely extras (home-made biscuits, board games, Scottish-made toiletries); most look out at Mull, Staffa, Iona and Jura. Just-landed lobsters, crabs, langoustines and dived scallops need little adornment on the daily specials board in the restaurant and the cosy bar, with its open fire, local photographs and nautical memorabilia. After sunset, the rooms' glow in the dark sky scopes and star maps allow guests to understand what they can see in a sky untainted by light pollution. Complimentary shuttle to the ferry pier. BEDROOMS 6. OPEN all year except Christmas, house parties only at New Year. FACILITIES lounge, 2 bars, restaurant, residents' lounge and dining room, free Wi-Fi, in-room TV (Freeview), garden, helipad, bicycles to borrow. BACKGROUND MUSIC none. LOCATION village centre. CHILDREN all ages welcomed. DOGS allowed in public bar. CREDIT CARDS MasterCard, Visa. PRICES per room B&B single £70, double £120 £150. À la carte £26.
25% DISCOUNT VOUCHERS

ARISAIG Highland
Map 5:C1

THE OLD LIBRARY LODGE AND RESTAURANT, PH39 4NH. Tel 01687 450651, www.oldlibrary.co.uk. In a couldn't-be-prettier Highland village, Mags and Allan Ritchie's 'friendly, casual' restaurant-with-rooms, forged from a 200-year-old stone stable, is a welcoming retreat for island-hopping travellers. It looks over a sheltered harbour with sweeping views across to the Small Isles. A daily specials board in the 'smart, bistro-style restaurant' presents a choice of modern Scottish dishes cooked with a French touch, perhaps butter-poached hake, mussels, butter beans, sauté asparagus. Garden gnomes dot the path to converted 200-year-old stables where most of the simply decorated, some a bit dated, bedrooms are housed; the rooms at the front have a 'wonderful view' across the bay. Scottish treats for a 'well-cooked breakfast' include black pudding and haggis. BEDROOMS 6, 4 in annexe. OPEN all year except Jan. FACILITIES residents' lounge, restaurant, free Wi-Fi, terraced garden. BACKGROUND MUSIC traditional, in restaurant. LOCATION in village, 19 miles W of Glenfinnan. CHILDREN all ages welcomed. DOGS allowed. CREDIT CARDS Amex, MasterCard, Visa. PRICES per room B&B single £75, double £120.

BALLYGRANT Argyll and Bute
Map 5:D1

KILMENY COUNTRY HOUSE, PA45 7QW. Tel 01496 840668, www.kilmeny. co.uk. At a handsomely furnished 19th-century house on the Isle of Islay, 'fabulous hosts' offers guests a sweet welcome with home-baked treats and tea. Margaret and Blair Rozga's 'superb' B&B is surrounded by Hebridean farmland. Country house decor and antiques style the traditional, individually designed bedrooms. A bonus in each: 'spectacular views' across hills, glen and countryside. Some rooms are pleasingly capacious (a generous suite with its own kitchen suits a family); others have access to a sheltered garden; all have tea, coffee, home-made biscuits; a fridge with fresh milk. A complimentary dram of whisky makes a thoughtful nightcap. Substantial farmhouse breakfasts with home-made bread, oatcakes and preserves are 'worth getting up for'. BEDROOMS 5, 2 on ground floor. OPEN Mar–Oct. FACILITIES drawing room, dining room, sun lounge, free Wi-Fi, in-room TV (Freeview), ½-acre garden. BACKGROUND MUSIC none. LOCATION ½ mile S of Ballygrant; 10 mins' drive to Port Askaig. CHILDREN over-4s welcomed. DOGS allowed in some bedrooms. CREDIT CARDS none accepted. PRICES per room B&B single £90–£120, double £125–£172.

BARCALDINE Argyll and Bute
Map 5:D1

ARDTORNA, The Mill Farm, PA37 1SE. Tel 01631 720125, www.ardtorna.co.uk.

Light, bright and full of life, Sean and Karen O'Byrne's super-modern, eco-friendly house is all Scandi style and floor-to-ceiling windows offering memorable views of Loch Creran. Afternoon pastries are part of a generous greeting, while a help-yourself home-made whisky cream liqueur remains a temptation. In the spruced-up bedrooms with bright splashes of colour, a king-size bed and underfloor heating, plus many extras: high-end toiletries, hand-made chocolates, complimentary treats in the fridge. Breakfast, served in the glass-fronted dining room, has home-baked soda bread, fresh-griddled waffles, Scottish platter with Stornoway black pudding and tattie scones. The hosts can help plan day trips; a traditional longbow lesson is an unexpected alternative – Sean is a former world champion. BEDROOMS 4. OPEN Mar–Nov. FACILITIES dining room, free Wi-Fi, in-room TV (Freeview), 1-acre farmland, parking. BACKGROUND MUSIC traditional in restaurant. LOCATION 12 miles N of Oban. CHILDREN over-12s welcomed. DOGS allowed. CREDIT CARDS MasterCard, Visa. PRICES per person B&B £60–£90.

BORVE Isle of Harris
Map 5:B1

PAIRC AN T-SRATH, HS3 3HT. Tel 01859 550386, www.paircant-srath.co.uk. On the crest of Borve's golden sand beach, Lena and Richard MacLennan's 'lovely, comfortable' guest house has 'superb views' over the sound of Taransay. It's all simply and unfussily done, without compromising comfort. Harris tweed blankets drape the bed in the neat, wood-floored bedrooms; fresh flowers and shelves of books bring lightness to a sitting room warmed by a peat fire.

Perhaps a surprising touch: a sauna in which to ease tired muscles after a day exploring the island. In the dining room, locally sourced produce (Uist scallops, Stornoway black pudding) are magicked into 'exceptionally good, well-presented' home-cooked dinners, served by candlelight, overlooking the sea. Breakfasts are a 'feast'. **BEDROOMS** 4. **OPEN** all year, except Christmas, New Year. **FACILITIES** sitting room, dining room, free Wi-Fi, sauna. **BACKGROUND MUSIC** none. **LOCATION** in village. **CHILDREN** all ages welcomed. **DOGS** allowed in 1 bedroom, by arrangement. **CREDIT CARDS** MasterCard, Visa. **PRICES** per person B&B £54. Set 3-course dinner £38.

BRAE Shetland
Map 5: inset A2

BUSTA HOUSE, ZE2 9QN. Tel 01806 522506, www.bustahouse.com. From the sheltered shores of Busta Voe, this white-painted hotel makes a pleasing base for island exploration. Itinerary inspiration is close to hand – each bedroom is named after a Shetland island. The house, originally built in 1588, has been much extended, leading to a quirky layout, with creaky floors, lots of stairs and a friendly ghost, Barbara. A homely lounge has bright carpets, wood floors, dignified seats by the window. Upstairs, traditionally styled bedrooms overlook the gardens or harbour. The bar has an extensive range of single malts; the restaurant, an unfussy menu with generous helpings of such dishes as pan-seared local king scallops, almond pesto cream. A surprise outside: the garden's gargoyles once graced the House of Commons. **BEDROOMS** 22. **OPEN** all year except 2 weeks over Christmas and New Year.

FACILITIES 2 lounges, bar/dining area, restaurant, free Wi-Fi, in-room TV, wedding facilities, garden, computer for guests' use. **BACKGROUND MUSIC** in restaurant. **LOCATION** 3 mins' drive S of Brae. **CHILDREN** all ages welcomed. **DOGS** allowed in some bedrooms. **CREDIT CARDS** All major cards. **PRICES** per room B&B £115–£160. À la carte £35.

BROADFORD Highland
Map 5:C1

TIGH AN DOCHAIS, 13 Harrapool, Isle of Skye, IV49 9AQ. Tel 01471 820022, www.skyebedbreakfast.co.uk. Across a galvanised footbridge, the huge windows of Neil Hope and Lesley Unwin's modern, architect-designed B&B bring those 'glorious views' of Broadford Bay and the Cuillin mountains right into the house. The book-lined bright, open-plan lounge/dining area has a log-burning stove and plump sofas enabling comfortable enjoyment of the panorama. On the floor below, a sliding door leads from each tartan-accented bedroom to larch decking. Neil Hope starts the day cooking a 'delicious' locally sourced breakfast, served communally: Skye sausages; Lewis cheeses; home-made bread, muffins and yogurt. An evening meal can be arranged at booking; restaurants are within walking distance. The 'friendly hosts' have plenty of 'helpful information' for planning local excursions. **BEDROOMS** 3, all on ground floor. **OPEN** Mar–Nov. **FACILITIES** lounge/dining area, free Wi-Fi, in-room TV (Freesat). **BACKGROUND MUSIC** 'traditional, occasionally, during breakfast'. **LOCATION** 1 mile E of Broadford. **CHILDREN** all ages welcomed (must take own room). **DOGS** not allowed. **CREDIT CARDS** MasterCard,

Visa. PRICES per room B&B £105. Set menu £25.

BRODICK Ayrshire
Map 5:E1

AUCHRANNIE HOUSE HOTEL, Auchrannie Road, Isle of Arran, KA27 8BZ. Tel 01770 302234, www. auchrannie.co.uk. South of Goat Fell's pyramidal peak, this large, child-friendly destination is the only resort on the Scottish isles. The 19th-century country house is one of two hotels established by the Johnston family on the sprawling estate. Rooms have tasteful earthy hues, hints of tweed; some of the spa hotel's large, contemporary rooms enjoy access to an outdoor terrace and hot tub. All rooms have Scottish smellies, fresh milk, tea- and coffee-making facilities. There are plush lounges, a well-stocked library, swimming pools; a huge playbarn for children. Dining options include grilled fare and West Coast seafood in informal Brambles; Scottish-themed tapas, perhaps haggis Scotch eggs, in a conservatory restaurant, eighteen69. Nearby, walks, bike and horse rides await. BEDROOMS 28, some suitable for disabled, plus Spa Resort rooms and 30 self-catering lodges. OPEN all year. FACILITIES bar, lounges, 3 restaurants, spa, indoor pool, gym, free Wi-Fi, in-room TV (Freeview), wedding/function facilities, 60-acre grounds, tennis, parking, complimentary shuttle bus to/from the ferry terminal. BACKGROUND MUSIC in public areas. LOCATION 1 mile from ferry terminal. CHILDREN all ages welcomed. DOGS allowed in some bedrooms, some public rooms. CREDIT CARDS Amex, MasterCard, Visa. PRICES per room B&B from £99, D,B&B from £139. Set dinner £35.

BRUICHLADDICH Argyll and Bute
Map 5:D1

LOCH GORM HOUSE, Isle of Islay, PA49 7UN. Tel 01496 850139, www. lochgormhouse.com. 'What a delightful place to stay.' On the northern shore of Islay, this 'charming, beautifully appointed' B&B is run by 'wonderfully welcoming' Fiona Doyle. The stone-built house is fronted by well-kept gardens, and has 'amazing views over the bay'. A florist, the hostess displays 'magnificent' flower arrangements in the large drawing room and the 'spotless', prettily furnished bedrooms that gaze seaward or inland across the fields. 'Our bright, comfortable bedroom had amazing views over the bay. Fiona made dinner reservations for us – a nice touch.' Breakfast ('such a feast') is a 'scrumptious' start to the day. Wellies, coats and beach towels are provided for coastal wanderings. BEDROOMS 3. OPEN Mar–Dec. FACILITIES drawing room, dining room, free Wi-Fi, in-room TV (Freeview), 1-acre garden, drying facilities. BACKGROUND MUSIC none. LOCATION outside village on seafront. CHILDREN all ages welcomed. DOGS well-behaved dogs allowed in bedrooms, bar. CREDIT CARDS Diners Club, MasterCard, Visa. PRICES per room B&B £135–£155.
25% DISCOUNT VOUCHERS

CRINAN Argyll and Bute
Map 5:D1

CRINAN HOTEL, PA31 8SR. Tel 01546 830261, www.crinanhotel.com. 'What an amazing location!' Seafood and sea views remain the two major draws at this 'friendly, informal' hotel in a 'spectacular position' where the Crinan canal meets the loch. Frances Macdonald is now at the helm, following the death of her husband, Nick Ryan. The two had run Crinan together for over 45 years. The staff remain 'hard working and very pleasant', wrote a Guide regular this year. Guests loved the 'marvellous' fresh seafood in the bar and restaurants but felt 'the whole needed updating; and housekeeping could be more thorough'. Bedrooms ('simply furnished') have views of the canal basin or across Loch Crinan towards the islands of Scarba and Mull. 'Wonderful art', much of it by Frances and son, Ross, is on display. **BEDROOMS** 21. **OPEN** Mar–20 Dec, 31 Dec–4 Jan. **FACILITIES** lift, 2 lounges, bar/bistro, 3 restaurants, coffee shop, art gallery, free Wi-Fi, in-room TV, ¼-acre garden, patio, wedding/function facilities, spa treatments. **BACKGROUND MUSIC** none. **LOCATION** village centre, waterfront. 6 miles from Lochgilphead. **CHILDREN** all ages welcomed. **DOGS** well-behaved dogs allowed by arrangement, not in Westward restaurant (£10 per night, own bedding required). **CREDIT CARDS** Amex, MasterCard, Visa. **PRICES** per room B&B £110–£290, D,B&B £150–£330. Set dinner (Westward) £45, à la carte (Seafood bar) £26. 25% DISCOUNT VOUCHERS

DALKEITH Midlothian
Map 5:D2

THE SUN INN, Lothianbridge, EH22 4TR. Tel 0131 663 2456, www.thesuninnedinburgh.co.uk. On the approach to Edinburgh, the humble, white-painted frontage of the Minto family's 'down-to-earth' roadside pub-with-rooms belies its zippy interiors. Stylish wallpaper, tweed scatter pillows and sassy bibelots jazz up the original fireplace and old beams. Updated pub classics in the popular dining room include Belhaven smoked haddock fishcakes, Musselburgh leeks, mature cheddar cheese sauce. Come summer, the covered courtyard opens for barbecues. Bold prints and handcrafted furniture characterise the bedrooms, well equipped with home-made biscuits, a Roberts radio, a DVD library; a suite has a lavish two-person copper bath, a modern four-poster bed. Quietest rooms face away from the street. The extensive breakfast menu includes home-made granola, fresh berries; a full Scottish including haggis, tattie scones. **BEDROOMS** 6. **OPEN** all year except 26 Dec–1 Jan. **FACILITIES** bar, gin bar, coffee shop, free Wi-Fi, in-room TV (Sky), garden, parking. **BACKGROUND MUSIC** in restaurant. **LOCATION** 8 miles SE of Edinburgh. **CHILDREN** all ages welcomed. **DOGS** assistance dogs accepted. **CREDIT CARDS** Amex, MasterCard, Visa. **PRICES** per room B&B single from £75, double from £95. À la carte £35.

DORNOCH Highland
Map 5:B2

2 QUAIL, Castle Street, IV25 3SN. Tel 01862 811811, www.2quail.com. Bright and inviting, a 'very pleasant' sandstone guest house provides homely, well-executed accommodation close to the cathedral and the Royal Dornoch Golf Club. The late-Victorian town house, owned by 'helpful hosts' Kerensa and Michael Carr, has a wood-burning stove, tartan carpet and well-stocked library in the cosy lounge; many family antiques are displayed throughout the property. Traditionally decorated bedrooms have a decent hospitality tray, a power shower in the bathroom. The evening's set menu takes into account guests' allergies, intolerances or dislikes (notify in advance). A 'delicious breakfast' is served from 7 am ('for those with an early tee time'). The sands of Dornoch Firth are nearby. BEDROOMS 3. OPEN all year except Christmas. FACILITIES lounge/library, dining room, free Wi-Fi, in-room TV (Freeview). BACKGROUND MUSIC none. LOCATION town centre. CHILDREN 'babes in arms', over-10s welcomed. DOGS well-behaved dogs allowed by arrangement, not in Westward restaurant (£10 per night, own bedding required). CREDIT CARDS Amex, MasterCard, Visa. PRICES per person B&B single from £85–£135, double £95–£140, D,B&B double £130–£170. Set dinners £22–£27.

DULNAIN BRIDGE Highland
Map 5:C2

MUCKRACH COUNTRY HOUSE HOTEL, Dulnain Bridge, PH26 3LY. Tel 01479 851227, www.muckrach.com. Surrounded by the Cairngorms national park, this restored Victorian shooting lodge has been given a zesty finish by the Cowap family. Local artwork, cheery modern furnishings and Scottish flourishes brighten the wood-panelled public areas; outside, the slated terrace overlooks pond and pastureland. Bright bedrooms have fluffy bathrobes, up-to-the-minute technology (smart TV, iPod dock, ceiling speakers). An all-day menu of cake, coffees and nibbles keeps you going, but dinner is a feast: 'home-style cooking with a twist', served in the candlelit conservatory restaurant, perhaps Calva brie, leek and potato Wellington. A nightcap requires due consideration, with a range of 70 whiskies. An extensive breakfast keeps the bar high: Inverawe smoked salmon, scrambled eggs; Muckrach kedgeree with peat smoked Peterhead haddock.

BEDROOMS 13, some in garden annexe, 2 interconnecting rooms suitable for a family. OPEN all year. FACILITIES drawing room, library, bar, conservatory restaurant/coffee shop, private dining room, free Wi-Fi, in-room TV (Freeview), 1-acre garden, terraced patio, weddings, meetings, drying room. BACKGROUND MUSIC in public areas. LOCATION outskirts of Dulnain Bridge, 5 miles from Grantown-on-Spey. CHILDREN all ages welcomed. DOGS well-behaved dogs allowed in some bedrooms, on lead in library. CREDIT CARDS Amex, MasterCard, Visa. PRICES per room B&B from £99, D,B&B from £159. À la carte £27.

EDINBURGH
Map 5:D2

THE BALMORAL, 1 Princes Street, EH2 2EQ. Tel 0131 556 2414, www.roccofortehotels.com/hotels-and-resorts/the-balmoral-hotel. An Edinburgh landmark for over a century, this Victorian railway stopover is today a thoroughly 21st-century luxury hotel (Rocco Forte Hotels). Greeted by a kilted doorman, visitors cross the threshold into grand public spaces. Most of the elegant bedrooms look towards Edinburgh Castle; all were designed by Olga Polizzi. Suites have Scottish flourishes, widescreen views. Guests who look further than the Michelin-starred restaurant or award-winning spa, might spend a sybaritic afternoon taking tea in the glass-domed Palm Court, or sampling some of the bar's 400-plus whiskies. Another option: informal dining in buzzy Brasserie Prince. A place where time waits: the hotel's iconic clock has been set three minutes fast since 1902, to ensure that no-one misses their train. BEDROOMS

188, 3 suitable for disabled. OPEN all year. FACILITIES drawing room, 3 bars, restaurant, brasserie, free Wi-Fi, in-room TV, civil wedding licence, conferences, indoor swimming pool, spa, gym, valet parking. BACKGROUND MUSIC in restaurant, brasserie, bars and lobby. LOCATION city centre. CHILDREN all ages welcomed. DOGS allowed in some bedrooms. CREDIT CARDS Amex, MasterCard, Visa. PRICES per room B&B from £224, 7-course set menu £89, 10-course set menu £120. À la carte £80.

BROOKS HOTEL EDINBURGH, 70–72 Grove Street, EH3 8AP. Tel 0131 228 2323, www.brooksedinburgh.com. Within easy reach of the city's sight-seeing trail, Andrew and Carla Brooks's spruced-up 1840s West End hotel has an elegant, clubby feel. The modern lounge is given a vintage edge with handpicked statement pieces including a black chandelier; deep leather seating, animal horns; periodicals, board games, an honesty bar and a DVD library are on hand. The well-appointed design carries into the unfussy bedrooms; some are suitable for a family. No need to rush at weekends: breakfasts, served until 11 am, include a full Scottish embracing haggis and a tati scone. A daily room-service comfort food menu (fish pie, pork and cider casserole) is available till 10 pm. See also Brooks Guesthouse, Bristol, and Brooks Country House, Ross-on-Wye (main entries). BEDROOMS 46, some in annexe, 1 suitable for disabled. OPEN all year except 23–27 Dec. FACILITIES lounge, breakfast room, dining room, free Wi-Fi, in-room TV, courtyard garden, paid parking nearby (£12 per day). BACKGROUND MUSIC in lounge (jazz/contemporary). LOCATION 10 mins' walk to Haymarket station. CHILDREN all ages welcomed. DOGS not allowed. CREDIT CARDS Amex, MasterCard, Visa. PRICES per room B&B single £65, double £75–£169.

CITYROOMZ EDINBURGH, 25–33 Shandwick Place, EH2 4RG. Tel 0131 229 6871, cityroomz.com. Ideal for city walkers on a budget, this affordable hotel, with its bright, pared-down style, makes a cheerful base for exploring the surrounding landmarks. Rooms on the upper floors look out at Old Town and New Town. Varying in size, rooms can be boxy or capacious, but they have all the essentials of a city stay: blackout curtains or blinds, an iron and ironing board, a laptop safe; a bedside nook for a cup of tea. BYO takeaway meals may be eaten in the communal dining area (crockery and cutlery provided). Breakfast – a continental buffet or a grab-and-go bag – is available at extra charge. BEDROOMS 45, 9 family rooms with bunk bed. OPEN all year. FACILITIES lift, dining room, free Wi-Fi, in-room TV, discounts for parking at Castle Terrace car park, nearby. BACKGROUND MUSIC in public areas. LOCATION city centre. CHILDREN all ages welcomed. DOGS well-behaved dogs allowed in some bedrooms, on lead in library. CREDIT CARDS MasterCard, Visa. PRICES room only from £63. Breakfast £9.

THE DUNSTANE HOUSES, 4 West Coates and 5 Hampton Terrace, EH12 5JQ. Tel 0131 337 6169, thedunstane.com. Heathery tones and tweedy fabrics bring a breath of fresh Orkney air to this family-run hotel in two Victorian villas just beyond the city centre. Luxurious suites have high ceiling, a deep copper bath. Rooms are simpler in Hampton House, opposite, but all are supplied with a comfortable bed, pampering products, home-made shortbread. In Ba' Bar, rich hues, leather bar stools, monochrome photographs and a wide selection of craft spirits; in the lounges, colourful velvet chairs and sofas. Modern Scottish dishes (crispy haggis bonbons, hand-dived scallops) are available through the day. Buses to the centre; those to the airport stop right outside. BEDROOMS 35, in 2 buildings. OPEN all year. FACILITIES bar, 2 lounges, conservatory, free Wi-Fi, in-room TV (Freeview), garden, parking. BACKGROUND MUSIC in public areas. CHILDREN all ages welcomed. DOGS not allowed. CREDIT CARDS Amex, MasterCard, Visa. PRICES per room B&B single from £149, double £154–£525, D,B&B double £204–£595. À la carte £30. 2-night min. stay preferred on Sat night.

94DR, 94 Dalkeith Road, EH16 5AF. Tel 0131 662 9265, 94dr.co.uk. Paul Lightfoot and John MacEwan may profess to have high-octane enthusiasm for all things, but their Southside Victorian town house is nothing but relaxing. 'Paul was very personable and helpful,' reports our inspector this year. Five minutes' walk from Holyrood Park, the stylish guest house's entrance hall, with beautiful period tiles, leads to a lounge with an eclectic library and honesty bar. The neat bedrooms bear Scottish heritage, from the period pieces to contemporary artworks; in the 'spotless' bathroom: underfloor heating, waffle bathrobes, upmarket toiletries. Front views stretch towards Salisbury Crags and Arthur's Seat; quieter, garden-view rooms lie at the rear. Home-cooked organic breakfasts including granola, apricot, vanilla,

honey; a 'pimped-up avocado' were 'a great start to the day'. BEDROOMS 6. OPEN all year except Christmas Day, 2 weeks in Jan. FACILITIES lounge, drawing room, breakfast room, free Wi-Fi, in-room TV (Freeview, Netflix), walled garden, bicycles available to borrow, pop-up dining event twice a month. BACKGROUND MUSIC none. LOCATION A 20-min. walk, or a 10-min. bus journey to all amenities. CHILDREN over-2s welcomed. DOGS not allowed. CREDIT CARDS Diners Club, MasterCard, Visa. PRICES per room B&B £150–£200. 2-night min. stay preferred.

TIGERLILY, 125 George Street, EH2 4JN. Tel 0131 225 5005, www. tigerlilyedinburgh.co.uk. Refreshingly spirited, this Georgian hotel in New Town does not go in for half measures. Every room has swagger, with rakish prints, jewel tones, wildly patterned wallpaper and shimmering mirror-ball surfaces; a lush living wall of greenery. Uncluttered bedrooms rein it in, thanks to a recent makeove, with soothing hues, stripped wooden floor, a sleek bathroom, but can't resist the odd splash of colour. All are packed with amenities: plush bathrobes, slippers, a pre-loaded iPod, an iPad concierge. The bars are popular with locals on a night out (the cocktail list numbers above 70); so are the brasserie-style plates served in the buzzy restaurant. Come morning, detox juices and breakfast baps are restorative fuel. BEDROOMS 33, some smoking. OPEN all year except 24–25 Dec. FACILITIES lift, 2 bars, restaurant, free Wi-Fi, in-room TV (Freeview). BACKGROUND MUSIC in bar and restaurant. LOCATION city centre. CHILDREN all ages welcomed. DOGS not allowed. CREDIT CARDS Amex, MasterCard, Visa. PRICES per room

B&B from £250, D,B&B from £310.
À la carte £30.

21212, 3 Royal Terrace, EH7 5AB. Tel
0345 22 21212, www.21212restaurant.
co.uk. Take a Michelin-starred kitchen,
throw in equally impressive bedrooms
and a soupçon of laid-back glamour,
and you have Paul Kitching and
Katie O'Brien's splendid restaurant-
with-rooms. Airy spaces within the
Georgian town house, which faces
the Royal Terrace Gardens, have been
given a light, quirky touch: a vast
copy of a painting by Caravaggio; a
sculpted Greek-style head; a dazzling
contemporary chandelier. An epicurean
evening begins in the handsome
first-floor drawing room with an
aperitif, followed by an accomplished
weekly-changing menu served in
the elegant dining room with clear
sight into the kitchen. The top-notch
dishes, with contemporary French
influences, include chicken, artichoke,
garlic-smoked figs. In the crisply styled
bedrooms, plush seating, city or firth
views, a soothing palette. **BEDROOMS**
4. **OPEN** all year except 12 days Jan, 12
days Sept, 25–26 Dec, 1 Jan. **FACILITIES**
drawing room, restaurant, private
dining rooms, free Wi-Fi, in-room
TV (Freeview). **BACKGROUND MUSIC**
none. **LOCATION** 5 mins' walk from city
centre. **CHILDREN** over-5s welcomed.
DOGS not allowed. **CREDIT CARDS** Amex,
MasterCard, Visa. **PRICES** per room B&B
£95–£295. Set menus £70–£85. 2-night
min. stay preferred.

23 MAYFIELD, 23 Mayfield Gardens,
EH9 2BX. Tel 0131 667 5806,
www.23mayfield.co.uk. A 'short
mile' from the city centre, the rather
unassuming exterior of Ross Birnie's
three-storey Victorian house belies
its handsome interiors and contented
atmosphere. Original stained-glass
windows, deep sofas and a well-stocked
honesty bar are relaxing combinations
in the panelled lounge; in the library,
some of the many books date back to
the 1740s. Handcrafted mahogany
furniture gives the bedrooms a
pleasingly masculine feel, softened by
the quality linen, high-end toiletries
and fresh coffee for the cafetière;
each bathroom has a shower rather
than a bath. An 'observatory' has a
telescope trained on Arthur's Seat.
Breakfasts, including a daily special,
are 'fabulously hearty'. Buses to the
centre stop frequently just outside.
BEDROOMS 7, 1 on ground floor. **OPEN**
all year except Christmas. **FACILITIES**
club room, breakfast room, free Wi-Fi,
in-room smart TV (Freeview), terrace,
garden, parking. **BACKGROUND MUSIC**
at breakfast. **LOCATION** 1 mile S of city
centre. **CHILDREN** over-2s welcomed.
DOGS assistance dogs allowed in hotel,
all dogs allowed in apartments. **CREDIT
CARDS** MasterCard, Visa. **PRICES** per
room B&B £120–£230.

THE WITCHERY BY THE CASTLE,
Castlehill, The Royal Mile, EH1 2NF.
Tel 0131 225 5613, www.thewitchery.
com. All is fair in the candlelit rooms of
James Thomson's enthralling 16th- and
17th-century buildings overlooking the
Royal Mile, with their hidden doors
and dramatic nooks and crannies. The
atmospheric restaurant-with-suites,
by the gates of Edinburgh Castle, is
swathed in tapestries and fine carvings.
An indulgent Scottish menu is served
in two theatrical dining rooms under a
painted ceiling, with such dishes as roast
loin of Cairngorm venison, honey-roast

root vegetables, parsnip mousseline, bramble jus. There's no lounge, but each of the eclectic, Gothic-style bedrooms has a bottle of champagne on arrival, a bath made for sharing, a huge four-poster, high-spec technology. Come morning, a breakfast hamper may be delivered to the room. See also Prestonfield (main entry). BEDROOMS 9 suites. OPEN all year except 24–25 Dec. FACILITIES 2 dining rooms, free Wi-Fi, terrace. BACKGROUND MUSIC in public areas. LOCATION by the castle, on the Royal Mile. CHILDREN all ages welcomed. DOGS not allowed. CREDIT CARDS Amex, MasterCard, Visa. PRICES per room B&B from £345. 3-course set menu £40.

ELIE Fife
Map 5:D3
THE SHIP INN, The Toft, KY9 1DT. Tel 01333 330246, www.shipinn.scot. Curling waves roll up to this smart pub/ restaurant-with-rooms in a picturesque former fishing village.Remodelled by Graham and Rachel Bucknall (see The Bridge Inn at Ratho, main entry), it has a comforting bar and dining area with tweed and leather seating, warming fires, hearty pub favourites with mostly local ingredients. The upstairs restaurant overlooks the water; the terrace above the sea wall is ideal for barbecues. Bedrooms, decorated in coastal tones, have a wool throw, coffee machine, plantation shutters and binoculars for studying passing ships. At low tide, the sand in front doubles as a cricket pitch for the country's only pub team to play on a beach (the MCC is an annual opponent). BEDROOMS 6. OPEN all year, except Christmas Day. FACILITIES bar, restaurant, beach bar, free Wi-Fi, in-room TV (Freeview),

beer garden/terrace. BACKGROUND MUSIC in public areas. LOCATION in town, on the bay. CHILDREN all ages welcomed. DOGS in bar, downstairs restaurant, 2 bedrooms (£15 per stay). CREDIT CARDS MasterCard, Visa. PRICES per person B&B £110–£185. À la carte £50.

FORT WILLIAM Highland
Map 5:C1
THE LIME TREE, Achintore Road, PH33 6RQ. Tel 01397 701806, www.limetreefortwilliam.co.uk. Quintessential loch views are a match for 'innovative food' and 'true hospitality' at David Wilson's former church manse – small wonder that the hotel, restaurant and modern art gallery attract returning guests year after year. Works by the host, a Highland artist, and others, are displayed throughout the building. Recently revamped, the 'comfortable, well-equipped bedrooms' have bright fabrics, solid furnishings and lots of natural light (loch-facing rooms book quickly). The 'cosy' dining room's modern Scottish dishes are 'tasty, and served in generous portions'. Breakfast is a feast: 'a very good buffet, followed by perfectly cooked hot dishes'. Along with contemporary Scottish artists, previous exhibitions at the gallery have included works from Goya, Matisse and Hockney. BEDROOMS 9, some in modern extension. OPEN all year except Christmas. FACILITIES 3 lounges, restaurant, gallery, free Wi-Fi, in-room TV (Freeview), garden, drying room, bicycle storage, parking. BACKGROUND MUSIC none. LOCATION edge of town centre (5-min. walk). CHILDREN all ages welcomed. DOGS allowed, separate dining area. CREDIT CARDS Amex, MasterCard, Visa. PRICES per room B&B £80–£150. À la carte £50.

GLASGOW Glasgow
Map 5:D2

15GLASGOW, 15 Woodside Place, G3 7QL. Tel 0141 332 1263, 15glasgow. com. As a former home of Glasgow merchants, Lorraine Gibson's listed B&B was built to provide rest and peace in a leafy neighbourhood – it still does this today. The 'well-located' late Victorian town house is an elegantly restored haven close to the city centre, minutes from galleries and museums. The sash windows, original fireplaces and intricate cornicing are complemented by a delicate Scottish design. Spacious, high-ceilinged bedrooms have a super-king-size bed, mood lighting; from two vast suites, huge windows overlook gardens front or rear. Ordered the night before, breakfast (eaten in the room, or communally in the lounge) includes the Angus stack: potato waffle, black pudding, fried egg, rocket, balsamic vinegar. Guests enjoy access to the private garden opposite. BEDROOMS 5. OPEN all year. FACILITIES lounge, free Wi Fi, in-room TV (Sky, Freeview), small garden, parking. BACKGROUND MUSIC none. LOCATION between town centre and West End. CHILDREN over-6s welcomed. DOGS allowed in bedrooms, not in public spaces. CREDIT CARDS MasterCard, Visa. PRICES per room B&B £130–£170.

GLENEGEDALE Argyll and Bute
Map 5:D1

GLENEGEDALE HOUSE, Isle of Islay, PA42 7AS. Tel 01496 300 400, www. glenegedalehouse.co.uk. Amid large gardens, Graeme and Emma Clark's well-placed white-washed house gazes across the Mull of Oa to the Atlantic beyond. Consummate hosts, the Clarks dispense local knowledge, freshly baked cakes, a dram each night in front of the fire, to appreciative B&B guests. Smart bedrooms, decorated with antiques and judicious plaid, are supplied with spoiling extras: toiletries, Scottish-blended teas, chocolates from a Highland chocolatier. The breakfast spread includes poached and fresh fruit, porridge laced with whisky (from one of the eight working distilleries on the island). Golden beaches and archaeological sites are nearby. Close to the small island airfield; ferry terminals a short drive away. BEDROOMS 4, plus 4-bed self-catering house. OPEN Jan–Nov. FACILITIES morning room, drawing room, bar, dining room, music room, free Wi-Fi, in-room TV (Freeview), garden, parking, public rooms wheelchair accessible. BACKGROUND MUSIC none. LOCATION 4 miles from Port Ellen, 6 miles from Bowmore. CHILDREN over-11s welcomed. DOGS not allowed. CREDIT CARDS MasterCard, Visa. PRICES per room B&B £115–£195.

GULLANE East Lothian
Map 5:D3

GREYWALLS, Muirfield, EH31 2EG. Tel 01620 842144, greywalls.co.uk. Flanked by the shoreline and Muirfield golf course, and with nine other courses nearby, the Weaver family's luxury hotel is a seaside haven for golfers. Managed by Duncan Fraser, the Edwardian honey-stone house stays true to the vision of its architect, Sir Edwin Lutyens, that it be a 'dignified holiday home'. Today, its plush rooms, afternoon teas, and well-maintained garden (attributed to Gertrude Jekyll) with croquet lawn, putting green and lawn tennis court, all create a civilised home-away-from-home feel. The restaurant deftly deploys locally sourced produce for classic French dishes; lighter meals are served in the bar/lounge. Broad views of the Firth of Forth or verdant fields are enjoyed from traditionally styled bedrooms. Fifteen minutes' walk to the sea. BEDROOMS 23, 4 on ground floor, 6 in lodges nearby. OPEN all year. FACILITIES bar/lounge, drawing room, library, restaurant, free Wi-Fi, in-room TV (Freeview), weddings/function facilities, spa treatments, 6-acre garden, tennis court. BACKGROUND MUSIC none. LOCATION 20 miles E of Edinburgh. CHILDREN all ages welcomed. DOGS allowed in cottage bedrooms, not in public rooms. CREDIT CARDS Amex, MasterCard, Visa. PRICES per room B&B single £95–£135, double £300–£420. Set dinner £40, à la carte £47. 25% DISCOUNT VOUCHERS

INNERLEITHEN Peebles
Map 5:E2

CADDON VIEW, Caddon View, EH44 6HH. Tel 01896 830208, www. caddonview.co.uk. Much praise this year for Stephen and Lisa Davies's 'good-value', 'highly recommended' Victorian guest house in the Tweed valley – 'a little patch of undiscovered Scotland'. Outdoorsy adventures in the Borders, many from the door, are plentiful. Indoor pursuits are well represented too, with books, board games, and a blazing fire in the drawing room where guests arrive to 'a friendly welcome' from the 'super hosts', including tea, home-baked treats. 'Our room was clean, pleasant, but quite small,' wrote a Guide inspector, 'with very few toiletries'. Five nights a week, Stephen Davies serves 'excellent' seasonal Scottish cuisine in the atmospheric dining room. 'Our marvellous venison was cooked to perfection.' Breakfast,

served until 10 am, is 'lovely, just the right amount.' BEDROOMS 8. OPEN all year except Christmas. FACILITIES drawing room, dining room, free Wi-Fi, in-room TV (Freeview), ½-acre mature garden, storage for bicycles and fishing gear, parking. BACKGROUND MUSIC in dining room. LOCATION 400 yards from the centre of Innerleithen. CHILDREN well-behaved children of all ages welcomed. DOGS allowed in 1 bedroom, drawing room 'if no other guests object' (£5 per night). PRICES per room B&B £70–£115, D,B&B £130–£170.

INVERNESS Inverness-shire
Map 5:C2

MOYNESS HOUSE, 6 Bruce Gardens, IV3 5EN. Tel 01463 236624, www. moyness.co.uk. The city's bustling centre is within a few minutes' stroll, yet Wilma and John Martin's B&B remains a restful retreat, within its own grounds on a quiet residential street. A modest Victorian villa, built in 1880, it was once home to Highland literary giant Neil M Gunn. His books line the peaceful sitting room overlooking the garden. Upstairs, the individually styled bedrooms – named after Gunn's works – are supplied with bathrobes, toiletries, a hospitality tray. The garden hens provide eggs for the 'tasty breakfasts'. The Martins have plentiful tips about the city and surrounding area, and happily help arrange tours. BEDROOMS 7. OPEN Feb–Dec. FACILITIES sitting room, dining room, free Wi-Fi, in-room TV (Freeview), ¼-acre garden, parking. BACKGROUND MUSIC at breakfast. LOCATION 10 mins' walk from the town centre. CHILDREN all ages welcomed. DOGS not allowed. CREDIT CARDS MasterCard, Visa. PRICES per room B&B £86–£125.

TRAFFORD BANK GUEST HOUSE, 96
Fairfield Road, IV3 5LL. Tel 01463
241414, www.traffordbankguesthouse.
co.uk. 'Careful attention to detail'
and 'a great breakfast' win praise at
Lorraine Pun's 'beautifully decorated'
sandstone Victorian B&B near the
Caledonian Canal. The 'helpful, very
friendly hostess', an interior designer,
has imbued the bay-windowed house –
a former bishop's home – with a casual
elegance. Tartan rugs and squashy sofas
dot the polished wood floors, antiques
mix with contemporary furniture. The
airy bedrooms have a wrought iron bed,
a silent mini-fridge, an iPod dock; some
have a Nespresso machine, a bathroom
with a free-standing roll-top or slipper
bath. Breakfast, ordered the night
before, is served in the conservatory.
The pretty garden has sheltered seating,
a sculpture collection. Local attractions
and the loch are a stroll away. BEDROOMS
5. OPEN Mar–Nov, 19 Jan–10 Feb.
FACILITIES 2 lounges, conservatory
breakfast room, free Wi-Fi, in-room
TV (Freeview), ½-acre garden, parking.
BACKGROUND MUSIC none. LOCATION 10
mins' walk from centre. CHILDREN over-
5s welcomed. DOGS allowed in cottage
bedrooms, not in public rooms. CREDIT
CARDS MasterCard, Visa. PRICES per
room B&B £110–£150.

KELSO Scottish Borders
Map 5:E3

THE OLD PRIORY BED AND BREAKFAST,
33/35 Woodmarket, TD5 7AT. Tel
01573 223030, www.theoldpriorykelso.
com. At their home in a cobbled
market town in the Scottish Borders,
the Girdwood family's 'traditional'
B&B receives generous praise from a
Guide regular in 2018. 'Even better than
our last visit. They are very friendly

hosts.' The late 18th-century house has
elegantly furnished bedrooms; there are
antiques, original shutters, silk-filled
duvets; 'a tray with good tea bags, a
teapot, fresh coffee and cafetiere'. The
modern bathroom has a double-size
shower. In the spacious, light-filled
dining room, fresh flowers, views over
the pretty enclosed garden, a 'very good
breakfast buffet, and plenty of cooked
choices too, even for vegetarians – a
vegetarian haggis!' Kelso Abbey is a
stroll away. BEDROOMS 4, 2 on ground
floor, 1 family suite. FACILITIES breakfast
room, garden, parking. CHILDREN all
ages welcomed. DOGS resident dogs.
CREDIT CARDS not accepted. PRICES per
room B&B £90–£120.

KIPPEN Stirlingshire
Map 5:D2

THE CROSS KEYS, Main Street,
FK8 3DN. Tel 01786 870293,
kippencrosskeys.com. A gateway to the
north for 300 years, Debby McGregor
and Brian Horsburgh's unassuming
inn – one of the oldest in Scotland –
stands in a village on the edge of Loch
Lomond and the Trossachs national
park. Today, its refined, award-winning
pub grub includes such dishes as guinea
fowl, tarragon mousse, mushroom and
pea barley risotto, greens. In summer,
locals, walkers, families and their dogs
head to the beer garden for views of
the Gargunnock and Fintry hills. In
winter, an open fire warms the rustic
bar with its exposed stone walls, antlers
and decent range of whiskies and real
ales. Neat, good-value bedrooms have
oak furnishings, crisp linens, a small
DVD library; underfloor heating in the
bathroom. BEDROOMS 3. OPEN all year
except Christmas Day, New Year's Day.
FACILITIES bar/dining areas, private

dining room, free Wi-Fi, in-room
TV (Freeview), civil wedding licence,
terrace, beer garden. BACKGROUND MUSIC
in bar. LOCATION 10 miles W of Stirling.
CHILDREN all ages welcomed. DOGS
allowed (£10 per night). CREDIT CARDS
MasterCard, Visa. PRICES per room
B&B single £59, double £79–£99.
À la carte £26.

LOCHMADDY Western Isles
Map 5: inset A1

HAMERSAY HOUSE HOTEL, Isle of
North Uist, HS6 5AE. Tel 01876 500
700, www.hamersayhouse.co.uk. A
paradise for wildlife and wilderness
lovers, Amanda and Niall Leveson
Gower's laid-back modern hotel sits
in a small village within an easy drive
of dazzling white sand beaches. It is
run with the 'same high standards and
very good food' as sister hotel Langass
Lodge, Locheport (see main entry). A
maritime air breezes through the bright
lounge and the modish brasserie, where
inventive menus use local game, just-
landed seafood, vegetables and herbs
from the garden. 'Cosy bedrooms' sport
tweedy touches; four rooms open on to
the garden. The landscaped grounds,
with a decked area for surveying the
bay, pose a striking contrast to the
rugged surroundings. Well placed
for the ferries; a village shop and
pub are close by. BEDROOMS 12, 6 in
extension. OPEN all year. FACILITIES
bar, lounge, restaurant, free Wi-Fi,
in-room TV, gym, garden, parking.
BACKGROUND MUSIC at low volume in
restaurant in evening. LOCATION on the
edge of the village. CHILDREN all ages
welcomed. DOGS not allowed. CREDIT
CARDS MasterCard, Visa. PRICES per
room B&B single £100, double £140.
À la carte £35.

MELROSE Scottish Borders
Map 5:E3

BURT'S, Market Square, TD6 9PL. Tel
01896 822285, www.burtshotel.co.uk.
Spend your day fishing on the River
Tweed, golfing or walking, then unwind
at this 'excellent', well-established 18th
century hotel on the High Street of a
pretty Borders town. The Henderson
family have been at the helm for nearly
50 years. It offers, a warm welcome,
unobtrusive staff and individually
styled bedrooms with earthy hues, and
a bathroom with Scottish toiletries.
In the restaurant, dark wood, light
tartans, trophy fish, and chef Trevor
Williams's modern Scottish dishes,
including Borders beef fillet, wild
mushroom gratin, heritage carrots,
pomme Anna, natural jus. Light bites
and 'mash' single malts are served in
the bar. The Hendersons also own The
Townhouse, across the street (see main
entry). BEDROOMS 20. OPEN all year, no
accommodation 24–26 Dec. FACILITIES
lobby lounge, residents' lounge, bistro
bar, restaurant, private dining room,
free Wi-Fi, in-room TV (Freeview),
wedding/function facilities, ½-acre
garden, parking. BACKGROUND MUSIC
none. LOCATION town centre. CHILDREN
all ages welcomed (restaurant over-8s
only). DOGS allowed in some bedrooms,
bar, not in restaurant. CREDIT CARDS all
major cards. PRICES per room B&B single
from £75, double from £140, D,B&B
double from £196. À la carte £39.

MOFFAT Dumfries and Galloway
Map 5:E2

HARTFELL HOUSE & THE LIMETREE
RESTAURANT, Hartfell Crescent,
DG10 9AL. Tel 01683 220153, www.
hartfellhouse.co.uk. A short detour
off the scenic Southern Upland Way

reveals a 'pleasant town' where Robert and Mhairi Ash's 'lovely Victorian house' overlooks the surrounding hills. Returning visitors 'come for the exquisite views, fantastic cooking, and good-value accommodation'. Each of the 'comfortable bedrooms' is supplied with a memory foam mattress and such pleasing extras as Scottish biscuits, fine toiletries. In the restaurant, chef Matt Seddon's short, frequently changing, Michelin-approved modern Scottish menu (vegetarians are well catered for, with advance notice) includes such 'delicious' dishes as roasted Cumbrian lamb, new potatoes, chargrilled courgette, peppers, salsa verde. 'Breakfast is equally excellent.' Easy access to the M74. BEDROOMS 7, plus self-catering cottage in the grounds. OPEN all year except Mon, Christmas. FACILITIES lounge, restaurant, free Wi-Fi, in-room TV (Freeview), garden, cooking classes, bicycle storage, parking. BACKGROUND MUSIC in restaurant. LOCATION 5 mins' walk from town centre. CHILDREN all ages welcomed. DOGS not allowed. CREDIT CARDS MasterCard, Visa. PRICES per room B&B single £50–£70, £75–£90, D,B&B double £134–£149. Set menu £29.50.

NAIRN Highland
Map 5:C2

SUNNY BRAE, Marine Road, IV12 4EA. Tel 01667 452309, sunnybraenairn.co.uk. On one of the sunniest stretches of the Scottish coast, John Bochel and Rachel Philipsen ensure that their 'good-value' B&B lives up to its name and catches every ray. 'The panorama of the sea' filters in through the south-facing building's glass front; pretty suntrap gardens have plentiful seating. Coastal sands and marine blues cheerfully decorate the bright, well-equipped bedrooms; each is provided with bottled water and bathrobes; four have views over the Moray Firth. A cheese board or charcuterie platter can be arranged for an evening meal. The owners have more than 100 malt whiskies waiting to be sampled. Minutes from the beach, the day might start with sand between the toes before heading back for a generous breakfast. BEDROOMS 8, 1 suitable for disabled. OPEN mid-Feb–mid-Dec. FACILITIES lounge, dining room, free Wi-Fi, in-room TV (Freeview), terrace, front and rear gardens, parking. BACKGROUND MUSIC none. LOCATION 5 mins' walk from the town centre, 2 mins from beach. CHILDREN all ages welcomed. DOGS only guide dogs. CREDIT CARDS MasterCard, Visa. PRICES per room B&B £85–£145. À la carte £35.

OBAN Argyll and Bute
Map 5:D1

GREYSTONES, Greystones, PA34 5EQ. Tel 01631358653, www.greystonesoban. co.uk. A fresh, bijou air wafts through Mark and Suzanne McPhillips's hillside B&B in a grand baronial pile offering epic views of Oban Bay. The hosts, both architects, retained the mansion's stained-glass windows, moulded ceilings and a fine wooden staircase, but kept it light and bright, adding modish furnishings and contemporary art. Uncluttered bedrooms have every amenity: fluffy bathrobes and Scottish toiletries in a spacious bathroom, tea-making facilities, wine glasses, a corkscrew; in most, superb views. Unusual breakfasts, served in the turreted dining room, may include porridge with raspberry cranachan or a cheesy spinach frittata. The helpful McPhillipses have ideas aplenty for trips around the Inner Hebrides. The town centre, harbour and seafood restaurants are within walking distance. BEDROOMS 5. OPEN Feb–Nov. FACILITIES sitting room, dining room, free Wi-Fi, in-room TV (Freeview), ½-acre garden, parking. BACKGROUND MUSIC none. LOCATION 5 mins' walk from town centre. CHILDREN not allowed. DOGS not allowed. CREDIT CARDS MasterCard, Visa. PRICES per room B&B £100–£180. 2-night min. stay preferred.

PEEBLES Scottish Borders
Map 5:E2

CRINGLETIE HOUSE, off Edinburgh Road, EH45 8PL. Tel 01721 725750, www.cringletie.com. A 'little jewel' in a secluded setting, Jacob and Johanna van Houdt's small baronial mansion crowns sweeping manicured lawns within acres of woodland. Inside, a fleet of 'friendly, well-trained staff'. Blazing log fires, a wooden staircase, hand-painted ceiling and an old service bell in each public room add to the grand ambience. 'Each of the comfortable, pristine bedrooms is fabulous, all beautifully appointed, with lovely toiletries.' Some are snug, some more modern; each has a sitting area, garden and hillside views. Outside, the extensive grounds include eclectic sculptures and a walled kitchen garden that supplies the restaurant's 'delicious' dishes including pan-roasted Atlantic cod, crushed Bombay potatoes, spring greens, smoked baba ganoush, lightly curried coconut sauce. BEDROOMS 13, 1 suitable for disabled, family cottage in grounds with hot tub. OPEN all year except 2–3 weeks Jan. FACILITIES bar, lounge, conservatory, garden room, restaurant, free Wi-Fi, in-room TV (Freeview), lift, wedding facilities, 28-acre fully accessible grounds,

parking. BACKGROUND MUSIC in public areas. LOCATION 2 miles N of Peebles. CHILDREN all ages welcomed. DOGS allowed in bedrooms, garden room. CREDIT CARDS MasterCard, Visa. PRICES per room B&B from £130, D,B&B from £200. À la carte £37.50.

THE TONTINE, High Street, EH45 8AJ. Tel 01721 720 892, www.tontinehotel. com. A welcoming sanctuary for outdoorsy types, Kate and Gordon Innes's town-centre hotel provides storage for fishing rods, guns and bicycles, as well as knowledgeable details on activities in the Scottish Borders. Built as a hotel in the early 19th century by French prisoners of war, it's now a popular spot for afternoon teas and cocktail evenings. Locals and residents mingle over real ales beside the lounge's open fire, or in the informal bistro. In the high-ceilinged, chandelier-lit restaurant, Alejandro Wunderlin's seasonal Scottish food includes braised lamb shank, ratatouille, mash, red wine jus. In both the main building and an annexe (connected by a glass-sided corridor), neat bedrooms have tweedy accessories; some overlook the river to the hills beyond. BEDROOMS 36, 20 in annexe. OPEN all year. FACILITIES lift, bar, lounge, bistro, restaurant, private dining/meeting room, free Wi-Fi, in-room TV (Freeview), civil wedding licence, 2 garden areas, drying room, secure bicycle storage, parking. BACKGROUND MUSIC in public rooms. LOCATION on the High Street in town centre. CHILDREN all ages welcomed. DOGS allowed in 10 annexe bedrooms, bar, bistro, garden (£10 per dog). CREDIT CARDS MasterCard, Visa. PRICES per room B&B single £55–£95, double £70–£130, D,B&B £98–£180.

PERTH Perth and Kinross
Map 5:D2

SUNBANK HOUSE, 50 Dundee Road,
PH2 7BA. Tel 01738 479888, www.
sunbankhouse.com. A tranquil retreat
within easy walking distance of the
bustling centre, Finlay and Agnes
Gillies's unfussy Victorian house stands
amid mature gardens. Traditional
by design, bedrooms are comfortably
furnished, unfussy and uncluttered,
with plenty of space to stretch out.
Two rooms suit a family; light sleepers
might request a room at the back.
Guests mingle over preprandial drinks
in the fire-lit lounge, before sampling
the dining room's locally sourced take
on classic dishes such as pan-fried
chicken breast in Parma ham, with
white wine, lemon and sage sauce, fresh
vegetables, baby potatoes. There is a
separate vegetarian menu. Breakfasts,
a feast, cater for everyone, and include
a buffet, smoked salmon, the full
Scottish. BEDROOMS 10, some on ground
floor, 2 suitable for disabled. OPEN
all year except Christmas. FACILITIES
lounge/bar, restaurant, free Wi-Fi,
in-room TV (Freeview), wedding/
function facilities, terrace, ½-acre
garden, parking. BACKGROUND MUSIC in
restaurant. CHILDREN all ages welcomed.
DOGS allowed in allocated rooms only
(£15 charge). CREDIT CARDS Amex,
MasterCard, Visa. PRICES per person
B&B single from £59, double from £40,
D,B&B from £65.

PITLOCHRY Perth and Kinross
Map 5:D2

PINE TREES, Strathview Terrace,
PH16 5QR. Tel 01796 472121, www.
pinetreeshotel.co.uk. High praise from
Guide regulars in 2018 for the 'friendly
service, imaginative food and lovely

room' at Valerie and Robert Kerr's
Victorian mansion on the outskirts
of town. With a 'beautiful setting
among mature trees', it has a 'relaxing
atmosphere', stately, dark wood, leather
sofas, and an impressive staircase
of wood and wrought iron; cosy
lounges are 'well supplied with board
games'. The traditionally furnished
bedrooms, two with four-poster, are
'comfortably appointed', with sweets,
bottled water, tea- and coffee-making
facilities; a shower room for most. The
garden-facing restaurant (ideal for
playing spot-the-red-squirrel) serves
'wonderful' Scottish dishes. Timing is
key: theatre, golf, fishing, everything
has its season. BEDROOMS 29, 3 in annexe,
6 in coach house, 7 on ground floor.
OPEN all year. FACILITIES 3 lounges, bar,
restaurant, free Wi-Fi (in lounge), in-
room TV (Freeview), 7-acre grounds,
parking. BACKGROUND MUSIC in bar and
restaurant. LOCATION ¼ mile N of town
centre. CHILDREN all ages welcomed.
DOGS well-behaved dogs allowed (£7.50
per night, only guide dogs allowed
in restaurant and bar lounge). CREDIT
CARDS Amex, MasterCard, Visa. PRICES
per person B&B from £75, D,B&B from
£95. À la carte £25.50.

PORTREE Highland
Map 5:C1

MARMALADE HOTEL, Home Farm Road,
IV51 9LX. Tel 01478 611711, www.
marmaladehotel.co.uk. Overlooking the
beautiful harbour town, a Georgian-
style country house (Perle Hotels) in
landscaped gardens has been given a
sleekly modern interior. Skye-crafted
natural fabrics, in soft greys and
heathered mustards, feature throughout,
alongside local materials and artworks.
Bedrooms vary in size, but all have

views of the garden, the bay, the outline of Cuillin hills beyond; extra touches: a sound system, capsule coffee machine, luxury toiletries. The light-filled, coolly contemporary restaurant is liked for its large period windows with far-reaching views, and its local specialities: a traditional char-grill; fresh oysters delivered daily. The bar opens on to an intimate courtyard. Breakfast includes porridge with cream, brown sugar, perhaps whisky, followed by a full Scottish. BEDROOMS 11, 2 ground-floor rooms in annexe, 1 suitable for disabled. OPEN all year. FACILITIES bar/restaurant, free Wi-Fi, in-room TV (Freeview), 2-acre grounds. BACKGROUND MUSIC none. LOCATION town centre. CHILDREN over-11s welcomed. DOGS not allowed. CREDIT CARDS Amex, MasterCard, Visa. PRICES per room B&B £120–£260. À la carte £35.

ST ANDREWS Fife
Map 5:D3

RUFFLETS, Strathkinness Low Road, KY16 9TX. Tel 01334 472594, www.rufflets.co.uk. Standing in tranquil, 'elegant gardens', this 'extremely welcoming', turreted 1920s mansion is owned by Mark and Christopher Forrester, grandsons of two of the original founders. It was one of Scotland's first country house hotels. Long-serving Stephen Owen manages the 'helpful staff'. The 'superb bedrooms' are packed with thoughtful touches (high-end toiletries, home-made shortbread, a hot-water bottle on a chilly night, a teddy bear); some have a huge four-poster, a private balcony. Seasons at Rufflets restaurant, opened in 2018, replaces the Terrace. Chef David Kinnes serves a seasonal Scottish menu, incorporating much home-grown produce. The ever-popular afternoon tea is taken on the terrace on clement days; more than 100 whiskies and 40 gins are an alternative. BEDROOMS 23, 4 on ground floor, 1 suitable for disabled, plus 3 self-catering cottages in gardens. OPEN all year. FACILITIES drawing room, library, bar, restaurant, free Wi-Fi, in-room TV (Freeview), wedding/function facilities, 10-acre grounds. BACKGROUND MUSIC in bar and restaurant. LOCATION 2 miles W of town. CHILDREN all ages welcomed. DOGS allowed in some bedrooms by arrangement. CREDIT CARDS Amex, MasterCard, Visa. PRICES per room B&B £145–£315, D,B&B £180–£385. À la carte £40.

SANQUHAR Dumfries and Galloway
Map 5:E2

BLACKADDIE HOUSE, Blackaddie Road, DG4 6JJ. Tel 01659 50270, www.blackaddiehotel.co.uk. A scenic approach leads to 'imaginative, well-cooked food' and 'especially comfortable bedrooms' at this 'lovely, small' restaurant-with-rooms' in an area ripe with history and hiking routes. Named after the 'black waters' flowing along the garden's edge, the 'quiet' and 'spotless' 16th-century manse by the River Nith is run by Jane McAndrew with 'attentive' staff. ('It's nice to be remembered,' said a returning Guide reader in 2018.) Her husband, patron/chef Ian McAndrew, produces 'top-of-the-scale' daily-changing menus in the 'charming dining room'. The recently refurbished bedrooms, each different (one has a baronial four-poster), come with home-made shortbread, Scottish tablet; an up-to-date bathroom, some with a hot-tub bath, most with a monsoon shower. More bathroom shelves would have been appreciated.

BEDROOMS 7, plus two 2-bed self-catering cottages. OPEN all year. FACILITIES bar, restaurant, breakfast/function room, library, conservatory, free Wi-Fi, in-room TV (Freeview), wedding/function facilities, 2-acre grounds, cookery school, fishing, parking. BACKGROUND MUSIC in public areas. LOCATION outskirts of village. CHILDREN all ages welcomed. DOGS allowed in some bedrooms (not in restaurant). CREDIT CARDS Amex, MasterCard, Visa. PRICES per room B&B single £105-£230, double £125–£250, D,B&B double £250–£365. Set menu £62.50, tasting menu £80.
25% DISCOUNT VOUCHERS

SCOURIE Highland
Map 5:B2

EDDRACHILLES HOTEL, Badcall Bay, IV27 4TH. Tel 01971 502080, www. eddrachilles.com. In 'a splendid location', Fiona and Richard Trevor's 18th-century church manse looks out at fishing boats bobbing on the water of a tranquil inlet. Visitors arriving at teatime are welcomed with a hot drink and home-baked cake. The modest bedrooms (most with spectacular sea views) have every amenity: crisp bedlinens, excellent toiletries, a good tea selection. Using locally landed shellfish and game, as well as vegetables and meat raised on local crofts, chef Per Soderberg's Scottish-Nordic dishes are 'superb'. At breakfast, 'excellent' cooked fare and 'equally good coffee'. The owners are gradually restoring ornamental and semi-formal gardens within the extensive grounds, leading to the seashore of Badcall Bay. BEDROOMS 10, 4 ground-floor rooms suitable for disabled. OPEN Mar–Nov, exclusive use over Christmas and New Year. FACILITIES large reception, bar/lounge, sun lounge, restaurant, free (slow) Wi-Fi in reception, lounge, in-room TV (Freeview), civil wedding licence, 3-acre grounds, parking. BACKGROUND MUSIC in public areas. LOCATION 2 miles S of Scourie. On the North Coast 500 route. CHILDREN all ages welcomed. DOGS well-behaved dogs allowed. CREDIT CARDS Diners, MasterCard, Visa. PRICES per room B&B single £80–£125, double £110–£160. Set dinner £33–£39, discounts for longer stays.

SOUTH GALSON Isle of Lewis
Map 5:B1

GALSON FARM GUEST HOUSE, HS2 0SH. Tel 01851 850492, www.galsonfarm. co.uk. In a 'peaceful area teeming with wildlife', Elaine and Richard Fothergill's sturdy guest house is maintaining its reputation for 'high-quality service and catering' on the dramatic north-west coast of Lewis. The 18th-century farmhouse was once part of a working farm; handsome belted Galloway cattle still tread the beach. Comfortable bedrooms have a silent mini-fridge. 'Our lovely king-sized room had coastal views to the Butt of Lewis,' reported Guide readers in 2018. The quiet reading lounge overlooks the surging Atlantic; hot drinks are available all day. Served communally, a simple two-course, Aga-fresh supper (arranged in advance) showcases local produce, alongside an extensive selection of tipples. 'Excellent' breakfasts, packed lunches fuel a day's exploration of beaches, mountains and burns. BEDROOMS 4. OPEN all year. FACILITIES 2 lounges, dining room, Wi-Fi access, garden, drying facilities, parking, bicycle storage., BACKGROUND MUSIC none. LOCATION around 8 miles S of Ness port, on NW coast, 20 miles from Stornaway. CHILDREN all ages welcomed. DOGS well-behaved dogs welcomed (animals on site). CREDIT CARDS MasterCard, Visa. PRICES per person B&B £47–£55. Set dinner £20.

SPEAN BRIDGE Inverness-shire
Map 5:C2

SMIDDY HOUSE, Roy Bridge Road, nr Fort William, PH34 4EU. Tel 01397 712335, www.smiddyhouse.com. A 'warm welcome' awaits at Robert Bryson and Glen Russell's highly regarded restaurant-with-rooms, in a former blacksmith's on the West Highland rail route. Arriving guests are served afternoon tea or, later in the day, sherry and home-made shortbread. 'Comfortable' bedrooms are 'beautifully decorated', but can be small; a family should book the more spacious Bryson suite with its 'nice lounge area and patio'. In the 'excellent restaurant', Glen Russell uses the best local produce (perhaps scallops from the Isle of Mull, salad and herbs from Skye) and his uncomplicated dishes focus on flavour and texture. 'Breakfast is to die for.' BEDROOMS 5, 1 suite in adjacent cottage. OPEN all year except 25–26, 31 Dec, restricted opening Nov–Mar. FACILITIES garden room, restaurant, free Wi-Fi, in-room TV (Freeview), golf, parking. BACKGROUND MUSIC in restaurant. LOCATION 9 miles N of Fort William. CHILDREN all ages welcomed. DOGS not allowed. CREDIT CARDS MasterCard, Visa. PRICES per room B&B £120–£195, D,B&B £200–£380. À la carte £40. 25% DISCOUNT VOUCHERS

STIRLING Stirlingshire
Map 5:D2

POWIS HOUSE, FK9 5PS. Tel 01786 460231, www.powishouse.co.uk.

Buffered by trees and fields, Jane and Colin Kilgour's secluded Georgian mansion has the feel of a sedate world, yet is just ten minutes' drive from the city centre. The house has been carefully preserved (there are records of every resident since it was built in 1746). In the gardens, a listed sundial and well-kept lawns are protected from resident sheep by a ha-ha. Inside, sash windows, high ceilings and polished wooden floors set the tone. Board games and DVDs are available in the sitting room. Harris tweed curtains and throws complement the bedrooms' original features (in one a cast-iron bath); broad views scan the horizon from each. Garden-fresh eggs for breakfast. BEDROOMS 3. OPEN Apr–Christmas. FACILITIES lounge, dining room, 9-acre garden, in-room TV (Freeview), free Wi-Fi. BACKGROUND MUSIC during breakfast. LOCATION 3 miles from town centre. CHILDREN all ages welcomed. DOGS not allowed. CREDIT CARDS MasterCard, Visa. PRICES per room B&B from £110.

VICTORIA SQUARE, 12 Victoria Square, FK8 2QZ. Tel 01786 473920, www. victoriasquareguesthouse.com. Within strolling distance of the city centre, Kari and Phillip Couser offer serene accommodation in their double-fronted Victorian house on leafy King's Park square. The elegant bedrooms, decorated in heritage hues, might have a king-sized wooden sleigh bed and views of Stirling Castle; perhaps a four-poster bed, a seating area in a bay window overlooking the square – a perfect spot for a 'room picnic'. Afternoon tea is no passing meal, but a sit-down indulgence in the orangery, with delicate finger sandwiches and toasted Osborne pudding loaf (a favourite of Queen Victoria's). Breakfast has a generous buffet plus cooked dishes (perhaps haggis with poached eggs), all taken beneath an original Commonwealth ceiling. BEDROOMS 10. OPEN all year except Christmas. FACILITIES lounge, breakfast room, orangery, free Wi-Fi, in-room TV (Freeview). BACKGROUND MUSIC none. LOCATION town centre ½ mile. CHILDREN over-11s welcomed. DOGS not allowed. CREDIT CARDS MasterCard, Visa. PRICES per room B&B £70–£145.

TONGUE Highland
Map 5:B2

THE TONGUE HOTEL, IV27 4XD. Tel 01847 611206, www.tonguehotel.co.uk. At the end of a long, single-track road, visitors to Lorraine and David Hook's 'wonderfully remote' small hotel find 'glorious' views of Ben Loyal, Loch Kyle and the ruins of Castle Varrich. Inside, the Victorian building is 'full of stags' heads and stuffed birds', with muted tweeds, wood panelling and cosy fireplaces. Service was 'perfectly charming but not yet up to speed', a Guide regular found in 2018. 'Characterful' bedrooms (some recently refurbished) might have a marble washstand or original fireplace; all have complimentary sherry. 'I had a very comfortable old bed, but the decor was tired.' The log fire-warmed restaurant serves 'tasty' home-made, locally sourced dinners. Breakfast, ordered the night before, has a full Scottish, home-made compotes, proper porridge. BEDROOMS 19. OPEN Valentine's Day to Christmas, not Mon Oct–Mar. FACILITIES lounge, 2 bars, restaurant, free Wi-Fi in public areas, in-room TV (Freeview), civil wedding licence, spa treatments, small garden. BACKGROUND MUSIC in public areas. LOCATION in village. CHILDREN all ages welcomed. DOGS allowed in bar, on lead, only. CREDIT CARDS Amex, MasterCard, Visa. PRICES per person B&B from £65, D,B&B from £95. À la carte £35.

ULLAPOOL Highland
Map 5:B2

THE SHEILING, Garve Road, IV26 2SX. Tel 01854 612947, www. thesheilingullapool.co.uk. The grounds of Lesley and Iain MacDonald's modern B&B border Loch Broom; on a clear day, views from the shore extend to the mountains beyond. Carla and Antonio Saenz are the new managers. The broad patio is tailor-made for a leisurely cuppa, while on chillier days, many board games await inside, along with an open fire. Bedrooms are simple but well equipped, with tea- and coffee-making facilities, a clock radio, complimentary sherry. Served in a light, bright room with sporrans on the wall, freshly cooked breakfasts (ordered the night before) include porridge with cream, fish from the Ullapool smokehouse, local sausages – all served to those views. Hebrides ferries are a stone's skip away. BEDROOMS 6, 2 on ground floor. OPEN Easter–mid-Oct. FACILITIES sitting room, dining room, free Wi-Fi, in-room TV (Freeview), 1-acre garden, drying room, sauna, fishing permits, parking. BACKGROUND MUSIC none. LOCATION 10 mins' walk S of Ullapool centre. CHILDREN all ages welcomed. DOGS allowed in ground-floor rooms, by arrangement (£10 per night). CREDIT CARDS MasterCard, Visa. PRICES per room B&B from £90.

WALES

ABERGELE Conwy
Map 3:A3

THE KINMEL ARMS, The Village, St George, LL22 9BP. Tel 01745 832207, www.thekinmelarms.co.uk. In the verdant Elwy valley, Lynn Cunnah-Watson and Tim Watson's handsome sandstone inn provides 'utter relaxation'. Home-baked cakes and loose-leaf tea, served in the tea room, are a sweet alternative to walking, swimming and playing golf, all nearby. In the popular bar, proper ales, local ciders (a reader in 2018 found the background radio 'rather noisy'); in the conservatory restaurant, 'excellent', seasonal brasserie-style meals, perhaps marinated lamb rump, beer-braised lamb faggot, potato fondant, texture of onions. Bedrooms ('beautifully appointed') display Tim Watson's striking artworks; perhaps a 'good walk-in shower', a vast slipper bath, a decked balcony. Overnight, a generous continental breakfast is delivered to the room; home-made and local treats are in the fridge. BEDROOMS 4, 2 on ground floor. OPEN all year except Mon, Christmas Day, New Year's Day. FACILITIES bar, restaurant, deli/shop, tea rooms, free Wi-Fi, in-room TV (Freeview), small garden, parking. BACKGROUND MUSIC in public areas. CHILDREN teenagers welcomed. DOGS allowed. CREDIT CARDS MasterCard, Visa. PRICES per room B&B £135–£175, D,B&B from £195. À la carte £32. 25% DISCOUNT VOUCHERS

AMROTH Pembrokeshire
Map 3:D2

MELLIEHA GUEST HOUSE,, SA67 8NA. Tel 01834 811581, www.mellieha.co.uk.

Off the beaten path, Julia and Stuart Adams's ranch-style B&B close to the sea is a tranquil change from nearby resort town Saundersfoot. Its peace is protected by the surrounding forested valley, on the edge of the National Trust's Colby Woodland Garden. Tea and home-baked cake are part of the 'generous welcome', served in the garden or conservatory – good spots for observing wildlife from birds to badgers. The pretty bedrooms have thoughtful extras (bathrobes, a torch for dark nights) and views across the garden to the sea. Laver bread and cockles might start the day. Easy access to the beach and the Pembrokeshire Coastal Path; restaurants and shops aren't far away. BEDROOMS 5. OPEN all year except 21 Dec–3 Jan. FACILITIES lounge, dining room, free Wi-Fi, in-room TV, 1-acre garden, parking. BACKGROUND MUSIC none. LOCATION 150 m from Amroth sea front. 2 miles E of Saundersfoot. CHILDREN over-12s welcomed. DOGS allowed in ground-floor rooms, by arrangement (£10 per night). CREDIT CARDS MasterCard, Visa. PRICES per room B&B £85–£108. 2-night min. stay at weekends preferred May–Sept. 25% DISCOUNT VOUCHERS

BALA Gwynedd
Map 3:B3

PALÉ HALL, Palé Estate, Llanderfel, LL23 7PS. Tel 01678 530285, www.palehall.co.uk. Rich in antiques, fine wood panelling and painted ceilings, this sumptuous, well-refurbished country house hotel, in an historic Victorian manor house, lies on the edge of Snowdonia national park. Sustainably run, the hotel is powered by one of the country's oldest running hydro-electric plants; it bottles its own spring water, and has the pick of local suppliers for Gareth Stevenson's seasonal fine-dining menus in the formal restaurant. Spacious bedrooms have original features, with added modern luxuries (a complimentary decanter of sherry, a television disguised as a gilt-framed mirror). Two suites are in a turret; another room has rich chinoiserie decor with oriental furnishings. Board games are in the library; lawn games, animals for petting, outside. Travelling dogs are properly pampered. BEDROOMS 18. OPEN all year. FACILITIES Grand Hall, 2 drawing rooms, library, 3 private dining rooms, free Wi-Fi, in-room TV (Freeview), civil wedding licence, 50-acre grounds, parking. BACKGROUND MUSIC in public areas. LOCATION 2 miles from Bala. CHILDREN all ages welcomed. DOGS allowed in 5 bedrooms, Grand Hall, library (£25 per dog). CREDIT CARDS all major cards. PRICES per room B&B £275–£860, D,B&B £385–£970. Set dinner £85, à la carte £60.

CAERNARFON Gwynedd
Map 3:A2

PLAS DINAS COUNTRY HOUSE,
Bontnewydd, LL54 7YF. Tel 01286 830214, www.plasdinas.co.uk. 'Delightful, hands-on' Neil and Marco Soares-Baines have transformed the former home of the Armstrong-Jones family into a luxurious B&B, set between the mountains and the sea. Bedrooms harmoniously merge vintage and modern pieces; each is thoughtfully supplied with 'all the things you might have forgotten to pack', high-end toiletries, a hot-water bottle. Some look across the Menai strait, others towards the peaks. Cosy spots before the drawing room's blazing log fire suit preprandial drinks; in warm weather, the terrace draws guests outside. Chef Daniel ap Geraint's country-house menus are served in the elegant new Gun Room restaurant, perhaps grilled lemon sole, samphire, capers, salt-baked turnip, wilted turnip tops, warm gooseberry marmalade. 'Great breakfasts.' Walking boots required: Snowdon is close. BEDROOMS 10, 1 on ground floor. OPEN all year except Christmas. FACILITIES drawing room, restaurant, private dining room, free Wi-Fi, in-room TV (Freeview), civil wedding licence, 15-acre grounds, parking. BACKGROUND MUSIC in drawing room and dining room. LOCATION 5-min drive S of town. CHILDREN over-12s welcomed. DOGS small, well-behaved dogs allowed in 2 bedrooms, by arrangement (£10 per night). CREDIT CARDS all major cards. PRICES per room B&B from £109. Set dinner 4-course £33, à la carte £43. 2-night min. stay at weekends. 25% DISCOUNT VOUCHERS

CARDIFF
Map 3:E4

CATHEDRAL 73, 73 Cathedral Road, CF11 9HE. Tel 02920 235005, www.cathedral73.com. The royal treatment awaits visitors to this stylishly refurbished Victorian town house hotel; a butler, personal chef and a chauffeur-driven vintage Rolls-Royce are at the ready, if required. Sitting across the park and the River Taff from Cardiff Castle, it has soothing soft grey interiors with the occasional flare of colour. Smart, pale-hued bedrooms and chic apartments (each with a kitchen) have top-shelf amenities: high-quality bedlinen, good toiletries, fresh milk. The tea room serves light lunches, afternoon tea with home-baked cakes; come evening (Thurs–Sat), it becomes a wine bar with Art Deco flourishes, food, live piano music. Alongside trips to the station, theatre, or opera, the bright yellow Rolls can be booked for a half-day tour. BEDROOMS 12, 1 on ground floor, suitable for disabled, 3 apartment suites, 2-bed coach house. OPEN all year, minimum housekeeping and no breakfast 25–26 Dec, 1 Jan. FACILITIES sitting room, bar/tea room, free Wi-Fi, in-room TV (Freeview), civil wedding licence, terrace, limited parking. BACKGROUND MUSIC in public areas. LOCATION ½ mile from city centre. CHILDREN all ages welcomed. DOGS allowed in ground-floor room. CREDIT CARDS MasterCard, Visa. PRICES per room from £130, cooked breakfast around £10.

HOTEL INDIGO CARDIFF, Dominions Arcade, CF10 2AR. Tel 08719 429104, www.hotelindigo.com. Inconspicuous amid shops, bars and restaurants, this late-Victorian hotel, alchemised out of an old office block, sits on a pedestrianised street, close to the station and castle. Inside, all things Welsh – heritage, industry and artistes – are celebrated with bright hand-woven textiles, slate signage, an upcycled miner's helmet light, and photographs of music icons (Shirley Bassey, Tom Jones, The Stereophonics). Stylish bedrooms are similarly inspired (the Industry rooms have a coal scuttle waste bin); there are dramatically tiled bathrooms, powerful showers. Many rooms have fabulous views. A lift ascends to the top-floor Marco Pierre White Steakhouse Bar & Grill, the rooftop terrace (well stocked with Welsh-made booze) overlooks the city skyline. BEDROOMS 122, 4 suitable for disabled. OPEN all year. FACILITIES lounge, restaurant, lift, free Wi-Fi, in-room TV, gym, discount at NCP car park nearby. BACKGROUND MUSIC in public areas. LOCATION city centre. CHILDREN all ages welcomed. DOGS not allowed. CREDIT CARDS all major cards. PRICES per room £122–£180. Breakfast £15.95.

COWBRIDGE Vale of Glamorgan Map 3:E3

THE BEAR, 63 High Street, CF71 7AF. Tel 01446 774814, www.townandcountrycollective.co.uk/thebear. Long a popular stopover, this well-located hotel has for centuries been the hub of a fashionable, cobbled market town surrounded by the cow-flecked fields of the Vale of Glamorgan. It once refreshed travellers heading from Swansea to Cardiff; today, locals and tourists rub shoulders, attracted in by its locally brewed drinks, updated pub grub and rejuvenating bedrooms. Individually designed, some are compact, others sprawling; in each: tea, coffee, Welsh toiletries. Local produce supplies the well-considered menus, served in the bar, lounge, courtyard or stylish Cellars dining room (vegetarians and vegans are well catered for, with such dishes as Glamorgan leek, carrot and cheddar hash, crème fraîche, spinach, minted peas). Mornings start with a buffet breakfast. BEDROOMS 33, some suitable for disabled, some in annexe, plus self-catering apartments. OPEN all year. FACILITIES lounge, restaurant, grill/bar, free Wi-Fi, in-room TV, wedding/conference facilities, courtyard, parking. BACKGROUND MUSIC in restaurant. LOCATION town centre. CHILDREN all ages welcomed. DOGS allowed. CREDIT CARDS MasterCard, Visa. PRICES per room B&B from £99. À la carte £30.

CWMBACH Powys
Map 3:D4

THE DRAWING ROOM, nr Builth Wells, LD2 3RT. Tel 01982 552493, www. the-drawing-room.co.uk. In the former summer retreat of a Victorian MP, Sir Marchant Williams, Melanie and Colin Dawson have created a 'truly wonderful little restaurant-with-rooms' where 'the food is a highlight'. Charming inside, the Georgian stone-built property, near the scenic Elan valley, has 'appealing', fresh flower-filled sitting rooms, and fine seasonal set menus. In the open-plan kitchen, the 'helpful hosts' use garden-fresh fruit and vegetables, along with meats from local farms, to produce 'ambitious, complex and delicious meals'; breads are home baked. Snug bedrooms are tastefully furnished; bathrooms (one with a large freestanding bath) have underfloor heating. At breakfast: fresh fruit, home made muesli, wild mushrooms with pancetta and duck egg. 'We had a beautiful day's walking between our two excellent dinners.' BEDROOMS 3. OPEN all year. FACILITIES lounge, restaurant, private dining room, in-room TV (Freeview), small garden. BACKGROUND MUSIC in restaurant. LOCATION 3 miles N of Builth Wells. CHILDREN over-11s welcomed. DOGS not allowed. CREDIT CARDS MasterCard, Visa. PRICES [2018] per room D,B&B £205–£230.

DOLGELLAU Gwynedd
Map 3:B3

Y MEIRIONNYDD, Smithfield Square, LL40 1ES. Tel 01341 422554, www. themeirionnydd.com. On the Mawddach trail, Marc Russell's stone-built restaurant-with-rooms stands at the southern gateway to Snowdonia national park. Days spent tramping up and down mountain paths end in cosy, tweedy rooms, where beds have luxurious linen and Welsh blankets; modern bathrooms have a walk-in shower or a bath, good toiletries, a slate floor. Guests and locals mingle in the friendly bar (perhaps over one of the vast selection of gins). Chef Robin Agnew creates comforting seasonal plates in the smart cellar restaurant, set within the exposed stone walls of the former county jail: the likes of oven-baked cod, sliced chorizo, chilli, garlic, tenderstem broccoli, baby potatoes. A hearty breakfast is fuel for hiking and biking in the surrounding hills. BEDROOMS 5. OPEN all year, except 22–26 Dec. FACILITIES bar, lounge, restaurant, in-room TV (Freeview), free Wi-Fi, terrace, bike storage. BACKGROUND MUSIC 'gentle music' in bar, restaurant. LOCATION town centre. CHILDREN over-6s welcomed. DOGS assistance dogs allowed. CREDIT CARDS Amex, MasterCard, Visa. PRICES per room B&B single £69–£85, double £75–£129, D,B&B double £99-£179, à la carte £28.

KNIGHTON Powys
Map 3:C4

MILEBROOK HOUSE, Milebrook,, LD7 1LT. Tel 01547 528632, www. milebrookhouse.co.uk. 'As good as ever', Beryl and Rodney Marsden's 'delightful' small hotel occupies an 18th-century stone dower house (once the home of Sir Wilfrid Thesiger), in extensive grounds leading to the River Teme. A three-generation enterprise: daughter Joanne manages 'well-trained' staff; granddaughter Katie is the chef. Locally reared meat, vegetables and fruit from the kitchen garden fuel her well-presented, 'good, if not exciting', dishes, served in the bar or the restaurant. Antiques, books, puzzles, an open fire in the sitting room foster a traditional country house atmosphere. Bedrooms are neatly furnished; those at the rear are quieter (the property fronts a busy road). One reader this year reported a fairly chaotic experience with booking. Guests arriving by train and walkers of Offa's Dyke can arrange a pickup. BEDROOMS 10, 2 on ground floor. OPEN all year. FACILITIES lounge, bar, 2 dining rooms, free Wi-Fi, in-room TV (Freeview), 3½-acre grounds. BACKGROUND MUSIC in bar and restaurant in evening. LOCATION on A4113, 2 miles E of Knighton. CHILDREN over-8s welcomed. DOGS not allowed. CREDIT CARDS MasterCard, Visa. PRICES per room B&B from £156, D,B&B from £199. À la carte £32.

LAUGHARNE Carmarthenshire
Map 3:D2

THE BOAT HOUSE, 1 Gosport Street, SA33 4SY. Tel 01994 427263, www.theboathouselaugharne.co.uk. In the centre of a small town described by resident scribe Dylan Thomas as a 'timeless, mild, beguiling island', visitors can stay in a former pub where the poet once told stories in exchange for a little refreshment. More usual forms of payment are accepted today at the 'comfortable, smart B&B' run by 'helpful hosts' Jane and Keith Nelson. The blue-painted property has spacious well-equipped rooms with large bed, a cafetière and freshly ground coffee, a selection of teas, home-baked biscuits, an umbrella for when it rains. Two rooms have views of the castle. An 'excellent breakfast spread' includes vanilla waffles, blueberry muffins and

vegetarian sausages – 'all home made and delicious'. BEDROOMS 4. OPEN all year. FACILITIES breakfast room, free Wi-Fi, in-room TV, parking. BACKGROUND MUSIC none. LOCATION in town centre. CHILDREN not allowed. DOGS in 1 room (£10 per night). CREDIT CARDS all major cards. PRICES per room B&B £85–£100.

LLANARTHNE Carmarthenshire
Map 3:D2

LLWYN HELYG, SA32 8HJ. Tel 01558 668778, www.llwynhelygcountryhouse. co.uk. Visitors to this 'glossy luxury B&B' are met with 'an unexpected wow factor, as you walk through the door'. In 'magnificent countryside', 'genuinely kind' hosts Fiona and Caron Jones have given their modern house a minimalist touch, all elegant granite, marble and honey-coloured wood – with an acoustically designed, vaulted listening room equipped with a sound system 'that's the best we've heard since the Royal Albert Hall'. A welcoming tea with home-made cake on one of the squashy sofas is accompanied by the sounds of the great composers. The 'very comfortable' bedrooms have a 'top-quality' bed, a 'luxurious' bathroom. 'Breakfast was very fresh.' Dining advice is readily supplied. The National Botanic Gardens of Wales are nearby. BEDROOMS 3. OPEN all year except 10 days over Christmas. FACILITIES 4 lounges, listening room, breakfast room, free Wi-Fi, in-room TV (Freeview), 3-acre garden. BACKGROUND MUSIC none. LOCATION 8 miles W of Llandeilo, 9 miles E of Carmarthen. CHILDREN over-15s welcomed. DOGS not allowed. CREDIT CARDS MasterCard, Visa. PRICES per room B&B single £99–£115, double £129–£155.

LLANDDEINIOLEN Gwynedd
Map 3:A3

Ty'n Rhos, Seion, LL55 3AE. Tel 01248 670489, www.tynrhos.co.uk. On a secluded farmstead, Hilary and Stephen Murphy and daughter Laura run this hotel 'in lovely countryside' overlooking the Isle of Anglesey. Sheep and cattle graze in fields beyond the gardens; binoculars are provided for watching the many varieties of birds. 'Staff were helpful and friendly without being pushy,' reported readers in 2018. Each named after a wildflower, bedrooms are in the creeper-covered house or the courtyard; some have patio doors opening on to the garden. Drinks and 'delicious' canapés are served in the conservatory, before 'large portions of a good dinner' including 'tasty pan-fired scallops in chicken velouté; locally reared, wonderfully flavourful lamb'. At breakfast, 'a decent buffet, very good cooked dishes, but too much background music'. BEDROOMS 19, 7 in converted outbuilding, 2 on ground floor, suitable for disabled. OPEN all year, except Christmas, New Year. FACILITIES lounge, bar, restaurant conservatory; free-Wi-Fi, in-room TV, 1-acre garden, parking. BACKGROUND MUSIC in public areas. LOCATION 12 mins from the Llanberis train, 4 miles from Bangor and Caernarfon. CHILDREN all ages welcomed. DOGS by arrangement, not in public areas. CREDIT CARDS MasterCard, Visa. PRICES room B&B single £78–£90, double £90–£185. D,B&B double £160–£250 (2-night min. stay).

LLANDUDNO Conwy
Map 3:A3

Escape, 48 Church Walks, LL30 2HL. Tel 01492 877776, www.escapebandb. co.uk. Urbane cool design and personal touches fill Sam Nayar and Gaenor Loftus's stylish B&B in a white-stucco Victorian villa just up the slopes of the Great Orme. Period features and oak-panelling are a well-maintained backdrop to modern and vintage furnishings and fabrics. Regularly updated bedrooms, each different, might have a copper bath, a pair of velvet-covered cocktail chairs, mood lighting in an overhead canopy. The Boudoir has wallpaper encrusted with crystals, an aubergine bed and black chandelier. In every room, high-end toiletries and high-spec technology. A DVD library and a piles of wool throws and crocheted granny-square blankets invite a cosy evening in. Occasional pop-up dining events; big breakfasts. A short stroll from the beach. BEDROOMS 9. OPEN all year except 18–26 Dec. FACILITIES lounge, breakfast room, free Wi-Fi, in-room TV (Freeview), front garden, limited parking. BACKGROUND MUSIC at breakfast. LOCATION 1 mile from town and coast. CHILDREN over-9s welcomed. DOGS allowed in some bedrooms, not in public rooms (£25 per night). CREDIT CARDS all major cards. PRICES per room B&B £99–£149.

LLANFERRES Denbighshire
Map 3:A4

The Druid Inn, Ruthin Road, CH7 5SN. Tel 01352 810225, www.druid-inn. co.uk. A lively gathering spot for locals, this 'lovely', unpretentious pub close to Offa's Dyke Path makes an ideal base for the area's many walks and bike trails. Promising 'a real taste of Wales', the 'friendly hosts' provide a welcoming atmosphere, and good beer in the cosy bar (low, beamed ceilings, roaring log fire), and tasty home-made fare in the traditional dining room. Neat bedrooms are a bit basic, but comfortable, with en-suite shower rooms; a separate guest bathroom has a tub for a relaxing soak. When the sun shines, guests spill outside to enjoy the gorgeous views of woods, fields and hills. The Grade II listed church of St Berris is next door. BEDROOMS 5, OPEN all year. FACILITIES bar, snug, restaurant, pool room, free Wi-Fi, in-room TV (Freeview), garden, parking. BACKGROUND MUSIC in public areas. LOCATION edge of village, close to Offa's Dyke Path. CHILDREN all ages welcome (but no family room). DOGS bar, pool room, not in bedrooms. CREDIT CARDS MasterCard, Visa. PRICES per room B&B single £72, double £85. À la carte £24.

LLANGAFFO Anglesey
Map 3:A2

THE OUTBUILDINGS, Bodowyr Farmhouse, LL60 6NH. Tel 01248 430132, www.theoutbuildings. co.uk. Glorious views to Snowdonia spill away from a cheerfully quirky restaurant-with-rooms surrounded by sheep-spotted fields on the Isle of Anglesey. Millie Mantle manages the 'much-enjoyed' place for Judith 'Bun' Matthews. Bright, modern and uncluttered, the well-appointed bedrooms in the converted stone-built barn and granary (one with a contemporary four-poster) have been playfully named (Pink Spotty Jug, Button's Room). The plentiful extras (a hot drinks tray, home-baked treats, a quality music system) are taken seriously. Equal in merit: a pink-painted shepherd's hut in the grounds. A communal breakfast initiates discussions of the evening's 'excellent' set menu, using local produce and foraged ingredients. Twenty-five minutes'

drive to the Holyhead ferry terminal; Llanddwyn beach is nearby. BEDROOMS 5, 1 on ground floor, 1 in garden. OPEN all year. FACILITIES 2 sitting rooms, restaurant with sitting area, free Wi-Fi, in-room TV (Freeview), civil wedding licence, private dining/function facilities, spa treatments, garden, tennis, parking. BACKGROUND MUSIC in sitting room and dining room, 'but we're happy to turn it off'. LOCATION 10 mins from Menai Bridge and 10 mins from Llanddwyn beach. CHILDREN babes-in-arms and over-12s welcomed. DOGS small, well-behaved dogs allowed in 1 bedroom (surrounding farmland has livestock). CREDIT CARDS Amex, MasterCard, Visa. PRICES per room B&B single £65–£75, double £85–£100. Set dinner £35.

LLANSTEFFAN Carmarthenshire
Map 3:D2

MANSION HOUSE LLANSTEFFAN, Pantyrathro, nr Carmarthen, SA33 5AJ. Tel 01267 241515, www. mansionhousellansteffan.co.uk. With extensive views over the Tywi estuary, David and Wendy Beaney's Georgian restaurant-with-rooms has brought 'stylish minimalism down to a fine art'. A tasteful recent refurbishment kept many original features: a marble-tiled entrance hall, grand staircase, stained glass, ornate plasterwork. Guide inspectors in 2018 received a 'warm, polite welcome', and were offered help with luggage to a 'large, comfortable bedroom with a capacious bathroom containing an efficient shower'. Eaves bedrooms lie up narrow stairs. All rooms have countryside or estuary views, home-made treats, luxury Welsh toiletries, bathrobes. Paul Owen's locally sourced seasonal menu was 'acceptably cooked, promptly served' in the garden-facing restaurant. Breakfast brings 'good fruit compote, first-rate tea, perfectly cooked scrambled eggs'. Drawbacks: 'repetitive muzak', slightly stark lighting. BEDROOMS 8, 2 on ground floor are inter-connecting, 1 suitable for disabled. OPEN all year. FACILITIES large open-plan bar/reception area, lounge, restaurant (closed Sun eve, Mon, Nov–Feb), free Wi-Fi, in-room TV (Freeview), civil wedding licence, conference facilities, 5 acre garden, parking. BACKGROUND MUSIC in public areas. LOCATION 2 miles to Llansteffan village, beach and castle. CHILDREN all ages welcomed (extra bed £25, children's menu). DOGS not allowed. CREDIT CARDS Amex, MasterCard, Visa. PRICES per room B&B from £109, D,B&B from £142. À la carte £30.

LLANTWIT MAJOR Vale of Glamorgan
Map 3:E3

THE WEST HOUSE, West Street, CF61 1SP. Tel 01446 792 406, www. townandcountrycollective.co.uk. In a restful setting, this recently renovated 17th-century country house is close to the centre of a historic village and the Glamorgan Heritage Coast. It has a peaceful bar and lounge, enlivened with the occasional antique, vintage typewriter, old portrait – good for a leisurely afternoon tea. The pristine bedrooms, some compact, have a comfortable bed and a breezy palette; dog-friendly rooms are provided with a towel, a dog bed, 'lovely doggie treats', and have hardwood flooring and easy access to the walled garden. All-day light bites and British classics (including good vegan and vegetarian options, perhaps oyster mushroom and champagne risotto, blue cheese) are served in the atmospheric restaurant; on fine days, the action moves out to the courtyard. BEDROOMS 22, 1 on ground floor. OPEN all year. FACILITIES bar, restaurant (closed Sun evenings), snug, conservatory, terrace, garden, civil wedding licence, parking, public areas wheelchair accessible. BACKGROUND MUSIC none. LOCATION close to Cardiff, Bridgend, Cowbridge. CHILDREN all ages welcomed. DOGS allowed. CREDIT CARDS Amex, MasterCard, Visa. PRICES per room from £85.

LLANWRTYD WELLS Powys
Map 3:D3

LASSWADE COUNTRY HOUSE, Station Road, LD5 4RW. Tel 01591 610515, www.lasswadehotel.co.uk. A gateway to the Cambrian mountains, this semi-rural Edwardian restaurant-with-rooms is a home-from-home with high green credentials. An electric vehicle charging point is available; incentives encourage visitors to arrive by public transport. 'Chatty' Roger and Emma Stevens are the hosts. Guide readers who visited in 2018 agreed with the Stevens's self-assessment ('boutique and high luxury we are not'), and reported that the overall decor – and their bathroom's shower – needed updating. The sitting room has squashy sofas, plenty of books and a log fire. The bedrooms have 'superb mountain views'. The host's breakfasts and daily-changing dinner menus are 'ample and very good'. 'He makes a mean zabaglione.' The Stevenses will help with day plans, if asked. BEDROOMS 8. OPEN 2 Mar–19 Dec. FACILITIES drawing room, restaurant, conservatory, free Wi-Fi, in-room TV (Freeview), function room, patio, small garden, parking. BACKGROUND MUSIC pianola in restaurant. LOCATION edge

of town. CHILDREN all ages welcomed, over-8s allowed in restaurant. DOGS allowed by arrangement (not in bedrooms, restaurant). CREDIT CARDS MasterCard, Visa. PRICES per room B&B £90–£135, D,B&B £160–£230, except during Royal Welsh Show week. Set menu £34.
25% DISCOUNT VOUCHERS

MONTGOMERY Powys
Map 3:C4
THE CHECKERS, Broad Street, SY15 6PN. Tel 01686 669822, www.checkerswales.co.uk. In a prettily conserved mid-Wales town, a 'charming' restaurant-with-rooms occupies this historic coaching inn, where refined dining is matched by elegantly Provençal-style accommodation. All beamed ceilings and sloping floors, it is owned by sisters Kathryn and Sarah Francis and Sarah's husband, Michelin-starred chef Stéphane Borie. Skilfully crafted tasting menus (perhaps including fennel and cumin velouté, smoked Blaenavon cheese soufflé) are served in the elegant, rustic dining room; vegetarian and pescatarian menus are 'no problem'. One of the well-appointed bedrooms is accessed via a roof terrace. At breakfast: home-made brioche toast, a full cooked plate with local sausages and bacon. One mile from Offa's Dyke. BEDROOMS 5, 1, in annexe, accessed via roof terrace. OPEN all year except 25, 26 Dec, 1 week in mid-autumn. FACILITIES lounge/bar (wood-burning stove), restaurant (closed Sun, Mon), free Wi-Fi, in-room TV, small terrace, cooking masterclasses. BACKGROUND MUSIC none. LOCATION centre of town. CHILDREN all ages welcomed, over-8s allowed in restaurant in evening. DOGS not allowed. CREDIT CARDS MasterCard, Visa. PRICES per room D,B&B £285–£350. 6-course tasting menu (Tues–Sat) £65.

MOYLEGROVE Pembrokeshire
Map 3:D2
THE OLD VICARAGE B&B, SA43 3BN. Tel 01239 881711, www.oldvicaragemoylegrove.co.uk. A walk through a wooded valley up from the sea leads to this imposing Edwardian vicarage above the village. Owners Meg and Jaap van Soest have refurbished the light-filled house in pared-back style, with wooden flooring and modern furniture draped with Welsh blankets. The airy sitting room has a horde of books; maps for walkers and cyclists. Unfussy bedrooms have a large bed, crisp linen, fresh milk and coffee, a shower room with Welsh toiletries. Organic breakfasts are served in a twin-aspect room with sea views. They include a veggie full Welsh; smoked salmon, dill pancakes, lemon and horseradish crème fraîche; apple and Pembrokeshire honey bircher muesli. Dinner available on request. BEDROOMS 5. OPEN all year, evening meals provided by request. FACILITIES sitting room, dining room, free Wi-Fi, in-room TV (Freeview), 1-acre garden. BACKGROUND MUSIC in dining room during the evening. LOCATION a few hundred yards outside village, 13 miles N of Fishguard. CHILDREN all ages welcomed. DOGS allowed, not in dining room. CREDIT CARDS Amex, MasterCard, Visa. PRICES per person B&B £90–£100. Dinner £35.

MUMBLES West Glamorgan
Map 3:E3
PATRICKS WITH ROOMS, 638 Mumbles Road, SA3 4EA. Tel 01792 360199, www.patrickswithrooms.com. There's

much to shout about at this long-established, family-run restaurant-with-rooms in a pretty village of artisan shops and galleries. Helmed by two husband-and-wife teams, Sally and Dean Fuller and Catherine and Patrick Walsh ('so friendly'), the 'huge, bright' bedrooms and 'excellent' cooking are praiseworthy – 'and the cucumber gin and tonic is a triumph'. Styled with verve, individually decorated bedrooms (some interconnecting) sprawl across a converted pub and boathouse. 'Ours had a colossal shower and a big bath in the spacious bathroom.' The monthly-changing menu, using Welsh produce, might have 'the best-ever rack of lamb'. Breakfast is 'delicious', perhaps home-made muesli and cockles and laver bread. BEDROOMS 16, 1 suitable for disabled, 6 in converted boathouse. OPEN all year except last 10 days in October, 25–26 Dec, 2 weeks in Jan. FACILITIES lift, lounge/bar, restaurant (closed Sun eve), free Wi-Fi, in-room TV (Freeview), civil wedding licence, meeting room, gym, on-street parking, public areas wheelchair accessible. BACKGROUND MUSIC in public areas. CHILDREN all ages welcomed. DOGS not allowed. CREDIT CARDS Amex, MasterCard, Visa. PRICES per room B&B single £100–£155, double £125–£185. À la carte £35.

NARBERTH Pembrokeshire
Map 3:D2

CANASTON OAKS, Canaston Bridge, SA67 8DE. Tel 01437 541254, www.canastonoaks.co.uk. Riverside ambles and 'by far the best breakfast of our holiday' draw fans to this 'very good' B&B in a well-restored Pembrokeshire longhouse, a short drive from a pleasant market town. Eleanor and David Lewis and daughter, Emma Millership, are the 'friendly owners, who go the extra mile', say Guide readers in 2018. Bedrooms, in converted barns or a lake-view lodge, have plenty of thoughtful extras (dressing gowns, candles; 'the fresh milk in the room was a lovely touch'). A family might request a suite of interconnecting rooms with a countryside-facing terrace. 'Our spotlessly clean room had an excellent bed.' Come morning, break the fast with smoked haddock fishcakes, a Welsh cheese omelette. 'We can't wait to return.' BEDROOMS 10, 3 in lodge, 2 suitable for disabled, plus 1-bed self-catering apartment. OPEN all year. FACILITIES lounge, dining room, free Wi-Fi, in-room TV (Freeview), 1-acre grounds, parking. BACKGROUND MUSIC at breakfast in the dining room. LOCATION 2 miles W of Narberth. CHILDREN all ages welcomed. DOGS assistance dogs allowed. CREDIT CARDS MasterCard, Visa. PRICES per room B&B £90–£175. 1-night bookings sometimes refused at peak times.
25% DISCOUNT VOUCHERS

NEWTOWN Powys
Map 3:C4

THE FOREST COUNTRY GUEST HOUSE, Gilfach Lane, Kerry, SY16 4DW. Tel 01686 621821, www.bedandbreakfastnewtown.co.uk. Home comforts and good value proliferate at Paul and Michelle Martin's family-friendly oasis amid undulating mid-Wales countryside. The peaceful, muzak-free, Victorian country house B&B is ringed by large, flower-filled gardens. Inside: books, maps and games, plus an antique Bechstein grand piano to play, and a suit of armour with a sword that children are allowed to brandish. Up the 19th-century oak staircase, pleasantly old-fashioned, county-style bedrooms have period pieces of furniture, views of fields graced by a herd of rare-breed sheep; one large room has a four-poster bed. DIY snacks and meals are easy in a kitchenette for guests' use. Eggs from the Martins' free-range hens supply the organic breakfasts. Powis Castle is nearby. BEDROOMS 5, plus 4 self-catering cottages (1 room adapted for limited mobility is accessed by stairs) OPEN all year except Christmas, New Year, self-catering cottages open all year. FACILITIES sitting room, dining room, kitchenette, games room, free Wi-Fi, in-room TV (Freeview), 4-acre garden, tennis, parking, secure bicycle storage. BACKGROUND MUSIC none. LOCATION 1 mile from Kerry village, 3 miles from Newtown. CHILDREN all ages welcomed. DOGS allowed in kennels in the grounds, and in cottages. CREDIT CARDS MasterCard, Visa. PRICES per room B&B single £65–£80, double £80–£115.

PENARTH Vale of Glamorgan
Map 3:E4

HOLM HOUSE, Marine Parade, CF64 3BG. Tel 029 2070 6029, www. holmhousehotel.com. High on a clifftop, overlooking Penarth Pier and the Bristol Channel, a nursing home in a Victorian suburb has been converted into a pleasant hotel with spa facilities. Trusted readers in 2018 wrote of 'very helpful, friendly staff' and a 'good dinner'. A pretty garden in front of the large house has well-spaced seating, decent views. In the bar, cocktails and mocktails; in the coastal-hued dining room and cosy snug, a steak menu and seasonal dishes (perhaps lemon, herb and pine nut crusted turbot fillet, Swiss chard, sorrel, roast fennel, parsley sauce) and 'delicious bread'. Understated bedrooms have 'every luxury' (soft bathrobes, home-baked Welsh cakes, teas and cafetière coffee); many have a sea view; two have a freestanding bath. BEDROOMS 13, 2 in annexe. OPEN all year. FACILITIES bar/lounge, snug, restaurant, free Wi-Fi, in-room TV (Sky), civil wedding licence, large garden, spa, gym. BACKGROUND MUSIC in public areas. LOCATION seafront location on the edge of town, 5 miles from Cardiff. CHILDREN all ages welcomed. DOGS allowed in annexe bedrooms, snug. CREDIT CARDS MasterCard, Visa. PRICES per room B&B from £120. À la carte from £30.

PORTMEIRION Gwynedd
Map 3:B3

HOTEL PORTMEIRION, Minffordd, Penrhyndeudraeth, LL48 6ER. Tel 01766 770000, www.portmeirion-village.com. Clustered on the edge of a spectacular tidal estuary, this mansion house hotel – the focal point of Sir Bertram Clough Williams-Ellis's Italianate village – has welcomed guests including HG Wells, George Bernard Shaw and Bertrand Russell. It 'combines old-world touches with stylish modernity'. Its traditional bedrooms have estuary and mountain views; more contemporary rooms in Castell Deudraeth overlook the walled garden; the bedrooms in the brightly coloured village cottages enjoy use of a fully equipped kitchen. Mealtime options include the informal brasserie, or the Art Deco dining room for 'very good, rather elaborate' cooking. A choice of preoccupations, too: a shell grotto, a bell tower, a dog cemetery, a pantiled temple. BEDROOMS 57, 14 in hotel, some on ground floor, 1 suitable for disabled, 11 in Castell Deudraeth, 32 in village. OPEN all year except 26–29 Nov. FACILITIES lift, 3 lounges, bar, restaurant, brasserie in Castell, free Wi-Fi, in-room TV, civil wedding licence, function facilities, 170-acre grounds, outdoor heated swimming pool (summer). BACKGROUND MUSIC in public areas. LOCATION 2 miles SE of Porthmadog. CHILDREN all ages welcomed. DOGS assistance dogs allowed. CREDIT CARDS Amex, MasterCard, Visa. PRICES per room B&B £124–£344, D,B&B £184–£404. Set menu £47–£55, à la carte £55. 2-night min. stay preferred.

ST DAVID'S Pembrokeshire
Map 3:D1

CRUG-GLAS, Abereiddy, Haverfordwest, SA62 6XX. Tel 01348 831302, www.crug-glas.co.uk. In the middle of their Pembrokeshire working farm, the Evans family 'warmly welcomes' visitors to their laid-back, pleasing restaurant-with-rooms. The Georgian farmhouse, perhaps austere on the outside, is a family home, filled with photographs and inherited pieces – the handsome, generations-old dresser houses the honesty bar. Janet Evans serves 'first-rate dinners' in the dining room, report Guide regulars in 2018. 'The view of sheep grazing added to our enjoyment of a beautiful twice-cooked Caerfai cheese soufflé and perfectly cooked duck.' Cottage-style bedrooms (in the main building, a converted milk parlour and a coach house) might have a double-ended copper bath; a separate sitting room. An 'excellent breakfast' has 'superb choice'. The coast is close. BEDROOMS 7, 2 in outbuildings, 1 on ground floor. OPEN all year except 24–26 Dec. FACILITIES drawing room, dining room, free Wi-Fi, in-room TV (Freeview), civil wedding licence, 1-acre garden. BACKGROUND MUSIC classical. LOCATION 3½ miles NE of St David's. CHILDREN babes in arms and over-11s welcomed. DOGS allowed in cottage (£10 per night). CREDIT CARDS MasterCard, Visa. PRICES per room B&B £150–£190. À la carte £35.

25% DISCOUNT VOUCHERS

CHANNEL ISLANDS

ST BRELADE Jersey
Map 1: inset E6
LA HAULE MANOR, La Neuve Route,
JE3 8BS. Tel 01534 741426, www.
lahaulemanor.com. It might be 550 miles
to the north, but a Provençal air breezes
through this white-painted Georgian
manor house overlooking St Aubin's
Bay. Ola Przyjemska runs the show,
supported by 'helpful and efficient' staff.
A complimentary glass of bubbly on
arrival also sets a warm tone. The high-
ceilinged sitting room has chandeliers
and ornate furnishings. Many of the
traditionally decorated bedrooms, each
different, mix whites, creams and Louis
XV-style pieces; some have broad sea
views. Parasol-shaded loungers encircle
the swimming pool. All-day light bites
are served in the bar. At dinner, free
transport takes guests to the restaurant
at sister hotel La Place; other eateries are
a short walk away. Ten minutes' drive
from airport; complimentary transfers.
BEDROOMS 16, some on ground floor,
plus 2 self-catering apartments. OPEN
all year except Christmas, New Year;
self-catering cottages open all year.
FACILITIES sitting room, bar, TV room,
breakfast room, free Wi-Fi, in-room
TV, terrace, garden, outdoor heated
swimming pool, hot tub, parking.
BACKGROUND MUSIC none. CHILDREN all
ages welcomed. DOGS allowed in kennels
in the grounds, and in cottages. CREDIT
CARDS MasterCard, Visa. PRICES per
room B&B £98–£217.

ST MARTIN Guernsey
Map 1: inset E5
BELLA LUCE HOTEL, La Fosse, GY4
6EB. Tel 01481 238764, bellalucehotel.

com. Renoir was once drawn to this
spot, above Moulin Huet Bay, to capture
the ever-changing scene in his Guernsey
paintings. Today, it's this luxurious small
hotel's 'delightful staff', 'comfortable
bedrooms' and 'outstanding food' that
attract visitors. The Wheadon family
has tastefully restored the handsome,
extended Norman manor house,
finishing the stylish bedrooms and suites
with superb bathroom, good technology;
some have a four-poster bed, a separate
lounge area. Diners tuck into 'ingenious'
modern European dishes by candlelight
in the garden-facing restaurant. While
praising the food, some guests found
the muzak 'a touch intrusive'. The
courtyard's shady tulip tree is perfect
for summer afternoons; the vaulted
cellar lounge's leather sofas overlook the
copper stills of the on-site gin distillery.
BEDROOMS 23, 2 on ground floor. OPEN
all year except Jan. FACILITIES snug, bar,
restaurant, cellar lounge, free Wi-Fi,
in-room TV (Freeview), civil wedding
licence, function facilities, 2-acre garden,
courtyard, outdoor swimming pool,
spa, parking. BACKGROUND MUSIC in
public areas. LOCATION 2 miles from the
town centre and airport. Above a valley,
with a beach below. CHILDREN all ages
welcomed. DOGS not allowed. CREDIT
CARDS Amex, MasterCard, Visa. PRICES
per room B&B from £130, D,B&B from
£167. À la carte £38.

ST PETER PORT Guernsey
Map 1: inset E5
LA COLLINETTE HOTEL, St Jacques,
GY1 1SN. Tel 01481 710331, www.
lacollinette.com. The Chambers clan
has encouraged a family-friendly
atmosphere at their white-painted,
flower-fronted Georgian hotel for
nearing 60 years. Fronted with

cheerful window boxes, the relaxed, unpretentious place near the waterfront is managed by the long-serving Cyril Fortier. Most of the bright, light bedrooms have splashes of ocean blue, glittering views of the sea beyond the grounds; all have a choice of pillow, a thick mattress topper and a hospitality tray with tea, coffee, biscuits. The informal restaurant serves uncomplicated dishes using much local produce. Breakfast brings a buffet; a Guernsey 'full house'; a grilled kipper. There's an activity for everyone: loungers by the swimming pool; on the other side of Candie Gardens, shops, the harbour, and island-hopping from the port. BEDROOMS 23. 14 self-catering cottages and apartments. OPEN all year. FACILITIES lounge, bar, restaurant, free Wi-Fi, in-room TV (Sky, Freeview), 2 acre garden, outdoor swimming pool, gym, spa treatments, restaurant and bar wheelchair accessible. BACKGROUND MUSIC in bar and restaurant. LOCATION 1 km W of town centre. CHILDREN all ages welcomed. DOGS not allowed. CREDIT CARDS MasterCard, Visa. PRICES per person B&B from £60. 25% DISCOUNT VOUCHERS

THE DUKE OF RICHMOND, Cambridge Park, GY1 1UY. Tel 01481 726221, www.dukeofrichmond.com. Trompe l'oeil flair and views as far as Herm and Sark beguile at this gracious hotel (Red Carnation Hotels) above the town. Copies of Impressionist masterpieces hang throughout the 19th-century building; a safari theme extends into the Leopard bar. Complimentary sweet snacks are replenished all day; an extensive range of loose-leaf teas is served for afternoon tea, in the conservatory or on the terrace.

Young travellers may decorate their own cupcakes with the chef. In the restaurant, fresh fish features heavily. Bedrooms might be modern or elegantly traditional, some feature strongly patterned wallpaper; rooms with a sea view may have a balcony. All come with twice-daily maid service, luxury smellies, a complimentary evening newspaper. At breakfast, perhaps kippers or waffles. BEDROOMS 73. OPEN all year except 24–26 Dec. FACILITIES lounge, bar, restaurant, free Wi-Fi, in-room TV, room service, wedding/function facilities, terrace, outdoor swimming pool. BACKGROUND MUSIC classical. CHILDREN all ages welcomed. DOGS allowed in 2 bedrooms, not in restaurant. CREDIT CARDS Amex, MasterCard, Visa. PRICES per room B&B from £162.

IRELAND

BALLINTOY Co. Antrim
Map 6:A6

WHITEPARK HOUSE, 150 Whitepark Road, BT54 6NH. Tel 028 2073 1482, www.whiteparkhouse.com. A cushion of mature trees surrounds Bob Isles's 'exemplary' B&B, a gentle buffer against the sound of the waves and birds that visit sandy Whitepark Bay. Guests at the crenellated 18th-century house are welcomed with home-baked treats, served in the 'delightful' lounge which displays art, artefacts and souvenirs collected from the host's adventures in Asia and Africa. In the spacious, traditionally decorated bedrooms, thoughtful details add comfortable charm: fluffy bathrobes, slippers, a hot-water bottle, 'a face cloth tied with a red ribbon'. One room has a brass four-poster bed; all have a large bathroom with power shower and separate bath. Restaurant advice and walking routes are readily supplied. Vegetarian and meaty Irish breakfasts start the day. BEDROOMS 3. OPEN Mar–Nov. FACILITIES sitting room, conservatory, free Wi-Fi, 1-acre garden. BACKGROUND MUSIC none. LOCATION 5 miles E of Bushmills. CHILDREN over-9s welcomed (must be able to take separate room). DOGS not allowed. CREDIT CARDS MasterCard, Visa. PRICES per room B&B single £90, double £130.

BALLYGALLY Co. Antrim
Map 6:B6

BALLYGALLY CASTLE, Coast Road, BT40 2QZ. Tel 028 2858 1066, www.hastingshotels.com/ballygally-castle. A 17th-century baronial pile, 'charmingly located' on the scenic Antrim Coast Road has received a 21st-century update. The sociable hotel (part of the Hastings Hotels group) sits in 'well-kept grounds', overlooking the beach. Each well-equipped room in the much-extended property is different: some trace the castle's original architecture, others are more modern; one has a ghost; all have a comfortable bed, iPod docking station; rubber duck in the bathroom. Many look across the water to Scotland. Provenance is important in the restaurant's classic Irish dishes including chicken fillet wrapped in Northern Irish dry-cured bacon, creamed leeks, Gracehill black pudding, champ croquettes, rich pan jus. An 'excellent' breakfast includes Bushmills whiskey porridge. Ten minutes' drive from the Larne ferry terminal. BEDROOMS 54, some suitable for disabled. OPEN all year. FACILITIES lounge, bar, restaurant, free Wi-Fi, in-room TV (Freeview), wedding/function facilities, 1½-acre walled gardens. BACKGROUND MUSIC none. LOCATION 6 miles N of the Port of Larne, on the Causeway Coastal Route. CHILDREN all ages welcomed. DOGS allowed in 2 bedrooms, not in restaurant. CREDIT CARDS Amex, MasterCard, Visa. PRICES per person B&B from £65, D,B&B from £90. À la carte £28.

BALLYLICKEY Co. Cork
Map 6:D4

SEAVIEW HOUSE. Tel 00 353 27 50073, www.seaviewhousehotel.com. While it has a brand-new seaweed bath house, treatment rooms, sauna and hot tub, this traditional hotel, at the head of Bantry Bay, preserves the aura of a bygone age. Run by the same family since the 1940s: nephew Ronan O'Sullivan is now at the helm. Spacious public rooms display family heirlooms, ornaments and objets d'art; a cosy library has acres of books and a crackling fire. Art-hung bedrooms (some snug) have mellow wood period furniture; a suite with a sofa bed can accommodate a family. Some rooms overlook the bay, others the landscaped, subtropical garden (a pleasant spot for afternoon tea). Guests gather for aperitifs in the lounge, before home-cooked country food in the garden-facing restaurant. BEDROOMS 25, 2 on ground floor, suitable for disabled. OPEN mid-Mar–mid-Nov. FACILITIES bar/lounge, residents' lounge, library, restaurant, free Wi-Fi in reception, in-room TV (Ericom), wedding facilities, 4-acre garden, parking. BACKGROUND MUSIC none. LOCATION 3 miles N of Bantry, 7 miles SE of Glengarriff. CHILDREN all ages welcomed. DOGS allowed in bedrooms, not in public rooms. CREDIT CARDS Amex, MasterCard, Visa. PRICES per person B&B from €70, D,B&B from €100. Set dinner menu €33–€48; à la carte €45. 25% DISCOUNT VOUCHERS

BELFAST Co. Antrim
Map 6:B6

THE OLD RECTORY, 148 Malone Road, BT9 5LH. Tel 028 9066 7882, www. anoldrectory.co.uk. Mary Callan provides a good-value base for the university at her Victorian guest house in a leafy residential suburb near the city centre. The well-maintained villa has books and board games in the drawing room; hot whiskey for cool days. Biscuits, reading material and (in some) views of the Belfast mountains feature in the comfortable bedrooms, each named after a local site of historic importance. Breakfast is an award-winning feast, with freshly squeezed

juices and good hot choices (a veggie or meaty fry-up, porridge with a dash of whiskey); raspberry jam, whiskey marmalade, bagels, soda and wheaten breads are all home made. Monday to Thursday, a small supper menu is available. Nearby Lagan Meadows has river walks. BEDROOMS 6, 1 on ground floor suitable for disabled. OPEN all year except Christmas, New Year, 2 weeks mid-July. FACILITIES drawing room, dining room, free Wi-Fi, in-room TV, garden, parking. BACKGROUND MUSIC 'quiet' at breakfast. LOCATION just under 2 miles from city centre CHILDREN all ages welcomed. DOGS not allowed. CREDIT CARDS MasterCard, Visa. PRICES per room B&B single from £55, double from £87, 2-night min stay May–Sept.

RAVENHILL HOUSE, 690 Ravenhill Road, BT6 0BZ. Tel 028 9020 7444, www. ravenhillhouse.com. Set back from the centre, this handsomely restored red-brick B&B is within easy reach of popular restaurants and independent shops, and a leafy park. Hosts Olive and Roger Nicholson provide a warm welcome for arriving guests, with tea and oven-fresh treats. Cosy bedrooms in the Victorian house are decorated with floral prints; in each, good seating, a spot to read, pleasing extras: home-baked shortbread; a vintage Hacker radio. Weekends are leisurely, with breakfast served till 10 am. In a dining room with wood-burning stove, parquet flooring and book-lined shelves, fuel for the day includes home-made marmalades and jellies, spiced fruit compote, freshly baked banana bread; good vegetarian options. BEDROOMS 4. OPEN Feb–mid-Dec. FACILITIES sitting room, dining room, free Wi-Fi, in-room TV (Freeview), small garden, parking. BACKGROUND MUSIC Radio 3 at breakfast. LOCATION 2 miles S of city centre. CHILDREN over-11s welcomed. DOGS not allowed. CREDIT CARDS Amex, MasterCard, Visa. PRICES per room B&B £85–£140. 2-night min. stay preferred on busy weekends.

BUSHMILLS Co. Antrim
Map 6:A6

BUSHMILLS INN, 9 Dunluce Road, BT57 8QG. Tel 028 2073 3000, www.bushmillsinn.com. A short stroll from the world's oldest distillery, this amiable 17th-century coaching inn on the Causeway Coastal Route is an eclectic jumble of ancient and modern. The public rooms have characterful wooden booths, higgledy-piggledy snugs, inglenook turf fires, a 'secret' library. Many of the spacious bedrooms in the mill house, each with its own sitting area, overlook the River Bush. In the bar, still lit by Victorian gas lights, whiskey cocktails and Irish music; in the garden-facing restaurant, modern Irish plates, perhaps slow-braised belted Galloway beef ragu, pappardelle pasta, aged parmesan. Suggested itineraries for days outdoors and indoors form well-considered top-ten lists ('Ten things to do when it's raining', '…as a family', etc). Two miles from the Giant's Causeway. BEDROOMS 41, some on ground floor, some suitable for disabled. OPEN all year, no accommodation 24–25 Dec. FACILITIES lift, lounge, restaurant, bar, gallery, loft, cinema, free Wi-Fi, in-room TV (Freeview), conference facilities, patio, 2-acre garden, parking. BACKGROUND MUSIC in public areas, live traditional Irish music sessions every Sat in bar. LOCATION village centre, on river. CHILDREN all ages welcomed. DOGS only permitted on outside patio area. CREDIT

CARDS Amex, MasterCard, Visa. PRICES per person sharing B&B £65–£105. À la carte £50.

CAHERSIVEEN Co. Kerry
Map 6:D4

QUINLAN & COOKE BOUTIQUE TOWNHOUSE, 3 Main Street, V23 WA46 Tel 00 353 66 947 2244, www.qc.ie. 'A brilliant base for a boat trip to the world heritage site of the Skellig Islands', Andrew and Kate Cooke's 'buzzing' destination restaurant has expanded to provide 'quirky, boutique-style' bedrooms. 'Kate is a charming owner/manager,' reports a Guide regular this year, 'service is friendly and efficient'. In the intimate restaurant, a short menu based on fresh, wild, local fish (supplied by the family business) is served 'in generous portions'. 'Spacious and comfortable' bedrooms have 'eclectic reading matter', a Nespresso machine, Barry's tea, and a fridge full of treat-bearing Kilner jars (fresh fruit salad, home-made fruit compote and yoghurt, granola, fresh milk). 'Come morning, freshly baked croissants and muffins appear in a bag on your door handle.' BEDROOMS 11. OPEN Apr–Oct; weekends only Nov–Mar; open Christmas/New Year. FACILITIES bar, lounge, free Wi-Fi, in-room TV (Sky), courtyard, gym, parking. BACKGROUND MUSIC in restaurant. LOCATION village centre. CHILDREN all ages welcomed. DOGS allowed. CREDIT CARDS Amex, MasterCard, Visa. PRICES per room B&B €119–€179, D,B&B €209–€269. À la carte €40.

CARLINGFORD Co. Louth
Map 6:B6

GHAN HOUSE. A91 DXY5. Tel 00 353 42 937 3682, www.ghanhouse.com. A tree's length from medieval Carlingford, this pretty Georgian house sits in mature walled gardens. It has been the Carroll family home for almost 30 years. Now Paul Carroll runs the hotel; his mother, Joyce, tends the garden and fills the rooms with freshly cut flowers. The house is filled with family photographs and heirlooms, squashy sofas, antique French beds and claw-footed baths. Log burners warm the drawing room and the 'elegant' dining room where menus based on abundant produce from lough and countryside include lapsang souchong smoked tea consommé, Lough Neal eel, beetroot, turnip. Traditionally decorated bedrooms have a modern bathroom and mountain views; most are in a garden annexe. A popular venue for private parties and weddings. BEDROOMS 12, 8 in annexe, 1 on ground floor. OPEN all year except 24–26 Dec. FACILITIES bar, lounge, restaurant, 2 private dining rooms, free Wi-Fi, in-room TV (Freeview), civil wedding licence, 3-acre garden, parking, charging point for electric cars. BACKGROUND MUSIC in public areas LOCATION near Carlingford. CHILDREN all ages welcomed. DOGS allowed in kennels in converted stables. CREDIT CARDS Amex, MasterCard, Visa. PRICES per person B&B €80–€125, D,B&B €135–£165. 6-course tasting menu from €50.

CASTLETOWN BEREHAVEN Co. Cork
Map 6:D4

BEARA COAST HOTEL, Cametringane Point. Tel 00 353 027 71446, www. bearacoast.com. 'A real discovery.' Overlooking a harbour brimming with fishing boats and big ships, this hotel has a 'first-rate setting' on the Beara peninsula. The contemporary interior

has been revamped by Mark Golden, who runs it with chef Mark Johnston. 'The owner is high-profile throughout, the staff are helpful and smiley,' reports a regular reader in 2018. Substantial, 'very good' food (scallops with orange and rocket; mussels, calamari, smoked salmon risotto) is served in the 'lively' Arches bar; an à la carte menu in the more formal plaid-seated dining room. 'Bright, comfortable bedrooms' have floral-patterned feature walls; many have a balcony with panoramic views of the harbour, the town, surrounding islands and mountains. 'Exceptional value for money.' BEDROOMS 16. OPEN all year. FACILITIES lift, lounge, bar, restaurant, function facilities, free Wi-Fi, in-room TV, terrace. BACKGROUND MUSIC in public areas. LOCATION on headland, overlooking harbour. CHILDREN all ages welcomed. DOGS allowed, by arrangement. CREDIT CARDS all major cards. PRICES per room B&B from €115. Cooked breakfast €15. Set menu dinner €39.50.

CLIFDEN Co. Galway
Map 6:C4

BLUE QUAY ROOMS, Seaview, H71 WE02. Tel 00 353 87 621 7616, www. bluequayrooms.com. An unmissably bright blue, Paddy and Julia Foyle's good-value B&B in a 200-year-old building above the harbour is minutes from the town centre. It is sister to The Quay House on the waterfront (see main entry), and managed by son Toby and Pauline Petit. The interiors are playfully decorated: white-painted antlers hang opposite gilt-framed portraits, close to a ship's wheel; a zebra skin is stretched across a wall. In cosy sitting areas, bold black-and-white flooring lies beneath blue ceilings;

a large metal lobster cooks atop the wood-burning stove. All but one of the pretty, modern bedrooms look across the harbour. Breakfasts are imaginative and plentiful. An ideal base for walkers and cyclists. BEDROOMS 8, plus 2-bed self-catering apartment. OPEN Apr–Oct. FACILITIES sitting area, breakfast room, free Wi-Fi, garden. BACKGROUND MUSIC none. LOCATION close to town centre. CHILDREN over-9s welcomed. DOGS not allowed. CREDIT CARDS not accepted. PRICES per room B&B single €60–€65, double €70–€85.

COBH Co. Cork
Map 6:D5
KNOCKEVEN HOUSE, Rushbrooke, P24E392. Tel 00 353 21 481 1778, www. knockevenhouse.com. High above Cork harbour, the flower-laden garden of this grand Victorian house creates a cheering welcome on the outskirts of a historic port town. Pam Mulhaire is the friendly hostess. Arriving guests are treated to a hot drink and home-baked scones in the elegant drawing room, where a blaze crackles on cool days. B&B accommodation is found in spacious, high-ceilinged bedrooms filled with period pieces, flower arrangements; bathrooms have thick towels, terry cloth robes, high-end toiletries. Communal, organic breakfasts, served at a mahogany table in the light-washed dining room overlooking the garden, have seasonal fruits, preserves and home-baked brown bread. The hostess has ready advice on local attractions and restaurants. BEDROOMS 5. OPEN 1 Jan–20 Dec. FACILITIES drawing room, dining room, free Wi-Fi, in-room TV, 2-acre grounds. BACKGROUND MUSIC at breakfast. LOCATION 1 mile W of centre. CHILDREN all ages welcomed. DOGS

allowed. CREDIT CARDS MasterCard, Visa. PRICES per room B&B single €90, double €120.

COLLINSTOWN Co. Westmeath
Map 6:C5
LOUGH BAWN HOUSE, Lough Bane. Tel 00 353 44 966 6186, www. loughbawnhouse.com. Four generations of Verity Butterfield's family have lived in this 'impressive' Georgian house, with 'divine' views down rolling meadow to the lough. The 'lovely hostess' welcomes guests with afternoon tea before an open fire in the homely drawing room packed with family heirlooms, books and an abundance of flowers. The 'excellent home-cooked dinner', served (by pre-arrangement) in an elegant dining room, 'is a real treat', report Guide inspectors in 2018. Pretty, country house-style bedrooms overlook the garden or lake; two share a 'wonderful' bathroom (wooden floors, a shuttered window, vast bathtub, 'glorious walk-in shower'). 'I could have happily moved into that bathroom and never left.' Free-ranging chickens provide the breakfast eggs. BEDROOMS 4. OPEN all year except over Christmas. FACILITIES sitting room, dining room, free Wi-Fi, 50 acres of parkland. BACKGROUND MUSIC none. CHILDREN over-2s welcomed. DOGS allowed (resident dogs). CREDIT CARDS MasterCard, Visa. PRICES per room B&B from €80. Dinner €40.

COLLON Co. Louth
Map 6:C6
COLLON HOUSE, Ardee Street, A92 YT29. Tel 00 353 87 235 5645, www. collonhouse.com. Painstakingly restored and maintained, Michael McMahon and John Bentley-Dunn's house in the Boyne valley 'exudes class, from bedroom to

table'. Built in 1740, it was once the home of John Foster, the last Speaker of the Irish House of Commons. It is filled with antiques, paintings and period furnishings. The enclosed gardens, with an intricate sunken box parterre and Greek-style summer house, are surrounded by mature trees and a ten-foot-high laurel hedge. Preprandials might be taken in the former ballroom; 'sumptuous' dinners (by arrangement for groups of six or more) are served in the panelled dining room. The richly decorated, well-equipped bedrooms – one with a four-poster, another a half-tester bed – have a subtly disguised bathroom. Thirty minutes' drive from Dublin airport. BEDROOMS 3, plus 2-room suite in adjacent mews house. OPEN New Year, Feb–Dec. FACILITIES 2 reception rooms, dining room, free Wi-Fi, TV in mews house, ¾-acre garden, parking. BACKGROUND MUSIC none. LOCATION middle of Collon village, near to the Boyne valley. CHILDREN over-13s welcomed. DOGS not allowed. CREDIT CARDS not accepted. PRICES per room B&B €150–€180. Set dinner €55.

DONEGAL TOWN Co. Donegal
Map 6:B5

ARD NA BREATHA, Drumrooske Middle. Tel 00 353 74 972 2288, www. ardnabreatha.com. Along the stretch of the Wild Atlantic Way outside Donegal, Theresa and Albert Morrow provide 'great value' at this coolly rustic B&B that stands within a working farm. A covered walkway leads to 'simple, cosy' bedrooms in a purpose-built annexe; there are king-size beds, wool rugs, pine furniture. The Morrows start their day at dawn (rising to lamb sheep when needed) but encourage guests to take their French toast and scrambled eggs (served in the main house, to order) at a more civilised hour. Books, an honesty bar and a fire create a peaceful atmosphere in the residents' lounge. Dinner is available only for groups of ten or more (by arrangement), but the hosts can advise on local eating options. BEDROOMS 6, all in converted barn. OPEN mid-Feb–end Oct. FACILITIES bar, lounge, restaurant, free Wi-Fi, in-room TV (Freeview), 1-acre grounds, unsuitable for disabled. BACKGROUND MUSIC in bar and restaurant at breakfast. LOCATION 1¼ miles NE of town centre. CHILDREN all ages welcomed. DOGS allowed in bedrooms (not unattended). CREDIT CARDS MasterCard, Visa. PRICES per room B&B €62–€134. .

HARVEY'S POINT, Lough Eske. Tel 00 353 74 972 2208, harveyspoint.com. A traditional hotel run with old-fashioned care between Lough Eske and the foothills of the Blue Stack mountains. Husband-and-wife team Marc Gysling and Deirdre McGlone are consummate hosts, ensuring that rare Irish whiskeys are ready for sipping by a peat fire, and sustaining supplies ready in the spacious bedrooms (fresh milk, fruit, biscuits). Lakeshore suites have a private entrance and lough-facing terrace. Modern Irish dishes are served in the restaurant overlooking the water, including pan-fried turbot, baby leek, mushroom, lemon. The day starts with freshly squeezed juices, buttermilk pancakes, a fish special, a grilled kipper. Stabling and grazing is available for equine travellers. Outdoorsy pursuits range from the active (archery, golf) to the passive (leisurely walks, loughside picnics). BEDROOMS 64, some suitable for disabled, plus 13 in lodge for group bookings. OPEN all year. FACILITIES lift, drawing room, bar, restaurant, ballroom, free Wi-Fi, in-room TV (Sky), wedding/conference facilities, 20-acre grounds. BACKGROUND MUSIC none. LOCATION 6 km outside Donegal Town. CHILDREN all ages welcomed. DOGS allowed. CREDIT CARDS MasterCard, Visa. PRICES per room B&B from €199. Set dinner €55, tasting menu €65. 2-night min. stay at weekends.

DUBLIN Co. Dublin
Map 6:C6
ARIEL HOUSE, 50–54 Lansdowne Road, Ballsbridge. Tel 00 353 1 668 5512, www.ariel-house.net. There's nothing ethereal about this 'warmly welcoming' guest house near Ballsbridge village; rather Jennie McKeown's 'helpful staff' encourages guests to feel solidly at home, day and night. An external stone staircase leads to the three interconnected Victorian town houses, sympathetically restored to retain plenty of original features including Flemish brickwork, ornate stained glass, sash windows. The best bedrooms are handsomely styled with antiques, Victorian-inspired fabrics; suites have a four-poster bed and Waterford crystal chandeliers. Guests mingle over complimentary afternoon tea in the 'comfortably grand lounge'. The day begins with an 'excellent' locally sourced breakfast, including home-made granola, potato-and-chive cakes; 'perfectly poached eggs'. The hall has a supply of umbrellas – it does rain in Dublin occasionally. BEDROOMS 37. OPEN all year except 23 Dec–4 Jan. FACILITIES drawing room, dining room, free Wi-Fi, garden. BACKGROUND MUSIC none. LOCATION 2 km from city centre. CHILDREN all ages welcomed. DOGS not allowed. CREDIT CARDS Amex,

MasterCard, Visa. PRICES per room B&B from €150.

WATERLOO HOUSE, 8-10 Waterloo Road, Ballsbridge. Tel 00 353 1 660 1888, waterloohouse.ie. The twin red doors to this 'attractive pair of houses' signal your arrival at Evelyn Corcoran's 'usefully located' Georgian B&B within walking distance of St Stephen's Green and many other city landmarks. Classically styled bedrooms, with warm earthy tones, and plenty of period-appropriate furnishings, can be snug, but they have 'everything one might require'. Light sleepers may wish to discuss room choice. The 'extensive breakfast', served in the dining room or the adjoining conservatory, is ideal fuel for steaming through the city: home-made muesli and soda bread, cold cuts, an omelette, a full Irish breakfast or 'catch of the day'. The 'very helpful' hostess has recommendations aplenty within the vicinity and further afield. BEDROOMS 19, some suitable for disabled. OPEN all year. FACILITIES lift, lounge, dining room, conservatory, free Wi-Fi, in-room TV, garden, parking, restaurant wheelchair accessible. BACKGROUND MUSIC all day in lounge, at breakfast in eating areas. LOCATION 1 mile to St Stephen's Green, Dublin city centre. CHILDREN all ages welcomed. DOGS not allowed. CREDIT CARDS MasterCard, Visa. PRICES per room B&B €99–€199. 2-night min. stay preferred on peak weekends.

DUNFANAGHY Co. Donegal
Map 6:A5
THE MILL, Figart. Tel 00 353 74 913 6985, www.themillrestaurant.com. 'Exceptional service' and 'well-crafted food' characterise this 19th-century flax mill on the Wild Atlantic Way,

now home to Susan and Derek Alcorn's friendly restaurant-with-rooms. Local seafood is prominent on the 'delicious' seasonal menu, served in the buzzy restaurant ('a real local hotspot – advance booking essential'); 'a food allergy was readily catered for'. A range of local craft beers is on hand for sipping before the turf fire. 'Modern, unfussy' bedrooms have 'every comfort', including home baked oatmeal cookies, thick woven blankets, extra seating. The studio of late watercolourist Frank Egginton (Susan Alcorn's grandfather) has been turned into an artful, spacious bedroom. 'Breakfast was excellent.' BEDROOMS 7. OPEN mid-Mar–mid-Dec. FACILITIES drawing room, restaurant (closed Mon all year, various other times throughout the year), conservatory, free Wi-Fi, in-room TV, garden. BACKGROUND MUSIC in public areas. LOCATION ½ mile W of Dunfanaghy. CHILDREN all ages welcomed. DOGS allowed. CREDIT CARDS Amex, MasterCard, Visa. PRICES per person B&B from €50.

GLASHABEG Co. Kerry
Map 6:D4

GORMAN'S CLIFFTOP HOUSE, Ballydavid. Tel 00 353 66 915 5162, www.gormans-clifftophouse.com. Backed by the mountainous spine of the Dingle peninsula, this 'great-value' guest house is 'full of warmth'. A family-run outfit, it's a haven of reliably 'excellent service', 'commendable meals' and 'beautiful views' of the sea. Sheelagh and Vincent Ó Gormáin, the 'fantastic, informative hosts', are the seventh generation to live in this 'wonderful spot'. Spacious, simple bedrooms have mountain or ocean views, a small library of local-interest books, a well-equipped

bathroom. (Some rooms on the top floor have a sloping ceiling.) Come evening, every table has a view at the 'excellent' residents-only suppers, home-cooked using just-landed fish and garden-fresh produce; 'great vegetarian choices'. Breakfasts are 'generous', and include Irish farmhouse cheeses, Burren smokehouse organic salmon, dropped pancakes. BEDROOMS 8. OPEN Mar–Oct. FACILITIES lounge, library, dining room (closed Sun), free Wi-Fi, in-room TV, 3-acre grounds. BACKGROUND MUSIC Irish or classical music in reception and dining room. LOCATION 8 miles W of Dingle on Wild Atlantic Way. CHILDREN all ages welcomed. DOGS allowed. CREDIT CARDS MasterCard, Visa. PRICES per room B&B from €130.

INIS MEÁIN Co. Galway
Map 6:C4

INIS MEÁIN RESTAURANT AND SUITES, Inis Meáin, H91 NX86. inismeain.com. Emerging from the landscape, Ruairí and Marie-Thérèse de Blacam's sustainably run stone-and-glass restaurant-with-suites is a design-led sanctum in a remote Gaelic stronghold. An exploration kit has all the essentials: bicycles, fishing rod, swimming towels, binoculars, nature guides, maps, hotpot lunch in a backpack. Appreciating the scene is only part of it; succinct menus exploit produce from the island, the restaurant greenhouse and the surrounding waters, with such dishes as lobster with aioli; beetroot carpaccio; lamb chop with salsa verde. Local materials – wood, lime, stone, and wool – form the linear architectural bedrooms; each has vast views from a private outdoor seating area. Breakfast is delivered to the door. 40-minute ferry from Ros a' Mhíl; 7-minute flight from

Connemara airport. **BEDROOMS** 5 suites. **OPEN** Apr–Sept. **FACILITIES** restaurant (closed Sun nights), free Wi-Fi, 3-acre grounds. **BACKGROUND MUSIC** none. **LOCATION** centre of a small island, 15 miles off the Galway coast. **CHILDREN** over-11s welcomed. **DOGS** not allowed. **CREDIT CARDS** MasterCard, Visa. **PRICES** per suite B&B from €280. Set dinner €73. 2-night min. stay.

KANTURK Co. Cork
Map 6:D5

GLENLOHANE, Tel 00 353 29 50014, glenlohane.ie. A home-from-home in the Blackwater valley. Visitors to this ivy-clad Georgian country house are invited to stay 'as if with friends' by the welcoming Sharp Bolster family. Meadows and farmland extend beyond the acres of landscaped gardens. Inside brims with heirlooms and memorabilia collected by more than ten generations of the family. Days might be spent in a fireside armchair in the book-lined study, and having tea in the airy drawing room. Spacious country-style bedrooms are pleasingly old-fashioned, with original fireplaces; one has a four-poster. The family has tips for decent nearby eateries; guests might alternatively give a day's notice and dine in. The hosts can help with organising vintage motorcycle or classic car tours. **BEDROOMS** 3, plus 2-bed self-catering cottage nearby, suitable for disabled. **OPEN** mid-Mar–mid-Dec. **FACILITIES** drawing room, library, dining room, free Wi-Fi, 250-acre gardens and farmland. **BACKGROUND MUSIC** none. **LOCATION** 1½ miles E of town. **CHILDREN** over-12s 'will be considered'. **DOGS** not allowed. **CREDIT CARDS** all major cards. **PRICES** per room B&B single €135–€150, double €235–€250, D,B&B €285–€300.

KENMARE Co. Kerry
Map 6:D4

SHEEN FALLS LODGE, Tel 00 353 64 664 1600, www.sheenfallslodge.ie. There are diversions aplenty at this much-refurbished 17th-century former fishing lodge on a tranquil estate overlooking Kenmare Bay and the Sheen waterfalls. Outdoorsy guests might cast for salmon on a private beat or walk trails with a guide; indoorsy guests may use the spa or sip a leisurely afternoon tea in the light-washed lounge. The main building's tasteful bedrooms mix peach and cream hues with colour from the estate, perhaps heather or oak. Some have an open fireplace, fabulous views; thatched self-catering cottages are in the grounds. The acclaimed restaurant's daily-changing menus use local produce, including estate-caught and -cured salmon, in such dishes as sea trout fillet, fennel, aubergine, olive. The vast cellar houses an impressive wine and whiskey collection. **BEDROOMS** 68, some suitable for disabled, plus 5 villas available for self-catering. **OPEN** Feb–Nov, Christmas, New Year, midweek only 19 Nov–22 Dec. Closed 2 Jan–8 Feb. **FACILITIES** 2 lounges, drawing room, library, study, bar, restaurant, free Wi-Fi, in-room TV (Sky), wedding/function facilities, 300-acre grounds, spa, indoor pool, terrace. **BACKGROUND MUSIC** in public areas. **LOCATION** 2 km from Kenmare, on the Ring of Kerry and the Beara peninsula. **CHILDREN** all ages welcomed. **DOGS** kennels available. **CREDIT CARDS** all major cards. **PRICES** per room B&B €190–€300. À la carte €65.

KILKENNY Co. Kilkenny
Map 6:D5

ROSQUIL HOUSE, Castlecomer Road, R95 P962. Tel 00 353 56 772 1419, www.rosquilhouse.com. Phil and Rhoda Nolan's friendly B&B is well located for exploring the medieval town with its castle and cathedral, just across the River Nore. Simple bedrooms are well equipped with a flat-screen TV and a hot drinks tray; larger rooms may have a seating area; families have a choice of rooms, including a separate self-catering apartment with its own entrance. The extensive, wholesome breakfast, made with locally sourced produce, is a point of pride: fruit (fresh and poached), house special granola, home-baked bread, local cheeses; cooked-to-order dishes include a full Irish, omelettes. The Nolans have plentiful, on-point advice on local hotspots and trips further afield. Kilkenny Golf Club is within reach of a decent 7 iron. **BEDROOMS** 7, 1 suitable for disabled, plus a self-catering apartment. **OPEN** Mar–21 Dec, 28 Dec–1 Jan, Feb (Thurs–Sun). **FACILITIES** lounge, dining room, free Wi-Fi, in-room TV. Smoking patio, ¼-acre garden. **BACKGROUND MUSIC** Irish or classical music in reception and dining room. **LOCATION** near town centre. **CHILDREN** all ages welcomed. **DOGS** allowed in self-catering apartment. **CREDIT CARDS** MasterCard, Visa. **PRICES** per person B&B double €40–€60.

KILLARNEY Co. Kerry
Map 6:D4
THE BREHON, Muckross Road, V93 RT22. Tel 00 353 64 663 0700, www.thebrehon.com. Peaceful repose greets travellers on the Wild Atlantic Way at the O'Donahue family's large spa hotel encircled by a spectacular mountainscape. Marble, dark wood and vast wall hangings greet visitors in the public spaces. Understated bedrooms, some small, some staid, have a bay window or balcony with views of the countryside or the purple-hued McGillycuddy Reeks mountains; some interconnecting rooms suit a family. Danú restaurant serves chef Chad Byrne's award-winning Irish fare, perhaps cannon of Irish lamb, aubergine, dates, hazelnut, mint; lighter bites in the bar. Well located for the town, Killarney national park (a short stroll away) and events at nearby INEC. Guests enjoy complimentary access to Angsana spa and the kids' club at sister, Gleneagle Hotel, next door. **BEDROOMS** 125, some suitable for disabled. **OPEN** all year. **FACILITIES** lift, lounge, bar, restaurant, private dining room, free Wi-Fi, in-room TV, wedding/function facilities, playroom, spa (12-metre indoor Vitality pool, steam room, herb sauna, spa bath, fitness centre, treatments), parking. **BACKGROUND MUSIC** in public areas. **LOCATION** ½ mile from town centre. **CHILDREN** all ages welcomed. **DOGS** allowed. **CREDIT CARDS** all major cards. **PRICES** per room B&B from €119, D,B&B from €199. À la carte €42.

LAHINCH Co. Clare
Map 6:C4
MOY HOUSE, Tel 00 353 65 708 2800, www.moyhouse.com. 'Great Atlantic views' and beach walks await at Antoin O'Looney's 'wonderfully hospitable' small hotel. Within large grounds with mature woodlands, the 18th-century house, built for Sir Augustine Fitzgerald, is 'fabulously located', between the coast road and Lahinch Bay. Inside, exposed stone walls, antiques, a characterful drawing room with an honesty bar, open fire, handcrafted furnishings. Bedrooms

have individual touches: a canopy bed, a turf-burning fire, a claw-foot bath. Produce from the hotel's farm and kitchen garden supplies chef Matthew Strefford's 'excellent' daily-changing menu, including Moy House shepherd's pie, garden vegetables, served to ocean views in the candlelit orangery restaurant. Next morning, home-made bread and granola, along with eggs from the hotel farm's chickens, set guests up for the day. BEDROOMS 9, 4 on ground floor. OPEN Apr–Oct. FACILITIES drawing room, library, restaurant (closed Sun, Mon), free Wi-Fi, computer provided, in-room TV (Sky), 15-acre grounds. BACKGROUND MUSIC in restaurant at mealtimes. LOCATION 2 miles outside Lahinch. CHILDREN all ages welcomed. DOGS allowed. CREDIT CARDS all major cards. PRICES per room B&B €160–€395, D,B&B €290–€525. À la carte €65.

MAGHERAFELT Co. Londonderry
Map 6:B6

LAUREL VILLA TOWNHOUSE, 60 Church Street, BT45 6AW. Tel 028 7930 1459, laurel-villa.com. Standing in deepest Seamus Heaney country, Eugene and Gerardine Kielt's elegant B&B is a haven for fans of the late Nobel prize-winning poet and playwright. Behind the villa's bright red door, guests find an intriguing collection of his books and memorabilia; in the grounds, a trail reveals his works' place alongside plants. Eugene Kielt, a Blue Badge guide, gives award-winning literary tours of the area. Bedrooms, each named after a great Ulster poet, including Longley and Kavanagh, display framed works and portraits of the writers. Breakfast (fresh scones, fruit salad, a full Ulster) is served in the wood-panelled dining room, beneath Heaney poems on scrolls. A large collection of genealogical and historic materials can help guests trace their Northern Irish heritage. BEDROOMS 4. OPEN all year. FACILITIES 2 lounges, dining room, patio, free Wi-Fi, in-room TV, ¼-acre garden, parking. BACKGROUND MUSIC none. LOCATION town centre. CHILDREN all ages welcomed. DOGS not allowed. CREDIT CARDS MasterCard, Visa. PRICES per person B&B single €75–€90, double €60–€90,

MOYARD Co. Galway
Map 6:C4

CROCNARAW COUNTRY HOUSE, H91 EF82. Tel 00 353 95 41068, www.crocnaraw.ie. Minutes from Connemara national park, Lucy Fretwell's 'fabulously located', creeper-clad Georgian guest house has mountain views, 'excellent food' and a homely, lived-in feel. The white-washed house stands in mature grounds fringed by a rustic stone wall. Quirky ornaments and comfy seating fill the airy public rooms. Afternoon tea with Aga-baked treats is served fireside in the flower-filled drawing room. Upstairs, bright and uncluttered bedrooms have more fresh flowers, a gloriously rustic outlook over a kitchen garden, an orchard and a meadow of donkeys. A generous breakfast of home-made soda bread and home-grown produce is served on sunshine-yellow crockery in the dining room. Private dinners by arrangement. Fishing, horse riding and golf are all on tap in the area. BEDROOMS 4. OPEN May–Oct, over Christmas and New Year by arrangement only. FACILITIES dining room, drawing room, snug, free Wi-Fi, 2-acre garden in 20-acre grounds. BACKGROUND MUSIC in public areas.

LOCATION by Ballinakill Bay, 5 miles N of Clifden on N59. CHILDREN all ages welcomed. DOGS allowed. CREDIT CARDS MasterCard, Visa. PRICES per person B&B from €45.

25% DISCOUNT VOUCHERS

NEWPORT Co. Mayo
Map 6:B4

NEWPORT HOUSE, F28 F243. Tel 00 353 98 41222, www.newporthouse.ie. Small wonder visitors linger at this inviting, creeper-covered Georgian mansion on the Clew Bay shoreline. The building is steeped in cosy country-house charm, thanks to Kieran Thompson, who has owned and meticulously maintained the property for over 30 years. Airy public rooms have gilt-framed artworks, antiques and trophy fish in glass cases; comfy fireside sofas, full bookshelves. Classically furnished bedrooms are in the main house and two courtyard buildings. In the elegant dining room, seafood from the bay, Irish beef and farmhouse cheeses. Dishes include wild salmon, garden spinach, champagne sauce. Anglers might cast their eye – and their line – at the extensive fishing rights; basket lunches, ghillies, and smoking/freezing facilities are available. BEDROOMS 14, 4 in courtyard, 2 on ground floor. OPEN mid-Mar–early Oct. FACILITIES drawing room, sitting room, bar, dining room, free Wi-Fi, in-room TV, 15-acre grounds, walled garden, private fishery, bicycle hire. BACKGROUND MUSIC none. LOCATION in village, 7 miles N of Westport. CHILDREN all ages welcomed. DOGS allowed in courtyard bedrooms. CREDIT CARDS Amex, MasterCard, Visa. PRICES B&B €115–€135, D,B&B €180–€195. 5-course dinner €58.

25% DISCOUNT VOUCHERS

RAMELTON Co. Donegal
Map 6:B5

FREWIN, Rectory Road. Tel 00 353 74 915 1246, www.accommodationdonegal. net. Restored with flair, Regina Gibson and Thomas Coyle's ivy-hung former rectory is a warm and welcoming outpost on the Wild Atlantic Way. The Victorian family home has been returned to its former glory by Thomas Coyle, an antiques collector and restorer who uplifted the stained-glass windows, open fires and an elegant staircase. In keeping with its period, the house has been kitted out with a candle-holding chandelier above the dining room table; antiques and comfy sofas in the sitting rooms. The spacious, country house-style bedrooms, each with a compact bathroom, might have a library, a four-poster bed, a roll-top bath. Communal breakfasts are praiseworthy. Golf, fishing, horse riding and guided hikes in the Bluestack mountains can be arranged. BEDROOMS 3, plus cottage in the grounds. OPEN Apr–Oct, by special arrangement for small groups in Feb and Nov. FACILITIES sitting room, library, dining room, free Wi-Fi, 2-acre garden, golf. BACKGROUND MUSIC none. LOCATION outskirts of town. CHILDREN over-12s welcomed. DOGS not allowed. CREDIT CARDS MasterCard, Visa. PRICES per person B&B single €90, double occupancy €85–€90.

RATHNEW Co. Wicklow
Map 6:C6

HUNTER'S HOTEL, Newrath Bridge, A67 TN30. Tel 00 353 404 40106, www.hunters.ie. With a claim to being Ireland's oldest coaching inn, this rambling property next to the River Varty has been owned by the same family for almost 200 years. The

brothers Gelletlie, the current stewards, have maintained its comfortably grand olde-worlde charm, with antiques, open fires and floral fabrics. 'Their determination to keep it close to the original 1825 inn has much to do with its evident success,' wrote a returning fan in 2018. 'On arrival we enjoyed coffee and good biscuits in the Victorian garden.' Most of the chintz-filled bedrooms overlook the grounds; in each, extra blankets for chilly nights. Housekeeping standards may not be perfect. The dining room has crisp linen, classic cuisine, 'slightly disjointed service'. Breakfast is 'up to the mark'. BEDROOMS 16, 1 on ground floor. OPEN all year except 24–26 Dec. FACILITIES drawing room, lounge, bar, dining room, private dining room, free Wi-Fi, in-room TV (Freeview), 5-acre grounds, golf, tennis, fishing nearby. BACKGROUND MUSIC none. LOCATION 1 mile SE of Ashford. CHILDREN all ages welcomed. DOGS allowed by arrangement. CREDIT CARDS Amex, MasterCard, Visa. PRICES per person B&B from €65, D,B&B from €95. Set dinner from €30.
25% DISCOUNT VOUCHERS

RECESS Co. Galway
Map 6:C4

LOUGH INAGH LODGE, Inagh Valley. Tel 00 353 95 34706, www. loughinaghlodgehotel.ie. In 'a spectacular position', cradled by a mountain range, this Victorian fishing lodge, once the retreat of a London brewer, is a remote and peaceful place. It has been owned by the O'Connor family for 30 years. A peat-fuelled fire burns in the cosy library and the well-appointed sitting room; both have warm hues, wood floors with rugs, antique furnishings and artworks. Dinner –

Irish food cooked with a French flair, underpinned by local seafood – is served on the dining room's white tablecloths; the wood-panelled bar has simpler fare. Upstairs, the comfortable bedrooms (each named after an Irish writer) are traditionally furnished, some with a four-poster. Lough view bedrooms 'are worth the extra'. BEDROOMS 13, 4 on ground floor, 1 suitable for disabled. OPEN Mar–Dec. FACILITIES sitting room, bar, library, dining room, free Wi-Fi, in-room TV (Freeview), 14-acre grounds, wedding facilities. BACKGROUND MUSIC none. LOCATION 3 miles N of Recess, on the lough's eastern shore. CHILDREN all ages welcomed. DOGS allowed. CREDIT CARDS all major cards. PRICES per room B&B €155–€220, D,B&B €250–€320. À la carte €50.
25% DISCOUNT VOUCHERS

THOMASTOWN Co. Kilkenny
Map 6:D5

BALLYDUFF HOUSE. Tel 00 353 56 775 8488, ballyduffhouse.ie. High praise from regular readers this year after returning to Brede Thomas's 'wonderful' B&B. His Georgian country house is admired for its 'glorious setting, genuine ambience' and 'very friendly, unaffected, efficient hospitality'; 'the result is pure magic'. Tea is served on guests' arrival in the 'remarkable' library ('the fruits of hundreds of years of reading of one family'). Fresh flowers, oil paintings, squashy sofas, open fires and Irish antiques fill downstairs. Upstairs, pretty, light-filled bedrooms have Georgian proportions, views of the gardens and countryside; one has a roll-top bath, another a four-poster. Full Irish breakfasts are served in the dining room. 'Everything works. What amazing value.' Golf, fishing, canoeing

are available on the doorstep. **BEDROOMS**
6. **OPEN** Apr–Oct, by arrangement
for groups of 4–6 in Feb, Mar, Nov.
FACILITIES drawing room, library, dining
room, free Wi-Fi, garden, fishing.
BACKGROUND MUSIC none. **LOCATION**
4 miles S of Thomastown. **CHILDREN**
all ages welcomed. **DOGS** allowed by
arrangement. **CREDIT CARDS** none
accepted. **PRICES** [2018] per person
B&B €50.

WATERVILLE Co. Kerry
Map 6:D4

BUTLER ARMS. Tel 00 353 66 947 4144,
www.butlerarms.com. On the edge of
Ballinskellig's bay, the Huggard sisters'
friendly, 'well-run', Victorian hotel
enjoys outstanding ocean views. Owned
by the same hands-on family since
1915, it has attracted such luminaries as
Walt Disney, JP Morgan and Michael
Douglas. Inside, cosy areas for seatingn
and blazing peat fires. Chef Craig
Newell's 'excellent' seafood is served in
Charlie's restaurant, including oysters,
local salmon and the hotel's signature
scallops with black pudding, parsnip
and apple purée; less formal dining is
found in Chaplin Lounge (named after
another famous guest). The 'very lively'
Fishermen's bar serves the family's own
pale ale and generous shots of local
folklore. 'Straightforward' bedrooms
overlook the Atlantic or hotel garden.
BEDROOMS 36, 10 on ground floor. **OPEN**
Mar–Nov. **FACILITIES** lounge, bar,
restaurant, coffee shop, free Wi-Fi,
in-room TV (Sky), wedding/function
facilities, garden, parking. **BACKGROUND
MUSIC** none. **LOCATION** village centre.
CHILDREN all ages welcomed. **DOGS**
allowed. **CREDIT CARDS** all major cards.
PRICES per room B&B from €120, D,B&B
from €180.

FREQUENTLY ASKED QUESTIONS

HOW DO YOU CHOOSE A GOOD HOTEL?

The hotels we like are relaxed, unstuffy and personally run. We do not have a specific template: our choices vary greatly in style and size. Most of the hotels in the Guide are family owned and family run. These are places where the needs and comfort of the guest are put ahead of the convenience of the management.

YOU ARE A HOTEL GUIDE – WHY DO YOU INCLUDE SO MANY PUBS AND B&BS?

Attitudes and expectations have changed considerably since the Guide was founded in the 1970s. Today's guests expect more informality, less deference. There has been a noticeable rise in the standards of food and accommodation in pubs and restaurants. This is demonstrated by the number of such places suggested to us by our readers. While pubs may have a more relaxed attitude than some traditional hotels, we ensure that only those that maintain high standards of service are included in our selections. The best B&Bs have always combined a high standard of accommodation with excellent value for money. Expect the bedrooms in a pub or B&B listed in the Guide to be well equipped, with thoughtful extras. B&B owners invariably know how to serve a good breakfast.

WHAT ARE YOUR LIKES AND DISLIKES?

We like
* Flexible times for meals.
* Two decent armchairs in the bedroom.
* Good bedside lighting.
* Proper hangers in the wardrobe.
* Fresh milk with the tea tray in the room.

We dislike
* Intrusive background music.
* Stuffy dress codes.
* Bossy notices and house rules.
* Hidden service charges.
* Packaged fruit juices at breakfast.

WHY DO YOU DROP HOTELS FROM ONE YEAR TO THE NEXT?

Readers are quick to tell us if they think standards have slipped at a hotel. If the evidence is overwhelming, we drop the hotel from the Guide or perhaps downgrade it to the Shortlist. Sometimes we send inspectors just to be sure. When a hotel is sold, we look for reports since the new owners took over, otherwise we inspect or omit it.

WHY DO YOU ASK FOR 'MORE REPORTS, PLEASE'?

When we have not heard about a hotel for several years, we ask readers for more reports. Sometimes readers returning to a favourite hotel may not send a fresh report. Readers often respond to our request.

WHAT SHOULD I TELL YOU IN A REPORT?

How you enjoyed your stay. We welcome reports of any length. We want to know what you think about the welcome, the service, the building and the facilities. Even a short report can tell us a great deal about the owners, the staff and the atmosphere.

HOW SHOULD I SEND YOU A REPORT?

You can email us at editor@goodhotelguide.com. Or you can write to us at the address given on the report form opposite, or send a report via the GHG's website: www.goodhotelguide.com.

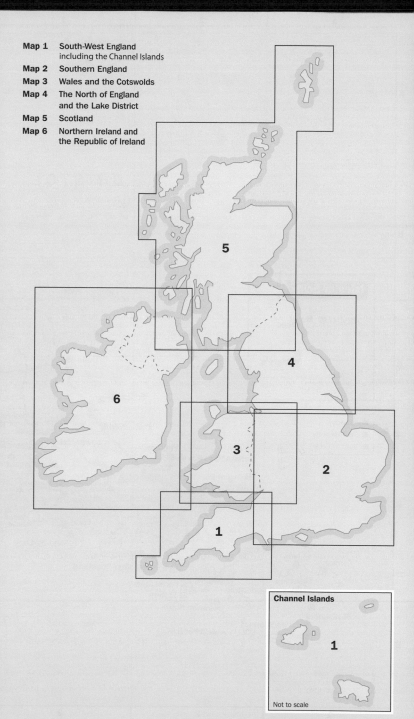

Map 1 South-West England
including the Channel Islands

Map 2 Southern England

Map 3 Wales and the Cotswolds

Map 4 The North of England
and the Lake District

Map 5 Scotland

Map 6 Northern Ireland and
the Republic of Ireland

Channel Islands

1

Not to scale

MAP 1 • SOUTH-WEST ENGLAND

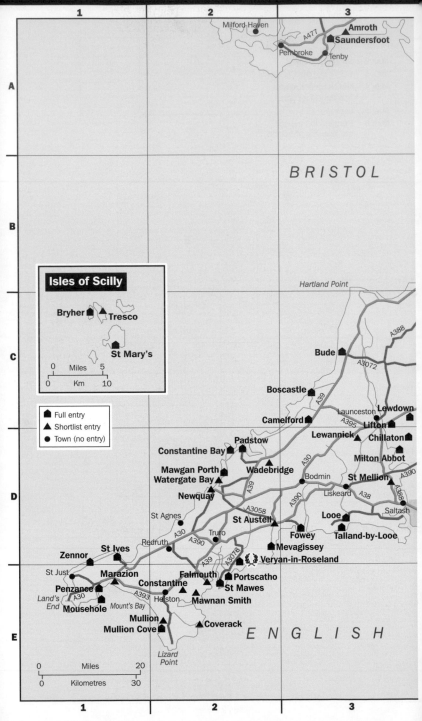

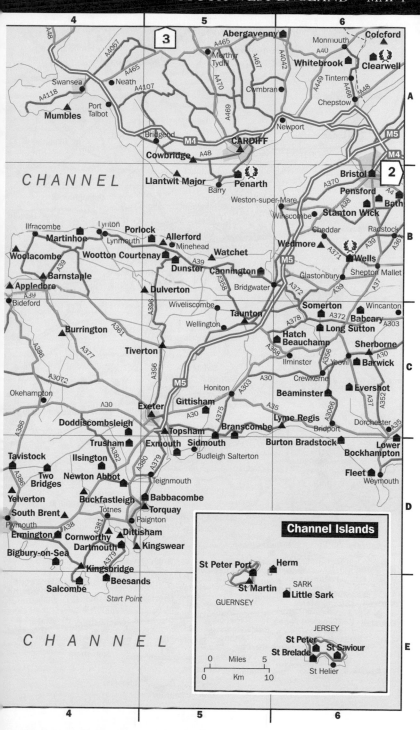

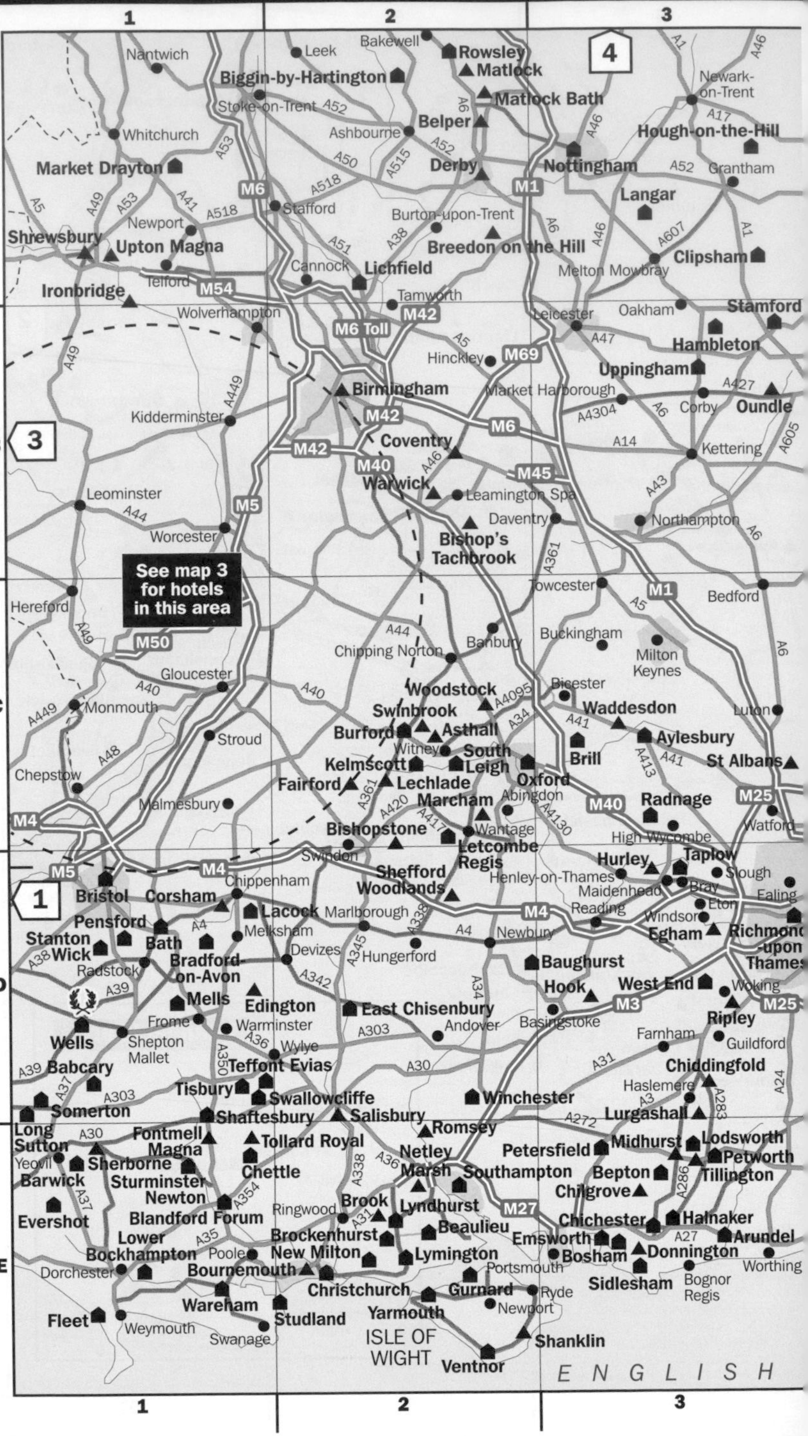

MAP 2 · SOUTHERN ENGLAND

See map 3 for hotels in this area

ENGLISH

ISLE OF WIGHT

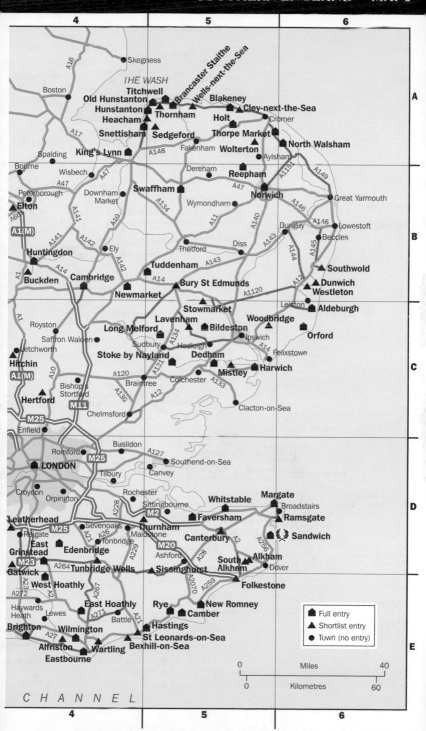

Legend:
- ■ Full entry
- ▲ Shortlist entry
- ● Town (no entry)

0 — Miles — 40
0 — Kilometres — 60

C H A N N E L

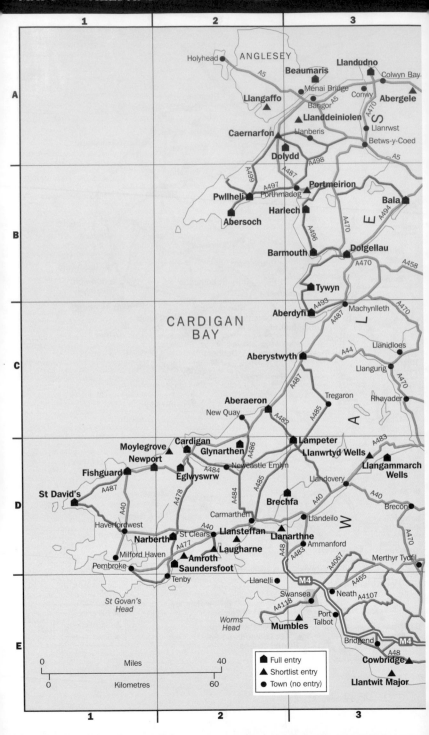

MAP 3 · WALES AND THE COTSWOLDS

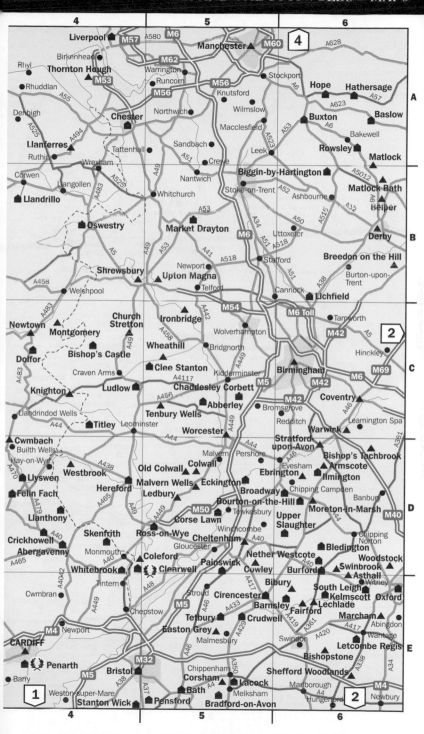

MAP 4 • THE NORTH OF ENGLAND AND THE LAKE DISTRICT

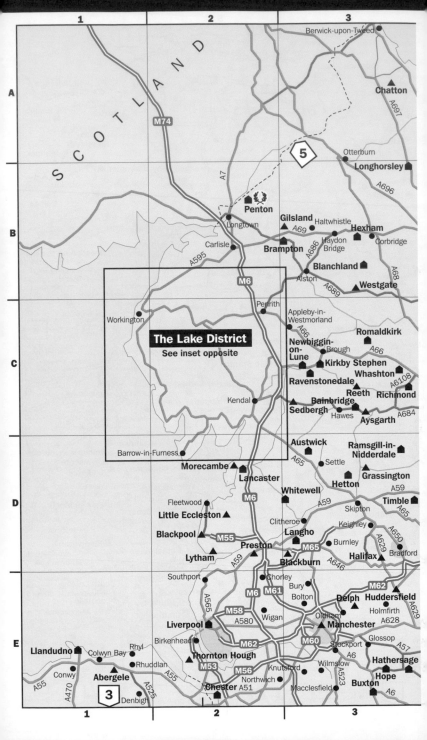

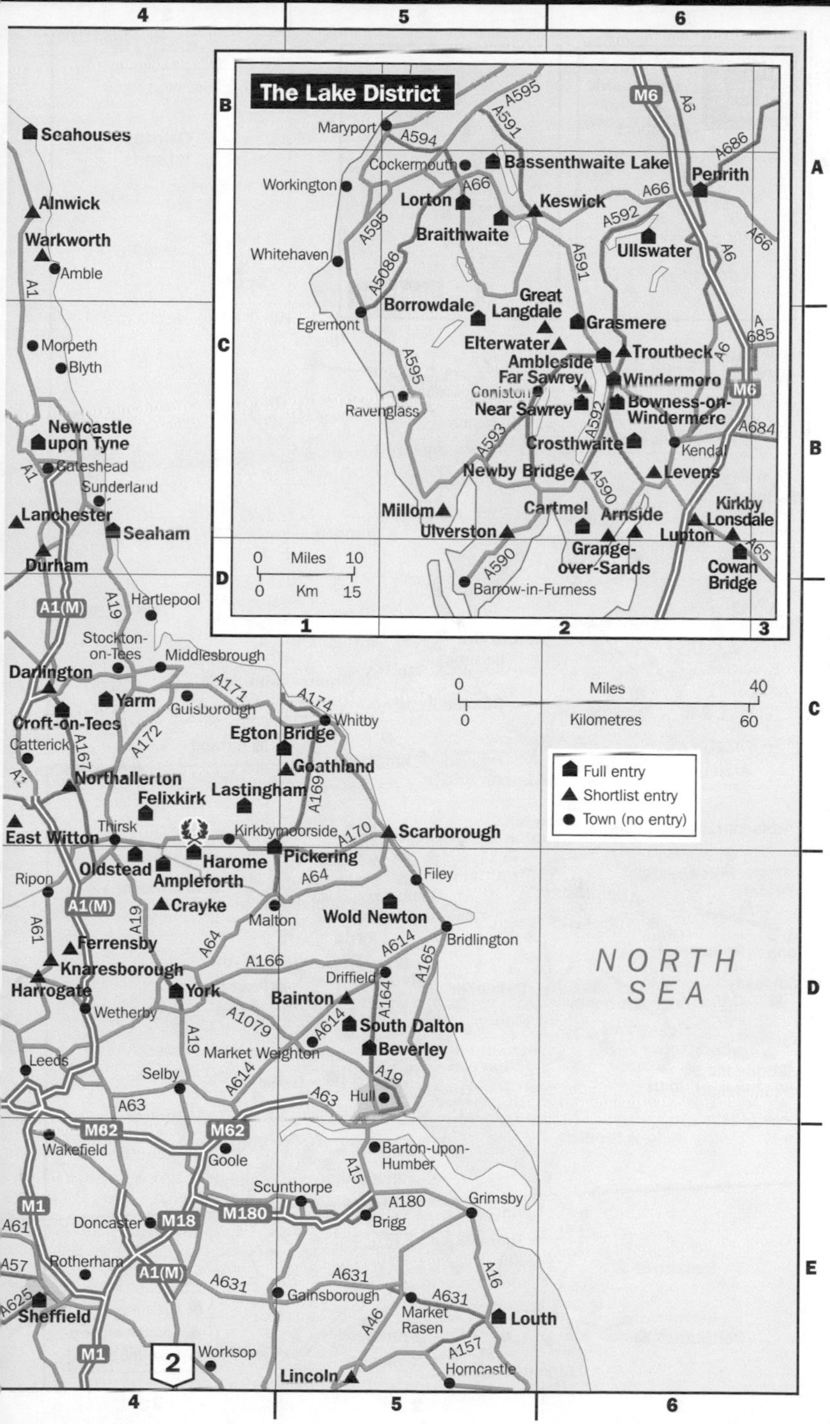

4   5   6

The Lake District

B

Maryport

Cockermouth   Bassenthwaite Lake

Workington

Lorton   Keswick   Penrith

A66

Braithwaite

Whitehaven   Ullswater

Borrowdale   Great Langdale   Grasmere

Egremont

Elterwater   Troutbeck

C   Ambleside   Windermere

Far Sawrey

Coniston   Bowness-on-Windermere

Ravenglass   Near Sawrey

Crosthwaite

Newby Bridge   Levels

Kendal

Millom   Cartmel   Arnside   Kirkby Lonsdale

Ulverston   Lupton

Grange-over-Sands   Cowan Bridge

D   Miles   0   10

Km   0   15

Barrow-in-Furness

1   2   3

A   Seahouses

Alnwick

Warkworth   Amble

Morpeth

Blyth

Newcastle upon Tyne

Gateshead

Sunderland

Lanchester

Seaham

Durham

Hartlepool

A1(M)

Stockton-on-Tees   Middlesbrough

Darlington   Yarm   Guisborough   Whitby

Croft-on-Tees   Egton Bridge

Catterick   Goathland

Northallerton   Lastingham

Felixkirk

Thirsk   Kirkbymoorside   Scarborough

East Witton

Oldstead   Harome   Pickering   Filey

Ripon   Ampleforth

A1(M)   Crayke   Malton   Wold Newton

Ferrensby   Bridlington

Knaresborough

Harrogate   York   Bainton   Driffield

Wetherby   South Dalton   Beverley

Leeds   Selby   Market Weighton   Hull

M62   M62

Wakefield   Goole   Barton-upon-Humber

M1   Scunthorpe   Grimsby

Doncaster   M18   M180   Brigg

Rotherham   A1(M)   Gainsborough   Market Rasen   Louth

Sheffield

M1   Worksop   Lincoln   Horncastle

Legend

■ Full entry
▲ Shortlist entry
● Town (no entry)

Miles   0   40

Kilometres   0   60

NORTH SEA

MAP 5 • SCOTLAND

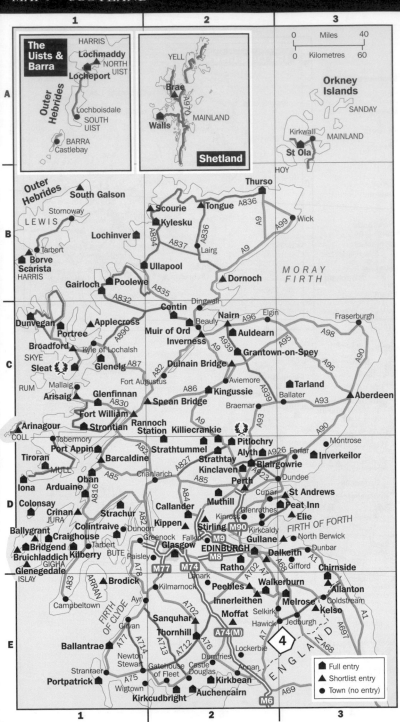

The Uists & Barra

HARRIS
Lochmaddy
NORTH UIST
Locheport
Outer Hebrides
Lochboisdale
SOUTH UIST
BARRA
Castlebay

YELL
Brae
A970
MAINLAND
Walls

Shetland

0 — Miles — 40
0 — Kilometres — 60

Orkney Islands

SANDAY

Kirkwall
MAINLAND
St Ola
HOY

Outer Hebrides
South Galson
Stornoway
L E W I S
Scourie **Tongue** A836 Thurso
Kylesku
A9 A99 Wick
Lochinver A894 A837 A836
Lairg A9
Borve Tarbert
Scarista
HARRIS
Ullapool A9
M O R A Y F I R T H
Gairloch **Poolewe**
A832 A835 **Dornoch**
Contin Dingwall
Dunvegan Beauly **Nairn** A96 Elgin Fraserburgh
Applecross A890 **Muir of Ord** **Auldearn** A95 A98
Portree **Inverness** A939 A95 A90
Broadford Kyle of Lochalsh A9 **Grantown-on-Spey** A96
SKYE A82 **Dulnain Bridge** A939
Sleat **Glenelg** A87 Aviemore **Tarland**
RUM Fort Augustus A86 **Kingussie** A939 Ballater **Aberdeen**
Mallaig **Glenfinnan** A830 Braemar A93
Arisaig **Spean Bridge** A9 A939
Fort William **Rannoch Station** **Killiecrankie** A93 A90
Arinagour **Strontian** **Pitlochry** Montrose
COLL Tobermory **Strathtummel** **Alyth** A926 Forfar **Inverkeilor**
Port Appin A85 **Strathtay** Blairgowrie
Tiroran **Barcaldine** A827 **Kinclaven** A23 Dundee
MULL Crianlarich A85 **Perth**
Oban A84 Cupar **St Andrews**
Iona **Arduaine** A816 **Muthill** Glenrothes **Peat Inn**
Colonsay **Strachur** **Callander** Kinross **Elie**
JURA **Kippen** **Stirling** M90 Kirkcaldy FIRTH OF FORTH
Crinan **Colintraive** Dunoon Falkirk M9 **Gullane**
Ballygrant **Craighouse** Greenock **EDINBURGH** North Berwick
Bridgend **Kilberry** Tarbert **Glasgow** M8 Dunbar
Bruichladdich GIGHA BUTE Paisley **Ratho** A702 A7 Gifford **Chirnside**
Glenegedale M77 M74 **Dalkeith** A68 A1 **Allanton**
ISLAY ARRAN **Brodick** Lanark A78 **Peebles** **Walkerburn** Coldstream
Campbeltown Kilmarnock **Innerleithen** **Melrose** **Kelso**
FIRTH OF CLYDE Ayr **Sanquhar** **Moffat** Selkirk **Kelso** A1
Ballantrae A77 A714 **Thornhill** A74(M) Hawick Jedburgh A697
Girvan A713 A712 A76 Lockerbie E N G L A N D A68
Portpatrick Newton Stewart Dumfries Annan A69
Stranraer A75 **Gatehouse of Fleet** Castle Douglas M6
Wigtown **Kirkbean**
Kirkcudbright **Auchencairn**

A836 A837 A894 A832 A835 A890 A87 A82 A830 A85 A84 A82 A816 A83 A77 A714 A713 A712 A76 A75 A702

4

Full entry
▲ **Shortlist entry**
● **Town (no entry)**

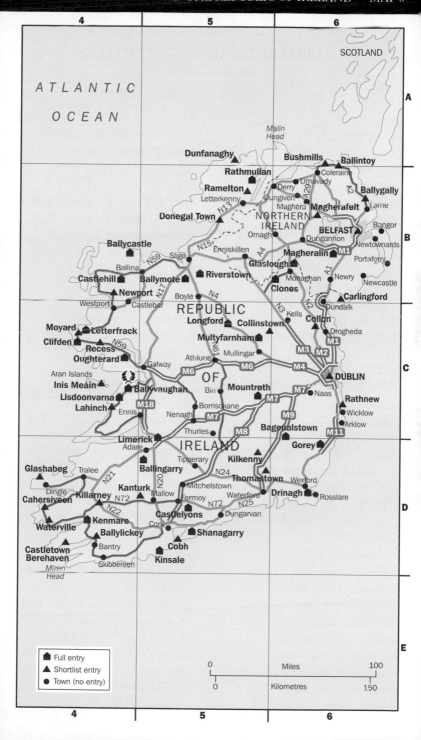

ALPHABETICAL LIST OF HOTELS
(S) indicates a Shortlist entry

Pheasant Harome 183

Pheasant Inn Shefford Woodlands (S) 593

Phoenix Court Scarborough (S) 592

Pier at Harwich Harwich 185

Pierhouse Port Appin 393

Pig near Bath Pensford 260

Pig on the Beach Studland 305

Pig at Combe Gittisham 177

Pig in the Forest Brockenhurst 127

Pig in the Wall Southampton 301

Pilgrm London (S) 501

Pilot London (S) 502

Pine Trees Pitlochry (S) 637

Pipe and Glass Inn South Dalton 299

Plantation House Ermington 169

Plas Bodegroes Pwllheli 447

Plas Dinas Country House Caernarfon (S) 643

Plough Kelmscott 200

Plough Lupton (S) 569

Plumber Manor Sturminster Newton 306

Pointer Brill 120

Polurrian Bay Mullion (S) 577

Pool House Poolewe 391

Poppies Callander 355

Porth Tocyn Abersoch 418

Portmeirion Portmeirion (S) 652

Portobello London 61

Powis House Stirling (S) 640

Prestonfield Edinburgh 362

Prince Hall Two Bridges 323

Prince's House Glenfinnan 368

Priory Wareham 330

Punch Bowl Crosthwaite 152

Q

Qbic London (S) 502

Quay House Clifden 469

Queensberry Bath 88

Quinlan & Cooke Boutique Townhouse Cahersiveen (S) 658

Quy Mill Cambridge (S) 528

R

Raeburn Edinburgh 363

Rathmullan House Rathmullan 485

Ravenhill House Belfast (S) 657

Reading Rooms Margate (S) 573

Read's Faversham 173

Rectory Crudwell 153

Red Lion Freehouse East Chisenbury 160

Red Lion Inn Babcary 79

Restaurant James Sommerin Penarth 445

Riverwood Strathtay 402

Riviera Sidmouth 296

Rock Inn Newton Abbot 243

Rocksalt Folkestone (S) 550

Romney Bay House New Romney 239

Rookery London 62

Room with a View Brighton (S) 524

Rooms Lytham (S) 570

Rose and Crown Romaldkirk 277

Rose & Crown Snettisham 297

Roseate House London (S) 502

Roseate Villa Bath (S) 516

Roseleigh Buxton 132

Rosemary Falmouth (S) 548

Rosleague Manor Letterfrack 477

Rosquil House Kilkenny (S) 664

Rothay Manor Ambleside 72

Roundwood House Mountrath 482

Royal Ventnor 328

Royal Crescent Bath 89

Royal Duchy Falmouth (S) 549

Royal Oak Swallowcliffe 308

Royal Oak Tetbury (S) 603